P9-CDX-971

Communication Mosaics

An Introduction to the Field of Communication

Eighth Edition

Julia T Wood

Lineberger Distinguished Professor of Humanities, Emerita
Caroline H. and Thomas S. Royster Distinguished Professor of Graduate Education, Emerita
The University of North Carolina at Chapel Hill

CENGAGE
Learning·

Australia • Brazil • Mexico • Singapore • United Kingdom • United States

CENGAGE
Learning®

Communication Mosaics: An Introduction to the Field of Communication, Eighth Edition
Julia T. Wood

Product Director: Monica Eckman

Product Manager: Kelli Strieby

Content Developer: Kate Scheinman

Associate Content Developer: Karolina Kiwak

Product Assistant: Colin Solan

Media Developer: Jessica Badiner

Marketing Manager: Kristin Davis

Content Project Manager: Dan Saabye

Art Director: Marissa Falco

Manufacturing Planner: Doug Bertke

IP Analyst: Ann Hoffman

IP Project Manager: Sarah Shainwald

Production Service: Lumina Datamatics

Compositor: Lumina Datamatics

Text and Cover Designer: Deborah Dutton

Cover Image: Shutterstock/Sukpaiboonwat

© 2017, 2014, 2011 Cengage Learning

WCN: 01-100-101

ALL RIGHTS RESERVED. No part of this work covered by the copyright herein may be reproduced, transmitted, stored, or used in any form or by any means graphic, electronic, or mechanical, including but not limited to photocopying, recording, scanning, digitizing, taping, web distribution, information networks, or information storage and retrieval systems, except as permitted under Section 107 or 108 of the 1976 United States Copyright Act, without the prior written permission of the publisher.

For product information and technology assistance, contact us at
Cengage Learning Customer & Sales Support, 1-800-354-9706

For permission to use material from this text or product, submit all requests online at **www.cengage.com/permissions**. Further permissions questions can be emailed to **permissionrequest@cengage.com**.

Library of Congress Control Number: 2015945976

Student Edition: 978-1-305-40358-1

Loose-leaf Edition: 978-1-305-65518-8

Cengage Learning
20 Channel Center Street
Boston, MA 02210
USA

Cengage Learning is a leading provider of customized learning solutions with employees residing in nearly 40 different countries and sales in more than 125 countries around the world. Find your local representative at **www.cengage.com**.

Cengage Learning products are represented in Canada by Nelson Education, Ltd.

To learn more about Cengage Learning Solutions, visit **www.cengage.com**.

Purchase any of our products at your local college store or at our preferred online store **www.cengagebrain.com**.

Printed in the United States of America
Print Number: 02   Print Year: 2016

Brief Contents

Contents

6 Listening and Responding to Others   108

Part III: Contexts of Communication

9 Communication and Personal Identity   173

10 Communication in Personal Relationships   193

List of Boxes

TAKE ACTION

Preface

I wrote *Communication Mosaics* to support survey courses that introduce students to the field of communication. Unlike other versions of the introductory course, the survey approach usually doesn't include performance assignments such as giving speeches. Instead, the survey course aims to provide a comprehensive view of the communication field, giving attention to topics beyond those that can be covered in performance-oriented introductory classes—such topics include mass communication, organizational communication, and digital communication—and focusing on conceptual understanding of the breadth and importance of communication in many spheres of our lives.

Responses to earlier editions of this book indicate that many faculty appreciate a textbook specifically designed to support a survey approach to the introductory course. Student response to previous editions and 15 years of class testing indicate that students, too, find *Communication Mosaics* useful in giving them an expansive introduction to the communication discipline. In addition to welcoming the approach of this book, faculty and students have been generous in offering suggestions, which I've used to improve this edition.

In the pages that follow, I explain my vision of this book and the features I've woven into it and then call attention to changes I made in preparing the current edition.

Communication as a Mosaic

As the title of the book suggests, communication is an intricate mosaic composed of parts that are distinct yet interrelated. All of the parts work together to create the whole of communication. This book increases students' awareness of the importance of basic communication skills and processes and shows students how those common elements surface in specific forms and contexts of communication.

The book is divided into three parts. Part I introduces students to the discipline of communication, discusses foundations for the study of communication, and describes careers for people who have strong communication backgrounds and skills. Chapter 1 introduces the book, identifies values of studying communication, defines and models communication, and describes careers for people who have strong academic training in communication. Chapter 2 surveys the discipline's evolution and methods of conducting research so that students understand the long and rich intellectual history of the field. This chapter also highlights the discipline's breadth by identifying its primary areas of research and teaching. Part II consists of six chapters, each of which focuses on one of the basic processes and skills that are central to a range of communication situations and goals. These basic communication skills and processes are:

- ◆ Perceiving and understanding
- ◆ Engaging in verbal communication
- ◆ Engaging in nonverbal communication

◆ Listening and responding

◆ Creating communication climates

◆ Adapting communication to cultures and social communities

These basic skills and processes shape the character and effectiveness of communication in a wide range of settings, although how each functions varies from one context to another. For example, we may use different listening skills when trying to understand a close friend and attending to television news.

Part III shows how the basic communication processes and skills covered in Part II function in seven specific contexts:

◆ Communication and personal identity

◆ Communication in personal relationships

◆ Communication in groups and teams

◆ Communication in organizations

◆ Public communication

◆ Mass media

◆ Computer-mediated communication

The MindTap for *Communication Mosaics* includes a chapter-length discussion of how the processes and skills covered in Part II apply to interviewing.

Features of *Communication Mosaics*

Accenting this book are six features that enhance students' learning and ensure the scholarly integrity of content.

Accessible, Conversational Style

I write in a conversational style that encourages students to engage the ideas in this book. I refer to myself as "I" rather than "the author," and I address students as "you" rather than "the student." I also use informal language, such as contractions, just as people do in everyday conversations. In the opening chapter of the book, I introduce myself to students so they know something about my view of communication and my motivations for writing this book.

Another way in which I've personalized my writing style is by including examples from a range of people. At times, I offer reflections from my own life. In addition, I enlarge the conversation beyond just the reader and me by including in all chapters reflective comments from students at my university and other campuses around the country. To protect privacy, I've changed the names of the students who wrote the commentaries.

Learning about communication should be enjoyable. I don't think textbooks have to be dry or burdened with unnecessary jargon. When it's necessary to use specialized terms, I define them so that students understand what they mean, but I've written this book in an accessible, personal style to make it more interesting to read.

Foundation in Research and Theory

A textbook is only as good as the research and theory on which it is built. *Communication Mosaics* draws on the impressive body of research and theory developed by scholars of communication as well as scholars in other fields.

Communication Mosaics reflects my belief that theory and practice go together. Years ago, renowned scholar Kurt Lewin said, "There is nothing so practical as good theory." His words remain true today. In this book, I blend theory and practice so that each draws on and enriches the other. Effective practice is theoretically informed: It is based on knowledge of how and why the communication process works and what is likely to result from different kinds of communication. At the same time, effective theories have pragmatic value: They help us understand experiences in our everyday lives. Each chapter in this book is informed by the impressive theories and research generated by scholars of communication and other fields. To ensure that the perspectives and skills in this book reflect current knowledge of effective communication practices, this edition includes more than 200 new references.

Integrated Attention to Social Diversity

Social diversity is a defining feature of our era. The United States and the world include people of different ages, sexual orientations, gender identities, races, ethnicities, sexes, abilities, spiritual commitments, and economic circumstances.

These differences affect how we communicate. Thus, the idea of universal communication goals and principles must be replaced with understandings of how diverse people use communication to accomplish goals and how they adapt communication to fit a range of contexts. *Communication Mosaics* emphasizes social diversity in three specific ways. First, Chapter 8 offers in-depth coverage of the relationships between communication and culture: how cultural factors influence communication style, how communication shapes culture, and how we adapt our ways of communicating to particular people and contexts. Second, I weave research on social diversity into all chapters of the book. For example, Chapter 10 explains differences in how women and men typically communicate in personal relationships, and Chapter 14 discusses differences in how mass media represent men and women and people of different races. Third, examples in the chapters, as well as photographs, feature a wide range of people and cultural contexts.

Coverage of Digital Media

Digital media increasingly infuse our lives, and this is reflected throughout this edition of *Communication Mosaics*. Every chapter includes examples and research related to both mass communication and social media we use for social, educational, professional, and political purposes. For example, Chapter 4 notes how language has changed in response to digital technologies. We have coined new words (*hypertext, IM*) and developed new meanings for existing words (*mouse, cyberspace, virtual reality*). Texting and tweeting have led to abbreviated ways of communicating: brb (be right back), h8 (hate), AYT (are you there?), 2G2BT (too good to be true), 9 (parent in room), 99 (parent is no longer watching or no longer in room), and dropping vowels in words (whl = while, nxt = next, tmrw or 2mrw = tomorrow). Chapter 10's coverage of personal relationships examines how social media affect the ways in which we meet and get to know friends and romantic partners and the means we have for maintaining long-distance relationships. You will also find a full chapter, Chapter 15, on CMC. In this chapter, I discuss the ways we use CMC—especially social media—and then explore the impact of CMC on how we think, relate, and act in personal, professional, and social contexts. Finally, every chapter in this edition includes a main section in which I discuss relationships between that chapter's topics and digital media.

I've also written digital activities to extend students' learning online in the Mind-Tap for *Communication Mosaics*—for details, see Resources for Students and Instructors, below.

Student Commentaries

Woven into each chapter are commentaries from students' journals and papers. Although students in my classes wrote many of these, students at other universities have also sent me their reflections, many of which are included in this edition. I include student commentaries because in more than 30 years of teaching I've learned that students have much to teach each other and their instructors. The commentaries show how different people relate communication principles and research to their own lives. I encourage students who use this edition to send me their comments and reflections so the next edition can reflect their perspectives and experiences too.

Pedagogical Features

A sixth focus of this book is features that are specifically designed to maximize learning.

Learning Objectives Opening each chapter are learning objectives that orient students to the chapter and help them organize how they read and study the material.

Engage! Featured in each chapter are "Engage!" boxes that highlight communication research and the role of communication in everyday life. I use these boxes to call students' attention to particularly interesting aspects of communication in a variety of settings.

Practical Application Every chapter in Parts II and III of this edition provides concrete guidelines for communicating effectively (appearing in a highlighted section under the heading "Guidelines for …"). In addition, each chapter includes "Take Action" exercises that invite students to apply skills and principles as they read about them. Some of these exercises encourage students to practice a particular skill, perhaps by engaging in civic life or service learning. Others invite students to observe how communication concepts and principles discussed in the text show up in everyday interactions. Still others ask students to reflect on the ways in which particular skills, theories, or concepts have shaped who they are and how they communicate. Finally, at the end of each chapter, I include questions that invite students to discuss and reflect on what they've learned in the chapter.

End-of-Chapter Resources Following each chapter are study resources gathered under the heading Review, Reflect, Extend. These resources include questions that encourage students to reflect on and discuss what they have read and to extend and apply the material presented in the chapter, as well as a list of key concepts (with page references), and further recommended resources, including articles, books, films, and online sites.

Highlighted Key Terms Within each chapter, I've boldfaced key terms that students should learn. All boldfaced terms are repeated in the margin of the page on which they first appear and in a list at the end of each chapter to encourage students to check their retention after they have read the chapter. By each term, I've noted the page on which the term first appears and is defined so that students can easily review concepts. Boldfaced terms are also defined in the glossary at the end of the book.

Experience Communication Case Study At the end of most chapters, I present a short case study that illustrates how ideas covered in the chapter show up in actual communication. To make the cases engaging and realistic, the MindTap for *Communication Mosaics* also provides videos of the scenarios presented in each case study and questions that ask students to apply chapter theories and principles.

The transcripts at the ends of Chapters 2 and 13, and the online videos available for each, are not case studies. Instead, the scenario for Chapter 2 features Tim Muehlhoff, a professor of communication at Biola University, being interviewed by a student about the relevance of ethics to communication, and the video for Chapter 13 is a speech by Elizabeth Lopez, a student in an introductory public speaking class.

Changes in This Edition

Teaching at a public university has made me sensitive to the cost of textbooks. I am not willing to publish new editions of my books with only cosmetic changes. Instead, I insist that a new edition offer substantive changes to justify the expense to students. Instructors who are familiar with previous editions of this book will notice significant changes in this edition that are responsive to generous feedback from reviewers, instructors, and students.

MindTap® for Wood's *Communication Mosaics*, 8th Edition

MindTap for Wood's *Communication Mosaics*, 8th Edition is a personalized teaching experience with relevant assignments that guide students to analyze, apply, and improve thinking, allowing you to measure skills and comprehension with ease. Mind-Tap allows you to set your course, elevate thinking, and promote better outcomes. Learn more in the Student Resources section, below.

Enhanced Coverage of Computer-Mediated Communication

Faculty who have adopted previous editions of this book will notice that I have updated Chapter 15, Digital Media and the Online World, with material on the ever-changing ways that we use digital media to craft identities; connect with others; and participate in education, work, and political and social organizing. I have also added information on best practices for managing digital media so that they enhance our lives.

In addition to revising Chapter 15, this edition further integrates attention to CMC with a new section in every chapter that focuses specifically on CMC in relation to the chapter's topics.

Condensed Coverage of the Communication Field

This edition heeds reviewers' suggestion to abridge Chapter 2, which introduces students to the field of communication. I continue to think it is important to discuss the field's origins so that students appreciate the rich intellectual history of the discipline. In this edition, however, my discussion of the field's history and current character is more concise.

The Latest Research about Human Communication

This edition includes more than 200 new references. The infusion of new research ensures that *Communication Mosaics* reflects up-to-date scholarship. For example, Chapter 12, Communication in Organizations, includes new information on the challenge of negotiating a balance between commitments to work and commitments to other facets of life. Chapter 14, Mass Media, includes recent research that demonstrates bias in mainstream media such as television and films. And, as noted above, I have rewritten Chapter 15, Digital Media and the Online World, to reflect the latest knowledge about how digital media affect our lives, including our communication and how we can best manage their roles in our lives.

Streamlined Presentation

I've worked to avoid the phenomenon of "page creep," which happens when authors add new material to each new edition of a book without condensing or eliminating any of the material in previous editions. Throughout the book, I've reduced the number of features, tightened prose, and eliminated dated research. This edition is slightly shorter than the previous one, yet it includes new information and features to encourage application of concepts and principles.

- FYI boxes have been renamed Engage! to better promote student interaction with the content. Many Engage! features contain interactive Critical Thinking Questions.

- Sharpen Your Skill boxes have been renamed Take Action. These exercises now appear in the end-of-chapter section.

- Critical Thinking Questions have also been added to select photo captions throughout.

Revised Coverage of Public Speaking

I have recast Chapter 13, Public Communication. As faculty know, it's difficult, if not impossible, to teach public speaking in a single chapter, yet that is all the space allotted in a book that surveys the broad field of communication. To offer students an interesting introduction to public communication, I have rewritten the chapter as an extended example in which a student body president named Harper prepares a speech to give at his graduation. Following Harper through the processes of thinking, research, organization, and practice, allows me to introduce principles of public speaking in an embodied, rather than abstract manner. In addition, adopters of this book have access to five chapters I have written that provide detailed instruction in preparing informative and persuasive speeches. Those additional chapters are available through Cengage Compose, Cengage Learning's customized learning materials program. Contact your local Cengage Learning consultant for more information on Cengage Compose.

Improved Order of End-of-Chapter Features

To facilitate improved student comprehension, I have reordered the end-of-chapter features as follows:

Summary

Experience Communication Case Study

Key Concepts

Review, Reflect, Extend

   Reflect and Discuss

   Take Action

Recommended Resources

New Interior Design

Finally, this edition has a more open, uncluttered design. Previous editions included many photos, cartoons, and in-text feature boxes. A number of students and faculty commented that all of these features made the pages feel crowded. In response, I have included fewer photos, cartoons, and feature boxes in this edition, and I have moved the skill-building exercises to the ends of chapters.

I hope that this edition of *Communication Mosaics* retains the strengths that instructors and students valued in previous editions while also benefiting from generous suggestions for improvement.

Resources for Students and Instructors

Accompanying this book is an integrated suite of resources to support both students and instructors.

Please note: If you want your students to have access to the online resources for this book, you can order them for your course. These resources can be bundled with every new copy of the text or ordered separately. If you do not order them, your students can purchase them directly from www.cengagebrain.com. Please consult your local Cengage Learning sales representative or **www.cengagebrain.com** for more information, user names and passwords, examination copies, or a demonstration of these ancillary products.

Instructor Resources

Instructors who adopt this book can request a number of resources to support their teaching.

◆ **The Instructor's Resource Manual** offers guidelines for setting up your course, sample syllabi, chapter-by-chapter outlines of content, suggested topics for lectures and discussion, and a wealth of class-tested exercises and assignments.

◆ **Instructor's Web site.** The password-protected instructor's Web site includes electronic access to the Instructor's Resource Manual and downloadable versions of the book's Microsoft® PowerPoint® slides. To gain access to the Web site, simply request a course key by opening the site's home page.

◆ **Cognero.** Cognero is Cengage's full-featured online testing system that allows users to create assessment questions and tests. Instructors have all of the features that are used to from Examview® with a number of valuable enhancements. These include: browser-based application, questions organized in a central database, real-time software and content updates, reordering of questions on a test automatically, feedback attached to questions or answers, and easy integration and exportation to an LMS platform.

◆ *The Teaching Assistant's Guide to the Basic Course* is available to instructors who adopt this textbook. Katherine G. Hendrix, who is on the faculty at the University of Memphis, prepared this resource specifically for new instructors. Based on leading communication teacher training programs, this guide discusses some of the general issues that accompany a teaching role and offers specific strategies for managing the first week of classes, leading productive discussions, managing sensitive topics in the classroom, and grading students' written and oral work.

Student Resources

Students have the option of utilizing a rich array of resources to enhance and extend their learning while using *Communication Mosaics*.

◆ **MindTap for Wood's *Communication Mosaics*, 8th Edition.** This edition's pedagogy is built on a strengthened learning architecture, based on skill building, application, and critical thinking, integrated carefully in MindTap—a personalized teaching experience with assignments that guide students to analyze, apply, and improve thinking, allowing instructors to measure skills and outcomes with ease. With MindTap, students are able to use dynamic technological resources, including interactive videos; find high-value gradable activities; and practice in an engaging, personalized online environment. MindApps that are provided support building a speaking outline, practicing, and presenting speeches.

◆ *The Art and Strategy of Service-Learning Presentations*, Second Edition, is available bundled with *Communication Mosaics*. Authored by Rick Isaacson and Jeff Saperstein of San Francisco State University, this handbook provides guidelines for connecting service-learning work with classroom concepts and advice for working effectively with agencies and organizations.

◆ *A Guide to the Basic Course for ESL Students* is available bundled with the book. Specifically for communicators whose first language is not English, it features FAQs, helpful URLs, and strategies for managing communication anxiety.

Acknowledgments

Although my name is the only one that appears as the author of this book, I could not have written it without the help of many people. I want to take a moment to acknowledge the support and assistance of a number of people who have influenced how I think and write.

I am deeply indebted to the Cengage Learning team. Everyone on that team has been extraordinarily professional and helpful throughout the evolution of this book. Leading the group is Nicole Morinon, senior product manager for speech communication, whose energy, support, and insight seem infinite. In addition to Nicole, I am grateful to other key members of the team: Monica Eckman, product director, and Kate Scheinman, senior content developer editor. Also integral to this edition were Kristin Davis, marketing manager; Colin Solan, product assistant; Jessica Badiner, media developer; Heather Preston, copy editor; Dan Saabye, content production manager; Sumathy Kumaran, project manager; Kathleen Shapiro, proofreader; Farah Fard, IP project manager; Jananie Kulasekaran, image permissions researcher; and Dharanivel Baskar, text permissions researcher.

This book is truly a collaborative effort that involved and reflects the contributions of everyone on the team.

I am particularly grateful to scholars and teachers of communication who contributed helpful comments and suggestions that guided this revision: Becki Bowman, McPherson College; Anita Chirco, Keuka College; Lynn Cockett, Juniata College; Katherine Dawson, University of Louisiana at Monroe; Mark Frederick, Regent University; Joe Habraken, University of New England; Zach Henning, University of Southern Indiana; Liliana Herakova, Holyoke Community College; Sarah Hill, Western Illinois University; Allison Holmes, Davidson County Community College; Patricia Linder, Middle Georgia State College; David Nelson, Valdosta State University; Clyde Remmo, Columbia College; Terri Russ, Saint Mary's College; Abbie Syrek, University of Nebraska Omaha; and David Zanolla, Western Illinois University.

The ideas in this book were also influenced by students in my classes and by students at other colleges and universities around the country. They provided insightful feedback and suggestions for ways to improve *Communication Mosaics*. In class discussions, conferences, e-mail, and written comments, students push me to do more and tell me which communication issues are prominent in their lives. Invariably, students teach me at least as much as I teach them. Because students are so thoughtful, I include many of their reflections as Student Voices in this book.

Finally, I thank those with whom I am closest. For more than 40 years, Robert (Robbie) Cox has been my partner in love, life, and work. Robbie is my greatest fan and my most rigorous critic, and both his support and his criticism shape all that I write. Special friends, Ruth, LindaBecker, Shelly, and Robin, sharpen my thinking and writing by testing my ideas against their experiences communicating with others. My sister Carolyn remains one of the most positive, perceptive, and delightful presences in my life, as do my youngest friends: Michelle, who is 25; Daniel, who is 21; and Harrison, who is 17. These young people continuously remind me of the magic and wonder in human relationships. And of course I must express my appreciation to the four-legged members of our family: our dog, Cassidy, and our cats, Always Rowdy and Rigby. When I am having a bad writing day, these three remind me that playing ball and brushing them are important parts of life.

1

A First Look at Communication

What we do in life is determined by how we communicate.

—Tony Robbins

How does communication affect your life?

 MindTap

Learning Objectives

Topics Covered in This Chapter	After studying this chapter, you should be able to . . .
The Value of Studying Communication	Differentiate among the three beneficial outcomes of studying communication: personal, professional, and civic.
Defining Communication	Discuss the importance of each of the four key terms in the definition of communication.
Models of Communication	Diagram elements in the transactional model of communication from your observation of a specific communication interaction.
Careers in Communication	Identify six careers that value the skills acquired by communication majors.
Digital Media and Communication	Adapt the four key terms in the definition of communication to the context of digital media.

MindTap™

Start with a quick engagement activity and **review** the chapter Learning Objectives.

Read, highlight, and take notes online.

◆ At the end of this term, the person you've been dating will graduate and take a job in a city a thousand miles away. You're concerned about sustaining the relationship when you have to communicate across the distance.

◆ At work, you're on a team that includes people from Mexico and Germany. You've noticed that in some ways they communicate differently from American-born workers. You aren't sure how to interpret their styles of communicating or how to interact effectively with them.

◆ You can't keep up with the e-mail, texts, and posts on your Facebook page. Although you love staying in touch with everyone, you sometimes feel overwhelmed by the sheer amount of communication that pours in.

◆ You volunteer at a literacy center where you teach children as well as adults to read. You believe the program would be more effective if the director did more to build a sense of community among volunteers. You want to encourage her to do that without seeming to criticize her.

◆ You want to advocate for a proposal to decrease waste that is put in the local landfill, but you don't have formal training in public speaking. You wonder how to organize your ideas to persuade others to support the proposal.

From the moment we arise until we go to bed, our days are filled with communication challenges and opportunities. Unlike some subjects you study, communication is relevant to every aspect of your life. We communicate with ourselves when we psych ourselves up for big moments and talk ourselves into or out of various courses of action. We communicate with others to build and sustain personal relationships, perform our jobs, advance in our careers, and participate in social and civic activities. Even when we're not around other people, we are involved in communication as we interact with mass media and social media. All facets of our lives involve communication.

Although we communicate continually, we aren't always effective. People who do not have strong communication knowledge and skills are limited in their efforts to achieve personal, social, professional, and civic goals. In contrast, people who communicate well have a strong advantage in all spheres of life. For this reason, learning about communication and developing your skills as a communicator are keys to a successful and fulfilling life.

Communication Mosaics is written for anyone who wants to learn about human communication. If you are a communication major, this book and the course it accompanies will give you a firm foundation for advanced study. If you are majoring in another discipline, you will gain a basic understanding of communication, and you will have opportunities to strengthen your skills as a communicator, which will help you throughout life.

This first chapter provides an overview of the book and the discipline of communication. To open the chapter, I first introduce myself and point out the perspective and features of the book. Second, I describe how communication is related to our personal, social, civic, and professional life. Third, I define communication and discuss progressively sophisticated models of the communication process. Fourth, I identify careers that people with strong backgrounds in communication are qualified to pursue. Finally, we discuss connections between communication and digital media.

An Introduction to the Author

As an undergraduate, I enrolled in a course much like the one you're taking now. In that course, I became fascinated by the field of communication, and my interest has endured for more than 40 years. Today, I am still captivated by the field—more than ever, in fact. I see communication both as a science that involves skills and knowledge and as an art that reflects human imagination and wisdom. Because communication is central to our lives, it is one of the most dynamic, fastest-growing fields.

When I was a student, I always wondered about the authors of my textbooks. Who were they? Why did they write the books I was assigned to read? Unfortunately, the authors never introduced themselves. I want to start our relationship differently by telling you something about myself. I am a middle-aged, middle-income, European-American woman who has strong spiritual beliefs and a deep commitment to education. For 40 years, I have been married to Robbie (Robert) Cox, a professor and a leader in the national Sierra Club.

As is true for all of us, who I am affects what I know and how I think, feel, and communicate. Therefore, some of what you'll read in this book reflects what I have learned in my research, teaching, and life. I grew up in a small rural town in the South. I also grew up in an era marked by movements for civil rights and women's rights, which shaped my values and fueled my commitment to civic engagement. I learned early that my experiences are not the only source of knowledge. I talk with others who have different perspectives than my own and I look to scholars to augment my direct observations and experiences. The hundreds of references at the end of this book have shaped both my understanding of human communication and the way I introduce you to the field.

Other facets of my identity also influence what I know and how I write. My thinking is influenced by my roles as a daughter, sister, romantic partner, friend, aunt, teacher, scholar, and member of civic groups. On a broader level, I am defined by the categories that Western culture uses to classify people—for instance, race, gender, socioeconomic level, and sexual orientation. The groups I belong to have given me certain experiences and insights and, conversely, I lack the experiences and insights that come with membership in other groups. As a woman, I understand discrimination based on sex because I've experienced it multiple times. Being middle class has shielded me from personal experience with hunger, poverty, and bias against the poor; and being heterosexual has spared me from being the direct target of homophobia and understanding how it feels to be marginalized because of my sexual identity. Because Western culture tends to treat whites as the norm, not as a distinct racial category, I was not socialized to think about my race and its meaning. However, critical race theorists have taught me to interrogate whiteness as fully as any other racial category.

Although I can use cultural categories to describe myself, they aren't as clear or definitive as we sometimes think. For instance, the category "woman" isn't as homogenous as the single noun suggests. Women differ from one another because of race–ethnicity, sexual orientation, socioeconomic status, ability and disability, and a range of other factors. Likewise, a particular race is not a homogenous category. Members of any race differ greatly as a result of factors such as ethnic background, gender, sexual orientation, socioeconomic status, spiritual and religious values, abilities and disabilities, and so forth. The same is true of people we can place in any category—they are alike in the particular way that defines the category, yet they are also different from one another in many ways.

Like me, your experiences and group memberships have shaped your identity and your perspectives. How are you similar to and different from others who belong to the same culturally defined groups in which you place yourself? If you are a man, for instance, how is your identity as a man influenced by your racial and ethnic background, socioeconomic status, sexual orientation, spiritual commitments, and so forth? What insights do your experiences and identity facilitate and hamper?

Although our identities limit what we personally know and experience, they don't completely prevent us from gaining insight into people and situations that are different from our own. As I mentioned before, critical race theorists have taught me to think analytically about whiteness as a racial category. Mass media and computer-mediated communication (CMC) give me knowledge of diverse people and situations all over the world. All of these resources allow me—and you, if you choose—to move beyond the limits of personal identity and experience to appreciate and participate in the larger world. What we learn by studying and interacting with people from different cultures and social communities expands our appreciation of the richness and complexity of humanity. In addition, interacting with people whose lives and communication differ from our own enlarges our repertoires of communication skills.

The Value of Studying Communication

Communication is one of the most popular undergraduate majors (McKinney, 2006; Schmitt, 2014). One reason for this popularity is the relevance of communication knowledge and skills to success in all aspects of life. In order to advance in professional life, you'll need to know how to present your ideas effectively, build good relationships with colleagues, monitor your perceptions, manage conflicts constructively, and listen thoughtfully. To have healthy, enduring personal relationships, you'll need to know how to communicate support, deal with conflicts, and understand communication styles that are different from your own. To be an engaged citizen, you'll need critical thinking skills and the verbal ability to express your own points of view. In short, communication skills are vital to personal and professional well-being and to the health of our communities and society.

Because you've been communicating all your life, you might ask why you need to study communication formally. One reason is that formal study can improve skill. Some people have a natural talent for music or athletics. Yet they can become even better musicians or athletes if they take voice lessons or study theories of offensive and defensive play. Likewise, even if you communicate well now, learning about communication can make you more effective.

Personal Life

We develop our personal identities through the process of interacting with others (Mead, 1934). In our earliest years, our parents told us who we were: "You're smart," "You're so strong," "You're such a clown." We first see ourselves through the eyes of others, so their messages form the foundations of our self-concepts. Later, we interact with teachers, friends, romantic partners, and co-workers who communicate their views of us. In addition, we learn who we are and how others perceive us as we engage mass communication and social media.

The profound connection between communication and identity is dramatically evident in children who are deprived of human contact. Case studies of children who

Ghadya Ka Bacha

Ghadya Ka Bacha, or the "wolf boy," was found in 1954 outside a hospital in Balrampur, India. He had callused knees and hands, as if he moved on all fours, and he had scars on his neck, suggesting he had been dragged about by animals.

Ramu, which was the name the hospital staff gave the child, showed no interest in others but became very excited once when he saw wolves on a visit to a zoo. Ramu lapped his milk instead of drinking as we do, and he tore apart his food.

Most doctors who examined Ramu concluded that he had been socialized by wolves and therefore acted like a wolf, not a person (Shattuck, 1980).

© Hulton Archive/Getty Images

 In this photo, Ramu is eating raw meat. What do Ramu's behaviors suggest about how we develop self-concepts? Would you define Ramu as a human or a wolf?

have been isolated from others for a long time show that they have no concept of themselves as humans, and their mental and psychological development is severely hindered by lack of language. The ENGAGE! box on this page presents a dramatic example of what can happen when human infants are deprived of interaction with other humans. A large body of research shows that social isolation is as dangerous to health as high blood pressure, smoking, obesity, or alcoholism (Holt-Lunstad, Smith, & Layton, 2010).

Substantial research shows that communicating with others promotes personal health, whereas social isolation is linked to stress, disease, and early death (Fackelmann, 2006; Kupfer, First, & Regier, 2002; McClure, 1997). College students who are in committed relationships have fewer mental health problems and are less likely to be obese (Braithwaite, Delevi, & Fincham, 2010). Heart disease is more common among people who lack strong interpersonal relationships (Ornish, 1998), and cancer patients who are married live longer than single cancer patients ("Cancer," 2009). Clearly, healthy interaction with others is important to our physical and mental well-being.

Personal Relationships

Daniel Goleman, author of *Social Intelligence* (2007), says humans are "wired to connect" (p. 4). And communication—verbal and nonverbal, face to face or mediated—is the primary way that we connect with others. For that reason, effective communication is the heart of personal relationships. We build connections with others by revealing our private identities, asking questions, working out problems, listening, remembering shared history, and making plans for the future. To learn more about Daniel Goleman's work, go to the online resources for this chapter.

A primary distinction between relationships that endure and those that collapse is effective communication. Couples who learn how to discuss their thoughts and feelings, listen mindfully, adapt to each other, and manage conflict constructively tend to sustain intimacy over time. Friends also rely on good communication to keep in touch, provide support, and listen sensitively, and families that practice good communication are more cohesive and stable (Galvin, Braithwaite, & Bylund, 2015). Communication in personal relationships does a lot more than solve problems or allow partners to make personal disclosures. For most of us, everyday talk and nonverbal interaction are the essence of relationships (Schmidt & Uecker, 2007; Wood & Duck, 2006a,b). Although dramatic moments affect relationships, it is our unremarkable, everyday interaction that sustains the daily rhythms of our intimate connections (Duck & McMahon, 2012; Goleman, 2011; Wood & Duck, 2006a,b). Partners weave their lives together through small talk about mutual friends, daily events, and other mundane topics. Couples involved in long-distance romances miss being able to share small talk.

In addition to studying how communication enhances relationships, interpersonal communication scholars investigate the role of communication in destructive relationship patterns such as abuse and violence. Teresa Sabourin and Glen Stamp (1995) have identified strong links between verbal behaviors and reciprocal violence between spouses. Other communication scholars (Lloyd & Emery, 2000; Wood, 2001b, 2004b) have documented a range of social and interpersonal influences on violence between intimates.

Sandy's comment is the first of many student voices you'll encounter in this book. In my classes, students teach me and each other by sharing their insights, experiences, and questions. Because I believe students have much to teach us, I've included reflections written by students at my university and other campuses. As you read these, you will probably identify with some, disagree with others, and be puzzled by still others. Whether you agree, disagree, or are perplexed, I think you will find that the student voices expand the text and spark thought and discussion in your class and elsewhere. I also welcome your comments about issues that strike you as you read this book. You may send them to me in care of Cengage Learning, 20 Channel Center Street, Boston, MA 02210.

 Sandy

When my boyfriend moved away, the hardest part wasn't missing the big moments. It was not talking about little stuff or just being together. It was like we weren't part of each other's life when we didn't talk about all the little things that happened or how we felt or whatever.

Professional Life

Communication skills are critical for success in professional life. The value of communication is clearly apparent in professions such as teaching, law, sales, and counseling, where talking and listening are central to effectiveness.

In other fields, the importance of communication may be less obvious, but it is nonetheless present. Leaders at organizations such as *The New York Times*, FedEx, and GlaxoSmithKline list communication as vital to their organizations' success (O'Hair & Eadie, 2009). Health-care professionals rely on communication skills to talk with patients about medical problems and courses of treatment and to gain cooperation from colleagues, patients, and families for continued care. Doctors who do not listen well are less effective in treating patients, and they're more likely to be sued than doctors who do listen well (Beckman, 2003; Levine, 2004; Milia, 2003). Further, good communication between doctors and patients and among medical staff is related to effective treatment of patients (Rosenbaum, 2011; Salas & Frush, 2012). The pivotal role of communication in healthcare makes it unsurprising that an increasing number of medical schools base admissions, in part, on applicants' communication skills, especially their ability to work in teams (Harris, 2011).

It's not surprising that most employers list communication skills as one of the top qualities in job candidates (Hart Research, 2013; Rhodes, 2010; Selingo, 2012). Even highly technical jobs require communication skills. Specialists have to be able to listen carefully to their clients and customers in order to understand their needs and goals. Specialists also need to be skilled in explaining technical ideas to people who lack their expertise. Ann Darling and Deanna Dannels (2003) asked engineers whether communication skills were important to their professional effectiveness. The engineers reported that their success on the job depended on listening well, presenting ideas clearly, and negotiating effectively with others. Fully 75 percent of the engineers said that communication skills had consequences for their career advancement. Sean, an older, returning student, makes this observation about the relevance of communication skills to his professional success:

Communication skills are critical for career success.

Sean

I'm taking this course because I need communication skills to do my job. I didn't think I would when I majored in computer science and went into technology development. But after two years, another guy and I decided to launch our own technical support company. We had trouble getting investors to provide start-up capital, because neither of us knew how to give an effective presentation. We had the tech skills but not the communication ones. Finally, we got our company launched and discovered that we didn't know much about how to supervise and lead either. Neither of us had ever taken courses in how to motivate and support people who work for you. So I'm taking this course as a night student, and I think it will make a major difference in how I do my job and whether our company succeeds.

Civic Life

Communication skills are vital to the health of our society. From painting on the walls of caves to telling stories in village squares to interacting on the Internet, people have found ways to communicate with each other to organize and improve their common social world (Keith, 2009). To be effective, citizens in a democracy must be able to express ideas and evaluate the ethical and logical strength of communication by public figures. To make informed judgments, voters need to listen critically to candidates' arguments and responses to questions. We also need to listen critically to proposals about goals for our communities, the institutions at which we work, and the organizations on which we depend for services.

Civic engagement is more than paying attention to politics and voting. It is also working with others—formally and informally, in small and large groups—to identify needs of communities and society and then to find ways of meeting those needs. John Dewey, a distinguished American philosopher, believed that democracy and communication are intricately connected. He argued that while democracy depends on citizens' voting, it is more basic and important that citizens interact. Dewey insisted

Bowling Together?

When Robert Putnam published *Bowling Alone* in 2000, it caused quite a stir. In it, he claimed that Americans are increasingly disconnected from one another and their communities. Putnam, a professor of public policy at Harvard, amassed evidence showing that Americans at the end of the 20th century were 25 to 50 percent less connected to others than they had been in the late 1960s.

Because he believed that diversity is a strength and that working together makes individuals and the country stronger, Putnam wanted to know what could bring us back together. Working with Lewis Feldstein, who has devoted his life to civic activism, Putnam began searching for examples of people who were connecting with each other to work on community and collective projects.

In *Better Together* (2003) Putnam and Feldstein present 12 stories of diverse people who are working together to build and strengthen their communities. Although the 12 examples are diverse—ranging from Philadelphia's Experience Corps, in which volunteers tutor children from impoverished backgrounds, to UPS: Diversity and Cohesion, which has changed the UPS company from one run almost exclusively by white males to one in which minorities and women have a strong presence in management—they have one thing in common: building and using social capital. The people involved in these efforts realize that they need to build networks of relationships and then draw on those networks to reach goals that are not attainable by individuals working (or bowling) alone.

To promote civic engagement, Putnam, Feldstein, and others established a Better Together initiative at Harvard University's Kennedy School of Government. If you'd like to learn more about building and using social capital, go to the Better Together website by going to the book's online resources for this chapter.

 To what extent do you agree with Putnam's claim that people are increasingly disconnected from one another?

that it's vital that citizens talk and listen to each other—they must share ideas, question each other's positions, debate and argue, and collaborate to build communities that are stronger than any individual could build. Without sustained, vigorous communication among citizens, democracy fails. To learn more about John Dewey and his philosophy, go to the book's online resources for this chapter.

Communication skills are especially important for effective interaction in an era of globalization, where we have daily encounters with people of different races, genders, sexual orientations, and traditions. Diversity in the United States, as elsewhere, is the norm. In 2000, 64 percent of Americans were Caucasian, but the prediction is that there will be no single majority race by 2043 (Cooper, 2012; Milbank, 2014). We live, work, and socialize with people who communicate differently than we do. Friendships and workplace relationships between people with different cultural backgrounds enlarge perspective and appreciation of the range of human values and viewpoints. Scott Page (2008), a professor of complex systems, points out that people with greatly different backgrounds and perspectives make for more productive, creative organizations. In much the same way that the health and evolution of a species depends on a rich genetic mixture, the well-being of human societies depends on diversity.

A recent survey shows that nearly half of first-year students at colleges and universities think that learning about other cultures is essential or very important (Hoover, 2010). Colleges and universities provide superb opportunities to get to know diverse people and to learn about their experiences, values, and cultural traditions.

The number of students from countries other than the United States who enroll in U.S. colleges and universities is at its all-time high (McMurtrie, 2011).

 **Luanne**

I used to feel it was hard to talk with people who weren't raised in the United States like I was. Sometimes it seems that they have a totally different way of talking than I do, and we don't understand each other naturally. But I've been trying to learn to understand people from other places, and it really is making me realize how many different ways of communicating people have. With so many cultures now part of this country, nobody can get by without learning how to relate to people from other cultures.

 **David**

As an African-American male, I sometimes feel as though I am a dash of pepper on top of a mountain of salt. I have attended many classes where I was the only African American out of 50 or even 100 students. In these classes, the feeling of judgment is cast down upon me for being different. Usually what I learn about is not "people," like the course says, but white people. Until I took a communication course, the only classes that included research and information on African Americans were in the African-American curriculum. This bothered me because white Americans are not the entire world.

Luanne was a student in one of my courses, and David wrote to me after taking a basic communication course at a college in the western United States. Luanne's reflection shows that she is aware of the importance of understanding the communication of people from cultures that differ from her own. David's comment illustrates the importance of weaving diversity into the study of communication. Communication, then, is important for personal, relationship, professional, and civic life. Because communication is a cornerstone of the human experience, your decision to study it will serve you well.

Defining Communication

We've been using the word *communication* for many pages, but we haven't yet defined it clearly. **Communication** is a systemic process in which people interact with and through symbols to create and interpret meanings. Let's unpack this definition by explaining its four key terms.

> **communication** A systemic process in which people interact with and through symbols to create and interpret meanings.

 **U.S. Demographics in the 21st Century**

The United States is home to a wide range of people with diverse ethnic, racial, cultural, and geographic backgrounds. And the proportions of different groups are changing. Currently, one in three U.S. residents is a minority. By 2043, non-Hispanic whites will be a minority. The following shifts in the ethnic makeup of the United States are predicted to take place between 2010 and 2050 ("Demographics," 2009; Milbank, 2014; "Quick Facts, 2011"):

	2010 (%)	2050 (%)
Black	12.6	13.0
Asians	4.8	8.0
White, non-Hispanic	63.7	46.0
Hispanics & Latino/a	16.3	30.0
Other	3.0	5.0

Numbers do not total 100 percent because some respondents marked multiple categories.

 How do you think the predicted demographic changes might affect facets of culture such as personal relationships and work?

Process

Communication is a **process**, which means that it is ongoing and dynamic. It's hard to tell when communication starts and stops, because what happens before we talk with someone may influence our interaction, and what occurs in a particular encounter may affect the future. That communication is a process means it is always in motion, moving forward and changing continually.

Systems

Communication takes place within **systems**. A system consists of interrelated parts that affect one another. In family communication, for instance, each family member is part of the system (Galvin, Dickson, & Marrow, 2006). The physical environment and the time of day also are elements of the system. People interact differently in a classroom than on a beach, and we may be more alert at certain times of day than at others. The history of a system also affects communication. If a workplace team has a history of listening sensitively and working out problems constructively, then when someone says, "There's something we need to talk about," the others are unlikely to become defensive. Conversely, if the team has a record of nasty conflicts and bickering, the same comment might arouse strong defensiveness.

Because the parts of a system are interdependent and continually interact, a change in any part of a system changes the entire system. When a new person joins a team, he or she brings new perspectives that, in turn, may alter how other team members behave. The team develops new patterns of interaction and forms new subgroups; thus, team performance changes. The interrelatedness of a system's parts is particularly evident in intercultural communication. When a corporation moves its operations to a new country, changes infuse everything from daily interaction on the factory floor to corporate culture.

Systems are not collections of random parts, but organized wholes. For this reason, a system operates as a totality of interacting elements. A family is a system, or totality, of interacting elements that include family members, their physical locations, and their jobs and schools. Before systems theory was developed, therapists who worked with disturbed members of families often tried to "fix" the person who supposedly was causing problems in a family. Thus, alcoholics might be separated from their families and given therapy to stay sober. Often, however, the alcoholic resumed drinking shortly after rejoining the family because the behavior of the "problem person" was shaped by the behaviors of other family members and other elements of the family system.

In a similar manner, organizations sometimes send managers to leadership training programs but do not provide training for the manager's subordinates. When the manager returns to the office and uses the new leadership techniques, subordinates are distrustful and resistant. They were accustomed to the manager's former style, and they haven't been taught how to deal with the new style of leadership.

Because systems are organized wholes, they are more than simple combinations of parts. As families, groups, organizations, and societies evolve, they discard or adapt old patterns, generate new patterns, lose some members, and gain new members. When new topics are introduced on blogs, new bloggers join, some established members go silent, and patterns of communication are reconfigured. Personal relationships grow beyond the two original parts (partners) to include trust or lack of trust, shared experiences, and private vocabularies. Systems include not only their original parts but also changes in those original elements and new elements that are created as a result of interaction.

process An ongoing continuity, the beginning and end of which are difficult to identify; for example, communication.

system A group of interrelated elements that affect one another. Communication is systemic.

Systems vary in how open they are. **Openness** is the extent to which a system affects and is affected by outside factors and processes. Some tribal communities are relatively closed systems that have little interaction with the world outside. Yet most cultures are fairly open to interaction with other cultures. This is increasingly true today as more and more people immigrate from one culture to another and as people travel more frequently and to more places. The more open the system, the more factors influence it. Mass media and communication technologies expand the openness of most societies and thus the influences on them and their ways of life.

A final point about systems is that they strive for but cannot sustain equilibrium. Systems seek a state of equilibrium, or **homeostasis**. That's why families create routines, organizations devise policies and procedures, individuals develop habits, groups generate norms, online communities develop conventions and abbreviations, and cultures generate rituals and traditions.

Yet no living system can sustain absolute balance or equilibrium. Change is inevitable and continuous. Sometimes, it's abrupt (a company moves all of its operations to a new country); at other times, it's gradual (a company begins to hire people from different cultures). Sometimes, influences outside a system prompt change (legislation affects importing and exporting in other countries). In other cases, the system generates change internally (an organization decides to alter its marketing targets). To function and survive, members of systems must continually adjust and change.

Communication is also affected by the larger systems within which it takes place. For example, different cultures have distinct understandings of appropriate verbal and nonverbal behaviors. Many Asian cultures place a high value on saving face, so Asians try not to cause personal embarrassment to others by disagreeing overtly. It is inappropriate to perceive people from Asian cultures as passive if they don't assert themselves in the ways that many Westerners do. Arab cultures consider it normal for people to be nearer to one another when talking than most Westerners find comfortable, and, in Bulgaria, head nods mean "no" rather than "yes." Different regions of the same country may also have different ways of communicating as Steve notes in his commentary. Even within a single region, there are differences based on ethnicity, religion, gender, and other factors. Therefore, to interpret communication, we have to consider the systems in which it takes place. In Chapter 8, we'll discuss different communication practices in diverse cultures.

 Steve

It took me a long time to get used to Southerners. I'm from the Midwest and there we don't chat everybody up like Southerners do. We talk if we have something to say, but we don't talk just to talk. When I first moved here, I thought most of the people I met were real busybodies because people I hardly knew would say things like "you should come to my church" or "mark your calendar for the supper to raise money for schools" like I wanted to go to those. Then I started dating a girl who was born near here and she "decoded" Southern culture for me. She explained that "you should come" is not a command, which is what it sounded like to me, but an invitation because Southerners want to be hospitable and include everyone. She also told me I was being perceived as very standoffish because I didn't chat back like Southerners do.

Symbols

Communication is symbolic. We don't have direct access to one another's thoughts and feelings. Instead, we rely on **symbols**, which are abstract, arbitrary, and ambiguous

openness The extent to which a system affects and is affected by its surrounding environment.

homeostasis A state of equilibrium that systems strive for but cannot sustain.

symbols Arbitrary, ambiguous, and abstract representations of phenomena. Symbols are the basis of language, much nonverbal behavior, and human thought.

meaning The significance we attribute to a phenomenon; what it signifies to us.

content level of meaning One of two levels of meaning; the literal information in a message.

relationship level of meaning One of the two levels of meaning in communication; expresses the relationship between communicators.

representations of other things. We might symbolize love by giving a ring, by saying "I love you," or by closely embracing someone. A promotion might be symbolized by a new title and a larger office (and a raise!). In Chapter 4, we'll look more closely at symbols. For now, just remember that human communication involves interaction with and through symbols.

Meanings

Finally, our definition focuses on **meanings**, which are at the heart of communication. Meanings are the significance we bestow on phenomena, or what they signify to us. Meanings are not inherent in experience itself. Instead, we use symbols to assign meanings to experience. We ask others to be sounding boards so we can clarify our thinking, figure out what things mean, enlarge our perspectives, check our perceptions, and label feelings to give them reality. In all these ways, we actively construct meaning by interacting with symbols.

Communication has two levels of meaning (Pinker, 2008; Watzlawick, Beavin, & Jackson, 1967). The **content level of meaning** contains the literal message. If a person knocks on your door and asks, "May I come in?" the content-level meaning is that the person is asking your permission to enter. The **relationship level of meaning** expresses the relationship between communicators. In our example, if the person who asks, "May I come in?" is your friend and is smiling, you would probably conclude that the person is seeking friendly interaction. But if the person is your supervisor and speaks in an angry tone, you might interpret the relationship-level meaning as a signal that your supervisor is not satisfied with your work and is going to call you on the carpet. The content-level meaning is the same in both examples, but the relationship-level meaning differs.

The relationship level of meaning is often more important than the content level. The relationship level of meaning may affirm connection with another person (Gottman & DeClaire, 2001). For example, this morning Robbie said to me, "I've got a meeting at noon, so I won't be home for lunch." The content-level meaning is obvious—Robbie is informing me of his schedule. The relationship-level meaning, however, is the more important message that Robbie wants to stay connected with me and is aware that we usually eat lunch together. Likewise, the content level of meaning of text messages is often mundane, even trivial: <waz up?> <not much here. U?> On the relationship level of meaning, however, this exchange expresses interest and a desire to stay in touch. The Engage box on the right invites you to pay attention to both levels of communication in your interactions.

Models of Communication

To build on our definition of communication, we'll now consider models of the human communication process. Over the years, scholars in communication have developed a number of models that reflect increasingly sophisticated understandings of the communication process.

Linear Models

Harold Laswell (1948) advanced an early model that described communication as a linear, or one-way, process in which one person acts on another person. This is also called a *transmission model* because it assumes that communication is transmitted in a

TAKE ACTION...activities are located at the end of this chapter and online.

straightforward manner from a sender to a receiver. This verbal model consists of five questions:

Who?

Says what?

In what channel?

To whom?

With what effect?

Claude Shannon and Warren Weaver (1949) refined Laswell's model by adding the concept of **noise**, which is anything that interferes with the intended meaning of communication. Noise may distort understanding. Figure 1.1 shows Shannon and Weaver's model. Although linear, or transmission, models such as these were useful starting points, they are too simplistic to capture the complexity of human communication.

Interactive Models

The major shortcoming of the early models was that they portrayed communication as flowing in only one direction, from a sender to a receiver. The linear model suggests that a person is only a sender or a receiver and that receivers passively absorb senders' messages. Clearly, this isn't how communication occurs.

When communication theorists realized that listeners respond to senders, they added **feedback** to their models. Feedback is a response to a message. Wilbur Schramm (1955) pointed out that communicators create and interpret messages within personal fields of experience. The more communicators' fields of experience overlap, the better they understand each other. Adding fields of experience to models clarifies why misunderstandings sometimes occur. You jokingly put down a friend, and he takes it seriously and is hurt. You offer to help someone, and she feels patronized (Figure 1.2).

Transactional Models

Although the interactive model was an improvement over the linear one, it still didn't capture the dynamism of human communication. The interactive model portrays

noise Anything that interferes with the intended meaning of communication; includes sounds (e.g., traffic) as well as psychological interferences (e.g., preoccupation).

feedback Verbal or nonverbal response to a message. The concept of feedback as applied to human communication appeared first in interactive models of communication.

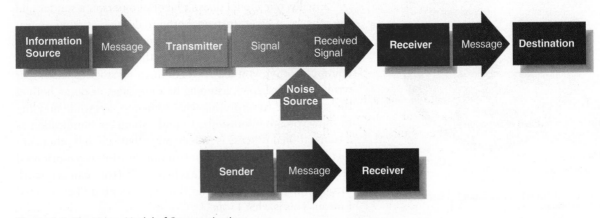

Figure 1.1 The Linear Model of Communication
Source: From Claude Shannon and Warran Weaver, *The Mathematical Theory of Communication.* Copyright 1949, 1998 by the Board of Trustees of the University of Illinois. Used with permission of the authors and the University of Illinois Press.

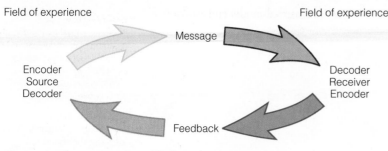

Field of experience   Field of experience

Figure 1.2 The Interactive Model of Communication
Source: Adapted from Schramm, 1955.

communication as a sequential process in which one person communicates to another, who then sends feedback to the first person. Yet people often communicate simultaneously. Also, the interactive model designates one person as a sender and another person as a receiver. In reality, communicators both send and receive messages. While handing out a press release, a public relations representative watches reporters to gauge their interest. The "speaker" is listening; the "listeners" are sending messages.

A final shortcoming of the interactive model is that it doesn't portray communication as changing over time as a result of what happens between people. For example, new employees are more reserved in conversations with co-workers than they are after months on the job, during which they get to know others and learn organizational norms. Figure 1.3 is a transactional model that highlights the features we have discussed.

Consistent with what we've covered in this chapter, our model includes noise that can distort communication. Noise includes sounds, such as a lawn mower or background chatter, as well as interferences within communicators, such as biases and preoccupation that hinder effective listening. In addition, our model represents communication as a continually changing process. How people communicate varies over time and in response to their history of relating.

The outer lines on our model emphasize that communication occurs within systems that affect what and how people communicate and what meanings they create. Those systems, or contexts, include the shared systems of the communicators (campus, town, culture) and the personal systems of each communicator (family, religious and civic associations, friends). Also note that our model, unlike previous ones, portrays each person's field of experience and his or her shared fields of experience as changing over time. As we encounter new people and grow personally, we alter how we interact with others.

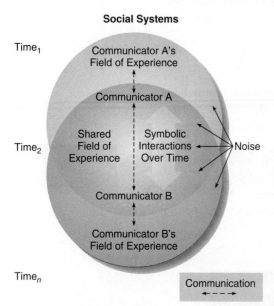

Figure 1.3 A Transactional Model of Communication
Source: Adapted from Wood, 1997, p. 21.

Finally, our model doesn't label one person a sender and the other a receiver. Instead, both are defined as communicators who participate equally, and often simultaneously, in the communication process. This means that at a given moment in communication, you may be sending a message (speaking or wrinkling your brow), listening to a message, or doing both at the same time (interpreting what someone says while nodding to show you are interested). To understand communication as a transactional process is to recognize that self and others are involved in a shared process: Communication is *we*-oriented (How can we understand each other? How can we work through this conflict?) rather than *me*-oriented (This is what I mean. This is what I want.).

In summary, the most accurate model of communication represents it as a transactional process in which people interact with and through symbols over time to create meaning.

Careers in Communication

You may wonder what kinds of careers are open to people with strong backgrounds in communication. As we've seen, communication skills are essential to success in most fields. Attorneys, accountants, bankers, doctors, and other professionals need communication skills to be effective. In addition, people who major in communication are particularly equipped for certain careers.

Research

Communication research is a vital and growing field of work. Many faculty members combine teaching and research. In this book, you'll encounter a good deal of academic research that helps us understand how communication works—or fails to work.

In addition to academic research, communication specialists help organizations by studying processes such as message production and marketing. Companies want to know how people respond to advertisements, logos, and product names. Communication researchers also assist counselors by investigating the ways in which communication helps and harms relationships.

Education

Teaching others about communication is another exciting career path for people with extensive backgrounds in the field. Across the nation, communication teachers at all levels are in demand. Secondary schools, junior colleges, colleges, universities, technical schools, and community colleges offer communication classes.

The level at which people are qualified to teach depends on how extensively they have pursued the study of communication. Generally, a bachelor's degree in communication education and a teaching certificate are required for teaching in elementary, middle, and high schools. A master's degree in communication qualifies a person to teach at community colleges, technical schools, and some junior colleges. The doctoral degree in communication generally is required of university faculty, although some universities offer nontenured, fixed term positions to people with master's degrees.

Although generalists are preferred for many teaching jobs, college-level faculty members often specialize in certain areas of communication. For instance, my research and teaching focus on interpersonal communication and gender and communication. Other college faculty members specialize in areas such as intercultural communication, family communication, health communication, and organizational dynamics.

Communication educators are not limited to communication departments. In recent years, more and more people with advanced degrees in communication have taken positions in medical and business schools. Doctors need training in listening sensitively to patients, explaining complex problems and procedures, and providing comfort, reassurance, and motivation. Similarly, good business people know not only their businesses but also how to explain their businesses to others, how to present themselves and their companies or products favorably, and so on.

The Nonprofit Sector

Communication skills and knowledge are vital to careers in the nonprofit sector. Former students of mine who are in nonprofit careers are working with homeless citizens, securing housing for poorer citizens, advancing environmental goals, and teaching literacy. Jobs such as these require strong communication skills. You have to be willing and able to listen and learn from people who are quite different from you in their backgrounds, goals, abilities, and dreams. You must know how to encourage, motivate, and support others and how to build strong teams of staff and volunteers. You must be able to establish a climate of mutual trust and respect with populations that—often for good reason—don't easily trust others. All of these are communication skills.

Mass and Digital Communication: Journalism, Broadcasting, Public Relations, and Advertising

Strong communication skills are necessary for careers in journalism, public relations, broadcasting, and advertising (Ihlen, Fredrikson, & van Ruler, 2009; Nerone, 2009; Smith, 2009). Good journalists know how to listen carefully and critically when conducting interviews. They also know how to write clearly, whether for newspapers or blogs, so that readers are drawn to their stories and speak effectively so viewers understand what their broadcast reports.

Effective public relations depend on understanding actual and potential clients and consumers and adapting messages to their interests, goals, and concerns. Effective advertising professionals help companies brand products so that consumers associate a product with a particular key message or theme. McDonald's advertising team has been effective in branding McDonald's as family-friendly; Porsche is branded as "the ultimate driving experience"; and Nike is identified with the "just do it" attitude.

Training and Consulting

Consulting is another career that welcomes people with backgrounds in communication. Businesses train employees in group communication skills, interview techniques, and interpersonal interaction. Some large corporations have entire departments devoted to training and development. People with communication backgrounds often join these departments and work with the corporation to design and teach courses or workshops that enhance employees' communication skills.

In addition, communication specialists may join or form consulting firms that provide communication training to governments and businesses. One of my colleagues consults with nonprofit organizations to help them develop work teams that interact effectively. Other communication specialists work with politicians to improve their presentational styles and sometimes to assist in writing their speeches. I consult with attorneys as an expert witness and a trial strategist on cases involving charges of sexual harassment and sex discrimination. Other communication consultants work with attorneys on jury selections and advise lawyers about how dress and nonverbal behaviors might affect jurors' perceptions of clients.

ENGAGE!

Careers in Communication

Learn more about careers open to people with strong training in communication. The National Communication Association publishes *Pathways to Careers in Communication*. In addition to discussing careers, this booklet provides useful information on the National Communication Association and its many programs. Visit the National Communication Association's website using the link provided in the online resources for this chapter.

Human Relations and Management

Because communication is the foundation of human relations, it's no surprise that many communication specialists build careers in human development or in the human relations departments of corporations. People with solid understandings of communication and good personal communication skills are effective in public relations, personnel management, grievance management, negotiation, customer relations, and development and fund-raising.

Communication degrees also open doors to careers in management. The most important qualifications for management are not technical skills but the abilities to interact with others and to communicate effectively. Good managers know how to listen, express ideas, build consensus, create supportive climates, and balance tasks and interpersonal concerns in dealing with others. Developing skills such as these gives communication majors a firm foundation for effective management. The ENGAGE! box on page 16 shows you how to learn about careers in communication that might appeal to you.

Digital Media and Communication

In every chapter, we will explore connections between chapter content and digital media. The ideas we have discussed in this introductory chapter are related to social and online media in several ways. First, consider how the values of communication that we identified are achieved using digital media. For instance, we rely on social media to maintain personal relationships. On social networking sites such as Facebook, we post updates and photos that let friends know what's happening in our lives and to learn what is happening in others' lives. We also use social media to establish and maintain professional ties. LinkedIn, for example, allows people to network professionally. We also use online and social media to engage in civic life—signing online petitions, blogging about issues that matter to us, and reading online newspapers and the blogs of others whose opinions we respect.

You might also consider what the definition of communication implies for interacting via digital media. When we talk with people face-to-face, we are aware of their immediate physical context, which is not the case with much online and digital interaction. We may not know who else is present and what else is happening around a person we text. When the systems within which communication occurs are unknown to us, it's more difficult to interpret others. For instance, does a delayed response mean the person you texted is angry, is thinking over what you said, or is talking with people he or she is with? Also, because nonverbal communication is restricted online and especially digitally, we may miss out on meaning, particularly on the relationship level.

Our definition also emphasizes process—changes in communication that happen over time. Think about how online and digital communication have evolved in the course of the

Social media can enrich or compete with face-to-face communication.

past two decades. When e-mail first emerged, most people treated it much like letter writing: An e-mail started with "Dear" or "Hello" and ended with a closing such as "Thank you" or "Sincerely." As e-mail became more popular and as all of us were flooded with e-mail messages, the opening and closing courtesies largely disappeared. As e-mail traffic continued to increase, abbreviations started being used: BRB (be right back), LOL (laughing out loud), and so forth. Texting and tweeting brought more innovation in use of symbols. Vowels are often dropped; single letters serve for some words (u for you, r for are); and phrases, rather than complete sentences, are acceptable. The rules of grammar, syntax, and spelling have also been loosened by digital natives who assume the autocorrect function edits correctly.

Overview of *Communication Mosaics*

To provide a context for your reading, let me share my vision for this book. Its title reflects the idea that communication is an intricate mosaic composed of basic processes and skills that are relevant to the range of situations in which we interact. Although all of the basic processes and skills affect communication in every situation, the prominence of each one varies according to context. For instance, in public speaking, presentation style stands out, and communication climate is less obvious. Conversely, in team interaction, communication that nurtures a productive climate may be more pronounced than a commanding presentational style.

Communication Mosaics is divided into three parts. Part I includes this and one additional chapter that introduces the discipline of communication by explaining its history, research methods, contemporary breadth, and career options.

Part II introduces you to six basic communication processes, concepts, and skills:

- Perceiving and understanding others

- Engaging in verbal communication

- Engaging in nonverbal communication

- Listening and responding to others

- Creating and sustaining communication climates

- Adapting communication to cultural contexts

Part III explores seven communication contexts that are common in our lives:

- Communication with yourself

- Interaction with friends and romantic partners

- Communication in groups and on teams

- Communication in organizations

- Public speaking

- Mass communication

- Digital media

Summary

In this chapter, we've taken a first look at human communication. We noted its importance in our lives, defined communication, and discussed models, the most accurate of which is a transactional model that emphasizes the dynamism of communication. Next, we discussed career paths for people who develop strong communication skills. We then traced relationships between the foregoing topics and digital media. Finally, we previewed the remainder of the book so that you have a clear overall sense of what lies ahead.

Experience Communication Case Study

The New Employee

Apply what you've learned in this chapter by analyzing the following case study, using the accompanying questions as a guide. These questions and a video of the case study are also available online with your MindTap Speech for *Communication Mosaics*.

Your supervisor asks you to mentor a new employee, Toya, and help her learn the ropes of the job. After two weeks, you perceive that Toya is responsible and punctual, and she takes initiative on her own. At the same time, you note that she is careless about details: She doesn't proofread reports, so they contain errors in spelling and grammar, and she doesn't check back to make sure something she did worked. You've also noticed that Toya seems insecure and wants a lot of affirmation and praise. You want to give her honest feedback so she can improve her job performance, yet you are afraid she will react defensively if you bring up her carelessness. You ask Toya to meet with you to discuss her first two weeks on the job. The meeting begins:

You: Well, you've been here for two weeks. How are you liking the job?

Toya: I like it a lot, and I'm trying to do my best every day. Nobody has said anything, so I guess I'm doing okay.

You: Well, I've noticed how responsible you are and how great you are about being a self-starter. Those are real strengths in this job.

Toya: Thanks. So I guess I'm doing okay, right?

You: What would you say if someone suggested that there are ways you can improve your work?

Toya: What do you mean? Have I done something wrong? Nobody's said anything to me. Is someone saying something behind my back?

© Cengage Learning

1. What would you say next to Toya? How would you meet your ethical responsibilities as her mentor and also adapt to her need for reassurance?

2. What responsibilities do you have to Toya, to your supervisor, and to the company? How can you reflect thoughtfully about potential tensions between these responsibilities?

3. How would your communication differ if you acted according to a linear model of communication, as opposed to a transactional one?

Key Concepts

Practice defining the chapter's terms by using online flashcards.

communication, 9
content level of meaning, 12
feedback, 13
homeostasis, 11
meaning, 12
noise, 13

openness, 11
process, 10
relationship level of meaning, 12
symbol, 11
system, 10

Reflect, personalize, and apply what you've learned

Review, Reflect, Extend

The Reflect and Discuss, and Take Action features that follow will help you review, reflect on, and extend the information and ideas presented in this chapter. These resources, and a diverse selection of additional study tools, are also available online at the MindTap Speech for *Communication Mosaics*.

Reflect and Discuss

1. Form groups of five to seven. Have one third of groups use the linear model of communication to describe communication in your class. Have one third of groups use the interactive model to describe communication in your class. The final third of groups should use the transactional model to describe communication in your class. As a class, identify what each model highlights and obscures. Which model best describes and explains communication in your class?

2. Interview a professional in your field of choice. Identify the communication skills that he or she thinks are most important for success. Which of those skills do you already have? Which skills do you need to develop or improve? How can you use this book and the course it accompanies to develop the skills you need to be effective in your career?

3. Go to the placement office on your campus and examine descriptions of available positions. Record the number of job notices that call for communication skills.

TAKE ACTION

1. Noticing Levels of Meaning in Communication

The next time you talk with a close friend, notice both levels of meaning.

- What is the content-level meaning?
- To what extent are liking, responsiveness, and power expressed on the relationship level of meaning?

Recommended Resources

1. Visit the website of the National Communication Association (NCA), which can be accessed by going to the book's online resources for this chapter. Click links to learn about the mission, history, and programs that the NCA offers. Click on Educational Resources and then on Communicating Common Ground under the Education tab to learn about NCA's service learning project in which many students are involved.

2. Watch the film *An Unfinished Life*. Analyze the communication among the four main characters, with a focus on the system within which they operate. What are the elements of the system? Identify two changes in the relationship system, and then trace how those changes affect all parts of the system as the film evolves.

3. Visit the Center for Communication and Civic Engagement, which can be accessed by going to this chapter's online resources. At this site, you'll find information about Seattle's Student Voices Project, a one-year curriculum focused on civic education. Consider talking with administrators on your campus about a curriculum in civic engagement.

2

The Field of Communication from Historical and Contemporary Perspectives

There is more than a verbal tie between the words common, community, and communication.
—John Dewey

What similarity can you identify among the words *common, community,* and *communication?*

MindTap

Learning Objectives

MindTap

Start with a quick engagement activity and **review** the chapter Learning Objectives.

Topics Covered in This Chapter	After studying this chapter, you should be able to . . .
The History of the Communication Field	Given historical milestones outlined in the text, explain how the field of communication responds to the changing character and needs of individuals and society.
Conducting Research in Communication	Recognize the four primary approaches to communication research.
The Breadth of the Communication Field	Identify the eight primary areas of the modern communication field.
Unifying Themes in the Communication Field	Discuss three themes that unify the diverse areas that comprise the field of communication.
Digital Media and Communication	Reflect on how the three unifying themes of communication relate to digital communication.

Read, highlight, and take notes online.

My father loved to tell me stories about my ancestors—his parents, grandparents, and great-grandparents. When I was seven years old and bored with his stories, I asked my father what any of that "ancient history" had to do with me. He responded by telling me that the family members who came before me shaped his identity and my own. He went on to tell me that I couldn't understand who I was without understanding the history of my family.

At the time, I didn't fully appreciate my father's wisdom, but I did start listening with more attention to his stories of our family history. In the years that followed, I realized he was right. My father's parents and grandparents had been farmers. Although he became an attorney, my father retained a deep love of animals and land, which he passed on to me and my siblings. I discovered that my impulsive personality was not new in the family; Charles Harrison Wood, my great-grandfather, had been known for being rash. Later, when it became clear that I had a keen talent for organizing, I felt a kinship with my father's mother, whose organizational skills had been well known in our home county.

Just as you can't fully appreciate who you are without knowing your family's history, you can't understand an academic discipline without learning about its history. This chapter introduces you to communication field's evolution. We first discuss the long and rich intellectual history of the discipline. Second, we discuss methods of conducting research that are used by communication scholars. The third section of the chapter surveys the major areas of the contemporary field and highlights themes that unify the different areas. The final section of the chapter applies what we've discussed to digital media.

The History of the Communication Field

As the title of this book suggests, communication is a mosaic, each part of which contributes to the overall character of the field. The mosaic has become more complex since the discipline's birth more than 2,500 years ago.

Classical Roots: Rhetoric and Democratic Life

One theme in the mosaic is that communication plays a vital role in democratic societies. The art of rhetoric was born in the mid-400s B.C. in the Grecian port city of Syracuse on the island of Sicily. At that time, the Sicilians had just overthrown the oppressive political regime led by a tyrant who had taken their land and impoverished them. After ousting the tyrant, the citizens established a democratic society. The first order of business was to regain property that the former government had taken from the people. A man named Corax, along with his pupil Tisias, taught citizens how to structure speeches, build arguments, and present cases for recovering their property in law courts. In other words, the communication field came into existence to answer a pressing need of citizens in a democracy.

Aristotle played a particularly key role in developing the first theories of rhetoric (Borchers, 2006). He understood that citizens could participate fully in democracy only if they were able to speak well and engage in discussion and debate about issues of the day. Building on the teachings of Corax and Tisias, other ancient teachers, notably Plato and Aristotle, taught their students how to analyze audiences, discover ideas and evidence to support claims, and organize and deliver speeches clearly and dynamically.

Learning from Ancient Theorists

You can study with great ancient rhetorical theorists online. To read *Gorgias,* one of Plato's most famous texts, and to read a summary of Aristotle's views of rhetoric, go to the book's online resources for this chapter.

One of the enduring contributions to our knowledge of rhetoric was Aristotle's thinking about how persuasion occurs. He theorized that there are three ways to persuade (Figure 2.1). **Ethos** is based on a speaker's credibility (trustworthiness, expertise, and good will). **Pathos** is appeals to listeners' emotions. **Logos** is logic and reasoning. If you think about your experiences in listening to speakers, you're likely to discover that, like people in Aristotle's time, you respond to ethos, pathos, and logos.

ethos One of the three forms of proof; proof based on the speaker's credibility (trustworthiness, expertise, and goodwill).

pathos One of the three forms of proof; proof based on appealing to listeners' emotions.

logos One of three forms of proof; proof based on logic and reasoning.

Liberal Education

Centuries after Aristotle taught, rhetoric held a premier spot in liberal education in Europe and the United States. By the 19th century, many of the most prestigious universities in the United States established chairs of rhetoric, held by distinguished scholars and civic leaders. Among these was President John Quincy Adams, who held the first Boylston Professor of Rhetoric Chair at Harvard University (Foss, Foss, & Trapp, 1991). In the 1800s and early 1900s, rhetoric was taught as a practical art that prepared people for responsible participation in civic life. The emphasis on teaching that marked this period explains why the first national professional organization, founded in 1914, was named the National Association of Teachers of Public Speaking.

In the 1900s, the communication discipline began to broaden beyond public speaking. In the early 20th century, philosopher John Dewey championed progressive thinking. For Dewey, this also meant championing communication in a broad sense. He realized that to have any impact on cultural life, progressive thinking must be communicated. In others words, people must be able to voice their ideas and to listen thoughtfully and critically to the ideas of others; they must talk, listen, debate, and discuss.

Dewey's interest in progressive thinking grew out of the political context of postwar America. After the two world wars, communication professionals felt an urgent need to understand the development of prejudice against social groups, willingness to follow authoritarian leaders such as Hitler, the effects of propaganda, and changes in attitudes and beliefs.

In the early 1900s, two major professional communication organizations were formed. The first was the Association for Education in Journalism and Mass Communication (AEJMC), which was founded in 1912. AEJMC promotes both academic and applied journalism, and it sponsors research journals and conferences on journalistic practice, scholarship, and teaching. Today, AEJMC has more than 3,500 members worldwide.

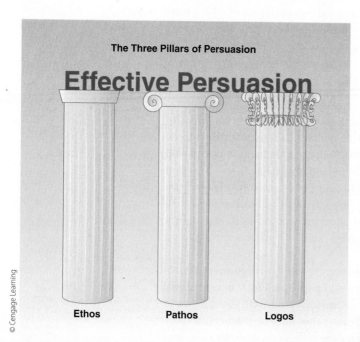

Figure 2.1 The Three Pillars of Persuasion

The second organization was founded in 1914. Because its original members were speech teachers, it was called Speech Teachers of America (STA). However, that name did not endure. The organization has changed its name three times, each change signaling evolution in the organization's scope and view of itself. The current name is the National Communication Association (NCA), and it has thousands of members in 20 countries.

In the mid-20th century, another part of the mosaic of communication was added: scientific, quantitative research, which gained prominence in almost all of the social sciences. The formation of the International Communication Association (ICA) in 1950 signaled a growing interest in scientific research in the communication field. Today, both NCA and ICA have international memberships, and both promote research of all types.

Broadening the Field

The 1960s and 1970s saw yet another addition to the communication mosaic. In the United States, this was a time of exceptional social and political upheaval. The civil rights movement and the second wave of the women's movement shook up long-standing patterns of personal and social relations. At the same time, youth culture ushered in new ideas about how people should interact and what was important in life. Many college students felt that personal relationships should receive more time and attention than the traditional curriculum provided. Responding to these currents in social life, the communication discipline expanded to include interpersonal communication. Many colleges and universities began to offer classes in family communication, nonverbal communication, and interaction in intimate relationships

Beginning in the 1960s and continuing to the present day, the relationship between communication and power in cultural life has become increasingly prominent in the communication mosaic. The tumultuous 1960s and 1970s were marked by social and political movements that questioned established power hierarchies. As mentioned above, two of the most notable of these movements were the civil rights movement, which challenged racial discrimination in the United States, and the women's movement, which challenged conventional gender roles in both public and private realms of life. Many scholars and teachers of communication embraced a critical focus on social movements and began to investigate the communicative

Communication is a primary tool in protests for social change.

dynamics that social movements employ and the ways in which social movements affect individuals and society.

The expansion of the field's interests to questions of power reflects the influence of French philosopher Michel Foucault (1970, 1972a, 1972b, 1978), who was deeply concerned with who is and who is not allowed to speak in a society. More specifically,

Foucault illuminated the ways in which culturally entrenched rules—often unwritten and unacknowledged—define who gets to speak, to whom we listen, and whose views are counted as important.

Building on Foucault's ideas, a number of communication scholars study the ways in which some people's communication is allowed and other people's communication is disallowed or disrespected. Equally, these scholars seek to empower people whose voices historically have been muted so that they can participate fully in public and private interactions that shape the character of personal and collective life. Consider one example. Historically, decisions about environmental issues that affect the health and environment of communities have been made almost entirely by privileged citizens: scientists and people in white-collar and technical professions. Left out of these vital discussions have been many blue-collar workers, unemployed or underemployed people, and citizens without formal education (Cox & Pezzullo, 2016; Martin, 2007). These citizens often are made voiceless by institutional barriers and administrative practices that define their concerns and their ways of speaking as inappropriate. Pezzullo (2007, 2008) and others (Agyeman, 2007; Norton, 2007; Sandler & Pezzullo, 2007) engage in research that increases our understanding of ways to empower those who suffer environmental hazards and who have not had a voice in their communities and the larger society.

Interest in the relationships between communication and power has reshaped many areas of the field. Rhetorical scholars have broadened their focus beyond individual speakers. Many of today's rhetorical scholars study gay rights, pro-life and pro-choice, environmental, and other social movements. They examine coercive tactics, symbolic strategies for defining issues (think of the power of terms such as *pro-choice* and *pro-life* compared with *pro-abortion* and *anti-abortion* or *pro-choice* and *anti-choice*), and how social movements challenge and change broadly held cultural practices and values.

Scholars in other areas of the field share an interest in how communication shapes and is shaped by the historical, social, and political contexts in which it occurs. Today, faculty in interpersonal and organizational communication conduct research and teach about how new technologies affect personal relationships and reshape societies, how organizational cultures and practices affect employees' productivity and job satisfaction, and how national trends such as downsizing and outsourcing affect workers' job commitment.

As this brief historical overview shows, the field of communication responds to the changing character and needs of individuals and society. Perhaps this is why the field has expanded, even during periods of downsizing at many colleges and universities. Just as Aristotle's students found that communication skills allowed them to participate in their society, today's communication faculty equip students with skills for understanding and participating in the present era.

Conducting Research in Communication

Like other scholarly disciplines, communication is based on knowledge gained from rigorous research (Baxter & Beebe, 2004; Carbaugh & Buzzanell, 2009; Reinhard, 2007). So that you can understand how scholars acquire knowledge, we'll discuss four primary approaches to communication research. These approaches are not incompatible; many scholars rely on multiple approaches. Further, even scholars who do not use multiple methods in their own research stay abreast of research that employs a range of methods.

Quantitative Research

Communication scholars rely on **quantitative research** to gather information in numerical form. One quantitative method, descriptive statistics, measures human behavior in terms of quantity, frequency, or amount. For example, researchers used descriptive statistics to show racial bias in children's books: Of 3,200 children's books published in 2013, only 93 were about black people (Myers, 2014).

A second method of quantitative research is surveys, instruments, questionnaires, or interviews that measure how people feel, think, act, and so forth. Surveys are valuable when a researcher wants to discover general trends among a particular group of people—members of an institution, for example, or Americans in general. Surveys often are used in organizations to gain information about employee morale, response to company policies, and job satisfaction. Once survey data are gathered, they may be analyzed using a variety of statistical methods.

A third method of quantitative research is experiment in which researchers measure how one variable (called the *independent variable*) that can be manipulated affects other variables (called *dependent variables*). Norman Wong and Joseph Cappella (2009) designed a series of experiments to test the effectiveness of different types of messages designed to persuade people to stop smoking. Some participants received messages that were high in threat and high in efficacy (claiming that smoking is dangerous and quitting is possible) whereas other participants received messages low in threat and efficacy. They found that the higher threat and efficacy message was more effective in motivating participants to seek help to quit smoking.

Qualitative Research

A second approach used by many scholars of communication is **qualitative research**, which provides nonnumerical knowledge about communication. Qualitative methods are especially valuable when researchers want to study aspects of communication that cannot easily be quantified, such as the meaning of experience, the function of rituals in organizational life, and how we feel about online communication (Schiebel, 2009). Three methods of qualitative research are most prominent in the communication discipline.

Textual analysis is the interpretation of symbolic activities—for example, how couples manage conflict or how attorneys interrogate witnesses. Texts are not limited to formal written texts or speeches, but also include AIDS quilt, community-building rituals among refugees, tours of toxic waste sites, self-disclosures in chat rooms on the Web, and stories told in families. In each case, communication practices are interpreted, rather than measured, to understand their significance.

Another qualitative method is *ethnography*, in which researchers try to discover what symbolic activities mean by immersing themselves in naturally occurring activities and natural contexts that have not been manipulated by researchers. By spending significant time in these contexts, ethnographic researchers are able to gain insight into the perspectives of those who are native to the context. At the center of ethnographic research is a commitment to understanding what communication means from the perspective of those involved rather than from that of an outside, uninvolved observer. Katy Bodey (Bodey & Wood, 2009) explored how girls in their late teens use social media to develop identities. She visited their blogs and sites, talked in-depth with girls about what they did online and why, and blogged herself. Bodey found that their blogs and pages on social sites are places where they talk about issues such as pressures to be

quantitative research
Techniques such as descriptive statistics, surveys, and experiments, used to gather quantifiable data.

qualitative research
Interpretive techniques, including textual analysis and ethnography, used to understand the character of experience, particularly how people perceive and make sense of communication.

skinny, drink (or not), have sex (or not), and dress particular ways. Bodey noticed that the girls were not just recording what they thought or did related to these pressures, but they were actually working out what they thought and wanted to do in the process of blogging or chatting online. In other words, social media were platforms for them to actively construct identities and get responses from others.

A third method of qualitative scholarship is *historical research*, which examines past events, people, and activities. Scholars rely on historical research to learn about the contexts in which ancient thinkers such as Aristotle developed their ideas. The data for historical scholarship include original documents, such as drafts of famous speeches and notes for revision, records that describe events and public reaction to them, and biographical studies of key figures.

Critical Research

A third approach to communication scholarship is **critical research,** in which scholars identify and challenge communication practices that oppress, marginalize, or otherwise harm individuals and social groups (Ono, 2009). In other words, critical research wrestles with power relationships and their impact.

Critical scholars perceive specific communication practices as means of reflecting, upholding, and sometimes challenging cultural ideology. For example, the practice of punching a time clock, used in many organizations, upholds the notion that workers must account for their time to those who have the means to own and run businesses. The meaning of punching a time clock is tied to an overall ideology that stipulates who has power over whom.

Some critical scholars contribute through original theorizing that helps us understand how certain groups and practices become dominant and how dominant ideologies sometimes are challenged and changed in a society. Other critical scholars engage in empirical work to reveal how particular practices function and whom they benefit and harm. For example, critical scholars have noted that women are underrepresented in films. Only 6 of 2013's 50 top-earning movies had a female lead character, and 20 percentage of all films in 2013 didn't have women as secondary characters (Duca, 2013). Critical media scholars also raise questions about how communication technologies shape individual thinking and social relationships and about who profits from digital media (Steiner-Adair, 2013).

Although the quantitative, qualitative, and critical approaches are distinct orientations to conducting research, they are not necessarily inconsistent or incompatible. In fact, scholars often rely on more than one research method in an effort to gain multifaceted understanding of what is being studied. Likewise, scholars often combine different kinds of data or theoretical perspectives to gain a fuller understanding of what is being studied than they would get from any single type of data or theoretical lens.

Studying phenomena in multiple ways is called **triangulation**. Communication researchers employ different types of triangulation. Data triangulation relies on multiple sources of data. For example, to study gender bias in sports reporting, researchers (Eastman & Billings, 2000) used three sources of data: *The New York Times,* CNN's *Sports Tonight,* and ESPN's *SportsCenter.* Researcher triangulation occurs when two or more researchers gather and analyze data so that the data are interpreted through multiple perspectives. Methodological triangulation involves using two or more methodologies to study a phenomenon. To study the relationship

critical research An approach to research that aims to identify, critique, or change communication practices that oppress, marginalize, or otherwise harm people.

triangulation Studying phenomena in multiple ways by relying on multiple sources of data, theories, researchers, and/or methodological approaches.

between stereotypical media messages about race and ethnicity, and consumers' social judgments of races and ethnicities, Dana Mastro (2003) employed both quantitative and critical methods.

Rhetorical Criticism

The final mode of research we will discuss, rhetorical criticism, dates back to the earliest teaching and research in the field. Rhetorical criticism is "the process of examining a text to see how it works communicatively" (Renegar & Malkowski, 2009, p. 51). However, as noted earlier, scholars have a broad view of what counts as a *message* or a *text*. In addition to speeches, texts include any and all symbolic activities—nonverbal actions and artifacts such as the Vietnam Veterans War Memorial, verbal but not vocal messages such as written messages and cartoons, films, images, web videos, and everyday performances of identity.

Rhetorical criticism aims to understand how particular texts work. How do they have impact—or fail to have impact—on listeners and viewers? Why do they have the impact they do, or not have the impact their creator intended? To answer such questions, a rhetorical critic first defines the object of criticism—what text is to be studied. Then, because all texts exist within contexts, the critic examines the context (social, economic, political, etc.) in which the text is situated.

Rhetorical critics have deepened our insight into pivotal texts, such as Elizabeth Cady Stanton's speech, "The Declaration of Sentiments," which was the keynote address at the first women's rights convention in 1848 (Campbell, 1989); Martin Luther King, Jr.'s 1963 "I Have a Dream" speech (Cox, 1989); and George W. Bush's on slavery at Goree Island (Medhurst, 2010).

In summary, communication scholars rely on quantitative and qualitative research, critical research, and rhetorical criticism. Each approach is valuable, and each has contributed to the overall knowledge that makes up communication as a scholarly discipline.

The Breadth of the Communication Field

As we have seen, the communication discipline has grown substantially since its beginnings in ancient Greece. The modern discipline can be classified into eight primary areas and a number of other areas that are part of curricula in some schools.

Intrapersonal Communication

Intrapersonal communication is communication with ourselves, or self-talk. You might wonder whether *intrapersonal communication* is another term for *thinking*. In one sense, yes. Intrapersonal communication does involve thinking because it is a cognitive process that occurs inside us. Yet because thinking relies on language to name and reflect on ideas, it is also communication (Vocate, 1994). Chiquella makes this point in her commentary.

 Chiquella

I figure out a lot of things by thinking them through in my head. It's like having a trial run without risk. Usually, after I think through different ideas or ways of approaching someone, I can see which one would be best.

intrapersonal communication
Communication with ourselves, or self-talk.

TAKE ACTION...activities are located at the end of this chapter and online.

One school of counseling focuses on enhancing self-esteem by changing how we talk to ourselves (Ellis & Harper, 1977; Rusk & Rusk, 1988; Seligman, 1990, 2002). For instance, you might say to yourself, "I blew that test, so I'm really stupid. I'll never graduate, and, nobody will hire me." This kind of talk lowers self-esteem by convincing you that a single event (blowing one test) proves you are worthless. Therapists who realize that what we say to ourselves affects our feelings urge us to challenge negative self-talk by saying, "One test is hardly a measure of my intelligence. I did well on the other test in this course, and I have a decent overall college record. I shouldn't be so hard on myself." What we say to ourselves can enhance or diminish self-esteem.

We engage in self-talk to plan our lives, to rehearse different ways of acting, and to prompt ourselves to do or not do particular things. Intrapersonal communication is how we remind ourselves to make eye contact when giving a speech, show respect to others ("I should listen to Grandmother's story"), check impulses that might hurt others ("I'll wait until I'm calmer to say anything"), and impress prospective employers ("I need to research the company before my interview").

Intrapersonal communication also helps us rehearse alternative scenarios and their possible outcomes. To control a disruptive group member, you might consider telling the person to "shut up," suggesting that the group adopt a rule that everyone should participate equally, and taking the person out for coffee and privately asking him or her to be less domineering. You think through the three options (and perhaps others), weigh the likely consequences of each, and then choose one to put into practice. We engage in internal dialogues continuously as we reflect on experiences, sort through ideas, and test alternative ways of acting.

Interpersonal Communication

A second major emphasis in the field of communication is interpersonal communication, which is communication between people. **Interpersonal communication** is not a single thing but rather a continuum that ranges from quite impersonal (interaction between you and a parking lot attendant) to highly interpersonal (interaction between you and your best friend) (Figure 2.2). The more we interact with a person as a distinct individual, the more interpersonal the communication is.

interpersonal communication
Communication between people, sometimes in close relationships such as friendship and romance.

Scholars of interpersonal communication study how communication creates and sustains relationships and how partners communicate to deal with the normal and extraordinary challenges of maintaining intimacy (Wood & Duck, 2006b). Researchers have shown that cross-sex friends engage in everyday talk less frequently than same-sex friends when communicating face-to-face and by phone. However, cross-sex and same-sex friends do not differ in how much they engage in everyday communication online (Ledbetter, Broeckelman-Post, & Krawsczyn, 2011).

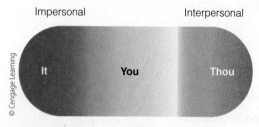

Figure 2.2 The Communication Continuum

Group and Team Communication

A third branch of the field is small-group and team communication. Research in this area focuses on leadership, member roles, group dynamics, agendas for achieving group goals, and managing conflict (Levi, 2010). Because groups involve more than one or two people, much teaching and research in this area focuses on how members coordinate their resources to arrive at collective decisions.

Public Communication

Public speaking remains an important branch of the communication field. Even though many people will not pursue careers that call for extensive formal speaking, many of us will be in situations where speaking up is a responsibility. My editor makes presentations to her sales representatives to explain what her books are about and how to spotlight important features to professors who may want to use them in their courses. I recently coached my doctor, who was asked to address her colleagues on a development in treatment of renal disease. My brother-in-law relies on public speaking skills to try cases in court, and my sister gives public speeches to raise money for a center for abused children. My editor, doctor, brother-in-law, and sister don't consider themselves public speakers, but public speaking is a part of their lives.

Within the area of public communication are subareas such as argumentation and political communication. Argumentation focuses on how to build effective arguments by using sound reasoning and strong evidence and by developing ideas in ways that respond to listeners' beliefs, concerns, and goals. Scholars of political communication are particularly interested in how politicians connect or fail to connect with voters, how political campaigns succeed or falter, how social movements build awareness of issues such as the environment (Cox & Pezzullo, 2016), and how rhetorical skills influence the process of policy making (Cox & McCloskey, 1996).

Organizational Communication

Communication in organizations is another growing area of interest. The work of communication scholars has identified communication skills that enhance professional success and traced the effects of various kinds of communication on morale, productivity, and commitment to organizations. Scholars of organizational communication focus substantial attention on **organizational culture**, which is understandings about an organization's identity and codes of thought and action that members of an organization share. Some organizations think of themselves as families. From this understanding emerge rules for how employees should interact and how fully they should commit to work.

Another area of increasing interest is personal relationships between co-workers. In addition to romantic relationships, co-workers may form friendships, which can become complicated if one person has higher status than the other or if one person is required to maintain confidentiality, which may be perceived as not trusting a friend.

 *Melbourne*

It was a real hassle when my supervisor and I started going out. Before, he gave me orders like he did all the other servers, and none of us thought anything about it. But after we started dating, he would sort of ask me, instead of tell me, what to do, like saying, "Mel, would you help out in section seven?" Another thing was that if he gave me a good station where tips run high, the other servers would give me trouble because they thought he was favoring me because we go out. And when he gave me a bad station, I'd feel he was being nasty for personal reasons. It was a mess being his employee and his girlfriend at the same time.

Mass Media

Mass media represent and influence cultural values. For instance, the use of young female models in ads and glamorous young women as reporters and news anchors perpetuates the cultural feminine ideal, which centers on youth and beauty. Films that

organizational culture
Understandings about identity and codes of thought and action that are shared by the members of an organization.

portray men as daring, brave, and violent perpetuate strength and boldness as masculine ideals.

As noted previously in this chapter, mass media sometimes reinforce cultural stereotypes about race and ethnicity. Communication scholars heighten awareness of how media shape—and sometimes distort—our perceptions of ourselves and society. Franklin's commentary addresses this point.

 Franklin

I hate the way television shows African Americans. Most of the time they are criminals or welfare cases or drunks or Uncle Toms. When I watch TV, I understand why so many people think blacks are dumb, uneducated, and criminal. We're not, but you'd never know it from watching television.

Computer-Mediated Communication

Scholars of computer-mediated communication study how newer technologies and the accompanying acceleration of the pace of interaction influence how we think and work and how we form, sustain, and end relationships. Some scholars caution that new technologies may undermine human community, whereas others celebrate the ways that mediated communication facilitates building community. Clearly, the verdict on digital media will not be in for some time. Meanwhile, we all struggle to keep up with our increasingly technological world. Today, students conduct much of their research on the Web or through specialized information services on the Internet, and friends and romantic partners text to stay in touch throughout the day. Communication scholars will continue to study whether emerging technologies merely alter how we communicate or actually change the kinds of relationships we build.

Intercultural Communication

Studying intercultural communication increases our insight into different cultures' communication styles and meanings. For example, an international student in one of my graduate classes seldom spoke up and wouldn't enter the heated debates that are typical of graduate classes. One day after class, I encouraged Mei-Ling to argue for her ideas when others challenged them. She replied that doing so would be impolite. Her culture considers it disrespectful to contradict others, particularly elders and teachers. In the context of her culture, Mei-Ling's deference did not mean that she lacked confidence.

One focus within intercultural communication research is different social communities within a single society. Cultural differences are obvious in communication between a Nepali and a Canadian. Less obvious are differences in communication between people who speak the same language. Within the United States there are distinct social communities based on race, gender, sexual orientation, and other factors. Members of social communities such as these often participate both in the overall culture of the United States and

© Andrew Rich/istockphoto.com

MindTap How do digital media change how we relate to others?

in the more specialized norms and practices of their communities. Recognizing and respecting different communication cultures increases personal effectiveness in a pluralistic society. Meikko's commentary reminds us of how cultural values are reflected in language.

 *Meikko*

What I find most odd about Americans is their focus on themselves. Here, everyone wants to be an individual who is so strong and stands out from everyone else. In Japan, it is not like that. We see ourselves as parts of families and communities, not as individuals. Here, I and my are the most common words, but they are not often said in Japan.

Scholars and teachers of intercultural communication do not limit their work to minority cultures and social communities. In addition, they study whiteness by examining what it means to be white. Members of dominant or majority groups often perceive their identities and communication as "standard" or "normal" and perceive the identities and communication of all other groups as different from those of majority groups. Studying whiteness as its own racial category helps us realize that white (and other dominant groups) is just as much a race–ethnicity as black or Native American, and that white communication practices are shaped by cultural influences as much as those of other groups are.

Other Curricular Emphases

The eight areas we have discussed are primary ones that are taught at most colleges and universities around the country. In addition to these widely accepted curricular offerings, there are other areas of communication that are emphasized at particular schools. These include ethics, health communication, journalism, performance studies, religious communication, and speech and hearing. Coursework in health communication is often offered at universities that have premier medical schools, and training in religious communication is desired at schools that have religious missions.

Blurring the Lines

The areas of the field that we've just discussed are not as discrete as they may seem. Just as technologies of communication have converged in significant ways, so, too, do areas of the communication discipline converge and interact. For example, my niece Michelle and I enjoy face time on our iPads. Our face time exchanges are both social media and interpersonal communication. Similarly, a CEO who hosts a company awards ceremony is simultaneously engaging in public speaking and team building.

The National Communication Association's magazine, *Communication Currents*, provides stories about research and teaching in many of the areas in the field of communication. The online resources for this chapter provide a link to this magazine.

Unifying Themes in the Communication Field

After reading about the many different areas of study in communication, you might think that the field is a collection of unrelated interests. That isn't accurate. Although there are distinct elements in the communication mosaic, common themes unify the diverse areas of the discipline, just as common colors and designs unify a tile mosaic.

Three enduring concerns—symbolic activities, meaning, and ethics—unify the diverse areas of communication.

Symbolic Activities

Symbols are the basis of language, thinking, and nonverbal communication. Symbols are arbitrary, ambiguous, and abstract representations of other phenomena. For instance, a wedding band is a symbol of marriage in Western culture, and a smile is a symbol of friendliness. Symbols allow us to reflect on our experiences and ourselves. Symbols also allow us to share experiences with others, even if they have not had those experiences themselves. We will discuss symbols in greater depth in Chapters 4 and 5, which deal with verbal and nonverbal communication, respectively.

Meaning

Closely related to interest in symbols is the communication field's concern with meaning. The human world is a world of meaning. We don't simply exist, eat, drink, sleep, and behave. Instead, we imbue every aspect of our lives with significance, or meaning. When I feed my cats, Rigby and Rowdy, they eat their food and then return to their feline adventures. However, we humans layer food and eating with meanings beyond the mere satisfaction of hunger. Food often symbolizes special events or commitments. For example, kosher products reflect commitment to Jewish heritage, and turkey is commonly associated with commemorating the first Thanksgiving in the United States (although vegetarians symbolize their commitment by *not* eating turkey). In some families meals are times for coming together and sharing lives, whereas in other families meals are battlefields where family tensions play out. Humans imbue eating and other activities with meaning beyond their functional qualities. Our experiences gain significance as a result of the values and meanings we attach to them.

Because we are symbol users, we actively interpret events, situations, experiences, and relationships. We use symbols to name, evaluate, reflect on, and share experiences, ideas, and feelings. In fact, as Benita's commentary points out, when we give names to things, we change how we think about them. Through the process of communicating with others, we define our relationships. Do we have a friendship, or something else? How serious are we? Do we feel the same way about each other? Is this conflict irresolvable, or can we work it out and stay together?

 Benita

It's funny how important a word can be. Nick and I had been going out for a long time, and we really liked each other, but I didn't know if this was going to be long term. Then we said we loved each other, and that changed how we saw each other and the relationship. Just using the word love transformed who we are.

To study communication, then, is to study how we use symbols to create meaning in our lives. As we interact with others, we build the meaning of friendship, team spirit, family, national identity, and organizational culture.

Ethics

ethics The branch of philosophy that deals with the goodness or rightness of particular actions. Ethical issues infuse all areas of the communication field.

A third theme that unifies the field of communication is concern with ethical dimensions of human interaction. **Ethics** is a branch of philosophy that focuses on moral principles and codes of conduct. What is right? What is wrong? What makes something right or wrong? Communication inevitably involves ethical matters because people affect each other when they interact (Makau, 2009). Therefore, it's important to think seriously about what moral guidelines we should follow in our communication and in our judgments of others' communication.

One ethical principle that is applicable to a broad range of situations is allowing others to make informed and willing choices. Adopting this principle discourages us from deceiving others by distorting evidence, withholding information, or coercing consent. Another important principle of ethical communication is respect for differences between people. Embracing this guideline deters us from imposing our ways and our values on others whose experiences and views of appropriate communication may differ from our own.

A third ethical principle is to take responsibility for our own communication and our responses to others' communication. You make choices when you communicate verbally and nonverbally. You choose whether to be diplomatic or blunt with a friend who asks your advice; you choose whether to listen carefully to a co-worker or zone out; you choose whether to be honest or deceptive in presenting yourself online. Each choice about communication has consequences, and those are your responsibility. We also choose how to interpret and respond to others' communication, so we should take responsibility for how we react. It is not ethical to say or think "he made me angry," or "she made me feel dumb." When we blame others for our own thoughts and feelings, we are not being ethical communicators.

Digital Media and Communication

The three unifying themes of communication are as relevant to digital media as to face-to-face communication. Symbols are the basis of digital communication just as they are of oral interaction. And symbols are just

 **Communication Ethics**

The National Communication Association encourages ethical communication. For that reason, the Association has a Credo for Ethical Communication. The Credo state: "Questions of right and wrong arise whenever people communicate. Ethical communication is fundamental to responsible thinking, decision making, and the development of relationships and communities within and across contexts, cultures, channels, and media. Moreover, ethical communication enhances human worth and dignity by fostering truthfulness, fairness, responsibility, personal integrity, and respect for self and others. We believe that unethical communication threatens the quality of all communication and consequently the well-being of individuals and the society in which we live. This chapter's online resources provide a link to three ethical statements, including the Credo.

 **Emoji**

The word *emoji* is a combination of two Japanese words: e (for picture) and moji (character). Although emoji are the latest social media graphics favored by tweeters, texters, and e-mailers, the use of pictures to communicate is certainly not new. Consider the following:

◆ 30,000 of years ago, people drew pictures on the walls of caves.

◆ In the 1400s, punctuation marks were standardized.

◆ By the Middle Ages, coats of arms were used to display familial heritage.

◆ Centuries ago, cartoons became popular.

◆ Computer icons first appeared in the 1980s.

◆ Emoticons were first used in 1982.

Emoji are the brainchild of Japanese telecommunications expert Shigetaka Kurita who based his social media characters on Japanese street signs (Steinmetz, 2014).

 Why do you think people have always found ways to express ideas through pictures as well as words?

as subject to ambiguity online as in face-to-face encounters. Have you ever had the experience of thinking a friend was angry because she or he sent a one-word reply to a text from you only to later discover the friend was simply rushed? Just as we share a language system for talking with others, we have a language for e-mails, texts, and tweets. Users quickly learn how to abbreviate, drop vowels, and adopt acronyms in order to "speak the language" of social media.

When we use digital media, we want to share meaning with others just as we do in face-to-face encounters. Because digital media don't allow many of the nonverbal cues that express feelings, we find ways to communicate emotions—emoticons, emoji, and stickers are symbols we've created to convey feelings.

The third unifying theme, ethics, applies to our use of digital media. In some ways, it is easier to be deceptive online than in face-to-face interaction. We can misrepresent our identities in chat rooms and social networking sites. Deceptions about age, appearance, race, and so forth are not immediately apparent. The fact that deception might not be detected doesn't free us of the ethical responsibility to be honest about who we are so that others can make free and informed choices about whether and how they want to interact with us.

Summary

Like most fields of study, communication includes many areas, which have evolved over a long and distinguished intellectual history. In this chapter, we reviewed the more than 2,500-year-old history of the discipline of communication and noted how it has changed over time. We also discussed types of research conducted by scholars of communication. We then described areas that are part of the modern field of communication, and we noted that these areas are unified by abiding interests in symbolic activities and meanings, as well as by a common interest in basic processes that form the foundations of personal, interpersonal, professional, civic, and mediated communication. The unifying themes of symbols, meaning, and ethics are as relevant to digital media as to our face-to-face communication. The foundations established in this chapter and in Chapter 1 prepare us for chapters that focus on basic processes and skills that pertain to a wide range of communication contexts.

Experience Communication Case Study

Communication Ethics

Apply what you've learned in this chapter by analyzing the following case study, using the accompanying questions as a guide. These questions and a video of the case study are also available online with your MindTap Speech for *Communication Mosaics*.

This case study differs from the others in this text because it is an actual interview, not an enacted fictional scenario. In the interview, Jenna Hiller asks Dr. Tim Muehlhoff some questions about communication and ethics, and Dr. Muehlhoff's responses elaborate on and clarify material covered in this chapter.

Student: In Chapter 2, Dr. Wood states that "ethical issues infuse all forms of communication." Can you explain what she means?

Professor: Well, in Chapter 2 she defines ethics as a branch of philosophy that's concerned with moral principles and conduct—what's right and

© Cengage Learning

Student: I'm still not sure I understand what you mean. I don't see how listening and responding to others involves ethical choices.

Professor: Well, my favorite quote about listening comes from Reuel Howe's book, *The Miracle of Dialogue*. In it, he says, "I cannot hear you because of what I expect you to say." And it's true, isn't it? We often judge people prematurely. We form unethical stereotypes of people, and then we respond to the stereotype rather than the person. For instance, when I was teaching at UNC-Chapel Hill with Julia Wood, there was a colleague of ours who was heavily criticized for using gangsta rap lyrics in a commencement address. And I was one of the critics. Even though I had not heard the speech, I thought to myself, "How can you use lyrics that are filled with anger, racism, and sexism?"—until I actually sat in on his class and listened to his rationale. I found out that this professor did not condone violence or sexism. He did argue that there's a lot we can learn about individuals by listening to their music. And I remember him saying once, "Hear the violence in those songs and condemn it. Hear the sexism, and condemn it. But also hear the pain and the hopelessness, and respond to it." You see, I had formed a caricature of this man, a stereotype—and that's unethical. Ethical communication means I allow you to speak for yourself, and then I respond to what you say—but I don't put words in your mouth and conform you to the image I want you to have.

what's wrong. But can you see how much personal choice is involved in that definition? Who gets to decide what is right and what is wrong? I was in Barnes & Noble a couple of months ago and saw a book called, *What Would Machiavelli Do? The Ends Justify the Meanness*. Now, you may remember that Machiavelli was one of the most ruthless politicians, and he lived in the early 1500s. He believed that success was the goal, and you should get it however you wanted to. And in the book, this author says, "This book is for people with the courage to leave decency and kindness behind, and seize the future by the throat and have it cough up money, power, and superior office space." So if Machiavelli is your ethical guide, then, when giving a speech, make up statistics. Plagiarize part of it, and say that it's your speech. When it comes to interpersonal communication, win an argument at all costs. Manipulate a person's emotions. If they've confided information to you, go ahead and use their words against them. In small-group communication, ignore a particular person you don't agree with. Every time they start to talk, you just interrupt them. But you know, Machiavelli's not our only choice. What would our communication look like if we asked the question, "What would Gandhi do?" or "What would Martin Luther King, Jr., do?" or "What would Jesus do?" How would that change how we communicate with people? We would choose what is right for everybody. We would choose to try to respect everybody. Machiavelli and Gandhi are some of the choices we have to make in all of our communication.

Student: Also in Chapter 2, Dr. Wood states that a principle for ethical communication is respecting differences between people. Am I supposed to just accept everyone and every value?

Professor: There's an old Jewish proverb that says, "It is folly and shame to speak before listening." The folly part I think we can understand. It's folly for me to respond to you if I don't know what you're saying. That's uninformed communication. The second part deals with ethics. It is shameful for me to respond to you before I listen. In other words, I view you as an inferior. I don't even need to listen to your perspective before I respond to it. Ethical communication does not mean that I have to accept the views of every person. It does mean that all my communication needs to be informed, and I treat people as equals, not as people who are inferior to me. In Chapter 7 Julia talks about communication climates—the overall mood between two people when they communicate. Now imagine what that communication climate would be like if our communication was both informed and respectful.

1. Dr. Tim Muehlhoff quoted the following statement from *The Miracle of Dialogue:* "I cannot hear you because of what I expect you to say." Recall some instances in your own life where you have been unable to hear what someone was saying because of your expectations and stereotypes of that person.

2. Dr. Muehlhoff also noted that he had seen a book entitled, *What Would Machiavelli Do? The Ends Justify the Meanness*. He then suggested that there are many people we might pick as our ethical guides. Whom would you pick as your guide for ethical communication? Fill in the blank in this sentence: What would ___ do? What ethical principles for communication follow from your choice of an ethical guide?

3. What ethical choices did Dr. Muehlhoff make in his conversation with Jenna Hiller about the relevance of ethics to communication?

4. Review "The New Employee," the case study for Chapter 1. What ethical choices did the senior employee make in communicating with Toya?

Key Concepts

Practice defining the chapter's terms by using online flashcards.

critical research, 28
ethics, 34
ethos, 24
interpersonal communication, 30
intrapersonal communication, 29
logos, 24

organizational culture, 31
pathos, 24
qualitative research, 27
quantitative research, 27
triangulation, 28

Reflect, personalize, and apply what you've learned

Review, Reflect, Extend

The Reflect and Discuss, and Take Action features that follow will help you review, reflect on, and extend the information and ideas presented in this chapter. These resources, and a diverse selection of additional study tools, are also available online at the MindTap Speech for *Communication Mosaics*.

Reflect and Discuss

1. Review the areas of communication discussed in the section on the breadth of the communication field. In which areas do you feel most competent as a communicator? In which areas do you feel less competent? Identify one goal for improving your communication competence that you can keep in mind as you read the rest of this book.

2. This chapter provides an overview of the field of communication and notes how it has evolved in response to social changes and issues. As a class, identify major changes you anticipate in U.S. society in the next 50 years. What kinds of changes in the field of communication might be prompted by the social changes you anticipate?

3. As a class, develop a survey to get experience collecting data. Develop a survey with two to three questions to learn about attitudes held by students on your campus toward a subject your class finds interesting. For instance, you might survey student attitudes regarding the values of college education (how important is college for (a) personal growth, (b) intellectual growth, and (c) career success?) or your campus's efforts to be environmentally responsible. After the class prepares the survey, each student should collect responses from 10 students. Then the class should tally all responses and discuss what the survey reveals.

TAKE ACTION

1. Analyze Your Self-Talk

Pay attention to the way you talk to yourself for the next day. When something goes wrong, what do you say to yourself? Do you put yourself down with negative messages? Do you generalize beyond the specific event to describe yourself as a loser or as inadequate? The first step in changing negative self-talk is to become aware of it. Try challenging negative self-talk and notice how doing so affects you.

2. Your Mediated World

How do personal and social media affect your relationships? How are texts and tweets different from face-to-face interactions? Have you made any acquaintances or friends through Facebook, Tumblr, Twitter, LinkedIn, or other social networks? Did those relationships develop differently from ones formed through face-to-face contact? Do you feel differently about people you have never seen and those you see face-to-face?

Recommended Resources

1. Josina Makau's thoughts on communication and ethics are important for all students in the field. An interview with her is available in this chapter's online resources.

2. Go to the book's online resources for this chapter and access NCA's online magazine, *Communication Currents*. You will find articles that reflect current research and teaching in the field.

3

Perceiving and Understanding

Reality is merely an illusion, albeit a persistent one.

—Albert Einstein

When the perceptions of you and a friend differ, how do you determine who is correct?

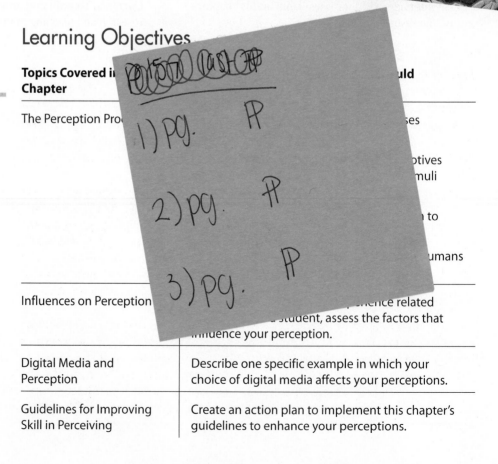

Learning Objectives

MindTap

Start with a quick engagement activity and **review** the chapter Learning Objectives.

Topics Covered in this Chapter	...you should...
The Perception Proc...	...ses
	...ptives ...muli
	...n to
	...umans
Influences on Perception	...ence related ...student, assess the factors that influence your perception.
Digital Media and Perception	Describe one specific example in which your choice of digital media affects your perceptions.
Guidelines for Improving Skill in Perceiving	Create an action plan to implement this chapter's guidelines to enhance your perceptions.

1) pg. ___
2) pg. ___
3) pg. ___

Read, highlight, and take notes online.

A few years ago, Robbie and I adopted a year-old dog who had been abandoned. Our new family member, whom we named Cassie, seemed small to us—she was fully grown and weighed just 35 pounds. Previously, we'd owned an Irish setter and a Lab mix, each of whom weighed about 70 pounds—twice Cassie's weight. A few weeks after Cassie joined us, my six-year-old nephew, Harrison, visited.

When Harrison walked into our home, Cassie ran to meet the new person and shower him with kisses. "She's so big!" Harrison shrieked as Cassie jumped on him, putting her paws on his shoulders so that her head was even with his. "She's a big, BIG dog," he announced. Because we were accustomed to dogs twice Cassie's size, and because Robbie and I are adults, Cassie seemed small to us. But to a boy who weighed 45 pounds and was less than 4 feet tall, she seemed large! Our perceptions reflected our distinct experiences and even our physical sizes.

This chapter focuses on perception, which is critical to our efforts to create meaning as we communicate with ourselves and others. Perception is the process by which we notice and make sense of phenomena. To explore the relationships between perception and communication, this chapter discusses three interrelated facets of perception and considers influences on how people perceive and why they sometimes differ in their perceptions. We will then discuss perception and digital media. To conclude the chapter, we will identify ways to improve perception.

The Perception Process

Perception is the active process of selecting, organizing, and interpreting people, objects, events, situations, and activities. The first thing to notice in this definition is that perception is an active process. We are not passive receivers of what is "out there" in the external world. Instead, we select certain things to notice, and then we organize and interpret what we have selectively noticed. What anything means to us depends on which aspects of it we attend to and how we organize and interpret what we notice.

Perception and communication influence each other. Perception shapes our understanding of others' communication and the choices we make in our own communication. For example, if you perceive a co-worker as hostile, you are more likely to notice his or her unfriendly behaviors than friendly ones and, as a result, to communicate defensively or to minimize interaction. Communication also influences our perceptions of people and situations. The language and nonverbal behaviors that other people use affect our perceptions of their intelligence, honesty, attractiveness, and so forth.

The second important aspect of the definition is that perception consists of three interrelated processes: selection, organization, and interpretation. These processes blend into one another. We organize perceptions even as we select what to perceive, and we interpret in an ongoing manner. Each process affects the other two. What we notice about people and situations influences how we interpret them. Also, our interpretation of a person or situation directs us to selectively notice certain, and not other, aspects of the person or setting.

perception An active process of selecting, organizing, and interpreting people, objects, events, situations, and activities.

Selection

Stop for a moment and notice what is going on around you right now. Is music playing in the background? Or do you perhaps hear several different kinds of music from different places? Is the room warm or cold, messy or clean, large or small, light or dark? Is laundry piled in the corner waiting to be washed?

Can you smell anything: food cooking, traces of cologne? Who else is in the room and nearby? Do you hear other conversations? Is a window open? Can you hear sounds of activities outside? Is it raining? Now, think about what's happening inside you. Are you tired or hungry? Do you have a headache or an itch anywhere? Is the type on this page large, small, easy to read?

Chances are that you weren't conscious of most of these phenomena when you began reading this chapter. Instead, you focused on reading and understanding the material. You selectively attended to what you defined as important, and you were unaware of many other things going on around you. This is typical of how we live our lives. We can't attend to everything in our environment, because far too much is there, and most of it isn't relevant to us at any given time.

A number of factors influence which stimuli we notice. First, some qualities of external phenomena draw our attention. For instance, we notice things that **STAND OUT** because they are larger, more **intense**, or unusual. We're more likely to hear a loud voice than a soft one and to notice a bright shirt more than a drab one. We also pay attention to what matters to us, so out of the 18 messages that appear when you check for text messages, you're likely to first notice those from people you want to hear from. Change also compels attention, which is why we become more attentive when a speaker shows a slide to enliven a speech or when a new person joins a dialogue in a chat room.

Sometimes, we deliberately influence what we notice by talking to ourselves. We tell ourselves to be alert if we have to drive when we're tired. We remind ourselves to speak loudly when we are addressing a large group without a microphone. We warn ourselves to stay in character when we have claimed an alternate identity in online chat rooms. Our self-concepts may also influence our perceptions. People who consider themselves attractive and desirable may perceive other attractive people as more available than do people with lower self-concepts. Researchers (Tsai & Reis, 2009) showed that lonely people tend to perceive others more negatively than people who are not lonely. It may be the case that lonely people are lonely, in part, because they see others as unattractive or unapproachable.

Our needs, interests, and motives influence what we choose to notice. If you're bored in your job, you're likely to notice ads for other jobs. If you've just broken up with a partner, you're more likely to notice attractive and available people than if you are in a satisfying relationship. Motives also explain the oasis phenomenon, in which thirsty people in a desert see an oasis although none is present. If we really want something, we may perceive it when it doesn't exist.

People tend to perceive desirable things as closer or more accessible than they really are. In one study, the researchers (Balcetis & Dunning, 2013) had people sit across the table from a full bottle of water and then had them either eat pretzels or drink water from an eight-ounce glass. The participants were then asked to estimate how many inches separated them from the bottle of water. Consistently, the participants who were thirsty from eating pretzels perceived the water bottle as being closer than the other participants. In another experiment, participants were given the chance to win a $25 gift card or a $0 gift card by tossing beanbags at it. The person whose beanbag landed closest won the gift card. Once again, the researchers found that people underestimated the distance between themselves and the desirable object.

Organization

We don't perceive randomly; instead, we organize our perceptions in meaningful ways. **Constructivism** is a theory that states that we organize and interpret experience by applying cognitive structures called **cognitive schemata**, or just **schemata** (the singular noun is *schema*). We rely on four schemata to make sense of phenomena: prototypes, personal constructs, stereotypes, and scripts (Burleson & Rack, 2008) (see Figure 3.1).

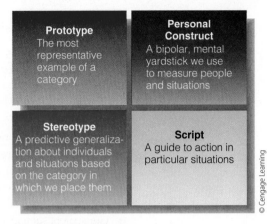

Prototype The most representative example of a category	Personal Construct A bipolar, mental yardstick we use to measure people and situations
Stereotype A predictive generalization about individuals and situations based on the category in which we place them	Script A guide to action in particular situations

© Cengage Learning

Figure 3.1 Cognitive Schemata

Prototypes   **Prototypes** are knowledge structures that define the clearest or ideal examples of some category (Fehr, 1993). For example, you probably have a prototype of a teacher, a friend, and a team leader. A prototype is an ideal, or best example, of a category: Jane is a model leader; Burt exemplifies a good friend; Ned is an ideal co-worker. The person who exemplifies a whole group, or category, is the category's prototype. We classify people by asking which of our prototypes they most closely resemble. Damion explains his prototype of a good friend.

 *Damion*

> *My ideal of a friend is my buddy Jackson. He stood by me when I got into a lot of trouble a couple of years ago. I got mixed up with some guys who used drugs, and I started using them. Pretty soon, the coach caught on to me, and he suspended me from the team. That made me feel like a total loser, and I got deeper into drugs. Jackson didn't give up on me, and he wouldn't let me give up either. He took me to a drug center and went with me every day for three weeks. He never turned away when I was sick or even when I cried most of one night when I was getting off the drugs. He just stood by me. Once I was straight, Jackson went with me to ask the coach about getting back on the team.*

Prototypes are useful to us because they allow us to group people, events, and situations into broad categories. However, when our prototypes don't match those of others, we may run into problems. For example, if your prototype of an ideal team member is a jokester, and the team leader's prototype of an ideal member is a task-focused worker, you may find your job on the line!

Personal Constructs   A **personal construct** is a mental yardstick that allows us to measure a person or situation along a bipolar dimension of judgment (Kelly, 1955). Examples of personal constructs are *intelligent–not intelligent, kind–not kind,* and *trustworthy–not trustworthy.* How intelligent, kind, and trustworthy is a speaker, journalist, friend, or co-worker? Whereas prototypes help us decide into which broad category a person, situation, or event fits, personal constructs allow us to make more detailed assessments of particular qualities of phenomena we perceive. Nai Lee's commentary offers an example of a personal construct.

constructivism A theory that holds that we organize and interpret experience by applying cognitive structures called schemata.

cognitive schemata Mental structures people use to organize and interpret experience. Four schemata have been identified: prototypes, personal constructs, stereotypes, and scripts.

schemata Cognitive structures we use to organize and interpret experiences. The four types of schemata are prototypes, personal constructs, stereotypes, and scripts. (Singular: *schema*)

prototype A knowledge structure that defines the clearest or most representative example of some category.

personal construct A bipolar mental yardstick that allows us to measure people and situations along bipolar dimensions of judgment, such as "honest—dishonest."

stereotype A predictive generalization about a person or situation.

 Nai Lee

One of the ways I look at people is by whether they are individualistic or related to others. In Korea, we think of ourselves as members of families and communities. The emphasis on individuals was the first thing I noticed when I came to this country, and it is still an important way I look at people.

Context influences which personal constructs are prominent in our assessments of others. If you are thinking about a person as a date, you're likely to rely on constructs such as *fun–not fun, intelligent–not intelligent,* and *attractive–not attractive.* When perceiving a co-worker, you're more likely to rely on constructs such as *reliable–not reliable, cooperative–not cooperative,* and *experienced–not experienced.* Constructs such as *fair–not fair, knowledgeable–not knowledgeable,* and *interesting–not interesting* may guide your perceptions of teachers. We assess people according to the constructs we use, not according to all the constructs that *could* be used. Thus, we may not perceive qualities that are not highlighted by the constructs we apply. This reminds us that the processes of selecting and organizing interact to affect our perceptions.

Stereotypes A **stereotype** is a predictive generalization about a person or situation. Based on the category (established by prototypes) in which we place something and how it measures up against personal constructs we apply, we predict what it will do. For instance, if you place someone in the category of "liberal people," you might stereotype the person as likely to vote Democratic, to support social services, and to oppose the death penalty. You may have stereotypes of fraternity and sorority members, professors, athletes, and people from other cultures.

 Winowa

People have a stereotype of Native Americans. People who are not Native Americans think we are all alike—how we look, how we act, what we believe, what our traditions are. But that isn't true. The Crow and Cherokee are as different as people from Kenya and New York. Some tribes have a history of aggression and violence; others have traditions of peace and harmony. We worship different spirits and have different tribal customs. All these differences are lost when people stereotype us all as Native Americans.

Stereotypes don't necessarily reflect actual similarities among phenomena that are put into a single category, as Winowa's commentary illustrates. Our stereotypes may keep us from seeing differences between people we have grouped into a category, as the ENGAGE! Box on the next page demonstrates.

Photofusion Picture Library/Alamy

🌐 **MindTap** What personal constructs do you rely on when perceiving the people in this photo?

Stereotypes may be accurate or inaccurate. In some cases, we have incorrect understandings of a group, and in other cases some members of a group don't conform to what is typical of the group as a whole. Although we need stereotypes in order to predict what will happen, we should remember that they are selective, subjective, and not necessarily accurate. In her commentary, Phyllis describes how a stereotype affects her.

script One of the four cognitive schemata; scripts define expected or appropriate sequences of action in particular settings.

 *Phyllis*

I'll tell you what stereotype really gets to me: the older student. I'm 38 and working on a B.A., and I'm tired of being treated like a housewife who's dabbling in courses. Some students treat me like their mother, not a peer. And some faculty are even worse. One professor told me that I shouldn't worry about grades because I didn't have to plan a career like the younger students. Well, I am planning a career, I am a student, and I am serious about my work.

Scripts   The final cognitive schema we use to organize perceptions is the script, which is a guide to action. A **script** is a sequence of activities that spells out how we and others are expected to act in a specific situation. If you run into a friend who is with someone you don't know, and your friend says, "Hi, this is Ben," you don't have to think about what you are supposed to say; your meeting-new-person script tells you that you should say, "Hi, I'm (your name)" and perhaps smile or offer to shake hands. Although we're often unaware of them, scripts guide many of our daily activities. You have scripts for greeting casual acquaintances as you walk around campus, texting friends to check in with them, and talking with professors. Scripts organize perceptions into lines of action.

 MindTap

TAKE ACTION…activities are located at the end of this chapter and online.

Dianne Holmberg and Samantha MacKenzie (2002) studied scripts for dating relationships. They found that partners who see their relationship as consistent with their perceptions of normative scripts for dating have generally positive evaluations of their relationships. Conversely, partners who perceive inconsistency between most people's perceptions of how dating relationships progress and what is happening in their own relationship tend to have less positive assessments of their relationship. Similarly, Sandra Metts (2006) has identified consistent scripts for heterosexual flirting.

Prototypes, personal constructs, stereotypes, and scripts are cognitive schemata that organize our thinking about people and situations. We use them to make sense of experience and to predict how we and others will act.

Interpretation

If you have ever been around a young child, then you know that "Why?" is an incessant question: Why is the sky blue? Why is the dog bigger

 **ENGAGE!**   ## The Census Bureau's Dilemma

Systems of organizing or classifying are arbitrary constructions invented by humans. Yet we sometimes act as if our classifications are objectively true. Consider the dilemma of the U.S. Census Bureau, which found that its method of classifying races no longer works. The mushrooming diversity of Americans has created problems for the bureau. The racial categories created in 1978 are no longer adequate to classify people with diverse languages, cultures, and ethnic heritages.

Lumping diverse groups into single categories such as Asian (which includes Japanese, Chinese, Taiwanese, Nepalese, etc.) or Native American (which includes Crow, Lumbee, Paiute, etc.) is inappropriate. The traditional classifications count Middle Easterners as white, and Alaskans as Alaskan Natives rather than as people born in the United States. Another deficiency of the standard categories is that they don't acknowledge multiracial identities, which many citizens have.

 MindTap Have you ever been lumped into a category that you felt erased your individuality?

interpretation The subjective process of creating explanations for what we observe and experience.

attribution An explanation of why things happen or why people act as they do; not necessarily correct interpretations of others and their motives.

self-serving bias The tendency to attribute our positive actions and successes to stable, global, internal influences that we control and to attribute negative actions and failures to unstable, specific, external influences beyond our control.

than the cat? Why do teachers have to give tests? Why can't I have the toy I want? Children's fascination with *why* is a search to figure out what causes things to happen and people to act as they do. Although adults are perhaps more sophisticated than children, we are no less interested in figuring out why things happen and why people behave as they do. To interpret experiences, we ask why something happens or why someone says, does, or doesn't do a particular thing.

Interpretation is the subjective process of creating explanations for what we observe and experience.

Attributions   Our quest to figure out the why of things brings us to the concept of **attribution**, which is the act of explaining why something happens or why a person acts a particular way (Manusov & Spitzberg, 2008; for the classic research in this area, see Heider, 1958; Kelley, 1967). We *attribute* our own and others' behaviors to causes.

Attributions have four dimensions. The first is the *internal–external* locus: the attribution of a person's behavior to internal factors ("He's short tempered") or external factors ("The traffic jam frustrated him"). The second dimension is *stability*, the explanation of actions as the result of stable, enduring factors that won't change over time ("She's a nervous person"; "This job is always stressful") or variable (unstable) temporary factors ("She's nervous right now because of a big deal she's closing"; "This is a stressful period at work"). The third dimension is *specificity*, the explanation of actions as the result of global factors ("She's intelligent") or specific factors ("She's gifted at math"). Finally, the dimension of *control* is the ascribing of responsibility for actions either to people themselves ("She doesn't try to control her temper") or to factors beyond their personal control ("She has a chemical imbalance"). In a recent study (Nagourney, 2008), volunteers were given a mild electric shock to their wrists. Some volunteers were told that another person chose to administer the shock. Other volunteers were told the shock was randomly selected by a computer. The volunteers who believed another person chose to shock them reported greater pain. Figure 3.2 illustrates the three dimensions of attribution.

The Self-Serving Bias   Although we develop explanations of our own and others' behaviors, the attributions we make aren't necessarily accurate. Research shows that we tend to construct attributions that serve our personal interests (Hamachek, 1992; Manusov & Spitzberg, 2008; Sypher, 1984). This phenomenon is known as the **self-serving bias**. Thus, we are inclined to attribute our positive actions and our successes to internal and stable factors. We're also likely to claim that good results come about because of the personal control we exerted. You might attribute making an *A* on a test to being a smart person (internal, stable, global) who studies hard (personal control). In her commentary, Chandra reflects on a self-serving attribution. The online resources for this chapter provide a link to additional information about, and examples of, self-serving bias.

Dimension

1. Locus	Internal	External
2. Stability	Stable	Unstable
3. Specificity	Specific	Global
4. Responsibility	Within personal control	Beyond personal control

© Cengage Learning

Figure 3.2 The Dimensions of Attribution

 *Chandra*

I wait tables to make money for school. It used to be that when I didn't make good tips, I would say that the customers were cheap or in bad moods or my manager assigned me to a slow station. When I made good tips, I always thought that it was because I am such a considerate server. Then we got a new manager, who told me that I made better tips when I was feeling good. He pointed out that I was really friendly and attentive to customers when I was in a good mood but that I could be careless when I felt down.

Conversely, we tend to avoid taking responsibility for negative actions and failures and instead attribute them to external and unstable events that are beyond personal control. To explain a failing grade on a test, you might say that you did poorly because the professor (external) put a lot of tricky questions on that particular test (unstable, specific) so that regardless of how hard you studied, you couldn't do well (outside personal control). The self-serving bias can distort our perceptions, leading us to take excessive credit for what we do well and to deny responsibility for our failings. It can also lead us to judge others less kindly than ourselves (Manusov, 2006; Sedikides, Campbell, Reede, & Elliot, 1998). The ENGAGE! box on this page shows how taking responsibility for problems may affect customers' perceptions and loyalty to companies.

In summary, perception involves three interrelated processes. The first—selection—involves noticing certain things and ignoring others within the total context. The second process is organization, wherein we use prototypes, personal constructs, stereotypes, and scripts to order what we have selectively perceived. Finally, we engage in interpretation to make sense of the perceptions we have gathered and organized. Attributions are a primary way that we explain what we and others do. Although we've discussed each process separately, they interact continually. Thus, our interpretations shape the knowledge schemata we use to organize experiences, and how we organize perceptions affects what we notice and interpret.

 **ENGAGE!**

We Failed and We're Sorry

Have you ever made a complaint about a product or service? If so, did you get a response and did it affect how you perceive the organization that made the product or offered the service? Communication researchers San Bolkan and John Daly (2009) had people write letters to organizations complaining about a product or service that had been unsatisfactory. When organizations responded to the complaints, Bolkan and Daly analyzed the responses and how they affected the perceptions of the people who wrote the letters. Bolkan and Daly identified three types of responses:

◆ *Excuses* deny responsibility for the problem ("Your flight was canceled, but it's not our fault.").

◆ *Justifications* accept responsibility, yet try to minimize the severity of the problem and blame ("Like all airlines, sometimes we have scheduling problems.").

◆ *Apologies* acknowledge blameworthiness, express sympathy, and ask for forgiveness ("We're sorry we cancelled your flight and caused you inconvenience. We hope you'll give us another chance.").

Bolkan and Daly found that the different types of responses to complaints affected consumers' perceptions of an organization and their intention to continue using its products and services. Excuses tended to result in negative perceptions of an organization whereas justifications did not have this effect unless they were extensive—that is, too many justifications led consumers to distrust the organizations. Apologies increased consumers' perceptions that the product or service was bad, yet also increased consumers' perception that the organization had responded well and increased consumers' intentions to do business with the organization in the future. Bolkan and Daly's advice to organizations: Take responsibility for problems, communicate respect and sympathy for consumers, provide justifications if appropriate, and apologize.

Influences on Perception

A few years ago, I went to a neighborhood cookout, at which a neighbor who did not attend was discussed. The absent person had been behaving oddly ever since he moved into our neighborhood. He had thrown a rock at one person's dog, had been seen going into another neighbor's house when the owners weren't home, had been verbally abusive to several members of the community, and had shot squirrels and birds, which nobody else in the neighborhood did.

At the picnic, neighbors were sharing stories of what he had done and what it meant. A woman who is a psychologist ventured the opinion that he was suffering from depression and needed help. The legal aspects of his behavior were the focus of an attorney's comments, who observed that the man could be arrested for breaking and entering and verbal harassment. A third person, who had recently left an abusive partner, was afraid that our neighbor posed a threat to all of us. Those of us who have dogs and cats in our families were concerned that the neighbor might shoot our pets. As this example illustrates, people don't always perceive situations in the same ways. How each of us perceived our neighbor was shaped by many factors in our backgrounds, training, and individual interests.

Physiological Factors

The most obvious reason perceptions vary among people is that we differ in our sensory abilities and physiologies. The five senses are not the same for all of us. Music that one person finds deafening is barely audible to another. On a given day, students wear everything from shorts and sandals to heavy jackets, a sign that they have different sensitivities to cold.

Our physiological states also influence perception. If you are tired, stressed, or sick, you're likely to perceive things more negatively than when you are well and rested. For instance, a playful insult from a friend might anger you if you were feeling down but might not bother you if you felt good. Each of us has biorhythms, which influence how alert we are at different times of day.

Expectations

Imagine that a friend tells you she wants you to meet a person whom she describes as "one of the coolest people I've ever met: He's funny and considerate and so interested in other people. You'll find him really easy to talk to and lots of fun." Chances are you would expect to like the new person and would in fact perceive the good qualities your friend led you to expect. If instead your friend had said, "This guy is a real drag. He's always telling bad jokes, and he's self-centered," you might expect not to like the man, and you might perceive only his shortcomings.

Based on a series of studies, John Bargh (1997, 1999) reports that how we act may be affected by subliminal priming of expectations. In one study, participants were told that they would be taking two tests. The researcher told each participant to go into a room and take a test and then to come out of the room and find the researcher to progress to the second test. One-half of the participants then took a test that presented them with a group of terms related to politeness. The other half of the participants took a test that presented them with a group of terms related to rudeness. When participants finished the test and went to look for the researcher, they found the researcher talking with another person. Of the participants who had worked with the terms related to rudeness, 63 percent interrupted the researcher's conversation, but only 17 percent of the participants who had worked with politeness terms interrupted the conversation. Apparently, their perceptions of appropriate behavior were affected by exposure to words that made rudeness or politeness salient to them.

Expectations affect our perceptions in a variety of communication situations. If we are told in advance that a new person on the job is "a real team player," we're likely to notice the new employee's cooperative behaviors and not likely to see competitive or self-serving behaviors that the new person may also present. If we're forewarned that a speaker tends to distort facts, we're likely to perceive misrepresentations in the speech. On the other hand, if we're told that the speaker is trustworthy, we may listen less critically and not perceive any slanting or distortions. Our sense of time has been radically reshaped by communication technologies that lead us to expect extremely quick exchanges. Just a decade ago, most people expected replies to business correspondence within a week to 10 days. Now, many people expect nearly instant responses, and we grumble if a friend isn't online when we IM her or him or if a text message isn't answered for several hours.

The influence of expectations on communication is the basis of **positive visualization**, which is a technique used to enhance success in a variety of situations by teaching people to visualize themselves positively. If you visualize yourself succeeding in an athletic contest or in an interview, you may increase your actual success.

What happens when our expectations are violated? That's the question asked by **expectancy violation theory**. Research shows that when our expectations are violated, we become more cognitively alert as we struggle to understand and cope with unexpected behaviors or events (Afifi & Metts, 1998; Bevan, 2003; Burgoon, 1993).

Three aspects of a violation of expectations influence how we will interpret it (Afifi & Metts, 1998). First, our interpretations are affected by whether the violation is positive (someone gives you a gift that you had not anticipated) or negative (your supervisor criticizes you). Second, our interpretations are influenced by the extent to which the behavior deviates from the expected behavior. If your supervisor has never criticized you before, harshly criticizing you now would be a significant deviation from expectations. Third, our interpretations are affected by the impact of the violation on a relationship. Think about the different impacts on a dating relationship if the person you are dating doesn't call when she or he promises and if she or he dates your best friend.

Cognitive Abilities

In addition to physiological, cultural, and social influences, perception is shaped by our cognitive abilities. How elaborately we think about situations and people, and the extent of our knowledge of others, affect how we select, organize, and interpret experiences.

positive visualization A technique used to enhance success in a variety of situations by teaching people to visualize themselves being effective and successful.

expectancy violation theory A theory claiming that when our expectations are violated, we become more cognitively alert as we struggle to understand and cope with unexpected behaviors.

Kitchin/Hurst/Age Fotostock

Seeing yourself as fierce and powerful boosts self-confidence.

Cognitive Complexity   People differ in the number and types of knowledge schemata they use to organize and interpret people and situations. **Cognitive complexity** is the number of personal constructs used (remember, personal constructs are bipolar dimensions of judgment), how abstract they are, and how elaborately they interact to shape perceptions. Most children have fairly simple cognitive systems. They rely on few schemata, focus more on concrete constructs (*tall–not tall*) than abstract psychological ones (*secure–not secure*), and often don't perceive relationships between different perceptions (How is security related to extroversion?).

Many adults have greater cognitive complexity, which affects the accuracy of perceptions. The older we get, the richer is our perspective for perceiving situations and people. Thus, compared with a person of 20, someone who is 60 has a more complex fund of experiences on which to draw. Throughout my 20s, I was easily upset when a class didn't go well or when a friend and I argued. Often, I became disheartened because I perceived these as significant problems. In my mid-30s, my father died. After his death, a less-than-perfect class or a minor argument with a friend didn't acutely distress me, because I had a very different perspective on what a serious problem was.

The extent of discrimination that is still experienced by women, people of color, and gays, lesbians, and transgender people understandably discourages many college students. I am more hopeful than some because I have seen significant changes in my lifetime. When I attended college, women and minorities were not admitted on an equal basis with Caucasian men, and almost all LGBTQ people concealed their sexual orientations. When I entered the job market, there were few laws to protect women, minorities, and LGBTQ people against discrimination in hiring, pay, and advancement. The substantial progress made during my life leads me to hold optimistic perceptions about society's ability to alleviate the inequities that still exist.

Cognitive complexity influences our perceptions of others. If you can think of people only as good or bad, you have limited ways of perceiving others. Similarly, people who focus on concrete data tend to have less sophisticated understandings than people who also perceive psychological data. For example, you might notice that a person is attractive, tells jokes, and talks a lot. At a more abstract psychological level, you might infer that the behaviors you observe reflect a secure, self-confident personality. This is a more sophisticated perception because it includes perceptions of why the person acts as she or he does.

What if you later find out that the person is quiet in classes? Someone with low cognitive complexity would have difficulty integrating the new information with earlier observations, and would be likely either to dismiss the new information because it doesn't fit or to replace the former perception with the more recent data and redefine the person as shy. A more cognitively complex person would integrate all the information into a coherent account. Perhaps a cognitively complex person would interpret the person as more confident in social situations than in academic ones. Research shows that cognitively complex people are flexible in interpreting complicated phenomena and are able to integrate new information into their thinking about people and situations. People who are less cognitively complex tend to ignore information that doesn't fit their impressions or to throw out old ideas and replace them with new impressions (Crockett, 1965; Delia, Clark, & Switzer, 1974). Either way, they screen out some of the nuances and inconsistencies that are part of human nature.

cognitive complexity The number of mental constructs an individual uses, how abstract they are, and how elaborately they interact to create perceptions.

Person-Centeredness **Person-centeredness** is the ability to perceive another as a unique individual. When we perceive distinctions among people, we can adapt our communication to particular individuals. Person-centeredness is linked to cognitive complexity (Zorn, 1991). People who are cognitively complex are able to perceive others and situations in more comprehensive and integrated ways than are less cognitively complex people. Thus, an effective politician may adopt a different speaking style and emphasize different topics when talking with elderly citizens, elementary school children, members of unions, and business executives. When texting or chatting online, we use common shorthand (for instance, *brb*, *lol*) with people who understand it, as Emma points out. The online resources for this chapter provide a link to an article on cultural differences in awareness of others' perspectives.

MindTap One gift of growing older is enriched perspective. What might these people be able to share that two 20-year-olds cannot?

 *Emma*

I talk differently when I'm e-mailing my parents and aunt than when I'm chatting online with friends. My parents and aunt don't know a lot of standard online lingo like myob *[mind your own business] and* OMG *[oh my gosh] or abbreviations like* r *for* are *and* u *for* you. *It takes more time to explain them to the family than it takes to just spell everything out.*

To adapt communication to others, we must understand something about them. In relationships that aren't highly personal, communicators sometimes tailor messages to the general characteristics of groups. For example, more educated people tend to be more critical and better informed, so effective speakers include strong evidence and show respect for listeners' knowledge when addressing people with high levels of education. Because uncertainty and change foster anxiety, effective managers communicate reassurance and provide maximum information to subordinates during times of organizational change. To be effective in a job interview, an interviewee should research the history and image of the company to find out what the company looks for in employees.

We have different degrees of insight into people with whom we interact. You need to know your intimates well to create satisfying relationships; you need to know professors and co-workers less well but well enough to converse with them; you need to know clerks only well enough to transact business. As we get to know someone better, we gain insight into how he or she differs from others in their group ("Rob's not like most conservatives"; "Carmen's more interested in people than most computer

person-centeredness The ability to perceive another as a unique and distinct individual apart from social roles and generalizations.

An Empathic Judge

On May 1, 2009, Justice David Souter announced he would be retiring from the Supreme Court. Immediately, people wanted to know whom President Obama would pick to replace Souter. Speaking in the White House press briefing room, the president told reporters that a key quality he was looking for in the next Supreme Court justice is empathy. He said he wanted a justice who can understand what it's like to be poor or gay or disabled or otherwise not privileged in America. According to President Obama, empathy is what allows a person to understand and identify with people's hopes and struggles, and this is essential to making sound decisions about justice.

 MindTap- In addition to judging in courts, what other occupations particularly require empathy?

science majors"). The more we interact with someone and the greater the variety of experiences we have together, the more we understand their motives, feelings, and behaviors. As we come to know others as individuals, we fine-tune our perceptions of them. Consequently, we rely less on stereotypes to perceive them.

Person-centeredness is not the same as empathy. **Empathy** is the ability to feel *with* another person—to feel what he or she feels in a situation. Person-centeredness, in contrast, is a cognitive skill—the ability to understand another person as a distinct individual, which allows adapting communication to his or her frames of reference (Muehlhoff, 2006). In his commentary, Steve explains how he developed person-centeredness with his girlfriend, Sherry.

 Steve

You really have to know somebody on an individual basis to know what he or she likes and wants. When I first started dating Sherry, I sent her red roses to let her know I thought she was special. That's the "lovers' flower," right? It turns out there were zillions of red roses at her father's funeral. Now, they make Sherry sad because they remind her he's dead. I also took her chocolates once, before I found out that she's allergic to chocolate. By now I know what she likes, but my experience shows that the general rules don't always apply to individuals.

Social Roles

Our social roles also shape our perceptions and our communication. Both the training we receive to fulfill a role and the actual demands of the role affect what we notice and how we interpret, evaluate, and respond to it. Teachers' perceptions of classes focus on how interested students seem, whether they appear to have read assigned material, and whether what they're learning is useful in their lives. Students have told me that they think about classes in terms of number and difficulty of tests, whether papers are required, and whether the professor is interesting. We have different ways of perceiving classes.

People's professions influence what they notice and how they think and act. In the earlier example, members of my community perceived our neighbor differently because of our distinct professional roles, as well as other factors. The attorney in the group focused on the legal—or illegal—nature of the neighbor's behavior, and the psychologist's training led her to perceive his behaviors as evidence of emotional problems.

Membership in Cultures and Social Communities

Membership in a culture influences perceptions. A **culture** consists of beliefs, values, understandings, practices, and ways of interpreting experience that are shared by a group of people (Klopf, 1991). Western culture's emphasis on technology and its

empathy The ability to feel with another person, to feel what he or she feels in a situation.

culture The beliefs, values, understandings, practices, and ways of interpreting experience that are shared by a group of people.

offspring, speed, leads us to expect things to happen fast—almost instantly. We e-mail memos, text friends, jet across the country, and microwave meals. In countries such as Nepal, Belize, and Mexico, life proceeds at a more leisurely pace, and people spend more time talking, relaxing, and engaging in low-key activities.

In addition to an overall culture, people may belong to social communities that shape their experiences, perspectives, and knowledge. A **social community** is a group of people who are part of an overall society (e.g., the United States) and are also distinct from the overall society in that they hold values, understandings, and practices that are not shared by people outside the group. Gender, race, religion, and sexual orientation often define social communities and may affect how members of the communities act, including how they communicate.

In summary, differences based on physiology, expectations, cognitive abilities, social roles, and membership in cultures and social communities affect how we perceive others and experiences. By extension, all these influences on perception affect how we communicate.

Digital Media and Perception

We now consider how ideas that we've discussed in the foregoing pages apply to social media and online communication. We'll focus on two connections between digital media and perception.

First, our choices of digital media shape our perceptions of events, issues, and people. If you follow Rush Limbaugh's tweets, you will get a conservative perspective on national and international issues and on the people involved in them. If you follow Rachel Maddow's tweets, you will get a liberal perspective on the same issues and people. Limbaugh frequently disparages feminists, by labeling them "feminazis"; Maddow identifies as a feminist and speaks favorably about feminist issues. Limbaugh sympathizes with corporate interests and tends to support lowering corporate taxes and boosting capitalism; Maddow is inclined to be distrustful of corporate interests, to think corporations should pay more taxes, and to favor reigning in some capitalist tendencies. Who's right? There is no objective answer to that question, but your views on such issues are shaped by the bloggers you follow.

Second, consider how membership in social communities affects what we say and post on social media. Try this experiment: Look at the social network profiles of people you know who belong to different ethnic groups. How often do their postings include boasting about individual accomplishments, which reflects Western but not Eastern values? Do people from communal and collectivist cultures post more photos of families and themselves with families than do people from individualist cultures? Now look at the profiles of women and men you know. To what extent does each sex tweet and post about relationships and sports, fashion, and politics? Are the trends that you note consistent with research we've discussed about Western and non-Western cultural values and feminine and masculine social communities?

Guidelines for Improving Skill in Perceiving

Four guidelines enhance skills in perceiving people and situations in ways that facilitate effective communication.

social community A group of people who live within a dominant culture yet also belong to another social group or groups that share values, understandings, and practices distinct from those of the dominant culture.

mind reading The assumption that we understand what another person thinks or how another person perceives something.

Avoid Mind Reading

Because perception is subjective, people differ in what they notice and in the meaning they attribute to it. One of the most common problems in communication is **mind reading**, which in this sense means assuming we understand what another person thinks or feels. When we mind read, we act as if we know what's on someone else's mind, and this can get us into trouble. For example, we can misinterpret a co-worker's absence from meetings if we assume that it signals disinterest instead of competing commitments. Mind reading is also a common cause of tension between spouses (Dickson, 1995; Gottman, 1993).

Consider a few examples of the problems mind reading can cause. One person might assume a friend is angry because the friend hasn't responded to a text message in 24 hours. This guess could well be wrong—the friend might be preoccupied or might have a dead phone battery. Mind reading also occurs when we say or think, "I know he's upset" (Has he said he is upset?) or "She doesn't care about me anymore" (maybe she is too preoccupied or worried to be attentive). In actuality, we seldom really know what others think, feel, or perceive. When we mind read, we impose our perspectives on others instead of allowing them to say what they think. This can cause misunderstandings and resentment because most of us prefer to speak for ourselves.

Check Perceptions with Others

The second guideline follows directly from our insight about the inadvisability of mind reading. Because perceptions are subjective, checking our perceptions with others is a good idea. In the earlier example, we could ask, "Why didn't you respond?" Rather than assuming a friend is angry, it might be valuable to ask, "Are you angry with me?" It's especially important to check perceptions when communicating online, because we don't have access to many of the nonverbal cues that help us interpret face-to-face communication. Sarcasm, irony, and other forms of communication may not be obvious online. Checking perceptions enhances clarity between people and invites productive dialogue, not blame and defensiveness.

Perception checking is an important communication skill because it helps people arrive at mutual understandings of each other and their interaction. To check perceptions, first state what you have noticed. For example, you might say, "Lately, you've given me less feedback on my work than in the past." Then, you check whether the other perceives the same thing: "Would you agree?" Finally, it's appropriate to invite the other person to help you understand her or his behavior. So in the example, if the other person agrees that he or she is less pleased with your work, you could say, "Can you give me some insight into why you're giving me less feedback?" If the other person doesn't agree that she or he is giving less feedback, a useful question might be, "Could you remind me of the feedback you've given me on the last few reports?"

When checking perceptions, it's important to use a tentative tone rather than a dogmatic or accusatory one. This minimizes defensiveness and encourages good discussion. Just let the other person know that you are perceiving something and would like that person to clarify his or her perceptions of what is happening and what it means.

Distinguish Facts from Inferences and Judgments

Effective communicators recognize the difference between factual statements and nonfactual statements such as inferences and judgments. A fact is based on observation or proof. For instance, "The student, Taylor, is late to class most days" is a factual statement. An **inference** is a deduction that goes beyond what you know or assume to be a fact. For instance, if Taylor's teacher has known other students who were late to class because they didn't care about the class, the teacher might generalize from them to infer, "Taylor doesn't care about this class." Note that the inference goes beyond facts that the teacher knows about Taylor.

A **judgment** is a belief or opinion that is based on observations, feelings, assumptions, or other phenomena that are not facts. In our example, the teacher might judge that "Taylor is an irresponsible student." But judging Taylor as irresponsible goes beyond the facts. Taylor's lateness to class may be due to a work shift that ends right before the class. The teacher might treat Taylor differently if a work schedule, rather than indifference, explained the tardiness. To communicate effectively, we need to avoid mistaking nonfactual statements for factual ones.

It's easy to confuse inferences with facts when we use language that makes inferences and judgments appear to be factual. When we say, "This person is rude," we've made a statement that sounds factual, and we may then perceive it as factual when it really isn't. To avoid this tendency, substitute a more tentative word for *is*. For instance, "This person seems rude" and "This person may be rude" are more tentative statements that keep us from treating an inference or judgment as a fact.

Checking perceptions is critical to effective parent–child communication.

Monitor the Self-Serving Bias

We discussed the self-serving bias earlier in this chapter. You'll recall that it involves attributing our successes and positive behaviors to internal, stable qualities that we control and attributing our failures and bad behaviors to external, unstable factors beyond our control. Because this bias can distort perceptions, we need to monitor it carefully. **Monitoring** is the process of calling behaviors or other phenomena to our attention so that we can observe and regulate them. Try to monitor the tendency to explain away your failures or adverse behaviors as not your fault and to take personal credit for accomplishments that were helped along by luck or situational factors.

Monitoring the self-serving bias also has implications for how we perceive others. Just as we tend to judge ourselves generously, we may judge others harshly. Monitor your perceptions to discover to what extent you attribute others' successes and admirable actions to external factors beyond their control and their shortcomings and blunders to internal factors they can (should) control. If you do this, substitute more

inference An interpretation that goes beyond the facts known but is believed to logically follow from them.

judgment A belief or opinion based on observations, feelings, assumptions, or other nonfactual phenomena.

monitoring The observation and regulation of one's own communication.

Attribution Patterns and Relationship Satisfaction

Investigations have shown that happy and unhappy couples have distinct attribution styles (Bradbury & Fincham, 1990; Fletcher & Fincham, 1991; Graham & Conoley, 2006; McNulty & Karney, 2001; Segrin, Hanzal, & Domschke, 2009). Happy couples make relationship-enhancing attributions. Such people attribute nice things a partner does to internal, stable, and global reasons. "She got the film for us because she is a good person who always does sweet things for us." They attribute unpleasant actions by a partner to external, unstable, and specific factors. "He yelled at me because all the stress of the past few days made him short with everyone."

Unhappy couples use reverse attribution patterns. They explain nice actions as resulting from external, unstable, and specific factors. "She got the tape because she had some extra time today." They see negative actions as stemming from internal, stable, and global factors. "He yelled at me because he is a nasty person who never shows any consideration to anybody else." Negative attributions encourage pessimistic views and sap motivation to improve a relationship. Whether positive or negative, attributions may be self-fulfilling prophecies.

generous explanations for others' behaviors, and notice how that affects your perceptions of them. The ENGAGE! box on this page discusses research that links different attributional tendencies to different levels of satisfaction with personal relationships.

Words crystallize perceptions. Until we label an experience, it remains nebulous and less than fully formed in our thinking. Only when we name our feelings and thoughts do we have a clear way to describe and think about them. But just as words crystallize experiences, they can freeze thought. Once we label our perceptions, we may respond to our labels rather than to the actual phenomena.

Summary

In this chapter, we've discussed perception, which is a basic communication process. It involves selecting, organizing, and interpreting experiences. These three facets of the perception process are not separate in practice; instead, they interact such that each affects the others.

What we selectively notice affects how we organize and interpret phenomena. At the same time, our interpretations influence what we notice in the world around us. Selection, organization, and interpretation interact continually in the process of perception. Our sensory capacities and physiological conditions affect what we perceive. In addition, expectations, cognitive abilities, social roles, and cultural context influence how we perceive experiences and how we communicate with ourselves and others. We also noted

that our choices of social and online media influence how we perceive issues, events, and people.

Skillful perception enhances communication. We discussed four guidelines for enhancing skills in perceiving. First, because people perceive differently, we should avoid mind reading. Extending this, we discussed the importance of checking perceptions, which involves stating how we perceive something and asking how another person perceives it. A third guideline is to distinguish facts from inferences in our perceptions and the symbols we use to label them. Finally, monitoring self-serving bias helps us perceive ourselves more accurately. We need to know when we are making factual descriptions and when we are making inferences that we should check.

Experience Communication Case Study
College Success

Apply what you've learned in this chapter by analyzing the following case study, using the accompanying questions as a guide. These questions and a video of the case study are also available online with your MindTap Speech for *Communication Mosaics*.

Your friend Jim tells you about a problem he's having with his parents. According to Jim, his parents have unrealistic expectations of him. He tends to be an average student, usually making *C*'s, a few *B*'s, and an occasional *D* in his courses. His parents are angry that his grades aren't better. Jim tells you that when he went home last month, his father said this:

Jim's father: I'm not paying for you to go to school so you can party with your friends. I paid my own way and still made Phi Beta Kappa. You have a free ride, and you're still just pulling *C*'s. You just have to study harder.

Jim [to you]: I mean, I like to hang out with my friends, but that's got nothing to do with my grades. My dad's this brilliant guy, I mean, he just cruised through college; he thinks it's easy. I don't know how it was back then, but all my classes are *hard*. I mean, no matter how much studying I do, I'm *not* gonna get all *A*'s. What should I do? I mean, how do I convince them that I'm doing everything I can?

© Cengage Learning

1. Both Jim and his parents make attributions to explain his grades. Describe the dimensions of Jim's attributions and those of his parents.

2. How might you assess the accuracy of Jim's attributions? What questions could you ask him to help you decide whether his perceptions are well founded or biased?

3. What constructs, prototypes, and scripts seem to operate in how Jim and his parents think about college life and being a student?

4. What could you say to Jim to help him and his parents reach a shared perspective on his academic work?

Key Concepts

Practice defining the chapter's terms by using online flashcards.

attribution, 46
cognitive complexity, 50
cognitive schemata, 43
constructivism, 43
culture, 52
empathy, 52

expectancy violation theory, 49
individualism, 59
inference, 55
interpretation, 46
judgment, 55
mind reading, 54

Reflect, personalize, and
apply what you've learned.

Review, Reflect, Extend

The Reflect and Discuss and Take Action features that follow will help you review, reflect on, and extend the information and ideas presented in this chapter. These resources, and a diverse selection of additional study tools, are also available online at the MindTap Speech for *Communication Mosaics*.

Reflect and Discuss

1. As a class, discuss how you communicate with people both online and face-to-face. What differences can you identify in how you communicate in each medium? What differences can you identify in how others communicate with you online and in person?

2. Read a local paper and pay attention to how the language in stories shapes your perceptions of events and people. Identify examples of how language shapes perceptions.

3. Think of someone you know who is person-centered. Describe the specific skills this person uses and how they affect his or her communication.

4. Go to a grocery store and notice how products are placed on shelves (at eye level, lower, or higher) and the colors and designs on product packaging. Identify factors discussed in this chapter that are used to make products stand out and gain shoppers' attention.

5. Volunteer to work in a context that allows you to interact with people you have not spent time with—for example, a homeless shelter. At the start of your work, make a list of schemata (prototypes, personal constructs, stereotypes, and scripts) you have about these people before you interact with them. After spending time interacting with them, review your list of schemata and evaluate how accurate they were.

TAKE ACTION

1. Sizing Up Others

a. Pay attention to the cognitive schemata you use the next time you meet a new person. First, notice how you classify the person. Do you categorize her or him as a potential friend, date, co-worker, and so on? Identify your prototype of the category into which you place the person.

b. Next, identify the constructs you use to assess the person. Do you focus on physical constructs (*attractive–not attractive*), mental constructs (*intelligent–not intelligent*), psychological constructs (*secure–not secure*), or interpersonal constructs (*available–not available*)? Would different constructs be prominent if you used a different prototype to classify the person?

c. Third, note how you stereotype the person. According to the prototype and constructs you've applied, what do you expect him or her to do? Would your expectations differ if you had placed him or her in a different category?

d. Finally, identify your script, or how you expect interaction to unfold between you according to the prototype, personal constructs, stereotypes, and scripts that you applied.

2. Appreciating Multiple Perspectives

Select a controversial issue that's in the news. Find two Web sites or blogs that have dramatically different, even opposing, perspectives on the issue. Monitor these for two weeks and compare how the issue is discussed on the different sites or blogs.

3. Noticing Individualism

The United States is a highly individualistic country that expects and rewards personal initiative and regards each person as unique and important. How do the individualistic values of our culture influence our perceptions and activities? Check it out by observing the following:

• How is seating arranged in restaurants? Are there large communal eating areas or private tables and booths for individuals or small groups?

• How are living spaces arranged? How many people live in the average house? Do families share homes? Does each member of the family have his or her own bedroom and/or other space?

• How many people share a car in your family and the families of your friends?

Other cultures, including Hispanic and Asian ones, are more collectivist and define identity in terms of membership in family and community rather than individuality. Because families are more valued in collectivist cultures, elders are given great respect and care. Rather than perceiving themselves as autonomous, as is typical in cultures that value **individualism**, people in communal cultures tend to think of themselves as members of and accountable to groups.

Differences between collectivist and individualistic cultures are also evident in child-care policies. More communal countries have policies that reflect the value they place on families. In every developed country except the United States, new parents, including adoptive parents, receive a period of paid parental leave, and some countries provide nearly a year's paid leave (Douglas, 2004; Wood & Fixmer-Oraiz, 2016).

4. Perception Checking

To gain skill in perception checking (and all communication behaviors), you need to practice. Try this:

a. Monitor your tendencies to mind read, especially in established relationships in which you feel you know your partners well.

b. The next time you catch yourself mind reading, stop. Instead, tell the other person what you are noticing and invite her or him to explain how she or he perceives what's happening. First, find out whether your partner agrees with you about

individualism A predominant Western value that regards each person as unique, important, and to be recognized for her or his individual qualities and behavior.

what you noticed. Second, if you agree, find out how your partner interprets and evaluates what is happening.

c. Engage in perception checking for two or three days so that you have lots of chances to see what happens. When you've done that, reflect on the number of times your mind reading was inaccurate.

d. Think about how your perception checking affected interaction with your friends and romantic partners.

5. Distinguishing Facts from Inferences and Judgments

Which of the following are factual statements?

a. There are 50 states in the United States.

b. People from small towns are friendly.

c. Actors are egotistical.

d. German shepherds tend to suffer from hip dysplasia.

e. Students who come to class late are disrespectful.

f. Acid rain can destroy trees.

g. College students take jobs to earn money for dating and clothes.

h. Older students aren't career oriented.

i. Evelyn made a total score of 690 on her SAT.

j. Evelyn would not do well in college.

Statements a, d, f, and i are facts; statements b, c, e, g, h, and j are inferences.

Recommended Resources

1. Learn more about fact–inference confusion and other ways in which language and perception affect our thinking by visiting the Web site of the Institute of General Semantics. You can access it by going to the book's online resources for this chapter.

2. Paul Watzlawick (1984). *The invented reality: How do we know what we believe we know?* Don't let the publication date of this book fool you. It is as useful today as when it was published in raising awareness of how our perceptions shape our sense of reality.

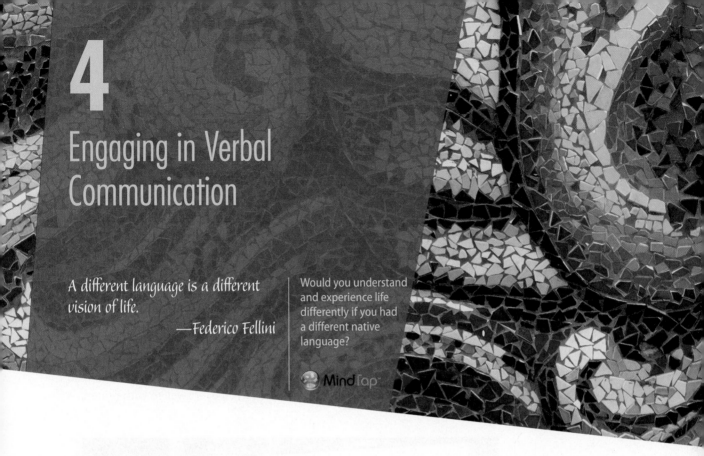

4
Engaging in Verbal Communication

A different language is a different vision of life.

—Federico Fellini

Would you understand and experience life differently if you had a different native language?

 MindTap

Learning Objectives

Topics Covered in This Chapter	After studying this chapter, you should be able to . . .
Language and Meaning	Explain what is meant by the statement, "Language is arbitrary, ambiguous, and abstract."
	Discuss the importance of the three principles that determine how we derive meaning from communication.
	Drawing on your personal experience, describe an example of demand–withdraw pattern.
Symbolic Abilities	Reflect on how each of the six symbolic abilities contributes to the constructive power of language.
Digital Media and Verbal Communication	Compare constituent rules you follow in face-to-face communication to those you follow in social media.
Guidelines for Effective Verbal Communication	Create an action plan to implement this chapter's guidelines to improve your verbal communication.

MindTap

Start with a quick engagement activity and **review** the chapter Learning Objectives.

Read, highlight, and take notes online.

Funerals are sad occasions, so why did hundreds of onlookers cheer as horses slowly pulled the pine coffin through downtown Detroit? Why did Julian Bond tell the onlookers, "The entity in this casket deserves to be dead" (Krolicki, 2007)? Who deserves to be dead? Who was in the casket?

Actually, nobody was in the casket; no person was being buried. This funeral was for the *N*-word. On Monday, July 9, 2007, the National Association for the Advancement of Colored People (NAACP) held a public burial for the *N*-word. This word had hurt many who attended its funeral. It was a mean, hateful word that "deserved to be dead."

Perhaps, as a child, you heard the nursery rhyme, "Sticks and stones can break my bones, but words can never hurt me." By now, most of us have figured out that the nursery rhyme would be more accurate if it were revised to say, "Sticks and stones can break my bones, but words can *really* hurt me." Words can harm us, sometimes terribly. Children often bully each other with name-calling. As children get older, the verbal bullying continues, with some of the cruelest verbal attacks hurled at people who do not conform to conventional social identities and rules. If you've ever been called hurtful names, you know how deeply words can wound.

Words can also enchant, comfort, teach, amuse, and inspire us. Have you ever read a poem or heard a song that captivated you? Have you ever swelled with pride at a

Bill Pugliano/Getty Images

"The entity in this casket deserves to be dead."

supervisor's praise? Have you ever felt bad and talked to a friend who said just the right thing—healing words? Have you ever been inspired to change something about yourself because of a great speech you heard?

Language is our most powerful tool. It allows us to plan, dream, remember, evaluate, reflect on ourselves and the world around us, and define who we are and want to be. Because language is so powerful, we need to understand it and use it in responsible, ethical ways.

In this chapter, we take a close look at verbal communication and explore its power. We begin by defining symbols and discussing principles of verbal communication. Next, we'll examine how language enables us to create meanings for ourselves, others, and our experiences. Third, we explore connections between verbal communication and digital media. Finally, we identify guidelines for effective verbal communication. In Chapter 5, we'll explore the companion system: nonverbal communication.

ENGAGE! Talking a Union into Existence

In Poland in the 1980s, the trade union Solidarity was born. The birth was not a dramatic event. There were no fireworks. There was no grand announcement of a powerful new union. Instead, the union grew out of words. It began with simple, face-to-face conversations among 10 or so workers in a Gdansk shipyard. They talked with each other about wanting freedom from oppressive conditions, about the need for change. Then, this handful of individuals talked with other workers who talked with others and so on. Within just a few months, the Solidarity trade union had more than 9 million members.

Language and Meaning

Language consists of **symbols**, which are representations of people, events, and all that goes on around us and in us. All language is symbolic, yet not all symbols are linguistic. **Nonverbal communication** includes symbols that aren't words, such as facial expressions, posture, and tone of voice. Art and music are also symbolic.

Features of Language

According to Harvard psychologist Steven Pinker (2000, 2008), humans are "verbivores"—a species that lives on words. **Verbal communication**, or language, consists of symbols in the form of spoken or written words. For instance, your name is a symbol that represents you. *Credit hour* is a term that refers to one unit in the total number of units required to graduate. *Love* represents an intense feeling. In combination with nonverbal symbols, verbal symbols form the core of the human world of meaning. As a first step in understanding the power of language, we'll examine three characteristics of symbols: arbitrariness, ambiguity, and abstraction.

Arbitrariness   Language is **arbitrary**, which means that verbal symbols are not intrinsically connected to what they represent. For instance, the term *twerk* has no natural relationship to provocative dancing. Certain words and terms seem right because as a society we agree to use them in particular ways, but they have no inherent correspondence to their referents.

Because meanings are arbitrary instead of necessary, language changes as we invent new words or imbue existing words with new meanings. TV commentators and bloggers have enlarged the political vocabulary with such terms as *Obamamania*, *gender gap*, and *political correctness*. *Cyberspace*, *hyperlink*, *tweet*, and *selfie* are terms we've created to refer to digital communication. To express feelings in online communication, people have invented *emoticons* (also a newly coined word) such as :) for "smile," :(for "frown," :D for "grin," <3 for "love or affection," and ;) for "wink."

symbols Arbitrary, ambiguous, and abstract representations of phenomena. Symbols are the basis of language, much nonverbal behavior, and human thought.

nonverbal communication All forms of communication other than words themselves; includes inflection and other vocal qualities as well as several other behaviors such as shrugs, blushing, and eye movements.

verbal communication Words and only words; does not include inflection, accent, volume, pitch, or other paralinguistic features of speech.

arbitrary Random or not necessary. Symbols are arbitrary because there is no need for any particular symbol to stand for a particular referent.

LOL dotcom BFF

Don't accuse the *Oxford English Dictionary* of being stuffy or old fashioned. Regarded by many as the standard for English usage, the *OED* has a new word team whose job is to consider which new words should be added to formal dictionaries. In the 2009 edition of the *OED*, words added included *ego-surfing* (searching the Internet for references to your name), *irritainment* (programming that irritates viewers but that viewers feel compelled to watch), and *fashionista* (a devotee of cutting-edge fashions). More recent editions include these new words: *smack talk* (banter), *man crush*, *IDC* (I don't care), *muffin top* (a new meaning was added that refers to flesh at the waistline), and *couch surfer* (someone who sleeps on friends' sofas rather than getting her or his own place) (http://www.oxforddictionaries.com/us /words/what-s-new, 2015).

The 2011 edition also includes symbols that arise from technologies and our use of them. In 2011, the *OED* added the following symbols: OMG, wiki, Google, dotcom, LOL, BFF, IMHO, TMI, and the heart symbol (OMG, 2011). And most recently Oxford added the Oxford Dictionaries Online (OIDO) (Dirda, 2013).

 MindTap What are the newest expressions you've noticed in social media?

Because language is dynamic, it changes as the people who use it change. In the United States, language continually incorporates words from people of diverse cultures and social communities. For example, terms from the hip-hop subculture such as *dis* (to disrespect) and words from non-U.S. cultures such as *machismo* and *karma* have been incorporated into English. In fact, English includes many words that originated in other cultures (Carnes, 1994): *cotton* comes from Arabic, *klutz* comes from Yiddish, *khaki* comes from Hindi, and *zombie* comes from language used by the Kongo group.

Ambiguity   Language is **ambiguous**, which means it doesn't have clear-cut, precise meanings. The term *good friend* means "someone to hang out with" to one person and "someone to confide in" to another. *Thanksgiving* may mean different things to Native Americans and European Americans. The meanings of these words vary according to cultural contexts and individuals' experiences. The language is the same, but what it means varies in relation to personal experiences, interests, identities, and backgrounds.

Although language doesn't mean exactly the same thing to everyone, within a culture or social community many words have an agreed-upon range of meanings. Thus, all of us know that the word *dogs* refers to four-footed creatures, but each of us also attributes personal meanings based on dogs we have known and how our families and cultures regard dogs. In some cultures, dogs are food for human consumption—not a meaning of *dogs* in the United States! Conversely, many Westerners eat beef, whereas cows are sacred in Hindu cultures.

The ambiguity of language can lead to misunderstandings. A friend recently told me of misunderstandings that arose when he tried to negotiate a contract with a Japanese firm. My friend, Erik, said that when he made his initial proposal, O-Young, who represented the Japanese company, nodded his head and said, "This is very good." Encouraged, Erik made additional suggestions, and O-Young smiled and responded, "This is a fine idea," and "I admire your work on the project." Yet O-Young consistently refused to sign the contract that contained Erik's proposals. Finally, another American businessperson explained to Erik that Japanese culture regards it as rude to refuse another person directly. To someone socialized in Japanese society, outright disagreement or rejection causes another person to lose face, and that is to be avoided at all costs. Once Erik understood that apparently favorable responses did not mean O-Young agreed with him, their negotiations became much more productive.

Consider other misunderstandings that are fueled by the ambiguity of language. A supervisor criticizes a new employee for "inadequate quality of work." The employee assumes the supervisor wants more productivity; the supervisor means that the employee

ambiguous Subject to multiple meanings. Symbols are ambiguous because their meanings vary from person to person, context to context, and so forth.

should be more careful in proofing material to catch errors. Spouses often have different meanings for "doing their share" of home chores. To many women, it means doing half the work, but to men it tends to mean doing more than their fathers did, which is still less than their wives do (Wood, 2011).

 Ron

A while ago, I told my girlfriend I needed more independence. She got all upset because she thought I didn't love her anymore and was pulling away. All I meant was that I need some time with the guys and some for just myself. She said that the last time a guy said he wanted more independence, she found out he was dating out on her.

Abstraction   Finally, language is **abstract**, which means that words are not the phenomena to which they refer. They stand for those phenomena—ideas, people, events, objects, feelings, and so forth, but they are not the things they represent. According to Steven Pinker (2008), who sees language as a window to human nature, the words we use say far more about us than the world outside of us. Pinker believes that words reflect our attitudes, values, and sense of relationship with others. In using language, we engage in a process of abstraction in which we move further and further away from external or objective phenomena. Words vary in their degree of abstractness. *Reading matter* is a very abstract term that includes everything from philosophy books to the list of ingredients on a cereal package. *Book* is a less abstract word. *Textbook* is even less abstract. And *Communication Mosaics* is the most concrete term because it refers to a specific textbook.

Our perceptions are one step away from the phenomena because perceptions are selective and subjective, as we learned in Chapter 3. We move a second step away from phenomena when we label a perception with language that is value laden. We abstract even further when we respond, not to behaviors or our perceptions of them, but to the labels we impose. This process can be illustrated as a ladder of abstraction (Figure 4.1), a concept developed by two early scholars of communication, Alfred Korzybski (1948) and S. I. Hayakawa (1962, 1964).

As language becomes increasingly abstract, the potential for confusion mushrooms. One way this happens is by overgeneralization. Mass communication often relies on highly general, abstract language to describe groups of people. Terms such as *inner-city youth*, *immigrants*, and *senior citizens* encourage us to notice distinctions

 **Language Creates Reality**

In naming things, language brings them into human consciousness. Here are a few examples of phenomena that all of us are aware of but which became social realities only when they were given names:

◆ *Blog* entered the language only in recent years. First there was the Web, and then there were *weblogs*, soon shortened to *blogs*. To see more social media vocabulary, go to the book's online resources for this chapter.

◆ *Domestic partners* refers to cohabiting, unmarried people who are gay, lesbian, transgender, or heterosexual.

◆ *Birth mother* designates a woman who gives birth but does not keep the child.

◆ *Date rape* is a term created to define as criminal an activity that for a long time took place without being named.

◆ *Environmental justice* refers to a movement to ensure that environmental dangers such as sites for storing toxic wastes are distributed fairly instead of being the burden of poor communities (Cox & Pezzullo, 2016; Pezzullo, 2007).

◆ *Blended family* refers to a family that includes children from one or both partners' previous relationships. Although such families have long existed, only in recent years were they named.

 What terms can you add to illustrate how naming things gives them a social reality that they do not otherwise have?

abstract Removed from concrete reality. Symbols are abstract because they refer to, but are not equivalent to, reality.

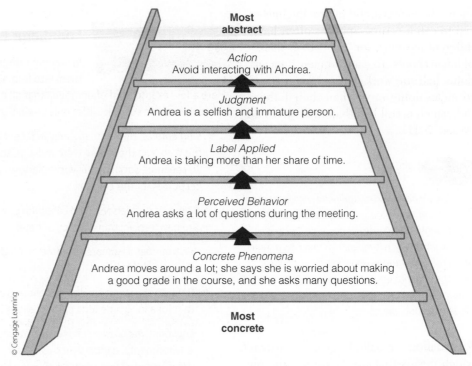

© Cengage Learning

Figure 4.1 The Ladder of Abstraction

between young people who live in the hearts of cities and young people who live else-where, between people who immigrate to the United States and those who were born here, and between people who are elderly and people who are not. At the same time, highly general terms for social groups, such as Asian American, Hispanic American, or African American, incline us to see commonalities among people within the categories but not to recognize distinctions among them. The ENGAGE! box on page 67 shows how labels for racial and ethnic groups have changed and how, with these changes, our perceptions of groups have evolved.

The language we attach to perceptions matters. Researchers have shown that we are more likely to recall behaviors that are consistent with how we've labeled peo-ple than to recall behaviors that are inconsistent (Fincham & Bradbury, 1987). When we say a friend is *insensitive*, we're likely to notice instances in which he is insensitive and to overlook times when he is sensitive. Similarly, if we label a co-worker *lazy*, we predispose ourselves to notice her lazy behaviors and not to perceive conscientious behaviors.

Principles of Communication

Three principles of communication explain how we create meaning for our interactions.

We Interpret Communication   Because language is abstract, ambiguous, and arbitrary, we have to interpret it to determine what it means. Interpretation is an active, creative process we use to make sense of experiences. Although we're usually not conscious of the effort we invest in interpreting words, we continually engage in the process of constructing meanings.

TAKE ACTION…activities are located at the end of this chapter and online.

John Searle (1976, 1995) distinguishes between **brute facts** and **institutional facts**. Brute facts are objective, concrete phenomena and activities. Institutional facts are the meanings of brute facts based on human interpretation. Borrowing an example from Searle (1976), during a football game one brute fact is that periodically people gather into roughly circular clusters. We name that activity the *huddle*, or *huddling*, and the institutional fact is that the players are planning their next play. Searle's point is that we create meaning by using language to represent institutional facts, or the social meanings we attribute to brute facts.

Yet language itself doesn't create meaning. Meaning also grows out of context. If someone says to you, "Get lost," you have to think about the context and the person who made the comment to decide whether it's an insult, friendly needling, or a colloquial way of saying you are out of line. Who the person is and where the interaction happens affect how we interpret the comment.

Rules Guide Communication   Although each of us draws on his or her individual experiences to interpret language, the process of interpretation is not entirely personal. Without realizing it, we learn how to interpret language in the process of being socialized into a particular culture (Argyle & Henderson, 1985; Shimanoff, 1980). People for whom English is a second language find English idioms such as "get lost," "easy as pie," and "dead right" very difficult to interpret (Lee, 2000). Go to the book's online resources for this chapter to learn more about idioms that can be confusing to people for whom English is a second language.

Communication rules are shared understandings among members of a particular culture or social group about what communication means and what behaviors are appropriate in various situations. Children often are taught that *please* and *thank you* are magic words that they should use. We learn that *sir* and *ma'am* are polite words to use when addressing our elders or people who have authority over us. In the course of interacting with our families and others, we unconsciously absorb rules that guide how we communicate and how we interpret others' communication. Research shows that children begin to understand and follow communication rules by the time they are one or two years old (Miller, 1993).

ENGAGE! The Languages of Race and Ethnicity

Our labels for races and ethnicities have changed over time (Davis, 1997; Delgado, 1998; Johnson, 1999; Martin, Krizek, Nakayama, & Bradford, 1996; Orbe & Harris, 2015; Tanno, 1997).

◆ In America's early years, Irish Catholic and Eastern European immigrants were not classified as *white*. Today they are.

◆ Historic and current labels for African Americans include *Negroes*, *coloreds*, *African Americans*, *people of color*, *blacks*, and *Afro-Americans*.

◆ Historic and current labels for indigenous people of Alaska include *Eskimo* and *Inuk*.

◆ Historic and current labels for Asians and Asian Americans include *Asians*, *Asian nationals*, and *Orientals*, as well as more specific ethnic labels such as *Japanese*, *Korean Americans*, and *Vietnamese Americans*.

◆ Native Americans may be called *Indians* or *Native Americans* or by labels that reference their specific nations, such as *Oneida* and *Sioux*.

◆ European Americans may be called *whites*, *Caucasians*, *European Americans*, or just plain *Americans*, which reflects the naive presumption that, in America, white is the "normal" race.

◆ Labels for South Americans include *Hispanics*, *Latinos* and *Latinas*, *Chicanos* and *Chicanas*, and more specific labels, such as *Cubanos* and *Mexicans*.

 MindTap   What do you perceive as the preferred terms today for ethnic groups?

brute facts Objective, concrete phenomena.

institutional facts Meanings people assign to brute facts (objective, concrete phenomena) that are based on human interpretation.

communication rules Shared understandings of what communication means and what behaviors are appropriate in various situations.

regulative rules
Communication rules that regulate interaction by specifying when, how, where, and with whom to talk about certain things.

constitutive rules
Communication rules that specify how certain communicative acts are to be counted.

Two kinds of rules guide our communication (Cronen, Pearce, & Snavely, 1979; Pearce, Cronen, & Conklin, 1979). **Regulative rules** regulate interaction by specifying when, how, where, and with whom to communicate about certain things. For instance, European Americans generally don't interrupt when someone is making a formal presentation, but in more informal settings interruptions may be appropriate. Some African Americans follow a different rule, which specifies that audience members should participate in public presentations by calling out responses. The rules of some cultures say that interrupting in any context is impolite.

Some families have a rule that people cannot argue at the dinner table, whereas other families regard arguments as a normal accompaniment to meals. Families also teach us rules about how to communicate in conflict situations (Honeycutt, Woods, & Fontenot, 1993; Jones & Gallois, 1989; Yerby, Buerkel-Rothfuss, & Bochner, 1990). Regulative rules also define when, where, and with whom it's appropriate to show affection and disclose private information. Regulative rules vary across cultures; what is considered appropriate in one society may be regarded as impolite or offensive elsewhere.

Constitutive rules define what a particular communication means or stands for. We learn that most people regard specific kinds of communication as showing respect (listening attentively, not correcting) and rudeness (talking over others). We also learn what communication is counted as friendship (sharing confidences, defending our friends when others criticize them), professionalism (making good contributions in group meetings, creating supportive climates), and intimacy (offering support, expressing affection). Like regulative rules, constitutive rules are shaped by cultures. A Take Action item at the end of this chapter allows you to reflect on rules that you follow in your communication.

Rules guide our everyday interactions by telling us when to communicate, what to communicate, and how to interpret others' verbal and nonverbal communication. Casual social interactions tend to adhere to rules that are widely shared in a society. Interaction between intimates also follows rules, but these are private rules that reflect special meanings partners have created (Duck, 2006; Wood, 2006). Television networks follow rules for what can and cannot be said and shown during specific times and rules for how often they insert commercials. Online chat rooms and forums develop specific and often unique rules for how people express themselves and respond to one another. Every organization develops a distinctive culture, which includes rules about how members interact.

Few rules are rigidly fixed. Like communication itself, most rules are subject to change. When we decide that a rule is not functional, we negotiate changes in it. A company may find that its rule for making decisions by consensus no longer works once the company triples in size, so voting becomes a constitutive rule to define decision making. When we don't have a rule for a particular kind of interaction, we invent one and often negotiate and refine it until it provides the assistance we want in structuring communication. When couples have a child, they often find that they don't have any guidelines for new communication situations, so they develop rules: "We take turns eating so one of us is free to hold the baby," or "Interrupting our conversation when the baby cries does not count as rudeness."

We don't have to be aware of communication rules in order to follow them. For the most part, we're really not conscious of the rules that guide how, when, where, and with whom we communicate about various things. We may not realize we have rules until one is broken, and we become aware that we had an expectation. Becoming aware of communication rules empowers you to change those that do not promote good interaction, as Emily's commentary illustrates.

 Emily

My boyfriend and I had this really frustrating pattern about planning what to do. He'd say, "What do you want to do this weekend?" And I'd say, "I don't know. What do you want to do?" Then he'd suggest two or three things and ask me which of them sounded good. I would say they were all fine with me, even if they weren't. And this would keep on forever. Both of us had a rule not to impose on the other, and it kept us from stating our preferences, so we just went in circles about any decision. Well, two weekends ago I talked to him about rules, and he agreed we had one that was frustrating. So we invented a new rule that says each of us has to state what we want to do, but the other has to say if that is not okay. It's a lot less frustrating to figure out what we want to do since we agreed on this rule.

Punctuation Affects Meaning   We punctuate communication to interpret meaning. Like the punctuation you studied in grammar classes, **punctuation** of verbal communication is a way to mark a flow of activity into meaningful units. Punctuation is our perception of when interaction begins and ends (Watzlawick, Beavin, & Jackson, 1967).

Before we can attribute meaning to communication, we must establish its boundaries. Usually this involves deciding who initiated communication and when the interaction began. If a co-worker suggests going out to lunch together, you might perceive the invitation as marking the start of the interaction. If you return another person's phone call, you might perceive the original call as the beginning of the episode. If someone insults you, you might define the insult as the act that marks the start of a quarrel.

When we don't agree on punctuation, problems may arise. If you've ever heard children arguing about who started a fight, you understand the importance of punctuation. Because people enter online discussions at different times, it's difficult to know who launched a particular topic or which messages initiate ideas and which are responses to earlier messages.

In personal relationships, a common instance of conflicting punctuation is the demand–withdraw pattern (Figure 4.2; Bergner & Bergner, 1990; Caughlin & Vangelisti, 2000; Christensen & Heavey, 1990; Wegner, 2005). In this pattern, one person demands something such as disclosure, and the other pulls away to avoid disclosing. The more the first person demands ("Tell me what's going on in your life"), the more the second person withdraws ("There's nothing to tell"). The people involved may be co-workers, friends, romantic partners, or a parent and an adolescent-child (Caughlin & Ramey, 2005). Each person punctuates the interaction as having started with the other: The demander thinks, "I demand because you withdraw," and the withdrawer thinks, "I withdraw because you demand." There is no objectively correct punctuation, because it depends on subjective perceptions.

Recent research (Shiffert & Schwartz, 2011) shows that men's, but not women's, sense of well-being is lowered when either they make

punctuation Defining the beginning and ending of interaction or interaction episodes. Punctuation is subjective and not always agreed on by those involved in the interaction.

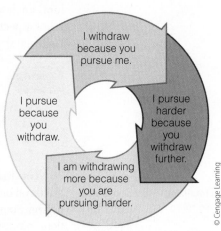

I withdraw because you pursue me.

I pursue harder because you withdraw further.

I am withdrawing more because you are pursuing harder.

I pursue because you withdraw.

© Cengage Learning

Figure 4.2 The Demand–Withdraw Pattern

demands of their spouses or their spouses make demands of them. To break out of unconstructive cycles such as demand–withdraw, people need to realize that they may punctuate differently and should discuss how each of them experiences the pattern. A Take Action item at the end of this chapter encourages you to check perceptions to see if you and another person are punctuating congruently.

Interpretation, communication rules, and punctuation influence the meaning we assign to language. These three principles highlight the creativity involved in constructing meaning to make sense of communication. We're now ready to explore the power of symbols by discussing uniquely symbolic abilities.

Symbolic Abilities

The ability to use language allows humans to live in a world of ideas and meanings. Instead of reacting without reflection to our concrete environments and experiences, we think about them and sometimes transform what they mean. Philosophers of language have identified six ways in which symbolic capacities affect our lives (Cassirer, 1944; Langer, 1953, 1979). As we discuss each, we'll consider how to recognize the constructive power of language and minimize the problems it can cause.

Language Defines Phenomena

The most basic symbolic ability is definition. We use words to define ourselves, others, experiences, relationships, feelings, and thoughts (Monastersky, 2002). In turn, the labels we use affect how we perceive what we have labeled. You see a car on the lot at a dealership and it is "a car." You test drive it, decide to buy it, and it becomes "my car," and you perceive it differently than when it was "a car." What has changed is not the car, but the meaning you attach to it and symbolize with the possessive label.

The labels we use to define others affect how we perceive them. When we label someone, we focus attention on particular aspects of that person and her or his activities. At the same time, we necessarily obscure other aspects of that person's identity. A person might be a loving father, a conservative, a concerned citizen, and a demanding supervisor, but we are unlikely to use all of those labels to define him. Each label directs our attention to certain aspects of the person and away from other aspects. This implies that we have an ethical responsibility to consider how our language shapes our perceptions of others. Orest's reflection makes this point.

 *Orest*

A lot of people relate to me as Asian, like that's all I am. Sometimes in classes, teachers ask me to explain the "Asian point of view," but they do not ask me to explain my perspective as a premed major or a working student. I am an Asian, but that is not all that I am.

Totalizing is responding to a person as if one label totally represents that person. We fix on one symbol to define someone and fail to recognize many other aspects of the person. Some people totalize gay men and lesbians by noticing only their sexual orientation. Interestingly, we don't totalize heterosexuals on the basis of *their* sexual orientation. Totalizing also occurs when we dismiss people by saying, "She's old," "He's just a jock," or

totalizing Responding to a person as if one aspect of that person were the total of who the person is.

"She's an illegal alien." Totalizing is not the same as stereotyping. When we stereotype someone, we define the person in terms of the characteristics of a group. When we totalize someone, we negate most of that person by spotlighting a single aspect of his or her identity. Reneé points out a form of totalizing that really bothers her.

 *Renée*

Okay, here's my issue. I love fashion—I mean I really love great clothes, jewelry, shoes, makeup—all of it! I'm always the first to wear a cool new style. So a lot of people brand me ditsy or silly. But I'm also Phi Beta Kappa and I've been accepted to law school. Why do people think that if you're into fashion, you can't also be smart and serious?

The symbols we use affect how we think and feel. If we describe our work in terms of frustrations, problems, and disappointments, we're likely to feel negative about it. On the other hand, if we describe rewards, challenges, and successes, we're likely to feel more positive about our work. The way we define experiences in relationships also affects how we feel about them. My colleagues and I asked romantically involved couples how they defined differences between them (Wood, Dendy, Dordek, Germany, & Varallo, 1994). We found that some people defined differences as positive forces that energize a relationship and keep it interesting. Others defined differences as problems or barriers to closeness. We noted a direct connection between how partners defined differences and how they acted. Partners who viewed differences as constructive approached their disagreements with curiosity, interest, and an expectation of growth through discussion. In contrast, partners who labeled differences as problems dreaded disagreements and tried to avoid talking about them.

People who consistently use negative labels to describe their relationships heighten their awareness of aspects of the relationships that they don't like and diminish their awareness of aspects that they do like (Cloven & Roloff, 1991). In contrast, partners who focus on good facets of relationships are more conscious of virtues in partners and relationships and are less bothered by flaws (Bradbury & Fincham, 1990; Fletcher & Fincham, 1991).

Conservative commentators in mass media and social media sometimes refer to "knee-jerk liberals" and "tree huggers," whereas liberal commentators refer to the same groups of people as "progressives" and "environmentalists." Depending on which commentators you listen to, you might have different perceptions of people in these groups.

ENGAGE! Don't Take This the Wrong Way, But...

Do you flinch when someone prefaces a comment to you with "Don't take this the wrong way, but …"? If so, there's a good reason. We know that what follows the phrase is not going to be pleasant to hear. How about "I'm only saying this because I care about you" or "I hate to be the one to break this to you"? Ouch—we know a verbal punch will follow those phrases. These are examples of what linguists call hedges that attempt to let the speaker avoid the consequences of what she or he says. In other words, the hedges say *don't blame me for what I'm saying.*

And then there are phrases that mean exactly the opposite of what they state. For example, "I'm not saying that you aren't doing the job well, Emma" means you *are* saying Emma is not doing the job well. "I'm not saying we can't still see each other" means you don't plan to see that person, at least not in the way you have been seeing her or him. We tend to use these verbal qualifiers because we are uncomfortable being direct about our intentions, thoughts, or feelings (Bernstein, 2014).

 MindTap Monitor your communication to see how often you use qualifying or hedging phrases. Could you find ways to speak more directly and honestly?

Language Evaluates Phenomena

As we noted when we discussed the ladder of abstraction, language is not neutral; it is laden with values. We describe people we like with language that accents their good qualities and downplays their flaws ("My friend is self-confident"). The reverse is true of our language for people we don't like ("My enemy is arrogant"). We might describe people who speak their minds as honest, assertive, outspoken, courageous, or authoritarian. Each word has a distinct connotation. Restaurants use words to enhance the attractiveness of menu entries. A dish described as "tender, milk-fed veal sautéed in natural juices and topped with succulent chunks of lobster" sounds more appetizing than one described as "meat from a baby calf that was kept anemic to make it tender, then slaughtered, cooked in blood, and topped with the flesh of a crustacean that was boiled to death."

The language we use also has ethical implications in terms of how it affects others. Most people with disabilities prefer not to be called "disabled," because that totalizes them in terms of a disability. The term *African American* emphasizes cultural heritage, whereas *black* focuses on skin color. *Hispanic* defines people by the Spanish language spoken in countries of origin, whereas *Latina* and *Latino* highlight the geographic origin of women and men, respectively.

Loaded language is words that slant perceptions, and thus meanings, exceedingly. Loaded language encourages extreme perceptions. Terms such as *geezer* and *old fogey* incline us to regard older people with contempt or pity. Alternatives such as *senior citizen* and *elder* reflect more respectful attitudes. In 2014, the U.S. Patent and Trademark Office canceled the Washington Redskins' trademark on the name *redskins* because the term disparages Native Americans ("A Victory," 2014).

An interesting communication phenomenon is the **reappropriation** of language. This happens when a group reclaims a term used by others to degrade its members and treats that term as a positive self-description. Reappropriation aims to remove the stigma from term that others use pejoratively. For instance, some gays, lesbians, and transgender people have reappropriated the term *queer* and use it as a positive statement about their identity. Southern writer Reynolds Price developed cancer of the spine that left him paraplegic. He scoffed at terms such as *differently abled* and *physically challenged*; he referred to himself as a *cripple* and to others who do not have disabilities as *temporarily able-bodied*. Perhaps the most controversial example of reappropriation is some African Americans' use of a word that was a racial epithet for years. In his book *Nigger: The Strange Career of a Troublesome Word* (2002), Harvard law professor Randall Kennedy traces the word's history and found that the word *nigger* is derived from *niger*, which is the Latin word for the color black. By the 18th century in America, it had become a particularly offensive racial slur. Today, Kennedy notes, the word is still a vile slur when used by non-blacks, but some blacks have reappropriated the term and use it among themselves.

loaded language An extreme form of evaluative language that relies on words that strongly slant perceptions and thus meanings.

reappropriation A group's reclamation of a term used by others to degrade the group's members; the treatment of those terms as positive self-descriptions. Aims to remove the stigma from terms that others use pejoratively.

Maynard

I'm as sensitive as the next guy, but I just can't keep up with what language offends what people anymore. When I was young, Negro *was an accepted term, then it was* black, *and now it's* African American. *Sometimes I forget and say* black *or even* Negro, *and I get accused of being racist. It used to be polite to say* girls, *but now that offends a lot of the women I work with. Just this year, I heard that we aren't supposed to say* blind *anymore, and we're supposed to say* visually impaired. *I just can't keep up.*

Probably many of us sympathize with Maynard, who was 54 when he took a course with me. Keeping up with changes in language is difficult, and occasionally we may offend someone unintentionally. Nonetheless, we should try to learn what terms hurt or insult others and avoid using them. We also should tell others when they've referred to us in ways we dislike. As long as you speak assertively but not confrontationally, others are likely to respect your ideas.

Language Organizes Experiences

Words organize our perceptions of events and experiences. As we learned in Chapter 3, the categories into which we place people influence how we interpret them and their communication. A criticism may be viewed as constructive if made by someone we categorize as a friend but insulting if made by someone we classify as an enemy. The words don't change, but their meaning varies depending on the category into which we place the person speaking those words. Because symbols organize our perceptions into broad categories, we don't have to consider each object and experience individually. This allows us to think about abstract concepts such as justice, integrity, and good family life. Our capacity to use broad concepts enables us to transcend specific concrete activities and enter the world of conceptual thought and ideals.

Our ability to abstract can also distort thinking. A primary way this occurs is by stereotyping, which is thinking unreflectively in broad generalizations about a whole class of people or experiences. Examples of stereotypes are "Management doesn't care about labor," "Teachers are smart," "Jocks are dumb," "Politicians lie," "Religious people are good," and "Conflict is bad." Notice that stereotypes can be positive or negative generalizations.

Common to all stereotypes is the classification of a phenomenon into a category based on general characteristics of members of the category. When we use terms such as *Native American*, *senior*, and *white collar workers*, we may see only what members of each group have in common and not perceive differences among individuals in the group. Clearly, we have to generalize; we simply cannot think about each and everything in our lives distinctly. However, stereotypes can obscure important differences among phenomena we lump together. Therefore, we have an ethical responsibility to monitor stereotypes and to stay alert to differences among things we place in any category.

Language Allows Hypothetical Thought

Where do you hope to be five years from now? What is your fondest childhood memory? What would you do if you won the lottery next week? To answer these questions, you must engage in **hypothetical thought**, which is thinking about experiences and ideas that are not part of your concrete, daily reality. Because we can think hypothetically, we can plan, dream, remember, set goals, consider alternative courses of action, and imagine possibilities.

Language allows us to name and imagine possibilities beyond what currently exists. Technology experts have conceived of many possibilities, such as implantable memory chips that will allow us to speak another language without having learned it. This kind of memory chip is still on the drawing boards of technology innovators, but we can think about it now because we have the term *implantable memory chip*. Not too many years ago, technology innovators imagined worldwide networks that connected people through computers; today that is a reality.

hypothetical thought
Thinking about experiences and ideas that do not exist or are not immediately present to the senses.

Alexander Raths/Shutterstock.com

Imagining the possibility of cures for diseases inspires scientists.

Hypothetical thought is possible because we are symbol users. Words give form to ideas so that we can hold them in our minds and reflect on them. We can contemplate things that have no real existence, and we can remember ourselves in the past and project ourselves into the future. Our ability to inhabit past, present, and future explains why we can set goals and work toward them, even though we do not realize the goal immediately (Dixson & Duck, 1993). For example, you've invested many hours in attending classes, studying, and writing papers because you have the idea of yourself as someone with a college degree. The degree is not real now, nor is the self that you will become once you have the degree. Yet the idea is sufficiently real to motivate you to work hard for many years. You can imagine yourself wearing academic regalia at your graduation, think of yourself as having a degree, and visualize yourself working in the career you plan to enter.

Hypothetical thought can enrich personal relationships by allowing intimates to remember shared moments. One of the strongest glues for intimacy is the ability to remember a history of shared experiences (Bruess, 2015; Bruess & Hoefs, 2006; Cockburn-Wootten & Zorn, 2006; Wood, 2006). Because they can remember rough times they have weathered, intimates can often get through trials in the present. Language that refers to a shared future ("When we're rocking on the porch at 80") also fuels intimacy. We interact differently with people we don't expect to see again and with those who are ongoing parts of our lives. Talking about future plans and dreams, another use of hypothetical thought, knits intimates together because it makes real the idea that more is yet to come (Acitelli, 1993; Wood, 2006).

Hypothetical thought also allows us to imagine being in places we have never visited. Television programs and Web sites show us faraway countries and expose us to people with different values, traditions, and ways of living. When we listen to or see programs or visit sites to learn about other cultures, we can think about these cultures and imagine visiting them.

Thinking hypothetically helps us improve who we are. We notice progress we have made when we can remember earlier versions of ourselves, and we motivate further self-growth when we envision additional improvements in ourselves. Your ability to think hypothetically enables you to chart a path of continuous growth. As Duk-Kyong points out, remembering ourselves at earlier times also allows us to notice progress we make toward achieving our goals.

 ## Duk-Kyong

Sometimes I get very discouraged that I do not yet know English perfectly and that there is much I still do not understand about customs in this country. It helps me to remember that when I came here 2 years ago I did not speak English at all, and I knew nothing about how people act here. Seeing how much progress I have made helps me to not be discouraged with what I do not yet know.

Language Allows Self-Reflection

Just as we use language to think about times in the past and future and to shape our perceptions of others, we use it to reflect on ourselves. We think about our existence and reflect on our actions. In his classic work in this area, George Herbert Mead (1934) noted that self-reflection is the foundation of human identity. Since Mead's original work, other scholars have developed his ideas and reaffirmed their importance (Atkinson & Housley, 2003; Leeds-Hurwitz, 2006; Sandstrom, Martin, & Fine, 2001).

According to Mead, the self has two aspects: the *I* and the *me*. The *I* is the spontaneous, creative self. The *I* acts impulsively in response to inner needs and desires, regardless of social norms. The *I* is the part of you that wants to send a really nasty e-mail message to a chat room visitor whom you find offensive.

The *me* is the socially conscious part of self that monitors and moderates the *I*'s impulses. The *me* reflects on the *I* from the social perspectives of others. The *me* is the part of you that says, "Hey, don't send that e-mail when you're so angry." The *I* is impervious to social conventions, but the *me* is keenly aware of them. If your supervisor criticizes your work, your *I* may want to tell that boss off, but your *me* censors that impulse and reminds you that subordinates have to defer to their bosses.

Because we have both spontaneous and reflective parts of ourselves, we can think about who we want to be and set goals for becoming the self we desire. We can feel shame, pride, and regret for our actions—emotions that are possible because we self-reflect. We can control what we do now by casting ourselves forward to consider how we might feel about our actions later—a point that Tiffany makes in her commentary.

Carolyn C. Wood/Julia T. Wood

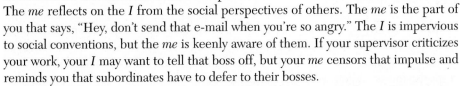

MindTap When my niece Michelle told me she had learned to read, she was bursting with pride. How might reflecting on this accomplishment affect how Michelle thinks about herself?

 *Tiffany*

My mother-in-law thinks it's wrong that I go to school instead of being a full-time homemaker and mother. She constantly criticizes me for neglecting my children and home. So many times I have wanted to tell her to butt out of my family, but I stop myself by reminding myself that in the long term it's important to me and my husband and the kids to maintain decent relations.

As Tiffany's commentary points out, self-reflection also empowers us to monitor ourselves. When we monitor ourselves, the *me* notices and evaluates the *I*'s impulses and may modify them based on the *me*'s awareness of social norms. For instance, during a discussion with a co-worker you might say to yourself, "I'm just sitting here like a lump on a log. I need to show that I'm interested in what he's saying." Based on your monitoring, you might listen more carefully, give feedback, and ask questions to show interest. Effective public speakers monitor audiences. If members of the audience start looking bored, speakers adapt by changing speaking pace or volume or by introducing a visual aid to add interest. When interacting with people from different

I The creative, spontaneous, impulsive aspect of the self. The *I* is complemented by the *me*.

me The reflective, analytical, socially conscious aspect of self. *Me* complements the *I* aspect of self.

cultures, we monitor by reminding ourselves that they may not operate by the same values and communication rules that we do. Self-reflection allows us to monitor our communication and adjust it to be effective and ethical.

Self-reflection also allows us to manage the image we present to others. When talking with teachers and supervisors, you may consciously use language that represents you as respectful, attentive, and responsible. When interacting with parents, you may repress some language that surfaces in discussions with your friends. When texting, you may use abbreviations and acronyms that are part of communication norms in social media. We continually use language to manage the images we project in particular situations and with specific people.

Language Defines Relationships and Interaction

A sixth way in which language creates meaning in our lives is by defining relationships and interaction. Our verbal communication conveys messages about how we perceive ourselves and others. "Mr. Buster" symbolizes a more formal relationship than "Phil." We also use language to regulate interaction. We signal that we want to speak by saying, "Excuse me" or "Let me jump in here." We invite others to speak by saying, "Do you have an opinion about this?" or "I'd like to hear what you think about the issue." You'll recall that in Chapter 1 we discussed two levels of meaning: the content level and the relationship level. There are three dimensions of relationship-level meaning (Mehrabian, 1981).

Responsiveness   One facet of relationship-level meaning is *responsiveness*. Through questions and statements of agreement or disagreement, we show attentiveness to others' communication. When we give thoughtful feedback to a colleague, we show responsiveness. When we ask an interviewee to elaborate ideas, we demonstrate interest in him or her. When we like or comment on a friend's post, we show interest. Different social and cultural groups learn distinct rules for showing responsiveness. For instance, women generally display greater verbal responsiveness than men do (Montgomery, 1988; Ueland, 1992), and Koreans tend to limit verbal responses more than Americans typically do.

Liking   A second dimension of relationship-level meaning is *liking*. We express liking verbally when we say, "I really enjoy being with you," "I'm glad we're working on the same team," and so forth. Conversely, we verbally communicate dislike by saying, "I don't want to spend time with you." In addition to these general rules shared in Western society, particular social groups instill more specific rules. Masculine socialization emphasizes emotional control and independence, so men are less likely than women to verbalize their feelings of affection for most other people. Feminine socialization encourages many women to verbalize feelings of warmth.

Power   The third aspect of relationship-level meaning is *power*. We use verbal communication to define dominance and to negotiate status and influence. Men typically exceed women in efforts to establish control over others. Research has shown that men are more likely than women to exert control verbally by controlling conversations, having the last word, interrupting, and correcting others (DeFrancisco, 1991). People in positions of power in organizations often express control with authoritative statements such as, "That's how it's going to be" and "I've heard all I want to hear."

Like many aspects of communication, the power dimension of relationship meaning is influenced by culture. Western cultures tend to favor competitiveness and overt displays of power more than many other cultures. For example, in negotiations Japanese tend to understate their initial position, stress areas of agreement with other negotiators, and work to avoid failure, or loss of face, for any of the negotiators. This is quite different from American negotiating tendencies, such as overstating initial positions to appear strong, being adversarial, and trying to make sure they win and other negotiators lose.

Summing up, we use language to define and evaluate phenomena, organize experiences, think hypothetically, self-reflect, and define relationships and interaction. Each of these abilities helps us create meaning in our personal, professional, and social relationships.

Digital Language

If you post a selfie and your friend tweets squee, you're good. And the whole reason you're online anyway is FoMo. Srsly.

Social media have prompted lots of new words such as the ones above: selfie = photo taken of yourself that is uploaded to a social media site; squee = delight, joy; FoMO = fear of missing out; srsly = seriously. If you've reached the end of this box, then you won't have to reply with TL:DR = too long didn't read (Dirda, 2013).

 To what extent do you think digital language enhances communication? To what extent does it hamper communication?

Digital Media and Verbal Communication

How does what we have learned about verbal communication apply to digital media? One of the most obvious ways is coining new words to describe experiences and modes of communication that are unique to digital media. Some of the words we invented are variations on words and phrases that already exist: *buddy list*, *netiquette*, and *cyberbullying*. Other words are wholly new, invented to describe what happens in cyberspace. For instance, *blog*, *virtual reality*, and *avatar* are words we have created to name experiences in computer-mediated communication (CMC).

The rules that we discussed apply to CMC just as they do to face-to-face communication. What regulative rules have evolved to govern when, where, and with whom it is appropriate to communicate online and digitally? Are there people you do not text, but instead call or e-mail? Are there people you do not e-mail but always text? Do you follow different rules for sharing personal information online and in face-to-face conversations?

Now think about constitutive rules you follow when using social media. What counts as a timely reply to a post? A tweet? A text? What counts as rudeness in texting? What counts as supportive in commenting on posts on social networking sites?

Guidelines for Effective Verbal Communication

Because language is arbitrary, abstract, and ambiguous, the potential for misunderstanding always exists. In addition, individual and cultural differences foster varying interpretations of language. Although we can't completely eliminate misunderstandings, we can minimize them by following four guidelines for using verbal communication effectively.

Urban Dictionary in the Courtroom

Is someone who calls himself a "jack boy" a thief? Is "catfishing" illegal? These are but two of many questions that confront contemporary courts (Kaufman, 2013). Conventional dictionaries aren't much help when courts are trying to understand slang, because those dictionaries seldom include the most current street language. Enter *Urban Dictionary* (www.urbandictionary.com), a crowdsourced site created by Aaron Peckham in 1999 when he was a first-year college student.

In 2013, a Wisconsin court had to rule on whether a convicted thief had to pay restitution to his victims. To decide, the court consulted *Urban Dictionary* to decode the term *jack boy*, which the thief had called himself. The definition, "to steal or take from an unsuspecting person or store," led the court to rule against the thief. *Urban Dictionary* defines *catfishing* as "Internet predators' fabricating online identities," which helped decide another case.

 Do you think crowdsourced documents are appropriate resources for deciding legal cases?

Engage in Person-Centered Communication

The single most important guideline for using language effectively is to be person-centered in your communication. Recall from Chapters 1 and 3 that person-centered communication is adapted to specific individuals. When I talk with colleagues about communication theories, I use language that is specialized and incomprehensible to people who aren't communication scholars. When I talk with undergraduate students about the same theories, I adapt my language to students' experiences and knowledge. Medical doctors need highly specialized vocabularies to discuss medical problems with other doctors, but they should translate that vocabulary into ordinary language when talking with patients. In public presentations, speakers adapt their language to the knowledge and attitudes of listeners. If listeners already favor what a speaker advocates, the speaker can use more impassioned language than if listeners are opposed to what he or she advocates. Person-centered communicators adapt to listeners.

Be Aware of Levels of Abstraction

We can reduce the likelihood of misunderstandings by being conscious of levels of abstraction. Much confusion results from language that is excessively abstract. For instance, a professor says, "Your papers should demonstrate a sophisticated conceptual grasp of material and its pragmatic implications in your subjective circumstances." Would you know how to write a paper to satisfy the professor? The language is so abstract that it is hard to figure out what the professor wants. Here's a more concrete description: "Your papers should include definitions of the concepts and specific examples that show how they apply to your personal life."

Abstract language is not always inadvisable. The goal is to use a level of abstraction that suits particular communication objectives and situations. Abstract words are appropriate when speakers and listeners have similar knowledge about what is being discussed. For example, long-term friends can say, "Let's just hang out" and understand the activities implied by the abstract term *hang out*. More-concrete language is useful when communicators don't have shared experiences and interpretations. For example, early in a friendship the suggestion to hang out would be more effective if it included specifics: "Let's hang out today—maybe watch the game and order pizza." Although abstract language is appropriate in some situations, it often contributes to misunderstandings. For example, online communication is easily misunderstood because it lacks many of the nonverbal cues that clarify meaning. Abstract language may also promote misunderstandings when people talk about changes they want in one another. For example, "I want you to show more initiative in your work" could mean that the person who is speaking wants the other person to work more hours, take on new projects, or seek less direction from supervisors. Vague abstractions promote misunderstanding when people don't share concrete referents for the abstract terms they use.

Qualify Language

Another strategy for increasing the clarity of communication is to qualify language. Two types of language require qualification. First, we should qualify generalizations so that we don't mislead ourselves or others into mistaking a general statement for an absolute one. "Politicians are crooked" is a false statement because it is overly general. A more accurate statement would be, "A number of politicians have been shown to be dishonest." Qualifying reminds us that our perceptions are tied to specific times, places, and circumstances.

We should also qualify language when describing and evaluating people. A **static evaluation** is an assessment that suggests that something is unchanging. Static evaluations are particularly troublesome when applied to people: "Ann is selfish," "Don is irresponsible," "Vy is rude." Whenever we use the word *is,* we suggest that something is fixed. In reality, we aren't static but continually changing. A person who is selfish at one time may be generous at other times. A person who is irresponsible on one occasion may be responsible in different situations. Ken's commentary illustrates that static evaluations can be both inaccurate and irritating.

 *Ken*

Parents are the worst for static evaluations. When I first got my license seven years ago, I had a fender bender and then got a speeding ticket. Since then, I've had a perfect record, but you'd never know it from what they say. Dad's always calling me "hot rodder," and Mom goes through this safety spiel every time I get ready to drive somewhere. You'd think I was the same now as when I was 16.

One technique for qualifying language is to index words. **Indexing** is a technique to remind us that our evaluations apply only to specific times and circumstances (Korzybski, 1948). To index, we would say "Ann $_{\text{June 6, 2014}}$ acted selfishly," "Don $_{\text{on the task committee}}$ was irresponsible," and "Vy $_{\text{in the meeting}}$ was rude." See how indexing ties description to a specific time and circumstance? Mental indexing reminds us that we and others change.

Own Your Feelings and Thoughts

We often use verbal language in ways that obscure our responsibility for how we feel, think, and act. For instance, people say, "You made me mad," or "You made me do that," as if what they felt or did were caused by someone else. When a person says, "You're so demanding," the person really means that she or he feels pressured by what someone else wants or expects. Feeling pressured is that person's response. Although others can influence us, they seldom determine how we feel. Our feelings and thoughts result from how we interpret others' communication. Although how we interpret what others say may lead us to feel certain ways, it is *our* interpretation that guides our responses.

In certain contexts, such as abusive relationships, others may powerfully shape how we think and feel. Yet even in these extreme situations, we need to remember

static evaluation An assessment that suggests that something is unchanging or static; e.g., "Bob is impatient."

indexing A technique of noting that every statement reflects a specific time and circumstance and may not apply to other times or circumstances.

You-Language	I-Language
You hurt me.	I feel hurt when you ignore what I say.
You're really domineering.	When you shout, I feel dominated.
You humiliated me.	I felt humiliated when you mentioned my problems in front of your friends.

© Cengage Learning

Figure 4.3 *I-* and *You*-Language

I-language Language that identifies the speaker's or perceiver's thoughts and feelings. (Compare with *you*-language.)

you-language Language that attributes intentions and motives to another person, usually the person to whom one is speaking. (Compare with *I*-language.)

that we, not others, are responsible for our feelings. We can disapprove of what others do without surrendering control of our thoughts, feelings, and actions. Telling others they make you feel some way is also likely to arouse defensiveness, which doesn't facilitate healthy personal or professional relationships. Effective communicators take responsibility for themselves by using language that owns their thoughts and feelings. They claim their feelings and do not blame others for what happens within themselves.

To take responsibility for your feelings, rely on **I-language**, not **you-language**. *I*-language identifies the speaker's or perceiver's thoughts and feelings, whereas *you*-language attributes intentions and motives to another person. Figure 4.3 gives examples of *I-* and *you*-language.

There are two differences between *I*-language and *you*-language. First, *I*-statements own responsibility, whereas *you*-statements project it onto another person. Second, *I*-statements are more descriptive than *you*-statements. *You*-statements tend to be accusations that are abstract and unspecific. This is one reason that *you*-language is ineffective in promoting change. *I*-statements provide concrete descriptions of behaviors without holding the other person responsible for how we feel.

Some people feel awkward when they first start using *I*-language. This is natural because most of us have learned to rely on *you*-language. With commitment and practice, however, you can learn to communicate using *I*-language. Once you feel comfortable using it, you will find *I*-language has many advantages. First, it is less likely than *you*-language to make others defensive, so *I*-language opens the doors for dialogue. Second, *I*-language is more honest. We deceive ourselves when we say, "You make me feel..." because others don't control how we feel. Finally, *I*-language is more empowering than *you*-language. When we say, "You did this" or "You made me feel that," we give control of our emotions, thoughts, and actions to others. This reduces our personal power and our motivation to change what is happening. Using *I*-language allows you to own your feelings while also explaining to others how you interpret their behaviors.

Summary

In this chapter, we've explored ways that verbal communication shapes who we are, what we do, and the meaning we attach to our experiences. Because they are arbitrary, ambiguous, and abstract, words do not have objective concrete meanings. Instead, the significance we give them reflects our life experiences and the regulative and constitutive rules of the culture and the social groups to which we belong.

Our ability to use symbols, whether in digital or face-to-face interactions, is a key part of the foundation of communication and human life. By defining, evaluating, and classifying phenomena, language allows us to order our experiences and feelings. In addition, we use language to think hypothetically, to self-reflect, and to define relationships and interactions. We increase the effectiveness of our verbal communication when we are person-centered and conscious of levels of abstraction, as well as own our thoughts and feelings, and when we qualify language appropriately. In Chapter 5, we'll see how nonverbal communication complements and extends verbal communication by allowing us to create meaning.

Experience Communication Case Study

The Roommates

Apply what you've learned in this chapter by analyzing the following case study, using the accompanying questions as a guide. These questions and a video of the case study are also available online with your MindTap Speech for *Communication Mosaics*.

Bernadette and Celia were assigned to be roommates a month ago when the school year began. Both were initially pleased with the match because they discovered commonalities in their interests and backgrounds. They are both sophomores from small towns, they have similar tastes in music and television programs, and they both like to stay up late and sleep in. Lately, however, Bernadette has been irritated by Celia's housekeeping—or lack of it!

Celia leaves her clothes lying all over the room. When they cook, Celia often leaves the pans and dishes for hours, and then it's usually Bernadette who cleans them. Bernadette feels she has to talk to Celia about this problem, but she hasn't figured out how or when to talk. When Celia gets in from classes, Bernadette is sitting on her bed, reading a textbook.

Celia: Hey, Bernie, how's it going?

[Celia drops her book bag in the middle of the floor, flops on the bed, and kicks her shoes off onto the floor. As Bernadette watches, she feels her frustration peaking and decides now is the time to talk to Celia about the problem.]

Bernadette: You shouldn't do that. You make me nuts the way you just throw your stuff all over the room.

Celia: I don't "throw my stuff all over the room." I just took off my shoes and put my books down, like I do every day.

Bernadette: No, you didn't. You dropped your bag right in the middle of the room, and you kicked your shoes where they happen to fall without ever noticing how messy they look. And you're right—that *is* what you do every day.

Celia: There's nothing wrong with wanting to be comfortable in my own room. Are we suddenly going for the Good Housekeeping Seal of approval?

Bernadette: Comfortable is one thing. But you're so messy. Your mess makes me really miserable.

Celia: Since when? This is the first I've heard about it.

Bernadette: Since we started rooming together, but I didn't want to say anything about how angry you make me. I just can't stand it anymore. You shouldn't be so messy.

Celia: Sounds to me like you've got a problem—you, not me.

Bernadette: Well it's you and your mess that are my problem. Do you have to be such a slob?

© Cengage Learning

1. Identify examples of *you*-language in this conversation. How would you change it to *I*-language?

2. Identify examples of loaded language and ambiguous language.

3. Do you agree with Celia that the problem is Bernadette's, not hers? Explain your answer.

4. To what extent do Celia and Bernadette engage in dual perspective to understand each other?

Key Concepts

Practice defining the chapter's terms by using online flashcards.

abstract, 65

ambiguous, 64

arbitrary, 63

brute facts, 67

communication rules, 67

constitutive rules, 68

hypothetical thought, 73

I, 75

I-language, 80

indexing, 79

institutional facts, 67

loaded language, 72

me, 75

nonverbal communication, 63

punctuation, 69

reappropriation, 72

regulative rules, 68

static evaluation, 79

symbol, 63

totalizing, 70

verbal communication, 63

you-language, 80

Reflect, personalize, and apply what you've learned

Review, Reflect, Extend

The Reflect and Discuss and Take Action features that follow will help you review, reflect on, and extend the information and ideas presented in this chapter. These resources, and a diverse selection of additional study tools, are also available online at the MindTap Speech for *Communication Mosaics.*

Reflect and Discuss

1. In the chapter, we learned that language names experiences and that language is continuously evolving. As a class, identify experiences, feelings, or other phenomena for which we don't yet have names. What is a good term to describe someone with whom you have a serious romance? *Boyfriend* and *girlfriend* no longer work for many people. Do members of your class prefer *significant other, romantic partner, special friend,* or another term?

2. Visit chat rooms and online forums and notice the screen names that people use. How do the names people create for themselves shape perceptions of their identities? What screen names do you use? Why did you choose them?

3. The national Student Voices Project was created in 2000 by the Annenberg Public Policy Center to encourage college-aged people to get involved with political issues. Over the years, it has been launched in multiple cities. Learn more about this project by going to the book's online resources for this.

TAKE ACTION

1. Communicating Clearly

To express yourself clearly, it's important to translate ambiguous words into concrete language. Practice translating with these examples:

Ambiguous Language	Concrete Language
You are rude.	I don't like it when you interrupt me.
We need more team spirit.	_____
I want more freedom.	_____
Your work is sloppy.	_____
That speaker is unprofessional.	_____

2. Communication Rules

Think about the regulative and constitutive rules you follow in your verbal communication. For each item listed here, identify two rules that guide your verbal behavior.

Regulative Rules

List rules that regulate your verbal communication when

a. Talking with elders

b. Interacting at dinnertime

c. Having first exchanges in the morning

d. Greeting casual friends on campus

e. Talking with professors

Constitutive Rules

How do you use verbal communication to show

a. Trustworthiness

b. Ambition

c. Disrespect

d. Support

e. Anger

After you've identified your rules, talk with others about their rules. Are there commonalities among your rules that reflect broad cultural norms? What explains differences in individuals' rules?

3. Punctuating Interaction

The next time you and another person enter an unproductive cycle, stop the conversation and discuss how each of you punctuates interaction.

a. What do you define as the start of interaction?

b. What does the other person define as the beginning?

c. What happens when you learn about each other's punctuation? How does this affect understanding between you?

4. Learning to Use *I*-Language

a. For the next 24 hours, pay attention to instances in which you use *you*-language. Catch yourself saying, "You made me angry," "You're being pushy," or engaging in other uses of *you*-language. Whenever you do so, change your language to *I*-language: "I feel angry when you…" or "I feel pressured when you…"

b. Do your thoughts and feelings about what is happening change when you substitute *I*-language for *you*-language?

Recommended Resources

1. Visit the Institute of General Semantics Web site by going to the book's online resources for this chapter.

2. Pinker, S. (1994). *The language instinct: How mind creates language.* New York: Harper Perennial; Pinker, S. (2008). *The stuff of thought: Language as a window to human nature.* New York: Penguin.

These books provide accessible discussions of how language works. Unlike some books on the subject of language, Pinker's books are written with clarity and a sharp sense of humor. Be warned that Pinker's ideas are controversial—some scientists do not agree with his theories of language and mind.

5

Engaging in Nonverbal Communication

What you do speaks so loud that I cannot hear what you say.
—Ralph Waldo Emerson

When a person's nonverbal and verbal communication are contradictory, which do you believe?

Learning Objectives

Topics Covered in This Chapter	After studying this chapter, you should be able to . . .
Principles of Nonverbal Communication	Discuss the importance of each of the five principles that clarify how nonverbal communication works.
	Drawing on your personal experience, describe an interaction in which nonverbal communication conveyed relationship-level meaning.
Types of Nonverbal Behaviors	Differentiate among the 10 types of nonverbal communication.
Digital Media and Nonverbal Communication	Comment on the use of emoticons or stickers in social media as a means of nonverbal expression.
Guidelines for Effective Nonverbal Communication	Create an action plan to implement this chapter's guidelines to strengthen your nonverbal communication.

MindTap™

Start with a quick engagement activity and **review** the chapter Learning Objectives.

Read, highlight, and take notes online.

Last summer my partner Robbie and I went to London with our friends Todd and Steve. One evening the four of us decided to visit a restaurant others had recommended. Dans le Noir, which is French for *in the dark*, is a restaurant staffed by blind servers, most of whom wear shirts emblazoned with the message *Ignorance is the only real blindness*. Diners have the experience of being sightless as they dine in pitch darkness. We could not see our food or plates or each other. Our server gave us a pitcher of water and told us to fill our glasses, which was a real challenge since we couldn't see the pitcher or glasses.

Without sight, conversation was awkward. I said something to Steve, but I couldn't see his face so I wasn't sure how he felt about my comment. Steve replied, and I was about to continue the conversational thread with him when Todd jumped in because he was unable to see that I was getting ready to speak. Robbie put his hand on my arm and I was startled because I didn't see the hand coming and, at first, didn't know it was his.

Our experience at Dans le Noir reminded me of how much we rely on nonverbal communication in our everyday interactions. Many of us grew up hearing "actions speak louder than words." The wisdom of this axiom is that nonverbal communication can be as powerful as or more powerful than words. Facial expressions can express love, suspicion, competitiveness, sorrow, interest, anger, and hatred. Body postures can convey relaxation, nervousness, boredom, and power. Dress can express social standing, cultural heritage, religious commitment, political values, and military rank. Physical objects can symbolize professional identity (stethoscope, briefcase), personal commitments (wedding band, school sweatshirt), and lifestyle (comfortable furniture casually arranged, stiff furniture in formal rooms).

In this chapter, we learn about the fascinating realm of nonverbal interaction. Like its verbal cousin, nonverbal communication powerfully affects our lives. We will identify principles of nonverbal communication and then explore types of nonverbal behavior. The third section of this chapter discusses relationships between nonverbal communication and digital media. As usual, the chapter concludes with guidelines for effectiveness.

Principles of Nonverbal Communication

Nonverbal communication includes all aspects of communication other than words. In addition to gestures and body language, nonverbal communication includes *how* we utter words (inflection, volume), features of environments that affect meaning (temperature, lighting), and objects that affect personal images and interaction patterns (dress, furniture). Nonverbal communication accounts for 65 to 93 percent of the total meaning of communication (Birdwhistell, 1970; Hickson, Stacks, & Moore, 2004; Mehrabian, 1981). Five principles clarify how nonverbal communication works.

Nonverbal Communication Is Ambiguous

Like verbal communication, nonverbal behavior is ambiguous. We can never be sure that others understand the meanings we intend to express with our nonverbal behavior. Conversely, we can't know whether they read meanings into our behaviors that

nonverbal communication All forms of communication other than words themselves; includes inflection and other vocal qualities as well as several other behaviors such as shrugs, blushing, and eye movements.

we do not intend. The ambiguity of nonverbal communication also arises because meanings change over time. Spreading apart the first two fingers meant victory during the world wars and came to stand for peace during the 1960s.

Nonverbal communication is guided by rules just as verbal communication is. These rules reduce the ambiguity of nonverbal communication by telling us what certain behaviors are understood to count as (constitutive rules) and when and where certain behaviors are appropriate and inappropriate (regulative rules). For example, most of us understand that people take turns speaking, and that we should whisper in libraries but it's appropriate to yell at ball games. We know that we are supposed to raise our hands if we want to ask a question during a lecture but don't need to raise our hands to speak when interacting with friends. We know we should dress differently for religious services, classes, and cookouts. Westerners know that a handshake is the standard greeting between business people whereas Japanese and Chinese business people often follow the constitutive rule of bowing as a respectful greeting (Samovar, Porter, McDaniel, & Roy, 2015). Culturally agreed-upon rules reduce but don't completely eliminate the ambiguity of nonverbal communication.

Nonverbal Behaviors Interact with Verbal Communication

Communication researchers have identified five ways in which nonverbal behaviors interact with verbal communication (Guerrero & Floyd, 2006; Knapp, Hall, & Horgan, 2013). First, nonverbal behaviors may repeat verbal messages. For example, you might say "yes" while nodding your head. In making a public presentation, a speaker might hold up one, two, and three fingers when saying "first," "second," and "third," to let listeners know she or he is moving from the first to the second to the third point of a speech.

Second, nonverbal behaviors may highlight verbal communication, as when you use inflection to emphasize certain words: "This is the *most* serious problem with the business plan." Third, nonverbal communication may complement, or add to, words. Speakers often emphasize verbal statements with forceful gestures and increases in volume; capital or boldfaced letters are used to symbolize the same emphasis in online communication.

Fourth, nonverbal behaviors may contradict verbal messages. For instance, a supervisor says, "Nothing's wrong" in a hostile tone of voice. Finally, we sometimes substitute nonverbal behaviors for verbal ones. You might roll your eyes to show that you disapprove of something or shrug your shoulders instead of saying, "I don't know." In all these ways, nonverbal behaviors interact with verbal communication.

Nonverbal Communication Regulates Interaction

Nonverbal communication can organize interaction between people (Guerrero & Floyd, 2006). Nonverbal cues tell us when someone else has finished speaking, when a professor wants discussion from students, and when interruptions are not welcome. By averting our eyes or by increasing our speaking volume and rate, we signal that we don't want to be interrupted. When we're finished talking, we look at others to signal, "Okay, now someone else can speak." Most Westerners invite specific people to speak by looking directly at them, yet eye contact is used less to regulate interaction in a number of cultures (Samovar et al., 2015). Although we're usually unaware of how nonverbal actions regulate interaction, we rely on them to know when to speak and when to remain silent.

Nonverbal Communication Establishes Relationship-Level Meanings

You'll recall that the relationship level of meaning defines relationships between communicators. Nonverbal communication can be powerful in expressing relationship-level meanings (Keeley & Hart, 1994). In fact, some communication scholars call nonverbal communication "the relationship language" because it so often expresses how people feel about one another (Richmond & McCroskey, 1995). We use nonverbal communication to convey the three dimensions of relationship-level meaning that we discussed in Chapter 4: responsiveness, liking, and power. Yet *how* people communicate responsiveness, liking and disliking, and power depends on the rules of their cultures and social communities.

Responsiveness   We use eye contact, inflections, facial expressions, and body posture to show interest in others. In formal presentations and casual conversations, Westerners signal interest by holding eye contact and assuming an attentive posture. However, all cultures do not have the same rules for eye contact. To express lack of interest, Westerners tend to avoid or decrease visual contact and adopt a passive body position or turn away from the other person. Members of some Asian cultures consider it rude to express lack of interest overtly, so they rely on more indirect indicators of lack of interest.

There are gender differences in responsiveness. As a rule, females tend to smile and to maintain eye contact and nod more in response to communication by others whereas males smile and nod less and often engage in less eye contact (Hall, 2006; Miller, 2011).

 *Maryam*

Americans do more than one thing at a time. In Nepal, when we talk with someone, we are with that person. We do not also write on paper or have television on. We talk with the person. It is hard for me to accept the custom of giving only some attention to each other in conversation.

Liking   Nonverbal behaviors are keen indicators of whether we feel positive or negative about others. Smiles and friendly touching among Westerners usually are signs of positive feelings, whereas frowns and belligerent postures express antagonism (Keeley & Hart, 1994). Political candidates shake hands, slap backs, and otherwise touch people whose votes they want. These are general rules of Western society; particular social groups instill more specific rules. For example, women generally sit closer together and engage in more eye contact and more friendly touching than men do (Atsuko, 2003; Knapp et al., 2013).

Harmony in people's postures and facial expressions may reflect how comfortable they are with each other (Guerrero & Floyd, 2006) and how much they support each other (Trees, 2000). In a cohesive team, many nonverbal behaviors typically signal that members are responsive to one another. In less cohesive groups, nonverbal behavior shows less responsiveness. In work settings people who like one another often sit together at meetings and during breaks.

Power   We use nonverbal behaviors to assert dominance and to negotiate status (Knapp et al., 2013; Remland, 2000). Compared with women, men generally assume more space and use greater volume and more forceful gestures to assert their ideas (Knapp et al., 2013; Major, Schmidlin, & Williams, 1990). Men are also more likely than women to move into others' spaces, touch others, and use eye contact to assert dominance.

Space also expresses power. The connection between power and space is evident in the fact that CEOs usually have large, spacious offices, entry-level and midlevel professionals have smaller offices or cubicles, and secretaries often have minuscule workstations, even though secretaries often store and manage more material than executives. A widely understood regulative communication rule is that people with status or power have the right to enter the space of people with less power, but the converse is not true. Similarly, more-powerful people are more likely to touch others, interrupt, and approach more closely than less-powerful people (Hall, Coats, & Smith-LeBeau, 2004). In families, adults usually have more space than children, and men are more likely than women to have their own rooms and to sit at heads of tables.

Jean-Louis Belluget/fotosearch

MindTap   Which person in this photo has greater power? How is it expressed?

 Ellen

Secretaries are the best decoders. They can read their bosses' moods in a heartbeat. I am a secretary, part-time now that I'm taking courses, and I can tell exactly what my boss is thinking. Sometimes, I know what he feels or will do before he does. I have to know when he can be interrupted, when he feels generous, and when not to cross his path.

Silence, a powerful form of nonverbal communication, can also be a means of exerting control. We sometimes use silence to stifle others' conversation in meetings. Silence accompanied by a glare is doubly powerful in conveying disapproval. Interviewers sometimes use silence to let interviewees know that they are not satisfied with answers given and to prompt interviewees to elaborate. In a number of Native American cultures and some Asian cultures, silence signals mindful attentiveness.

Nonverbal Communication Reflects Cultural Values

Like verbal communication, nonverbal patterns reflect rules of specific cultures (Andersen Hecht, Hoobler, & Smallwood, 2002; Guerrero & Farinelli, 2009; Samovar, Porter, & McDaniel, 2013; Samovar et al., 2015). This implies that most nonverbal communication isn't instinctual but is learned in the process of socialization. For instance, most Westerners consider it inappropriate to touch or hold hands with same-sex friends, especially male friends, but this is an acceptable way of showing closeness in some non-Western cultures (Orbe & Harris, 2015; Samovar et al., 2013).

The United States is a highly individualistic culture in which people want private spaces, and we resent and sometimes fight anyone who trespasses on what we consider our territory. We want private homes, and our own rooms within those homes. We don't want others to get too close to us, unless they are intimates. In more collectivist cultures, people tend to be less territorial. For instance, Brazilians routinely stand close to one another in shops, buses, and elevators, and when they bump into each other, they don't apologize or draw back, as U.S. citizens do. In other countries, such as Hong Kong, people are used to living and working in very close quarters (Chan, 1999).

Western culture prizes time, and that is evident in the presence of clocks in most or all rooms of homes and public spaces and in the nearly universal use of wristwatches, which are not worn by people in many other cultures. Westerners' time consciousness is also reflected in the technological devices that are now part of many people's daily attire. We carry pagers, iPads, and smartphones to maintain nearly instant contact with others. Orientations toward time are more fluid and flexible among some cultural groups, such as Hispanics.

TAKE ACTION…activities are located at the end of this chapter and online.

 *Yumiko*

> *I try to teach my daughter to follow the customs of my native Japan, but she is learning to be American. I scold her for talking loud and speaking when she has not been addressed, but she tells me all the other kids talk loud and talk when they wish. I tell her it is not polite to look directly at others, but she says everyone looks at others here. She communicates as an American, not a Japanese.*

Patterns of eye contact also reflect cultural values. U.S. society values frankness and assertion, so meeting another's eyes is considered appropriate and a demonstration of personal honesty. Yet in many Asian and northern European countries, direct eye contact is considered abrasive and disrespectful (Axtell, 2007; Samovar et al., 2013, 2015). Many Latinos and Latinas express attentiveness and respect by avoiding direct eye contact, whereas European Americans express attentiveness and respect by maintaining it (Orbe & Harris, 2015). In Brazil, eye contact often is so intense that many Northern Europeans consider it staring, which they find rude.

Sensory perception—our experience of touch, smell, taste, sight, and sound—is shaped by culture to a surprising degree. Recent research (Howes & Classen, 2013; Luhrmann, 2014) shows that how keenly we perceive particular sensations depends on the culture in which we live. For example, English-speaking people are quite adept at sensing color but far less skilled in differentiating smells. Conversely, rain-forest people in the Jahai on the Malay Peninsula are keenly tuned to smells.

The five principles of nonverbal communication we have discussed provide a foundation for a closer look at specific kinds of nonverbal communication.

Types of Nonverbal Behaviors

Because so much of our interaction is nonverbal, this symbol system includes many kinds of communication. In this section, we will discuss 10 forms of nonverbal behavior that we use to create and interpret meanings:

◆ Kinesics (face and body motion)

◆ Haptics (touch)

- Physical appearance

- Olfactics (smell)

- Artifacts (personal objects)

- Proxemics (personal space)

- Environmental factors

- Chronemics (perception and use of time)

- Paralanguage (vocal qualities)

- Silence

Kinesics

Kinesics refers to body position and body motions, including those of the face. Our bodies communicate a great deal about how we see ourselves. A speaker who stands erect and appears confident announces self-assurance, whereas someone who slouches and shuffles may seem to say, "I'm not very sure of myself." We also communicate moods with body posture and motion. For example, someone who walks quickly with a resolute facial expression appears more determined than someone who saunters along with an unfocused gaze. Similarly, people whose nonverbal behaviors indicate they have sufficient vigor to take care of themselves and move quickly are less likely to be attacked than people whose posture and movements indicate less vitality (Gunns, Johnston, & Hudson, 2002). We sit rigidly when we are nervous and adopt a more relaxed posture when we feel at ease. Audiences show interest by alert body posture and good eye contact with speakers, and they signal disinterest by slumped posture and lack of eye contact.

Body postures and gestures may signal whether we are open to interaction. Speakers who stay behind podiums and read notes often are perceived as less open than speakers who speak without notes or barriers between them and audiences. Someone who sits with arms crossed and looks downward may be perceived as saying, "Don't bother me." That's also a nonverbal strategy students sometimes use to dissuade teachers from calling on them in class. To signal that we'd like to interact, we look at others and sometimes smile. We use gestures to express how we feel about others and situations. We use one hand gesture to say "okay" and a different hand gesture to communicate contempt.

Our faces are intricate messengers. Our eyes can shoot daggers of anger, issue challenges, express skepticism, or radiate love. The face is particularly powerful in conveying liking and responsiveness (Keeley & Hart, 1994; Patterson, 1992). Many speakers smile to suggest that they are open and friendly. Smiles and warm gazes signal that we like others and are happy being around them (Gueguen & De Gail, 2003). Americans often cross their legs while seated, but this is highly offensive according to cultural rules in Ghana and Turkey (Samovar et al., 2013, 2015).

Poets call the eyes the "windows to the soul" for good reason. Our eyes communicate important and complex messages about how we feel, and we often look at others' eyes to judge their emotions, honesty, and self-confidence. This explains why strong eye contact tends to heighten the credibility of public speakers in Western societies. Yet eye contact is not universally regarded as positive. Among traditional Hasidic Jews, for example, boys are taught not to look into women's eyes.

kinesics Body position and body motions, including those of the face, that may be used to communicate or may be interpreted as communicating.

I Can Tell You're Lying by Your Eyes

Have you ever looked into someone's eyes to decide if the person is telling the truth? If so, you're not alone. Most of us think we can spot liars by their shifty eyes or nervous gestures. The Transportation Screening Authority (TSA) shares the belief that deceptive people can be identified by their body language. The evidence, however, suggests otherwise.

TSA has invested roughly a billion dollars training "behavior detection officers" to discern nonverbal behaviors that indicate a person is a terrorist. When the TSA's program was evaluated in 2013, the Government Accountability Office recommended discontinuing the program because there was no proof it was effective (Tierney, 2014). Scientific research supports the recommendation to cut funds. A large number of studies show that people correctly identify liars only 47 percent of the time, which is less than random picking would have accomplished (Hartwig & Bond, 2011).

According to Nicholas Epley (2014), professor of Behavioral Science at the University of Chicago, most people vastly overestimate their ability to decipher what others think based on others' nonverbal behaviors. Like the TSA, most of us think people betray their deceptions with body language that we can read. And like the TSA, we're probably wrong.

 MindTap Do you believe you can read others' nonverbal behaviors?

Weighty Matters

Getting a job is a weighty matter. Literally. Researchers have conducted experiments on the impact of touch on decisions we make (Schmid, 2010). In one experiment, people were asked to evaluate a job candidate's résumé. For half of the people, the résumé was attached to a lightweight clipboard that weighed three-fourths of a pound. The other half of the people read the résumé attached to a four and one-half pound clipboard. People holding the heavy clipboard evaluated the job candidate more highly.

Intrigued by how the sense of touch affected judgments of the job candidate, the researchers devised another experiment. They told 86 people who were trying to buy a car that their first offer had been rejected and they should make a second offer. Some of the would-be car buyers were seated on stiff, hard chairs whereas others were seated on comfortable, cushioned chairs. The people seated in the hard chairs raised their offer by an average of $896.50 whereas the people in the more comfortable chairs raised their offer by an average $1,243.60.

Haptics

Haptics is a term for nonverbal communication involving physical touch. Many communication scholars believe that touching and being touched are essential to healthy life (Ackerman, 1990; Whitman, White, O'Mara, & Goeke-Morey, 1999). In disturbed families, parents sometimes push children away and handle them harshly, nonverbally signaling rejection. Conversely, researchers have learned that babies who are massaged thrive more than babies who are touched less (Miller, 2006; Mwakalye & DeAngelis, 1995).

Touch lies at the heart of much of human experience. Touch is everything from the first caress a newborn feels to the embrace of a lover, from a healer's hands on a broken body to a vicious punch, from the sensual pleasure of stroking velvet to the pain of being pricked by a thorn, and from a helping hand to being kicked while down. Cultural anthropologist Constance Classen (2012) refers to touch as the "deepest sense" because it is so basic to human life throughout history. We long to touch what and whom we consider beautiful and desirable: kittens, puppies, babies, luxurious clothes, and sculpture.

Research suggests some general sex differences in touching behavior. Compared to men, women are more likely to engage in touch to show liking and intimacy

haptics Nonverbal communication involving physical touch.

(Andersen, 1999), whereas men are more likely than women to use touch to assert power and control (Jhally & Katz, 2001).

Physical Appearance

Western culture places an extremely high value on **physical appearance** and on specific aspects of appearance. We first notice obvious physical qualities such as sex, skin color, and size. Based on physical qualities, we may make inferences about others' personalities. Although these associations may have no factual basis, they can affect personal and social relationships as well as decisions about hiring, placement, and promotion.

Cultures prescribe ideals for physical form, and these vary across cultures and over time. Currently, Western cultural ideals emphasize thinness in women and muscularity and height in men (Kimmel, 2013; Lamb & Brown, 2006; Levin & Kilbourne, 2008; Spar, 2013). Appearance is a more significant concern for girls and women than boys and men because it is more central to how women are judged. Three out of four women say their appearance is a main factor affecting their self-image, and a third of women rank appearance as more important to self-image than job performance or intelligence (Rhode, 2010). As a result, many women tend to become preoccupied with dieting and other means of weight control (Buss, 2001; Davies-Popelka, 2015). If you'd like to learn more about eating disorders and help for people who have them, go to the book's online resources for this chapter. In her commentary, Cass makes a point that will be familiar to many women.

ENGAGE! ## Kissing: Two Weeks of a Lifetime

Kissing is usually not considered a science, but hold on! Sheril Kirshenbaum's (2011) new book, *The Science of Kissing*, provides some facts about kissing.

◆ About two-thirds of people tilt their head to the right when kissing.

◆ The racing heart and elevated blood pressure that often accompany kissing are caused by the neurotransmitter dopamine, which is related to pleasure and emotional responses.

◆ Passionate, smoldering kissing burns 6.4 calories a minute.

◆ Over a lifetime, the average person spends approximately 2 weeks kissing.

◆ Men tend to like sloppy, wet kisses more than women, perhaps because those kisses transfer men's saliva, which contains testosterone and may enhance women's interest in further intimacy.

◆ Closed-lip kisses require only two facial muscles whereas French kisses involve all 34 facial muscles.

◆ How many bacteria are exchanged in kissing? You don't want to know: millions—yes, millions!

 *Cass*

I've been dieting since I was in grammar school. I'm 5' 5" and weigh 102 pounds, but I want to weigh less. I look at the models in magazines and the women in films, and they are so much slimmer than I am. I have to watch everything I eat and exercise all the time, and I'm still too fat.

This general cultural standard for attractiveness is modified by ethnicity and socioeconomic class. Traditional African societies perceive full-figured bodies as symbols of health, prosperity, and wealth, all of which are desirable (Bocella, 2001). African Americans who embrace this value accept or prefer women who weigh more than the ideal for European American women (Berry, 2014; Mernissi, 2004; Schooler, Ward, Merriwether, & Caruthers, 2004; Walker, 2007). But ethnicity doesn't operate in isolation. Socioeconomic class modifies ethnic views about weight. Research shows that middle-income African American women who are upwardly mobile may deemphasize their ethnic identities and become more susceptible to mainstream culture's ideal of very thin women and to eating disorders (Bocella, 2001).

physical appearance A form of nonverbal communication; how we look, including the cultural meanings, values, and expectations associated with looks.

Pictorial Press Ltd/Alamy

©Anton Oparin/Shutterstock.com

 MindTap™   What is your perspective on changes in cultural ideals for the female body from that of Marilyn Monroe in the 1950s to top models today?

Physical appearance includes physiological characteristics, such as eye color and height, as well as ways in which we manage, or even alter, our physical appearance. For instance, many people control their physical appearance by dieting, using steroids and other drugs, coloring their hair, wearing colored contact lenses, and using makeup. People also manage appearance through cosmetic surgeries and procedures, which increasing numbers of both men and women have. Women most often have breast augmentation, tummy tuck, liposuction, eyelid surgery, and breast lift (American Society of Plastic Surgeons, 2014). The most popular surgeries for men are liposuction, eyelid surgery, rhinoplasty, and face lifts (American Society of Plastic Surgeons, 2014). Both sexes also increasingly rely on less invasive treatments such as soft tissue filler, chemical peels, and laser hair removal (American Society of Plastic Surgeons, 2014).

Olfactics

Olfactics (from the word *olfactory*, which refers to the sense of smell) is a term for odors and scents—or, more precisely, our perception of them. As we've noted, perceptions are shaped by culture, and our sense of smell is no exception. Westerners are less able to identify particular smells such as cinnamon, peanut butter, and coffee than people in many other cultures (Luhrmann, 2014). The smell of freshly baked bread or cookies often makes us feel happy (and hungry!). Also, as Andy notes, scents we choose to wear can be personal signatures.

olfactics The perception of scents and odors; one form of nonverbal communication.

 *Andy*

I dated this one girl for two years, and then we broke up last year. By now, I pretty much don't think about her unless I pass somebody who is wearing the cologne she wore. One sniff of that transports me back to when she and I were together.

Andy is not alone in responding strongly to smells. Natalie Angier (2008), Pulitzer-prize-winning science columnist and science reporter, points out that olfaction is the first of our senses to develop and that it remains the quickest—we register and respond to smells faster than to sights or sounds. Further, smells are processed in the brain's ancient limbic system where emotional memories are stored. That's why the smell of cinnamon takes me back to baking cookies with Mom when I was six years old. Body odors produced by pheromones, the sex-specific chemicals our bodies produce, may affect sexual attraction. Male sweat contains a pheromone derived from progesterone, whereas female sweat contains a phero-

 **ENGAGE!**

Kangaroo Care

Kangaroo Care is the title of Susan Ludington-Hoe's 1993 book. In it, she tells the story of an accidental discovery about the importance of touch to human survival. Until recently, it was typical for Western hospital workers to take newborn babies to nurseries where sophisticated monitoring devices could be used to ensure the babies' health.

The wisdom of separating newborns from mothers was challenged by an accidental finding from a hospital in Bogotá, Colombia. In the 1980s, the hospital experienced a serious lack of resources, including blankets used to wrap newborns. To keep the babies warm, hospital workers placed the naked babies on their mothers' naked chests. The babies thrived—more than they had when wrapped in blankets (Miller, 2006). Because the skin-to-skin contact between mothers and babies is similar to that of kangaroo moms and babies, the technique was dubbed "kangaroo care." Since the accidental discovery in Bogotá, hospitals in the United States have reported that premature babies who experience skin-to-skin contact with their moms are less fussy and calmer than premature babies who do not (Miller, 2006).

mone linked to estrogen (Bakalar, 2006). Heterosexual men and women respond to the pheromones of the opposite sex with increased activity in the hypothalamus, which is linked to sexual behavior. Interestingly, lesbians respond with elevated hypothalamic activity to the estrogen-like pheromone of other women (Bakalar, 2006).

Artifacts

Artifacts are personal objects we use to announce our identities and to personalize our environments. More women than men wear makeup and jewelry. Women are also more likely than men to wear form-fitting clothes and high-heeled shoes. Typically, men wear less jewelry, clothes with less adornment, and functional shoes (Johnson, Roberts, & Warell, 2002; Klein, 2001). Men's clothing is looser and less binding, and it includes pockets for wallets, change, keys, and so forth. In contrast, women's clothing often doesn't include pockets, so women need purses to hold personal items.

Artifacts reflect distinct organizational identities: Bankers, attorneys, and many other professionals are expected to wear business suits or dresses to work, whereas employees at many high-tech companies wear jeans and other informal attire. Each way of dressing reflects a particular organizational ethos. Nurses and doctors usually wear white and often drape stethoscopes around their necks; many executives carry briefcases, whereas students more often tote backpacks. White-collar professionals tend to wear tailored outfits and dress shoes, whereas blue-collar workers often dress in jeans or uniforms and boots. The military requires uniforms that define individuals as members of the group. In addition, stripes, medals, and insignia signify rank and accomplishments.

artifact Any personal object with which one announces one's identities or personalizes one's environment.

Branded

The artifacts we choose increasingly announce political commitments. A baseball hat says, "End Sweatshop Labor"; a T-shirt proclaims, "Save the Planet"; a bumper sticker reads, "Biodiesel is the future"; a button says, "Free Choice" and another declares, "Pro Life." More and more people seem to want their clothes, cars, coffee mugs, and other objects to send messages about their political values.

Artifacts that announce our values are different than those that serve as free ads for commercial companies when we wear T-shirts with their brands on us. To watch a video on commercial interests in having us advertise for them, go to book's online resources for this chapter.

 MindTap® Do you wear clothes that have messages? If so, what do they say about your identity?

Individuals' fashion choices may put their personal stamps on positions. When George W. Bush was president, he insisted on formal dress—coat and tie—at all times in the Oval Office. He once chewed out a staff person who dared to wear khakis and a buttoned-down shirt on a Saturday, and the staff person was not allowed to enter the Oval Office (Stolberg, 2009). When he became president, Barack Obama created a less formal working culture in the White House. He sometimes takes off his jacket while working in the Oval Office, and he often skips the tie on weekends. Similarly, Michelle Obama opted for bolder and often less expensive ensembles than most previous first ladies.

We use artifacts to define settings and personal territories (Bateson, 1990; Wood, 2006). When national leaders speak, the setting usually is decked with symbols of national identity and pride, such as flags. At annual meetings of companies, the chair usually speaks from a podium that bears the company logo. In much the same manner, we claim our private spaces by filling them with objects that matter to us and that reflect our experiences and values. Lovers of art adorn their homes and offices with paintings and sculptures that reflect their interests. Religious families often express their commitments by displaying pictures of holy scenes and the Bible, the Koran, or other sacred text. Professionals may decorate their offices with expensive furniture and framed awards to announce their status or with pictures of family to remind them of people they cherish. MySpace and Facebook pages include songs, photos, and images aimed at conveying specific personalities. Like other kinds of nonverbal communication, artifacts' meanings vary across cultures, as the ENGAGE! Feature on the next page illustrates.

We also use artifacts to express cultural and ethnic identities. Indians may wear saris, Native Americans may wear jewelry with tribal symbols, and African Americans may wear clothes and jewelry of traditional African design. Further, as any college student knows, school symbols adorn everything from T-shirts and sweatshirts to car bumpers and notebooks. Wearing something with a symbol of your school on it declares your membership in or loyalty to that campus community.

Sam Gosling (2008) published an interesting book on artifacts: *Snoop: What Your Stuff Says About You*. Gosling refers to bumper stickers, tattoos, posters, and so forth as "identity claims," which give signals about how we want others to perceive us and also remind ourselves of who we are. For instance, when moving out of her home state, one woman Gosling studied tattooed the outline of her state on her inside forearm. It was intended for her eyes to remind her of her home state.

Proxemics and Personal Space

proxemics A form of non-verbal communication that involves space and how we use it.

Proxemics refers to space and how we use it. The classic research on proxemics was done by Edward Hall in 1968. At the time, Hall reported that every culture has norms for using space and for how close people should be to one another. In the

United States, we interact with social acquaintances from a distance of 4 to 12 feet but are comfortable with 18 inches or less between us and friends or romantic partners (Hall, 1968). Most people who were born and raised in the United States consider it normal for individuals to have separate spaces or rooms. As Sucheng points out, however, what is considered a normal amount of individual space varies from culture to culture.

 *Sucheng*

In the United States, each person has so much room! Every individual has a separate room to sleep and sometimes another separate room to work. Also, I see that each family here lives in a separate house. People have much less space in China. Families live together, with sons bringing their families into their parents' home and all sharing the same space. At first, when I came here, it felt strange to have so much space, but now I sometimes feel very crowded when I go home.

Cultural Rules About Artifacts

Giving gifts can lead to misunderstandings when giver and recipient are from different cultures (Axtell, 2007).

◆ A Chinese person might not appreciate the gift of a clock, because clocks symbolize death in China.

◆ Giving a gift to an Arab person on first meeting would likely be interpreted as a bribe.

◆ Bringing flowers to a dinner hosted by a person from Kenya would cause confusion because in Kenya flowers express sympathy for a loss.

◆ The Swiss consider even numbers of flowers bad luck, so never give a dozen roses.

Space also announces status, with greater space and more desirable space assumed by those with higher status in a culture. It's no coincidence that industries expose our most vulnerable communities to pollutants and carcinogens that they seldom foist on middle- and upper-class people. The meaning of this pattern is very clear: "The space of minorities and poor people is often invaded and contaminated, but the territory of more affluent citizens is respected" (Cox, 2014).

How people arrange space may reflect closeness and desire, or lack of desire, for interaction. Highly formal businesses often have private offices with doors that are usually closed and little common space. Couples who are highly interdependent tend to have more common space and less individual space in their homes than do couples who are more independent (Fitzpatrick, 1988; Werner, Altman, & Oxley, 1985). Similarly, families who enjoy interaction arrange furniture to invite conversation and eye contact. In families who seek less interaction, chairs may be far apart and may face televisions instead of each other (Keeley & Hart, 1994).

The ways that offices are arranged may invite or discourage interaction and may foster equal or unequal power relationships. Some professors and executives have desks that face their office doors and a chair beside the desk to promote open communication with people who come to their offices. Other professors and executives turn their desks away from the door and place chairs opposite to their desks, which configures the space hierarchically. Whether office doors are open or shut may also indicate willingness to interact.

Environmental Factors

Environmental factors are elements of settings that affect how we feel, think, and act. We feel more relaxed in rooms with comfortable chairs than in rooms with stiff, formal furniture. Candlelit dining tables may promote romantic feelings, and churches,

environmental factor
Any nonverbal element of a setting that affects how we think, feel, act, and communicate.

synagogues, and temples use candles to foster respect. A New Jersey hospital recently redesigned rooms to increase natural light and otherwise create more attractive environments. Patients in the redesigned rooms asked for 30 percent less medication and rated food better than patients in the unremodeled rooms even though the food was the same (Kimmelman, 2014). A recent study found that color affects cognitive functions. Red stimulates accuracy, recall, and attention to detail whereas blue stimulates creativity (Belluck, 2009). Perhaps we should have blue computer screens when doing creative writing and red screens when working on math problems.

Restaurants use environmental features to control how long people spend eating. For example, low lights, comfortable chairs or booths, and soft music often are part of the environment in upscale restaurants. On the other hand, fast-food eateries have hard plastic booths and bright lights, which encourage diners to eat and move on. To maximize profit, restaurants want to get people in and out as quickly as possible. Music with a fast tempo speeds up the pace of eating in restaurants; on average, people eat 3.2 mouthfuls a minute when the background music is slow and 5.1 mouthfuls a minute when music with a faster tempo is played ("Did You Know?" 1998). Restaurants use a variety of environmental cues to create the atmosphere they want—to encourage customers to linger, or to encourage them to eat and run. You can identify some of the environmental features that affect a restaurant's atmosphere by completing the Take Action feature at the end of this chapter.

In the same way that restaurants and other public places use environmental factors to influence mood and behavior, we choose colors, furniture arrangements, lighting, and other objects to create the atmosphere we desire in our home.

Chronemics

Chronemics refer to how we perceive and use time to define identities and interaction. We use time to negotiate and convey status (Levine & Norenzayan, 1999). In Western societies, there seems to be an unwritten but widely understood cultural rule stipulating that people with high status can keep people with less status waiting. Conversely, people with low status are expected to be punctual. Subordinates are expected to report punctually to meetings, but bosses are allowed to be tardy.

Chronemics express cultural attitudes toward time. In some cultures, people saunter whereas in others they dash from place to place. In some cultures business is conducted quickly by staying on task whereas in other cultures it is conducted more slowly by intermingling task and social interaction. According to a study of pace of life (Levine & Norenzayan, 1999), the countries with the fastest pace of life are Switzerland (#1), Ireland, Germany, and Japan. The countries with the slowest pace of life are Mexico (#31), Indonesia, Brazil, and El Salvador. The United States was 16th—right in the middle of the list. Notice that the slowest pace of life is in countries that have warm climates while the fastest pace of life is in countries with colder climates.

Western societies value time and its cousin, speed (Calero, 2005; Honoré, 2005). We want computers, not typewriters, and many of us replace our computers and software as soon as faster versions become available. We often try to do several things at once to get more done, rely on the microwave to cook faster, and take for granted speed systems such as instant copying and photos (McGee-Cooper, Trammel, & Lau, 1992). The value that Westerners place on time is evident in everyday expressions: "You're *wasting* my time," "This new software program will *save* time," "That

chronemics Nonverbal communication involving the perception and use of time to define identities and interaction.

mistake *cost* me three hours," "I've *invested* a lot of time in this class," "I can't *afford* to go out tonight," "I can make up for *lost* time by using a shortcut," and "I'm *running out* of time."

Many other cultures have far more relaxed attitudes toward time and punctuality (Samovar et al., 2013). In many South American countries, it's normal to come to meetings or classes after the announced time of starting, and it's not assumed that people will leave when the scheduled time for ending arrives. In the Philippines, punctuality has never been particularly valued, but that may be changing. In 2009, the Philippine Department of Education launched a 10-year campaign to instill in students the value of being on time (Overland, 2009).

The length of time we spend with different people reflects the extent of our interest in them and affection for them. A manager is inclined to spend more time with a new employee who seems to have executive potential than with one who seems less impressive. A speaker usually gives a fuller answer to a question from a high-status member of the audience than to one from a person with less status. In general, we spend more time with people we like than with those we don't like or who bore us. Researchers report that increased contact among college students is a clear sign that a relationship is intensifying, and reduced time together signals decreasing interest (Baxter, 1985; Dindia, 1994; Tolhuizen, 1989).

Chronemics also involves expectations of time, which are influenced by social norms. For example, you expect a class to last 50 or 75 minutes. Several minutes before the end of a class period, students often close their notebooks and start gathering their belongings, signaling the teacher that time is up. A similar pattern often is evident in business meetings. We expect religious services to last approximately an hour, and we might be upset if a rabbi or minister talked for two hours.

Paralanguage

Paralanguage is communication that is vocal but not actual words. Paralanguage includes sounds, such as murmurs and gasps, and vocal qualities, such as volume, rhythm, pitch, and inflection. Vocal cues signal others to interpret what we say as a joke, a threat, a statement of fact, a question, and so forth. Effective public speakers modulate inflection, volume, and rhythm to enhance their presentations.

We use vocal cues to communicate feelings to friends and romantic partners. Whispering, for instance, signals confidentiality or intimacy, whereas shouting conveys anger or excitement. Depending on the context, sighing may communicate empathy, boredom, or contentment. Research shows that tone of voice is a powerful clue to feelings between marital partners. Negative vocal tones often reveal dissatisfaction or dislike in social interaction. Negative intonation may also signal dissatisfaction or disapproval in work settings. A derisive or sarcastic tone can communicate scorn clearly, whereas a warm voice conveys friendliness.

Our voices affect how others perceive us. To some extent, we control vocal cues that influence image. For instance, we can deliberately sound confident in job interviews or when asking for a raise. The president adopts a solemn voice when announcing military. Most of us know how to make ourselves sound apologetic, seductive, or angry when those images suit our purposes. In addition to the ways we intentionally use our voices, natural and habitual vocal qualities affect how others perceive us. For instance, people who speak at slow to moderate rates are perceived as having greater control over interaction than people who speak more rapidly (Tusing & Dillard, 2000).

paralanguage Communication that is vocal but not verbal. Paralanguage includes accent, inflection, volume, pitch, and sounds such as murmurs and gasps.

 **Leah**

Everyone in my family knew that when Mother raised her voice we were in trouble, but when our father lowered his, we were in trouble. His voice would drop to this low volume and get very slow and deep. It was a signal to take cover FAST!

Our ethnic heritage and identification influence how we use our voices. In general, African American speech has more vocal range, inflection, and tonal quality than European American speech (Garner, 1994). In general, African Americans are also more likely than European Americans to signal interest in what another person is saying by making listening sounds ("um hmm," "yeah, yeah") (Brilhart & Galanes, 1995). Paralanguage also reflects gender. Men's voices tend to have louder volume, lower pitch, and less inflection, features that conform to cultural views of men as assertive and emotionally controlled. Women's voices typically have higher pitch, softer volume, and more inflection, features consistent with cultural views of women as emotional and deferential. Socioeconomic level influences pronunciation, rate of speech, and accent.

Silence

A final type of nonverbal behavior is **silence**, which is a lack of communicated sound. Although silence is quiet, it can communicate powerful messages. "I'm not speaking to you" speaks volumes. Silence can convey contentment when intimates are so comfortable they don't need to talk. Silence can also communicate awkwardness, as you know if you've ever had trouble making conversation on a first date. Yet the awkwardness that many Westerners feel when silence falls is not felt by people from some other cultures, as Jin Lee explains.

 **Jin Lee**

In the United States, people feel it is necessary to talk all of the time, to fill in any silence with words and more words. I was not brought up that way. In my country, it is good to be silent some of the time. It shows you are listening to another, you are thinking about what the other says, you are respectful and do not need to put in your words.

Some parents discipline children by ignoring them. No matter what the child says or does, the parents refuse to acknowledge the child's existence. The silencing strategy may also surface later in life. We sometimes deliberately freeze out others when we're angry with them (Williams, 2001). In some military academies, such as West Point, silence is a method of stripping a cadet of personhood if the cadet is perceived as having broken the academy's honor code. On the job, silence may signal disapproval, as peers often ostracize whistle-blowers and union-busters. People who violate the rules of chat rooms may be silenced by getting no responses to their messages.

Audiences sometimes shout down speakers they dislike; when angry, romantic partners may refuse to speak; and the Catholic Church excommunicates people who violate its canons. Like other forms of communication, silence—and what it means—is linked to culture. European Americans tend to be talkative; they are inclined to fill in silence with words. Among Native Americans, however, historically silence conveys respect, active listening, and thought about what others are saying (Braithwaite, 1990; Carbaugh, 1998).

silence Lack of sound. Silence can be a powerful form of nonverbal communication.

We've seen that nonverbal communication includes kinesics, haptics, physical appearance, olfactics, artifacts, proxemics, environmental factors, chronemics, paralanguage, and silence.

Digital Media and Nonverbal Communication

Nonverbal communication is more restricted in digital and online communication than in face-to-face interaction. Words in an e-mail, tweet, or text don't tell us whether the person who wrote them is serious, sarcastic, or playful. The need to signal others how to interpret our words and to understand how we should interpret their words compelled invention of emoticons such as:

(::( )::) = band aid to symbolize comfort

;) = smile + wink to symbolize playfulness

=^.^= = cat to symbolize friskiness

<3 = heart

But emoticons aren't expressive enough for some people, which led to the development of stickers, which are cartoon-like icons that people send to replace text messages. First used in Japan, stickers are gaining popularity among Westerners, who find words and even emoticons insufficient for what they want to express. Now that stickers have caught on, the race for super-cute is on, with startups trying to come up with the cutest stickers. Path offers Willa, a playful wombat; Facebook offers Pusheen, a cat that sometimes presents itself as a unicorn, and Napoli, a very emotional ice cream cone (Rusli, 2013). Facebook founder Mark Zuckerberg sends a blue thumbs-up sign to symbolize approval. An undergraduate sends a sleepy bunny cartoon to signal that she's tired (Rusli, 2013). And stickers don't need translation when shared between users who have different languages.

A second interesting facet of nonverbal communication in digital media is the size of a person's electronic footprint. Some people tweet continuously and update their Facebook pages at least daily and sometimes more often, whereas others tweet less often and update their Facebook pages infrequently. Some people comment on nearly everything posted by others, whereas other people comment more selectively. There is no research to tell us what it means when people have small or large electronic footprints, but there are noticeable differences in how much space people take. Electronic footprints don't go away just because we delete texts or photos, so you should exercise caution in what you post online and what text messages you send.

© Pixel Embargo/Shutterstock.com

When and why do you use emoticons or stickers in your social media communication?

Third, as we noted earlier in this chapter, digital communication can compete with, and sometimes interfere with, face-to-face communication. Do you send or check texts while talking with others face-to-face? (And don't think people don't notice just because you have eye contact while texting!) If so, does that convey the level of responsiveness you want to convey? Dual perspective might lead you to think about the person with whom you are in face-to-face contact. Is he or she someone who is as wired to social media as you are? If not, you might want to focus on the face-to-face interaction.

The presence of social media in our lives has not been lost on furniture manufacturers. Traditional home offices are out, and chairs and chaises specifically designed for mobile computing are in (Hrabi, 2013). Dubbed the "lifestyle work-at-home collection," this furniture has wide arms for laptops and allows people to adjust them infinitely. Conversely, office designers should rethink the open-plan workspace that relies on cubicles. People who work in cubicles are interrupted 29 percent more often than people who work in private offices, and interruptions are not just irritating; they are costly: They increase workers' exhaustion, error rates, and stress-related illnesses (Shellenbarger, 2013).

Guidelines for Effective Nonverbal Communication

Nonverbal communication, like verbal communication, can be misinterpreted. Following these two guidelines should reduce nonverbal misunderstandings in your interactions.

Monitor Your Nonverbal Communication

Think about the preceding discussion of ways we use nonverbal behaviors to announce our identities. Are you projecting the image you desire? Do others interpret your facial and body movements in ways consistent with the image you want to project? Do friends ever tell you that you seem uninterested when really you *are* interested? If so, you can monitor your nonverbal actions to more clearly communicate your involvement and interest in conversations. To reduce the chance that work associates will think you're uninterested in meetings, use what you've learned in this chapter to engage in nonverbal behaviors that others associate with responsiveness and attention.

Think also about how you arrange your personal spaces. Have you set up your room, office, apartment, or home to invite the kind of interaction you prefer, or are they arranged in ways that undercut your goals as a communicator? Paying attention to the nonverbal dimensions of your world can empower you to use them more effectively to achieve your interpersonal goals.

Interpret Others' Nonverbal Communication Tentatively

Although popular advice books promise to show you how to read nonverbal communications, no surefire formula exists. It's naive to think we can decode something so complex and ambiguous.

In this chapter, we've discussed findings about the meanings people attach to nonverbal behaviors. We can never be sure what a particular behavior means to specific people in a particular context. For instance, we've said that sitting close together indicates liking. As a general rule, this is true. However, sometimes contented friends and couples like to have physical distance between them. Partners may also avoid physical closeness when one has a cold or flu.

People socialized in non-Western cultures learn distinct rules for proxemics. Because nonverbal communication is ambiguous and personal, we should not assume we can interpret it with precision. An ethical principle of communication is to qualify interpretations of nonverbal behavior with awareness of personal and contextual considerations.

Personal Qualifications   Generalizations about nonverbal behavior state what is usual or common. They don't tell us about the exceptions to the rule. For instance, although eye contact generally is a sign of responsiveness, some people close their eyes to concentrate when listening. Sometimes people who cross their arms and condense into a tight posture are expressing hostility or lack of interest in interaction. However, the same behaviors might mean that a person is cold and trying to conserve body heat. Most people use less inflection and adopt a slack posture when they're not really interested in what they're talking about. However, the same behaviors may mean that we're tired.

Because nonverbal behaviors are ambiguous and vary between people, we need to be cautious about how we interpret these behaviors. A key principle is that we construct the meanings we attach to nonverbal communication. A good way to keep this in mind is to rely on *I*-language, not *you*-language, which we discussed earlier. *You*-language might lead us to inaccurately say of someone who doesn't look at us, "You're communicating lack of interest." A more responsible statement would use *I*-language to say, "When you don't look at me, I feel you're not interested in what I'm saying." Using *I*-language reminds us to take responsibility for our judgments and feelings. In addition, we become less likely to make others defensive by inaccurately interpreting their nonverbal behavior.

Contextual Qualifications   Like the meaning of verbal communication, the significance of nonverbal behaviors depends on the contexts in which they occur. Our nonverbal communication reflects the various settings we inhabit. We are more or less formal, relaxed, and open depending on context. Most people are more at ease and confident in their own territories than in someone else's, so we tend to be more relaxed in our homes and offices than in business places; teams often win games when they have the "home turf" advantage. We also dress according to context—a suit for a job interview, jeans or casual slacks and a shirt for a game.

Immediate physical settings are not the only factor that affects nonverbal communication. As we have seen, all communication reflects the values and understandings of particular cultures. We are likely to misinterpret people from other cultures when we impose the norms and rules of our culture on them. This suggests that we have an ethical responsibility not to assume that our rules and norms apply to the behaviors of others.

Even within the United States, we have diverse social communities, and each has its rules for nonverbal behavior. Ethical communicators try to adopt dual perspective when interpreting others, especially when they and we belong to different cultures. To enhance your awareness of cultural influences on communication, Chapter 8 deals with that topic in detail.

Summary

In this chapter, we've explored the fascinating world of nonverbal communication. We learned that nonverbal communication is symbolic and functions to supplement or replace verbal messages, regulate interaction, reflect and establish relationship-level meanings, and express cultural membership. These five principles of nonverbal behavior help us understand the complex ways in which nonverbal communication operates and what it may mean.

We discussed 10 types of nonverbal communication, each of which reflects cultural rules and expresses our personal identities and feelings toward others. We use nonverbal behaviors to announce and perform our identities, relying on actions, artifacts, and contextual features to embody what our culture has taught us is appropriate for our gender, race, class, sexuality, and ethnicity. We also noted that nonverbal communication is more restricted in digital environments than in face-to-face interactions. Because nonverbal communication is ambiguous, we need to be aware of the potential for misunderstandings both in face-to-face interactions and those on social media. Effectiveness requires that we learn to monitor our nonverbal communication and to exercise caution in interpreting that of others.

Experience Communication Case Study

Teamwork

Apply what you've learned in this chapter by analyzing the following case study, using the accompanying questions as a guide. These questions and a video of the case study are also available online with your MindTap Speech for *Communication Mosaics*.

A project team is meeting to discuss the most effective way to present its recommendations for implementing a flextime policy on a trial basis. Members of the team are Jason (the team leader), Erika, Victoria, Bill, and Jensen. They are seated around a rectangular table with Jason at the head.

Jason: So we've decided to recommend trying flextime for a two-month period and with a number of procedures to make sure that people's new schedules don't interfere with productivity. There's a lot of information to communicate to employees, so how can we do that best?

Victoria: I think it would be good to use PowerPoint to highlight the key aspects of the new procedures. People always seem to remember better if they see something.

Bill: Oh, come on. PowerPoint is so overused. Everyone is tired of it by now. Can't we do something more creative?

Victoria: Well I like it. It's a good teaching tool.

Bill: I didn't know we were teaching. I thought our job was to report recommendations.

Victoria: So what do you suggest, Bill? [She nervously pulls on her bracelet as she speaks.]

Bill: I don't have a suggestion. I'm just against PowerPoint. [He doesn't look up as he speaks.]

Jason: Okay, let's not bicker among ourselves. [He pauses, gazes directly at Bill, then continues.] Lots of people like PowerPoint, lots don't. Instead of arguing about its value, let's ask what it is we want to communicate to the employees here. Maybe talking about our goal first will help us decide on the best means of achieving it.

Erika: Good idea. I'd like for us to focus first on getting everyone excited about the benefits of flextime. If they understand those, they'll be motivated to learn the procedures, even if there are a lot of them.

Jensen: Erika is right. That's a good way to start. Maybe we could create a handout or PowerPoint slide—either would work—to summarize the benefits of flextime that we've identified in our research.

Jason: Good, okay now we're cooking. Victoria, will you make notes on the ideas as we discuss them?

Victoria opens a notebook and begins writing notes.

Noticing that Bill is typing into his personal digital assistant (PDA), Jason looks directly at Bill and says, "Are you with us on how we lead off in our presentation?"

Bill: Sure, fine with me. [He puts the PDA aside but keeps his eyes on it.]

Erika: So maybe then we should say that the only way flextime can work is if we make sure that everyone agrees on procedures so that no division is ever missing more than one person during key production hours.

Jensen: Very good. That would add to people's motivation to learn and follow the procedures we've found are effective in other companies like ours. I think it would be great if Erika could present that topic because she did most of the research on it.

He smiles at Erika, and she pantomimes tipping her hat to him.

Jason: [He looks at Erika with a raised brow, and she nods.] Good. Okay, Erika's in charge of that. What's next?

Victoria: Then it's time to spell out the procedures and….

Bill: You can't just spell them out. You have to explain each one—give people a rationale for them or they won't follow them.

Victoria glares at Bill, then looks across the table at Erika, who shrugs as if to say, "I don't know what's bothering Bill today."

Jason: Bill, why don't you lead off, then, and tell us the first procedure we should mention and the rationale we should provide for it.

Bill looks up from his PDA, which he's been using again. He shrugs and says harshly, "Just spell out the rules, that's all."

Victoria: Would it be too much trouble for you to cut off your gadget and join us in this meeting, Bill?

Bill: Would it be too much trouble for you to quit hassling me?

Jason: [He turns his chair to face Bill squarely.] Look, I don't know what's eating you, but you're really being a jerk. If you've got a problem with this meeting or someone here, put it on the table. Otherwise, be a team player.

© Cengage Learning®

1. Identify nonverbal behaviors that regulate turn taking within the team.

2. Identify nonverbal behaviors that express relationship-level meanings of communication. What aspects of team members' nonverbal communication express liking or disliking, responsiveness or lack of responsiveness, and power?

3. How do artifacts affect interaction between members of the team?

4. If you were the sixth member of this team, what kinds of communication might you enact to help relieve tension in the group?

Key Concepts

Practice defining the chapter's terms by using online flashcards.

artifacts, 95	olfactics, 94
chronemics, 98	paralanguage, 99
environmental factors, 97	physical appearance, 93
haptics, 92	proxemics, 96
kinesics, 91	silence, 100
nonverbal communication, 86	

Reflect, personalize, and apply what you've learned

Review, Reflect, Extend

The Reflect and Discuss and Take Action features that follow will help you review, reflect on, and extend the information and ideas presented in this chapter. These resources, and a diverse selection of additional study tools, are also available online at the MindTap Speech for *Communication Mosaics*.

Reflect and Discuss

1. Attend a gathering of people from a culture different from yours. Observe nonverbal behaviors of the people there: How do they greet one another? How much eye contact accompanies interaction? How close to one another do people sit?

2. Describe the spatial arrangements in the home of your family of origin. Was there a room in which family members interacted a good deal? How was furniture arranged in that room? Who had separate space and personal chairs in your family? What do the nonverbal patterns reflect about your family's communication style?

3. As a class, discuss current gender prescriptions in the United States. How are men and women "supposed" to look? How are these cultural expectations communicated? How might you resist and alter unhealthy cultural gender prescriptions for appearance?

TAKE ACTION

1. Noticing Spatial Clues to Power Relations

Observe a business setting—an office or other work context. To sharpen your insight into spatial indicators of power, answer the following questions:

a. Who has more space? Who has less?

b. Who enters the space of others? Who does not?

c. Who touches others?

d. Who uses commanding gestures? Who does not?

2. Increasing Awareness of Environmental Factors

Observe a restaurant in which you feel rushed and another restaurant in which you feel like taking your time. Answer the following questions about each restaurant:

a. How much space is there between tables?

b. What kind of lighting is used?

c. What sort of music and sound are in the place?

d. How comfortable are the chairs?

e. What colors and art do you see?

Can you make any generalizations about environmental features that promote relaxation and those that do not?

3. Using *I*-Language About Nonverbal Behaviors

This exercise extends principles of *I*-language we discussed in Chapter 4 to the context of nonverbal communication. Practice translating *you*-language into *I*-language to describe nonverbal behaviors.

Example   *You*-language   You're staring at me.
               I-language   When you look at me so intensely,
                                  I feel uncomfortable.

You-Language	*I*-Language
You're lying—I can tell because you won't look me in the eye.	_____
Your dress is unprofessional	_____
Your perfume stinks.	_____
Don't you smirk when I'm talking.	_____
You have lazy posture.	_____

Recommended Resources

1. Sandra Metts. (2006). Gendered Communication in Dating Relationships. In B. Dow & J. T. Wood (Eds.), *Handbook of Gender & Communication* (pp. 25–40). Thousand Oaks, CA: Sage. This chapter offers a wealth of information on gendered patterns of nonverbal communication. Especially interesting are the detailed descriptions of nonverbal flirting behaviors.

2. Amy Cuddy's Ted talk provides excellent information about how body posture can affect not only how others see us, but how we see ourselves. To view the talk, go to this chapter's online resources.

6

Listening and Responding to Others

It was impossible to get a conversation going, everybody was talking too much.

—*Yogi Berra*

How do you feel when you are in conversations in which everyone is talking and nobody is listening?

MindTap

Learning Objectives

Start with a quick engagement activity and **review** the chapter Learning Objectives.

Topics Covered in This Chapter	After studying this chapter, you should be able to . . .
The Listening Process	Describe the role of each of the six elements in the listening process.
Obstacles to Effective Listening	Drawing on personal experience, assess common external and internal obstacles to mindful listening.
Digital Media and Listening	Evaluate how your use of digital media affects your ability to practice mindful listening.
Guidelines for Effective Listening	Create an action plan to implement this chapter's guidelines to improve your listening skills.

🔵 MindTap

Read, highlight, and take notes online.

"**G**ot a minute?" Jackson asks as he enters Sophia's office. "Sure," Sophia agrees, without looking up from her laptop. (She's reading a report that is the main topic at a meeting later today. Lately, her supervisor has criticized her for being unprepared for meetings, and she wants to be on top of information today.)

"I'm concerned about Frank. He's missed several days lately, and he's late half the time when he does come into work," Jackson begins. "He hasn't given me any explanation for his absences and tardiness, and I can't keep overlooking it."

"Yeah, I know that routine," Sophia says with irritation. "Last month, Barton missed two days in a row and left early several other days."

"That's exactly what I'm talking about," agrees Jackson. "I can't let Frank disregard rules that everyone else follows, but I don't want to come down too hard on him, especially when I don't know why he's missing so much time."

"I told Barton that from now on he could either be at work when he should be or give me a darned good reason for why he wasn't," Sophia says forcefully. Her mind wanders back to relive the confrontation with Barton.

"I wonder if the two situations are really similar," Jackson says.

Sophia realizes she was lost in her own thoughts. "Sorry, I didn't catch what you said," she says.

"I was wondering if you're saying that I should handle Frank like you handled Barton," he repeats.

"You have to enforce the rules, or he'll walk all over you." Sophia's eyes drift back to the laptop screen.

"I hate to be so hard on Frank," Jackson says.

"Remember last year when Cheryl kept missing work? Well, I tried to be subtle and hint that she couldn't skip work. In one ear and out the other. You have to be firm."

"But Frank's not like Barton or Cheryl," he notes. "He's never tried to run over me or shirk his work. I have a hunch something is going on that's interfering with his work. Cheryl and Barton both had patterns of irresponsibility."

"I don't think my staff is any less responsible than yours. I'm a good supervisor, you know," Sophia snaps.

"That's not what I meant. I just don't think I need to hit Frank over the head with a two-by-four," Jackson says.

"And I suppose you think that's what I did?"

"I don't know. I wasn't there. I'm just thinking that maybe our situations are different," says Jackson.

When we think about communication, we usually focus on talking. Yet, in the communication process, listening is at least as important as talking. As obvious as this seems, few of us devote as much energy to listening as we do to talking.

In the conversation between Jackson and Sophia, poor listening is evident in several ways. First, Sophia is preoccupied with a report she is reading. If she really wants to listen to Jackson, she should put the report aside. Also, Jackson might have asked if Sophia would rather talk later. A second problem is Sophia's tendency to monopolize the conversation, turning it into an occasion to discuss *her* supervisory problems instead of Jackson's concerns about Frank's behavior. Third, Sophia listens defensively,

Who Listens?

We might do well to heed wisdom offered by Mother Teresa. Here's an excerpt from Dan Rather's interview with Mother Teresa shortly before her death in 1997 (Bailey, 1998).

Rather: What do you say to God when you pray?
Mother Teresa: I listen.
Rather: Well, what does God say?
Mother Teresa: He listens.

interpreting Jackson as criticizing her when he suggests that his situation might call for different action than hers. Like Sophia, most of us don't listen as well as we could much of the time. When we listen poorly, we communicate ineffectively.

Studies of people ranging from college students to professionals show that the average person spends 45 to 55 percent of waking time listening to others; that's more time than we spend in any other communication activity (Buckley, 1992; Nichols, 1996; Weaver, 1972; Wolvin, 2009). We listen in classes, at public lectures, to television and radio, in conversations, during interviews, on Skype, to videos on YouTube, on the job, and when participating in groups. If we add the time we listen while doing other things, the total listening time is even greater.

We may listen a lot, but we don't necessarily listen effectively. When people don't listen well on the job, they may miss information that can affect their professional effectiveness and advancement (Darling & Dannels, 2003; Gabric & McFadden, 2001; Landrum & Harrold, 2003). Skill in listening is also linked to resolving workplace conflicts (Van Styke, 1999). Doctors who don't listen fully to patients may misdiagnose or mistreat medical problems (Christensen, 2004; Richtel, 2011; Scholz, 2005; Underwood & Adler, 2005). Ineffective listening in the classroom diminishes learning and performance on tests. In personal relationships, poor listening can hinder understanding of others, and not listening well to public communication leaves us uninformed about civic issues. Learning to listen well enhances personal, academic, social, civic, and professional effectiveness.

This chapter explores listening, which is the fourth basic communication process. First, we'll consider what's involved in listening and discuss obstacles to effective listening. Next, we'll examine common forms of ineffective listening. Third, we'll consider how listening applies to Computer-mediated communication. Finally, we'll identify ways to improve listening.

hearing A physiological activity that occurs when sound waves hit our eardrums. Unlike listening, hearing is a passive process.

listening The process of receiving, constructing meaning from, and responding to spoken and/or nonverbal messages. The process consists of being mindful, hearing, selecting and organizing information, interpreting communication, responding, and remembering.

The Listening Process

Although we often use the words *listening* and *hearing* as if they were synonyms, actually they're not. **Hearing** is a physiological activity that occurs when sound waves hit functioning eardrums. Hearing is not the only way we receive messages. We also receive them through sight, as when we notice nonverbal behaviors, read lips, or interpret American Sign Language (ASL).

Listening is more complex than hearing. The International Listening Association (http://www.listen.org, 2011) defines listening as the "process of receiving, constructing meaning from, and responding to spoken and/or nonverbal messages." This means that, in addition to hearing, or physically receiving messages, listening involves being mindful, selecting and organizing information, interpreting communication, responding, physically receiving messages, and remembering (Figure 6.1).

Being Mindful

Mindfulness is focusing on what is happening in the moment (Wood, 1997, 2004a). When you are mindful, you don't think about what you did yesterday or the paper you need to write or a problem at work or your response to a text someone sent. Instead, mindful listeners focus on the people with whom they are interacting.

One reason that many people have difficulty focusing mindfully on what another is saying is that we listen at a faster rate than we talk. The average person can understand approximately 300 words a minute, yet the average person speaks at a rate of approximately 100 words a minute. This leaves a lot of free time for listeners' minds to drift if they aren't committed to being mindful.

Mindfulness enhances communication in two ways. First, attending mindfully to others increases our understanding of their thoughts and feelings. Second, mindfulness promotes more complete communication by others. When we really listen to others, they tend to elaborate their ideas and express their feelings in greater depth. Simone's commentary highlights the impact of mindfulness on communication.

 *Simone*

The best listener I've ever met was Nate, a guy I worked with on the campus newspaper. He wrote the best stories on special speakers who came to campus. At first, I thought he just got more interesting personalities to interview than I did. But then he and I had a couple of joint interviews, and I saw how he listened. When an interviewee was talking, Nate gave the person his undivided attention—like there was nobody else and nothing else around. People really open up when you treat them like the most interesting person in the world.

Obviously, mindfulness is important in personal relationships. It is equally important in professional life. Pamela Kruger (1999) talked with business executives and concluded that "leaders must know how to listen. . . . But first, and just as important, leaders must *want* to listen" (p. 134).

Mindfulness isn't a talent that some people naturally have and others don't. It's an ethical commitment to attend fully to others in particular moments. No techniques will make you a good listener if you don't choose to be mindful. Thus, your choice of whether to be mindful is the foundation of how you listen—or fail to. A Take Action activity at the end of this chapter provides guidelines for developing mindfulness.

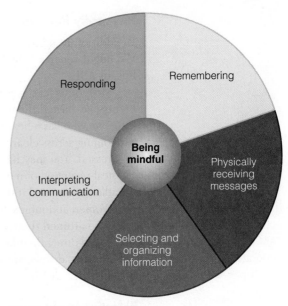

Figure 6.1 The Listening Process
Source: Adapted from Wood, 1997, p. 21.

mindfulness Being fully present in the moment; the first step of listening and the foundation of all the other steps.

 **ENGAGE!**

The Power of Responsive Listening

According to a story told on campuses, students proved the power of responsive listening by experimenting with a professor. The professor was a boring lecturer who read his notes in a monotone, seldom gestured, and did little to engage students. After the first few minutes of class, the students changed their postures, kept greater eye contact, nodded, and so forth. Shortly after the students began giving cues of active listening, the lecturer started using gestures, increased his speaking rate and inflection, and began to interact with students visually and verbally. Then the students stopped showing interest. Within a few minutes, the lecturer returned to his old lecture style.

Physically Receiving Communication

In addition to mindfulness, listening involves physically receiving communication. We might receive it by hearing sounds, interpreting nonverbal behaviors, reading lips, or ASL.

Most of us take hearing for granted. However, people who have hearing impairments may have difficulty receiving oral messages (Carl, 1998). When we speak with someone who has a hearing impairment, we should face the person and verify that we are coming across clearly. Our ability to receive messages also declines if we are tired or stressed. You may have noticed that it's hard to sustain attention in long classes. Physical reception of messages is also hampered if others are talking around us, if TVs or radios are on, and if there are competing visual cues.

Women and men seem to differ somewhat in how they listen. As a rule, women are more attuned than men to all that is going on around them. Men tend to focus, shape, and direct their hearing in specific ways, whereas women are more likely to notice contexts, details, and digressions, as well as major themes in interaction (Wood & Fixmer-Oraiz, 2016).

Selecting and Organizing Communication

The third element of listening is selecting and organizing material. As we noted in Chapter 3, we don't perceive everything around us. Instead, we selectively attend to some aspects of communication and disregard others. What we attend to depends on many factors, including physiological influences, expectations, cognitive structures, social roles, and membership in cultures and social communities. If we are preoccupied, we may not notice, select, and organize material effectively. In the example that opened this chapter, Sophia's involvement with her report impeded her ability to listen to Jackson. If you want to communicate effectively, you should take responsibility for controlling thoughts and concerns that can interfere with listening. Choosing to be mindful doesn't guarantee that our minds won't stray, but it does mean that we will bring ourselves back to the moment.

As you'll recall from Chapter 3, we use cognitive schemata to organize our perceptions. As you listen to other people, you decide how to categorize them by deciding which of your prototypes they most closely resemble: friend, professional rival, colleague, supervisor, and so forth. You then apply personal constructs to assess whether they are smart or not smart, honest or not honest, reasonable or not reasonable, open to advice or not open, and so on. Next, you apply stereotypes to predict what they will do. Finally, you choose a script that seems appropriate to follow.

Listeners actively define the listening situation and construct its meaning. When we define someone as emotionally upset, we're likely to rely on a script that tells us to back off and let him air his feelings. On the other hand, when a co-worker comes to you with a problem that must be solved quickly, you assume she might welcome concrete advice. It's important to realize that *we construct others and their communication* by the schemata we use to organize our perceptions of them. Because our perceptions can be wrong, we should be ready to revise them in the course of interacting.

Interpreting Communication

The fourth aspect of listening is **interpretation**. When we interpret, we put together all that we have selected and organized to make sense of communication. Effective interpretation depends on your ability to understand others on their terms. Certainly,

TAKE ACTION…activities are located at the end of this chapter and online.

interpretation The subjective process of organizing and making sense of perceptions.

you won't always agree with other people's feelings and thoughts. Recognizing others' viewpoints doesn't mean you agree with them, but it does mean you make an earnest effort to grasp what they think and feel. This is an ethical responsibility of listening.

 *Maggie*

Don and I didn't understand each other's perspective, and we didn't even understand that we didn't understand. Once, I told him I was really upset about a friend of mine who needed money for an emergency. Don told me she had no right to expect me to bail her out, but that had nothing to do with what I was feeling. He would have seen the situation in terms of rights, but I didn't, and he didn't grasp my take. Only after we got counseling did we learn to listen to each other instead of listening through ourselves.

As Maggie notes in her commentary, to respect another person's perspective is to give a special gift. What we give is regard for the other person and a willingness to open ourselves to that person's way of looking at the world. Too often, we impose our meanings on others, we try to correct or argue with them about what they feel, or we crowd out their words with ours. To listen effectively, we need to focus on understanding others on their own terms.

Responding

Effective listening involves **responding**, which includes expressing interest, asking questions, voicing our own ideas on a topic, and otherwise communicating attentiveness. As we noted in Chapter 1, communication is a transactional process in which we simultaneously receive and send messages. Skillful listeners give signs that they are involved in interaction, even though they are not speaking at the moment (Hutchby, 2005; ILA, 2008, 2011). We respond not only when others finish speaking but also throughout interaction. At public presentations, audience members show interest by looking at speakers, nodding their heads, and adopting attentive postures. Nonverbal behaviors, such as looking out a window and slouching, signal that you aren't involved. We also show lack of involvement or interest by yawning, looking bored, or staring blankly.

responding Symbolizing interest in what is being said with observable feedback to speakers during interaction; the fifth of six elements of listening.

remembering The process of recalling what one has heard; the sixth element of listening.

Good listeners show that they're engaged. The only way that others know we are listening is through our feedback. Indicators of engagement include attentive posture, head nods, eye contact, and vocal responses such as "Mmhmm" and "Go on." When we demonstrate involvement, we communicate interest in the other person's ideas and they are likely to offer more details and information (Beukeboom, 2009).

Remembering

Many listening experts regard **remembering** as the final part of the listening process. We forget a lot of what we hear. Eight hours after receiving a message, we recall only about 35 percent of our interpretations of the message. Because we

 **ENGAGE!** ## Listening Is an Act of Love

Perhaps you sometimes listen to *The Story*, a regular program on National Public Radio. Each story is part of a large project called StoryCorps. Dave Isay set out to make an oral history of America by listening to the stories of everyday people—not politicians, celebrities, or CEOs, but regular people. By January 2009, StoryCorps had recorded more than 40,000 stories of ordinary Americans—what they value, how they understand life. Dave Isay gathered a number of these stories into a book, which he titled *Listening Is an Act of Love* (2008). To learn more about StoryCorps, go to the book's online resources for this chapter.

forget about two thirds of the meanings we construct from others' communication, it's important to make sure we hang on to the most important third (Adler & Proctor, 2013). Selectively focusing our attention is particularly important when we listen to presentations that contain a great deal of information. Later in this chapter, we'll discuss strategies for improving retention.

In summary, listening is a complex process that involves being mindful, physically receiving messages, selecting and organizing information, interpreting communication, responding, and remembering. We're now ready to consider hindrances to the listening process so we can recognize and manage them.

Obstacles to Effective Listening

There are two broad types of obstacles to listening well: situational obstacles that are in communication contexts, and internal obstacles that are within communicators.

Situational Obstacles

Incomprehensibility
A few years ago, I traveled to Pennsylvania to attend a week-long teaching by the Dalai Lama. For eight hours each day, I sat trying to learn from this wise Tibetan monk. He always began by speaking in English, but it was heavily accented English that I had difficulty understanding. As he went into greater depth on a topic, he switched to Tibetan, which I did not understand at all. The Dalai Lama would speak for one to five minutes, and then his translator would convey the gist of the message in English.

Incomprehensibility exists when a message is not clearly understandable because of language or transmission problems. In my case, the lack of clarity resulted from an accent unfamiliar to me and use of a language that I didn't know. Other causes for unclear messages may be use of jargon that listeners don't understand, lack of a microphone when one is needed for audibility, fading in and out on cell calls, mumbling by a speaker, and syntax or grammar that makes it difficult to grasp what a communicator means to say.

Message Overload
The sheer amount of communication in our lives makes it difficult to listen fully to all of it. **Message overload** occurs when we receive more messages than we can effectively process. For good reason, our era has been dubbed "the information age." Each day, we are inundated by messages—face-to-face and mediated. We simply can't attend mindfully to all the messages that come our way (Jackson, 2008; Klingberg, 2008; Zuckerberg, 2013).

Message overload often occurs in educational contexts. Students who take four or five classes each term deal with four or five sets of readings, class lectures, and online materials—a load that can overwhelm even the most conscientious student. Message overload may also happen when communication occurs simultaneously in multiple channels. For instance, you might suffer information overload if a speaker is presenting information orally while showing a slide with complex statistical data. In such a situation, it's difficult to decide whether to focus on the visual message or the oral one. Similarly, when we try to text or check eBay while having a conversation with a friend, we may suffer message overload.

incomprehensibility When a message is not clearly understandable due to language or transmission problems; one of four situational obstacles to listening.

message overload The receiving of more messages than we can interpret, evaluate, and remember; can interfere with effective listening.

Message Complexity   Listening may also be impeded by **message complexity**, which exists when a message is highly complex, is packed with detailed or technical information, or involves intricate reasoning. The more detailed and complicated the ideas, the more they tax short-term memory (Janusik, 2007). Effective speakers make an effort to reduce the complexity of their messages. In addition, good listeners try to break down complex information or invest extra effort to understand complicated messages.

Environmental Distractions   **Environmental distractions** are a fourth impediment to effective listening. These are occurrences in the communication setting that interfere with effective listening (Keizer, 2010). Distractions exist in all communication situations. It might be a television in the background, side comments during a conference, or muffled traffic sounds from outside. Increasingly, we are interrupted by the buzzes of pagers and the ringtones of smartphones.

Cognitive psychologists have found that text and alerts distract people and undermine their ability to give full attention to any task (Begley, 2009). Interruptions fragment concentration so we have trouble resituating ourselves in whatever we were doing before the interruption. We may miss something, particularly if we were interrupted while performing a sequential task. In the summer of 2008, an airliner taking off from Madrid crashed and killed 153 people. Postcrash investigations revealed the error resulted from interruption in the preflight check (Begley, 2009).

If you want to listen effectively, reduce environmental distractions. Turn your phone off and lower the volume of music if someone wants to talk with you. Shut your laptop to attend more fully to a conversation. Even when we can't eliminate distractions, we can usually reduce them or move to a location that is more conducive to good listening.

Internal Obstacles

In addition to situational impediments to effective listening, five internal obstacles hinder our efforts to listen well.

Preoccupation   One of the most common hindrances to listening is **preoccupation**. When we are absorbed in our thoughts and concerns, we can't focus on what someone else is saying. Perhaps you've attended a class right before taking a test in another class and later realized you got almost nothing out of the first class. That's because you were preoccupied with the upcoming test. If you turn on your phone and find 20 text messages, you may be preoccupied by a sense of obligation to read and respond to all of them, so you are not fully, mindfully focused on reading and responding to each one as you open it. In the example that opened this chapter, Sophia's preoccupation with a report impeded her ability to listen to her colleague. When we are preoccupied with our thoughts, we aren't mindful.

Supersaturation

Continuous advances in technology mean we have greater access to information and people than was possible in any previous era. Smartphones, pagers, televisions, radios, laptops, tablets, iWatches, . . . there's no end to the information and engagement that comes our way throughout the day.

Media scholar Todd Gitlin (2005) refers to the never-ending flow of information as a "media torrent" that leads to supersaturation, or being constantly in touch, constantly informed, and constantly overloaded with information, whether we want it or not. Two other media scholars, Jane Brown and Joanne Cantor (2000), use the term *perpetual linkage* to refer to always being connected to others.

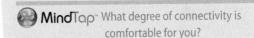 What degree of connectivity is comfortable for you?

message complexity The amount of detailed information or intricate reasoning in a message; can interfere with effective listening.

environmental distractions In communication situations, any occurrence that interferes with listening.

preoccupation Absorption in our own thoughts or concerns.

Environmental distractions can interfere with both hearing and listening.

Prejudgment   A second internal obstacle to good listening is **prejudgment**—the tendency to judge others or their ideas before we've heard them. Sometimes we think we already know what someone will say, so we don't listen carefully. In other cases, we decide in advance that others have nothing to offer us, so we tune them out. A study of doctor–patient communication found that, on average, doctors interrupted patients 23 seconds into patients' explanations of medical problems (Levine, 2004). Doctors who assume they already know what a patient has to say are likely to miss information that is needed to understand a patient's concerns. Keeping an open mind when listening to speakers with whom you disagree is also advisable. Keith's commentary provides an example of the negative impact of prejudgments on listening.

 Keith

My parents are so quick to tell me what I think and feel or should think and feel that they never listen to what I do feel or think. Last year, I told them I was thinking about taking a year off from school. Before I could explain why I wanted to do this, Dad was all over me about the need to get ahead in a career. Mom said I was looking for an easy out from my studies. What I wanted to do was work as an intern to get some hands-on experience in media production, which is my major. I wasn't after an easy out, and I do want to get ahead, but they couldn't even hear me through their own ideas about what I felt.

When we prejudge, we mind read. As we noted in Chapter 3, mind reading is assuming we know what others feel, think, and are going to say, and we may then fit their messages into our preconceptions. This can lead us to misunderstand what they mean because we haven't really listened to them on their terms. When we impose our prejudgments on others' words, at the relationship level of meaning we express a disregard for them and what they say. Prejudgments also affect the content level of meaning because we may not grasp important content when we decide in advance that someone has nothing of value to say. This can be costly on the job, where we are expected to pay attention and understand information even if we don't like it or the person expressing it.

Lack of Effort   Listening is hard work: We have to be mindful, focus on what others say, interpret and organize messages, remember, and respond. We also have to control distractions inside ourselves and in situations. Sometimes we aren't willing to invest the effort to listen well. In other instances, we want to listen, but we're tired, ill, hungry, or unable to focus for other reasons (Isaacs, 1999). When this happens, it's effective to postpone interaction until you can listen mindfully. If you explain that you want to listen well, the other person is likely to appreciate your honesty and your commitment to listening.

prejudgment Judging others or their ideas before one has heard them.

Reacting to Emotionally Loaded Language   A fourth internal obstacle to effective listening is the tendency to react to emotionally loaded language—words that evoke very strong positive or negative responses. You may find some words and phrases very soothing or pleasant. Certain other words and phrases may summon up strongly negative feelings and images. When we react to words that are emotionally loaded for us, we may fail to grasp another person's meaning. One way to guard against this is to be aware of words and phrases that tend to trigger strong emotional reactions in us. If we bring these to a conscious level, then we can monitor our tendencies to respond unthinkingly.

Not Recognizing Diverse Listening Styles   A final hindrance to effective listening is not recognizing and adjusting to different listening styles that reflect diverse cultures and social communities (Brownell, 2002; Samovar, Porter, & McDaniel, 2013; Samovar, Porter, McDaniel, & Roy, 2015). For example, in general, women are more active than men in giving verbal and nonverbal feedback, using head nods, facial expressions, and responsive questions to show interest (Wood & Fixmer-Oraiz, 2017). Some African Americans call out responses to a speaker or preacher as a way to show interest in what the speaker is saying. A speaker who doesn't understand this pattern is likely to misinterpret the responses as interruptions. Conversely, some African Americans may perceive European-American listeners as uninterested because they don't participate by calling out during a speech or sermon. Nancy's reflections on her perceptions as a white person at a black church illustrate the importance of recognizing and respecting diverse listening styles.

 *Nancy*

I was amazed the first time I went to a black church. Members of the congregation kept speaking back to the minister and exclaiming over what they liked. At first, I was alienated, but after a while I got into the spirit, and I felt a whole lot more involved in the service than I ever had in my own church.

Forms of Ineffective Listening

Now that we've discussed obstacles to effective listening, let's identify six common forms of ineffective listening. Some may seem familiar because you and people you know probably engage in them at times.

Pseudolistening   **Pseudolistening** is pretending to listen. When we pseudolisten, we appear attentive, but our minds are really elsewhere. We pseudolisten when communication bores us but we feel it is important to appear attentive. Superficial social interaction and boring lectures are communication situations in which we may consciously choose to pseudolisten so that we seem polite even though we really aren't involved. On the job, we may need to appear interested in what others say because of their positions. Pseudolistening is inadvisable, however, when we really want to understand another's communication.

Monopolizing   **Monopolizing** is hogging the stage by continually focusing communication on ourselves instead of on the person who is talking. Two tactics are typical of monopolizing. One is *conversational rerouting*, in which a person shifts the topic of talk to himself or herself. For example, if Ellen tells her friend Marla that she's having trouble with her roommate, Marla might reroute the conversation by saying, "I know what you mean. My roommate is a real slob." And then Marla launches into an extended description of her roommate problems. In the workplace, people may shift conversations to their accomplishments and concerns. In both personal and work relationships, rerouting takes the conversation away from the person who is talking and focuses it on oneself (Donoghue & Siegel, 2005).

pseudolistening Pretending to listen.

monopolizing Hogging the stage by continuously focusing communication on oneself instead of on the person who is talking.

© 1989 Peanuts Worldwide LLC. Dist. By UNIVERSAL UCLICK. Reprinted with permission. All rights reserved.

A second monopolizing tactic, *interrupting*, can occur in combination with rerouting: A person interrupts and then introduces a new topic. In other cases, diversionary interrupting involves questions and challenges that disrupt or challenge the person who is speaking. Monopolizers may fire questions that express doubt about what a speaker says ("What makes you think that?" "How can you be sure?" "Did anyone else see what you did?") or prematurely offer advice to establish their command of the situation and perhaps to put down the other person ("What you should do is . . ."; "You really blew that. What I would have done is . . ."). Both rerouting and diversionary interrupting monopolize conversations. They are the antithesis of good listening.

It's important to realize that not all interruptions are attempts to monopolize communication (Goldsmith & Fulfs, 1999). In some situations, we interrupt the flow of others' talk to show interest, to voice support, and to ask for elaboration. Interrupting for these reasons doesn't divert attention from the person speaking; instead, it affirms that person and keeps the focus on her or him.

Selective Listening   A third form of ineffective listening is **selective listening**, which involves focusing only on particular parts of communication. One form of selective listening is focusing only on communication that interests us or corresponds to our opinions and feelings. If you are worried about a storm, you may listen selectively to weather reports and disregard news. Students often become highly attentive in classes when teachers say, "This will be on the test." In the workplace, we may become more attentive when communication addresses topics such as raises, layoffs, and other matters that may affect us directly.

Selective listening also occurs when we reject communication that bores us or is inconsistent with our values, opinions, or choices. We may selectively filter out a co-worker's criticisms of our work.

Defensive Listening   **Defensive listening** involves perceiving a personal attack, criticism, or hostile undertone in communication when none is intended. When we listen defensively, we assume others don't like, trust, or respect us, and we read these motives into whatever they say, regardless of how innocent their communication actually is (Donoghue & Siegel, 2005). Some people are generally defensive, expecting insults and criticism from all quarters. They hear threats and negative judgments in almost anything said to them. Thus, an innocent remark such as, "Have you finished the report yet?" may be perceived as criticism that the report hasn't been turned in yet.

In other instances, defensive listening is confined to areas where we judge ourselves inadequate or to times when we feel negative about ourselves. A woman who fears she is not valued in her job may interpret committee assignments as signs that she is not well regarded. Someone who has been laid off may perceive work-related comments as personal criticism of his or her unemployment.

selective listening Focusing only on selected parts of communication; e.g., screening out parts of a message that don't interest us or with which we disagree, or riveting our attention on parts of communication that interest us or with which we agree.

defensive listening The perception of a personal attack, criticism, or hostile undertone in communication when none is intended.

Ambushing **Ambushing** is listening carefully for the purpose of gathering ammunition to use in attacking a speaker. Ambushing often relies on an extreme form of monopolizing in which interruptions are constant and intentionally disruptive. Political candidates routinely listen carefully to their opponents in order to undercut them.

Ambushing may also plague work life, especially in organizations that encourage employees to compete with one another in order to stand out. These employees display no openness, make no effort to understand the other's meaning, take no interest in recognizing value in what another says, and do not want genuine dialogue. Eric provides another example of ambushing.

 *Eric*

One brother at my [fraternity] house is a real ambusher. He's a pre-law major, and he loves to debate and win arguments. No matter what somebody talks about, this guy just listens long enough to mount a counterattack. He doesn't care about understanding anybody else, just about beating them. I've quit talking when he's around.

Literal Listening **Literal listening** involves listening only to the content level of meaning and ignoring the relationship level of meaning. When we listen literally, we do not listen to what's being communicated about the other person or about our relationship with that person. For example, one member of a work team might avoid eye contact, shrug his shoulders, and say in a flat voice, "I guess I can go along with this decision." If other group members listen only to his literal message, they will assume the group has reached a decision. However, the relational level of meaning, conveyed nonverbally, suggests the member is not happy with the decision. It's likely that this member will not be fully committed to the decision and will not be enthusiastic about implementing it. Literal listening neglects others' feelings and our relationship with them.

> **ambushing** Listening carefully to a speaker in order to attack her or him.
>
> **literal listening** Listening only to the content level of meaning and ignoring the relationship level of meaning.

Digital Media and Listening

There are at least three ways that the ideas in this chapter are relevant to digital media. First, some online communication requires listening. When you Skype or have FaceTime with a friend or family member, you need the same mindfulness and listening skills that you do to listen to someone face to face.

Second, our increasing engagement with digital media can be an obstacle to effective listening. Leslie Perlow, who is on the faculty of Harvard's Business School, is the author of *Sleeping with Your Smartphone* (2013) in which she asserts that our devices threaten to overtake our lives. She recommends that professionals need blocks of time when they are entirely disconnected so that they can

Listen Up, Doc

Cookbook medicine is what Doctors Leana Wen and Joshua Kosowsky (2013) think is causing a lot of misdiagnoses and unnecessary tests. In their book, *When Doctors Don't Listen*, Wen and Kosowsky point out that doctors increasingly rely on algorithms, or flow charts, to diagnose patients. A patient who has chest pain will be treated by a heart attack algorithm; a patient with fever and cough is treated by a pneumonia algorithm (Zuger, 2013). This makes sense in many cases, and it increases efficiency in treating patients.

But sometimes a rock that fell on a person caused the chest pain; sometimes fever and a cough are caused by bronchitis. The problem, say Wen and Kosowsky, is that algorithms depersonalize medicine. They urge doctors to spend more time listening to patients before prescribing diagnosis tests or assuming what the problem is. Just as good cooks don't unthinkingly follow recipes, good doctors don't let cookbook medicine substitute for listening to individual patients.

concentrate on listening and working together. Randi Zuckerberg (2013) also urges people to disconnect from devices periodically and engage in real life. People need to get back to talking face to face, really looking at each other and getting energy from each other. Highly creative work environments depend on listening—truly listening (Brady, 2013; Korkki, 2013).

Third, we need to exercise critical thinking when communicating online. As we have noted earlier, anyone can post anything online, so accuracy is not guaranteed. When you read blogs and tweets, you should ask critical thinking questions such as: What qualifies this person to have an informed stance on this issue? Does this person have any vested interest or any ties to others who have stakes in the issue? What is this person's track record of accuracy? Another way to keep your critical thinking sharp is to check other sources of information on the same issue to see if there is a consistent opinion. Consistency doesn't necessarily equal right, but it gives you one way of assessing what you read online.

It's also wise to be thoughtful about what you communicate on social media. As Randi Zuckerberg (2013) notes, the fact that you can post pictures and comments about every moment of your life doesn't mean you should. People who are more discriminating about what they put online are likely to be more interesting to those who follow them.

informational listening
Listening to understand information and ideas.

critical listening Listening to analyze and evaluate the content of communication or the character of the person speaking.

relationship listening
Listening to support another person or to understand how another person thinks, feels, or perceives some situation, event, or other phenomenon.

Guidelines for Effective Listening

Our discussion of listening and the obstacles to it provides a foundation for improving our effectiveness as listeners. The key guideline is to adapt listening to specific communication goals and situations. Two kinds of listening, **informational and critical listening** and **relationship listening**, require specific skills and attitudes. We'll discuss how to be effective when engaging in these two kinds of listening and briefly discuss other types of listening.

 **ENGAGE!**

Laptop versus Lecture

Many colleges and universities that require students to have laptops are having second thoughts. The problem? It seems that instead of using laptops to enhance what they learn from lectures, some students are using them to find alternatives to listening to lectures—net surfing, shopping and texting friends, checking blogs, online shopping, or working on assignments (Young, 2006). Some students claim that they can multitask and therefore can attend to lectures while doing other tasks. Yet, research indicates that not only may laptops distract from focusing on classes, but also may be less effective for taking notes than old fashioned handwritten notes (Pappano, 2014).

 MindTap· Do you use a laptop or tablet in classes? If so, does it enhance what you learn?

Develop Skills for Informational and Critical Listening

Much of our listening is to gain and evaluate information. We listen for information in classes and professional meetings, when we are learning a new job, during important news stories, when we need to understand a medical treatment, and when we are getting directions. In all these cases, the primary purpose of listening is to gain and understand information.

Closely related to informational listening is critical listening: We listen to make judgments about people and ideas. Like informational listening, critical listening requires attending closely to the content of communication. Yet critical listening goes beyond gaining information to analyze and evaluate it and the people who express it. We decide whether a speaker is credible and ethical by judging the thoroughness of a presentation, the accuracy of evidence, the carefulness of reasoning, and personal confidence and trustworthiness. Informational and critical listening call for skills that help us gain and retain information. Critical listening also calls for skill in evaluating information.

Be Mindful   The first step in listening to information critically is to make a decision to attend carefully, even if the material is complex and difficult. This may mean that you time your conversations, whether phone, online, or face to face, so that you have the mental energy to be mindful. Don't let your mind wander if information gets complicated or confusing. Avoid daydreaming, and stay focused on learning as much as you can. Later, you may want to ask questions if material isn't clear or if you have reservations about evidence or logic.

Control Obstacles   You can also minimize distractions. You might shut a window to block out traffic noises or adjust a thermostat so that the room's temperature is comfortable. In addition, you should minimize psychological distractions by emptying your mind of the many concerns, ideas, and prejudgments that can interfere with attending to the communication at hand.

Ask Questions   Asking speakers to clarify their messages or to elaborate allows you to understand information you didn't grasp at first and to deepen your insight into content you did comprehend. Recently, I listened to a fairly technical talk on national economic issues. After the speech, audience members asked these questions: "Could you explain what you meant by the M2 money supply?" "How does inflation affect wages?" and "Can you clarify the distinction between the national debt and the deficit?" These questions showed that the listeners had paid attention and were interested in further information. Questions compliment a speaker because they show that you are interested and want to know more.

Critical listening often calls for asking probing questions. "What is the source of your statistics on the rate of unemployment?" "Is a seven-year-old statistic on Welfare current enough to tell us anything about Welfare issues today?" "Have you met with any policy makers who hold a point of view contrary to yours? What is their response to your proposals?" "All the sources you quoted in your presentation are fiscal conservatives. Does this mean your presentation and your conclusions are biased?"

Use Aids to Recall   To remember important information, we can apply principles of perception we discussed in Chapter 3. For instance, we learned that we tend to notice and recall stimuli that are repeated. To use this principle to increase your retention, repeat important ideas to yourself immediately after hearing them. This moves new information from short-term to long-term memory. Repeating the names of people when you meet them can save you the embarrassment of having to ask them to repeat their names.

Another way to increase retention is to use mnemonic (pronounced *"knee monic"*) devices, which are memory aids that create patterns that help you remember what you've heard. For instance, ROB is a mnemonic for remembering that Robert from

© mangostock/Shutterstock.com

Listening to a Second Language

Asking questions is especially important and appropriate for nonnative speakers of the speaker's language. People who have learned English as a second language may not understand idioms such as *in a heartbeat* (fast), *not on your life* (very unlikely), or *off the wall* (wacky) (Lee, 1994, 2000). Another listening difficulty for nonnative speakers of a language is the ability to distinguish between sounds. Research shows that this ability is learned, not innate. By the age of one, if not sooner, babies can distinguish between sounds of languages they hear spoken (Monastersky, 2001). Non-Chinese people have difficulty distinguishing between two distinct sounds in Mandarin Chinese: *qi*, which is approximately like the English *ch* sound, and *xi*, which is approximately like the English *sh* sound. People who are native to Japan have a hard time distinguishing between the English sounds *ra* and *la*. To read more about learning English as a second language, go to the book's online resources for this chapter.

Ohio, is studying Business. A well-known mnemonic is HOMES for the Great Lakes: Lakes Huron, Ontario, Michigan, Erie, and Superior.

Organize Information   Another technique for increasing your retention is to organize what you hear. Because people seldom order what they hear, the information isn't coherently organized and so it's hard to retain or recall. We can impose order by regrouping what we hear. For example, suppose a friend tells you that he's confused about long-range goals, doesn't know what he can do with a math major, wants to locate in the Midwest, wonders whether graduate school is necessary, likes small towns, needs some internships to try out different options, and wants a family eventually. You could organize this stream of concerns into two categories: academic issues (careers for math majors, graduate school, internship opportunities) and lifestyle preferences (Midwest, small town, family). Remembering these two categories allows you to retain the essence of your friend's concerns, even if you forget many of the specifics.

Develop Skills for Relationship Listening

Listening for information focuses on the content level of meaning in communication. Yet, often we are as concerned or even more concerned with the relationship level of meaning, which has to do with feelings and relationships between communicators. We engage in relationship listening when we listen to a friend's worries, let a romantic partner tell us about problems, counsel a co-worker, or talk with a parent about health concerns. Specific listening attitudes and skills enhance our ability to listen supportively (Nichols, 1996).

Be Mindful   The first requirement for effective relationship listening is mindfulness, which is also the first step in informational listening. When we're listening to give support, however, we focus on feelings that may not be communicated explicitly. Thus, mindful relationship listening involves looking for feelings and perceptions that are "between the words." As listening scholar Gerald Egan notes, "Total listening is more than attending to another person's words. It is also listening to the meanings that are buried in the words and between the words and in the silences in communication" (1973, p. 228).

Suspend Judgment   When listening to provide support, it's important to avoid judgmental responses. When we judge, we add our evaluations to other people's experiences, and this moves us away from them and their feelings. Our judgments may also lead others to become defensive and unwilling to talk further with us. To curb judgment, we can ask whether we really need to evaluate right now. José's commentary illustrates the value of suspending judgment when listening relationally.

 José

My best friend makes it so easy for me to tell whatever is on my mind. She never puts me down or makes me feel stupid or weird. Sometimes, I ask her what she thinks, and she has this way of telling me without making me feel wrong if I think differently. What it boils down to is respect. She respects me and herself, and so she doesn't have to prove anything by acting better than me.

Only if someone asks for our evaluation should we offer it. Even if our opinion is sought, we should express it in a way that doesn't devalue others. Sometimes people excuse strongly judgmental comments by saying, "You asked me to be honest" or "I mean this as constructive criticism." Too often, however, the judgments are not constructive and are harsher than candor requires.

Strive to Understand the Other's Perspective   One of the most important principles for effective relationship listening is to concentrate on grasping the other person's perspective by being person-centered (Nichols, 1996). This means we have to step outside of our point of view at least long enough to understand another's perceptions. We can't respond sensitively to others until we understand their perspective and meanings. To do this, we must put aside our views and focus on their words and nonverbal behaviors for clues to others feelings and thoughts.

One communication skill that helps us gain insight into others is the use of **minimal encouragers**. These are responses that gently invite another person to elaborate. Examples of minimal encouragers are "Tell me more," "Really?" "Go on," "I'm with you," "Then what happened?" "Yeah?" and "I see." We can also use nonverbal minimal encouragers, such as a raised eyebrow to show that we're involved, a nod to signal that we understand, or vocalizations such as "um," and "uh huh." Keep in mind that these are *minimal* encouragers; they shouldn't take the focus away from the other person. Effective minimal encouragers are brief interjections that prompt, rather than interfere with, the flow of another's talk.

Paraphrasing is a second way to gain insight into others' perspectives. To paraphrase, we reflect our interpretations of others' communication back to them. For example, a friend might confide, "With all the news on teenagers and drugs, I wonder if my kid brother is messing around with drugs." You could paraphrase this way: "It sounds as if you think your brother may be taking drugs." This paraphrase allows us to clarify whether the friend has any evidence of the brother's drug involvement. The response might be, "No, I don't have any reason to suspect him, but I just worry because drugs are so pervasive in high schools now." Paraphrasing can also be a way to check perceptions to see whether we understand another person's meaning: "Let me see if I followed you. I think what you're saying is . . . ."

 Lynette

I discovered something really interesting when I practiced paraphrasing for class. I found out that knowing I needed to rephrase what someone else was saying forced me to listen more carefully to what they were saying. I understood people better than I usually do when I'm not so focused on what they are saying. I hadn't even realized that I wasn't listening well before.

A third way to enhance understanding of others is to ask questions. For instance, we might ask, "How do you feel about that?" or "What do you plan to do?" Another

minimal encouragers Communication that gently invites another person to elaborate by expressing interest in hearing more.

paraphrasing A method of clarifying another's meaning by reflecting one's interpretation of the other's communication back to that person.

reason we ask questions is to find out what a person wants from us. Sometimes it isn't clear whether someone wants advice, a shoulder to cry on, or a safe place to vent feelings. If we can't figure out what's wanted, it's appropriate to ask, "Are you looking for advice or a sounding board?" Asking directly signals that we really want to help and allows others to tell us how we can best do that. A Take Action feature at the end of this chapter will help you develop your skills in paraphrasing.

Express Support   Once you have understood another's meanings and perspective, relationship listening should focus on communicating support. This doesn't necessarily require us to agree with another's perspective or ideas. It does call upon us to communicate support for the person. To illustrate how we can support someone even if we don't agree with his or her position, consider the following exchange between a son and his father:

Son: Dad, I'm changing my major to acting.

Father: Oh.

Son: Yeah, I've wanted to do it for some time, but I hesitated because acting isn't as safe as accounting.

Father: That's certainly true.

Son: Yeah, but I've decided to do it anyway. I'd like to know what you think about the idea.

Father: The idea worries me. Starving actors are a dime a dozen. It just won't provide you with any economic future or security.

Son: I understand acting isn't as secure as business, but it is what I really want to do.

Father: Tell me what you feel about acting—why it matters so much to you.

Son: It's the most creative, totally fulfilling thing I do. I've tried to get interested in business, but I just don't love that like I do acting. I feel like I have to give this a try, or I'll always wonder if I could have made it. If I don't get somewhere in 5 or 6 years, I'll rethink career options.

Father: Couldn't you finish your business degree and get a job and act on the side?

Son: No. I've got to give acting a full shot—give it everything I have to see if I can make it.

Father: Well, I still have reservations, but I guess I can understand having to try something that matters this much to you. I'm just concerned that you'll lose years of your life to something that doesn't work out.

Son: Well, I'm kind of concerned about that too, but I'm more worried about wasting years of my life in a career that doesn't excite me than about trying to make a go of the one that does.

Father: That makes sense. I wouldn't make the choice you're making, but I respect your decision and your guts for taking a big gamble.

This dialogue illustrates several principles of effective relationship listening. First, note that the father's first two comments are minimal encouragers that invite his son to elaborate on his thoughts and feelings. The father also encourages his son to explain how he feels. Later, the father suggests a compromise solution, but his son rejects that, and the father respects the son's position. It is important that the father makes his position clear, but he separates his personal stance from his respect for his son's right to make his own choices. In this way, the father disagrees without negatively evaluating his son.

Develop Skills for Other Listening Goals

In addition to listening for information, to make critical evaluations, and to provide support, we listen for pleasure and to discriminate.

Listening for Pleasure   Sometimes we listen for pleasure, as when we attend concerts or comedy shows or listen to friends tell jokes. When listening for pleasure, we don't need to concentrate on organizing and remembering as much as we do when we listen for information, although retention is important if you want to tell the joke to someone else later. Yet listening for pleasure does require mindfulness, hearing, and interpretation.

Listening to Discriminate   In some situations, we listen to make fine discriminations in sounds in order to draw accurate conclusions and act appropriately in response. For example, doctors listen to discriminate when they use stethoscopes to assess heart function or chest congestion. Parents listen to discriminate a baby's cries for attention, food, reassurance, or a diaper change. Skilled mechanics can distinguish engine sounds far more keenly than most other people. Mindfulness and keen hearing abilities are skills that assist listening to discriminate.

Mindfulness is a prerequisite for effective listening of all types. With the exception of mindfulness, each listening purpose tends to emphasize particular aspects of the listening process and to put less weight on others. Whereas evaluating content is especially important in listening critically, it is less crucial when listening for pleasure. Hearing acoustic nuances is important when listening to discriminate but not vital to listening for information. Selecting, organizing, and retaining information matter more when we are listening for information than when we are listening for pleasure. Deciding on your purpose for listening allows you to use the most pertinent communication skills.

Summary

Listening is a major and vital part of communication, yet too often we don't consider it as important as talking. In this chapter, we've explored the complex and demanding process of listening. We began by distinguishing between hearing and listening. The former is a straightforward physiological process that doesn't take effort on our part. Listening, in contrast, is a complicated process involving being mindful, hearing, selecting and organizing, interpreting, responding, and remembering. Listening well takes commitment and skill. Attending effectively when using digital media

requires the same mindfulness and listening skills that we use in face-to-face conversations.

Obstacles in ourselves as well as in situations and messages jeopardize effective listening. Incomprehensibility, message overload, complexity of material, and environmental distractions are external obstacles to listening. In addition, preoccupations, prejudgments, reacting to emotional language, lack of effort, and not recognizing differences in listening styles can hamper listening. The obstacles to listening often lead to various forms of ineffective listening, including pseudolistening, monopolizing, selective listening, defensive listening, ambushing, and literal listening. Each form of ineffective listening prevents us from being fully engaged in communication. Another obstacle to effective listening is the online environment. Our increasing enmeshment in social media has the potential to impoverish in-person interaction.

We also discussed different purposes for listening and identified the skills and attitudes that advance each

purpose. Informational and critical listening require us to adopt a mindful attitude and to think critically, to organize and evaluate information, to clarify understanding by asking questions, and to develop aids to retention of complex material. Relationship listening also requires mindfulness, but it calls for other distinct listening skills. Suspending judgment, paraphrasing, giving minimal encouragers, and expressing support enhance the effectiveness of relationship listening.

Experience Communication Case Study

Family Hour

Apply what you've learned in this chapter by analyzing the following case study, using the accompanying questions as a guide. These questions and a video of the case study are also available online with your MindTap Speech for *Communication Mosaics*.

Over spring break, 20-year-old Josh visits his father. He wants to convince his family to support him in joining a fraternity that has given him a bid. On his second day home, after dinner, Josh decides to broach the topic. His dad is watching the evening news on television when Josh walks into the living room. Josh sits down and opens the conversation.

Josh: Well, something pretty interesting has happened at school this semester.

Dad: I'll bet you found a girlfriend, right? I was about your age when your mother and I started dating, and that was the best part of college. I still remember how she looked on our first date. She was young then, and she was very slender and pretty. I saw her and thought she was the loveliest thing I'd ever seen. Before long, we were a regular item. Yep, it was about when I was 20, like you are now.

Josh: Well, I haven't found a girlfriend, but I did get a bid from Sigma Chi.

Dad: Sigma Chi. What is that—a fraternity?

Josh: Yeah, it's probably the coolest fraternity on campus. I attended some rush parties this semester—mainly out of curiosity, just to see what they were like.

Dad: Why'd you do that? Before you ever went to college, I told you to steer clear of fraternities. They cost a lot of money, and they distract you from your studies.

Josh: Well, I know you told me to steer clear of fraternities, but I did check a few out. I'd be willing to take a job to help pay the membership fee and monthly dues. Besides, it's not that much more expensive when you figure I'd be eating at the house.

© Cengage Learning

Dad: Do you realize how much it costs just for you to go to that school? I'm paying $14,000 a year! When I went to school, I had to go to state college because my parents couldn't afford to send me to the school of my choice. You have no idea how lucky you are to be going to the school you wanted to go to and have me footing all of the bills

Josh: But we could work it out so that a fraternity wouldn't cost you anything. Like I said, I. . . .

Dad: If you want to take a job, fine. I could use some help paying your tuition and fees. But you're not taking a job just so you can belong to a party house.

Josh: I thought they were just party houses too, until I attended rush. Now, I went to several houses that were that way, but Sigma Chi isn't. I really liked the brothers at Sigma Chi. They're interesting and friendly and fun, so I was thrilled when. . . .

Dad: I don't want to hear about it. You're not joining a fraternity. I told you what happened when I was in college. I joined one, and pretty soon my Dean's List grades dropped to Cs and Ds. When you live in a fraternity house, you can't study like you can in your dorm room or the library. I should know. I tried it and found out the hard way. There's no need for you to repeat my mistake.

Josh: But, Dad, I'm not you. Joining a fraternity wouldn't necessarily mean that my grades. . . .

Dad: What do you mean, you're not me? You think I wasn't a good student before I joined the fraternity? You think you're so smart that you can party all the time and still make good grades? Let me tell you something, I thought that too, and, boy! Was I ever wrong. As soon as I joined the house, it was party time all the time. There was always music blaring and girls in the house and poker games—anything but studying. I wasn't stupid. It's just not an atmosphere that encourages academic work.

Josh: I'd like to give it a try. I really like these guys, and I think I can handle being in Sigma Chi and still. . . .

Dad: Well, you think wrong!

1. What examples of ineffective listening are evident in this dialogue?

2. If you could advise Josh's father on listening effectively, what would you tell him to do differently?

3. What advice would you offer Josh on listening more effectively to his father?

Key Concepts

Practice defining the chapter's terms by using online flashcards.

ambushing, 119
critical listening, 120
defensive listening, 118
environmental distractions, 115
hearing, 110
incomprehensibility, 114
informational and critical listening, 120
interpretation, 112
listening, 110
literal listening, 119
message complexity, 115
message overload, 114

mindfulness, 111
minimal encouragers, 123
monopolizing, 117
paraphrasing, 123
prejudgment, 116
preoccupation, 115
pseudolistening, 117
relationship listening, 120
remembering, 113
responding, 113
selective listening, 118

Review, Reflect, Extend

The Reflect and Discuss and Take Action features that follow will help you review, reflect on, and extend the information and ideas presented in this chapter. These resources, and a diverse selection of additional study tools, are also available online at the MindTap Speech for *Communication Mosaics*.

Reflect, personalize, and apply what you've learned

Reflect and Discuss

1. Review the types of ineffective listening discussed in this chapter. Do any describe ways in which you attend (or don't attend) to others? Select one type of ineffective listening in which you engage and work to minimize it in your interactions.

2. As a class, identify ethical principles that guide different listening purposes. What different moral goals and responsibilities accompany informational and critical listening and relationship listening?

3. Spend time with people you do not usually interact with. If you are engaged in a service learning project, your community partners would be a good choice. Practice using minimal encouragers and paraphrasing to increase the depth of your understanding of their perspectives.

TAKE ACTION

1. Developing Mindfulness

Mindfulness develops with commitment and practice. Four guidelines will help you develop mindfulness.

a. Empty your mind of thoughts, ideas, and plans so that you are open to listening to another.

b. Concentrate on the person with whom you are communicating. Say to yourself, "I want to focus on this person and what she or he is saying and feeling."

c. Don't be surprised if distracting thoughts come up or you find yourself thinking about your responses instead of what the other person is saying. This is natural. Just push away diverting thoughts and refocus on the person with whom you are talking.

d. Evaluate how well you listened when you were focusing on being mindful. If you aren't as fully engaged as you want to be, remind yourself that mindfulness is a habit of mind and a way of living. Developing your ability to be mindful is a process that requires time and practice.

2. Improving Recall

Apply the principles we've discussed to enhance what you remember.

a. The next time you meet someone, repeat his or her name to yourself three times after you are introduced. Do you find that the name sticks better?

b. After your next communication class, take 15 minutes to review your notes in a quiet place. Read them aloud so you hear as well as see the main ideas. Does this increase your retention of the material?

c. Invent mnemonics that help you remember basic information from messages.

d. Organize complex ideas by grouping them into categories. To remember the main ideas of this chapter, you might use major subheadings to form categories: listening process, obstacles to listening, and listening goals. Creating the mnemonic POG (process, obstacles, goals) could help you remember those topics.

3. Practice Paraphrasing

Learning to paraphrase enhances communication. You can develop skill in paraphrasing by creating paraphrases of the following comments:

a. "I don't know how they expect me to get my work done when they don't give me any training on how to use this new software program."

b. "I've got three midterms and a paper due next week, and I'm behind in my reading."

c. "My parents don't understand why I need to go to summer school, and they won't pay my expenses."

d. "My son wants to go to summer school and expects us to come up with the money. Doesn't he understand what we're already paying for the regular school year?"

Recommended Resources

1. The film *Erin Brockovich* dramatically illustrates the power of listening. Watch the film, and pay attention to how Julia Roberts, in the role of Erin Brockovich, shows she is listening carefully to people who have been harmed by toxic chemicals and not heard by others.

2. To learn more about taking good notes to improve recall, visit the Web page created by the Office of Academic Advising at the College of St. Benedict/ St. John's University, which is available through this book's online resources.

3. The International Listening Association (ILA) is a rich resource for learning more about listening and networking with others who recognize its importance in everyday life. Its Web site features exercises to test and improve listening, factoids about listening, Internet discussion groups, quotes about the nature and value of listening, and a bibliography for those who want to read more. You may access this site through this book's online resources.

7

Creating Communication Climates

Kind words may be short . . . but their echoes are endless.
— *Mother Teresa*

How do you handle excessive insults and hostility in online communication?

MindTap

Learning Objectives

MindTap

Start with a quick engagement activity and **review** the chapter Learning Objectives.

Topics Covered in This Chapter	After studying this chapter, you should be able to . . .
Levels of Confirmation and Disconfirmation	Describe the three levels of confirmation: recognition, acknowledgment, and endorsement.
Defensive and Supportive Climates	Contrast the six types of communication that build supportive climates with the corresponding six types of communication that build defensive climates.
Conflict and Communication	Discuss how each of the four components in the conflict process can contribute to healthy conflict management.
Digital Media and Communication Climate	Apply the levels of confirmation to communication via digital media. Explain three constructive ways to respond to flaming in social media.
Guidelines for Creating and Sustaining Healthy Communication Climates	Create an action plan to implement this chapter's five guidelines for building and sustaining healthy climates.

◆ You have scheduled a performance review with an employee, who began working for you six months ago. You need to call his attention to some problems in his work while also showing that you value him and believe he can improve his performance.

◆ Your friend Olivia just decided to drop out of school and you're worried about her. You disagree with the decision but still want to support your friend.

◆ You're concerned that your younger brother's friends may be using drugs. You want to find a way to talk openly with your brother and to warn him about using drugs without making him feel that you are judging him or his friends.

In each of these situations, achieving your goals depends on your ability to create an effective **communication climate**, which is the emotional tone of a relationship between people. In much the same way that physical climate influences our moods, communication climate affects how people feel and interact with one another.

This chapter focuses on the basic skill of creating effective communication climates. We begin by discussing *confirmation* as a keystone of positive communication climates. Next, we identify specific kinds of communication that foster defensive and supportive communication climates. In the third section of the chapter, we discuss creating healthy communication climates as a foundation for managing conflict constructively. We then consider how this chapter's topics apply to social media. Finally, we identify guidelines for creating and sustaining healthy communication climates.

Levels of Confirmation and Disconfirmation

Philosopher Martin Buber (1957, 1970) believed that each of us needs interpersonal *confirmation* to be healthy and to grow. Communication scholars (Anderson, Baxter, & Cissna, 2004; Arnett, 2004; MacGeorge, 2009; Stewart, Zediker, & Black, 2004) have drawn on Buber's work to develop philosophies of communication that emphasize confirmation as a basis of meaningful dialogue. The essence of **confirmation** is the expressed valuing of another person. We all want to feel we are valued by colleagues in our workplace, by audiences in public speaking settings, and by intimates in personal relationships. When others confirm us, we feel appreciated and respected. When they disconfirm us, we feel discounted and devalued.

Few climates are purely confirming or purely disconfirming. Many relationships include a mix of the two climate types. It's not unusual for relationships to cycle between periods that are relatively confirming and other periods that are relatively disconfirming (Figure 7.1). Over the course of time, confirming communication outweighs disconfirming communication in healthy, positive relationships. Communication scholars (Cissna & Sieburg, 1986) have identified three levels of confirmation that affect communication climates: recognition, acknowledgment, and endorsement.

Recognition

The most basic form of interpersonal confirmation is **recognition**, the expression of awareness of another person's existence. We recognize others by nonverbal behaviors (a smile, a handshake, looking up when someone enters your room) and by verbal communication ("Hello," "Good to meet you," "Welcome home"). We disconfirm

MindTap

Read, highlight, and take notes online.

communication climate
The overall feeling, or emotional mood, between people.

confirmation The expressed valuing of another person.

recognition The most basic level of interpersonal confirmation; the communication of awareness that another person exists and is present.

© Cengage Learning

Figure 7.1 The Continuum of Communication Climates

others at a fundamental level when we don't recognize their existence. For example, you might not speak to a person when you enter a room, or you might not look at a teammate who comes late to a meeting. People often refuse to recognize homeless individuals. Notice how often drivers and passers-by refuse to make eye contact with people holding signs that say, "Homeless. Please help." Failing to give even basic eye contact says, "You don't exist." Not responding to another's comments is also a failure to give recognition. As we noted in Chapter 5, silence is sometimes used to disconfirm another's existence.

 Erika

Last year I was diagnosed with cancer and had to go through chemotherapy. I lost my hair and a huge amount of weight so I looked like a skeleton. It was amazing how people treated me like I was invisible. Even people who knew me would look away and not talk to me like I wasn't there.

Dr. Michael Kahn (2008) points out that some doctors fail to recognize patients as human beings. Kahn notes that doctors often enter patients' rooms without knocking, don't introduce themselves, and don't greet patients. Such actions fail to recognize patients, which is highly disconfirming.

 Nikki

I work at a fast-food restaurant, and I'm often assigned to the drive-through window. On my last shift, four drivers were talking on their cells when they got to the window. They made gestures to order their food and never said a word to me—not "hello," not "I'd like the chicken melt," not "thank you." Nothing. They acted like a person was not there, like I was just a machine.

Acknowledgment

A second, more powerful level of interpersonal confirmation is **acknowledgment**: attentiveness to what a person feels, thinks, or says. Nonverbally, we acknowledge others by nodding our heads or by making eye contact to show we are listening. Verbal acknowledgments are direct responses to others' communication. If a friend says, "I'm really worried that I blew the LSAT exam," you could acknowledge that by responding, "So the exam made you anxious, huh?" This paraphrasing response acknowledges the thoughts and feelings of the other person. Communication researcher René Dailey (2006) found that adolescents talk more openly with parents if they perceive that the parents acknowledge their feelings.

We disconfirm others when we don't acknowledge their feelings, thoughts, or words. For instance, if you responded to your friend's statement about the LSAT by saying, "Want to go out and catch a film tonight?" your response would ignore what your friend said. We also fail to acknowledge others if we deny the feelings they communicate: "You did fine on the LSAT." Lack of acknowledgment may also take the form of nonresponse to a friend's comment or nonresponse to ideas expresses in a meetings (Conrad & Poole, 2012). Lisa explains how she feels when others refuse to acknowledge her statements about her abilities.

acknowledgment The second of three levels of interpersonal confirmation; communicating that you hear and understand another's expressed feelings and thoughts.

Table 7.1   Levels of Confirmation and Disconfirmation

	Confirming Messages	*Disconfirming Messages*
Recognition	You exist.	You don't exist.
	Hello.	Silence
Acknowledgment	Listening	Not listening
	I'm sorry you're hurt.	You'll get over it.
	I know you're worried.	Let's drop the subject.
Endorsement	What you think is true.	You are wrong.
	What you feel is okay.	You shouldn't feel what you do.
	I feel the same way.	Your feeling doesn't make sense.
	What you feel is normal.	It's stupid to feel that way.

© Cengage Learning

 **Lisa**

I'm amazed by how often people won't acknowledge what I tell them. A hundred times, I've been walking across campus, and someone's come up and offered to guide me. I tell them I don't need help, but they put an arm under my elbow to guide me. I am blind, but I can think just fine. I know if I need help. Why can't they acknowledge that?

Endorsement

The highest level of interpersonal confirmation is **endorsement**—accepting a person's feelings or thoughts as valid. This doesn't necessarily mean agreeing with the person's thoughts or feelings, but it does mean accepting them as real for that person. You could endorse the friend who is worried about the LSAT by saying, "It's natural to be worried about the LSAT when you have so much riding on it." We fail to endorse others when we reject their thoughts and feelings. For example, it would be disconfirming to say, "How can you worry about your LSAT score when people around the world are starving?" This response rejects the validity of the other person's expressed feelings and may close the lines of communication between the two of you. Table 7.1 provides examples of communication at each level of confirmation.

In her commentary, Jennie provides an example of how hurtful it can be not to feel endorsed by friends.

 **Jennie**

My father died two years ago. We were very close, so I was upset and sad for a long time. After a couple of months, some of my friends said things like, "You need to move on," or "It's time to quit mourning for your father." Those comments made me feel like I was crazy to still be grieving. I felt like they were saying what I was feeling wasn't right or something.

It's important to realize that disconfirmation is not the same as disagreement. After all, disagreements can be productive and healthy. What is disconfirming is to be told that we don't exist or matter or that our feelings and thoughts are crazy, wrong, stupid, or deviant. A Take Action activity at the end of this chapter encourages you to notice confirming and disconfirming communication in online conversations.

 MindTap

TAKE ACTION . . . activities are located at the end of this chapter and online.

endorsement The third of three levels of interpersonal confirmation; the communication of acceptance of another's thoughts and feelings. Not the same as agreement.

Interpersonal confirmation is a key to building supportive, trusting communication climates.

If you think about what we've discussed, you'll probably find that the relationships in which you feel most valued and comfortable are those with high degrees of recognition, acknowledgment, and endorsement. We'll now consider other forms of communication that affect climates.

Defensive and Supportive Climates

Communication researcher Jack Gibb (1961, 1964, 1970) studied the relationship between communication and climate. He began by noting that in some climates we feel defensive whereas in others we feel supported. Gibb identified six types of communication that promote defensive climates and six contrasting types of communication that foster supportive climates. Since Gibb published his findings, other communication scholars have confirmed them (Barge, 2009; Becker, Halbesleben, & O'Hair, 2005).

Evaluation versus Description

As we noted in Chapter 4's discussion of the evaluative nature of language, we tend to feel defensive when others evaluate us, particularly when they evaluate us negatively (Caughlin, Afifi, Carpenter-Theune, & Miller, 2005; Conrad & Poole, 2012; Reis, Clark, & Holmes, 2004). Examples of evaluative statements are "It's dumb to feel that way" and "That's a stupid idea."

Descriptive communication doesn't evaluate what others think and feel. Instead, it describes behaviors without passing judgment. In Chapter 4, we discussed *I*-language, in which a speaker takes responsibility for what she or he feels and avoids judging others. For example, "I feel upset when you scream" describes what the person speaking feels or thinks, but it doesn't evaluate another. On the other hand, "You upset me" evaluates the other person and holds her or him responsible for what you feel. "I felt hurt when you said that" describes your feelings, whereas "You hurt me" blames another for your feelings.

Descriptive language may refer to others, but it does so by describing, not evaluating, their behavior (for example, "I notice you are speaking less in team meetings lately" versus "You're uninvolved in team meetings"). Nonverbal communication can also convey evaluation—a raised eyebrow expresses skepticism, shaking your head communicates disapproval.

Certainty versus Provisionalism

The language of certainty is absolute and often dogmatic. It suggests there is only one valid answer, point of view, or course of action. Because certainty proclaims an absolutely correct position, it slams the door on further discussion. Leaders can stifle creativity if they dogmatically state what the team should do (Covey, 2013; Hackman & Johnson, 2013). There's no point in talking with people who demean any point of view but their own. Certainty is also communicated when we repeat our positions instead of considering others' ideas. Monika provides an example of certainty and its impact on her relationship with her father.

 Monika

My father is totally closed-minded. He has his ideas, and everything else is crazy. I told him I was majoring in communication studies, and he said I'd never get a job as a speechwriter. He never asked what communication studies is, or I would have told him it's a lot more than speechwriting. He always assumes that he knows everything about whatever is being discussed. He has no interest in information or other points of view. I've learned to keep my ideas to myself around him—there's no communication.

One form of certainty communication is **ethnocentrism**. Ethnocentrism is a perspective based on the assumption that our culture and its norms are the only right ones. For instance, someone who says, "It's always disrespectful to be late" reveals insensitivity to societies that are less time conscious than the United States. Certainty is also evident when we say, "My mind can't be changed because I'm right," "Only a fool would think that," or "There's no point in further discussion."

An alternative to certainty is *provisionalism*, which relies on tentative language to signal openness to other points of view. Provisional language indicates that we are willing to consider alternative positions, and this encourages others to voice their ideas. Provisional communication includes such statements as, "The way I tend to see the issue is . . . ," and "One way to look at the problem is . . . ." Note that each comment shows that the speaker realizes that other positions also could be reasonable. Tentative communication reflects an open mind, which is why it invites continued conversation.

Strategy versus Spontaneity

Strategic communication aims at manipulating a person or group for the benefit of the person manipulating. In work situations, employees may become defensive if they feel management is trying to trick them into thinking their jobs are more important than they are (Conrad & Poole, 2012). We may also feel that someone is trying to manipulate us with a comment such as, "Remember how I helped you with that project you were behind on last month?" After a preamble like that, we suspect a trap of some sort. Nonverbal behaviors may also convey strategy, as when a speaker pauses a long time before answering a question or refuses to look at listeners. A sense of deception pollutes the communication climate.

Spontaneity stands in contrast to strategy. Spontaneous communication is open, honest, and not manipulative. To be ethical, spontaneous communication must not be used against others. For instance, it may be spontaneous to be verbally abusive, but it is not ethical because it does not show respect for the other communicator. "I really need your help with my computer" is more spontaneous than "Would you do something for me if I told you it really mattered?" Likewise, it is more spontaneous to ask for a favor in a straightforward way ("Would you help me?") than to preface a request by reciting everything you've done for someone else.

Control versus Problem Orientation

Controlling communication attempts to coerce others. In response, others often feel defensive, and they may respond with resentment or even rebellion. For example, a woman who earns a higher salary than her partner might say, "Well, I like the Honda more than the Ford you want, and it's my money that's going to pay for it." The speaker not only pushes her preference but also implies that her salary gives her greater power.

ethnocentrism The tendency to assume that one way of life is normal and superior to other ways of life.

Whether the issue is trivial (which movie to see) or important (which policy a group will recommend), controllers try to impose their points of view on others. Winning an argument or having the last word is more important than finding the best solution. Controlling communication prompts defensiveness because the relationship-level meaning is that the person exerting control thinks she or he has greater power, rights, or intelligence than others.

Rather than imposing a preference, problem-oriented communication focuses on resolving problems. The goal is to work collaboratively to come up with something that everyone finds acceptable. Here's an example of problem-oriented communication: "It seems that we have really different ideas about how to get started on this task. Let's talk through what each of us wants and see if we can find a way for all of us to achieve what we need." Note how this statement invites collaboration and confirms the other people and a team focus by expressing a desire to meet all members' needs.

Problem-oriented communication tends to reduce conflict and foster an open interaction climate (McKinney, Kelly, & Duran, 1997; McNutt, 1997). The relationship level of meaning in problem-oriented interaction emphasizes that the communicators care about and respect each other. In contrast, controlling behaviors aim for one person to triumph over others, an outcome that undercuts harmony.

Neutrality versus Empathy

We tend to become defensive when others act in a neutral manner, especially if we are discussing something about which we feel strongly. Neutral communication implies indifference to others and what they say. Consequently, others may feel hurt or defensive.

In contrast to neutrality, expressed empathy confirms the worth of others and shows concern for their thoughts and feelings. We communicate empathy when we say, "I can understand why you feel that way," "It sounds like you feel uncomfortable with your job," or "I don't blame you for being worried about the situation." Gibb stressed that empathy doesn't necessarily mean agreement; instead, it conveys respect for others and what they think and feel. Especially when we don't agree with others, it's important to show that we respect them as people. Doing so fosters a supportive climate and keeps lines of communication open, even if differences continue to exist.

Superiority versus Equality

Most of us resent people who act as if they are better than we are. Consider several messages that convey superiority: "I know a lot more than you"; "You don't have my experience"; "You really should go to my hairdresser." Each of these messages says loudly and clearly, "You aren't as good (smart, experienced, attractive) as I am." Predictably, the frequent result is that we try to save face by shutting out the people and messages that belittle us. Carl's experience in his job provides an example of the impact of communication that conveys superiority.

 *Carl*

I am really uncomfortable with one of the guys on my team at work. He always acts like he knows best and that nobody else is as smart or experienced. The other day, I suggested a way we might improve our team's productivity, and he said, "I remember when I used to think that." What a put-down! You can bet I won't go to him with another idea.

We feel more relaxed and comfortable communicating with people who treat us as equals. At the relationship level of meaning, expressed equality communicates respect. This promotes an open, unguarded climate for interaction. We can have special expertise in certain areas and still show regard for others and what they think, feel, and say. Creating a climate of equality encourages everyone to be involved without fear of being judged inadequate.

We've seen that confirmation, which may include recognizing, acknowledging, and endorsing others, is the basis of healthy communication climates. Our discussion of defensive and supportive communication enlightens us about specific kinds of communication that express confirmation or disconfirmation. A Take Action activity at the end of this chapter invites you to apply what you've learned about communication that fosters defensiveness and supportiveness. Our discussion of communication climates is a good foundation for considering the role of conflict in human relationships and how building and sustaining affirming communication climates creates a foundation for managing conflict productively.

Conflict and Communication

Conflict exists when people who depend on each other have different views, interests, values, responsibilities, or objectives and perceive their differences as incompatible. The presence of conflict doesn't mean a relationship is in trouble, although how people manage conflict does affect relationship health. Typically, conflict is a sign that people are involved with each other. If they weren't, differences wouldn't matter and wouldn't need to be resolved (Cahn & Abigail, 2013; Parker-Pope, 2010). When tensions arise, it's good to remember that engaging in conflict is a signal that we have to work something out in order to keep a relationship on course.

Conflict Can Be Overt or Covert

Conflict can be overt or covert. **Overt conflict** exists when people express differences in a straightforward manner. They might discuss a disagreement, honestly express different points of view, or argue heatedly about ideas. In each case, differences are out in the open.

 *Carlotta*

> *My roommate doesn't tell me when she's mad or hurt or whatever. Instead, she plays these games that drive me crazy. Sometimes, she refuses to talk to me and denies that anything is wrong. Other times, she "forgets" some of my stuff when she gets our groceries. I have to guess what is wrong because she won't tell me. It strains our friendship.*

Yet, as Carla points out, not all conflict is overt. **Covert conflict** exists when people express disagreement or difference only indirectly. For instance, if you're annoyed that your roommate left the kitchen a mess, you might play the stereo when she or he is sleeping. It's almost impossible to resolve conflicts when we don't communicate openly about our differences.

Components in the Conflict Process

Because conflict is inevitable and can be productive, we need to understand how to manage conflict so that it is healthy for us, for our relationships, and for

conflict The expression by people who depend on each other of different views, interests, or goals and the perception of differences as incompatible or in opposition.

overt conflict Conflict expressed directly and in a straightforward manner.

covert conflict Conflict that is expressed indirectly; generally more difficult to manage constructively than overt conflict.

ENGAGE!   Crisis = Danger + Opportunity

The Chinese word for *crisis* is made up of two characters. The character on the left means "danger." The character on the right means "opportunity." Like the Chinese word for *crisis*, we should remember that conflict can be both dangerous and an opportunity.

© Cengage Learning

MindTap Identify the opportunity and danger that were present in a conflict you experienced.

decision making. The process of conflict includes four key components (Feldman & Ridley, 2000):

◆ Conflicts of interest: Goals, interests, or opinions that seem incompatible

◆ Conflict orientations: Individuals' attitudes toward conflict

◆ Conflict responses: Overt behavioral responses to conflict

◆ Conflict outcomes: How conflict is resolved and how the process of conflict affects relationships between people

Conflicts of Interest   The first component of conflict is goals, interests, or views that are perceived as incompatible. You want to set up a time each day when you and a co-worker will both be online, but your co-worker wants to work face-to-face. You believe money should be enjoyed, and your partner believes in saving for a rainy day. When we find our interests at odds with people who matter to us or with whom we must maintain working relationships, we need to resolve conflicts of interest, preferably in a way that doesn't harm the relationship.

Conflict Orientations   The second component is how we perceive conflict. Do you view conflict as a positive process that allows people to work out differences? Do you assume that everyone is bound to lose in conflict situations? Your answers to these questions reflect your orientation toward conflict and thus how you approach it. One of the greatest influences on orientations toward conflict is cultural background. Societies such as the United States accept conflict and assertive competition. Other societies consider it demeaning to engage in open conflict. In these cultures, many of which are Eastern, differences are generally handled indirectly and privately (Martin & Nakayama, 2007; Oetzel & Ting-Toomey, 2013).

Three basic conflict orientations are *lose–lose, win–lose,* and *win–win.* Each of these is appropriate in some situations; the challenge is to know when each view is constructive.

The **lose–lose** approach to conflict assumes that conflict results in losses for everyone. This orientation presumes that conflict cannot produce positive outcomes. One of my colleagues avoids conflict whenever possible because he feels that everyone loses when there is disagreement. As a result, honest differences that need to be aired and resolved are avoided or are superficially patched over. Although the lose–lose perspective usually is not beneficial, it has merit in specific circumstances. Some issues aren't worth the effort of conflict. In order to maintain a positive working relationship, co-workers may avoid discussing issues on which they disagree strongly, as long as those differences are not relevant to job performance.

lose–lose One of three orientations to conflict; assumes that everyone loses when conflict occurs.

The **win–lose** orientation to conflict assumes that one person wins at the expense of the other. A person who perceives conflict as a win–lose matter thinks that whatever one person gains is at the other's expense and that what one person loses benefits the other. Partners who disagree about whether to move to a new location that provides better job prospects for only one of them might lock into a yes–no mode in which they can see only two alternatives: move or don't move. They are unlikely to make an effort to find a mutually acceptable solution, such as moving to a third place that meets both partners' needs adequately, or temporarily having a long-distance relationship so each person can maximize professional opportunities. Eventually, one partner "wins," but at the cost of the other and the relationship.

© wavebreakmedia/Shutterstock.com

MindTap° What do the nonverbal behaviors in this photo suggest to you?

A win–lose orientation tends to undermine relationships because someone has to lose. There is no possibility that both can win, much less that the relationship can. For this reason, win–lose orientations should really be called win–lose–lose because when one person wins, both the other person and the relationship can lose.

Before you dismiss win–lose as a totally unconstructive orientation to conflict, let's consider when it might be effective. Win–lose can be an appropriate orientation when we have low commitment to a relationship and little desire to take care of the person with whom we disagree. When you're buying a car, for instance, you want the best deal you can get, and you have little concern for the dealer's profit.

The **win–win** orientation to conflict assumes that there are usually ways to resolve differences so that everyone gains. People who have this orientation engage in conflict with the goal of coming up with a resolution that is acceptable to everyone. A person is willing to make some accommodations in order to build a solution that lets others win, too. When people adopt win–win views of conflict, they often find solutions that neither had thought of previously. This happens because they are committed to their own and the other's satisfaction. Sometimes win–win attitudes result in compromises that satisfy enough of each person's needs to provide confirmation and to protect the health of the relationship (Canary, Lakey, & Sillars, 2013). Tess describes a situation in which she and her partner worked to find a way for both of them (and their relationship) to win.

 Tess

One of the roughest issues for Jerry and me was when he started working most nights. The time after dinner had always been "our time." When Jerry took the new job, he had to stay in constant contact with the California office. Because of the time difference, at 6 p.m., when Jerry and I used to do something together, it's only 3 p.m. on the West Coast, and the business day is still going. I was hurt that he no longer had time for us, and he was angry that I wanted time he needed for business. We kept talking and came up with the idea of spending a day together each weekend, which we'd never done. Although my idea would still be to share evenings, this solution keeps us in touch with each other.

win–lose One of the three orientations toward conflict; assumes that in any conflict one person wins and the other(s) loses.

win–win One of the three orientations to conflict; assumes that everyone involved in a conflict can gain.

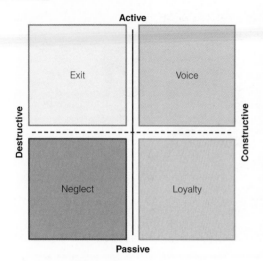

Figure 7.2 Responses to Conflict
Source: Adapted from Wood, 1997, p. 21.

What we learned about perception in Chapter 3 reminds us that how we perceive and label conflict powerfully affects what it means to us and how we craft resolutions. We're unlikely to find a win–win solution when we conceive conflict as win–lose or lose–lose.

Conflict Responses   The third component of conflict is how we respond to it. A series of studies identified four responses to conflict (Rusbult, 1987; Rusbult, Johnson, & Morrow, 1986; Rusbult & Zembrodt, 1983; Rusbult, Zembrodt, & Iwaniszek, 1986). Figure 7.2 summarizes these responses to conflict, which are active or passive, depending on whether they address problems. Responses are also constructive or destructive in their effect on relationships.

The *exit response* involves leaving conflict, either by physically exiting or by psychologically withdrawing. "I am not going to talk about it" is an exit response. Because exit is forceful, it is active; because it fails to resolve tension, it can be destructive. However, there are situations in which exit can be a positive response, especially if it is only temporary. For instance, if you know that you will say or do something you will regret if you don't walk away from an argument, exiting may be a wise short-term response.

The *neglect response* occurs when a person denies or minimizes problems. "You're making a mountain out of a molehill" is a neglect response that denies that a serious issue exists. The neglect response is also disconfirming because it fails to acknowledge and respect how another feels. Neglect can be destructive because it evades difficulties, and it is passive because it doesn't actively promote discussion.

The *loyalty response* is staying committed to a relationship despite differences. Loyalty involves hoping that things will get better on their own. Loyalty is silent allegiance, so it is passive. Because loyalty doesn't end a relationship and preserves the option of addressing tension later, loyalty can be constructive. However, loyalty may result in the partner who expresses it feeling ignored and unappreciated (Overall, Sibley, & Travaglia, 2010).

Finally, *voice* is potentially the most active, constructive response to conflict because it focuses on dealing directly with problems and helps the relationship by managing differences (Overall et al., 2010). A person who says to a co-worker, "I want to talk about the tension between us" exemplifies the voice response to conflict.

You may have noticed that I wrote voice is *potentially* the most active, constructive response to conflict. To achieve that potential, the voice response needs to embody good communication skills. For instance, it's important to confirm others and to rely on communication that cultivates supportive climates. It's also wise to consider others' perspectives, rely on *I*-language, and listen mindfully.

When conflict arises, it is easy to become self-centered—to focus on your feelings, ideas, and goals, and to want to express your needs and emotions (Lewis, Haviland-Jones, & Barrett, 2008). Yet, if you are so busy expressing yourself that you do not listen to, recognize, and acknowledge others, interaction is unlikely to be productive for the issues or the relationship. As Buddhist teacher Thubten Chodron (2001) notes, "Good communication involves expressing ourselves in a way that the other person understands. It is not simply dumping our feelings on the other" (p. 23).

Although most of us have one or two customary responses to conflict, we can develop skill in other responses. Once you understand your current ways of responding to conflict, you can consider whether you want to develop skill in additional styles.

Conflict Outcomes   The final component of conflict is the outcome. When most people think of conflict outcomes, they think of the decision that has resulted. Although this is indeed an outcome of conflict, it isn't the only one nor necessarily the most important outcome.

A conflict's impact on a relationship may be a more significant and enduring outcome than the actual decision (Cahn & Abigail, 2013; Canary et al., 2013). Relationship outcomes are influenced more by how we manage conflict than by the resolution itself. Conflicts can strengthen relationships when people build a supportive interpersonal climate and work to sustain that climate as a part of managing conflict. Harm to relationships is most likely when people disconfirm each other and cultivate defensive communication climates. Because our choices of how to manage conflict have an impact on relationships, we need to be especially careful to communicate in respectful and affirming ways when conflicts arise.

Third-Party Assistance in Resolving Conflict

So far, our discussion has assumed that the people who have a conflict manage it themselves. Yet there are times when the people having conflict seek others' help to resolve their differences. They make lack the necessary communication skills or motivation. They may have locked themselves into opposing positions. They may have personal animosity that undermines constructive discussion. In cases such as these, it is often wise to turn to a third party.

Sometimes a co-worker or a friend can help people resolve differences. Two co-workers who are at loggerheads may gain insight and perspective from a colleague who is not invested in the positions they have staked out (Myers & Larson, 2005). A good friend who knows a couple well may be able to help one or both of the partners see a way to meet the other partner's interests.

Third parties may also be outsiders: individuals who do not have personal relationships with any of the parties who are in conflict. The most common types of third parties from the outside are mediators and arbitrators.

A **mediator** works with people who are in conflict to reach a decision but has no power to make a decision. Typically, mediators focus on helping parties in conflict communicate more productively. Mediators often begin by working with parties to create an agenda and rules for discussion: what will be covered and in what sequence, who may speak when (regulative rules), and how parties are expected to speak (constitutive rules for respect and politeness). Once an agenda and communication rules are established, mediators may clarify each party's views through paraphrasing, ask questions to make sure that all relevant information is known to all, and make direct recommendations ("You could each take half of the royalties from the invention you each claim to have made"). Mediators also try to maintain a good communication climate by introducing humor, thanking parties for constructive participation, intervening if parties engage in behavior outside of the agreed upon rules, and helping each person recognize the other's point of view. Mediators are most advisable when the parties in conflict have relatively equal power and so feel equally able to speak up (Murphy & Rubinson, 2005). Unions often rely on mediation to resolve conflicts between union members and management.

Unlike a mediator, an **arbitrator** has the authority to make decisions. After gathering information from all parties and listening to evidence, argument, and proposals, an arbitrator announces a decision that is typically binding on participants. Sports teams often submit disputes to arbitrators.

mediator Outside third party who facilitates discussion between two or more parties who are in conflict but who does not have the power to make a decision.

arbitrator Outside third party who has the authority to make a decision on a conflict between two or more people.

An Attorney's Perspective

Leigh Wilco (2014) is an attorney who works in Atlanta, where he has been named one of the city's top litigators. Although he's a skilled trial lawyer, Mr. Wilco often encourages his clients to try mediation or arbitration as alternatives to trial. Following are his thoughts on the values of these third-party modes of resolving conflict.

"While jury trials are the foundation of our legal system, there are problems with them. First, because of the number of cases filed, it can often take years to get to trial. Second, even after a trial, the appeals process can take a year or more. Third, jury trials have become increasingly expensive and time consuming. Finally, while we still claim everyone has a right to trial by a "jury of your peers," it is rare that the actual jury has the same life experiences as the parties.

"The advantages of mediation are that it can be done at any time during the conflict process, it is much quicker and less expensive than trial, and, if an agreement is reached, it is final and binding. The most important advantage, however, is that the parties have control over the decision. With a jury trial one side (or sometimes both sides) might be grossly unhappy with the verdict. In mediation, if you think what is offered by the other side is not fair, you can refuse it and go to trial. Mediation empowers the parties with decision-making ability that is absent from a trial.

"Arbitration, like a trial, does not allow the parties to be the decision makers, but it can have some advantages over a jury trial. The two main advantages are speed and expertise. An arbitration should take less time than a trial. Second, an arbitration is usually conducted by an individual with expertise in the area of the dispute that most jurors don't have. This makes it particularly suitable for complex cases.

"A possible disadvantage of arbitrations is that they are usually conducted by either one or three arbitrators. This gives more control and power to a single person than a 12-person jury does.

"My experience is that most people do not enjoy the cost, time, and stress of a jury trial, even if they win. Mediation and arbitration allow the parties to have more control over the process, resolve the dispute sooner, and get on with their lives."

Digital Media and Communication Climate

Climate matters when we communicate using digital media just as it does in face-to-face interaction. Perhaps you have visited some sites and blogs that seem friendly and inviting and others that seem less so. If you review the communication on these sites and blogs, you may discover there is more confirming communication on the sites that seem inviting.

Another connection between this chapter's content and digital communication concerns acknowledgment, which is the most basic level of confirmation. When you say hello to someone you see, that person is likely to acknowledge your greeting with a smile, head nod, or return "hello." It's not the same in digital environments. When you text or send an e-mail, how do you know whether and when another receives it? If a friend doesn't reply to your text within a few minutes, it's hard to tell whether the person is ignoring you or simply hasn't received the message.

The more limited access to nonverbal cues in digital media may reduce our ability to interpret others' communication. In person, we can see a wink or twinkle that indicates a friend is kidding with us. In online and digital environments, that's more difficult, even with emoticons. It's hard to tell whether a text message that says

<heard enough from you> indicates that the sender values what you've texted and now gets your perspective; is irritated by something you texted; or is being dogmatic, saying the door to more conversation is closed. Because online and digital communication tends to be more abbreviated than face-to-face communication, offering extra cues is useful as is being tentative about how we interpret online and digital messages.

Our discussion of conflict is also relevant to digital media. In digital environments, we can pause or step away from heated exchanges in order to cool down. In face-to-face communication, it's difficult to call a time out because the person we are arguing with is present with us and often as engaged as we are in the conflict. With online and digital communication, by contrast, we can step aside. We can choose to delay replying or to not reply to a quarrelsome e-mail, a provocative comment on a blog, or an insulting text message. We can give ourselves time to cool off before responding, if we choose to respond at all. In addition, social media allow us to reflect on our messages and to edit our communication before hitting the send button.

Digital and online communication can also exacerbate conflict. When hostilities intensify in online environments and people do not step away to cool off, the result may be **flaming**, which is excessively insulting another person online, often using language that is derogatory or obscene. Someone who disagrees with a comment you post may respond with "You are ruining the gene pool." It is tempting to send a reciprocal insult, which is likely to up the ante and lead the other person to send an even more offensive insult. Because the two people are not physically in each other's presence and may not even know each other personally, it's easy to exchange messages you would never say to a person's face. Flame wars are generally unproductive.

There are several ways to respond to flaming:

◆ First, you can just ignore it. Refusing to reply deprives the flamer of knowing she or he upset you, so the flamer is not encouraged to continue.

◆ Second, if you think a flamer is offending others by engaging in hate speech or other truly harmful behavior, consider asking the system administrator or chat room moderator to intervene.

◆ A third option is to move the conversation out of a public space, such as to a chat room or social network. Ask the flamer to continue the discussion privately through e-mail or another medium.

Guidelines for Creating and Sustaining Healthy Communication Climates

To translate what we've covered in this chapter into practical information, we'll discuss five guidelines for building and sustaining healthy climates.

Communicate in Ways That Confirm Others

Although confirmation is important, it isn't always easy to give. When we disagree with what others think or do, it may be difficult to confirm them. However, confirmation is not the same as agreement. You can confirm someone as a person even if you don't admire or condone the person's ideas or actions.

flaming Excessively insulting another person online, often using language that is derogatory or obscene.

 **Dean**

My supervisor did an excellent job of letting me know I was valued when I got passed over for a promotion last year. He came to my office to talk to me before the promotion was announced. He told me both I and the other guy were qualified but that he had seniority and also field experience I didn't have. Then he assigned me to a field position for six months so I could get the experience I needed to get promoted. His talk made all the difference in how I felt about staying with the company.

Communication can express both confirmation of another person and disagreement with that person. In fact, research tells us that people expect real friends to give honest feedback, even if it isn't always pleasant to hear (Rawlins, 1994). Similarly, in the workplace, managers who give honest feedback, including criticism, are more likely to build strong working relationships with subordinates than are managers who avoid criticism and conflict (Covey, 2013). This implies that we have an ethical responsibility to be honest in our communication. It is false friends who tell us only what we want to hear. We can offer honest feedback within a context that assures others we value and respect them, as Dan's commentary illustrates.

 **Dan**

When I first came to school here, I got in with a crowd that drank a lot. At first, I drank only on weekends, but pretty soon I was drinking every night and drinking more and more. My grades were suffering, but I didn't stop. Then my friend Betsy told me she wanted to help me stop drinking. The way she talked to me, I knew that she was being honest because she cared. She was a better friend than all my drinking buddies because she cared enough not to let me hurt myself. All my buddies just stood by and said nothing.

Communicate in Ways That Confirm Yourself

It is just as important to confirm yourself as others. You are no less valuable than others, your needs are no less important, and your preferences are no less valid. It is a misunderstanding to think that the interpersonal communication principles we've discussed apply only how we behave toward others. They pertain equally to how we should treat ourselves. Thus, it is ethical to confirm others and ourselves equally.

You confirm yourself when you express your thoughts and feelings honestly. By doing that, you show that you respect yourself. You also give others a chance to understand who you are. You communicate ethically when you assert your feelings, ideas, and preferences while honoring those of others. If you don't assert yourself in the workplace, you give up the possibility of influencing the quality of work produced and how it is organized. If you don't assert yourself in personal relationships, you undercut your own and your partner's respect for your ideas, feelings, and needs, as Maria points out in her commentary.

 **Maria**

Ever since I was a kid, I have muffled my own needs and tried to please others. I thought I was taking care of relationships, but actually I was hurting them, because I felt neglected. My resentment poisoned relationships in subtle but potent ways. Now, I'm learning to tell others what I want and need, and that's improving my relationships.

Table 7.2   Aggression, Assertion, and Deference

Aggressive	Assertive	Deferential
I demand that we spend time together.	I'd like to create more time for us.	If you don't want us to spend time with each other, that's okay with me.
Get this report done today. I need it.	I'd like to get this report today. Can you manage that?	I need this report today, but if you can't get it done, that's all right.
Tell me what you're feeling; I insist.	I would like to understand more how you feel.	If you don't want to talk about how you feel, okay.

© Cengage Learning

Assertive communication is not aggressive. Aggressive communication occurs when one person puts herself or himself ahead of others or derides others' thoughts, feelings, goals, or actions. In contrast, assertive communication simply expresses the speaker's thoughts, feelings, preferences, and goals without disparaging anyone else. You communicate assertively when you express yourself firmly and unapologetically.

Assertive communication is also not deferential. Unlike deference, assertion doesn't subordinate your needs to those of others. Assertion also differs from passive aggression, in which a person blocks or resists while denying that she or he is doing so. Assertion is a matter of clearly stating what you feel, think, or want. This should be done without disparaging others and what they feel, think, or want. You should simply state your feelings in an open, descriptive manner. Table 7.2 illustrates how aggression, assertion, and deference differ. Even when people disagree or have conflicting needs, each person can state her or his feelings and confirm the other's perspective. Usually, there are ways to acknowledge multiple viewpoints.

Respect Diversity among People

Just as individuals differ, so do relationships in personal and professional life. There is tremendous variety in what people find comfortable, affirming, and satisfying. For this reason, it's counterproductive to try to force all people and relationships to fit into a single mode. For example, you might know one co-worker who enjoys a lot of verbal banter and another who is offended by it. There's no need to try to persuade the second co-worker to engage in verbal teasing or the first one to stop doing so. To build and sustain supportive, confirming climates, we need to adapt our communication to people's differences.

Because people and relationships are diverse, we should respect a range of communication choices and relationship patterns. In addition, we should be cautious about imposing our meaning on others' communication. People from different social groups, including distinct groups in the United States, have learned different communication styles. What Westerners consider to be open, healthy self-disclosure may feel offensively intrusive to people from some Asian societies. European Americans can misinterpret the dramatic, assertive speaking style of some African Americans. Especially in the workplace, it's important to understand that people vary widely in communication styles. To communicate effectively, we need to respect diversity among people. Valaya makes this point in her commentary.

 Valaya

One of the most hard adjustments for me has been how Americans assert themselves. I was very surprised that students argue with their teachers. We would never do that in Taiwan. It would be extremely disrespectful. I also see friends argue, sometimes very much. I understand this is a cultural difference, but I have trouble accepting it. I learned that disagreements very much hurt relationships.

It's also appropriate to ask others to explain behaviors that are not familiar to you. For instance, Valaya might ask other students what it means to them when they argue with teachers, and other students might ask Valaya what it means to her not to argue with teachers. Asking others what their communication means lets them know that they matter to you, and it allows us to gain insight into perspectives other than our own.

Time Conflict Effectively

A fourth guideline for creating effective communication climates is to time them so that each person can be mindful and so that the context and available time allow for constructive discussion. Most of us are irritable when we are sick, tired, or stressed, so conflict is unlikely to be managed well. It's also generally more productive to discuss problems in private rather than in public settings. It takes time to manage conflict constructively, so it's wise not to engage in conflict when we have limited time. It's impossible to express ourselves clearly, to listen well, to be confirming, and to respond sensitively when a stopwatch is ticking in our minds.

Be flexible about when you engage in conflict. Some people prefer to tackle problems as soon as they come up, whereas other people need time to reflect before interacting. If one person feels ready to talk about a problem but the other doesn't, it's wise to delay discussion if possible. Of course, this works only if the person who is ready agrees to talk about the issue at a later time. In his book *Anger at Work* (1996), Dr. Hendrie Weisinger recommends taking a "time out" if emotions are raw or tempers are flaring. For instance, suppose someone says something to you that makes you very angry. What would you do? Dr. Weisinger suggests you tell the other person that you want to discuss the issue but you need 10 minutes. You might say you have to make a phone call first or explain that you'd prefer to cool down.

A third way to use timing to promote positive conflict is **bracketing**, which marks off (or brackets) peripheral issues for later discussion. In the course of conflict, multiple issues often surface. If we try to deal with each one as it arises, we get sidetracked from the immediate or main issue. Bracketing other concerns for later discussion lets us keep conflict focused productively. Keep in mind, however, that bracketing works only if people actually do return to the issues they set aside.

Show Grace When Appropriate

Finally, an important principle to keep in mind during conflict is that **grace** is sometimes appropriate. Although the idea of grace has not traditionally been discussed in communication texts, it is an important part of spiritual and philosophical thinking about ethical communication. You don't have to be religious or know philosophy to show grace. All that's needed is a willingness to sometimes excuse someone who has no right to expect your compassion or forgiveness. Showing grace when appropriate is equally important in personal and professional relationships.

Grace is granting forgiveness, putting aside our needs, or helping another save face when no standard says we should or must do so. Rather than being prompted by rules or expectations, grace springs from a generosity of spirit. Grace isn't forgiving when we *should* do so (for instance, excusing people who aren't responsible for their actions). Nor is grace allowing others to have their way when we have no choice (deferring when our supervisor insists, for example). Instead, grace is kindness that is neither earned nor required. For instance, two roommates agree to split chores, and one doesn't do her share during a week when she has three tests. Her roommate might

bracketing Identifying and setting aside for later discussion the issues peripheral to a current conflict.

grace Granting forgiveness, putting aside our own needs, or helping another save face when no standard says we should or must do so.

do all the chores even though there is no expectation of this generosity. It's also an act of grace to defer to another person's preference when you could impose yours. Similarly, when someone hurts you and has no right to expect forgiveness, you may choose to forgive anyway. We do so not because we have to, but because we want to.

Grace is given without strings. We show kindness, defer our needs, or forgive a wrong *without any expectation of reward or reciprocity*. Grace isn't doing something nice to make a co-worker feel grateful or indebted to us. Nor is it grace when we do something with the expectation of a payback. For an act to be one of grace, it must be done without conditions or expectation of return.

Grace is not always appropriate. Generosity of spirit can be exploited by people who take advantage of kindness. Some people repeatedly abuse and hurt others, confident that pardons will be granted. When grace is extended and then exploited, extending it again may be unwise. However, if you show grace in good faith and another takes advantage, you should not fault yourself. Kindness and a willingness to forgive are worthy moral precepts. Those who abuse grace, not those who offer it, are blameworthy.

Because Western culture emphasizes the assertion and protection of self-interest, grace is not widely practiced or esteemed. We are told to stand up for ourselves, to not let others walk on us, and to refuse to tolerate transgressions. It is important to honor and assert ourselves, as we've emphasized throughout this book. Yet self-assertion can work in tandem with generosity toward others.

None of us is perfect. We all make mistakes, hurt others with thoughtless acts, fail to meet responsibilities, and occasionally do things we know are wrong. Sometimes there is no reason others should forgive us when we wrong them; we have no right to expect exoneration. Yet human relations must have some room for redemption, for the extension of grace when it is not required or earned.

The guidelines we've discussed combine respect for self, others, relationships, and communication. Using these guidelines should enhance your ability to foster healthy, affirming climates in your relationships with others.

Summary

In this chapter, we've explored communication climate as a foundation of interaction with others. A basic requirement for healthy communication climates is confirmation. Each of us wants to feel valued, especially by those for whom we care most deeply. We discussed particular kinds of communication that foster supportive and defensive climates in relationships.

Communication that fosters supportive climates also helps us manage conflict constructively. We discussed lose–lose, win–lose, and win–win approaches to conflict and explored how each affects interaction. In addition, conflict patterns are influenced by whether people respond by exiting, neglecting, being loyal, or giving voice to tensions. In most cases, voice is the preferred response because it is the only response that allows people to deal with conflict actively and constructively. Conflicts that occur in the online world provide greater opportunities to pause and step away and, at the same time, greater potential for escalation into flaming wars.

To close the chapter, we considered five guidelines for building healthy communication climates. The first one is to accept and affirm others, communicating that we respect them even though we may not always agree with them or share their feelings. A companion guideline is to accept and assert ourselves. Each of us is entitled to voice our thoughts, feelings, and needs. Doing so honors ourselves and helps others understand us. A third guideline is to respect diversity. Humans vary widely, as do their preferred styles of communicating. When we respect differences between people, we gain insight into the fascinating array of human interactions.

The fourth and fifth guidelines concern communicating when conflicts arise. We learned that we can make choices about timing that increase the likelihood of constructive climate. In addition, we discussed the value of showing grace—unearned, unrequired compassion—when that is appropriate.

Experience Communication Case Study
Cloudy Climate

Apply what you've learned in this chapter by analyzing the following case study, using the accompanying questions as a guide. These questions and a video of the case study are also available online with your MindTap Speech for *Communication Mosaics*.

Andy and Martha married five years ago when they completed graduate school. Last week, Andy got the job offer of his dreams—with one problem: He would have to move 1,500 miles away. Martha loves her current job and has no interest in moving or in living apart. Andy sees this job as one that could really advance his career. For the past week, they have talked and argued continually about the job offer. Tonight, while they are preparing dinner in their kitchen, they have returned to the topic once again. We join them midway in their discussion, just as it is heating up.

© Cengage Learning

Andy: So, today I was checking on the costs for flights from here to Seattle. If we plan ahead for visits, we can get round-trip flights for around $300. That's not too bad.

Martha: While you're thinking about finances, you might consider the cost of renting a second apartment out there. We agreed last night that it would be too expensive to live apart.

Andy: I never agreed to that. Martha, can't you understand how important this job is to my career?

Martha: And what about our marriage? I suppose that's not important?

Andy: [He grabs a knife and begins cutting an onion.] I never said that! If you'd pull with me on this, our marriage would be fine. You're just not. . . .

Martha: [She slams a pot on the stove.] Not what? Not willing to be the traditional supportive wife, I assume.

Andy: [He grimaces, puts down the knife, and turns to face Martha.] That isn't what I was going to say. I never asked you to be a traditional wife or to be anything other than who you are, but I want you to let me be myself, too.

Martha: If you want to be yourself, then why did you get married? Marriage is about more than just yourself—it's about both of us and what's good for the two of us. You're not thinking of us at all.

Andy: And I suppose you are? You're only thinking about what you want. You don't seem to give a darn what I want. You're being incredibly selfish.

Martha: [She slams her hand against the counter and shouts.] Selfish! I'm selfish to care about our marriage?

Andy: You're using that to manipulate me, as if I don't care about the marriage and you do. If you really cared about it, maybe you'd consider moving to Seattle so we could be together.

Martha: [She raises her eyebrows and speaks in a sarcastic tone.] And just a minute ago, you said you weren't asking me to be a traditional wife. Now you want me to be the trailing spouse so you can do what you please. Dandy!

Andy: I didn't say that. You're putting words in my mouth. What I said was—

Martha: What you said was I should move to Seattle and support whatever it is you want to do.

Andy: [He slams the knife into the cutting board.] I did not say that. Quit telling me what I said!

[He takes a deep breath, lowers his voice, then continues.] Look, Martha, can we just step back from this argument and try to look at the options with a fresh eye?

Martha: I've looked all I want to look. I've heard all I want to hear. You know where I stand on this, and you know I'm right even if you don't want to admit it.

1. Identify examples of mind reading, and describe their impact on Martha's and Andy's discussion.

2. Identify communication that fosters a defensive interpersonal climate.

3. To what extent do you think Andy and Martha feel listened to by the other?

4. Do you perceive any relationship-level meanings that aren't being addressed in this conversation?

Key Concepts

Practice defining the chapter's terms by using online flashcards.

acknowledgment, 132
arbitrator, 141
bracketing, 146
confirmation, 131
communication climate, 131
conflict, 137
covert conflict, 137
endorsement, 133
ethnocentrism, 135

flaming, 143
grace, 146
lose–lose, 138
mediator, 141
overt conflict, 137
recognition, 131
win–lose, 139
win–win, 139

Review, Reflect, Extend

The Reflect and Discuss and Take Action features that follow will help you review, reflect on, and extend the information and ideas presented in this chapter. These resources, and a diverse selection of additional study tools, are also available online at the MindTap Speech for *Communication Mosaics*.

Reflect, personalize, and apply what you've learned

Reflect and Discuss

1. Think about the most effective work climate you've ever experienced. Describe the communication in that climate. How does the communication in that situation reflect the skills and principles discussed in this chapter?

2. As a class, discuss the ethical principles reflected in the communication behaviors discussed in this chapter. What ethical principles underlie confirming communication and disconfirming communication?

3. Interview a professional in the field you plan to enter or return to after completing college. Ask your interviewee to describe the kind of climate

that is most effective in his or her work situation. Ask what specific kinds of communication foster and impede a good working climate. How do your interviewee's perceptions relate to the material covered in this chapter?

4. When do you find it most difficult to confirm others? Is it hard for you to be confirming when you disagree with another person? After reading this chapter, can you distinguish disagreement from disconfirmation?

5. As a class, identify ways in which faculty at your school confirm and disconfirm students. Be specific in naming particular types of communication (and examples) that are confirming and disconfirming.

TAKE ACTION

1. Confirmation and Disconfirmation in Online Communication

Confirming and disconfirming communication is not limited to face-to-face interactions. It also establishes climates in online communication.

To gain insight into the particular forms of communication that create confirming and disconfirming climates, visit a chat room, forum, or blog of your choosing. Take notes on communication that expresses or denies recognition, acknowledgment, and endorsement of others. What differences can you identify between confirming and disconfirming communication in online interactions?

2. Using Descriptive Language

To develop skill in supportive communication, translate the following evaluative statements into descriptive ones:

Evaluative	Descriptive
This report is poorly done.	This report doesn't include background information.
You're lazy.	_____
You are such a know it all.	_____
You're obsessing about the problem.	_____
You're too involved.	_____
You're dominating the team.	_____

3. Assessing Communication Climates

Use the behaviors we've discussed as a checklist for assessing communication climates. The next time you feel defensive, ask yourself whether others are communicating superiority, control, strategy, certainty, neutrality, or evaluation. In a communication climate that you find supportive and open, ask yourself whether the following behaviors are present: spontaneity, equality, provisionalism, problem orientation, empathy, and description.

4. Communicating Assertively

The following statements are deferential or aggressive. Revise each one so that it is assertive.

a. I'm going to the party regardless of what you want.

b. I'll lend you the money, even though I may have to work an extra shift to get it.

c. We're getting the car that I like, and that's it!

d. They don't have vegetarian entrees at the restaurant you want to go to, but I can just eat a salad.

Recommended Resources

1. Redford Williams, M.D., and Virginia Williams, Ph.D. (1993). *Anger kills: Seventeen strategies for controlling the hostility that can harm your health.* New York: Harper Perennial. This is a very readable book that details the harm that anger and hostility cause us and provides practical advice on ways to own and manage your anger to interact more effectively with others.

2. To see a video presentation of Jack Gibb's classic research on defensive and supportive communication, go to the book's online resources for this chapter.

3. Use the online resources for this chapter to visit the site of Powerful Non-Defensive Communication.

8

Adapting Communication to Cultures and Social Communities

All human activity takes place within a culture and interacts with culture.

—Pope John Paul II

If you woke up tomorrow as a different race or gender than you are, how would your life change?

MindTap

Learning Objectives

MindTap

Start with a quick engagement activity and **review** the chapter Learning Objectives.

Topics Covered in This Chapter	After studying this chapter, you should be able to …
Understanding Cultures and Social Communities	Given two distinct cultures, compare each of the five dimensions of cultural life.
Relationships between Culture and Communication	Reflect on how the four central relationships between culture and communication influenced your formative development.
Digital Media, Cultures, and Social Communities	Discuss digital media's role in disseminating perceptions of cultures and social groups.
Guidelines for Adapting Communication to Diverse Cultures and Social Communities	Create an action plan to implement this chapter's four guidelines for adapting communication to diverse cultures and social communities.

◆ Is it more important for society to be well-ordered or to provide personal freedom to its members?

◆ Does winning an honor reflect more on the person who receives it or the person's family?

◆ Should you attempt to stand out as best in your class, on your team, and so on?

How you answer those questions is influenced by the culture to which you belong. If you were socialized in a culture that emphasizes individualism, you probably rank personal freedom as more important than social order and think an honor reflects primarily on the individual who wins it. However, if you were raised in a culture that emphasizes collective well-being, you probably think an orderly society is more important than personal freedom and believe an honor reflects primarily on the family of the individual who receives it (Hofstede, 1991, 2001; Hofstede, Hofstede, & Minkov, 2010; Jandt, 2012). Likewise, individualistic societies celebrate outstanding individuals (Best Actor, MVP) whereas collectivist cultures encourage individuals to be part of a team or group and not stand out from others.

MindTap

Read, highlight, and take notes online.

The value people assign to individualism and collectivism influences how they communicate. For instance, in cultures that emphasize collective goals and harmony, people generally do not state their positions directly or strongly and do not promote themselves. They are also less likely to compete or express differences directly than are people raised in individualistic cultures. These opening topics introduce us to the many ways in which communication and culture are linked.

The most culturally diverse nation that exists, the United States, becomes home to more immigrants every year than any other nation (Qin, 2014). To participate effectively in the United States and to be part of the global society, we need to understand cultural differences and the ways they affect communication. Effectiveness in social and professional life demands that you adapt your communication to people of varied cultural backgrounds and customs. The competitive and direct style of negotiation customary among Westerners may offend Korean businesspeople (Kim & Meyers, 2012). Friendly touches that are comfortable to most U.S. citizens may be perceived as rude and intrusive by Germans or suggestive by Ugandans (Muwanguzi & Musambira, 2013). In some cultures, direct eye contact is interpreted as honesty whereas in other cultures it is interpreted as disrespect.

In this chapter, we discuss the sixth and final basic communication process: adapting communication to cultures and social communities. We first discuss dimensions of cultures and social communities. Next, we explore four important relationships between culture and communication. The third section of the chapter explores how digital media are related to cultures and social communities. We close the chapter with guidelines for adapting communication effectively to diverse cultures and social groups.

Understanding Cultures and Social Communities

Although the word *culture* is part of our everyday vocabulary, it's difficult to define. Culture is part of everything we think, do, feel, and believe, yet we can't point to a thing that is culture. Most simply defined, **culture** is a way of life—a system of ideas, values, beliefs, customs, and language that is passed from one generation to the next and that reflects and sustains a particular way of life.

culture The beliefs, understandings, practices, and ways of interpreting experience that are shared by a group of people.

 How would this photo be different if the two people were both Americans?

TAKE ACTION…activities are located at the end of this chapter and online.

social community A group of people who live within a dominant culture yet also belong to another social group or groups that share values, understandings, and practices distinct from those of the dominant culture.

standpoint theory A theory that holds that a culture includes a number of social groups that differently shape the perceptions, identities, and opportunities of members of those groups.

standpoint The social, symbolic, and material conditions common to a group of people that influence how they understand themselves, others, and society.

Cultures Are Systems

In Chapter 1, we discussed systems, which are made up of interacting, interrelated parts. Because cultures are systems, the interconnected parts of a culture affect one another and the whole. For example, the technological revolution has had multiple and far-reaching implications for cultural life. Computer-mediated communication allows us to interact with people who are not geographically close. Today many people rely on social media to form and sustain friendships, family ties, and romantic relationships. Telecommuting allows people who previously worked in physical offices to do their jobs in their homes or while traveling. Multinational organizations hold virtual conferences that allow employees around the world to communicate in real time and with full audio and visual contact. As an aspect of culture, technology doesn't just affect technology; rather, it affects other factors, such as how, where, and with whom we communicate, as well as the boundaries of work and personal life. Because cultures are holistic, no change is isolated from the overall system.

Multiple Social Communities May Coexist in a Single Culture

National borders are not the only lines that mark different groups of people. Groups with distinct ways of life can coexist in a single society or geographic territory. Individuals are affected not only by the culture as a whole, but also by membership in groups outside of mainstream culture, which are called **social communities** (also called co-cultures) (Jandt, 2012; Samovar, Porter, & McDaniel, 2013; Samovar, Porter, McDaniel, & Roy, 2015).

Most societies have a dominant, or mainstream, way of life with which most members of a culture identify. European, heterosexual, landowning, able-bodied men who were Christian in heritage, if not always in actual practice, developed mainstream Western culture. Yet, Western society includes many groups that are outside of, or are not exclusively identified with, this mainstream culture. Gay men, lesbians, bisexuals, and transgender people experience difficulty in a society that does not grant them the social standing and legal rights given to heterosexuals. Mainstream customs in America often ignore or marginalize American citizens who are Muslim, Buddhist, Hindu, or other non-Christian religions. Despite substantial progress, women still face discrimination as do people who are not white. A Take Action activity at the end of this chapter encourages you to notice that many U.S. calendars reflect mainstream culture and marginalize social communities outside of it.

Standpoint theory illuminates the importance of social communities. Standpoint theory claims that social groups within a culture distinctively shape members' perceptions, identities, expectations, knowledge, and so forth. However, belonging to a particular social community does not necessarily lead to a **standpoint**, which is political awareness of the social, symbolic, and material circumstances of the community and the larger power dynamics that hold those circumstances in place (Wood, 2005). One can be a member of a social community and have perspective and experience shaped by that community without becoming conscious of the social structures and practices

 **Racial Bias Starts Early**

Is racial bias still a problem in America? According to an ABC News and *Washington Post* poll reported in January 2009, that depends on whom you ask. Twice as many blacks as whites think racism is still a problem, whereas twice as many whites as blacks think racial equality has been achieved (Blow, 2009).

What can explain the major discrepancy between blacks' and whites' views? One explanation is that most whites believe they are not racially biased but still hold implicit biases. That's the idea behind Project Implicit, a virtual lab managed by scholars at Harvard, the University of Virginia, and the University of Washington. After six years of testing people's biases, the findings are clear: 75 percent of whites have an implicit pro-white/anti-black bias. While some blacks also harbor implicit racial biases—some pro-black and some pro-white—blacks are the least likely of all races to have any racial bias (Blow, 2009).

Another question studied by scientists at Project Implicit is when racial prejudice starts. According to Mahzarin Banaji, a professor at Harvard, it starts at much earlier ages than most of us think. She has devoted her career to studying hidden and often subtle biases and attitudes. According to Banaji's research, children as young as 3 years old have the same level of bias as adults (Fogg, 2008). If you'd like to learn more about Project Implicit or take tests to determine if you harbor implicit racial biases, go to the book's online resources for this chapter.

 Which theory discussed in this book offers insight into reasons that blacks perceive more racial bias than whites in the United States?

that define the community as outside of the mainstream. When a member of a social community develops political awareness of the forces that create inequity, then that person has a standpoint. For example, being black does not give one a black standpoint nor does being female make one a feminist. If a black person or a woman becomes politically aware of sexist and racist practices and policies that were part of the U.S. history and still persist, then the person may develop a standpoint. Race, gender, class, and sexual orientation are primary social communities in Western culture.

In an early discussion of standpoint, philosopher Georg Wilhelm Friedrich Hegel (1807) pointed out that standpoints reflect power positions in society. To illustrate, he noted that masters and slaves perceive slavery very differently. Extending Hegel's point, we can see that those in positions of power have a vested interest in preserving the system that gives them privileges. Therefore, they are unlikely to perceive its flaws and inequities. On the other hand, those who are disadvantaged by a system are able to see inequities and discrimination (Wood, 2005; Wood & Fixmer-Oraiz, 2016).

Like verbal communication, nonverbal communication often reflects the perspective of the mainstream group (Muwanguzi & Musambira, 2013). For example, the dominance of people without disabilities is

 **If You Woke up Tomorrow**

How would your life change if you woke up tomorrow and discovered you were of a different race or sex or gender identity or sexual orientation than you were when you went to sleep?

That's pretty much what happened to Gregory Howard Williams. Until age 10, Gregory lived in Virginia with his white middle-class family. At age 10, however, he learned he was black—his father was a light-skinned man of African descent, which was why Gregory also appeared white. When Gregory learned he was black and began living as a black man, his whole life changed.

Read his stirring account of the changes in his life in his autobiography, *Life on the Color Line: The True Story of a White Boy Who Discovered He Was Black*. Go to the book's online resources for this chapter to learn more about Gregory Williams' life.

reflected in the number of buildings that do not have ramps or bathroom facilities for people who use wheelchairs, and public presentations that do not include signers for people with hearing limitations. Many campus and business buildings feature portraits of white men but few of women or people of color. Mostafa's commentary illustrates how his standpoint affects his perceptions of his school.

 Mostafa

I went to a black college for two years before transferring here, and it's like two different worlds. There, I saw a lot of brothers and sisters all the time, and I had black teachers. There were portraits of black leaders in buildings and black magazines in the bookstore. Here, I've had only one black teacher, and I see 50 whites for every one black on campus. I've yet to see a black person's portrait hung in any campus building, and I have to go to specialty stores to buy black magazines. The whole atmosphere on this campus communicates, "White is right."

Of the many social communities, gendered communities have been most extensively studied. Because we know more about gender than about other social communities, we'll explore gender as a particular example of a social community. However, the principles and patterns that characterize gendered social communities also apply to other social communities.

Scholars have investigated the communication of people socialized in different gender communities. One of the earliest studies reported that children's play is sex segregated, that boys and girls tend to play different kinds of games (Maltz & Borker, 1982). Games that girls favor, such as house and school, involve few players, require talk to negotiate how to play because there aren't clear-cut guidelines, and depend on cooperation, sensitivity, and communication among players. Baseball, soccer, and war, which are typical boys' games, require more players and have clear goals and rules, so less talk is needed to play. Most boys' games are competitive, both between teams and for individual status within teams (Rudman & Glick, 2010; Terlecki et al., 2011). Interaction in games teaches boys and girls distinct understandings of why, when, and how to use talk.

Research on gendered patterns of communication reveals that the rules we learn through play remain with many of us as we grow older. For instance, women's talk generally is relatively expressive and focused on feelings and relationships, whereas men's talk tends to be more instrumental, assertive, and competitive (Guerrero, Jones, & Boburka, 2006; Kimbrough, Guadagno, Muscanell, & Dill, 2013; Leaper & Ayres, 2007; Mulac, 2006; Wood & Fixmer-Oraiz, 2016; Ye & Palomares, 2013). Many women favor management styles that are more collaborative than those typical of men. In personal relationships, women tend to be more interested in talking about relationship issues than men are.

Another general gender difference is what each gender tends to perceive as the center of a relationship. For many men who were socialized in masculine communities, activities tend to be a key foundation of friendships and romantic relationships (Inman, 1996; Swain, 1989; Wood & Inman, 1993). Thus, men who are socialized in masculine communities typically build and sustain friendships by doing things together (playing soccer, watching sports) and doing things for one another. For many women who are socialized in feminine communities, communication is the crux of relationships. Communication is not only a means to other ends but also an end in itself (Acitelli, 1993; Duck & Wood, 2006; Riessman, 1990; Terlecki et al., 2011; Ye & Palomares, 2013).

Although we have focused on gender to illustrate how social communities shape communication, gender isn't the only social community that affects how people communicate. Research finds that communication patterns vary among social classes. For example, racial and ethnic groups also teach their members distinctive ways of interacting. African Americans generally communicate more assertively than European Americans (Gonzalez, Houston, & Chen, 2012; Johnson, 2000; Orbe & Harris, 2015). What some African Americans perceive as authentic, powerful exchanges may be viewed as confrontational by people from different social communities because the latter learned different rules for what counts as wit and what counts as antagonism. Keep in mind that these are generalizations; they do not describe the communication of all blacks or all whites.

 ## Michelle

I'm offended when I read that blacks communicate differently from whites. I don't, and neither do a lot of my black friends. Both of my parents were professionals, and I attended good schools, including a private one for two years. I speak the same way whites do. When the author of our book says blacks engage in call and response or talk differently from whites, it makes it sound like blacks are different from whites—like we don't know how to communicate like they do. If the author isn't black, how does she know how we communicate?

Michelle wrote her comment after reading a previous edition of this book. She's correct that not all blacks communicate the same way and not all blacks communicate differently from whites, who also don't communicate in a uniform way. What you've read about the communication patterns of African Americans or other social groups is based on research, much of which was conducted by scholars who are members of the groups described. I include this research because many minority students have complained to me about textbooks that present only middle-class white communication patterns and present those as standard or correct. This point of view is reflected in Jason's comment, which he wrote after reading the same book Michelle criticized.

 ## Jason

This is the first time since being at this school that I've seen blacks really included in a textbook or a class, other than my African American classes. I think that's good, like it affirms my identity as a black. If I have to study how whites communicate, why shouldn't they learn how I communicate and why I communicate that way? I think we're all broadened if we know more about more kinds of people and how they think and act and talk.

In this book, I include credible research on a variety of social groups so that we understand a range of ways in which people communicate. Yet it's critical to remember that statements about any group's communication are generalizations, not universal truths. Each of us communicates in some ways that are consistent with the patterns of particular social communities to which we belong, and in other ways our communication departs from norms for those communities. In part, that is because we belong to many groups. Michelle is not only black (a racial–ethnic group) but also upper-middle class (a socioeconomic group). Jason is also black, and he is from a working-class family. This may shed light on why Jason identifies with what African American scholars report as traditional black communication patterns and why Michelle does not.

Dimensions of Cultures and Social Communities

Geert Hofstede (1991, 2001; Hofstede et al., 2010), a Dutch anthropologist and social psychologist, provided insight into the perspectives, attitudes, and behavioral patterns that distinguish cultures. Before becoming a faculty member, Hofstede worked at IBM where he trained managers and supervised personnel research. In this role, he conducted more than 100,000 employee opinion surveys at IBM branches in countries all over the world. Hofstede noticed that there were clear differences among IBM employees in different cultures. He left IBM to study the data and was able to identify five key dimensions that vary among cultures.

Individualism/Collectivism

The dimension of **individualism/collectivism** refers to the extent to which members of a culture understand themselves as part of and connected to their families, groups, and cultures. In cultures high in collectivism (Pakistan, China), people's identity is deeply tied to their groups, families, and clans. In cultures high in individualism (United States, Australia), people tend to think of themselves as individuals who act relatively independently.

Communication scholar, Stella Ting-Toomey has studied cultural differences in what she calls face, which includes individual and cultural facets of identity. For instance, individual facets of your identity include your major or profession and your tastes in music whereas cultural facets of identity include whether you see yourself more as an individual or a member of families, groups, and your culture. Ting-Toomey (2005) reports that in collectivist cultures, the face of the group is more important than the face of any individual. In individualist cultures, the face of the individual is often more important than the face of the group (Neuliep, 2014).

Uncertainty Avoidance

Uncertainty avoidance refers to the extent to which people want to avoid ambiguity and vagueness. In some cultures (Poland, South Korea), people like to have everything spelled out very explicitly in order to avoid misunderstandings. Yet, in other cultures (Hong Kong, Sweden), uncertainty is more tolerated and expectations are less set since surprises may happen.

Power Distance

The third dimension of culture is **power distance**, which refers to the size of the gap between people with high and low power and the extent to which that is regarded as normal. Social hierarchies exist in all cultures, but how they are understood and whether they are accepted varies widely. In some cultures (India, China), the distance between high and low power is wider than others, making for a society in which people respect the powerful, and there is lower expectation of movement between classes, castes, or levels. In cultures where power distance is low (New Zealand, Norway), people tend to expect that those in power will have earned it, rather than simply gaining power by virtue of position.

Cultural differences in power distance may lead to misunderstandings. A Ugandan immigrant to the United States interpreted the relatively casual and egalitarian relationships between professors and students as rudeness by the students. The immigrant commented that, "The students drink, eat in class, talk back to professors … all this is unacceptable behavior in Uganda. No wonder Americans are losing their jobs to outsourcing because they are not respectful" (Muwanguzi & Musambira, 2013, n. p.).

Masculinity/Femininity

The fourth dimension of culture is **masculinity/femininity** (sometimes called aggressiveness). This dimension refers to the extent to which a culture values aggressiveness, competitiveness, looking out for yourself, and dominating others and nature, which are typically associated with men, versus gentleness, cooperation, and

---

individualism/collectivism Dimension of cultures that refers to the extent to which members of a culture understand themselves as part of and connected to their families, groups, and cultures.

uncertainty avoidance Dimension of culture that refers to the extent to which people want to avoid ambiguity and vagueness.

power distance Dimension of culture that refers to the size of the gap between people with high and low power and the extent to which that is regarded as normal.

masculinity/femininity Dimension of culture that refers to the extent to which a culture values aggressiveness, competitiveness, looking out for yourself, and dominating others, which are typically associated with men, versus gentleness, cooperation, and taking care of others and the natural world, which tend to be associated with women. Also called aggressiveness.

taking care of others and living in harmony with the natural world, which tend to be associated with women. In cultures that are higher in femininity (Netherlands, Norway), men and women are more gentle, cooperative, and caring. In cultures that are higher in masculinity (Japan, Germany), however, men are more aggressive and competitive. In highly masculine cultures, women may also be competitive and assertive, but generally they are less so than men.

Long-Term/Short-Term Orientation   The final dimension was not included in Hofstede's original work, but he added it later when it became clear to him that cultures varied how long term their orientations are. **Long-term/short-term orientation** refers to the extent to which members of a culture think about long term (history and future) versus short term (present). Long-term planning, thrift, and industriousness and respect for elders and ancestors are valued in cultures with a long-term orientation (most Asian countries). In contrast, living for the moment, not saving for a rainy day, and not having as much respect for elders and ancestors are more likely to be found in cultures with a short-term orientation (Australia, Germany). The long-term end of the continuum is associated with what are sometimes called Confucian values, although cultures not historically connected with this influence can also have a long-term orientation. This value is not just about future—it is also about respect for one's ancestors and plans and hopes for those who follow.

These five dimensions help us understand key differences among cultures and social communities.

long-term/short-term orientation Dimension of culture that refers to the extent to which members of a culture think about long-term (history and future) versus short-term (present).

Relationships between Culture and Communication

Communication is closely linked to culture because communication expresses, sustains, and alters culture (Callahan, 2010; Jandt, 2012; Neuliep, 2014). Your culture directly shapes how you communicate, teaching you whether and when interrupting is appropriate, how much eye contact is polite, and how much distance should be kept between people. We are not born knowing how, when, and to whom to speak, just as we are not born with attitudes about cooperating or competing. We acquire attitudes as we interact with others, and we then reflect cultural teachings in the way we communicate.

To gain a deeper understanding of how culture and communication influence each other, we will discuss four central relationships between culture and communication.

We Learn Culture in the Process of Communicating

We don't study our native culture to learn how to behave appropriately. Instead, we learn a culture's perspectives and rules during the process of

ENGAGE!   Adages Express Cultural Values

Every culture has adages, or sayings, that express its values and pass them from one generation to the next. Following are some adages that reflect values in particular cultures (Samovar, Porter, & McDaniel, 2013).

◆ "A zebra does not despise its stripes." Among the Masai of Africa, this saying encourages acceptance of things and oneself as they are.

◆ "Know the family and you will know the child." This Chinese proverb reflects the belief that individuals are less important than families.

◆ "The child has no owner." "It takes a whole village to raise a child." These African adages express the idea that children belong to, and are socialized by, whole communities, not just biological parents.

◆ "Better to be a fool with the crowd than wise by oneself." "A solitary soul neither sings nor cries." These Mexican proverbs reflect a strong commitment to collectivism.

 MindTap·   Identify an adage that you heard often when you were growing up.

communicating. By observing and interacting with others and being exposed to mass communication, we learn language (the word *dog*) and what it means (a pet to love, a working animal, or food to eat). In other words, in learning language we learn our culture's meanings and values. Children aren't born knowing that they should respect their elders or worship youth; they aren't born thinking that women should wear dresses or saris; at birth, they don't perceive piercing or tattoos as attractive or ugly; they don't enter the world thinking of themselves as individuals or members of groups. We learn all of these values and norms in the process of communicating with others.

From the moment of birth, we begin to learn the beliefs, values, and norms of our society. You learn to respect your elders or not by how you see others communicate with older people, how you hear others refer to older people, and how the media portray older citizens. We learn what ideal bodies are from media and from others' talk about people of various physical proportions. As Intan points out, we also learn nonverbal communication from the culture into which we are socialized.

 **Intan**

Eye contact is the hardest part of learning American culture. In my home, it would be very rude to do that. We look away or down when talking so as not to give insult. In America, if I look down, it is thought I am hiding something or am dishonest. So I am learning to look at others when we talk, but it feels very disrespectful still to me.

Both conscious and unconscious learning are continuous processes through which we learn language and internalize culture so that it is seamlessly part of who we are and how we see the world. As we learn language and nonverbal codes, we learn cultural values that are encoded in language.

Communication Reflects Cultural Values

One of the best indicators that a culture or social community exists is communication (Jandt, 2012; Samovar et al., 2015). Because we learn to communicate in the process of interacting with others, people from different cultures use communication in different ways and attach different meanings to communicative acts.

To illustrate how communication reflects and expresses culture, we'll discuss the individualism/collectivism dimension of culture. Communication reflects and expresses the individualistic or collectivist values of cultures. For example, many Asian languages include numerous words to describe particular relationships: my grandmother's brother, my father's uncle, my youngest son, my oldest daughter. This linguistic focus reflects the cultural emphasis on collective life and family relationships. Reflecting the Western emphasis on individualism, the English language has fewer words to describe the range of kinship bonds. As Maria points out in her commentary, people from individualistic cultures often misunderstand the values and choices of people from collectivist cultures.

 **Maria**

I get hassled by a lot of girls on campus about being dependent on my family. They say I'm too close to my folks and my grandparents and aunts and uncles and cousins. But what they mean by "too close" is I'm closer with my family than most whites are. It's a white standard they're using, and it doesn't fit me. Strong ties with family and the community are important, good values we learn in Mexico.

Individualistic and collectivist cultures tend to cultivate distinct communication styles (Jandt, 2012; Neuliep, 2014; Samovar et al., 2013, 2015). Individualistic cultures generally rely on a **low-context communication style**, which is very direct, explicit, and detailed. Because people are regarded as distinct individuals, communicators do not assume that others will share their meanings or values. Instead, everything must be spelled out carefully and clearly. Because self-expression and personal initiative are valued in individualistic cultures, argument and persuasion are perceived as appropriate.

Collectivist cultures typically rely on a **high-context communication style**, which is indirect and undetailed and which conveys meanings more implicitly than explicitly (Samovar et al., 2013). Because people are regarded as interconnected, it is assumed they are alike in terms of their values and understandings. Thus, there is no need to spell everything out. Instead, communicators assume that others will understand what isn't stated and will be able to use shared knowledge of situations and relationships to interpret vague statements. Also, in high-context cultures, a person's history (family, status in community) forms a context for understanding what a person says. This context is generally considered more important than the message itself.

low-context communication style Language that is very explicit, detailed, and precise; generally used in individualistic cultures.

high-context communication style An indirect and undetailed way of speaking that conveys meanings implicitly rather than explicitly; typical of collectivist cultures.

Consider a concrete example of the difference between high-context and low-context communication styles. A man using low-context communication style might invite friends to dinner this way: "Come to our home at 7 P.M. tomorrow, and we'll eat around 8:30. Feel free to bring your baby with you. When he gets tired, you can put him to bed in the guest room." A woman using a high-context communication style might invite the same friends to dinner this way: "Please come to our home tomorrow evening." The speaker using low context spelled out everything— when to arrive, when to expect a meal, that the baby is invited, and that there is a place for the baby to sleep, even that the invitation is for dinner. By contrast, the high-context speaker assumed that the guests would share her understandings—being invited into a home in the evening implies that dinner will be served, that 7 P.M. is an appropriate time to arrive, that 8:30 is a typical time to eat dinner, that the baby is welcome, and that there will be a place for the baby to sleep. For people who have learned a high-context communication style, the low-context style seems overly literal and seems to belabor the obvious. (Who wouldn't serve dinner to guests in the evening? Guests' families are always included in invitations.)

 **Doesn't Translate**

Most languages have some words that do not have single word equivalents in other languages. When we try to translate these terms into our own language, we require lots of words to approximate the meaning of a single word in the culture that coined the word.

◆ *Iktsuarpok* (Inuit): The frustration of waiting for someone to turn up

◆ *Schadenfreude* (German): Enjoyment obtained from the misery of others

◆ *Utepils* (Norwegian): To sit outside on a sunny day enjoying a beer

◆ *Mamihlapinatapei* (Yagán): a wordless yet meaningful look shared by two people who both want to initiate something but are both reluctant to do so.

◆ *Age-otori* (Japanese): To look worse after having your hair cut

To learn more words that have no easy equivalent in English, go to the online resources for this chapter.

 Can you identify a feeling, experience, or other phenomenon for which there is no word in the English language?

© Bill Aron/PhotoEdit

Passing tradition from one generation to the next is how cultures sustain themselves. In this photo, a Jewish elder instructs a young boy in Jewish traditions.

Communication Expresses and Sustains Cultures

Communication simultaneously reflects and sustains cultural values. Each time we express cultural values, we also perpetuate them. When some Asian Americans avoid overt display of emotions, they fortify and express the value of self-restraint and the priority of reason over emotion. When some Westerners argue, speak up for their ideas, and compete in conversations, they uphold the values of individuality and assertiveness. Communication, then, is a mirror of a culture's values and a primary means of keeping them woven into the fabric of everyday life.

The Western preoccupation with time and efficiency is evident in the abundance of words that refer to time (*hours, minutes, seconds, days, weeks*) and in common phrases such as "Let's not waste time." The value Westerners place on productivity may explain why Americans average only 13 days of vacation yearly while Italians average 42, British average 28, and Japanese average 25 (Love, 2011). In the United States, "The early bird gets the worm" implies that initiative is valuable, and "Nice guys finish last" suggests that winning is important and that it's more important to be aggressive than nice.

Communication Is a Source of Cultural Change

In addition to reflecting culture, communication is a source of change in cultures and social communities. Within in the United States, social communities have used communication to resist the mainstream's efforts to define their identity. Whenever a group says, "No, the way you describe me is wrong," that group initiates change in the cultural understandings.

Communication helps propel change by naming things in ways that shape how we understand them. For instance, the terms *environmental racism* and *environmental justice* were coined to name the practice of locating toxic waste dumps and other environmental hazards in communities where people tend to be poor and nonwhite. The verbal use of *google* grew out of the noun, Google, which refers to a particular online search engine. The term *sexual harassment* names a practice that certainly is not new, but for many years it was not labeled and not given social reality. Mary's commentary explains how important the label is.

 Mary

It was 15 years ago, when I was just starting college, that a professor sexually harassed me, only I didn't know to call it that then. I felt guilty, like maybe I'd done something to encourage him, or I felt maybe I was overreacting to his kissing me and touching me. But I later learned the term. Now I have a name for what happened—a name that said he was wrong, not me. It was only then that I could let go of that whole business.

As a primary tool of social movements, communication prompts changes in cultural life. The civil rights and black power movements motivated black Americans to assert the value and beauty of black culture. Simultaneously, African Americans used communication to persuade nonblack citizens to rethink their attitudes and practices. Gay pride marches challenge social attitudes about gay men and lesbians just as demonstrations for immigrants' rights challenge attitudes toward immigrants.

In addition to instigating change directly, communication accompanies other kinds of cultural change. Scientists had to explain antibiotics to medical practitioners and to a general public that believed infections were caused by fate, not by viruses and bacteria. Ideas and practices borrowed from one culture must be translated into other cultures; for example, the Japanese system of management has been adapted to fit the culture of many U.S. companies. Calamities also must be defined and explained: Are increasing natural disasters such as tsunamis and flooding the result of global climate change or the anger of the gods? Did we lose the war because we had a weak military or because our cause was wrong? Do technologies enrich cultural life or diminish it? Cultures use communication to define what change means and implies for social life.

Both an overall culture and particular social communities shape our perceptions and ways of communicating. Yet we can learn to appreciate different cultural systems and the diverse forms of communication they foster, as well as the ways in which multiple social identities shape our communication. Doing so enables us to adapt our communication effectively in response to the diverse people with whom we interact.

Digital Media, Cultures, and Social Communities

The Internet allows access to and interaction among members of different cultures and social communities. Just a few clicks on your computer yield a wealth of sites that provide you with information on any religion, sexual orientation, gender identity, race, or ethnicity. You can learn a great deal about other cultures and social communities by visiting online sites. The online world also allows us to interact with members of other cultures and social communities. Before computers, the only methods of interacting with people who did not live in our community were phone, mail, or travel.

Digital media also have a dark side related to cultures and social communities. The virtual world provides a thriving home for **hate groups**, which are collections of people that advocate and engage in hatred, aggression, or violence toward members of a particular race, ethnicity, gender, sexual orientation, gender identity, religion, or any other selected segment of society. Hate groups stoke stereotypes, ethnocentrism, and violence. These groups specialize in degrading social communities and cultures that they dislike. They also encourage hateful attitudes and, in some cases, violence toward members of particular communities and cultures. In the United States, the FBI follows hate groups, and two organizations have taken the lead in monitoring online hate groups: the Anti-Defamation League and the Southern Poverty Law Center. This chapter's online resources provide links to both of these groups so that you may learn about the work they do.

hate groups Collections of people who advocate and engage in hatred, aggression, or violence toward members of a particular race, ethnicity, gender, sexual orientation, gender identity, religion, or any other selected segment of a society.

Guidelines for Adapting Communication to Diverse Cultures and Social Communities

To participate effectively in a culturally diverse world, we must adapt our communication to different contexts and people. Effective adaptation occurs when we tailor our verbal and nonverbal symbols and our ways of perceiving, creating climates, listening, and responding. We'll consider four guidelines for adapting communication in ways that are sensitive to different cultures and communities.

Engage in Person-Centered Communication

When we encounter unfamiliar customs, we experience uncertainty—what does this behavior mean? What's going to happen next? What should I do in response? **Uncertainty reduction theory** explains that because we find uncertainty uncomfortable, we try to reduce it. To do this, we seek information—we ask questions, we listen and observe others, we look for patterns in interaction. As we learn more about values and norms in a culture or social community, we become more comfortable interacting with members of that culture or community. In turn, as we interact more, we learn more about what members of a culture believe and value and the kind of behaviors that are appropriate in the context.

Reducing uncertainty by learning about other people and cultures allows us to engage in person-centered communication. From our discussion in Chapter 3, you'll recall that person-centeredness involves recognizing another person's perspective and taking that into account as you communicate. For instance, it's advisable to refrain from using idioms when talking with someone for whom English is a second language. Competent communicators adapt to the perspectives of those with whom they interact.

Person-centeredness requires us to negotiate between awareness of group tendencies and equal awareness of individual differences. For example, we should realize that Asian Americans generally are less assertive than European Americans, yet we shouldn't assume that every Asian American will be deferential or that every European American will be assertive. What describes a group accurately may not apply equally to every member of the group. A good guideline is to assume that each person with whom you communicate fits some, but not other, generalizations about his or her social communities.

uncertainty reduction theory The theory that people find uncertainty uncomfortable and so are motivated to use communication to reduce uncertainty.

Interacting with people from other cultures enlarges our perspectives.

Respect Others' Feelings and Ideas

Has anyone ever said to you, "You shouldn't feel that way"? If so, you know how infuriating it can be to be told that your feelings aren't valid, appropriate, or acceptable. Equally destructive is to be told our thoughts are wrong. When someone says, "How can you think something so stupid?" we feel disconfirmed.

One of the most disconfirming forms of communication is speaking for others when they are able to speak for themselves (Alcoff, 1991; Wood, 1998). Marsha Houston (2004, p. 124), an accomplished communication scholar, explains how claiming understanding can diminish a person. She writes that white women should never tell African American women that they understand their experiences as black women. Here's Houston's explanation:

> I have heard this sentence completed in numerous, sometimes bizarre, ways, from "because sexism is just as bad as racism," to "because I watch *The Cosby Show*," to "because I'm also a member of a minority group. I'm Jewish . . . Italian . . . overweight. . . ." Similar experiences should not be confused with the same experience; my experience of prejudice is erased when you identify it as "the same" as yours.

Generally, it's rude and disempowering to speak for others. Just as we should not speak for others, we should not assume we understand how they feel or think. As we have seen, distinct experiences and cultural backgrounds make each of us unique. We seldom completely grasp what another person feels or thinks. Although it is supportive to make an effort to understand others, it isn't supportive to presume that we understand experiences we haven't had, as Susan's commentary points out.

 *Susan*

I hate it when people tell me they understand what it's like to have a learning disability. For one thing, there are a lot of learning disabilities, and I resent being lumped in a broad category. For another thing, if someone doesn't have dyslexia, which is my problem, they don't know what it means. They have no idea what it's like to see letters scrambled or wonder if you are seeing words right. People shouldn't say "I understand" what they haven't experienced.

Respecting what others say about their thoughts and feelings is a cornerstone of effective communication. Ethical communicators do not attempt to speak for others and do not assume they fully understand others' experiences. If you don't understand what others say or do, ask them to explain. This shows that you are interested and respect their experience. It also paves the way for greater understanding between people of different backgrounds.

Resist Ethnocentric Bias

Without thinking, most of us rely on our home culture and social communities as the standards for judging others. This can interfere with good communication. Ethnocentrism is the tendency to regard ourselves and our way of life as normal and superior to other people and other ways of life. Literally, ethnocentrism means to put our ethnicity (*ethno*) at the center (*centrism*) of the universe.

Ethnocentrism encourages negative judgments of anything that differs from our ways. In extreme form, ethnocentrism can lead one group of people to feel it has the right to dominate other groups and suppress other cultures. An abhorrent example of ethnocentrism was Nazi Germany's declaration that Aryans were the "master race," followed by the systematic genocide of Jewish people. Yet we need not look to such dramatic examples as Nazi Germany to find ethnocentrism. It occurs whenever we judge someone from a different culture as less sensitive, honest, ambitious, good, or civilized than people from our culture.

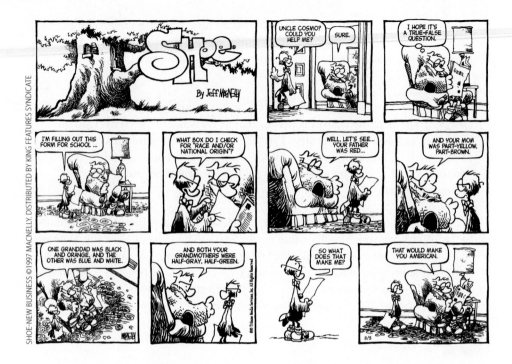

SHOE-NEW BUSINESS ©1997 MACNELLY. DISTRIBUTED BY KING FEATURES SYNDICATE

To reduce ethnocentrism, we should remember that what is considered normal and right varies between cultures. **Cultural relativism** recognizes that cultures vary in how they think and behave as well as in what they believe and value. Cultural relativism is not the same as moral relativism. We can acknowledge that a particular practice makes sense in its cultural context without approving of it. Cultural relativism reminds us that something that appears odd or even wrong to us may seem natural and right from the point of view of a different culture. This facilitates respect, even when differences exist.

Recognize That Adapting to Cultural Diversity Is a Process

Developing skill in intercultural communication takes time. We don't move suddenly from being unaware of how people in other cultures interact to being totally comfortable and competent in communication with them. Adapting to cultural diversity is a gradual process that takes time, experience with a variety of people, and a genuine desire to know and appreciate cultural differences.

Responses to diversity range from total rejection and disapproval to full participation in a different culture's communication styles. At particular times in our lives, we may find ourselves adopting different responses to diversity or to specific forms of diversity. We may also find that our responses to people with different cultural backgrounds evolve over the course of our relationships with them. That's natural in the overall process of recognizing and responding to diversity in life.

Resistance   A common response to diversity is **resistance**, which occurs when we reject the beliefs of particular cultures or social communities. Without reflection, many people evaluate others based on the standards of their own culture. Some people, including Maggie (see her commentary), think their judgments reflect universal truths. They aren't aware that they are imposing the arbitrary yardstick of their particular

cultural relativism
The recognition that cultures vary in thought, action, and behavior as well as in beliefs and values; not the same as moral relativism.

resistance A response to cultural diversity; attacking the cultural practices of others or proclaiming that one's own cultural traditions are superior.

culture and ignoring the yardsticks of other cultures. Devaluing whatever differs from our ways limits human experience and diminishes cultural life.

 *Maggie*

I'm tired of being told I should "appreciate" difference. In most cases, I don't. If people from other countries want to live in America, they should act and talk like Americans. They should adapt, not me.

Resistance may be expressed in many ways. Hate crimes pollute campuses and the broader society. Denial of other cultures leads to racial slurs, anti-Semitic messages, and homophobic attacks. Resistance may also motivate members of a culture or social community to associate only with each other and to remain unaware of commonalities among people with diverse backgrounds. Insulation within a single culture occurs in both majority and minority groups.

Members of social groups may also resist and deny their group identities in an effort to fit into the mainstream. **Assimilation** occurs when people give up their ways and adopt the ways of the dominant culture. Philosopher Peter Berger (1969) calls this *surrendering* because it involves giving up an original cultural identity for a new one. For many years, assimilation was the dominant response of immigrants to the United States. The idea of America as a "melting pot" encouraged newcomers to melt into the mainstream by surrendering whatever made them different from native-born citizens.

More recently, the melting pot metaphor has been criticized as undesirable because it erases the unique heritages of people who come to America. Jesse Jackson proposed the alternative metaphor of the family quilt. This metaphor portrays the United States as a country in which diverse groups' values and customs are visible, as are the individual squares in a quilt, and at the same time each group contributes to a larger whole, just as each square contributes to a quilt's overall beauty.

Some people use another form of resistance to provoke change in cultural practices and viewpoints. For example, heterosexuals who refuse to refer to their partners as "spouses" are resisting mainstream culture's refusal to grant legal status to gay and lesbian commitments. When culturally advantaged people resist and challenge the devaluation of disadvantaged groups, they can be powerful agents of change.

Tolerance   A second response to diversity is **tolerance**, which is an acceptance of differences whether or not one approves of or even understands them. Tolerance involves respecting others' rights to their ways even though we may think their ways are wrong, bad, or offensive. Judgment still exists, but it's not actively imposed on others. Tolerance is open-mindedness in accepting the existence of differences, yet it is less open-minded in perceiving the value of alternative lifestyles and

assimilation The giving up of one's native ways to take on the ways of another culture.

tolerance A response to diversity in which one accepts differences, although one may not approve of or even understand them.

World Traveling

María Lugones is a professor of philosophy at the State University of New York's Binghamton campus. Throughout her career, she has emphasized the value of what she calls "world travelling" (1992). By this, she means traveling to worlds other than our own. Lugones (2006) notes that many people are "border dwellers." They live in the borderlands in between cultures. For instance, Hispanics, Latinas, and Latinos who have moved to the United States often live between the culture in which they were born and raised and the culture where they now live. Students who study abroad are border dwellers for a short period of time. Lugones emphasizes the importance of world traveling, or "border crossing," as a way to experience diversity in values, material conditions, people, and so forth. She believes that we are all enriched by traveling to others' worlds.

values. Although tolerance is not as divisive as resistance, it does not actively foster a community in which people appreciate diversity and learn to grow from encountering differences.

Understanding

Understanding   Actor Matt Damon recently commented, "I think many of our problems as a country would be solved if people had thick passports." Currently approximately 20 percent of Americans have passports (Overheard, 2008, p. 3E). What Damon meant is that traveling to other cultures and experiencing different perspectives would give us greater understanding of differences. Damon's comment reflects a third response to diversity, which is **understanding** that differences are rooted in cultural teachings and that no cultural teachings are intrinsically best or right. This response builds on the idea of cultural relativism, which we discussed earlier. Rather than assuming that whatever differs from our ways is a deviation from a universal standard (ours), a person who understands realizes that diverse values, beliefs, norms, and communication styles are rooted in distinct cultural perspectives.

People who respond to diversity with understanding might notice that a Japanese person doesn't hold eye contact but would not assume that the Japanese person was devious. Instead, an understanding person would try to learn what eye contact means in Japanese society in order to understand the behavior in its native cultural context. Curiosity, rather than judgment, dominates in this stage, as we make active efforts to understand others in terms of the values and traditions of their cultures.

Respect

Respect   Once we move beyond judgment and begin to understand the cultural basis for ways that differ from ours, we may come to **respect** differences. We can appreciate the distinct validity and value of placing family above self, of arranged marriage, and of feminine and masculine communication styles. We don't have to adopt others' ways in order to respect them on their terms.

Respect allows us to acknowledge genuine differences between groups yet remain anchored in the values and customs of our culture (Simons, Vázquez, & Harris, 1993). Learning about people who differ from us increases our understanding of them and thus our ability to communicate effectively with them. What is needed to respect others is the ability to see them and what they do on their terms, not ours. In other words, respect avoids ethnocentrism.

Participation

Participation   A final response to diversity is **participation**, in which we incorporate some practices and values of other groups into our own lives. More than other responses, participation encourages us to develop skills for participating in a multicultural world in which all of us can take part in some of each other's customs. Harvard professor Henry Louis Gates (1992) believes that the ideal society is one in which we build a common civic culture that celebrates both differences and commonalities.

People who respond to diversity by participating learn to be **multilingual**, which means they are able to speak and understand more than one language or more than one group's ways of using language. Many people are already at least bilingual (also termed *code switching*). Many African Americans know how to operate in mainstream Caucasian society and in their distinct ethnic communities. Bilingualism, or code switching, is also practiced by many Asian Americans, Mexican Americans, lesbians, gay men, and members of other groups that are simultaneously part of a dominant and a minority culture.

understanding A response to cultural diversity that assumes that differences are rooted in cultural teachings and that no traditions, customs, or behaviors are intrinsically better than others.

respect A response to cultural diversity in which one values others' customs, traditions, and values even if one does not actively incorporate them into one's life.

participation A response to cultural diversity in which one incorporates some practices, customs, and traditions of other groups into one's life.

multilingual Able to speak and understand more than one language or communication style used in a social group or culture.

My partner, Robbie, and I have learned how to use both feminine and masculine communication styles. He was socialized to be assertive, competitive, and analytical in conversation, whereas I learned to be more expressive, cooperative, and relationship oriented. When we were first a couple, we were often frustrated by differences in our communication styles. I perceived him as insensitive to feelings and overly linear in his conversational style. He perceived me as being too focused on relationship issues and inefficient in moving from problems to solutions. Gradually, each of us learned to understand and then respect the other's ways of communicating. Still later, we came to participate in each other's styles, and now both of us are fluent in both languages. Not only has this improved communication between us, but it has made us more competent communicators in general.

People reach different stages in their abilities to respond to particular cultures and social communities. The different responses to cultural diversity that we've discussed represent parts of a process of learning to understand and adapt to diverse cultural groups. In the courses of our lives, many of us will move in and out of various responses as we interact with people from multiple cultures. At specific times, we may find we are tolerant of one cultural group, respectful of another, and able to participate in yet others.

Summary

In Chapter 1, we learned that communication is systemic. Because it is systemic, it must be understood as existing within and influenced by multiple contexts. In this chapter, we've focused on cultures and social communities as particularly important systems that shape and are shaped by communication.

Five principles summarize the relationships between culture and communication. First, we learn a culture in the process of communicating with others. Second, language is a primary indicator that a culture exists. Third, multiple social communities may coexist within a single culture, and people may belong to multiple cultures and social communities. Fourth, communication both reflects and sustains cultures. Fifth, communication is a potent force for changing cultural life.

We noted that digital media allow more access to and interaction among social communities, yet also provide a venue for hate groups to form and disperse their messages. The final section of this chapter identified four guidelines for communicating effectively in a socially diverse world. Moving beyond the belief that our ways are the only right ways allows us to understand, respect, and sometimes participate in a diverse world and to enlarge ourselves in the process.

Although this chapter has focused on differences between people, it would be a mistake to be so aware of differences that we overlook our commonalities. No matter what culture we belong to, we all have feelings, dreams, ideas, hopes, fears, and values. Our common humanity transcends many of our differences.

Experience Communication Case Study

The Job Interview

Apply what you've learned in this chapter by analyzing the following case study, using the accompanying questions as a guide. These questions and a video of the case study are also available online with your MindTap Speech for *Communication Mosaics*.

Mei-ying Yung is a graduating senior. Like many college students, Mei-ying loves technologies. Unlike many of her peers, however, she is particularly fascinated by programming. In her senior year, she developed and installed complex new programs to make advising more efficient and to reduce the frustration and errors in registration for courses. Although she has been in the United States for six years, in many ways Mei-ying reflects the Chinese culture where she was born and where she spent the first 15 years of her life. Today, Mei-ying is interviewing for a position at New Thinking, a fast-growing tech company that specializes in developing programs tailored to the needs of individual companies. The interviewer, Barton Hingham, is 32 years old and a native of California, where New Thinking is based. As the scenario opens, Ms. Yung walks into the small room in which Mr. Hingham is seated behind a desk. He rises to greet her and walks over with his hand outstretched to shake hers.

Hingham: Good morning, Ms. Yung. I've been looking forward to meeting you. Your résumé is most impressive.

[Ms. Yung looks downward, smiles, and limply shakes Mr. Hingham's hand. He gestures to a chair, and she sits down in it.]

Hingham: I hope this interview will allow us to get to know each other a bit and decide whether there is a good fit between you and New Thinking. I'll be asking you some questions about your background and interests. And you should feel free to ask me any questions that you have. Okay?

Yung: Yes.

Hingham: I see from your transcript that you majored in computer programming and did very well. I certainly didn't have this many *A*s on *my* college transcript!

Yung: Thank you. I am very fortunate to have good teachers.

Hingham: Tell me a little about your experience in writing original programs for business applications.

Yung: I do not have great experience, but I have been grateful to help the college with some of its work.

Hingham: Tell me about how you've helped the college. I see you designed a program for advising. Can you explain to me what you did to develop that program?

Yung: Not really so much. I could see that much of advising is based on rules, so I only need to write the rules into a program so advisers could do their jobs more better.

Hingham: Perhaps you're being too modest. I've done enough programming myself to know how difficult it is to develop a program for something with as many details as advising. There are so many majors, each with different requirements and regulations. How did you program all of that variation?

Yung: I read the handbook on advising and the regulations on each major, and then programmed decision trees into an advising template. Not so hard.

Hingham: Well, that's exactly the kind of project we do at New Thinking. People come to us with problems in their jobs, and we write programs to solve them. Does that sound like the kind of thing you would enjoy doing?

Yung: Yes. I very much like to solve problems to help others.

Hingham: What was your favorite course during college?

Yung: They are all very valuable. I enjoy all.

Hingham: Did you have one course in which you did especially well?

Yung: [blushing, looking down] I would not say that. I try to do well in all my courses, to learn from them.

Later Barton Hingham and Molly Cannett, another interviewer for New Thinking, are discussing the day's interviews over dinner.

Cannett: Did you find any good prospects today?

Hingham: Not really. I thought I was going to be bowled over by this one woman—name's Mei-ying Yung—who has done some incredibly intricate programming on her own while in college.

Cannett: Sounds like just the kind of person we're looking for.

Hingham: I thought so, too, until the interview. She just didn't seem to have the gusto we want. She showed no confidence or initiative in the interview. It was like the transcript and the person were totally different.

Cannett: Hmmm, that's odd. Usually when we see someone who looks that good on paper, the interview is just a formality.

Hingham: Yeah, but I guess the formality is more important than we realized: Yung was a real dud in the interview. I still don't know what to make of it.

© Cengage Learning

1. How does Mei-ying Yung's communication reflect her socialization in Chinese culture?

2. How could Mei-ying be more effective without abandoning the values of her native culture?

3. What could enhance Barton Hingham's ability to communicate effectively with people who were raised in non-Western cultures?

Key Concepts

Practice defining the chapter's terms by using online flashcards.

assimilation, 167

cultural relativism, 166

culture, 153

hate groups, 163

high-context communication style, 161

individualism/collectivism, 158

long-term/short-term orientation, 159

low-context communication style, 161

masculinity/femininity, 158

multilingual, 168

participation, 168

power distance, 158

resistance, 166

respect, 168

social communities, 154

standpoint, 154

standpoint theory, 154

tolerance, 167

uncertainty avoidance, 158

uncertainty reduction theory, 164

understanding, 168

Review, Reflect, Extend

The Reflect and Discuss, and Take Action features that follow will help you review, reflect on, and extend the information and ideas presented in this chapter. These resources, and a diverse selection of additional study tools, are also available online at the MindTap Speech for *Communication Mosaics*.

Reflect, personalize, and apply what you've learned.

Reflect and Discuss

1. Identify ways that you do and do not fit generalizations for communication by members of your sex that were discussed in this chapter. What about you—your race, ethnicity, sexual orientation, and so forth—might explain the ways in which you depart from general tendencies identified by researchers?

2. Continue the exercise started on page 166 by listing common sayings or adages in your culture. Decide what each saying reflects about the beliefs, values, and concerns of your culture.

3. As a class, discuss the tension between recognizing individuality and noting patterns common in specific social groups. Is it possible to recognize both that people have standpoints in social groups and that members of any group vary? You might recall the concept of totalizing from Chapter 4 to assist your consideration of this issue.

1. Communicating Culture

Locate a standard calendar and an academic calendar for your campus. Which of the following holidays of different cultural groups are recognized and treated as holidays by suspension of normal campus and community operations?

Christmas	Passover	Saka
Yom Kippur	Kwanzaa	Hegira
Elderly Day	Seleicodae	Martin Luther King, Jr. Day
Hanukkah	Easter	

What do calendars communicate about the place of different groups in a culture?

2. Becoming Self-Reflective about Your Culture

We can't resist ethnocentric bias unless we understand our own culture and social communities and the values that they attempt to instill in us. Earlier in this chapter, we identified proverbs that express values in non-Western cultures. Now, we'll do the reverse by looking at common sayings and proverbs in the United States. Read the adages below, and identify what they reflect about cultural values in the United States.

- "You can't be too rich or too thin."
- "A stitch in time saves nine."
- "A watched pot never boils."
- "It's the squeaky wheel that gets the grease."
- "You've made your bed, now lie in it."

What other sayings can you think of that express key U.S. values?

Recommended Resources

1. Edward Schieffelin and Robert Crittenden's classic story, *Like People in a Dream,* is a richly detailed account of first contact between two cultures. In 1935, white explorers went into interior parts of New Guinea where the indigenous people still used Stone Age tools.

2. Jess Row's novel *Your Face in Mine* (2014) follows characters who change their races. The two primary characters are a white American who becomes black and a white American who becomes Chinese. The story illuminates white privilege in ways that invite thinking and self-reflection.

9

Communication and Personal Identity

The true voyage of self–discovery lies not in seeking new landscapes but in having new eyes.

—Marcel Proust

How do social networking sites affect your sense of identity?

MindTap™

Learning Objectives

Topics Covered in This Chapter	After studying this chapter, you should be able to ...
Understanding the Self	Describe the four key social categories considered important to identity in America today.
The Self Arises in Communication with Others	Give at least one example from your life of social comparison that shaped your self-concept.
Social Media and Personal Identity	Examine the role of social networking sites in providing you with direct definitions and reflected appraisals.
Guidelines for Communicating with Ourselves	Create an action plan to implement the three chapter guidelines for communicating with ourselves.

MindTap™

Start with a quick engagement activity and **review** the chapter Learning Objectives.

Read, highlight, and take notes online.

When I was eight years old, I thought I would grow up to be a novelist. By age 12, my parents had taught me to bake, I was sure that I would be a pastry chef. When I was 20 and in love with my college sweetheart, I realized I would be a stay-at-home wife and mother. When I was 22 years old and had parted ways with my college sweetheart, I was sure that I would be single. Then I began graduate school and met Robbie, and I started to define myself as a scholar and teacher and a partner to Robbie. Today, I am not single, not a novelist, not a stay-at-home wife and mother, and not a pastry chef. My sense of who I am has changed as a result of experiences and people who have affected how I define myself.

Your sense of who you are has probably also changed over the years. How you define yourself today is shaped by your interactions with others throughout your life. Similarly, the self you become in the future will change in response to people and experiences that lie ahead.

In this chapter, we will explore how the self is formed and how it changes in the process of communicating with others. First, we will define the self and discuss how interaction with others shapes who we are and how we see ourselves. Second, we will examine particular types of communication that influence our identities. The final section of the chapter discusses guidelines for continuing to enrich who you are.

Understanding the Self

The **self** is an ever-changing system of perspectives that is formed and sustained in communication with others and ourselves. This definition highlights several important aspects of personal identity. First, it points out that the self consists of perspectives that grow out of communication. Second, this definition emphasizes that the self is not static or fixed, but dynamic. Each of us evolves and changes throughout life. Third, the definition calls attention to the idea that perspectives on the self are a system, which, you will recall, means that all parts are interrelated. If one perspective on yourself changes—for instance, how your professor assesses your academic ability—then other perspectives will also change—for instance, how you view your professional options. Finally, the definition highlights communication as a critically important influence on who we are and how we see ourselves.

 Tim

When I became a Christian, everything about me changed. I realized I had not been as Jesus would want in my relationships with my parents or my girlfriend. I also saw that I had not chosen a profession that served Christ, so I changed my major from business to education. I gave up some of the friends I had and made some new friends who share my beliefs.

The Self Is Multidimensional

There are many facets to the self. You have a physical self that includes your height, weight, body type, abilities and disabilities, and the color of your skin, hair, and eyes. You also have an emotional self that reflects how sensitive you are, whether you have a temper, and so forth. Your cognitive self includes your intelligence and intellectual aptitudes. Roles such as son, daughter, brother, sister, friend, aunt, parent, and

self A multidimensional process that involves forming and acting from social perspectives that arise and evolve in communication with others and ourselves.

neighbor are part of your social self, and roles such as manager, entrepreneur, and collaborator may be part of your professional self.

The self is not innate; we aren't born with clear understandings of who we are. Instead, we develop these understandings in the process of communicating with others who tell us who we are, what we should and should not do, and how valuable we are. As we internalize others' perspectives, we come to perceive ourselves through their eyes.

There are two kinds of others whose perspectives influence how we see ourselves and what we believe is possible and desirable for us (Mead, 1934). The first perspective is that of society, as a whole (called the **generalized other**). The second perspective is that of particular individuals who are significant in our lives (**particular others**).

Society Shapes the Self

All societies have ways of classifying people, but the particular ways differ across cultures. In the United States, we do not categorize people into castes, although some cultures do. Westerners recognize only two sexes and genders, but an increasing number of countries, including New Zealand, Australia, and Nepal, recognize multiple sexes (Bendavid, 2013) and some societies regard sex as changeable so a man can become a woman and vice versa (Baird, 2014; Bilefsky, 2008). Four key social categories recognized and considered important to identity in the United States today are race, gender, sexual orientation, and socioeconomic class.

generalized other The perspective that represents one's perception of the rules, roles, and attitudes endorsed by one's group or community.

particular others Specific people who are significant to the self and who influence the self's values, perspectives, and esteem.

Race   In North America, race is considered a primary aspect of personal identity (González, Houston, & Chen, 2012). It is one of the first aspects of a person that we notice, and it is an aspect of identity that is shaped by broad cultural views. The race that has been privileged historically in the United States is Caucasian. In the early years of this country's life, some people considered it normal and right for white men to own black women, men, and children and to require them to work for no wages and in poor conditions. At that time, people also considered it natural that white men could vote but white women and black men and women could not.

Although discrimination against people of color has declined since America's early days, Caucasian privilege continues (Gallagher, 2012; Higginbotham & Andersen, 2012). White children often have access to better schools with more resources than do children of African American or Hispanic/Latino/a heritage. The upper levels of government, education, and business are dominated by white men, whereas people of color and white women continue to fight for equal rights in admission, hiring, and advancement.

One key indication of white privilege is the assumption that white is the standard or normal race. People who are not white are often identified by their race (black congressman, Indian student, Latina businesswoman), but whites seldom are. A relatively new area of scholarship

Race is one of the categories of personal identity considered important in Western culture.

Jupiterimages/Stockbyte/Thinkstock/Getty Images

and teaching is Critical Whiteness Studies, which aims to make whiteness as visible and as open to analysis as any other race (Delgado & Stefanic, 2012).

The ways we classify people into races are based more on social ideas than skin color or other characteristics of people. What counts as "black" or "white" or any other racial category does not depend exclusively on genes or skin color (Delgado & Stefanic, 2012; Morning, 2011; Ore, 2013). The word *white* wasn't used to describe race or identity until Europeans colonized the United States. They invented the label *white* as a way to increase solidarity among European settlers, who actually had varied ethnic backgrounds. By calling themselves white, these diverse people could gloss over differences among themselves and distinguish themselves from people they defined as nonwhites. The first generations of Irish immigrants were not considered white (Negra, 2006; Painter, 2010).

Growing numbers of people have multiple racial and ethnic identities. More and more, multiracial individuals are challenging limited categories of race and changing the cultural fabric of the nation (Brunsma, 2006; "Quick Facts," 2011). After a number of applicants to colleges complained about having to check a single category of race, the Common Application for colleges began allowing students to check all racial categories with which they identify (Schwartz & Dash, 2011).

Gender Gender, which is the meaning society attaches to sex, is another category that is important in Western culture. Historically, Western society valued men more than women and considered men more rational, competent, and entitled to various social advantages and opportunities. In the 1800s, women in the United States as well as other Western cultures were not allowed to own property, enter professions, or vote.

Western society's gender prescriptions are less rigid today than they were in the past. Many men wear jewelry, tweeze their eyebrows, and use gels and spray to style their hair; many women wear workout clothes and don't use makeup; and members of both sexes pursue high-power careers and child rearing. Despite relaxation in social views, many gender prescriptions persist. Girls and women are expected to be caring, deferential, and cooperative, whereas boys and men are supposed to be independent, assertive, and competitive. Beth's commentary indicates how others respond to her refusal to conform to social expectations for women. Men who refuse to conform to social views of masculinity and who are gentle and caring risk being called wimps.

Multiracialism

For many people, the question is not "Which race or ethnicity are you?" but "Which races or ethnicities are you?" Below are a few well-known Americans with multiracial heritage. You can probably add other names to the list.

Jennifer Beals —Actress, her father is black; her mother is white.
Mariah Carey —Singer/actress, her father is Venezuelan/African American; her mother is Irish.
Naomi Campbell —Model, her mother is Jamaican; her father is multiracial, at least partly Chinese.
Johnny Depp —Actor, he has acknowledged German, Irish, and Cherokee lineage.
Soledad O'Brien —Reporter/news anchor, her father is Australian (his parents are Irish, hence the surname O'Brien); her mother is a black Cuban.
Barack Obama —U.S. president, his father was Kenyan; his mother was white American.
Alicia Keys —Singer, her father is black; her mother is Italian.
Derek Jeter —Baseball player, his father is black; his mother is white.

 How many of your acquaintances have multiple ethnic heritages?

 Beth

*I get along with kids, but I don't want to have any of my own. I don't really like kids. Everyone—
my parents, my friends, my boyfriend—thinks that is so weird. But I know a lot of guys who don't
like kids, and nobody thinks they're weird or anything.*

Sexual Orientation   A third aspect of identity that is salient in Western culture is sexual orientation. Historically and today, heterosexuals are viewed as normal, and people who have other sexual orientations are often regarded as abnormal. Society communicates this viewpoint not only directly but also through privileges given to heterosexuals but denied to gay men, lesbians, bisexuals, and transgender people. Most of us don't have to worry about where we go to the bathroom, but transgender people often experience anger or resistance if they enter men's or women's bathrooms. Most of us can find clothes that fit, but women's blouses are too tight in the shoulders for transgender women and men's pants are too tight in the hips for masculine-presenting women (Italie, 2014).

A transgender woman whom I know wrote the following reflection on what it felt like growing up biologically male when she felt female and how she feels now that she lives as a woman.

Socioeconomic Class   Socioeconomic class is a fourth facet of identity that Western society considers important (Acker, 2013, Scott & Leonhardt, 2013). Socioeconomic class is difficult to pinpoint because it is not straightforwardly visible, as sex and race usually are. Even though we can't see or point to socioeconomic class, it profoundly shapes how we see ourselves and the lives we live. It affects the kinds of schools, jobs, friends, and lifestyle choices we see as possibilities for ourselves.

Socioeconomic class isn't just the amount of money a person has. It's a basic part of how we understand our place in the world and how we think, feel, and act Lawless, 2012). Socioeconomic level affects which stores we shop in, the restaurants we patronize, the neighborhoods in which we live, and the schools we attend. It influences how we dress, including our views of what it means to be well dressed. It also influences who our friends are, what forms of recreation we enjoy, where we live and work, and what kind of vehicles we drive.

Particular Others Shape the Self

In addition to the perspective of society as a whole, the self is shaped by the perspectives of specific individuals who matter to us. These people, called particular others, are especially significant to us and shape how we see ourselves. Mothers, fathers, siblings, peers, and, often, day-care providers are others who are significant to us in our early years. For some of us, particular others also include aunts, uncles, grandparents, and friends. In general, Hispanics, Latinas and Latinos, Indians, Asians and Asian Americans, and African Americans often have closer and larger extended families than European Americans (Ferrante, 2013). As Eugenio points out in his commentary, people other than parents can affect how children see themselves, others, and the social world.

Views of self

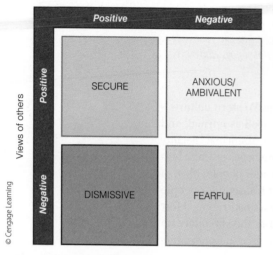

Figure 9.1 Attachment Styles

© Cengage Learning

attachment styles The patterns of interaction between child and primary caregiver that teach the child who he or she is, who others are, and how to approach relationships. Four attachment styles have been identified: anxious/ambivalent, dismissive, fearful, and secure.

secure attachment style One of the four styles of attachment; a style fostered by a caregiver who communicates with an infant in consistently loving and attentive ways and which inclines people to view themselves and others as worthy and to be comfortable both alone and in intimate relationships.

fearful attachment style One of the four styles of attachment; characterized by the perception of self as unworthy of love; fostered by dismissive, rejecting, or abusive treatment by a caregiver.

dismissive attachment style One of the four attachment styles; characterized by a view of others as unworthy of love and the self as adequate yet removed from intimate relationships; fostered by disinterested, rejecting, or abusive treatment by a caregiver.

 *Eugenio*

My father was not at home much when I was growing up. He worked in Merida, where the tourists go and spend money. My grandfather lived with us, and he raised me. He taught me to read and to count, and he showed me how to care for our livestock and repair the roof on our house after the rains each year. He is the one who talked to me about life and what matters. He is the one who taught me how to be a man.

Attachment Styles   One way that particular others shape our understanding of ourselves is through their **attachment styles**, patterns of care giving that teach us how to view ourselves and personal relationships. From his studies of interaction between parents and children, John Bowlby (1973, 1988) concluded that we learn attachment styles in our earliest relationships. These early relationships are especially important because they form expectations for later relationships (Bartholomew & Horowitz, 1991; Miller, 1993; Mooney, 2009; Trees, 2006). Four distinct attachment styles have been identified (see Figure 9.1).

A **secure attachment style** develops when a child's primary caregiver responds in a consistently attentive and loving way to a child. In response, the child develops a positive sense of self-worth ("I am lovable") and a positive view of others ("People are loving and can be trusted"). People with secure attachment styles tend to be outgoing, affectionate, and able to handle the challenges and disappointments of close relationships without losing self-esteem. A majority of middle-class children in the United States are securely attached, but fewer children in lower economic classes are (Domingue & Mollen, 2009; Greenberg, 1997).

A **fearful attachment style** is cultivated when the primary caregiver communicates in negative, rejecting, or abusive ways with a child. Children who are treated this way often infer that they are unworthy of love and that others are not loving. Thus, they learn to see themselves as unlovable and others as rejecting. Not surprisingly, this leads them to be apprehensive about relationships. Although they often want close bonds with others, they fear others will not love them and that they are not lovable. Thus, as adults they may avoid others or feel insecure in relationships.

 *Zondi*

In South Africa, where I was born, I learned that I was not important. Most daughters learn this. My name is Zondomini, which means between happiness and sadness. The happiness is because a child was born. The sadness is because I am a girl, not a boy. I am struggling now to see myself as worthy as a woman.

A **dismissive attachment style** is also promoted by caregivers who are uninterested in, rejecting of, or abusive toward children. People who develop this style do not accept the caregiver's view of them as unlovable. Instead, they dismiss others as unworthy. Consequently, children develop a positive view of themselves and a low regard for others and relationships. This prompts a defensive tendency to view relationships as unnecessary and undesirable.

The final pattern is the **anxious/ambivalent attachment style**, which is the most complex of the four. Each of the other styles results from some consistent pattern of treatment by a caregiver. The anxious/ambivalent style, however, is fostered by inconsistent treatment from the caregiver. Sometimes the adult is loving and attentive, yet at other times she or he is indifferent or rejecting. The caregiver's communication is not only inconsistent but also unpredictable. He or she may respond positively to something a child does on Monday and react negatively to the same behavior on Tuesday. Naturally, this unpredictability creates great anxiety in a child (Miller, 1993). Because children tend to assume that adults are right, children often assume that they themselves are the source of any problem. In her commentary, Noreen explains how inconsistent behaviors from her father confused and harmed her as a child.

Life Scripts   Family members also shape our self-concepts by communicating **life scripts**, which are rules for living and identity (Berne, 1964; Harris, 1969, Steiner, 1994). Like scripts for plays, life scripts define our roles, how we are to play them, and the basic elements of what our families see as the right plot for our lives. Think back to your childhood to recall some of the identity scripts that your family communicated to you. Were you told, "Save your money for a rainy day," "Always help others," "Look out for yourself," or "Don't live on credit"? These are examples of identity scripts people learn in families.

Our basic identity scripts are formed early, probably by age five. This means that fundamental understandings of who we are and how we are supposed to live are forged when we have almost no control. We aren't allowed to coauthor or even edit our initial life scripts, because adults have power. As children, we aren't even conscious of learning scripts. It is largely an unconscious process by which we internalize scripts that others write and assign to us, and we absorb them with little if any awareness. As adults, however, we are no longer passive recipients of others' scripts. We have the capacity to review the life scripts that were given to us and to challenge and change those that do not fit the selves we now choose to be. The Take Action feature on page 192 invites you to review your life scripts and challenge those that no longer work for you.

The Self Arises in Communication with Others

We've seen that our understanding of who we are is shaped by the perspectives of particular others and the society in which we live. But how do we learn those perspectives? How are they imparted to us? We learn them in the process of communicating with others—both individuals who matter to us (particular others) and society as a whole (generalized other). Scholars have identified four communication processes that explain how we come to know the perspectives of others and how those shape our understandings of who we are and can be.

Reflected Appraisal

The process of seeing ourselves through the eyes of others is called **reflected appraisal**, or the "looking-glass self" (Cooley, 1912). As infants interact with others, they learn how others see them—they see themselves in the looking glass, or mirror, of others' eyes. This is the beginning of a self-concept. Note that the self starts outside

MindTap

TAKE ACTION…activities are located at the end of this chapter and online.

anxious/ambivalent attachment style One of the four styles of attachment; a style, characterized by preoccupation with relationships, in which intimacy is both wanted and feared. It is fostered by inconsistent treatment from a caregiver.

life scripts Guides to action based on rules for living and identity. Initially communicated in familie; scripts define our roles, how we are to play them, and the basic elements in the plot of our lives.

reflected appraisal The image and estimate of ourselves that we perceive others communicate to us.

© Leigh M. Wilco

MindTap Who are your looking glasses? For whom are you a looking glass?

of us with others' views of who we are. In other words, we first see ourselves from the perspectives of others. If parents and other care givers communicate to children that they are special and cherished, the children will probably see themselves as worthy of love. On the other hand, children whose parents and other care givers communicate that they are not wanted or loved may come to think of themselves as unlovable.

Reflected appraisals are not confined to childhood but continue throughout our lives. Sometimes, a teacher is the first to see potential in a student that the student has not recognized in herself or himself. Peers also provide reflected appraisals, telling us if we are good at sports, attractive, and so forth. Later, in professional life we encounter co-workers and bosses who reflect their appraisals of us (we're on the fast track, average, or not suited to our positions). The friends and romantic partners we choose throughout life become primary looking glasses for us.

Direct Definition

As the term implies, **direct definition** is communication that explicitly tells us who we are by labeling us and our behaviors. Parents and other family members are usually the first people to offer direct definitions to us. They define us by the symbols they use to describe us. For instance, parents might say, "You're my sweet little girl" or "You're a big, strong boy" and thus communicate to the child which sex she or he is and what the sexual assignment means (girls are sweet, boys are big and strong). Children who hear such messages may internalize their parents' views of the sexes and use those as models for themselves.

Family members provide direct communication about many aspects of who we are. Positive labels enhance our self-esteem: "You're so smart," "You're sweet," "You're great at soccer." Negative labels can damage children's self-esteem: "You're a troublemaker," "You're stupid," and "You're impossible" are messages that can demolish a child's sense of self-worth. Direct definition also takes place as family members respond to children's behaviors. If children clown around and parents respond by saying, "What a cut-up; you really are funny," the children are likely to perceive themselves as funny. From direct definition, children learn how others see them and what others value and expect of them, and this influences how they regard themselves and what they expect of themselves.

Peers also offer direct definitions of us: "You're smart," "You're clumsy," "You don't belong in our group." The ways that peers define us often have pivotal impact on how we perceive ourselves and our worth. Peers are particularly strong in commenting directly on conformity to expectations of gender. Men who are not interested in drinking and hooking up may be ridiculed and excluded for not being real men (Kimmel & Messner, 2012). Women who don't wear popular brands of clothing or who weigh more than what is considered ideal may be ridiculed as unfeminine (Spar, 2013).

direct definition Communication that tells us who we are by explicitly labeling us and reacting to our behaviors; usually occurs first in families and later in interaction with peers and others.

One particularly powerful way in which reflected appraisals and direct definitions affect the self is through **self-fulfilling prophecies**—expectations or judgments of ourselves that we bring about through our own actions. If you have done poorly in classes where teachers didn't seem to respect you and have done well with teachers who thought you were smart, you know what a self-fulfilling prophecy is. Because we internalize others' perspectives, we may label ourselves as they do and then act to fulfill the labels we have internalized. We may try to live up or down to the ways we and others define us.

When I was seven years old, I took a swimming class. No matter how hard I tried to follow the teacher's directions, I couldn't swim; I couldn't even float. After three weeks, the teacher told me that I would never learn to swim and I should stay away from water. For the next 43 years, I accepted the teacher's label of *nonswimmer*. When I was 50, Robbie challenged my view of myself as a nonswimmer. He said I could learn to swim if I wanted to, and he volunteered to coach me. After just a few days of one-on-one coaching, I was swimming and floating.

Am I Pretty?

Most of us care how others see us. For many young girls, one of the key issues is whether others see them as attractive. Whereas girls once asked friends "am I pretty?" they are now likely to post the question in a YouTube video of themselves. And the responses can be extremely cruel. One-on-one evaluations between girls who are friends usually include some diplomacy, even tenderness, but comments posted as replied to YouTube videos observe no boundaries. When 13-year-old Sammie posted an Am I Pretty? video, one male responded comments, "Yes, you are really ugly. Now go cry to someone that actually cares" (Quenqua, 2014).

Am I Pretty? videos are not rare. More than 23,000 videos, mostly from 13- to 15-year-olds, have been posted, and they keep pouring in (Quenqua, 2014). Some psychiatrists consider these videos an alarming new form of self-mutilation, not unlike cutting. Other observers regard the ubiquity of the videos further evidence that popular culture is obsessed with superficial qualities rather than substantive ones.

 How would you compare the value of direct definition from friends in face-to-face conversation and strangers' comments on a YouTube posting?

Like me, many of us believe inaccurate things about ourselves. In some cases, the labels were once true but aren't any longer, yet we continue to apply them to ourselves (remember indexing, which we discussed in Chapter 4). In other cases, the labels were never valid, but we believed them anyway. Sometimes, children are mislabeled as slow when the real problem is that they have physiological difficulties such as impaired vision or they are struggling with a second language. Even when the true source of difficulty is discovered, the children already may have adopted a destructive self-fulfilling prophecy. If we accept others' judgments, we may fulfill their prophecies.

Social Comparison

Communication with others also affects self-concept through **social comparison**, rating of ourselves relative to others with respect to our talents, abilities, qualities, and so forth. Whereas reflected appraisals are based on how we think others view us, social comparisons are our comparisons of ourselves to others.

We gauge ourselves in relation to others in two ways. First, we compare ourselves with others to decide whether we are like them or different from them. Are we the same age, color, or religion? Do we have similar backgrounds, interests, political beliefs, and social commitments? Assessing similarity and difference allows us to

self-fulfilling prophecies
Acting in ways that bring about others' or our own expectations or judgments of ourselves.

social comparison
Comparing ourselves with others to form judgments of our talents, abilities, qualities, and so forth.

© Peter Bernik/Shutterstock.com

 MindTap™   How did your parents' communication with you influence your self-concept?

decide with whom we fit. However, this can deprive us of diverse perspectives of people whose experiences and beliefs differ from ours.

Second, we engage in social comparisons to assess specific aspects of ourselves. Because there are no absolute standards of beauty, intelligence, musical talent, athletic ability, and so forth, we measure ourselves in relation to others. Am I as good a goalie as Hendrick? Am I as smart as Maya? Through comparing ourselves to others, we decide how we measure up on various criteria. This is normal and necessary if we are to develop realistic self-concepts. However, we should be wary of what psychologists call upward comparison, which is the tendency to compare ourselves to people who exceed us in what they have or can do (Luttmer, 2005; Tugend, 2011). For most of us, it isn't realistic to judge our attractiveness in relation to models, or our athletic ability in relation to professional players. Likewise, we won't have valid assessments of ourselves if we compare ourselves to people who are clearly less attractive, athletic, and so forth (Buunk, Groothof, & Siero, 2007).

Social comparison can lead us to be dissatisfied if we compare ourselves to others who are doing better or have more. Would you feel better about yourself if you made $100,000 a year in a community where most people make $75,000 or made $150,000 in a community where most people make $200,000? Research shows that most people prefer the former—they feel better about themselves if they are making more than their neighbors (Halvorson, 2010; Luttmer, 2005; Tugend, 2011). In other words, we tend to feel better about ourselves if we are doing better than those around us, regardless of how well we are doing in absolute terms.

ENGAGE!

Virtual Identity Development

Many children have make-believe friends. Today, technologies allow children to create their own make-believe friends and even their own identities. One popular game, The Sims, allows players to create families and living spaces and then to direct interactions among family members. Marjorie Taylor (1999), a psychologist who has studied imaginary playmates, says that children create Sims characters who are just like themselves or characters who allow them to experiment with different identities. Researchers who study both children and technology think such games are great resources that help children learn to think about relationships and ways of interacting with others (Schiesel, 2006).

MindTap™   Did you have imaginary friends when you were a young child? What do you remember about them and their value to you?

Self-Disclosure

Finally, our self-concepts are also affected—challenged, changed, reinforced, enlarged—by our self-disclosures and others' responses to them. **Self-disclosure** is the revelation of personal information about ourselves that others are unlikely to learn on their own. We self-disclose when we express private hopes and fears, intimate feelings, and personal experiences, perceptions, and goals.

Self-disclosures vary in how personal they are. To a co-worker who is upset about not receiving a promotion, you might disclose your experience in not getting a

self-disclosure The revelation of personal information about ourselves that others are unlikely to discover in other ways.

promotion some years ago. To your best friend, you might disclose more intimate feelings and experiences. Although we don't reveal our private selves to everyone and don't do it a great deal of the time even with intimates, self-disclosure is an important kind of communication. How others respond to our self-disclosures can profoundly affect how we see and accept ourselves, as Seth's commentary shows. Self-disclosure is most likely to take place when the communication climate is affirming, accepting, and supportive.

 Seth

Ever since I was a kid, my dad told me I was going to be a doctor like him and join his practice after medical school. I never really thought about it until I got to college and found I didn't like the pre-med classes. Then I took an introductory sociology class and loved it. I took more classes and decided to major in soc. I was so scared to tell my dad, but I finally did the fall of my junior year. I was afraid he would be disappointed in me and he was—at first. But as I told him more about why I loved sociology, he became more accepting, and that made me feel better about myself.

A number of years ago, Joseph Luft and Harry Ingham created a model that describes different kinds of knowledge and perceptions that are related to self-concept and personal growth (Luft, 1969). They called the model the Johari Window, which is a combination of their first names, Joe and Harry (Figure 9.2). The panes, or areas, in the Johari Window refer to four types of information and perceptions that are relevant to the self:

◆ The open, or free, area contains information that is known both to ourselves and to others. Your name, your major, and your tastes in music are probably information that you share easily with others.

◆ The blind area contains perceptions of us that others have but we don't. For example, others may perceive us as leaders, even though we don't see ourselves that way. Co-workers and supervisors may recognize strengths, weaknesses, and potentials of which we are unaware. The hidden area contains information that we have about ourselves but choose not to reveal to others. You might not tell most people about your vulnerabilities or about traumas you've experienced. You might conceal self-doubts when interviewing for a job. Even with our closest intimates, we may preserve some areas of privacy.

◆ The unknown area is made up of information about ourselves that neither we nor others know. The unknown area is the most difficult to understand because, as the area's name implies, it contains information that is not known. We cannot know how we will handle a job layoff unless we experience one; we cannot know if we're good at bridge unless we try playing it. The unknown area includes your untapped resources, untried talents, and unknown reactions to experiences you've never had. David, who started college after serving in the Army, provides an example of what had been an unknown to him.

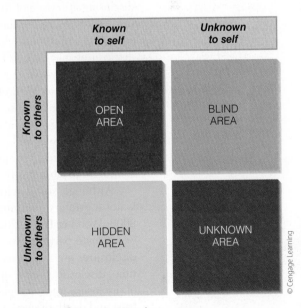

Figure 9.2 The Johari Window

 David

*I was shipped out to Iraq shortly after American troops were assigned there. Talk about scared—
I was terrified. I was also really unsure of how I would do. Could I stand up to the physical
challenges? Would I freeze up in battle? Could I kill someone if I had to? Being a soldier in Iraq
taught me some things about myself I don't think I could have learned any other way.*

Because a healthy self-concept requires knowledge of yourself, it's useful to gain access to information in our blind and unknown areas. To reduce your unknown area, you might enter unfamiliar situations. You might also try novel activities, interact with people whose cultural backgrounds differ from yours, and experiment with new ways of communicating. To decrease your blind area, you could ask others how they perceive you, or you could pay attention to how they act toward you. To diminish your hidden area, in carefully chosen relationships you might disclose information that you do not share with most people.

Uncertainty reduction theory, which we mentioned in Chapter 8, asserts that people find uncertainty uncomfortable and so are motivated to use communication to reduce uncertainty. Uncertainty is very high during initial encounters. Because we find uncertainty uncomfortable, we use both indirect and direct strategies to reduce it (Berger, 1977, 1988; Gudykunst, 1995; Kim, 1995). We gain information indirectly by observing the person: How does Chris react to various people and situations? Does Chris like spicy foods? How flexible is Chris in adapting when there is a change in plans? We also use direct communication to gain information and reduce our uncertainty about a new acquaintance: Where are you from? What's your major? Do you follow politics?

Self-disclosure is another way to reduce uncertainty early in relationships. We want to share our private selves and see how others respond to our disclosures. We may also hope that if we disclose something personal, others will reciprocate by disclosing to us, which would reduce our uncertainty. Because there are risks in self-disclosing, it's wise not to disclose too much too quickly. Initial self-disclosures should involve limited risk to the discloser: I'm afraid of heights; I hope I get accepted to law school. If low-level disclosures are met with respect and confidentiality, higher-level disclosures may follow: I have a difficult relationship with my father; I was seriously depressed a few years ago.

According to researchers, careful self-disclosure not only fosters personal growth but also tends to increase closeness, at least among Westerners (Derlega & Berg, 1987; Greene, Derlega, & Mathews, 2006). Yet people vary in their perceptions of the link between disclosure and intimacy. For some people, talk is a primary way of developing intimacy, whereas other people regard sharing experiences and being together as more conducive to closeness than talking intimately.

Although self-disclosure is important in the early stages of a relationship, it is not a primary communication dynamic in most enduring relationships (Dindia, 2000; Wood & Duck, 2006b). When we're first getting to know colleagues, friends, or intimate partners, we have to reveal parts of ourselves and learn about them, so disclosures are necessary and desirable. However, in relationships that endure over time, disclosures make up little of the total communication. Although the frequency of disclosure tends to decline over time, partners continue to reap the benefits of the trust and depth of personal knowledge created by early disclosures. Also, partners do

uncertainty reduction theory The theory that people find uncertainty uncomfortable and so are motivated to use communication to reduce uncertainty.

continue to disclose new experiences and insights to one another; it's just that mature relationships usually see less disclosure than embryonic ones.

Although infrequent self-disclosures do not necessarily indicate a lack of closeness, a noticeable decline in the level of disclosure that has become standard in a relationship may be a sign that intimacy is waning. When a friendship, a romance, or a close working relationship wanes, typically the depth of disclosure decreases (Duck & Wood, 2006).

Research shows that there are some sex differences in self-disclosure. In general, women engage in more verbal self-disclosures than men (Wood, 2015). While women tend to perceive greater levels of intimacy in face-to-face friendships, online friendships are more likely to be satisfying to women when they include high levels of self-disclosure (Bane, Cornish, Erspamer, & Kampman, 2010).

The human self originates in communication. From interaction with family members, peers, and society as a whole, we learn the prevailing values of our culture and of particular people who are significant to us. What we learn guides how we perceive ourselves and how we communicate. We're now ready to discuss three challenges related to personal growth.

Digital Media and Personal Identity

We'll discuss three of many ways that this chapter's focus on personal identity is pertinent to social media. First, consider the importance of social media in providing us with direct definitions and reflected appraisals. A 2013 survey ("The Social Scene") reports that nearly 30 percent of Americans 12 years or older have a profile on at least one social networking site, and 60 percent of Americans 12 years or older are heavy users of social networks. That implies we get and give a lot of appraisals through online and digital communication. When you post a photo on Facebook, others respond by saying, "You look great!" and "Very cool outfit." Knowing that others think you look attractive probably elevates your own sense of your attractiveness. But what if others' comments are less positive? "Have you gained weight?" "What did you do to your hair?" Those reflected appraisals are likely to make you feel less good about yourself (Quenqua, 2014).

Girls and women are more likely than boys to use social media as a venue for self-development. Teen girls use their blogs and pages on social networking sites to talk about issues such as pressures to be skinny, drink (or not), have sex (or not), and dress particular ways (Bodey, 2009; Bodey & Wood, 2009). As girls work out what they think and want to do in their online communities, they count on comments from others to clarify their own thinking and gain confidence in their ability to reject gender norms they find troubling.

Social networks can be—and too often are—used for **cyberbullying**, which includes text messages, comments, rumors, embarrassing pictures, videos, and fake profiles that are meant to hurt another person and are sent by e-mail or posted on social networking sites. Direct definitions, such as "You are ugly" or "You look like a wimp," are very hurtful, regardless of whether they are true. Fully 43 percent of teenagers are subject to some form of cyberbullying. For LGBTQ teenagers, the percentage is even higher: 53 percent (Burney, 2012). When asked why people were so cruel online, one young boy explained, "You can be as mean as you want on Facebook" (Hoffman, 2010, p. A12). Cyberbullying has no necessary stopping point.

cyberbullying Text messages, comments, rumors, embarrassing pictures, videos, and fake profiles that are meant to hurt another person and are sent by e-mail or posted on social networking sites.

School yard bullying pretty much stays on the school yard. Thus, a victim can escape by going home or visiting a friend. Online bullying, on the other hand, can follow the victim anywhere, 24-7. It is unremitting.

Second, social media are also key sources for social comparison. We read others' updates and compare our accomplishments to theirs, our activities to theirs, our number of friends to theirs, and so on. On social networking sites, many, perhaps most, people emphasize what is positive in their lives and downplay or omit mention of what is not so positive (Krasnova, Wenninger, Widjaja, & Buxmann, 2013; Tierney, 2013). This suggests that we might be wise to be cautious in comparing ourselves to the selves others present online.

Third, social media are platforms for skilled facework. In fact, social media allow us more time to plan and sculpt our self-presentation than we have in most face-to-face encounters. We can edit, reedit, and re-reedit our profile until it is exactly the way we want it. We can choose only our best photos for posting, and we can photoshop them to make ourselves appear more attractive. Also, we can take time to compose new posts to our home page and to reply to friends' postings. This means that online communication has great potential for strategic manipulation and even misrepresentation. Of course, we can be strategic and manipulative in face-to-face encounters too, but we don't always have as much time to prepare our self-presentations and we don't have the luxury of editing what we say.

Guidelines for Communicating with Ourselves

We will discuss three guidelines for communicating with ourselves in ways that foster personal growth and a healthy society.

Reflect Critically on Social Perspectives

We've seen that people tend to internalize the perspectives of their society. In many ways this is useful, even essential, for collective life. If we all made up our own rules about when to stop and go at traffic intersections, wrecks would proliferate. If each of us operated by our own inclinations, we would have no shared standards regarding tax payment, robbery, and so forth. Life would be chaotic.

Yet not all social views are as constructive as traffic regulations and criminal law. Each of us has an ethical responsibility to exercise critical judgment about which social views we personally accept and which ones we will allow to guide our behaviors, attitudes, and values. In addition, we have an ethical obligation to use our communication to contribute to constructive change in our society.

Society's perspectives are not fixed, nor are they based on objective, absolute truths. Instead, the values and views endorsed by a society at any given time are arbitrary and subject to change. The arbitrary nature of social values becomes especially obvious when we consider how widely values differ between cultures. For example, the Agta people in the Philippines and the Tini Aborigines in Australia view hunting skill as a feminine ideal (Estioko-Griffin & Griffin, 1997). Also, some groups in India have a category of identity for female men (Nanda, 2004).

Social views also change over time in a single society. As we have seen, Western society's perspectives on race, gender, sexual orientation, and gender identity are not what they were 50 or even 10 years ago. Social perspectives change in response to individual and collective efforts to revise social meanings. Each of us has an ethical responsibility to speak out against social perspectives that we perceive as wrong or harmful. By doing so, we participate in the ongoing process of refining our society.

Commit to Personal Growth

Most of us perceive ways we could improve as communicators. Maybe you want to be more assertive, more mindful when listening, or more confident as a public speaker. Following three suggestions will help you nurture your own personal growth.

Set Realistic Goals   Although willpower can do marvelous things, it has limits. We need to recognize that trying to change how we see ourselves works only if our goals are realistic. It's not realistic and usually not effective to expect dramatic growth immediately. If you are shy and want to be more extroverted, it's realistic to decide that you will speak up more often and attend more social functions. On the other hand, setting the goal of being the life of the party may not be reasonable.

Realistic goals require realistic standards. In a culture that emphasizes perfectionism, it's easy to be trapped into expecting more than is humanly possible. If your goal is to be a totally perfect communicator in all situations, you set yourself up for failure. More reasonable and more constructive is to establish a series of small goals that you can meet. You might focus on improving one communication skill. When you are satisfied with your ability at that skill, you can focus on a second one.

Assess Yourself Fairly   Being realistic also involves making fair assessments of ourselves. This requires us to make reasonable social comparisons, place judgments of ourselves in context, realize that we are always in process, and assess ourselves in the perspective of time. Remembering our discussion of social comparison, we know that selecting reasonable yardsticks for ourselves is important. Comparing your academic work with that of a certified genius is not appropriate. It is reasonable to measure your academic performance against others who have intellectual abilities and life situations similar to yours.

To assess ourselves effectively, we also should appreciate how our individual qualities and abilities fit together to form the whole self. Recall systems theory, which we discussed in Chapter 1. It reminds us that we treat ourselves unfairly if we judge specific aspects of our communication outside their overall context. Most often, we do this by highlighting our shortcomings and overlooking what we do well. This leads to a distorted self-perception.

It's more realistic to judge yourself from an overall perspective. Babe Ruth hit 714 home runs, and he also struck out 1,330 times. If he had defined himself only in terms of his strikeouts, he probably would never have become a world-renowned baseball player. One of my colleagues faults himself for being slow to grade and return students' papers. He compares himself with others in my department who return students' work more quickly. However, this man has twice as many office hours as any of his colleagues. His judgment that he is slow in returning papers is based on comparing himself with colleagues who spend less time talking with their students than he does. However, he doesn't compare himself with them when thinking about his office hours. In our efforts to improve self-concept, then, we should acknowledge our strengths and virtues as well as parts of ourselves we want to change.

To create and sustain a healthy self-concept, we also need to be attentive to unfair assessments of us that others may make. Others, including parents and bosses, sometimes have unreasonable expectations. If we measure our abilities by their unreasonable standards, we may underestimate our effectiveness. We should consider others' views of us, but we should not accept them uncritically.

A key foundation for improving self-concept is to accept yourself as someone in process. The human self is continuously in process, always changing, always becoming. This implies several things. First, it means that it's healthy to accept who you are now as a starting point. You don't have to like or admire everything about yourself, but accepting who you are today allows you to move forward. The person you are today has been shaped by all the experiences, interactions, reflected appraisals, and social comparisons during your life. Only by realizing and accepting who you are now can you grow in new ways.

Accepting yourself as in process also implies that you realize you can change. Who you are today is not who you were 10 years ago or who you will be 10 years from now. Don't let yourself be hindered by negative self-fulfilling prophecies or by the belief that you cannot change (Rusk & Rusk, 1988). You can change if you set realistic goals, make a genuine commitment, and work for the changes you want. Just remember that you are not fixed as you are but always in the process of becoming.

Create a Supportive Context for the Change You Seek

Just as it is easier to swim with the tide than against it, it is easier to promote changes in ourselves in contexts that support our efforts. You can do a lot to create a climate that nurtures your personal growth by choosing contexts and people who help you become who you want to be.

First, think about settings. If you want to improve your physical condition, it makes more sense to participate in intramural sports than to hang out in bars. If you want to lose weight, it's better to go to restaurants that serve healthful foods and offer light choices than to go to cholesterol castles. If you want to become more outgoing, you need to put yourself in social situations rather than in libraries. But libraries are a better context than parties if your goal is to improve academic performance. Bob's commentary illustrates the influence of setting on personal behavior.

 Bob

I never drank much until I got into this one group at school. All of them drank all the time. It was easy to join them. In fact, it was pretty hard not to drink and still be one of the guys. A while ago, I decided I was drinking too much. It was hard enough not to drink, because the guys were always doing it, but what really made it hard was the ways the guys got on me for abstaining. They let me know I was being uncool and made me feel like a jerk. Finally, I had to get a different apartment to stop drinking.

Second, the people we are with have a great deal to do with how we see ourselves and how worthy we feel we are. This means you can create a supportive context by consciously choosing to be around people who believe in you and encourage your personal growth. It's equally important to steer clear of people who pull you down or say you can't change. In other words, people who reflect positive appraisals of us

Uppers, Downers, and Vultures

Uppers are people who communicate positively about us and who reflect positive appraisals of our self-worth. They notice our strengths, see our progress, and accept our weaknesses and problems without discounting us. When we're around uppers, we feel more upbeat and positive about ourselves. Uppers aren't necessarily unconditionally positive in their communication. A true friend can be an upper by recognizing our weaknesses and helping us work on them.

Instead of putting us down, an upper believes in us and helps us believe in our capacity to change.

Downers are people who communicate negatively about us and our worth. They call attention to our flaws, emphasize our problems, and put down our dreams and goals. When we're around downers, we tend to feel down about ourselves. Reflecting their perspectives, we're more aware of our weaknesses and less confident of what we can accomplish. Downers discourage belief in ourselves.

Vultures are extreme downers. They attack our self-concepts. Sometimes vultures initiate harsh criticism of us. In other cases vultures discover our weak spots and exploit them, picking us apart by focusing on sensitive areas in our self-concept. By telling us we are inadequate, vultures demolish our self-esteem.

 MindTap™ Who are the uppers in your life? Do you have any downers or vultures?

enhance our ability to improve. One way to think about how others' communication affects how we feel about ourselves is to recognize that people can be uppers, downers, or vultures (Simon, 1977). The ENGAGE! feature on page 189 explains uppers, downers, and vultures.

Other people are not the only ones who can be uppers, downers, and vultures. We also communicate with ourselves, and our messages influence our self-esteem. One of the most crippling kinds of self-talk in which we can engage is **self-sabotage**. This involves telling ourselves we are no good, we can't do something, there's no point in trying to change, and so forth. We may be repeating judgments others made of us or inventing negative self-fulfilling prophecies. Either way, self-sabotage defeats us because it undermines our belief in ourselves. Self-sabotage is poisonous; it destroys our motivation to grow.

We can be downers or even vultures to ourselves, just as others can be. In fact, we can probably do more damage to our self-concept than others can because we are most aware of our vulnerabilities and fears. This may explain why vultures were originally described as people who put themselves down (Simon, 1977). We can also be uppers for ourselves. We can affirm our worth, encourage our growth, and fortify our sense of self-worth. Positive self-talk is a useful way to interrupt and challenge negative messages from yourself and others. The next time you hear yourself saying, "I can't do this," or someone else says, "You'll never change," challenge the self-defeating message by saying out loud to yourself, "I can do it. I will change." Use positive self-talk to resist counterproductive communication about yourself.

Before leaving this discussion, we should make it clear that improving your self-concept is not facilitated by uncritical positive communication. None of us grows and improves when we listen only to praise, particularly if it is less than honest. The true uppers in our lives offer constructive criticism to encourage us to reach for better versions of ourselves.

self-sabotage Self-talk that communicates that we are no good, that we can't do something, that we can't change, and so forth; undermines belief in ourselves and motivation to change and grow.

upper A person who communicates positive messages about us and our worth.

downer A person who communicates negatively about us and our worth.

vulture A person who attacks a person's self-esteem; may attack others or himself or herself.

Summary

In this chapter, we explored the self as a process that evolves over the course of our lives. We saw that the self is not present at birth but develops as we interact with others. Through communication, we learn the perspectives of particular others and the broad social community. Attachment style, reflected appraisals, direct definitions, and social comparisons further shape how we see ourselves and how we change over time. By interacting with society overall, we also learn society's views of aspects of identity, including race, gender, sexual preference, and income level. However, these are arbitrary views that we can challenge if we find them unethical. In doing so, we participate in the continuous evolution of our collective world.

The last part of the chapter focused on concrete ways to facilitate personal growth. You can foster your personal growth by setting realistic goals and assessing yourself fairly. Creating contexts that support the changes you seek makes it easier to promote those changes. Transforming how we see ourselves is not easy, but it is possible. We can make amazing changes in who we are and who we will become when we embrace our human capacity to make choices.

Experience Communication Case Study

Parental Teachings

Apply what you've learned in this chapter by analyzing the following case study, using the accompanying questions as a guide. These questions and a video of the case study are also available online with your MindTap Speech for *Communication Mosaics*.

Kate McDonald is in the neighborhood park with her two children, seven-year-old Emma and five-year-old Jeremy. The three of them walk into the park and approach the swing set.

Kate: Jeremy, why don't you push Emma so she can swing? Emma, you hang on tight.

Jeremy begins pushing his sister, who squeals with delight. Jeremy gives an extra-hard push that lands him in the dirt in front of the swing set. Laughing, Emma jumps off, falling in the dirt beside her brother.

Kate: Come here, sweetie. You've got dirt all over your knees and your pretty new dress.

Kate brushes the dirt off Emma, who then runs over to the jungle gym set that Jeremy is now climbing. Kate smiles as she watches Jeremy climb fearlessly on the bars.

Kate: You're a brave little man, aren't you? How high can you go?

Encouraged by his mother, Jeremy climbs to the top bars and holds up a fist, screaming, "Look at me, Mom! I'm king of the hill. I climbed to the very top!"

Kate laughs and claps her hands to applaud him. Jealous of the attention Jeremy is getting, Emma runs over to the jungle gym and starts climbing. Kate calls out, "Careful, honey. Don't go any higher. You could fall and hurt yourself." When Emma ignores her mother and reaches for a higher bar, Kate walks over and pulls her off, saying, "Emma, I told you that is dangerous. Time to get down. Why don't you play on the swings some more?"

Once Kate puts Emma on the ground, the girl walks over to the swings and begins swaying.

© Cengage Learning®

1. Identify examples of direct definition in this scenario. How does Kate define Emma and Jeremy?

2. Identify examples of reflected appraisal in this scenario. What appraisals of her son and daughter does Kate reflect to them?

3. What do Emma's and Jeremy's responses to Kate suggest about their acceptance of her views of them?

4. To what extent does Kate's communication with her children reflect normative gender expectations in Western culture?

Key Concepts

Practice defining the chapter's terms by using online flashcards.

anxious/ambivalent attachment style, 179
attachment style, 178
cyberbullying, 185
direct definition, 180
dismissive attachment style, 178
downer, 189
fearful attachment style, 178
generalized other, 175
life script, 179
particular others, 175

reflected appraisal, 179
secure attachment style, 178
self, 174
self-disclosure, 182
self-fulfilling prophecy, 181
self-sabotage, 189
social comparison, 181
uncertainty reduction theory, 184
upper, 189
vulture, 189

Review, Reflect, Extend

The Reflect and Discuss and Take Action features that follow will help you review, reflect on, and extend the information and ideas presented in this chapter. These resources, and a diverse selection of additional study tools, are also available online at the MindTap Speech for *Communication Mosaics*.

MindTap

Reflect, personalize, and apply what you've learned.

Reflect and Discuss

As a class, discuss society's views (the generalized other) of women and men. What are current social expectations for each sex? What behaviors, appearances, and attitudes violate social prescriptions for gender? Do you agree or disagree with these social expectations?

1. If you could revise the generalized other, how would you do it? Would race/ethnicity, gender, sexual orientation, and socioeconomic class be important aspects of self in your revision?

2. Write one or two paragraphs to describe of how you defined yourself when you were 6, 10, and 16. How is your current self different from and an extension of those earlier views of yourself? Now, write a one- to two-paragraph description of how who you think you will be in 10 years. Tuck it away and reread it a decade from now.

TAKE ACTION

1. Reflecting on Your Life Scripts

To take control of our lives, we must first understand influences that shape it currently. Identify the life scripts your parents taught you.

- First, recall explicit messages your parents gave you about "who we are" and "who you are." Can you hear their voices telling you codes you were expected to follow?
- Next, write down the scripts. Try to capture the language your parents used in teaching the scripts.
- Now review each script. Which ones make sense to you today? Are you still following any that have become irrelevant or nonfunctional for you? Do you disagree with any of them?
- Commit to changing scripts that aren't productive for you or that conflict with values you now hold.
- In some cases, we can rewrite scripts. To do so, we must become aware of the scripts we were taught and take responsibility for scripting our lives.

2. Identifying Social Values in Media

Select four popular magazines, and read the articles and advertisements in them.

- What do the articles and ads convey about what and who is valued in the United States?
- What do articles convey about how women or men are regarded and what they are expected to be and do?
- How many ads aimed at women focus on beauty, looking young, losing weight, taking care of others, and attracting men?
- How many ads aimed at men emphasize strength, virility, success, and independence?

To extend this exercise, note the cultural values conveyed by television, films, billboards, and news stories. Pay attention to who is highlighted and how different genders, races, and professions are represented.

Recommended Resources

If you would like to learn more about how the attachment styles discussed in this chapter affect romantic relationships, go to the book's online resources for this chapter.

1. The film *Nell* dramatizes the impact of communication with others on self-concept. View the film, and notice how Nell's world changes as she begins to communicate with others.

2. Some societies have more rigid lines for class membership than the United States does. One of the most rigid systems is the caste system in India. To learn about how a person's caste affects his or her opportunities in life, go to the book's online resources for this chapter.

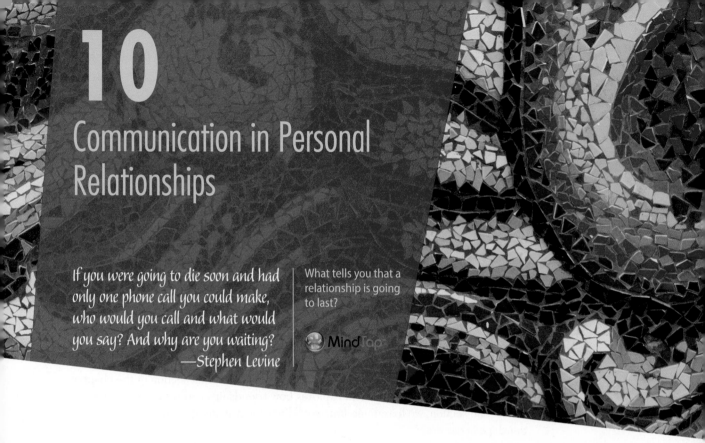

10

Communication in Personal Relationships

If you were going to die soon and had only one phone call you could make, who would you call and what would you say? And why are you waiting?
—Stephen Levine

What tells you that a relationship is going to last?

 MindTap

Learning Objectives

Topics Covered in This Chapter	After studying this chapter, you should be able to ...
Understanding Personal Relationships	Drawing on examples from your experience, describe the four features of personal relationships.
	Identify four strategies for negotiating dialectical tensions in personal relationships.
	Describe a significant turning point in one of your personal relationships.
	Drawing examples from well-known romantic relationships in film and literature, illustrate the three broad stages of romantic relationship evolution.
Digital Media and Personal Relationships	Given what you've learned about the four features of personal relationships, compare the intimacy you have with online and face-to-face friends.
Guidelines for Communicating in Personal Relationships	Given what you've learned about the four features of personal relationships, compare the intimacy you have with online and face-to-face friends.

MindTap

Start with a quick engagement activity and review the chapter Learning Objectives.

Read, highlight, and take notes online.

When my mother could no longer live alone, Robbie (my partner) and I invited her into our home where she lived for the final 14 months of her life. As you might imagine, during this period I felt much sadness. What you might not realize is that I also experienced a great deal of joy and personal growth as important relationships in my life gained greater depth. Mother and I grew close in new ways, and my ties with Robbie, my sister Carolyn, and close friends were deepened as I shared with them the fears and feelings that accompany losing a parent.

My experience is not unusual. All of us count on family, close friends, and romantic partners in hard times as well as good times. Our intimates help us get through sorrows and disappointments, and they celebrate our joys and victories. Try to imagine that suddenly you have no close friends or family and no romantic partner. How would your life be different? What would be missing? If you're like most people, a great deal would be missing. Personal relationships are important sources of growth, pleasure, comfort, and fulfillment

Healthy, effective communication is the heartbeat of strong personal relationships. In previous chapters, we've discussed basic communication processes. In this chapter, we focus on how those apply to personal relationships. The first section of the chapter defines personal relationships and explores how friendships and romances evolve. In the second section, we'll examine four guidelines for sustaining healthy personal relationships in our era.

Understanding Personal Relationships

A **personal relationship** is a voluntary commitment between irreplaceable individuals who are influenced by rules, relationship dialectics, and surrounding contexts. This definition highlights important features that distinguish personal relationships from other kinds of human connections. We'll discuss each of these features and then explore typical evolutionary paths of friendships and romantic relationships.

Features of Personal Relationships

Personal relationships are unique: Each one is distinct as a result of commitment, rules, surrounding contexts, and relationship dialectics.

Uniqueness   Most of our relationships are social, not personal. A **social relationship** is one in which participants interact according to general social roles rather than unique individual identities. For instance, you might talk about a course and professor with a classmate and talk return policies with store clerks. In each case, the person could be replaced by someone else in the same role. In social relationships, the individual people are less important than the roles they fulfill.

In personal relationships, however, the particular people and what they create between them define the connection (Norwood & Duck, 2009). Others cannot replace intimate partners, best friends, or family members we love. When one person in a personal relationship leaves or dies, that relationship ends, although it may remain strong in memory. We may later have other intimates, but a new partner or best friend will not duplicate the former one.

Voluntary Commitment   The sparks and the emotional high of being in love or discovering a new friend stem from **passion**, an intense feeling based on the rewards of

personal relationship
A relationship defined by uniqueness, rules, relationship dialectics, commitment, and embeddedness in contexts. Personal relationships, unlike social ones, are irreplaceable.

social relationship
Replaceable relationships that tend to follow broad social scripts and rules and in which participants tend to assume conventional social roles in relation to one another. Contrast with *personal relationship*.

involvement with another person. Passion is why we have the sensations of butterflies in the stomach and giddiness. As exciting as passion is, it isn't the basis of enduring relationships.

Commitment is the decision to remain with a relationship. The hallmark of commitment is the intention to share the future (Lund, 1985; Ragan, 2003). Committed friends and romantic partners assume they will stay together. Because commitment assumes a shared future, partners are unlikely to bail out if the going gets rough. Instead, they stay together despite trouble, disappointments, sporadic restlessness, and lulls in emotional depth (Badiou, 2012).

Commitment grows out of **investment**, which is what we put into a relationship that we could not retrieve if the relationship were to end (Rusbult, Drigotas, & Verette, 1994). When we care about another person, we invest time, energy, thought, and feelings in interaction. In doing this, we invest *ourselves* in others. We also make material investments that can't be recovered if a relationship ends. Gifts, money spent on dates, and so forth cannot be recovered fully if the relationship ends. Investments are powerful because they are personal choices to give things that can't be recovered. The more we invest in a relationship, the more difficult it is to end it (Dainton, 2006; Guerrero, Andersen, & Afifi, 2008). Sarah points out that investing heavily in a relationship can sometimes trap a person.

 Sarah

When Sean and I were first married, I was so happy I didn't care about anything else. My friends tried to talk me out of quitting school, but I wanted to work to put Sean through medical school. Then, we had one baby and another and a third, and I was a stay-at-home mom who was totally involved in family. Then things started unraveling between Sean and me. I thought about a divorce. But then I thought, "Where could I go? How could I support myself and the kids?" I hadn't finished college, so I couldn't earn a decent income. My job skills were rusty because I'd been out of the job market for 10 years. It was like I was trapped because I'd put too much in the marriage to leave.

Relationship Rules   All relationships have **rules** that guide how partners communicate and interpret each other's communication (Argyle & Henderson, 1984). Typically, relationship rules are unspoken understandings between partners. Although friends and romantic partners may never explicitly discuss rules, they learn how important rules are if they violate one, as Miguel's commentary illustrates.

 Miguel

Sherry and I had been dating for about six months when some of my friends from another school came to visit on their spring break. We decided to go out on Saturday night to hear a local band. It never occurred to me to check with Sherry, because we hadn't made plans for that night. But she was so mad at me. She said, "We always go out on Fridays and Saturdays"— like it was written in stone or something.

As we noted in Chapter 4, two kinds of rules guide our communication. *Constitutive rules*

Shared time and experiences are important investments that fuel commitment.

passion Intensely positive feelings and desires for another person. Passion is based on the rewards of involvement and is not equivalent to commitment.

commitment The decision to remain in a relationship. One of three dimensions of enduring romantic relationships, commitment has more influence on relationship continuity than does love alone. An advanced stage in the process of escalation in romantic relationships.

investment Something put into a relationship that cannot be recovered should the relationship end. Investments, more than rewards and love, increase commitment.

rules Patterned ways of behaving and interpreting behavior. All relationships develop rules.

define how to interpret communication. For instance, some people count listening to problems as caring, whereas others count engaging in activities to divert attention from problems as caring (Tavris, 1992; Wood, 2001c). Families often have constitutive rules that define what kinds of communication symbolize love and commitment (visiting at least three times a year, remembering birthdays). Constitutive rules are worked out over time as people in personal relationships learn what things mean to each other and what each of them needs and wants.

Regulative rules govern interaction by specifying when and with whom to engage in various kinds of communication. For example, many people operate according to a regulative rule that says it's okay to criticize a personal friend in private but to do so in front of others is not acceptable. Some romantic partners limit physical displays of affection to private settings.

Equally important are "shalt not" rules that define what each won't tolerate. For example, most Westerners would consider it a betrayal if a friend became sexually involved with their romantic partner. Some families have strong "shalt not" rules that members cannot marry outside their race, religion, or ethnic group. Rules regulate both trivial and important aspects of interaction. Not interrupting may be a rule, but breaking it probably won't wreck a good friendship. On the other hand, deceitful communication or divulging confidences may sound the death knell of a friendship.

 Kiran

Nobody in my family has ever married a non-Indian, and I am expected to follow this tradition. If my parents find out I even dated someone who is not Indian, they get very upset. My father has told me that if I marry outside of our ethnicity, he will disown me.

Because rules reflect our cultures and social communities, friends and romantic partners from different racial and ethnic backgrounds may not understand each other's relationship rules. Communication scholar Mary Jane Collier (1996) found that Latinas and Latinos regard supportive communication and respect as key norms in friendship whereas African Americans place more priority on showing respect and consideration, Asian Americans emphasize exchanging ideas, and European Americans place highest priority on honesty, disclosure, and advice.

Affected by Contexts   Personal relationships are not isolated from the social world. Instead, the surroundings of relationships influence interaction between people (Dainton, 2006; Felmlee, 2001). Our families of origin influence what we look for in people with whom we want close relationships. Our social circles establish norms for such activities as religious involvement, drinking, political activism, participation in community groups, studying, working, and socializing. Circumstances in the larger society may also influence interaction between intimates. For instance, during deep recessions people who are laid off may experience a diminished sense of self-worth. Because personal relationships are systems, shifts in one partner's earning power and self-worth reverberate, causing ripples of change throughout a relationship (Coontz, 2014). The many social contexts of our lives affect what we expect of relationships and how we communicate in them.

Speed dating and online sites such as OkCupid maximize the number of potential partners you can screen in a short time (Samp & Palevitz, 2009). The growing number of dual-career couples is revising traditional expectations about how much each partner participates in earning income, homemaking, and child care ("Choose Your Parents,"

2014; Galvin, 2006; Wood, 2010). Increasingly, people have friends and romantic partners of races, religions, and cultures different than their own (Angier, 2013a,b; Jensen, 2014). Thus, our social circles and the larger society as well are contexts that influence the relationships we form and the ways we communicate within them.

Relationship Dialectics   A final quality of personal relationships is the presence of **relationship dialectics**. These are opposing and continuous tensions that are normal in all close relationships. Of the many possible dialectics, we will discuss three that are particularly prominent in close relationships (Anderson, Baxter, & Cissna, 2004; Baxter, 2010).

Staying in Touch

Today's college students tend to stay in touch with their parents. On average, college students call, e-mail, Skype, or text their parents 13 times a week (Lourogos, 2010)—up from 10.4 times a week in 2006 (Setoodeh, 2006). Not surprisingly, the main topic of communication is finances (30.6 percent of students), but that's not the only topic. College students also talk with parents about career planning (19.9 percent), academics (12.6 percent), health and safety (7.7 percent), and personal relationships (7.2 percent) (Setoodeh, 2006).

 How often do you talk with members of your family?

The **autonomy/connection** dialectic involves the desires to be separate, on the one hand, and to be connected, on the other. Because we want to be deeply linked to others, we cherish spending time with our intimates, sharing experiences, and feeling connected. At the same time, we don't want relationships to swallow our individuality, so we seek some distance and time apart, even from our intimates.

Most people in personal relationships experience friction as a result of the contradictory desires for autonomy and connection (Erbert, 2000). Friends and romantic partners may vacation together and be with each other constantly for a week or more. They're often surprised when they return home and crave time apart. Intense immersion in togetherness prompts us to reestablish independent identity. When we get together with our families during holidays, we're often excited about catching up and talking intensely. Yet we often feel glad when the visit is over and we can part from families for a time. Both autonomy and closeness are natural human needs. The challenge is to nurture both individuality and intimacy.

The dialectic of **novelty/predictability** reflects tension between the desire for familiar routines and the desire for novelty. We like a certain amount of routine to provide security and predictability in our lives. Friends often have standard times to get together, families develop rituals for holidays and birthdays, and romantic couples settle on preferred times and places for going out (Bruess, 2015; Bruess & Hoefs, 2006; Duck, 2006; Wood, 2006a). Yet too much routine is boring, so we seek novel experiences. Friends may take up a new sport together, families may plan unusual vacations, and romantic partners might explore a new hobby or do something spontaneous and different to introduce variety into their customary routine.

 *Meg*

Craig and I have been together for ten years, so it's no surprise that we've settled into a lot of routines—too many! Last summer, I started biking to get some exercise. After a while, Craig decided to join me, and that's led to so many new experiences for us—places we go for great rides, mishaps we've had with flat tires and the like. These new experiences are a booster shot for our relationship.

relationship dialectics The tensions between opposing forces or tendencies that are normal parts of all relationships: autonomy/connection, novelty/predictability, and openness/closedness.

autonomy/connection One of three relationship dialectics; the tension between the need for personal autonomy, or independence, and connection, or intimacy.

novelty/predictability One of three relationship dialectics; the tension between the desire for spontaneous, new experiences, and the desire for routines and familiar experiences.

The third dialectic, **openness/closedness**, involves the desire for openness in tension with the desire for privacy. Although intimate relationships sometimes are idealized as totally open and honest, complete openness would be intolerable (Baxter, 2006; Petronio & Caughlin, 2006). Most of us want to share our inner selves with our intimates, yet there are times when we don't feel like disclosing and topics we don't want to discuss with anyone. Families often share deep feelings and thoughts but don't discuss sexual activities and attitudes. Friends and romantic partners, on the other hand, may talk about sex and other personal topics but may not share family secrets.

Researchers have identified four ways in which friends and romantic partners deal with dialectical tensions (Baxter & Simon, 1993). One response, called **neutralization**, negotiates a balance between the opposing dialectical forces. This involves striking a compromise in which both needs are met to an extent, but neither is fully satisfied. A couple might agree to be generally open but not highly disclosive.

Separation addresses one need in a dialectic and ignores the other. For example, friends might agree to make novelty a priority and suppress their needs for routine. Research suggests that separation, which denies one natural, human need, is generally the least satisfying response.

There is a form of separation that doesn't require denying either need in a dialectic. Cyclic alteration occurs when partners cycle between dialectical poles to favor each pole alternately. Couples involved in long-distance relationships often spend weekends in close contact and don't see each other during the week.

A third way to manage dialectics is **segmentation**, in which partners assign each pole to certain spheres, issues, activities, or times. For instance, friends might be open about many topics but respect each other's privacy and refrain from prying in one or two areas. Romantic partners might be autonomous in their professional activities yet connected in their interaction in the home and in their involvement with children. Jessica's commentary explains how segmentation surfaces in her relationship with her father.

Jessica

I can talk about anything with my mom. She's like my best friend. She knows all about every part of my life. With my dad, it's a different story. We can talk about my classes and my job and cars and stuff like that. What we never, never talk about is dating and my boyfriends. Mom says he doesn't like to think about his "little girl" being romantically involved. Maybe that's it. All I know is that we don't ever talk about boys in my life.

The final method of managing dialectics is **reframing**. This is a complex strategy that redefines apparently contradictory needs as not really in opposition. My colleagues and I found clear examples of reframing in a study of intimate partners (Wood, Dendy, Dordek, Germany, & Varallo, 1994). Some couples said that their autonomy enhances closeness because knowing they are separate in some ways allows them to feel safer about being deeply connected in other ways. Instead of viewing autonomy and closeness as opposing, these partners transcended the apparent tension between the two to define the needs as mutually enhancing.

The Evolutionary Course of Personal Relationships

Every personal relationship develops at its own pace and in unique ways. Yet many friendships and romances generally follow common patterns of growth and, sometimes,

---

openness/closedness
One of three relationship dialectics; the tension between the desire to share private thoughts, feelings, and experiences with intimates and the desire to preserve personal privacy.

neutralization One of four responses to relationship dialectics; balancing or finding a compromise between two dialectical poles.

separation One of the four responses to relationship dialectics, in which friends or romantic partners assign one pole of a dialectic to certain spheres of activities or topics and assign the contradictory dialectical pole to distinct spheres of activities or topics.

segmentation One of the four responses to relationship dialectics; segmentation responses meet one dialectical need while ignoring or not satisfying the contradictory dialectical need.

reframing One of the four responses to relationship dialectics; transcends the apparent contradiction between two dialectical poles and reinterprets them as not in tension.

decline. Scholars who study relationships have developed models that describe typical growth and decline trajectories for friendships and romantic relationships.

As we discuss relationship evolution, keep in mind that changes in relationships do not just happen automatically. Rather, particular experiences and events cause relationships to become more or less intimate. These events and experiences are called turning points. A **turning point** moves a relationship toward or away from intimacy. In romantic relationships, turning points that propel a relationship toward intimacy might include first kiss, first "I love you," and meeting parents. Turning points that move a relationship away from closeness might include learning a person has a drug problem or discovering infidelity (Baxter & Bullis, 1986). Turning points that move friendships toward increased closeness include taking a trip together, participating in a common activity, and sharing personal information. Turning points that decrease closeness between friends include moving apart and conflict (Johnson, Wittenberg, Haigh, & Wigley, 2004). As you read about friendship and romantic relationship development, think about turning points that might propel movement.

Friendships   Although friendships can jump to life quickly, usually they unfold through a series of fairly predictable stages. Based on extensive study of friendships, Bill Rawlins (1981, 1994) developed a model of how friendships develop. His model broke friendships into six distinct stages. Rather than enumerating specific stages, however, our discussion will highlight the general flow of friendship as people move from being strangers to friends and—sometimes—back to less personal relationships.

Most friendships begin with interactions based on social roles. We meet potential friends in classes, at work, through membership in teams or clubs, or in an airport, a store, or public event. We might also meet a new person online. In initial interactions, we tend to rely on standard social rules. Generally, we stick with safe topics and exercise care in making disclosures. Disclosures sometimes are made more quickly online than in person because people seem willing to take more risks when not interacting face-to-face.

If we enjoy initial interactions, we're likely to try to get to know them better, so we see if there are sufficient common ground and interests to develop a friendship. A businessperson mentions aspects of family life to see whether an associate wants to get more personal. People on social networking sites often talk about experiences, books, and ideas. Although friendly exchanges are not dramatic, they allow us to explore the potential for a deeper relationship.

Friendships may also form as a result of being in the same environment. For instance, individuals who work in the same office will see each other, engage in conversation, and share colleagues and organizational rules. People who join a chorus or political group will interact and discuss issues that affect the group. The Seeds of Peace program brings together teenagers from regions experiencing conflict such as Israel and Palestine. The teenagers attend a three-week camp where they eat, sleep, play, and engage in discussions with one another. At the end of three weeks, the campers report feeling more positive toward people on "the other side" (Schroeder & Risen, 2014).

If both people enjoy interacting, they may begin to move outside of conventional social roles. Two co-workers might schedule a dinner after work. People who have gotten to know each other over the Internet sometimes develop enough interest to meet

turning point Particular experiences and events that cause relationships to become more or less intimate.

Friends of the Heart and Friends of the Road

Lillian Rubin (1985) has made a career of studying close relationships, particularly friendships. One of her more interesting findings is that there are two basic kinds of friends: friends of the heart and friends of the road.

Friends of the heart are people we meet who become part of us in enduring ways. They are soul mates with whom we feel deeply and permanently connected. If friends of the heart move far away from each other, they often stay in touch and visit. Even if they don't maintain regular contact, they feel deeply woven into each other's lives.

Friends of the road are friends we make and from whom we part as we travel the road of life. We make friends wherever we are, and we provide support, companionship, fun, and so forth. When they or we move, we make no effort to stay in touch or maintain any continuing sense of connection. Friends of the road are people we enjoy for a time, then leave behind.

 MindTap What roles do friends of the road and the heart play in your life?

in person. As people interact more personally, they begin to talk about feelings, values, goals, and attitudes (Yost, 2004). This personal knowledge forms the initial foundation of friendship.

Friendship grows as people show increased involvement and caring. At this point, friends often begin to work out their private ways of relating. When my friend Sue and I were in graduate school, we developed the ritual of calling each day between 6 and 7 P.M. to catch up while we were each fixing dinner. Some friends settle into patterns of getting together for specific things (watching games, shopping, racquetball, Saturday brunch, walking).

The benchmark of an established friendship is the assumption of continuity. Whereas earlier in the relationship people didn't count on getting together unless they made a specific plan, established friends don't have to ask whether they'll get together.

Trust is another criterion of established friendship. Through disclosing private information and responding with acceptance, friends earn each other's trust. In turn, they feel safe sharing even more intimate information and revealing vulnerabilities that they conceal from most people (Galupo & Gonzalez, 2013; Hruschka, 2010; Monsour, 2002). Good friendships may continue indefinitely, in some cases for a lifetime.

Friendships wane when one or both people cease to be committed to them. Sometimes friends drift apart because each is pulled in a different direction by career demands or personal circumstances (Guerrero et al., 2008). This reminds us of the influence of surrounding contexts on relationships. The common interests and experiences that once fueled the friendship begin to dissolve. Casey's commentary illustrates how changes can cause friendships to wither.

 *Casey*

Molly and I became friends our first day in middle school. We were best friends through high school and for our first year at college when we roomed together. Then she got really into the social scene—parties, hookups—and I got into campus-community partnerships. After a while, we were just into such different things that we didn't share any interests and didn't have anything to talk about.

Friendships may also deteriorate because they've run their natural course and become boring or are no longer enriching (Grayling, 2013; Norwood & Duck, 2009). The fact that some friendships don't last a lifetime doesn't mean that they aren't special and important. The ENGAGE! feature on this page points out that friends at a particular time and place in our lives are important to us, even though they aren't forever friends. A third reason friendships end is the violation of rules. Telling a friend's secrets to a third person is a violation if you and your friend had an agreement to keep confidences. Deterioration doesn't always lead to the end of the friendship. Even when serious violations occur, friendships can sometimes be repaired if both friends are committed to rebuilding the relationship.

Friends share activities that allow them to get together regularly.

Romantic Relationships   Like friendships, many romantic relationships follow a similar evolutionary path. Researchers have identified as many as 12 specific stages, but we don't need to know all of these. It's more useful to think of romantic relationships as including three broad stages: escalating, navigating, and deteriorating.

Before forming romantic relationships, each of us has figured out some things about who we are and what qualities we look for in romantic partners. The self that we have developed influences our choice of romantic partners.

The earliest interaction in romantic relationships involves expressing interest (Metts, 2006). This stage involves both taking the initiative with others and responding to invitations they make to us. "I love this kind of music" is an example of an invitation to interact. We may also signal interest nonverbally by smiling or holding eye contact. The meaning of invitational communication is found on the relationship level, not the content level. "I love this kind of music" literally means that a person loves the music. On the relationship level of meaning, however, the message is "I'm interested in talking with you."

The two greatest influences on initial attraction are proximity and similarity. Proximity, or physical nearness, influences initial attraction. We can interact only with people we meet, whether in person or online. Consequently, where we live, work, and socialize and our online social communities constrain the possibilities for relationships. This reminds us that communication is systemic. From our discussion in Chapter 1, recall that the systemic character of communication means that context affects what happens when people transact. Some contexts, such as college campuses, promote meeting potential romantic partners, whereas other contexts are less conducive to meeting and dating.

Similarity is also important in romantic relationships. In the realm of romance, "birds of a feather flock together" seems truer than "opposites attract" (Levin, Taylor & Caudle, 2007; Samp & Palevitz, 2009). The **matching hypothesis** predicts that people will seek relationships with others who closely match their own values, attitudes, social background, and physical attractiveness (Kurt & Sherker, 2003). We may fantasize about relationships with stunning people, but in reality we're likely to pass them by for someone at our level of attractiveness. We also tend to be attracted to people whose values, attitudes, interests, and lifestyles are similar to ours.

matching hypothesis
The prediction that people will seek relationships with others who closely match their values, attitudes, social background, and physical attractiveness.

The Eye of the Beholder

You've heard the expression, "beauty is in the eye of the beholder." When it comes to judging people's desirability, that expression turns out to be accurate—at least once we get beyond first impressions. Researchers who study relationships report that people usually agree on how desirable—handsome, pretty, charismatic—a stranger is when first seeing or meeting the individual. However, if people interact with that individual over time, their judgments of her or his desirability vary widely: The consensus evaporates. That's because interaction with another person allows us to appreciate that person's unique qualities and those outweigh first impressions of desirability (Eastwick & Hunt, 2014). In other words, your unique appeal counts most in the long run.

 MindTap   Has your perception of a person's attractiveness ever changed after you got to know her or him?

As we continue to interact with others, both breadth and depth of disclosure increase. People may talk about difficulties in their lives, reasons for ending previous relationships, dreams for the future, and so forth. Increasingly, couples who are developing intimacy text and talk often as they get to know each other (Samp & Palevitz, 2009).

If increased interaction intensifies attraction, the relationship may escalate. A turning point that signals greater intimacy is that two people begin to spend more and more time together and to rely less on external structures such as movies or parties. During this phase, some couples are almost inseparable. They immerse themselves in the budding relationship and may feel they can't be together enough.

As a romantic relationship heats up, partners often idealize each other. Idealizing occurs when we see a relationship and partner as more wonderful, exciting, and perfect than they really are (Guerrero et al., 2008; Hendrick & Hendrick, 1988, 1996). Yet not everyone idealizes a new romantic partner. A person who is calm and prefers to get to know someone gradually and as a friend first will not experience relationship escalation in the same way as a person who is impulsive and likes to move quickly in relationships. The ENGAGE! feature on page 203 elaborates different styles of loving.

As a relationship escalates, partners also begin to develop relationship vocabularies that include nicknames and private codes. Private language heightens partners' sense of being a special couple. Partners invent words and nicknames for each other, and they develop ways to send private messages in public settings. Private language both reflects and enhances intimacy (Wood, 2006a).

Although online romantic relationships and face-to-face romantic relationships are alike in many respects, they also differ in some ways. Compared to face-to-face relationships, online ones tend to form more rapidly, and they allow more deliberate and sometimes deceptive attempts to control self-presentation. Also, online relationships foster idealized perceptions, so people involved in them may be more likely than partners in face-to-face relationships to see each other in terms of what they want or need. Third, because physical presence is not part of online relationships, partners cannot experience the kind of closeness that is fueled by touch, smell, and taste.

Some couples move onto commitment. Others discover that the magic fades and they part ways. A third option is for couples to reflect and perhaps discuss their relationship's strengths, problems, and potential for the future. After the exhilaration of falling in love is over, partners consider whether they want to transform love into commitment. If so, they work through problems and obstacles to long-term viability. Couples may need to work out differences in religions and conflicts of location and career goals. As the ENGAGE! feature on the next page points out, some couples have additional issues to work through in forming a long-term relationship.

Styles of Loving

Just as people differ in their tastes in food and dress, so do we differ in how we love. Researchers have identified six different styles of loving, each of which is valid, although not all styles are compatible with one another (Hendrick & Hendrick, 1996; Hendrick, Hendrick, Foote, & Slapion-Foote, 1984; Lee, 1973, 1988). Although these researchers refer to styles of "love," you will notice that both love and commitment characterize the styles. See whether you can identify your style of loving in the descriptions that follow:

◆ **Eros** is a style of loving that is passionate, intense, and fast moving. Not confined to sexual passion, eros may be expressed in spiritual, intellectual, or emotional ways.

◆ **Storge** (pronounced "store-gay") is a comfortable, "best friends" kind of love that grows gradually to create a stable, even-keeled companionship.

◆ **Ludus** is a playful, sometimes manipulative style of loving. For ludic lovers, love is a challenge, a puzzle, a game to be relished but not to lead to commitment.

◆ **Mania** is an unsettling style of loving marked by emotional extremes. Manic lovers often are insecure about their value and their partners' commitment.

◆ **Agape** is a selfless kind of love in which a beloved's happiness is more important than one's own. Agapic lovers are generous, unselfish, and devoted.

◆ **Pragma** is a pragmatic and goal-oriented style of loving. Pragmas rely on reason and practical considerations when initially selecting people to love.

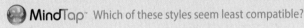

MindTap Which of these styles seem least compatible?

Partners who decide to stay together have options for their long-term commitments. Marriage is the traditional form for long-term romantic commitments. Historically, marriage was available only to heterosexuals, but that is changing rapidly.

But marriage is less popular than it once was in the United States. Whereas 72 percent of U.S. adults were married in 1960, only 51 percent are married today (Jensen, 2014). Many same-sex and different-sex couples cohabit without being married. Between 1996 and 2012, cohabitation rose 170 percent to 7.8 million couples (Angier, 2013b). A good number of married and cohabiting couples, as well as singles, have children. Only 5 percent of reported births were to unmarried women in 1960, yet today 41 percent of reported births were to unmarried women (Jensen, 2014). Increased social acceptance of same-sex couples has allowed more to adopt. Approximately 19 percent of same-sex couples raising children have adopted a child, more than double the number in 2000 (Angier, 2013a). The most stable of all families are headed by gay men who have children together (Angier, 2013a; Stacey, 2011).

Not everyone marries, and not everyone who marries stays married. Approximately 25 percent of households in the United States consist of one person—the greatest number of people living alone in this country's history (Olds & Schwartz, 2010). Marriage is also occurring later than it once did. Between 1970 and 2013, the average age at which men enter a first marriage rose from just over 23 to just under 29; for women, it rose from 21 to 26 ½ (Angier, 2013c). Not being married or cohabiting doesn't necessarily mean

eros One of the six styles of loving; passionate, intense, and erotic.

storge One of the six styles of loving; based on friendship; even-keeled.

ludus One of the six styles of loving; playful and sometimes manipulative.

mania One of the six styles of loving; an obsessive style that often reflects personal insecurity.

agape One of the six styles of loving; it is selfless and focused on the other's happiness.

pragma One of the six styles of loving; based on practical considerations and criteria for attachment.

© karelnoppe/Shutterstock.com

Trust and comfort characterize established friendships.

not having a family. Increasing numbers of people are creating social networks that function as families (Braithwaite et al., 2010; Galupo & Gonzalez, 2013; Galupo et al., 2014). Susan Brown, who directs the National Center for Family and Marriage Research, says that Americans today have a flexible concept of family that includes "whomever we view to be part of our families" (Jensen, 2014). Because we don't all have to try to fit into one form or one model of a family, we are able to create families that suit our values and needs.

For many committed romantic relationships, the longest stage involves maintaining intimacy over time and in the face of changes in partners, the relationship, and surrounding contexts. Couples continuously work through new problems, revisit old ones, and accommodate changes in their individual and joint lives. To use an automotive analogy, maintaining a relationship involves both preventive maintenance and periodic repairs (Galvin, Braithwaite, & Bylund, 2015; Stafford, 2009). In her study of older couples who have stayed together, therapist Maggie Scarf (2008) found that the later years in very long-term marriages can be the happiest, in part because couples have learned to focus on what matters and not to sweat the small stuff. Other research shows that couples who talk issues through and make decisions thoughtfully have higher quality relationships than couples who are less communicative (Parker-Pope, 2014). The nucleus of an established intimate relationship is its **relationship culture**, which is the private world of rules, understandings, meanings, and patterns of interacting that partners create (Wood, 1982).

relationship culture
A private world of rules, understandings, and patterns of acting and interpreting that partners create to give meaning to their relationship; the nucleus of intimacy.

ENGAGE! Stages in the Escalation of Interracial Relationships

Romantic relationships between people of different races and ethnicities are increasing (Angier, 2013b; Jensen, 2014; Rosenfeld, 2009; Smith & Hattery, 2013). In addition to the stages generally followed in developing intimacy, partners in interracial relationships often deal simultaneously with relationship stages prompted by external pressures, such as bias against interracial dating and disapproval by friends and family. The following model (Foeman & Nance, 1999) describes four stages experienced by many interracial romantic partners.

1. Racial awareness: Each partner becomes conscious of his or her racial identity and views of the partner's racial identity. In addition, partners heighten awareness of broad social perspectives on their own and the other's racial groups.

2. Coping: The couple struggles with external pressures, including families' and friends' disapproval, and develops strategies to protect their relationship from external damage.

3. Identity emergence: Partners reject external definitions of who they are and declare their couple identity to others. Partners also develop a definition of the relationship for themselves.

4. Relationship maintenance: The couple works to preserve the relationship as it incorporates new challenges, such as having children, moving to new areas, and entering new social circles.

By the time a couple commits to an intimate relationship, there is a well-established relationship culture, but it is not static. Instead, it continues to evolve throughout the life of the relationship. Especially important in navigating is ongoing small talk, through which partners weave the fabric of their history and their current lives, experiences, and dreams.

The concept of the relationship culture includes how a couple manages relationship dialectics. Chris and Jimmy may do a great many things together, whereas Lana and Brittany emphasize autonomy. Brent and Carmella may be open and expressive, whereas Jacob and Paige prefer more privacy in their marriage. There aren't right and wrong ways to manage dialectics, because individuals and couples differ in their needs and in their preferences for managing tensions between autonomy and connection, openness and privacy, and novelty and routine.

Not all committed relationships endure. Often the first sign that a relationship is in trouble is that one or both partners individually dwells on problems in the relationship and dissatisfactions with the partner. It's easy for focusing on problems to become a self-fulfilling prophecy: As gloomy thoughts snowball and awareness of positive features of the relationship ebbs, partners may actually bring about the failure of their relationship.

There are some general sex and gender differences in what partners brood about during intrapsychic processes (Barstead, Bouchard, & Shih, 2013; Duck & Wood, 2006). For women, unhappiness with a relationship most often arises when communication declines in quality or quantity. Men are more likely to be dissatisfied by specific behaviors or the lack of valued behaviors. In other words, many women feel a relationship is breaking down if "we don't really communicate with each other anymore," whereas men are more likely to feel dissatisfied if "we don't do fun things together anymore."

Our era is witnessing increasing variety in long-term romantic relationships.

There are also sex differences in sources of jealousy. In general, women are more jealous of emotional commitments and men are more jealous of sexual involvements. These gender differences also show up in reactions to online relationships. Women are more jealous of a partner's emotional investment in another relationship whereas men are more jealous of a partner's sexual infidelity (cybersex) (Burchell & Ward, 2011; Groothof, Dijkstra, & Bareids, 2009).

Deteriorating relationships often experience the breakdown of established patterns, understandings, and rules. Partners may stop talking during dinner, no longer bother to call when they are running late, and in other ways depart from rules and patterns in their relational culture. As the fabric of intimacy weakens, dissatisfaction mounts. Because many women are socialized to be sensitive to interpersonal nuances, they are generally more likely than men to notice tensions and early symptoms of relationship distress (Wood, 2015). Whether a troubled relationship ends depends on how committed partners are, whether they perceive attractive alternatives to the relationship, and whether they have the communication skills to resolve problems.

TAKE ACTION...activities
are located at the end of
this chapter and online.

If partners elect to part ways, they decide, either separately or in collaboration, how to explain their problems to friends, co-workers, children, in-laws, and social acquaintances. In addition, each partner must individually make sense of the relationship: what it meant, why it failed, and how it affected them. Typically, we mourn a relationship that has died. Even the person who initiates a breakup often is sad about the failure to realize what seemed possible at one time. Yet sadness may be accompanied by other, more positive outcomes from breakups. Ty Tashiro and Patricia Frazier (2003) surveyed undergraduates who had recently broken up with a romantic partner. They found that breakups generate not only distress but also personal growth. People reported that breaking up gave them new insights into themselves, improved family relationships, and clarified their ideas about future partners.

Our discussion describes how many people experience the evolution of romantic relationships. However, not everyone follows the pattern presented here. Some long-term partners experience falling in love again or experience problems that lead to brooding and dissatisfaction. Couples may slide into deterioration and then invest to revive intimacy.

Digital Media and Personal Relationships

In the foregoing pages, we have already noted some of the ways in which digital media affect personal relationships. Before digital media existed, our choices of friends and romantic partners were largely limited to the people we encountered face-to-face. In addition, the face-to-face process of getting to know others requires time and money to learn what we can now learn quickly through online profiles and searches. Once friends and couples in long-distance relationships relied on letters, expensive plane tickets, and long-distance calls to maintain contact, whereas today we can Skype and text to stay in touch (Tong & Walther, 2011). In many ways, social media have made it far easier to form and maintain romantic relationships.

At the same time, social media have introduced new challenges for people seeking romance. Both sexes tend to misrepresent themselves when posting online profiles (Hall, Park, Song, & Cody, 2010). People may give false information about their physical attractiveness, and people who are less attractive are more likely to embellish their photographs and self-descriptions (Toma & Hancock, 2010).

Another concern about social media is the potential for cyberstalking. Former boyfriends and girlfriends may monitor your online communication and harass you or interfere with your communication with other people. In addition, someone you meet online can become obsessed with you and, in extreme cases, can engage in stalking you online, following your every move and imposing himself or herself into your life.

It's easy to friend someone on Facebook, but some media observers question whether online friendships are as rich and close as face-to-face friendships. William Deresiewicz (2009) asks, "If we have 768 'friends,' in what sense do we have any?" And he then suggests that "once we decided to become friends with everyone, we would forget how to be friends with anyone" (p. B6). Contrasting online friendships with traditional, face-to-face ones, Deresiewicz notes that the former are less personal and less adapted to individuals. He thinks many online friendships are "just broadcasting our stream of consciousness to all 500 of our friends at once" because "we're too busy to spare our friends more time than it takes to text" (p. B9). Deresiewicz may be exaggerating, but it might be worth your time to reflect on the intimacy you have with online and face-to-face friends.

Guidelines for Communicating in Personal Relationships

To sustain fulfilling personal relationships, partners rely on communication to deal with internal tensions and external pressures. We'll consider four specific guidelines to help friends and romantic partners sustain satisfying relationships.

Adapt Communication to Manage Distance

Geographic separation can be difficult for friends and romantic couples. Two of the greatest problems for long-distance commitments are the lack of daily communication about small events and issues, and unrealistic expectations about interaction when partners are geographically together. Greg's commentary offers an example of both of these problems.

 *Greg*

When Annie and I first moved to different cities, I don't know whether it was harder being apart or together. I missed her so much when we were apart for weeks at a time, and I really missed just being together in a laid-back kind of way. But whenever we were together, we both felt really pressured to be together every minute and not to have any disagreements or bad times. That's just not possible, and expecting it really caused us a lot of grief. Now, we are careful to call and stay in touch with e-mail so that we feel part of each other's regular lives. And we've learned that it's okay to have some private time even when we're together for only a few days.

The first problem—not being able to share small talk and daily routines—is a major loss, especially for people who can't afford phone plans with unlimited text and talk. As we have seen, communication about ordinary topics weaves partners' lives together. Mundane conversations between friends and romantic partners are the foundation of relationships.

A second common problem is unrealistic expectations for time together. Because partners have so little time when they are physically together, they often believe that every moment must be perfect. They feel there should be no conflict and that they should spend every minute together. Yet this is an unrealistic expectation. The need for autonomy may even be greater for long-distance couples because partners are used to living alone and have established independent rhythms that may not mesh well.

The good news is that these problems don't necessarily sabotage long-distance romance. Many couples maintain satisfying commitments despite geographic separation. Digital media have greatly enhanced our ability to stay in touch despite distance.

Ensure Equity in Family Relationships

Today, most adults work outside the home. Therefore, partners in a relationship must balance investments in two careers with investments in maintaining the relationship. According to **equity theory**, people are happier and more satisfied with equitable relationships than with inequitable ones. In equitable relationships, partners perceive that the benefits and costs of being in the relationship are about equal for each of

equity theory The theory that people are happier and more satisfied with equitable relationships than inequitable ones. In equitable relationships, partners perceive the benefits and costs of the relationship as about equal for each of them.

them. When we think we are investing more than our partner is, we tend to be resentful and angry; when it seems our partner is investing more than we are, we're likely to feel guilty (Guerrero, La Valley, & Farinelli, 2008).

Although few partners demand moment-to-moment equality, most of us want our relationships to be equitable over time (Wood, 2011). Equity has multiple dimensions. We may evaluate the fairness of financial, emotional, physical, and other contributions to a relationship. One area that strongly affects satisfaction of spouses and cohabiting partners is equity in housework and child care. Inequitable division of domestic obligations fuels dissatisfaction and resentment, both of which harm intimacy (Coontz, 2013, 2014).

Traditionally, women were assigned care of the home and family because men were more likely to be the primary or only wage earners. That is no longer true. Today, nearly two thirds of women in the United States work outside of the home (Peters & Wessel, 2014), and approximately one fourth of women in heterosexual partnerships earn more money than their male partners (Adams, 2014; Ream, 2012). Unfortunately, divisions of family and home responsibilities inadequately reflect changes in employment. Even when both partners in heterosexual relationships work outside the home, in most dual-career families women do most of the child care and homemaking (Bianchi, Sayer, Milkie, & Robinson, 2012; Wood, 2015b). In her commentary, Molly gives us insight into the resentment that can grow when both partners work outside the home but one does most of the work in and for the home.

 **Molly**

It really isn't fair when both spouses work outside the home but only one of them takes care of the home and kids. For years, that was how Jake's and my marriage worked, no matter how much I tried to talk with him about a fairer arrangement. Finally, I had just had it, so I quit doing everything. Groceries didn't get bought, laundry piled up, and he didn't have clean shirts, he didn't remember his mother's birthday (and for the first time ever, I didn't remind him), bills didn't get paid. After a while, he suggested we talk about a system we could both live with.

How do gay and lesbian partners manage domestic responsibilities? According to existing research, they strive for and achieve more balanced power than heterosexual couples. Gay and lesbian couples report a greater desire for shared power and decision making than do heterosexual couples (Hunter, 2012).

Not only do women usually do more of the actual labor of maintaining a home and caring for children, they also tend to assume a greater portion of **psychological responsibility**, which involves remembering, planning, and coordinating domestic activities (Hochschild, 2003). Parents may alternate taking children to the doctor, but it is usually the mother who remembers when the kids need checkups, makes the appointments, and reminds the father to take the children. Both partners sign cards and give gifts, but in many families it is women who assume responsibility for remembering the birthdays and buying the cards and gifts. Successful long-term relationships in our era require partners to communicate collaboratively to design equitable divisions of responsibility.

The consequences of inequity are substantial. Women who do most of the homemaking and child-care tasks are often stressed, fatigued, and susceptible to illness (Hochschild, 2003), and they are at a disadvantage in their paid work because they have such heavy responsibilities at home (McDonald, Phipps, & Lethbridge, 2005). In addition, the inequity of the arrangement is a primary source of relationship dissatisfaction and instability.

psychological responsibility The obligation to remember, plan, and coordinate domestic work and child care. In general, women assume psychological responsibility for child care and housework even when both partners share in the actual doing of tasks.

SALLY FORTH © 1998 KING FEATURES SYNDICATE

To work out an equitable division of domestic labor requires more than agreeing that each partner will do a fair share. Partners must also agree on a standard of housekeeping. Many couples argue because one person wants floors vacuumed and beds changed more often than the other person. The person with the higher standard may feel frustrated that her or his partner doesn't do more while the person with the lower standard resents being nagged to do work he or she considers unimportant (Wood, 2011). There's no right or wrong standard for domestic labor, but family members need to agree on one.

Avoid Intimate Partner Violence

Intimate partner violence is experienced and perpetrated by both sexes and by gays, lesbians, straights, and transgender people (Douglas, 2012; Pear, 2012). It is also experienced and perpetrated by members of all races and economic classes. Twenty-five percent of U.S. women have been violently attacked by husbands or boyfriends, and one U.S. woman dies every six hours from a partner's violence (Kristof, 2014). Worldwide, at least 30 percent of women have been victims of intimate partner violence ("Prevalence of," 2013). Violence is high not only in marriages but also in dating and cohabiting relationships (Hoffman, 2012). In addition to physical abuse, verbal and emotional brutality poison altogether too many relationships.

Among heterosexuals, intimate partner violence is inflicted primarily by men against women. In fact, intimate partner violence is the most common form of violence committed against women in the United States (Haynes, 2009). Men make up an estimated 15 percent of all victims of intimate partner violence (France, 2006). Although a majority of perpetrators of intimate partner violence are men, we need to

ENGAGE!

A New Job for Dad

The recession that began in 2008 has propelled changes in men's involvement in home life. Between 2008 and 2010, millions of Americans lost jobs, and the majority of them were men. Although some of these men are again employed, others are not. In 2014, one in six men in prime earning years is out of work in the United States (Peters & Wessel, 2014). For many of these men, the jobs they once had no longer exist due to globalization and technological innovation that are altering work opportunities (Peters & Wessel, 2014).

According to a recent study by the Pew Research Center, 2 million fathers are now stay-at-home dads by choice or necessity (Ludden, 2014). Laid off after 20 years in a Fortune 500 company, Andrew Emery says, "It was a big part of my identity; it's who you are. It took me a long time to fill in the blank when people asked me what I do" (Kershaw, 2009, p. E6). Yet, after the initial adjustment, many men discover opportunities and satisfaction in being full-time fathers. In fact, many of them are hoping to find reemployment in careers that enable them to spend more time with their children (Ludden, 2014; Noelle, 2011).

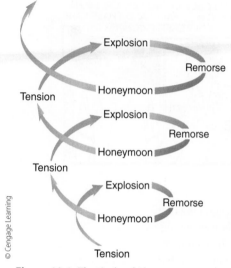

Figure 10.1 The Cycle of Abuse

© Cengage Learning

remember that the vast majority of men do not inflict violence on girl-friends and wives, and they would not consider doing so.

A rising form of intimate partner violence is stalking, which is repeated, intrusive behavior that is uninvited and unwanted, that seems obsessive, and that makes the target afraid or concerned for her or his safety. Stalking is particularly easy on campuses because it isn't difficult to learn others' routines. Social networking sites such as MySpace and Facebook give stalkers more ways to learn about (potential) victims' habits and patterns (Spitzack & Cupach, 2015).

Violence seldom stops without intervention. Instead, in most cases it follows a predictable cycle: Tension mounts in the abuser; the abuser explodes, becoming violent; the abuser then is remorseful and loving; the victim feels loved and reassured that the relationship is working; then tension mounts anew, and the cycle begins again (Figure 10.1). Often, the level of violence increases with each new iteration of the cycle.

Communication and violence are related in two ways. Most obviously, patterns of communication between couples, and abusers' patterns of intrapersonal communication, can fuel tendencies toward violence. Some partners deliberately annoy and taunt each other, a pattern that can lead to extreme violence. Also, the language that abusers use to describe physical assaults on partners includes denial, trivializing the harm done, and blaming the partner or circumstances for "making me do it" (Johnson, 2006; Wood, 2004b). These communication patterns allow abusers to deny their offenses, justify unjustifiable actions, and cast responsibility outside themselves.

Violent relationships are *not* the fault of victims. Nobody deserves violence. If you know or suspect that someone you care about is a victim of abuse, don't ignore the situation, and don't assume it's none of your business. It is an act of friendship to notice and offer to help. Victims of violence must make the ultimate decision about what to do, but the support and concern of friends can help them.

Insist on Safer Sex

In the HIV/AIDS era, sexual activities pose serious, even deadly, threats. To date, 617,000 people in the United States have died of AIDS (Notable Numbers, 2011). The most common ways to contract the virus are through sex with a hookup, casual date, or serious romantic partner or through sharing of needles. Worldwide, the numbers are even more startling. Every single day, an estimated 7,000 people become infected with HIV (Notable Numbers, 2011). And HIV/AIDS is not the only STD. Chlamydia cases are increasing as are cases of genital warts (Dennis & Wood, 2012).

Despite these dangers, a great many people still don't practice safer sex, which includes abstinence, restricting sexual activity to a single partner who has been tested and found to be free of HIV and other STDs, and using latex condoms.

Communication scholars have found two primary reasons why people don't practice safer sex. First, ironically, many people find it more embarrassing to talk about sex than to engage in it (Collins & Fauci, 2010). They find it awkward to ask direct questions of partners ("Have you been tested for HIV?" "Are you having sex with anyone else?") or to make direct requests of partners ("I want you to wear a condom," "I would like you to be tested for HIV before we have sex"). Because about 25 percent of people who are HIV positive are not aware of their medical infection, tests are imperative before having sexual relationships (Centers for Disease Control and Prevention, 2011). Naturally, it's difficult to talk explicitly about sex and the dangers of STDs. However, it is far more difficult to live with HIV or another disease or the knowledge that you infected another person.

A second reason people sometimes fail to negotiate safer sex is that alcohol or other drugs have diminished their rational thought and control. Alcohol and other drugs loosen inhibitions, including appropriate concerns about personal safety.

Good communication skills facilitate negotiating safer sex. It is more constructive to say, "I feel unsafe having unprotected sex" than "Without a condom, you could give me an STD" (note that the first statement uses *I*-language, whereas the second one uses *you*-language). Relationship language fosters a positive communication climate; for example, talk about *our safety* and *our relationship* when negotiating sexual activity. People who care about themselves and their partners are honest about their sexual histories and assertive about safer sex practices.

Test Your Knowledge about Sexually Transmitted Diseases

Many people hold dangerous misunderstandings about sexually transmitted diseases (STDs). Here's a chance for you to test your knowledge against the facts (Centers for Disease Control and Prevention, 2011, 2014; Dennis & Wood, 2012; "Notable Numbers," 2011).

- **Misconception:** If I'm tested for HIV and make sure any sexual partner is, I'm safe.
- **Get the Facts:** HIV is not the only STD, and it's not the most common. Other STDs are genital warts, genital herpes, hepatitis B, chlamydia, gonorrhea, human papillomavirus (HPV), syphilis, and trichomoniasis. One in 20 people will get hepatitis B in his or her lifetime, and 15 to 25 percent of those who do will die from liver disease.
- **Misconception:** I'm not taking much of a chance because few people have STDs.
- **Get the Facts:** By age 25, one of two sexually active youths will contract an STD. More than 65 million Americans are currently living with an STD, and 15 million new cases are diagnosed each year.
- **Misconception:** STDs affect older people.
- **Get the Facts:** Half of all new STDs occur in people 15 to 24 years old. Each year, one in four teens contracts an STD. Among blacks, 50 percent of 14- to 19-year-olds contract an STD.
- **Misconception:** The incidence of STDs is declining.
- **Get the Facts:** Some STDs, such as genital warts, are actually increasing.
- **Misconception:** I can't catch an STD if I have only oral sex.
- **Get the Facts:** Think again. You can catch STDs from oral, anal, or vaginal sexual activity.
- **Misconception:** I could tell if someone had an STD because there are symptoms.
- **Get the Facts:** Many STDs have no symptoms or no early ones. For instance, HPV, which 50 percent of sexually active people will contract at some point, often has no symptoms.
- **Misconception:** STDs can be treated, so there aren't serious consequences even if I do get one.
- **Get the Facts:** Some can be treated. Some are resistant to treatment. And because some have no symptoms, people may not seek treatment until it's too late.
- **Misconception:** I see a doctor regularly, so I am tested for STDs.
- **Get the Facts:** Most doctors do not routinely test for STDs.
- **Misconception:** Other than HIV, STDs don't have major consequences.
- **Get the Facts:** Because STDs often have no symptoms, they may go untreated for some time. Effects of STDs include infertility, blindness, liver cancer, increased vulnerability to HIV, and death.

Learn more about STDs by going to the book's online resources for this chapter.

Summary

In this chapter, we've explored communication in personal relationships, which are defined by commitment, uniqueness, relationship dialectics, relationship rules, and interaction with surrounding contexts. We traced the typical evolutionary paths of friendships and romances by noting how partners communicate during escalating, stabilizing, and declining trajectories of personal relationships. We noted that social media facilitate relationships in many ways, yet can also be used to harm relationships in other ways.

In the final section of the chapter, we considered four guidelines for friends and romantic partners. The communication principles and skills we have discussed in this and previous chapters can help us meet the challenges of sustaining intimacy across geographic distance, creating equitable relationships, resisting violence, and negotiating safer sex. Good communication skills are essential to managing these challenges so that we, our intimates, and the relationships we create survive and thrive over time.

Experience Communication Case Study

Abuse

Apply what you've learned in this chapter by analyzing the following case study, using the accompanying questions as a guide. These questions and a video of the case study are also available online with your MindTap Speech for *Communication Mosaics*.

Amy met Hailley at the beginning of the school year. Amy was drawn to Hailley because she seemed confident and positive. Over several months, the two of them became good friends, sharing high and low points about school, family, and dates.

Two months ago, Hailley started dating Dan, a man who dropped out of college after two years and who now works as a waiter. At first, Hailley seemed happy with Dan, but then she started changing. She's become less extroverted and a lot less positive.

Often, when Amy suggests doing something together, Hailley says she can't because Dan might come over or call, and he doesn't like her not to be available to him. When Amy sees them together, she notices that he doesn't treat her with respect and often criticizes her harshly. For example, when Hailley said something to Dan when he was on his cell phone, he shouted, "Don't talk to me. I'm on the phone." Later, when Hailey dropped some papers, Dan said harshly, "You are so clumsy!"

Amy is concerned that Hailley may be in a relationship that is verbally and physically abusive. Amy thinks that Dan is damaging Hailley's self-concept, and she wants to help.

Amy: I'm just worried about you. I don't like the way he treats you.

Hailley: Because he called me clumsy? I am clumsy, and besides, if I do something stupid, I can't expect him not to notice.

Amy: But he doesn't show any respect for you at all.

Hailley: Well, he's a guy. He says what he's thinking. I know a lot of people's boyfriends like that. Besides, I don't think there's anything wrong with Dan. I think I just have to stop doing things that make him mad.

© Cengage Learning

1. If you were Hailley's friend, what responsibilities would you have, if any, for helping her?

2. If you were Dan's friend, what might you say to alter his behaviors?

3. How does the concept of reflected appraisal, discussed in Chapter 9, apply to this case?

Key Concepts

Practice defining the chapter's terms by using online flashcards.

agape, 203
autonomy/connection, 197
commitment, 195
equity theory, 207
eros, 203
investment, 195
ludus, 203
mania, 203
matching hypothesis, 201
neutralization, 198
novelty/predictability, 197
openness/closedness, 198
passion, 195

personal relationship, 194
pragma, 203
psychological responsibility, 208
reframing, 198
relationship culture, 204
relationship dialectics, 197
rules, 195
segmentation, 198
separation, 198
social relationship, 194
storge, 203
turning point, 199

Review, Reflect, Extend

The Reflect and Discuss and Take Action features that follow will help you review, reflect on, and extend the information and ideas presented in this chapter. These resources, and a diverse selection of additional study tools, are also available online at the MindTap Speech for *Communication Mosaics*.

Reflect, personalize, and apply what you've learned

Reflect and Discuss

1. Think about the distinction between love and commitment and the role each plays in personal relationships. Describe relationships in which commitment is present but love is not. Describe relationships in which love exists but not commitment. What can you conclude about the impact of each?

2. As a class, discuss differences in the goals and rules for friendships and romantic relationships. Does comparing the two kinds of relationships give you any insight into the difficulties that commonly arise when two people who have been friends become romantically involved? What are the difficulties of trying to be friends with someone with whom you've been romantically involved?

TAKE ACTION

1. Good Endings[1]

We've all been through bad breakups. Anger, frustration, confusion, and a sense of betrayal are feelings that can prompt us to behave less well than we should when ending a relationship. But what would a good breakup look like? As a class, create a script for effective and ethical communication during the breakup of a serious romantic relationship.

2. Connect with Others in Long-Distance Relationships

If you are in a long-distance relationship, you can learn a lot from others who are or have been in one. There are Web sites and online communities devoted to long-distance relationships. Most of them offer advice, and some feature stories in which people who are in or have been in long-distance relationships share experiences and ideas about what worked and didn't work. The online resources for this chapter provide a link to a site that offers apps specifically designed for long-distance relationships.

Recommended Resources

1. Visit an online dating service. Identify qualities men and women claim they have and qualities men and women are looking for in romantic partners. What similarities and differences can you identify?

2. Many men as well as women are committed to ending violence against women. To learn more about men who are committed to stopping violence, go to the online resources for this chapter.

3. View the film *About a Boy* (2002), directed by Paul and Chris Weitz. The story is about a surprising and unusual friendship between a selfish single man and a lonely boy. The central themes are friendship and support.

---

[1]I am indebted to Emily Brooke Anzicek, who is on the faculty at Bowling Green State University, for developing this exercise and allowing me to include it in this chapter.

11

Communication in Groups and Teams

Never doubt that a small group of thoughtful, committed people can change the world. Indeed, it is the only thing that ever has.

—Margaret Mead

What is the most important key to effective group work?

 Mind Tap

Learning Objectives

Topics Covered in This Chapter	After studying this chapter, you should be able to …
Understanding Communication in Groups and Teams	Differentiate between the six types of groups and teams included in this chapter.
Potential Limitations and Strengths of Groups	Contrast potential group limitations with potential group strengths.
Features of Small Groups	Use examples from a small group of which you are or were a member to describe the five features of groups presented in this chapter.
Methods of Group Decision Making	Given a small group problem to solve, determine which of the two common methods to use: the standard agenda or the nominal group technique.
Digital Media and Groups	List six best practices for working in virtual groups or teams.
Guidelines for Communicating in Groups and Teams	When called upon to participate in a work group, create an action plan to implement this chapter's guidelines for communicating in groups and teams.

Mind Tap

Start with a quick engagement activity and **review** the chapter Learning Objectives.

◆ If a patient wants to die when medical procedures could save her or him, should doctors follow the patient's wishes?

◆ A woman whose health makes carrying a fetus dangerous to her nonetheless wants to become pregnant, and she asks doctors for fertility treatment. Should doctors provide the treatment?

Imagine trying to answer these questions. Imagine that you have only eight minutes to consider each question and come up with a response. And imagine that how you handle these questions determines whether you get into medical school. For many people aspiring to attend medical school, this is reality, not imagination. A number of medical schools, including those at Stanford, Los Angeles, and Cincinnati, have decided that the standard criteria for admissions decisions to med school—grades, test scores, and the traditional interview—are ineffective in screening out applicants who lack the communication skills to be good doctors (Harris, 2011). No longer is a doctor the sole and unquestioned expert. Instead, most doctors today are members of health-care teams, so the ability to work collaboratively is critical. Doctors who bully nurses, don't listen to patients, and are too dogmatic to consider other points of view are poor team members. In fact, as many as 98,000 preventable deaths each year have been traced to poor communication among doctors, nurses, and other members of health-care teams (Gupta, 2012; Harris, 2011).

To assess communication skills for teamwork, applicants have nine eight-minute interviews in which they discuss specific situations with interviewers. There are no right or wrong answers to the questions. Rather, applicants are assessed on how well they communicate with interviewers. Are they overly opinionated? Do they listen well to others? Are they comfortable working collaboratively? Do they encourage others to offer ideas? How do they handle disagreement, which is common among members of health-care teams? Teamwork is so critical to effective patient-care today that a number of medical schools not only consider the ability to collaborate in making admissions decisions, but also require students to take courses in teamwork.

Do you enjoy working on groups and teams? If so, you have lots of company. If not, you also have lots of company. For every person who is enthusiastic about group work, there is another person who dreads or merely tolerates it. Regardless of how much you enjoy working in groups, chances are groups will be part of your life. Pick up any newspaper, and you will see announcements for social groups, volunteer service committees, personal support groups, health teams, focus groups run by companies trying out new products, and political action coalitions. If you go online, you'll encounter a range of groups that you can join to give and get personal support, exchange information, and share interests. Most workplaces have both ongoing groups or committees and short-term ones that form to address a particular issue and disband when the job is done.

In this chapter, we'll see how basic communication skills covered in Part II apply to interaction in groups and teams. We begin by defining groups and teams and tracing their rising popularity. Second, we identify potential strengths and weaknesses of groups and teams. Third, we consider aspects of groups that affect communication. Fourth, we identify two effective methods of group decision making. The fifth section of this chapter considers how groups and teams make use of digital media. Finally, we discuss guidelines for effective participation in groups.

Understanding Communication in Groups and Teams

There are many kinds of groups, each with distinctive goals and communication patterns. Social groups provide us with conversation and recreation with people we enjoy. Communication in social groups tends to be relaxed, informal, and more focused on interpersonal climate than tasks. Personal growth and therapy groups enable people to deal with significant issues and problems in a supportive context. Communication aims to help members clarify and address issues in their lives. Task groups exist to solve problems, develop policies, or achieve other substantive goals. The communication of task groups concentrates on evidence, reasoning, and decision making, as well as on organizing and maintaining a healthy climate for interaction.

Groups and teams are central to work life in our era.

Although different types of groups have distinct primary purposes, most groups include three kinds of communication: *climate communication*, *procedural communication*, and *task communication*. For example, social groups devote the bulk of their talk to climate communication, yet they often move into task discussion, as when one friend asks another for help in solving a problem. Task groups typically include some climate communication and a good deal of procedural communication, and personal growth and therapy groups include task communication to deal with members' issues, climate communication to create and sustain support and trust, and procedural communication to manage time and move conversation along.

Communication in groups and teams involves the basic processes we discussed in earlier chapters. For example, constructive group communication requires that members use effective verbal and nonverbal communication, check perceptions with one another, listen mindfully, build good climates, and adapt communication to each other and various group goals and situations.

Defining Groups and Teams

What is a group? Are six people standing in line to buy tickets a group? Are four businesspeople in an airport lounge a group? Both examples describe collections of individuals but not groups. Unless people are interacting and involved in a collective endeavor, a group does not exist.

For a group to exist, the people must interact, be interdependent, have a common goal, and share some rules of conduct (Harris & Sherblom, 2010; Lumsden, Lumsden, & Wiethoff, 2009; Rothwell, 2015). Thus,

ENGAGE!

Virtual Teams

Increasingly, teams do their work virtually. Communication researchers Erik Timmerman and Craig Scott (2006) point out that the degree of virtualness varies. Some teams work face-to-face part of the time and online part of the time. Some teams rely entirely on videoconferencing, whereas other teams never even see each other but communicate via e-mail and groupware. Across teams with different degrees of virtualness, those that communicate effectively, especially in terms of members' responsiveness to one another, have the highest cohesiveness and greatest member satisfaction.

Mark Edward Atkinson/Jupiter Images

we can define a **group** as three or more people who interact over time, depend on one another, and follow shared rules of conduct to reach a common goal. In some instances, individual members' goals are in tension with the collective goal, but a common goal still exists. Group members are interdependent—they need one another to achieve something, such as develop a policy for the workplace, play a sport, or promote personal growth.

A **team** is a special kind of group characterized by different, complementary resources of members and by a strong sense of collective identity (Rothwell, 2015). Like all groups, teams involve interaction, interdependence, shared rules, and common goals. Yet teams are distinct from groups in two respects. First, teams consist of people who bring different and specialized resources to a common project. Second, teams develop greater interdependence and a stronger sense of collective identity than many groups (Lumsden et al., 2009).

Groups and teams develop rules that members understand and follow. You will recall from Chapter 4 that constitutive rules state what counts as what. For example, in some groups disagreement counts as a positive sign of involvement and critical thinking, whereas other groups regard disagreement as negative. Regulative rules regulate how, when, and with whom we interact. For instance, a group might have the regulative rules that members do not interrupt each other and that disagreements within the group are not discussed with outsiders.

 *Mieko*

When I first came here to go to school, I felt very alone. I met some other students from Japan, and we formed a group to help us feel at home in America. For the first year, that group was most important to us because we felt uprooted. The second year, it was not so important, because we'd all started finding ways to fit in here, and we felt more at home. The third year, we decided not to be a group anymore. The reason we wanted a group no longer existed.

The Rise of Groups and Teams

Today, groups and teams are more than ever a part of work life (Fujishin, 2013; Harris & Sherblom, 2010). Whether you are an attorney working with a litigation team, a healthcare professional on a medical team, or a teacher on a team assigned to reduce drop outs, your professional success and advancement will be linked to how effectively you communicate in groups. Because task groups and teams are especially common, we'll concentrate on them in this chapter. Of course, much of the information we'll discuss pertains to other types of groups as well. We'll identify six kinds of task groups that are prevalent in professional and civic life.

Project Teams   Many professions rely on project teams, which consist of people who have expertise related to different facets of a project and who combine their knowledge and skills to accomplish a common goal. For example, to launch a new product, pharmaceutical companies often put together product teams that include scientists and doctors who understand the technical character of the new drug, along with other personnel who have expertise in marketing, product design, advertising, and customer relations. Working together, team members develop a coherent, coordinated plan for testing, packaging, advertising, and marketing the new product.

group More than two people who interact over time, who are interdependent, and who follow shared rules of conduct to reach a common goal. A team is one type of group.

team A special kind of group characterized by different and complementary resources of members and by a strong sense of collective identity. All teams are groups, but not all groups are teams.

Focus Groups   Focus groups are used to find out what people think about a specific idea, product, issue, or person. Focus groups are a mainstay of advertisers who want to understand attitudes, preferences, and responses of people whom they want to buy their product, vote for their candidate, and so forth. How do 21- to 25-year-olds respond to a name that might being considered for a new microbrew? How do retirees respond to a planned advertising campaign for cruises? What do middle-income citizens think of a mayoral candidate's environmental record? A focus group is guided by a leader or facilitator who develops a list of questions in advance and uses these to encourage participants to express ideas, beliefs, feelings, and perceptions relevant to the topic.

Brainstorming Groups   When idea generation is the goal, brainstorming groups are appropriate. The goal of **brainstorming** is to come up with as many ideas as possible. Because criticism tends to stifle creativity, brainstorming groups bar criticism and encourage imaginative, even wild, thinking. (Rules for brainstorming appear in Figure 11.1.)

Perhaps you are concerned that brainstorming might produce unrealistic ideas. That's not really a problem, because evaluative discussion follows brainstorming. During evaluation, members work together to appraise the ideas generated through brainstorming. Members discard impractical ideas, refine weak or undeveloped contributions, consolidate related suggestions, and further discuss promising ones. To set a tone for creative communication, leaders or facilitators of brainstorming groups express energy, stoke members' imaginations, and respond enthusiastically to ideas.

Advisory Groups   The solitary manager, president, or CEO who relies only on his or her own ideas is not functional in modern life. Instead, most high-level decision makers rely on advisory groups to provide expert briefing on the range of issues relevant to decisions they must make. Advisory groups allow decision makers to benefit from other experts' information and advice pertinent to developing effective policies and making informed decisions.

Teamwork Lacking in the Operating Room

Reports of errors in surgery are not uncommon. Have you ever wondered how a sponge could be left inside a patient or the wrong limb operated on? One contributor to surgical errors is poor teamwork among those working in the operating room. A survey of more than 2,100 surgeons, anesthesiologists, and nurses at 60 hospitals showed that many teams suffer from weak teamwork (Nagourney, 2006). Doctors' disregard for nurses' expertise was one of the most commonly cited dynamics that undermined effective teamwork.

brainstorming A group technique for generating potential solutions to a problem; the free flow of ideas without immediate criticism.

- ◆ Do not evaluate ideas in any way. Both verbal and nonverbal criticism are inappropriate.

- ◆ Record all ideas on a board or easel so that all members of the group can see them.

- ◆ Go for quantity: The more ideas, the better.

- ◆ Build on ideas. An idea presented by one member of the group may stimulate an extension by another member. This is desirable.

- ◆ Encourage creativity. Welcome wild and even preposterous ideas. An idea that seems wacky may lead to other ideas that are more workable.

© Cengage Learning

Figure 11.1 Rules for Brainstorming

Young Presidents Organization

In 1950, Ray Hickok opened the first meeting of the Young Presidents' Organization (YPO). Today, there are more than 300 YPO chapters, which include 20,000 members in 100 countries. Members have included politicians such as Lloyd Bentsen and Bo Callaway, financial superstars such as Sir John Templeton and Steve Forbes, and U.S. postmaster general Bob Tisch (McNees, 1999). The premise of YPO is simple: By engaging each other, peers can help each other become better leaders. In YPO meetings, members share experiences, help one another cope with the unusual pressures and pleasures of early business success, and coach one another through career stages and challenges. To learn more about YPO, go to the book's online resources for this chapter.

Quality Improvement Teams   **Quality improvement teams** (also called *continuous quality improvement teams*) include three or more people who have distinct skills or knowledge and who work together to improve quality in an organization (Lumsden, Lumsden, & Wiethoff, 2009). These teams mix not only people with differing expertise but also people at different levels in an organization's hierarchy. Thus, a secretary may contribute as much as a manager to a team charged to improve office productivity.

For quality improvement teams to be effective, management must support their work and recommendations. Nothing is more frustrating than to be asked to invest energy in making recommendations and then to have the recommendations ignored. When given support, quality improvement teams often generate impressive and creative solutions to organizational problems such as high costs, on-the-job accidents, and low worker morale.

Decision-Making Groups   A sixth kind of task group has authority to make decisions. What should be the company's policy on medical leave? What benefits and personnel should be cut to achieve a 15 percent decrease in annual expenses? Some decision-making groups are ongoing; they meet on a regular basis to make decisions about training and development, public relations, budgets, and other matters. Later in this chapter, we'll discuss two methods commonly used by decision-making groups.

Potential Limitations and Strengths of Groups

A great deal of research has compared individual and group decision making. As you might expect, the research identifies potential weaknesses and potential strengths of groups.

Potential Limitations of Groups

One significant disadvantage of group discussion is the time needed for the group process. Operating solo, an individual can think through ideas quickly. In group discussion, however, all members have an opportunity to voice ideas and respond to the ideas others put forward. It takes substantial time for each person to express thoughts, clarify misunderstandings, and respond to questions or criticisms. In addition, groups take time to deliberate about alternative courses of action. Therefore, group discussion generally isn't a wise choice for routine or formulaic work or for emergency tasks. When creativity and thoroughness are important, however, the value of groups may be more important than the time they take.

Groups also have the potential to suppress individuals and encourage conformity. This can happen in two ways. First, conformity pressures may exist when a majority

quality improvement teams A group in which people from different departments or areas in an organization collaborate to solve problems, meet needs, or increase the quality of work life. Also called *continuous quality improvement team*.

has an opinion different from that of a minority or a single member. Holding out for your point of view is difficult when most or all of your peers have a different one. In effective groups, however, all members understand and resist conformity pressures. They realize that the majority is sometimes wrong and the minority, even just one person, is sometimes right. Members have an ethical responsibility to encourage expression of diverse ideas and open debate about different views.

Conformity pressures may also arise when one member is extremely charismatic or has more power or prestige than other members. Even if that person is all alone in a point of view, other members may conform to it. Sometimes a high-status member doesn't intend to influence others and may not overtly exert pressure. However, the other members still perceive the status, and it may affect their judgments. Often neither the high-status person nor other members are consciously aware of pressures to conform. Lance's commentary illustrates how a member who is perceived to have special status can suppress others' individual thought and creativity.

 ## Lance

I used to belong to a creative writing group where all of us helped each other improve our writing. At first, all of us were equally vocal, and we had a lot of good discussions and even disagreements that helped us grow as writers. But then one member of the group got a story accepted by a big magazine, and all of a sudden we thought of her as a better writer than any of us. She didn't act any different, but we saw her as more accomplished, so when she said something, everybody listened and nobody disagreed. It was like a wet blanket on our creativity because her opinion just carried too much weight once she got published.

Another potential disadvantage of group work is the possibility of **social loafing**, which exists when members of a group exert less effort than they would if they worked alone (Hoon & Tan, 2008). If an individual is charged with a task and the task doesn't get done, the individual can be held accountable. When a group is charged with a task, however, members may have less of a sense of accountability for the end product. They may work less hard because each member thinks that no one will notice if she or he slacks off. Scott Snook (2000), a professor at West Point, asserts that social loafing contributed to the accidental shooting down of two U.S. Army Black Hawk helicopters in Iraq. Snook's analysis of records led him to conclude that the team that was assigned to keep track of helicopters to prevent shooting them was ineffective because no single member of the team felt compelled to take responsibility.

Potential Strengths of Groups

The primary potential strengths of groups in comparison to individuals are greater resources, more thorough thought, heightened creativity, and enhanced commitment to decisions. A group obviously exceeds any individual in the ideas, perspectives, experiences, and expertise it can bring to bear on solving a problem. One member knows the technical aspects of a product, another understands market psychology, a third is talented in advertising, and so forth. Health-care teams consist of specialists who combine their knowledge to care for a patient.

Groups also can be more thorough than individuals. Greater thoroughness by groups isn't simply the result of more people. When conformity pressures are controlled, discussion can promote critical and careful analysis because members propel

social loafing Exists when members of a group exert less effort than they would if they worked alone.

Einstein's Mistakes

That's the title of a book by Hans Ohanian (2008). As brilliant as Einstein may have been, he didn't make his great discoveries alone. He is most famous for $E = mc^2$, the equation expressing the law of relativity. However, math wasn't Einstein's strong suit and his proof of the law contained a number of mathematical mistakes. Another physicist, Max Von Laue, worked out a complete and correct proof, at which point $E = mc^2$ was on scientifically solid ground.

The myth of the individual genius is popular in Western societies, in part because they place high value on individualism. However, great innovations, discoveries, and inventions usually reflect the work of many people (Rae-Dupree, 2008). In his book *Group Genius*, Keith Sawyer (2008) shows that most creativity is the product of groups and teams. One person may get the credit—the raise, the patent, the Nobel Prize—but it took many to do the work.

 Are there accomplishments for which you individually receive credit which others helped you accomplish?

each other's thinking. **Synergy** is a special kind of collaborative vitality that enhances the efforts, talents, and strengths of individual members (Furnham & Xenikou, 2013; Rothwell, 2015).

A third value of groups is that they are generally more creative than individuals. Again, the reason seems to lie in the synergy of groups. Any individual eventually runs out of new ideas, but groups seem to have almost infinite generative ability. As members talk, they build on each other's ideas, refine proposals, and see new possibilities in each other's comments.

Finally, an important strength of groups is their ability to generate commitment to outcomes. The greater commitment fostered by group discussion arises from two sources. First, participation enhances commitment to decisions. Groups in which all members participate tend to generate greater commitment among members, which is especially important if members will be involved in implementing the decision. Second, because groups have greater resources than individual decision makers, their decisions are more likely to take into account the points of view of the various people needed to make a decision work. This is critical because a decision can be sabotaged if people dislike it or feel that their perspectives weren't considered.

Greater resources, thoroughness, creativity, and commitment to group goals are powerful values of group process. To incorporate these values, members must be willing to invest the time that discussion takes and must resist pressures to conform or engage in social loafing.

Features of Small Groups

What happens in groups and teams depends largely on members' abilities to participate effectively. If members are not skilled in basic communication processes, groups are unlikely to achieve their potential for productivity and creativity. We'll consider five features of small groups that affect and are affected by participation.

Cohesion

synergy A special kind of collaborative vitality that enhances the energies, talents, and strengths of individual members.

cohesion Closeness, or feeling of *esprit de corps*, among members of a group.

Have you ever felt really connected to others and excited about working to achieve a common goal? If so, then you know what **cohesion** is. Cohesion is the degree of closeness among members and the sense of group spirit. In highly cohesive groups, members see themselves as tightly linked and committed to shared goals. This heightens satisfaction with group membership. High cohesion and the satisfaction it generates tend to increase members' commitment to a group and its goals. Consequently, cohesion is important for effective and satisfying group communication. The online resources for this chapter provide a link to an article on team cohesion among athletes.

Cohesion is fueled by communication that builds group identity and creates a climate of inclusion for all members. Comments that stress pulling together and collective interests build cohesion by reinforcing group identity. Cohesion is also fostered by communication that highlights similarities between members—common interests, values, goals, experiences, and ways of thinking. A third way to enhance cohesion is for members to be responsive to one another so that everyone feels valued by the group.

Cohesion and participation are reciprocal in their influence. Cohesion is promoted when all members are involved and communicating in the group. At the same time, cohesiveness generates a feeling of identity and involvement; once established, it fosters participation. Thus, high levels of participation tend to build cohesion, and strong cohesion generally fosters vigorous participation. Encouraging all members to be involved and responding to each person's contributions fuels cohesion and continued participation. Although cohesion is important for effective group communication, excessive cohesion can actually undermine sound group work. When members are too close, they may be less critical of each other's ideas and less willing to engage in analysis and arguments that are necessary to develop the best outcomes.

© Franck Fife/AFP/Getty Images

How do you explain the high cohesion that marks successful athletic teams?

Extreme cohesion sometimes leads to **groupthink**, in which members cease to think critically and independently. Groupthink has occurred in high-level groups such as presidential advisory boards and national decision-making bodies (Hart, 1994; Janis, 1977; Young, Wood, Phillips, & Pedersen, 2001). Members tend to perceive their group so positively that they assume it cannot make bad decisions. Consequently, members do not critically screen ideas generated in deliberations. The predictable result is low-quality group outcomes that often fail.

America's invasion of Iraq was based on intelligence that Iraq had weapons of mass destruction. An in-depth investigation by the Senate concluded that the decision to go to war was propelled by members of the CIA and other agencies who unintentionally engaged in groupthink (Isikoff, 2004) so that critical thinking was suspended. Groupthink is not restricted to presidential boards and Senate committees. It can occur in any group if members suspend critical thinking. The online resources for this chapter include a link to research on online groupthink.

Group Size

The number of people in a group affects the amount and quality of communication. In a group of five people, each idea must be received and interpreted by four others, each of whom may respond with comments that four others must receive and interpret. As group size increases, the contributions of each member tend to decrease. You may have experienced frustration when participating in large online chat rooms and blogs. It can be hard to get your ideas in, and the sheer number of people contributing ideas can mean that no idea receives much response.

groupthink The absence of critical and independent thought on the part of group members about ideas generated by the group.

power The ability to influence others; a feature of small groups that affects participation.

power over The ability to help or harm others. Power over others usually is communicated in ways that highlight the status and influence of the person exerting the power.

power to The ability to empower others to reach their goals. People who use power to help others generally do not highlight their own status and influence.

Because participation is linked to commitment, larger groups may generate less commitment to group outcomes than smaller groups do. Because participation also affects cohesion and satisfaction, larger groups may also be less cohesive and less satisfying than smaller ones (Benenson, Gordon, & Roy, 2000; DeCremer & Leonardelli, 2003).

 ### Harrison

The worst group I was ever in had three members. We were supposed to have five, but two dropped out after the first meeting, so there were three of us to come up with proposals for artistic programs for the campus. Nobody would say anything against anybody else's ideas, even if we thought they were bad. For myself, I know I held back from criticizing a lot of times because I didn't want to offend either of the other two. We came up with some really bad ideas because we were so small we couldn't risk arguing.

As Harrison's commentary shows, groups can be too small as well as too large. With too few members, a group has limited resources, which diminishes a primary value of group decision making. Also, members of small groups may be unwilling to criticize each other's ideas, because alienating one member would dramatically weaken the group. Five to seven members is an ideal size for a group (Lumsden et al., 2009).

Power Structure

Power structure is a third feature that influences participation in small groups. **Power** is the ability to influence others (Rothwell, 2015). There are two distinct kinds of power.

Power over is the ability to help or harm others. This form of power usually is expressed in ways that emphasize and build the status of the person wielding influence. A team leader might exert positive power over a member by providing mentoring, giving strong performance reviews, and assigning the member high-status roles on the team. A leader could also exert negative power by withholding these benefits, assigning unpleasant tasks, and responding negatively to a member's contributions to meetings.

Power to is the ability to empower others to reach their goals (Boulding, 1990; Conrad & Poole, 2012). People who empower others do not emphasize their status. Instead, they act behind the scenes to enlarge others' influence and visibility and help others succeed. Power to creates opportunities for others, recognizes achievements, and helps others accomplish their goals.

If all members of a group have roughly equal power, the group has a *distributed*

 **ENGAGE!**

Five Bases of Power

What is power? How does a person get it? There is more than one answer to each of these questions because there are different sources of power (Arnold & Feldman, 1986).

◆ **Reward Power:** The ability to give people things they value, such as attention, approval, public praise, promotions, and raises

◆ **Coercive Power:** The ability to punish others through demotions, firing, and undesirable assignments

◆ **Legitimate Power:** The organizational role, such as manager, supervisor, or CEO, that results in others' compliance

◆ **Expert Power:** Influence derived from expert knowledge or experience

◆ **Referent Power:** Influence based on personal charisma and personality

 MindTap   Which base or bases of power would you prefer to have? Why?

power structure. On the other hand, if one or more members have greater power than others, the group has a *hierarchical power structure.* Hierarchy may take the form of one person who is more powerful than all the others, who are equal in power to one another. Alternatively, hierarchy may involve multiple levels of power. A leader might have the greatest power, three others might have power equal to each other's but less than the leader's, and four other members might have little power. The ENGAGE! feature on p. 224 summarizes the primary sources of power.

How is power related to participation? First, members with high power tend to be the centers of group communication; they talk more, and others talk more to them. **Social climbing** is the attempt to increase personal status in a group by winning the approval of high-status members. If social climbing doesn't increase the status of those doing it, they often become marginal participants in groups. Members with more power tend to find discussion more satisfying than members with less power (Young et al., 2001). This makes sense because those with power get to participate more and get their way more often.

Power influences communication and is influenced by it. In other words, how members communicate affects how much power they acquire. People who make good substantive comments, cultivate a healthy climate, and organize deliberations tend to earn power quickly. These are examples of earned power that is conferred because a member provides skills valued by the group. Members who demonstrate that they have done their homework and respond thoughtfully likewise gain power.

social climbing The attempt to increase personal status in a group by winning the approval of high-status members.

norms An informal rule that guides how members of a culture or group think, feel, and act. Norms define what is normal or appropriate in various situations.

Interaction Patterns

Another important influence on communication in groups is interaction patterns (Figure 11.2). In centralized patterns, one or two people hold central positions, and most or all communication goes directly to them or is funneled through them.

Decentralized patterns promote more balanced communication. As you might suspect, the power of individual members often affects interaction patterns. If one or two members have greater power, a centralized pattern of interaction is likely to emerge. Decentralized patterns are more typical when members have roughly equal power.

Group Norms

A final feature of small groups is the presence of **norms**—guidelines that regulate how members act as well as how they interact with each other. Group norms control everything from the most trivial to the most critical aspects of a group's life. Relatively inconsequential norms may regulate meeting time and whether eating

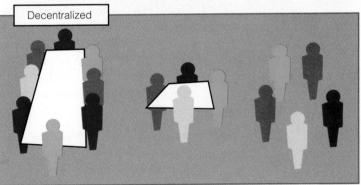

Figure 11.2 Patterns of Interaction in Groups

© Cengage Learning

is allowed during meetings. More substantive norms govern how members express and analyze ideas, listen to one another, and manage conflict.

Norms grow directly out of interaction. For example, at an initial meeting some members might check messages on their smartphones when others are speaking. If this continues, a norm of disrespect will develop, and members will form the habit of listening poorly. On the other hand, one member might say, "I think we need to put our phones away during meetings so we can attend to the discussion." If other members heed this suggestion, a norm of respectful communication may develop.

 Baxter

When our team first formed, everyone was pretty casual. There was a lot of kidding around before we got down to work at each meeting, and members often drifted in late. I didn't want to crack down at the beginning, because I thought that might dampen group spirit. With 20–20 hindsight, I now see I should have imposed some rules at the outset. I've tried to get members to get to meetings on time and buckle down to work, but I'm fighting against a history of being laid back.

As Baxter's commentary demonstrates, norms often become entrenched early in a group's life, so it's important to pay attention to them from the outset. By noticing patterns and tendencies, you can exert influence over the norms that govern conduct in a group. Cohesion, size, power structure, interaction patterns, and norms are features of groups that affect participation, productivity, and satisfaction.

Methods of Group Decision Making

Many groups are charged either to make decisions or to give recommendations to an individual or other group that has the authority to implement them. Because decision making is a primary goal of groups, we'll discuss two methods of group decision making.

Standard Agenda

The standard agenda is a time-tested and logical, six-step method for solving problems and making decisions (Rothwell, 2015).

1. Stage 1: Define the problem. Is the problem a matter of fact (What are the current requirements for a major in communication?) or value (What are the most useful courses to prepare communication majors for careers?) or policy (What can be done to encourage communication majors to take a broad range of courses in the major?)? Defining the problem also requires reaching agreement on what terms mean. For instance, what is meant by "a broad range of courses" or "prepare for careers"?

2. Stage 2: Gather and analyze evidence and information. Groups gather and examine information related to the defined problem. How many communication majors are there? How many majors take each of the courses offered by the department? What do communication departments at peer institutions require for majors? How do communication majors fare in the job market?

3. Stage 3: Establish criteria for a solution. Criteria are standards that the group can use to evaluate alternative solutions. Here are criteria that might be appropriate for a group deciding the policy issue of requirements for communication majors: Students must be able to complete the major in four years. Faculty must be qualified to teach the required classes. The requirements must be consistent with university requirements for all majors.

4. Stage 4: Generate and evaluate solutions. Members may brainstorm solutions and may also derive solutions from the research completed during Stage 2. Once the group has a number of solutions to consider, each one is measured against the criteria established in Stage 3.

5. Stage 5: Select and implement the best solution or decision. (Some versions of standard agenda separate this stage into two separate stages: selecting and implementing.) Ideally, a clearly preferred decision emerges when all options are tested against criteria. If no single solution is clearly best, group members must deliberate about the advantages and disadvantages of competing solutions. Once a group makes a choice by consensus or voting, then the group implements its decision. If it is a decision-making group, it authorizes the decision and personnel to implement it. If the group is advisory, it forwards its recommendation to the person or group that has the power to implement.

6. Stage 6: Monitor the decision. The final stage is critical and often overlooked by decision-making groups. The goal of this stage is to monitor the solution once it has been implemented. Too often groups end their work with implementing a decision or recommending a decision to someone who implements it. But how do you know if the solution works? How do you know if there are unintended consequences of the solution? The only way to know is to monitor the decision and, if necessary, modify it. A good monitoring plan spells out how effectiveness will be assessed: More majors will complete in four years. Majors will get more job interviews. Majors will evaluate their classes at a designated level of quality.

The standard agenda guides groups through stages that allow members to understand problems and issues and develop, implement, and assess decisions to remedy the problems and respond to issues.

Nominal Group Technique

A second widely used method of making decisions is the nominal group technique (NGT) (Delbecq & VandeVen, 1971; Potter, Gordon, & Hamer, 2004). This method is appropriate when a group wants to make a decision quickly and wants every member's opinions taken into account. NGT typically has a facilitator, who may or may not be a member of the group. The facilitator guides a group through five stages.

1. Stage 1: Introduction and explanation. The goals of this stage are to welcome the participants, clarify the purpose of meeting, outline the process or procedures that will be followed, and establish a healthy climate for group interaction.

2. Stage 2: Silent generation of ideas. The facilitator gives each group member a sheet of paper or an index card on which to record all of the ideas she or he has in relation to the question, problem, or topic posed by the facilitator. As the name of the stage indicates, this is a silent process; members don't discuss ideas with one another. This stage is a form of individual brainstorming.

3. Stage 3: Sharing ideas. When all members are through writing, the facilitator invites participants to share their ideas with the group. Using a flip chart, board, or computer-projected system, the facilitator lists ideas for all to see. As ideas are shared, participants write down any new ideas that are sparked by other members' contributions. A major benefit of this process is that all members have equal ability to participate, which is a corrective in groups where some members tend to be more vocal.

4. Stage 4: Group discussion. The facilitator encourages group members to elaborate on ideas and to ask questions of one another to gain clarification on what the idea is and what benefits it might have. The facilitator should also monitor group climate, making sure that all ideas are given respectful consideration. Finally, the facilitator encourages group members to think about ways that the ideas might be combined to create additional ideas.

5. Stage 5: Voting and ranking. Members individually rank each idea, giving a "1" to the most favored idea. The typical way of reaching a decision is to total all members' rankings for each item and the group's decision is the idea with the lowest total ranking. (There are variations on computing a final decision.) The group's decision is announced immediately so that members have a sense of closure when the meeting ends.

Both standard agenda and NGT provide procedural structure for moving a group through stages of discussion that encourage thoughtful analysis and careful decision making.

Digital Media and Groups

Whereas physical copresence was once required for groups and teams to exist and work together, that is no longer the case. Today, groups may operate through virtual conferences or through computer networking. In fact, one report found that 46 percent of people who work on virtual teams have never met face-to-face ("Virtual Team Challenges," n.d.). It's easy to understand why virtual teams have soared in popularity. They save travel expenses for members who live in different locations, they don't require physical meeting space, and they save members' time by not requiring packing and travel. Yet, virtual teams also pose challenges. To be effective, virtual teams must adapt to the CMC environment in which they operate. In other words, effective leadership and participation in virtual teams requires adjustments from face-to-face style.

The two greatest challenges for virtual teams are limited nonverbal cues and constraints on building relationships and group climate ("Virtual Team Challenges," n.d.). Many of the nonverbal cues we take for granted in face-to-face interaction are absent or limited in virtual groups. How do members know when it's their turn to speak? How do they know how others interpret their ideas? How do they know whether others are listening? Missing also are some of the informal interactions that build relationships among members of face-to-face groups. There is no water cooler where people get comfortable with each other through casual conversations. The literal pat on the back or smile that builds report may not be possible in virtual groups.

Those who have studied best practices in virtual groups recommend the following strategies for meeting the key challenges of virtual groups (Harvard Business Press, 2010; Kurtzberg, 2014; "Virtual Team Challenges," n.d.):

1. Have regular (weekly or monthly) nontask meetings. These allow members to get to know each other and build a group climate.

2. Establish a rule against multitasking during group meetings. This increases the likelihood that members are attending to group discussion and listening to one another.

3. Use multiple forms of CMC to connect. E-mail, tweets, Skyping, and individual conversations with group members build rapport.

4. Post information about all members on a group site so that each member's accomplishments and expertise are highlighted and so that members become familiar with each other.

5. Take time zones into account when scheduling meetings. When it is 9 A.M. Eastern Daylight Saving Time, it is 6 A.M. in California, and 10 P.M. in Tokyo.

6. If at all possible, arrange for occasional face-to-face meetings. Especially when starting a group, an opportunity for members to see, hear, and be with each other is important. The online resources for this chapter provide a link to an article on challenges for virtual teams.

Guidelines for Communicating in Groups and Teams

To realize the strengths of group work and avoid its potential weaknesses, members must participate constructively, provide leadership, and manage conflict so that it benefits the group and its outcomes.

Participate Constructively

Because interaction is the heart of groups and teams, communication skills are vital to effectiveness. There are four kinds of communication in groups (Figure 11.3). The first three—task communication, procedural communication, and climate communication—are constructive because they foster healthy group climate and quality outcomes. The fourth kind of communication is egocentric communication, which detracts from a positive group climate and effective decision making.

Task Communication   **Task communication** provides ideas and information, clarifies members' understanding, and critically evaluates ideas. Task contributions may initiate ideas, respond to others' ideas, or provide critical evaluation of information. Task comments also include asking for ideas and feedback.

Procedural Communication   If you've ever participated in a disorganized group, you understand the importance of **procedural communication**. It helps a group get organized and stay on track. Procedural contributions establish agendas, coordinate members' comments, and record group progress. In addition, procedural contributions curb digressions and tangents, summarize progress, and regulate participation so that everyone has opportunities to speak and nobody dominates.

Climate Communication   A group is more than a task unit. It is also people involved in a relationship that can be more or less pleasant. **Climate communication** focuses on creating and maintaining a constructive climate that encourages members to

task communication One of three constructive forms of participation in group decision making; focuses on giving and analyzing information and ideas.

procedural communication One of three constructive ways of participating in group decision making; orders ideas and coordinates contributions of members.

climate communication One of three constructive forms of participation in group decision making; the creating and sustaining of an open, engaged atmosphere for discussion.

Task Communication	Initiates ideas
	Seeks information
	Gives information
	Elaborates on ideas
	Evaluates, offers critical analysis
Procedural Communication	Establishes agenda
	Provides orientation
	Curbs digressions
	Guides participation
	Coordinates ideas
	Summarizes others' contributions
	Records group progress
Climate Communication	Establishes and maintains healthy climate
	Energizes group process
	Harmonizes ideas
	Recognizes others
	Reconciles conflicts
	Builds enthusiasm for the group
Egocentric Communication	Is aggressive toward others
	Blocks ideas
	Seeks personal recognition (brags)
	Dominates interaction
	Pleads for special interests
	Confesses, self-discloses, seeks personal help
	Disrupts task
	Devalues others
	Trivializes the group and its work

© Cengage Learning

Figure 11.3 Types of Communication in Groups

contribute and evaluate ideas critically. Climate comments emphasize a group's strengths and progress, recognize members' contributions, reconcile conflicts, add humor, and build enthusiasm for the group's work.

Egocentric Communication   I was once on a committee that had one member who was continuously negative. If one person suggested an idea for our task, this member would say, "We've already tried that" or "That will never work." The member's negativity undermined the committee. Perhaps you've been in groups where one person was always negative, argumentative, or domineering. **Egocentric communication**, or dysfunctional communication, blocks others and productive discussion and sabotages a healthy climate. It detracts from group progress because it is self-centered rather than group-centered. Examples of egocentric talk are devaluing a member's ideas, trivializing group efforts, being aggressive toward others, bragging about personal accomplishments, dominating, disrupting group work, and pleading for special causes that aren't in the group's interests.

Figure 11.4 provides a transcript of a group discussion that includes the four kinds of communication we've discussed. Notice how skillfully Ann communicates to defuse tension between Bob and Jan before it disrupts the group. You might also notice that Ed provides the primary procedural leadership for the group, and Bob is effective in

egocentric communication
An unconstructive form of group contribution that is used to block others or to call attention to oneself.

Ed:	Let's start by talking about our goals. [procedural]
Jan:	That's a good idea. [climate]
Bob:	I think our goal is to come up with a better meal plan for students on campus. [task]
Ed:	What do you mean by "better"? Do you mean cheaper or more variety or more tasteful? [task]
Ann:	I think it's all three. [task]
Ed:	Well, we probably do care about all three, but maybe we should talk about one at a time so we can keep our discussion focused. [procedural]
Bob:	Okay, I vote we focus first on taste—like it would be good if there were some taste to the food on campus! [task and climate (humor)]
Jan:	Do you mean taste itself or quality of food, which might also include nutrition? [task]
Bob:	Pure taste! When I'm hungry, I don't think about what's good for me, just what tastes good. [task and possibly climate (humor)]
Jan:	Well, maybe we want the food service to think about nutrition because we don't. [task]
Bob:	If you're a health food nut, that's your problem. I don't think nutrition is something that's important in the food service on campus. [task; may also be egocentric if his tone toward Jan is snide]
Ed:	Let's do this: Let's talk first about what we would like in terms of taste itself. [procedural] Before we meet next time, it might be a good idea for one of us to talk with the manager of the cafeteria to see whether they have to meet any nutritional guidelines in what they serve. [task]
Ann:	I'll volunteer to do that. [task]
Ed:	Great. Thanks, Ann. [climate]
Bob:	I'll volunteer to do taste testing! [climate (humor)]
Jan:	With your weight, you'd better not. [egocentric]
Bob:	Yeah, like you have a right to criticize me. [egocentric]
Ann:	Look, none of us is here to criticize anyone else. We're here because we want to improve the food service on campus. [climate] We've decided we want to focus first on taste, [procedural] so who has an idea of how we go about studying that? [task]

© Cengage Learning

Figure 11.4 Coding Group Communication

interjecting humor to enhance the climate. Several members recognize contributions to the discussion. You can further improve your ability to recognize different kinds of group communication by completing the Sharpen Your Skill exercise on this page.

Provide Leadership

All groups need leadership. However, leadership is not necessarily one individual. Instead, leadership is a set of behaviors that helps a group maintain a good climate and accomplish tasks in an organized way. Sometimes one member provides guidance on task and procedures, and another member focuses on building a healthy group climate by recognizing and responding to members' ideas and feelings (Covey,

MindTap

TAKE ACTION…activities are located at the end of this chapter and online.

2012; Goleman, McKee, & Boyatzis, 2002) as well as by encouraging cohesion. It's also not uncommon for different people to provide leadership at different times in a group's life. The person who guides the group at the outset may not be the one who advances the group's work in later phases. Even when an official leader exists, other members may contribute much of the communication that provides the overall leadership of a group.

Leadership is the process of establishing and maintaining a good working climate, organizing group processes, and ensuring that discussion is substantive. Whether a group has one or multiple leaders, the primary responsibilities of leaders are to organize discussion, to ensure sound research and reasoning, to promote norms for mindful listening and clear verbal and nonverbal communication, to create a productive climate, to build group morale, and to discourage egocentric communication that detracts from group efforts. Krystal's commentary provides an example of effective shared leadership.

 Krystal

The most effective group I've ever been in had three leaders. I was the person who understood our task best, so I contributed the most to critical thinking about the issues. But Belinda was the one who kept us organized. She could get us off tangents, and she knew when it was time to move on from one stage of work to the next. She also pulled ideas together to coordinate our thinking. Kevin was the climate leader. He could always tell a joke if things got tense, and he was the best person I ever saw for recognizing others' contributions. I couldn't point to any one leader in that group, but we sure did have good leadership.

Manage Conflict Constructively

In Chapter 7, we learned that conflict is natural and can be productive. In groups and teams, conflict stimulates thinking, helps members consider diverse perspectives and avoid groupthink, and enlarges members' understanding of issues involved in making decisions and generating ideas (McClure, 2005; Rothwell, 2015). To achieve these goals, however, conflict must be managed skillfully. Although many of us may not enjoy conflict, we can nonetheless recognize its value—even its necessity—for effective group work. Trey's experience illustrates what can happen when a group puts conflict avoidance ahead of high-quality work.

leadership A set of behaviors that helps a group maintain a good climate and accomplish tasks in an organized way.

ENGAGE!   Servant Leadership

We often think of leaders as individuals whom others serve, but, in some cases, it's the reverse. For servant leaders, the decision to lead arises from a humble desire to serve others and causes bigger than themselves. Their leadership isn't motivated by desire to increase their personal power or comfort, but rather a wish to help others. As a result, servant leaders focus on the needs and aspirations of their followers whom they serve.

Although contemporary leadership experts such as Stephen Covey (2012, 2013) extol servant leadership, esteem for servant leaders has much older roots in spiritual and religious teachings such as those of the Buddha, Lao-Tzu, Chanakya, and Jesus.

 Trey

I used to think conflict was terrible and hurt groups, but last year I was a member of a group that had no—I mean, zero—conflict. A couple of times, I tried to bring up an idea different from what had been suggested, but my idea wouldn't even get a hearing. The whole goal was not to disagree. As a result, we didn't do a very thorough job of analyzing the issues, and we didn't subject the solution we developed to critical scrutiny. When our recommendation was put into practice, it bombed. We could have foreseen and avoided the failure if we had been willing to argue and disagree in order to test our idea before we put it forward.

Disruptive Conflict   Effective members promote conflict that is constructive for the group's tasks and climate and discourage conflict that disrupts healthy discussion. Conflict is disruptive when it interferes with effective work and a healthy communication climate. Typically, **disruptive conflict** is marked by egocentric communication that is competitive as members vie with each other to wield influence and get their way. Accompanying the competitive tone of communication is a self-interested focus in which members talk about only their own ideas, solutions, and points of view. The competitive and self-centered communication in disruptive conflict fosters diminished cohesion and a win–lose orientation to conflict.

Group climate deteriorates during disruptive conflict. Members may feel unsafe volunteering ideas because others might harshly evaluate or scorn them. Personal attacks may occur as members criticize one another's motives or attack one another personally. Recall the discussion in Chapter 7 about communication that fosters defensiveness; we saw that defensive climates are promoted by communication that expresses evaluation, superiority, control orientation, neutrality, certainty, and closed-mindedness. Just as these forms of communication undermine healthy climates in personal relationships, they also interfere with group climate and productivity (Fujishin, 2013).

Constructive Conflict   **Constructive conflict** occurs when members understand that disagreements are natural and can help them achieve their shared goals. Communication that expresses respect for diverse opinions reflects this attitude. Members also emphasize shared interests and goals. The cooperative focus of communication encourages a win–win orientation. Discussion is open and supportive of differences, and disagreements focus on issues, not personalities.

To encourage constructive conflict, communication should demonstrate openness to different ideas, willingness to alter opinions when good reasons exist, and respect for the integrity of other members and the views they express. Also, keep in mind that conflict grows out of the entire system of group communication. Thus, constructive conflict is most likely to occur when members have established a supportive, open climate of communication. Group climate is built throughout the life of a group, beginning with the first meeting. It is important to communicate in ways that build a strong climate from the start so that it is already established when conflict arises.

disruptive conflict In groups, disagreement characterized by competitive communication, self-interested focus on the part of members, and a win–lose orientation.

constructive conflict In groups, disagreement that is characterized by respect for diverse opinions, emphasis on shared interests and goals, and a win–win orientation.

Summary

In this chapter, we've considered small groups and how they operate. To be effective, group members, whether in virtual or face-to-face groups, must recognize and manage the potential weaknesses of group discussion in order to realize the benefits of group decision making. Many factors, including cohesion, size, power, norms, and interaction patterns, influence communication in task groups and teams. Each of these features shapes the small group system within which communication transpires. Following time-tested decision-making models, such as the standard agenda or nominal group technique, further enhances a task groups' efficiency and effectiveness.

After considering best practices for virtual groups, we discussed three guidelines for effective communication in groups and teams. Developing skill in task, procedural, and climate communication and avoiding egocentric comments will make you a valuable member of any group. The second guideline for effective communication in groups and teams is to ensure leadership, which may be provided by one or more members. Good leadership exists when members communicate to organize discussion, ensure careful work on the task, and build cohesion, morale, and an effective climate for collective work. A third guideline is to manage conflict so that it enhances, rather than detracts from, group processes.

Experience Communication Case Study

Group Communication

Apply what you've learned in this chapter by analyzing the following case study, using the accompanying questions as a guide. These questions and a video of the case study are also available online with your MindTap Speech for *Communication Mosaics*.

As members of the Student Government Financial Committee, Davinia, Joyce, Thomas, and Pat make decisions on how much funding, if any, to give various student groups that request support from the funds collected from student fees. They are meeting for the first time in a campus cafeteria.

Thomas: Well, we've got 23 applications for funding and a total of $19,000 that we can distribute.

Davinia: Maybe we should start by listing how much each of the 23 groups wants.

Joyce: It might be better to start by determining the criteria that we'll use to decide if groups get any funding from student fees.

Davinia: Yeah, right. We should set up our criteria before we look at applications.

Thomas: Sounds good to me. Pat, what do you think?

Pat: I'm on board. Let's set up criteria first and then review the applications against those.

Joyce: Okay, we might start by looking at the criteria used last year by the Financial Committee. Does anyone have a copy of those?

Thomas: I do. [He passes out copies to the other three people.] They had three criteria: service to a significant number of students, compliance with the college's nondiscrimination policies, and educational benefit.

Davinia: What counts as "educational benefit"? Did last year's committee specify that?

Joyce: Good question. Thomas, you were on the committee last year. Do you remember what they counted as educational benefit?

Thomas: The main thing I remember is that it was distinguished from artistic benefit—like a concert or art exhibit or something like that.

Pat: But can't art be educational?

Davinia: Yeah, I think so. Thomas, Joyce, do you?

Thomas: I guess, but it's like art's primary purpose isn't to educate.

Joyce: I agree. It's kind of hard to put into words, but I think educational benefit has more to do with information and the mind, and art has more to do with the soul. Does that sound too hokey? [Laughter.]

Pat: Okay, so we want to say that we don't distribute funds to any hokey groups, right? [More laughter.]

Davinia: It's not like we're against art or anything. It's just that the funding we can distribute is for educational benefit, right? [Everyone nods.]

Joyce: Okay, let's move onto another criterion. What is a significant number of students?

Thomas: Last year, we said that the proposals for using money had to be of potential interest to at least 20 percent of students to get funding. How does that sound to you?

Pat: Sounds okay, as long as we remember that something can be of potential interest to students who aren't members of specific groups. Like, for instance, I might want to attend a program on Native American customs even though I'm not a Native American. See what I mean?

Davinia: Good point; we don't want to define student interest as student identity or anything like that. [Nods of agreement.]

Thomas: Okay, so are we agreed that 20 percent is about right, with the understanding that the 20 percent can include students who aren't in a group applying for funding? [Nods.] Okay, then do we need to discuss the criterion of compliance with the college's policies on nondiscrimination?

© Cengage Learning

1. Classify each statement in this scenario as one of the forms of group communication (task, procedural, climate, egocentric). Is the balance among forms appropriate for a decision-making group?

2. Based on this discussion, does this group seem to have a single leader, or do different members provide leadership to the group?

3. How do you perceive the interaction pattern between members? Does everyone seem to be involved and participating?

4. Are any of the potential values of group versus individual decision making evident in this discussion?

Key Concepts

Practice defining the chapter's terms by using online flashcards.

brainstorming, 219

climate communication, 229

cohesion, 222

constructive conflict, 233

disruptive conflict, 233

egocentric communication, 230

group, 218

groupthink, 223

leadership, 232

norm, 225

power, 224

power over, 224

power to, 224

procedural communication, 229

quality improvement team, 220

social climbing, 225

social loafing, 221

synergy, 222

task communication, 229

team, 218

MindTap™

Reflect, personalize, and apply what you've learned.

Review, Reflect, Extend

The Reflect and Discuss, and Take Action features that follow will help you review, reflect on, and extend the information and ideas presented in this chapter. These resources, and a diverse selection of additional study tools, are also available online at the MindTap Speech for *Communication Mosaics*.

Reflect and Discuss

1. Interview a professional in the field you hope to enter after college. Ask her or him to identify how various groups and teams discussed in this chapter are used on the job. If you are already employed in a career, reflect on your experiences with groups on the job.

2. In your class, form groups of five to seven. Select a topic for discussion such as "What is the best method of assessing learning in this class?" or "How can our campus be more environmentally responsible?" Have half of the groups follow standard agenda and the other half follow NGT to discuss the question. When the groups have finished the task, discuss your impression of each method of decision making.

 MindTap™

TAKE ACTION

1. Noticing Communication in Groups

Observe a group meeting—either a group you belong to or one you visit. For 10 minutes of group discussion, keep track of the communication, noting whether each comment is task, procedural, climate, egocentric, or a combination of two or more. Do the patterns of communication give you insight into why the group is effective or ineffective?

2. Evaluating the Impact of Group Communication

Observe a meeting of a campus governing group—for instance, the Board of Trustees. Do the communication patterns you observe explain the effectiveness or ineffectiveness of the group?

Recommended Resources

1. Although *Twelve Angry Men* was produced many years ago, it remains an excellent film about group dynamics in a decision-making group, in this case a jury.

2. Ken Blanchard, John Carlos, and Alan Randolph wrote *Empowerment Takes More Than a Minute* (1998) to give working tools to people who want to be empowering leaders. The book is organized in story form, relying on an extended case study to provide hands-on advice, tools, and exercises for increasing employees' sense of empowerment. They emphasize the importance of personal contact, encouragement, and feedback between leaders and employees.

12

Communication in Organizations

Like a human being, a company has to have an internal communication mechanism, a "nervous system," to coordinate its actions.

—Bill Gates

If internal communication is the nervous system of a company, what would be a company's heart and mind?

MindTap

Learning Objectives

Topics Covered in This Chapter	After studying this chapter, you should be able to ...
Key Features of Organizational Communication	Describe how the three key features of structure, communication networks, and links to external environments influence organizational communication.
Organizational Culture	Draw on your workplace experience to provide examples of each of the four kinds of communication that aid in developing and conveying organizational culture: vocabularies, stories, rites and rituals, and structures.
Digital Media and Organizational Communication	Given that digital media has both potential benefits and liabilities in the workplace, comment on how digital media has impacted your work experience.
Guidelines for Communicating in Organizations	When participating in an organizational environment, create an action plan to implement this chapter's guidelines to improve your skills for communicating in organizations.

 MindTap

Start with a quick engagement activity and **review** the chapter Learning Objectives.

◆ Josh is a senior systems analyst at MicroLife, an innovative technology firm in Silicon Valley. Although he typically works more than 40 hours a week, his schedule varies according to his moods and his responsibilities for caring for his daughter, Marie. Some days Josh is at his desk before 8 A.M., other days he gets to the office around noon, and sometimes he works from home. Life on the job is casual, as is dress. Sneakers, T-shirts, and jeans are standard attire for all employees at MicroLife. People drop by each other's offices without appointments and sometimes even without specific business to conduct. When Josh first joined MicroLife, drop-by chats with longer-term employees gave him insight into the company. He can still remember hearing stories about Wayne Murray—fondly called "Wild Man Wayne"—who launched the company from a makeshift workstation in his garage. He also heard tale after tale of oddball ideas the company backed that became highly profitable. Josh really enjoys the creative freedom at MicroLife: Everyone is encouraged to think innovatively, to try new ways of doing things. Weekly soccer games provide friendly competition between the Nerds (the team of systems analysts) and the Words (the team of software writers).

◆ Khloe slips her shoes off under her desk, hoping nobody will see, because Bankers United has a strict dress code requiring suits, heels (for women), and clean-shaven faces (for men). On her first day at work, a manager took her out to lunch and mentioned a recent hire who "just didn't work out" because she didn't dress professionally. Khloe got the message. From other employees, she heard about people who had been given bad performance reviews for being late more than once in a six-month period. When Khloe suggested a way to streamline mortgage applications, she was told, "That's not how we do things here." She quickly figured out that Bankers United expected everyone to follow rules rigidly. Although she sometimes feels constrained by the authoritarian atmosphere of Bankers United, Khloe also likes having clear-cut guidelines to follow. For her, rules provide a kind of security.

Would you rather work for MicroLife or Bankers United? If you're a relaxed person who enjoys informality and does well in unstructured environments, MicroLife may appeal to you. MicroLife is one of many businesses and professions that are flexible about dress and hours. As long as the work gets done—programs debugged, products developed—it doesn't matter how people dress and when or where they work.

On the other hand, if you like clear-cut rules and a traditional working environment, Bankers United may be more attractive to you. Like many organizations that serve the public, Bankers United employees need to be in place during standard business hours to take care of customers. Although organizations differ in many ways, common to them is the centrality of communication (Putnam & Mumby, 2013).

This chapter focuses on organizational communication. In the first section, we'll identify key features of organizational communication. Next, we'll discuss the overall culture of the organization, which is what creates the social and task climate for employees. As we will see, organizational culture is created and expressed through communication. Every organization has a distinct culture that consists of traditions, structures, and practices that reflect and reproduce a particular form of work life and on-the-job relationships. In the third section of the chapter, we'll consider how computer-mediated communication (CMC) can improve and interfere with organizational life. As usual, we close the chapter by discussing guidelines.

Key Features of Organizational Communication

Much of what you've learned in previous chapters applies to communication in organizations. For instance, successful communication on the job requires listening skills, care in making attributions and checking perceptions, verbal and nonverbal competence, awareness of and adaptation to differences among people, and the abilities to build supportive climates and manage conflict. In addition, organizational communication has three distinct features: structure, communication networks, and links to external environments.

Structure

Organizations are structured. As Charles Conrad and Marshall Scott Poole (2012) point out, the very word *organization* means structure. In organizations, structure provides predictability about roles, procedures, and expectations.

Many organizations rely on a hierarchical structure that assigns different levels of power and status to different members and specifies the chain of command that says who is to communicate with whom about what. Not all hierarchies are rigid, but a loose chain of command doesn't mean there isn't one. Many academic departments have loose structure in which members generally interact as equals. However, faculty are ultimately responsible to the chair of the department who can reprimand or assign tasks to any faculty member, but faculty can't do the same to the chair.

Communication Networks

A second characteristic of organizational communication is that it occurs in **communication networks**, which are formal and informal links between members of organizations (Modaff, Butler, & DeWine, 2011). In most organizations, people belong to multiple networks. For example, a faculty member belongs to a social network that includes colleagues, students, and staff. In addition, most faculty participate in task networks made up of people concerned about teaching, research, and departmental life and ad hoc networks that arise irregularly in response to specific crises or issues. Faculty also belong to networks outside their departments yet within the university. Overlaps among networks ensure that people will communicate in various ways with many people in any organization.

In addition to networks in physical places of work, virtual networks are becoming more common in the workplace (Kurtzberg, 2014; Rothwell, 2015). Today, it is commonplace for professionals to e-mail and text colleagues across the country or in different countries. The growth in telecommuting also means that employees may interact with proximate co-workers more by CMC than face-to-face communication. In 2014, an estimated 3.3 million U.S. employees telecommute half of the time, and an estimated 25 million telecommute part of the time. This is an 80 percent increase since 2005 (Global Analytics Workplace, n.d.). Using computers, smartphones, tablets, faxes, and other devices, telecommuters do their work and

communication network
The links among members of an organization. May be formal (e.g., as specified in an organizational chart) or informal (friendship circles).

maintain contact with colleagues and clients without being at a central, physical workplace. As we noted in Chapter 11, virtual workplaces pose challenges, but the benefits are substantial.

Links to External Environments

In Chapter 1, we discussed systems as interdependent, interacting wholes. Like other communication systems, organizations are embedded in multiple contexts that affect how they work and whether they succeed or fail (Siebold, Hollingshead, & Yoon, 2013). In other words, an organization's operation cannot be understood by looking only within the organization. We must also look outside it to grasp how the organization is related to and affected by its contexts.

Consider the impact on a few U.S. businesses of the recession that began in 2008:

◆ As the housing industry slumped, construction workers were laid off, and home supply stores lost business.

◆ Legal firms laid off attorneys who specialize in closings on home sales.

◆ As the economy continued to weaken, financial institutions lowered the interest they pay on savings, giving consumers less reason to save.

◆ U.S. companies relied more on outsourcing to countries where labor costs are lower.

◆ Luxury products and services such as cruises and massages suffered as many people struggled to pay for necessities.

◆ As people lost jobs, they had less income, forcing retailers in all spheres to lower prices, have more sales, and lure customers with special promotions.

Although internal factors may have contributed to how specific businesses fared, clearly many organizations suffered because of factors outside their organizational boundaries. When economic times are good, when war is not a threat, and when inflation is in check, even mediocre companies survive and sometimes thrive. When external conditions are bad, even good companies can be hurt or driven out of business. All organizations are linked to and influenced by the contexts in which they are embedded.

Systems in which organizations exist influence communication in organizations. Directors, CEOs, board members, and other leaders who feel pressured by economic problems may tighten controls, demand greater efficiency and productivity, and curtail raises, bonuses, and social events for employees.

Organizational Culture

organizational culture
Values, behaviors, practices, and forms of communication that are shared by the members of an organization and that reflect an organization's identity.

In Chapter 8, we noted that cultures are characterized by shared values, behaviors, practices, and forms of communication. Extending the idea of culture to organizations, communication scholars focus on **organizational culture**, which consists of values, behaviors, practices, and forms of communication that are shared by members of an organization and that reflect an organization's identity.

Just as ethnic cultures consist of meanings shared by members of the ethnic groups, organizational cultures consist of meanings shared by members of organizations. Just as new members of ethnic cultures are socialized into a particular culture's preexisting meanings and traditions, new members of organizations are socialized into a particular organization's preexisting meanings and traditions (Argyris, 2012; Eisenberg, Goodall, & Trethewey, 2013; Miller, 2014). Just as a culture's way of life continues even though particular people leave or die, an organization's culture persists despite the comings and goings of particular individuals.

Scholars have gained insight into the ways in which communication creates, sustains, and expresses the culture of organizations (Pacanowsky, 1989; Pacanowsky & O'Donnell-Trujillo, 1982, 1983; Riley, 1983; Scott & Myers, 2005; Smircich, 1983). The relationship between communication and organizational culture is reciprocal: Communication between members of organizations creates, sustains, and sometimes alters the culture. At the same time, organizational culture influences patterns of communication between members.

As employees interact, they create, sustain, and sometimes change their organization's culture (Argyris, 2012; Pacanowsky, 1989). Four kinds of communication that are particularly important in developing and conveying organizational culture are vocabularies, stories, rites and rituals, and structures.

© wavebreakmedia/Shutterstock.com

MindTap Based on this photo, what can you infer about this organization's culture?

Vocabulary

The most obvious communication dimension of organizational culture is vocabulary. Just as the language of an ethnic culture reflects and expresses its history, norms, values, and identity, the language of an organization reflects and expresses its history, norms, values, and identity.

Hierarchical Language   Many organizations and professions have vocabularies that designate status. The military, for example, relies on language that continually acknowledges rank ("Yes, sir;" "Captain;" "Major;" "General"), which reflects the close ties among rank, respect, and authority. Salutes, as well as stripes and medals on uniforms, are part of the nonverbal vocabulary that emphasizes rank and status.

Unequal terms of address also communicate rank. For instance, the CEO may use first names ("Good morning, Jan") when speaking to employees. Unless given permission to use the CEO's first name, however, lower-status members of an organization typically use Mr., Ms., Sir, or Ma'am in addressing the CEO. Colleges and universities use titles to designate faculty members' rank and status: instructor, assistant

Not Exactly a Slam Dunk

The prevalence of sports-related terms in U.S. business culture is not generally a problem within the United States. However, it can be baffling when used in international contexts. Consider these examples (Jones, 2007):

◆ At a global leadership meeting in Italy, the CEO of an electronics company wanted to alter the agenda, so he said, "I'm calling an audible."

◆ In a meeting with Indian executives, a U.S. CEO wanted to modify a clause in a contract, so he asked for "a jump-ball scenario."

◆ AFLAC CEO Dan Amos assured Japanese executives that using the AFLAC duck in ads in Japan would be a "slam dunk."

professor, associate professor, full professor, and distinguished (or chaired) professor. Faculty generally use students' first names, whereas students tend to use titles to address their teachers: Dr. Matthews or Professor Matthews.

Masculine Language   Because organizations historically were run by men, and men held most or all of the high-level positions, it's not surprising that many organizations have developed and continue to use language reflecting men's traditional interests and experiences (Ashcraft & Mumby, 2004; Mumby, 2007). Consider the number of phrases in the work world that are taken from sports (*home run, ballpark estimate, touchdown, develop a game plan, be a team player, take a time out, the starting lineup*), from military life (*battle plan, mount a campaign, plan of attack, under fire, get the big guns, offensive strike*), and from male sexual parts and activities (a troublesome person is a "prick"; you can "hit on" a person, "screw" someone, or "stick it" to them; bold professionals have "balls").

Less prevalent in most organizations is language that reflects traditionally feminine interests and experiences (*put something on the back burner, percolate an idea, stir the pot, give birth to a plan*). Whether intentional or not, language that reflects traditionally masculine experiences and interests can bind men together in a community in which some women may feel unwelcome or uncomfortable (Wood, 1992b, 1994c).

Stories

Scholars of organizational culture recognize that humans are storytellers by nature. We tell stories to create meaning in our lives, and that includes the lives we live in organizations. Furthermore, the stories we tell do some real work in establishing and sustaining organizational cultures. Three kinds of stories are important in organizational contexts.

Corporate Stories   Corporate stories convey the values, style, and history of an organization. Just as families have favorite stories about their histories and identities that they retell often, organizations have favorite stories that reflect their collective visions of themselves (Conrad & Poole, 2012; Gargiulo, 2005; Mumby, 1993, 2006).

One important function of corporate stories is to socialize new members into the culture of an organization. For example, both Levi Strauss and Microsoft are known for an informal style of operation. Veteran employees regale new employees with tales about the laid-back character of the companies: casual dress, relaxed meetings, fluid timetables, and nonbureaucratic ways of getting things done. In some workplaces, corporate stories teach employees to regard the company as a family. When told and retold among members of an organization, stories vitalize organizational values and foster feelings of connection. You've heard the term *war stories*, which refers to frequently retold stories about key moments such as crises, successes, and takeovers. When long-term members of organizations rehash pivotal events in their shared history, they cement the bonds between them and their involvement with the organization and bring newer members of the organization into the cultural history. Jed's commentary provides a good example of how stories express and reinforce organizational culture.

 Jed

I sing with the Gospel Choir, and we have a good following in the Southeast. When I first joined the group, the other members talked to me. In our conversations, what I heard again and again was the idea that we exist to make music for God and about God, not to glorify ourselves. One of the choir members told me about a singer who had gotten on a personal ego trip because of all the bookings we were getting, and he started thinking he was more important than the music. That guy didn't last long with the group.

Personal Stories Members of organizations also tell stories about themselves. Personal stories are accounts that announce how people see themselves and how they want to be seen by others (Cockburn-Wootten & Zorn, 2006). For example, if Sabra perceives herself as a supportive team player, she could simply tell new employees, "I am a supportive person who believes in teamwork." On the other hand, she could define her image by telling a story: "When I first came here, most folks were operating in isolation, and I thought a lot more could be accomplished if we learned to collaborate. Let me tell you something I did to make that happen. After I'd been on staff for three months, I was assigned to work up a plan for downsizing our manufacturing department. Instead of just developing a plan on my own, I talked with several other managers, and then I met with people who worked in manufacturing to get their ideas. The plan we came up with reflected all of our input." This narrative gives a concrete, coherent account of how Sabra sees herself and wants others to see her.

Collegial Stories The third type of organizational story offers accounts of other members of the organization. When I first became a faculty member, a senior colleague took me out to lunch and told me anecdotes about people in the department and university. At the time, I thought he was simply sharing some interesting stories. Later, however, I realized he had given me valuable information about the players in my new context.

Collegial stories told by co-workers forewarn us about what to expect from whom. "If you need help getting around the CEO, Jane's the one to see. A year ago, I couldn't finish a report by deadline, so Jane rearranged his calendar so he thought the report wasn't due for another week." "Roberts is a real stickler for rules. Once when I took an extra 20 minutes on my lunch break, he reamed me out." "Pat trades on politics, not performance. Pat took several of the higher-ups out for lunch and golfed with them for the month before bonuses were decided." Whether positive or negative, collegial stories assert identities for others in an organization. They are part of the informal network that teaches new members of an organization what to expect from other members of the organization.

 What type of rite is commencement?

Rites and Rituals

Rites and rituals are verbal and nonverbal practices that express and reproduce organizational cultures (Islam & Zyphur, 2009). They do so by providing standardized ways of expressing organizational values and identity.

Rites   **Rites** are dramatic, planned sets of activities that bring together aspects of cultural ideology in a single event. Harrison Trice and Janice Beyer (1984) identified six kinds of organizational rites. *Rites of passage* are used to mark moving into different levels or parts of organizations. For example, a nonverbal symbol of promotion may be the moving of an employee's office from the second to the fourth floor after a promotion. A desk plaque with a new employee's name and title is a rite that acknowledges a change in identity. *Rites of integration* affirm and enhance the sense of community in an organization. Examples are holiday parties, annual picnics, and graduation ceremonies.

Organizational cultures also include rites that blame or praise people. Firings, demotions, and reprimands are common *blaming rites*. The counterpart is *enhancement rites*, which praise individuals and teams that embody the organization's goals and self-image. Campuses bestow awards on faculty who are especially gifted teachers or outstanding scholars. Many companies give awards for productivity (most sales of the month, quarter, or year). Organizations use organizational newsletters to inform employees of new policies and other news related to the organization and to congratulate employees on accomplishments. Audrey describes an enhancement rite in her sorority.

Audrey

In my sorority, we recognize sisters who make the dean's list each semester by putting a rose on their dinner plates. That way everyone realizes who has done well academically, and we can also remind ourselves that scholarship is one of the qualities we all aspire to.

Organizations also develop rites for managing change. *Renewal rites* aim to revitalize and modernize organizations. Training workshops serve this purpose, as do periodic retreats at which employees discuss the organization's mission, goals, and health. Finally, *conflict resolution rites* are standard methods of dealing with differences and discord. Examples are arbitration, collective bargaining, mediation, executive fiat, voting, and ignoring or denying problems. The conflict resolution rite that typifies an organization reflects the values of its overall culture.

Rituals   **Rituals** are forms of communication that occur regularly and that members of an organization perceive as familiar and routine parts of organizational life.

rite A dramatic, planned set of activities that brings together aspects of cultural ideology in a single event.

ritual A form of regularly occurring communication that members of an organization perceive as a familiar, routine part of organizational life and that reflects a particular value or role definition.

© Armadillo Stock/Shutterstock.com

Rituals differ from rites in that rituals don't necessarily bring together a number of aspects of organizational ideology into a single event. Rather, rituals are repeated communication performances that express a particular value or role definition.

Organizations have personal, task, and social rituals. *Personal rituals* are routine behaviors that individuals use to express their organizational identities. In their study of organizational cultures, Pacanowsky and O'Donnell-Trujillo (1983) noted that Lou Polito, the owner of a car company, opened all the company's mail every day. Whenever possible, Polito hand-delivered mail to the divisions of his company to communicate his openness and his involvement with the day-to-day business.

Social rituals are standardized performances that affirm relationships between members of organizations (Mumby, 2006). Some organizations have a company dining room to encourage socializing among employees. In the United Kingdom and Japan, many businesses have afternoon tea breaks. E-mail chatting and forwarding jokes are additional examples of socializing rituals in the workplace. Tamar Katriel (1990) identified a social ritual of griping among Israelis. *Kiturim*, the name Israelis give to their griping, most often occurs during Friday night social events called *mesibotkiturim*, which translates as "gripe sessions." Unlike griping about personal concerns, *kiturim* typically focuses on national issues, concerns, and problems. Sharon provides an example of an office griping ritual.

Workplace Bullying

The term *schoolyard bully* reflects the common experience of being bullied—or being a bully—in elementary school. Most of us expect bullying to be left behind as we move into adult life. But that doesn't always happen. According to a 2010 survey (Workplacebullying.org, 2010), at least 35 percent of employees in the United States report they have experienced **workplace bullying**, which is recurring hostile behaviors often used by people with greater power against people with lesser power (Keashly & Neuman, 2005; Tracy, Lutgen-Sandvik, & Alberts, 2006; Yamada, 2010).

Bullying is most harmful when enacted by people with power. When a person devalues a person with less power, the person with less power lacks the authority to protect herself or himself by stopping the bullying. Bullying includes ridicule, spreading untrue and hurtful rumors, insults, and making false accusations. Both sexes engage in workplace bullying, but men do so more frequently: 62 percent of bullies are male and 38 percent are female (Workplace-bullying.org, 2010). The costs of bullying are high: decreased morale, weak or broken employee networks, increased turnover, lowered commitment, and reduced productivity (Yamada, 2010).

Workers' rights advocates have been campaigning for years to get states to enact laws against workplace bullying. Many labor analysts predict that laws against workplace bullying will soon be passed.

 Would you support laws against bullying? Why or why not?

 *Sharon*

Where I work, we have this ritual of spending the first half-hour or so at work every Monday complaining about what we have to get done that week. Even if we don't have a rough week ahead, we go through the motions of moaning and groaning. It's kind of like a bonding ceremony for us.

Task rituals are repeated activities that help members of an organization perform their jobs. Perhaps a special conference room is used for particular tasks, such as giving marketing presentations or making sales proposals. Task rituals are also evident in forms and procedures that members of organizations are expected to follow. These forms and procedures standardize task performance in a manner consistent with the organization's view of itself and how it operates. In their study of a police

workplace bullying
Recurring hostile behaviors often used by people with greater power against people with lesser power.

TAKE ACTION…activities are located at the end of this chapter and online.

unit, Pacanowsky and O'Donnell-Trujillo (1983) identified the routine that officers are trained to follow when they stop drivers for traffic violations. Officers are taught to ask a series of questions right after stopping a motorist: "May I see your license, please?" "Do you know why I stopped you?" "Do you know how fast you were going?" These opening questions allow officers to size up traffic violators and decide whether to give them a break or ticket. A Take Action exercise at the end of this chapter invites you to notice rituals in an organization to which you belong.

Structures

Organizational cultures are also represented through structural aspects of organizational life. As the name implies, **structures** organize relationships and interaction between members of an organization. We'll consider four structures that express and uphold organizational culture: roles, rules, policies, and communication networks.

Roles   **Roles** are responsibilities and behaviors expected of people because of their specific positions in an organization. Most organizations formally define roles in job descriptions:

◆ Training coordinator: Responsible for assessing needs and providing training to Northwest branches of the firm; supervise staff of 25 professional trainers, coordinates with director of human relations. Supervisory experience required.

◆ Assistant professor: Duties include teaching three classes per term, supervising graduate student theses, serving on departmental and university committees, and conducting research. Ph.D. and experience required.

A role is not tied to any particular person. Rather, it is a set of functions and responsibilities that could be performed by any number of people who have particular talents, experiences, and other relevant qualifications. If one person quits or is fired, another replaces the first. Regardless of who is in the role, the organization will continue with its structure intact. Organizational charts portray who is responsible to whom and clarify the hierarchy of power among roles in the organization.

Rules

Rules, which we discussed in Chapters 1, 4, and 10, are patterned ways of interacting. Rules are present in organizational contexts just as they are in other settings. As in other contexts, organizational rules may be formal (in the contract or organizational chart) or informal (norms for interaction).

Within organizations, constitutive rules specify what various kinds of communication symbolize. Some firms count working late as evidence of commitment. Socializing with colleagues after work may count as showing team spirit. Taking on extra assignments, attending training sessions, and dressing like upper management may communicate ambition.

 Lyle

I found out the hard way that a company I worked for was dead serious about the organizational chart. I had a problem with a co-worker, so I talked with a guy in another department I was friends with. Somehow my supervisor found out, and he blew a gasket. He was furious that I had "gone outside of the chain of command" instead of coming straight to him.

structure Organize relationships and interaction among members of an organization. Structures include roles, rules, policies, and communication networks.

role The responsibilities and behaviors expected of a person by virtue of his or her position.

rules Patterned ways of behaving and interpreting behavior. All relationships develop rules.

Regulative rules specify when, where, and with whom communication should occur. Organizational charts formalize regulative rules by showing who reports to whom. Other regulative rules may specify that problems and proprietary information should not be discussed with people outside the organization. Some organizations have found that employees spend so much time online that productivity suffers, so rules regulating online activity are established. Lyle's commentary points out what counted as violating the chain of command in his company.

Policies   **Policies** are formal statements of practices that reflect and uphold the overall culture of an organization. Most organizations codify policies governing such aspects of work life as hiring, promotion, benefits, grievances, and medical leave. The content of policies in these areas differs among organizations in ways that reflect the distinct cultures of diverse work environments.

Organizational policies also reflect the larger society within which organizations are embedded. For example, as public awareness of sexual harassment increased and laws were passed to hold individuals and corporations accountable, most organizations developed formal policies that define sexual harassment, state the organization's attitude toward it, and detail the procedure for filing and resolving grievances. Because of the prevalence of dual-career couples, many organizations have created procedures to help place the spouses of people they want to hire.

Communication Networks   As we noted earlier in this chapter, networks link members of an organization together. These networks play key roles in expressing and reinforcing an organization's culture.

Job descriptions and organizational charts, which specify who is supposed to communicate with whom about what, are formal networks. Formal networks provide the order necessary for organizations to operate. They define lines of upward communication (subordinates to superiors; providing feedback, reporting results), downward communication (superiors to subordinates; giving orders, establishing policies), and horizontal communication (peer to peer; coordinating between departments).

Informal networks are more difficult to describe because they are neither formally defined nor based on fixed organizational roles. Friendships, alliances, carpools, and nearby offices can be informal networks through which a great deal of information flows. Communication outside the formal channels of an organization is sometimes called the *grapevine*, a term that suggests its free-flowing character. Although details often are lost or distorted as messages travel along a grapevine, the general information conveyed informally has a surprisingly high rate of accuracy: 75 to 90 percent (Hellweg, 1992). If details are important, however, the grapevine may be a poor source of information.

Digital Media and Organizational Communication

It is not an exaggeration to state that technologies have revolutionized how organizations operate. We'll discuss four of the many ways that digital media have changed the workplace.

Digital media have the potential to increase productivity and efficiency. We count on e-mail and text messages from supervisors and co-workers to keep us informed, expect material we need to come to us as attachments or scans, and assume computers will do the majority of calculating and record keeping. Virtual conferences

policy A formal statement of practice that reflects and upholds an organization's culture.

Tomorrow's Organizations

Work groups and teams will increasingly work virtually, with people connecting from different places and even different countries (Rothwell, 2015; Siebold et al., 2013). Technologies such as text messaging, VoIP, audio- and videoconferencing, and webinars allow groups to work across time and distance. In future years, we're sure to see additional technologies that further facilitate virtual group work.

One of the best ways to learn about social and organizational trends that are reshaping the world of work is to read online magazines. Links to *Entrepreneur*, which discusses emerging trends and resources for entrepreneurs, and idea café, which was created by business owners, are available in the online resources for this chapter.

are increasingly preferred to more costly and time-intensive physical meetings. Instead of spending hours inputting data manually, much data can now be scanned into computers. Cut and paste and Track Changes programs mean that we no longer have to retype entire reports to incorporate changes. Much of the information we need—from company reports to research in libraries—is available online, saving us time in tracking it down. Scans and attachments allow us to send information rapidly instead of waiting for mail or even fax. These and other time savers mean that CMC can boost productivity (Ean, 2011; Kendrick & Sooknanan, 2014; Luttrell, 2014; Rice & Leonardi, 2013).

Second, technologies increase organizational flexibility. As we noted in Chapter 11, technologies allow people to work in places other than brick and mortar offices and at times other than 9 to 5. Most professionals have computers, smartphones, printers, and often fax machines in their homes. For many jobs, that's all the equipment that's needed to conduct business. Employees who have mobility limitations may be able to meet all of their job requirements without going to an office. Similarly, if a child is ill, the nanny is sick, or the day-care center is closed, employees may be able to stay home with their child while still doing their work.

Third, digital media enlarge the range of professional contacts. LinkedIn began as a tool to link entrepreneurs and has expanded to be a networking hub for professionals in many fields. In addition, professional networks are increasingly used for job seeking and job recruiting. Active job seekers may survey job opportunities posted on these sites. Recruiters pay LinkedIn for the privilege of trawling the network to find professionals suited to jobs they are trying to fill. Before deciding where to locate new offices, some companies review profiles on LinkedIn to see where qualified workers are grouped ("Workers of the World," 2014).

The fourth impact of CMC on the workplace is not beneficial. CMC, especially social media, can be a powerful distraction from work. We all know how tempting it is to post updates on our lives and check Facebook and LinkedIn for updates from friends; to tweet friends; and to shop, watch videos, and play games. Never before have we had such easy access to nonwork activities while at work. And that can cause problems. The most obvious problem is that all of these activities interfere with our productivity and, ultimately, our job performance and success. A second problem is that, unless there is a policy allowing personal CMC, it's unethical to engage in personal communication via your computer, tablet, or phone during the time that your employer is paying you a salary. And third, substantial use of social media while at work can cost you your job. Employers are becoming increasingly intolerant of employees who engage in personal and social communication via CMC during work hours. As the ENGAGE! feature on page 249 indicates, many employers rely on sophisticated systems to monitor employees' CMC activity.

Keeping Track of Employees

◆ A majority of today's employers monitor their employees (Staples, 2014). Two thirds of employers monitor their employees' Web site visits and 43 percent monitor e-mail, sometimes with dire consequences: 28 percent of employers have fired workers for e-mail misuse ("Workplace Privacy," 2011). Here are a few facts to keep in mind:

◆ In most cases, employers have the right to monitor employees' computer screens while they are working and to see what is stored in computers terminals and hard disks.

◆ Employers have the right to monitor employees' Internet usage, including e-mail.

◆ In most cases, employers have the right to monitor employees' phone calls and to obtain records of calls made. Personal calls are an exception; employers are supposed to cease monitoring if they realize a call is personal.

◆ In most cases, employers have the right to videotape employees. Videotaping is not allowed in bathrooms, locker rooms, and other places where courts have ruled it would be intrusive.

◆ A 2010 legal ruling broadened employers' rights. This ruling states that an employer's policy regarding monitoring need not specify every means of communication subject to the policy. In other words, employees should assume they, as well as their phones and computers, are subject to monitoring.

To learn more about privacy (or lack thereof) in the workplace, visit the online resources for this chapter.

Guidelines for Communicating in Organizations

We'll discuss three guidelines that are particularly relevant to organizational communication in our era.

Expect to Move in and out of Teams

Effective communication in today's and tomorrow's organizations requires interacting intensely with members of face-to-face and virtual teams that form and dissolve quickly (Siebold et al., 2013). Whereas autonomous workers—single leaders, mavericks, and independent professionals— were prized in the 1940s, the team player is most highly sought today (Rothwell, 2015). John, who returned to school in his mid-40s, describes the changes in his job over the past 13 years on page 250.

Employee Mistreatment in Culturally Diverse Organizations

We hear a lot about the increasing diversity of the workforce in the United States and elsewhere.

What we hear less about is emerging as a serious problem that seems more prevalent in culturally diverse workplaces than in culturally homogeneous ones. The problem is employee mistreatment, particularly against minorities and women.

Mistreatment ranges from unlawful activities, such as harassment and inequitable benefits, to more subtle activities, such as stereotyping, ridicule, and exclusion from informal networks (Carter & Silva, 2010).

Individuals who are treated unfairly in the workplace tend to withdraw, leave, become resentful, or experience anger, which may be expressed in a variety of ways. Clearly, these consequences are not limited to individual employees—they affect organizations' health and productivity. If employees are not contributing constructively on the job, the entire organization suffers.

 John

My job is entirely different today than when I started it 13 years ago. When I came aboard, each of us had his own responsibilities, and management pretty much left us alone to do our work. I found authors and helped them develop their ideas, Andy took care of all art for the books, someone else was in charge of marketing, and so forth. Each of us did our job on a book and passed the book on to the next person. Now the big buzzword is team. Everything is done in teams. From the start of a new book project, the author and I are part of a team that includes the art editor, marketing director, manuscript designer, and so forth. Each of us has to coordinate with the others continually; nobody works as a lone operator. Although I had reservations about teams at first, by now I'm convinced that they are superior to individuals working independently. The books we're producing are more internally coherent, and they are developed far more efficiently when we collaborate.

The skills we discussed in Part II of this book will help you perceive carefully, listen well, use verbal and nonverbal communication effectively, promote constructive climates, and adapt your style of interacting to the diverse people on your teams. The challenge is to be able to adjust your style of communicating to the expectations and interaction styles of a variety of people and to the constraints of a range of situations. The greater your repertoire of communication skills, the more effectively you will be able to move in and out of teams on the job.

Balance Investments in Life and Work

Nobody is just a worker. We are also people with children and parents and passions outside of the workplace. Each of us needs to find ways to balance commitments to work with commitments to other aspects of life, including family, recreation, civic engagements, hobbies, and community involvement.

Many workplaces do not make it easy to balance life and work. Too often organizations make few or no accommodations for employees' lives outside of work (Buzzanell & Kirby, 2013). The most blatant example of this is the lack of universal family leave. The United States is the only Western country and one of only three countries in the world that do not provide paid family leave to all workers. Of 185 countries in the United Nation's most recent study, 182 offer some level of financial payment to new mothers on maternity leave. The three that do not are Oman, Papua New Guinea, and the United States (Rowe-Finkbeiner, 2014; Zarocostas, 2014). Further, at least 70 countries provide paid leave to fathers (Coontz, 2013; Weber, 2013; Zarocostas, 2014). U.S. law also mandates fewer weeks of unpaid leave than other Western countries (Zarocostas, 2014).

In addition to institutional barriers, social norms can also constrain efforts to balance work and life. Some men subscribe to traditional views of masculinity and are unwilling to let family responsibilities affect their careers, which often means a female partner's career suffers from her commitment to family. Men who would like to take family leave often do not because they fear that doing so would reduce their status at work (Parker & Wang, 2013; Weber, 2013) or because their partners expect them to be breadwinners.

Organizations with the best chance of thriving in the future will adapt to the realities of contemporary workers and their families (Williams, 2013). Recognizing this, many organizations are becoming more flexible and generous in supporting employees' nonwork commitments. Doing so reduces turnover and increases employees' commitment to organizations.

Manage Personal Relationships on the Job

A third guideline is to find ways to deal with relationships that are simultaneously personal and professional. You probably will be involved in a number of such relationships during your life.

Friendships between co-workers or supervisors and subordinates often enhance job commitment and satisfaction. This is not surprising, because work is more enjoyable when we work with people we like. Yet workplace friendships also have drawbacks. On-the-job friendships may involve tension between the role expectations for friends and for colleagues. A supervisor may have difficulty rendering a fair evaluation of a subordinate who is also a friend. The supervisor might err by overrating the subordinate–friend's strengths or might try to compensate for personal affection by being especially harsh in judging the friend–subordinate. Friendship may also make it awkward to give negative feedback, which is essential to effective performance on the job. Workplace friends often talk about organizational issues, but when one friend enters management, she or he may not be able to discuss those issues with friends who are not in management. Also, workplace friendships that deteriorate may create stress in the workplace.

 *Anna*

> It's hard for me now that my best friend has been promoted over me. Part of it is envy, because I wanted the promotion, too. But the hardest part is that I resent her power over me. When Billie gives me an assignment, I feel like as my friend she shouldn't dump extra work on me. But I also know that as the boss she has to give extra work to all of us sometimes. It just doesn't feel right for my best friend to tell me what to do and evaluate my work.

Romantic relationships between people who work together are also increasing. Most women and men work outside the home, sometimes spending more hours on the job than in the home. In Chapter 10, we learned that proximity is a key influence on the formation of romantic relationships. It's no surprise, then, that people who see each other almost every day sometimes find themselves attracted to each other. Yet on-the-job romances pose challenges (Sias, 2013). They are likely to involve many of the same tensions that operate in friendships between supervisors and subordinates. In addition, romantic relationships are especially likely to arouse co-workers' resentment and discomfort. Romantic breakups also tend to be more dramatic than breakups

The workplace creates opportunities to interact with people who we may find attractive romantically.

Clerkenwell Images/iStockphoto.com

between friends. As Eugene points out, when a workplace romance dies, tension and discomfort may arise.

 *Eugene*

Once I got involved with a woman where I was working. We were assigned to the same team and really hit it off, and one thing led to another, and we were dating. I guess it affected our work some, since we spent a lot of time talking and stuff in the office. But the real problem came when we broke up. It's impossible to avoid seeing your "ex" when you work together in a small office, and everyone else acted like they were walking on eggshells around us. She finally quit, and you could just feel tension drain out of everyone else in our office.

It's unrealistic to assume we can avoid personal relationships with co-workers. The challenge is to manage those relationships so that personal bonds don't jeopardize professionalism. Friends and romantic partners may need to adjust their expectations and styles of interacting so that personal and work roles do not conflict. It's also advisable to make sure that on-the-job communication doesn't reflect favoritism and privileges that could cause resentment in co-workers. It's important to invest extra effort to maintain an open communication climate with other co-workers.

Summary

In this chapter, we've seen that the culture of an organization is created, sustained, and altered in the process of communication between members of an organization. As they talk, interact via digital media, exchange stories, develop policies, and participate in the formal and informal networks, they continuously weave the fabric of their individual roles and collective life. Digital media facilitate organizational communication in many ways, yet they also may allow members of organizations to engage in personal and social interaction while at work. In addition, digital media reduce individual privacy by creating multiple ways that employers can monitor employees.

Organizations, like other contexts of communication, involve a number of challenges. To meet those challenges, we discussed three guidelines. One is to be prepared to move in and out of teams rapidly, which is required in many modern organizations. A second guideline is to find ways to achieve balance between work and the other aspects of your life. Finally, we discussed ways to manage personal relationships in the workplace. It's likely that you will form friendships and perhaps romantic relationships with people in the workplace. The communication skills we've discussed throughout this book will help you navigate the tensions and challenges of close relationships on the job.

Experience Communication Case Study

 MindTap

Ed Misses the Banquet

Apply what you've learned in this chapter by analyzing the following case study, using the accompanying questions as a guide. These questions and a video of the case study are also available online with your MindTap Speech for *Communication Mosaics*.

Ed recently began working at a new job. Although he's been in his new job only five weeks, he likes it a lot, and he's told you that he sees a future for himself with this company. But last week, a problem arose. Along with all other employees, Ed was invited to the annual company banquet, at which everyone socializes and awards are given for outstanding performance. Ed's daughter was in a play the night of the banquet, so Ed chose to attend his daughter's play rather than the company event. The invitation to the banquet had stated only, "Hope to see you there" and had not been RSVP, so Ed didn't mention to anyone that he couldn't attend. When he arrived at work the next Monday morning, however, he discovered the case was otherwise and had the exchange that follows with his manager. Later, when Ed talked with several co-workers who had been around a few years, he discovered that top management sees the annual banquet as a "command performance" that signifies company unity and loyalty.

Ed's manager: You skipped the banquet last Saturday. I had really thought you were committed to our company.

Ed: My daughter was in a play that night.

Ed's manager: I don't care *why* you didn't come. We notice who is really with us and who isn't.

© Cengage Learning®

1. How does the concept of constitutive rules, which we first discussed in Chapter 4, help explain the misunderstanding between Ed and his manager?

2. How might Ed use the informal network in his organization to learn the normative practices of the company and the meanings they have to others in the company?

3. How do the ambiguity and abstraction inherent in language explain the misunderstanding between Ed and his manager?

4. How would you suggest that Ed repair the damage done by his absence from the company banquet? What might he say to his manager? How could he use *I*-language, indexing, and dual perspective to guide his communication?

5. Do you think the banquet is a ritual? Why or why not?

Key Concepts

Practice defining the chapter's terms by using online flashcards.

communication network, 239
organizational culture, 240
policy, 247
rite, 244
ritual, 244

role, 246
rules, 246
structure, 246
workplace bullying, 245

Review, Reflect, Extend

The Reflect and Discuss, and Take Action features that follow will help you review, reflect on, and extend the information and ideas presented in this chapter. These resources, and a diverse selection of additional study tools, are also available online at the MindTap Speech for *Communication Mosaics*.

Reflect, personalize, and apply what you've learned.

Reflect and Discuss

1. Think about an organization to which you belong. It may be a company you work for or a social organization such as a fraternity or an interest club. Describe some common rites and rituals in this organization. What do these rites and rituals communicate about the organization's culture?

2. Talk with a person who has worked in a profession for at least 20 years. Ask her or him how technologies, especially digital ones, have affected relationships and job productivity.

TAKE ACTION

1. Noticing Your School's Culture

Like all organizations, your school has an organizational culture. Based on material in this chapter, see if you can identify aspects of that culture. You might start by reading your college's policies governing students. From its policies concerning class attendance, drug use, and dishonorable conduct, what can you infer about the culture the college wants to promote? (Note how dishonorable conduct is defined; this differs among schools.)

Next, think about stories about campus life and people that you were told during your first weeks on campus. How did these stories shape your understandings and expectations of the school? Finally, identify rites and rituals at your school. What values do they convey and uphold?

If you belong to particular campus groups (political, athletic, social), identify policies, stories, rites, and rituals that are part of these groups.

2. Get Informed about On-the-Job Relationships

Workplace relationships—whether romances or friendships—can enhance professional life and jeopardize careers. Before you get involved in a workplace romantic relationship or friendship, take the time to get informed so you can make informed choices.

The online resources for this chapter provide a link to an article that gives advice about how employers should handle workplace romances.

Recommended Resources

1. Visit the Web site of an organization you think you might like to join. Explore different links on the site to learn about the organization's policies and the image it presents. From the material on its site, what can you infer about the organization's culture?

2. The film *Remember the Titans* provides a dramatic account of a man who was assigned to coach a group of athletes in a recently integrated school. The players didn't work together well, largely because of ethnic differences and ethnocentric attitudes. This film provides rich insights into leadership and the development of a cohesive organizational culture for the team.

3. Interviews are a common form of communication in organizations. Among the types of interviews that are part of organizational life are hiring interviews, problem-solving interviews, reprimand interviews, and appraisal interviews. A chapter on interviewing is available in the MindTap.

13
Public Communication

Speech belongs half to the speaker,
half to the listener.
　　　　　—Michel de Montaigne

What makes a public
speech compelling
to you?

MindTap

Learning Objectives

Topics Covered in This Chapter	After studying this chapter, you should be able to ...
Choosing a Speaking Purpose	When presented with a public speaking occasion, determine which of the three general purposes is appropriate.
Earning Credibility	Drawing from your experience listening to public speakers, provide examples of the three types, or levels, of credibility.
Finding Evidence	Given a chosen topic, conduct research to find examples of the four types of evidence.
Organizing Speeches	Given an identified speech purpose, selected topic, and researched evidence, determine which of the recognized patterns of organizing speeches will be most effective.
Developing Effective Delivery	Distinguish among the four modes of delivery.
Digital Media and Public Speaking	Identify three ways that digital media can assist speakers.
Guidelines for Public Speaking	To improve your public speaking and your critical listening to others' public speeches, create an action plan to implement the chapter's guidelines

 MindTap

Start with a quick
engagement activity
and **review** the chapter
Learning Objectives.

Read, highlight, and take notes online.

When he was elected Student Body President, Harper hadn't considered one aspect of the job: giving a graduation speech. Now it's late March of his senior year and commencement is only six weeks away. Harper knows he has to get serious about his speech. Fortunately, he took several communication courses, including public speaking, so he has some knowledge of how to prepare a speech. What he needs to do is figure out what he wants to say and how to say it.[1]

Speaking to entertain is something most of us will do in our lives.

Moved to Speak

Candace Lightner had never thought of herself as a public speaker. She had never sought the limelight and had seldom been required to speak out to others. Then, in 1980, her 13-year-old daughter was killed by a teenage drunk driver. Once she recovered from the immediate grief of her daughter's untimely death, Lightner began a crusade for stricter laws against drunk driving (Lightner, 1990; Sellinger, 1994).

She founded Mothers Against Drunk Driving (MADD), which now has thousands of members. In addition, Lightner persuaded state and federal legislators to approve stiffer laws and penalties for drunk driving and to raise the age for drinking to 21. Although not an experienced speaker when she began her crusade, Lightner became a skillful speaker in order to get her message across.

Like Harper, many of us do not consider ourselves public speakers, but we are called upon to speak publicly on occasion. You might be asked to give a toast at a friend's wedding, to present a plan to clients, to introduce a keynote speaker at a banquet, or you might feel compelled to speak up in favor of a development proposal at a community meeting. Knowing the basics of public speaking enables you to be an active citizen, an effective professional, and an advocate for people and causes that matter to you.

In this chapter, we'll follow Harper as he prepares and practices his graduation speech. As we observe him, we'll note key principles of effective public speaking that he is embodying. We will then consider how digital media assist Harper's preparation and presentation. As usual, the chapter closes with guidelines for effectiveness.

Harper begins by thinking back to his public speaking class. His professor emphasized the idea that good public speeches are not stilted, but are what she called "enlarged conversation." Remembering this calms Harper's nerves. He's not going to make a stiff, formal speech; he's going to have a conversation with his classmates.

The other thing his professor emphasized was adapting a speech. Over and over, she said that a good speech is not removed from its context, but rather is responsive to the people and situation in which it is

---

[1] Harper's thoughts are printed in brown font.

Fuse/Jupiter Images

presented. His teacher so often stressed the tailoring of speeches to occasion and audience that Harper and other students joked this was her mantra.

"What is distinctive about this occasion?" Harper asks himself. He thinks about the word *commencement*, which means beginning. He also thinks about the fact that the occasion marks an ending, the conclusion of undergraduate school. "Beginnings and endings," Harper muses. "That's what this occasion means." As Harper continues to reflect on the occasion, he realizes everyone will be in a festive, happy mood, ready to celebrate a big achievement. He notes to himself that the speech can't be too somber, given the happy mood and context.

His thoughts turn to his classmates. Who are they? What do members of the graduating class have in common that can help him develop a good speech that speaks to them? Most of us entered in 2011, Harper thinks. What has happened in the four years since we started? When he runs out of ideas from his own memory, he googles each year and the phrase *major events*.

Ancient rhetoricians called this part of speech preparation *inventio*, the Latin word for *invention*, because speakers invent ways to connect their topics with their listeners. This is usually the first step in the process of preparing a speech—generating ideas, which the speaker later culls to select those that will go into the speech.

MindTap

TAKE ACTION…activities are located at the end of this chapter and online.

2011
* Osama Bin Laden is killed by U.S. military.
* Kim Kardashian and Chris Humphries get engaged.
* Kim Kardashian and Chris Humphries marry.
* Prince William and Kathryn marry.
* Steve Jobs dies.
* Kim Kardashian and Chris Humphries separate.

2012
* Barack Obama is elected to a second term.
* Usain Bolt becomes the first person to win the 100-m and 200-m sprint in back to back Olympics.
* Three members of Russian punk band Pussy Riot are jailed for two years.
* Barack Obama issues an official statement favoring same-sex marriage.
* The USADA strips Lance Armstrong of his seven Tour de France titles.
* Hurricane Sandy devastates the northeastern United States.

2013
* Lance Armstrong admits to doping in all seven of his Tour de France victories.
* Oscar Pistorius, a South African amputee sprint runner, is charged with the murder of Reeva Steenkamp.
* A two-year-old U.S. girl becomes the first child born with HIV to be cured.
* Grand Theft Auto takes the record for being fastest entertainment product to reach $1 billion in sales.
* Netflix releases the first season of Orange Is the New Black.
* Boston Marathon terror attack happens.

2014
* Ebola outbreak threatens to become a pandemic.
* ISIS beheads journalists.
* The largest march for climate justice in history is held.
* Oscar Pistorius is found not guilty of murder but guilty of a lesser crime.

2015
* Hillary Clinton is the Democratic nominee for the president of the United States.
* NASA's Dawn probe enters orbit around the dwarf planet of Ceres.
* ISIS (the Islamic State of Iraq) shocks the world with its brutality.
* Ireland becomes the first country to legalize same-sex marriage by popular vote.

As he looks over events that have happened in the past four years, Harper notices that some people have done amazing things with their lives: Usain Bolt's dedication to training allowed him to win double Olympic medals; Barack Obama became the first black president and then won re-election; scientists came up with an in utero treatment for HIV. Just as clearly, Harper sees, some people have made poor choices or engaged in evil: The Boston bombers; Lance Armstrong. Steve Jobs's premature death reminds Harper how important it is to make your time count. Harper shakes his head thinking of Kim Kardashian—engaged, married, and divorced in a single year. "Oh well," he thinks, "I can mention her for comic appeal to keep the speech from getting too serious."

An idea for the overall thesis of his speech emerges: *How will each of us use our time?* Harper's always felt that everyone should try to make life a little better for others and for those who come next. Now he sees that his speech can be a vehicle for expressing this passion. Contrasting people like Steve Jobs, who used his talents to create systems that billions of people rely on, with people like Lance Armstrong, who doped and lied, will help him paint the dramatic choices that lie before the graduating class. He had been thinking that he'd probably give a humorous speech, but, in this moment, Harper decides he is going to give a persuasive speech.

Choosing a Speaking Purpose

There are three general purposes of public communication: To entertain, to inform, and to persuade (Griffin, 2015; Hamilton, 2015). You probably realize that these purposes often overlap. For example, persuasive communication generally includes information. Some of your professors include stories and interesting examples to enliven informational lectures. Speeches to entertain may also teach listeners something new.

In a **speech to entertain**, the primary objective is to engage, interest, amuse, or please listeners. You might think that only accomplished comics and performers present speeches to entertain. Actually, many of us will be involved in speaking to entertain during our lives. You might be asked to give an after-dinner speech, present a toast at a friend's wedding, or roast a colleague at a retirement party.

Humor, although often part of speeches to entertain, is not the only way we engage others. We also entertain when we tell stories to share experiences, build community, pass on history, or teach a lesson. Parents share with children stories of family history and mentors share stories of an organization's history with new employees.

A **speech to inform** has the primary goal of increasing listeners' understanding, awareness, or knowledge of some topic. For example, a speaker might want listeners to understand the rights guaranteed in the Bill of Rights or to make listeners aware of recycling programs. In both cases, the primary purpose is to enrich listeners' knowledge, although each topic has persuasive implications. A speech to inform may also take the form of a demonstration, in which the speaker shows how to use a new computer program or how to distinguish between poisonous and nonpoisonous species of mushrooms. As Gladys points out, however, speaking to inform may be more successful when speakers also entertain or otherwise capture listeners' interest.

speech to entertain
A speech intended to amuse, interest, and engage listeners.

speech to inform A speech intended to increase listeners' understanding, awareness, or knowledge of some topic.

 **Gladys**

I've taught second grade for eight years, and there's one thing I've learned: If you don't get the students' interest, you can't teach them anything. My education classes taught me to focus on content when planning lessons. But working in real classrooms with real children taught me that before a teacher can get content or information across to students, she has to first capture their interest.

A **speech to persuade** aims to influence attitudes, change practices, or alter beliefs. Rather than primarily an entertainer or teacher, the persuasive speaker is an advocate who argues for a cause, issue, policy, attitude, or action. In one of my classes, a student named Chris gave a speech designed to persuade other students to contribute to the Red Cross blood drive. He began by telling us that he was a hemophiliac, whose life depended on blood donations. He then explained the procedures for donating blood (a subordinate informational purpose) so that listeners would not be deterred by fear of the unknown. Next, he described several cases of people who had died or had become critically ill because adequate supplies of blood weren't available. In the two weeks after his speech, more than one third of the students who had heard his speech donated blood.

Earning Credibility

"But what gives me the right to advise others to use their time well?" Harper asks himself. "I'm not a brilliant scientist who has invented a cure for cancer. I'm not a Nobel Prize winning novelist. What makes *me* qualified to urge my peers to commit to making a difference? How can I persuade them that I am a responsible source for this message?"

In asking this question, Harper is considering the concept of speaker credibility. Effective public speaking (and, indeed, communication of all types) depends on credibility. **Credibility** exists when listeners believe in a speaker and trust what the speaker says. Credibility is based on listeners' perceptions of a speaker's position, authority, knowledge (also called *expertise*), dynamism, and trustworthiness (also called *character*). Therefore, to enhance credibility, speakers, especially those who do not have impressive titles and accomplishments, should demonstrate that they are informed about their topics, that they are dynamic communicators, and that they are ethical in using evidence and reasoning (Jaffe, 2016; Verderber, Sellnow, & Verderber, 2015).

A speaker's credibility is not necessarily static (Griffin, 2015). Some speakers have high **initial credibility**, which is the expertise, dynamism, and character that listeners attribute to them before they begin to speak. Initial credibility is based on titles, experiences, and achievements that are known to listeners before they hear the speech. For example, Michelle Obama has high initial credibility on the issue of children's health and the Pope has high initial credibility on Catholicism.

 **Ricardo**

Last month, I went to a lecture about getting started in financial planning. I figured the speaker just wanted to sell me something, so I didn't have too high a regard for him. But during his talk, he quoted lots of information from unbiased sources, so I saw that he really knew his stuff. He also didn't try to sell us anything, so I began to trust what he said. And he made the ideas really easy to follow with charts and handouts. By the time he was through, I thought he was excellent.

speech to persuade A speech intended to change listeners' attitudes, beliefs, or behaviors or to motivate listeners to action.

credibility The ability of a person to engender belief in what he or she says or does. Listeners confer or refuse to confer credibility on speakers.

initial credibility The expertise and trustworthiness listeners attribute to a speaker before a presentation begins. Initial credibility is based on the speaker's titles, positions, experiences, or achievements that are known to listeners before they hear the speech.

As Ricardo points out, a speaker without much initial credibility may earn strong credibility in the process of presenting a speech. Speakers may gain **derived credibility**, which listeners grant as a result of how speakers communicate during presentations. Speakers may earn derived credibility by providing clear, well-organized information and convincing evidence, and by an engaging delivery style. Speakers may also increase credibility during a presentation if listeners regard them as likable and as having goodwill toward the listeners (McCroskey & Teven, 1999).

Terminal credibility is a cumulative combination of initial and derived credibility. Terminal credibility may be greater or less than initial credibility, depending on how effectively a speaker has communicated.

> Harper realizes he won't have high initial credibility, so he will have to develop, or derive, credibility by showing that he has experience, by presenting support for his ideas, and by delivering his speech with conviction and dynamism. Since his first year spring break, he has gone on service breaks—Nicaragua to build silos for farmers' crops, New Orleans to build a Habitat house, Nepal to lay pipes for a water system to a remote village. Harper decides he will offer brief descriptions of these service trips and the difference they made. He has letters from some of the people he met in each of the countries; he can quote from those letters to bring the people alive to his audience.

Finding Evidence

Evidence is material used to support claims, such as those made in a public speech. Evidence serves a number of important functions in speeches. First, it can be used to make ideas clearer, more compelling, and more dramatic. Second, evidence fortifies a speaker's opinions, which are seldom sufficient to persuade intelligent listeners. Finally, evidence heightens a speaker's credibility. A speaker who supports ideas well comes across as informed and prepared. Therefore, including strong evidence allows speakers to increase credibility during a presentation.

The effectiveness of evidence depends directly on whether listeners understand and accept it. This reinforces the importance of adapting to listeners. Even if a speaker quotes the world's leading authority, it won't be effective if listeners don't find the authority credible (Olson & Cal, 1984). Consequently, speakers' choices of evidence should take listeners' perspectives into account. The goal is to include support that they find credible, while also making sure the evidence is valid. Before including any form of evidence, speakers have an ethical responsibility to check the accuracy of material and the credibility of sources.

Four forms of support are widely respected, and each tends to be effective in specific situations and for particular goals (Hamilton, 2015; Verderber et al., 2015): **statistics**, **examples**, **comparisons**, and **quotations**. In addition, **visual aids**, which are not technically a form of evidence, allow speakers to present and enhance other forms of evidence. For instance, a graph (visual aid) of statistics (evidence) enhances the impact of a speaker's point.

---

derived credibility The expertise and trustworthiness attributed to a speaker by listeners as a result of how the speaker communicates during a presentation.

terminal credibility The cumulative expertise and trustworthiness listeners attribute to a speaker as a result of initial and derived credibility; may be greater or less than initial credibility, depending on how effectively a speaker has communicated.

evidence Material used to support claims: statistics, examples, comparisons, and quotations.

statistics A form of evidence that uses numbers to summarize a great many individual cases or to demonstrate relationships between phenomena.

example A form of evidence in which a single instance is used to make a point, to dramatize an idea, or to personalize information. The four types of examples are undetailed, detailed, hypothetical, and anecdotal.

comparison A form of evidence associating two things that are similar or different in some important way or ways.

quotation A form of evidence that uses exact citations of others' statements. Also called *testimony*.

visual aid A visual image, such as a chart, graph, photograph, or physical object, that reinforces ideas presented verbally or provides information.

Figure 13.1 summarizes the types of evidence and their uses.

Examples provide concrete descriptions of situations, individuals, problems, or other phenomena.

Types: Short (instance)
Detailed
Hypothetical
Anecdotal

Uses: To personalize information and ideas
To add interest to a presentation
To enhance dramatic effect

Comparisons (analogies) compare two ideas, processes, people, situations, or other phenomena.

Types: Literal analogy (A heart is a pump.)
Figurative analogy (Life is a journey.)
Metaphor (The company is a family.)
Simile (The company is like a family.)

Uses: To show connections between phenomena
To relate a new idea to one that is familiar to listeners
To provide interest

Statistics summarize quantitative information.

Types: Percentages and ratios
Demographic data
Frequency counts
Correlations
Trends

Uses: To summarize many instances of some phenomenon
To show relationships between two or more phenomena (cause or correlation)
To demonstrate trends or patterns

Quotations (testimony) restate or paraphrase the words of others, giving appropriate credit to the sources of the words.

Types: Short quotation
Extended quotation
Paraphrase

Uses: To add variety and interest
To support a speaker's claims
To draw on the credibility of people whom listeners know
To include particularly arresting phrasings of ideas

Visual aids reinforce verbal communication and provide visual information and appeals.

Types: Handmade charts and graphs
Overheads/transparencies
Computer-created charts and graphs
PowerPoint slides
Objects, pictures, handouts, film clips

Uses: To strengthen and underscore verbal messages
To translate statistics into pictures that are understandable
To add variety and interest
To give listeners a vivid appreciation of a topic, issue, or point

© Cengage Learning

Figure 13.1 Types of Evidence and Their Uses

Harper thinks he remembers that the founder of Teach for America dreamed up the idea while she was a college student and focused on building the organization immediately after her graduation. He googles Teach for America and discovers that his memory is correct. He notes the name of the founder is Wendy Kopp and learns that she started Teach for America with fewer than 500 teachers and now has over 12,000. "That's a great example of what someone our age can do," Harper says to himself. I'll use that to support my theme. Harper continues to conduct research using online libraries and making a few trips to the campus library to get information from reference works not available online. He also interviews two classmates who were on his service trips to have examples of college students other than himself who have decided to make a difference.

Organizing Speeches

Now Harper faces the question of how to organize his speech. He grabs the notebook he kept in his public speaking class to review organizational patterns.

Organization increases speaking effectiveness in several ways (Griffin, 2015; Verderber et al., 2015). First, organization affects comprehension of ideas. Listeners can understand, follow, and remember a speech that is well planned and well ordered. Listeners are less likely to retain the key ideas in a poorly organized speech. Second, experimental evidence shows that listeners are better persuaded by an organized speech than by a disorganized one. Finally, organization enhances speakers' credibility, probably because a carefully structured speech reflects well on a speaker's preparation and respect for listeners. When a person gives a disorganized speech, listeners may regard the speaker as incompetent or unprepared, which reduces derived and terminal credibility.

The Body

The body of a speech develops the thesis by organizing content into points that are distinct yet related. In short speeches of 5 to 10 minutes, two or three points usually are all that a speaker can develop well. Longer speeches may include more points. You can organize speeches in many ways, and each organizational pattern has distinct effects on the overall meaning (see Figure 13.2).

Chronological patterns or *time patterns* organize ideas chronologically. They emphasize progression, sequences, or development. Harper could focus on (1) the year most of his classmates were born, (2) the year they are graduating, and (3) 20 years after graduation. *Spatial patterns* organize ideas according to physical relationships. They are useful in explaining layouts, geographic relationships, or connections between parts of a system. For instance, Harper could have three points that move from making a difference at (1) local, (2) national, and (3) international levels.

Topical patterns (also called *classification patterns*) order speech content into categories or areas. This pattern is useful for speeches in which topics break down into two or three areas that aren't related temporally, spatially, or otherwise. Harper could

Topic: Literacy

Speech 1: Chronological Organization

Thesis: As America changes, so must our ways of teaching literacy.

Claim 1:   When America was founded, reading was restricted primarily to the aristocratic class.

Claim 2:   By the late 1800s, more members of working class and African Americans were also taught to read.

Claim 3:   Today, America must find ways to provide literacy education to immigrants.

Speech 2: Spatial Organization

Thesis: Teaching literacy happens in homes, schools, and volunteer-run literacy programs.

Claim 1:   The home is where many children first learn to read.

Claim 2:   Schools teach literacy to many students.

Claim 3:   When home and school don't teach literacy, volunteer-run programs can teach literacy.

Speech 3: Cause–Effects

Thesis: Literacy programs will increase productivity, enhance citizens' engagement with society, and reduce incarceration rates.

Claim 1:   People who can read are more economically stable and productive than people who cannot read.

Claim 2:   Citizens who can read more actively engage civic and social issues.

Claim 3:   Literate citizens are less likely to break the law and go to prison.

© Cengage Learning

Figure 13.2 Organizing Speeches

have three topical areas for his three main points: contributing with your mind, your labor, and your wallet.

Wave patterns feature repetitions; each "wave" repeats the main theme with variations or extensions (Jaffe, 2016). *Comparative patterns* compare two or more phenomena (people, machines, planets, situations). This pattern demonstrates similarities between phenomena ("Steve Jobs and Usain Bolt are alike in dedicating themselves to a goal.") or differences between phenomena ("People like President Obama use their time to serve others while people like Lance Armstrong use their time to serve themselves.").

Persuasive speeches typically rely on organizational patterns that encourage listeners to change attitudes or behaviors. *Problem–solution patterns* allow speakers to describe a problem and propose a solution: There is much need in the world that we can address with your minds, hearts, and hands. *Cause–effect* and *effect–cause patterns* order speech content into two main points: cause and effect. This structure is useful for persuasive speeches that aim to convince listeners that certain consequences will follow from particular actions. Harper might show beneficial outcomes of service and mission trips.

A final way to organize a persuasive speech is the *motivated* sequence pattern (Gronbeck McKerro, Ehninger, & Monroe, 1994; Jaffe, 2016; Monroe, 1935). This pattern is effective in diverse communication situations, probably because it follows a natural order of human thought. The motivated sequence pattern includes five sequential steps.

- The *attention step* focuses listeners' attention on the topic with a strong opening ("Imagine a mother with three young children and no home to live in").

- The *need step* shows that a real and serious problem exists ("Poverty makes it impossible for some people to afford homes").

- Next is the *satisfaction step*, in which a speaker recommends a solution to the problem described ("Habitat for Humanity was founded to assist people in building homes for themselves").

- The *visualization step* intensifies listeners' commitment to the solution by helping them imagine the results that the recommended solution would achieve ("Here is a photo of Vivian Murphy standing in front of the home that she and 10 other students built in 2013").

- Finally, in the *action step* the speaker appeals to listeners to take concrete action to realize the recommended solution ("I urge you to call Habitat today and volunteer to help another Vivian have a home").

Organizing an effective speech is not the same as organizing a paper. Oral communication requires more explicit organization, greater redundancy, and simpler sentence structure. Unlike readers, listeners cannot refer to an earlier passage if they become confused or forget a point already made. For the same reason, they may not follow long, complex sentences that are delivered orally. Providing signposts to highlight organization and repeating key ideas increase listeners' retention of a message (Coopman & Lull, 2015; Hamilton, 2015).

Consistent with the need for redundancy in oral communication, good speeches tell listeners what the speaker is going to tell them, present the message, and then remind listeners of the main points. This means preparing an introduction, a body, and a conclusion. In addition, speakers should include transitions to move listeners from point to point in the speech.

> Harper thinks over the theme he's decided on and the meaning of the commencement occasion. Beginnings and endings and four years of college suggest a chronological pattern, starting in 2011 and then each of the successive three college years. He can talk about one of his service trips for each year, which will build his credibility. In the outline he writes three events in cultural life for each year of college and adds one of his personal experiences from a service trip. Then he adds one additional piece of evidence from his research for each of the four years.

The Introduction

"Now, how do I introduce the speech?" Harper asks himself. Thinking about the chronological pattern for the body of the speech gives Harper an idea. Why not open with something about the year most of his classmates were born? Quickly, he googles 1993 major events, and finds lots of things happened that provide a perspective on how quickly time moves.

1993

* *Bill Clinton inaugurated as the 42nd U.S. president.*
* *Police officers found guilty of violating Rodney King's civil rights.*
* *The World Wide Web is born at CERN.*
* *Lorena Gallo Bobbitt amputates husband John Wayne Bobbitt's penis.*
* *Nelson Mandela and South Africa president F. W. de Klerk awarded Nobel Peace Prize.*
* *Vatican recognizes Israel.*

Harper decides to open with a question: Guess what was born the same year that most of us were born? The Web. *He'll then note how quickly the cumbersome initial Web has evolved into the nearly seamless system that he and his classmates consider just part of the air they breathe. After that, he'll note that time passes quickly and then present his thesis as a short, clear sentence:* Each of us can use our time to make a difference. *Then he'll offer a succinct preview so his audience can follow his speech:* In the next few minutes, I'll review with you some of the defining events of each of our four years in college and ask what difference your life meant in each of those years.

The introduction is the first thing an audience hears, and a good introduction does a lot of work. It should gain listeners' attention, give them a reason to listen, establish the credibility of the speaker, and state the thesis and how it will be developed.

The first objective of an introduction is to gain listeners' attention, which may also provide them with a motivation to listen. You might open with a dramatic piece of evidence, say, a startling statistic: Most of you in the graduating class have lived 192,816 hours in your 22 years. Other ways to gain attention are to present a striking visual aid (a photo of the silo that Harper's service group built in Nicaragua) or a dramatic example (the detailed story of the single mom for whom his service group built a Habitat house).

You could pose a question that invites listeners to think actively about the topic: "What have you accomplished in your 192,816 hours on planet earth?" Speakers may also gain listeners' attention by referring to personal experience with the topic: "Last year I made friends with four Nepalese teens while we were building a water system for their village." Notice that an example of the speaker's involvement in the topic helps in developing credibility.

The introduction should also include a **thesis statement**. Your thesis should be a clear, short sentence that captures the main idea of your talk and the key points supporting that idea. A good thesis statement presents the principal claim of a speech and the main points by which it will be developed: "In my talk, I will take you through the four years you've been in college to show how much has happened and how much need still exists in our world." In summary, a good introduction:

* Captures listeners' attention
* Motivates listeners to listen
* States the main idea (thesis) of the speech and the key points supporting that idea
* Enhances the speaker's credibility

thesis statement The main idea of an entire speech; should capture the key message in a concise sentence that listeners can remember easily.

The Conclusion

With a preliminary outline of his introduction and the body of the speech, Harper *turns* his attention to the conclusion. From his public speaking class, he remembers that he should end on a strong note, but he can't recall what else a conclusion should do. Once again, he reviews his notes from the class.

A good speech ends on a strong point. The conclusion is a speaker's last chance to emphasize ideas, increase credibility, and gain listeners' support or approval. An effective conclusion accomplishes two goals. First, it summarizes the main ideas of the speech. Second, it leaves listeners with a memorable final idea such as a dramatic quote or example, a challenge, or an unforgettable computer graphic.

Harper outlines summaries of the four main points—each of the years of college—and then works on the final idea, which he wants to be really strong. The chronological organization and the introduction suggest a good way to close the speech. He writes out the exact words he wants for the closing: Imagine who you will be when 22 more years have passed. Will you be proud of how you've spent those years? Will your 44 years on earth have made a difference?

Transitions

The last aspect of organization that Harper needs to consider is **transitions**, which are words, phrases, and sentences that connect ideas in a speech. Transitions signal listeners that you have finished talking about one idea and are ready to move to the next one. Within the development of a single point, speakers usually rely on such transitional words and phrases as *therefore, and so, for this reason*, and *as the evidence suggests*. To make transitions from one point to another within a speech, speakers may use phrases: *"First, consider what happened in 2011.... Second, think about the big events of 2012...."* Speakers also provide transitions within points of a speech: *"Now that we have seen how much time we have, let's consider how long it takes to build the average Habitat house."* Finally, speakers typically use one or more sentences to create transitions between the major parts of a speech (introduction, body, conclusion). *"I have shown how quickly time passes and argued that we need to spend our time wisely. Before I leave you, let me summarize the key ideas I've presented."*

Developing Effective Delivery

"What about delivery?" Harper asks himself. He thumbs through the notes from his public speaking class, looking for information on delivery.

transition A word, phrase, or sentence that connects ideas and main points in a speech so that listeners can follow a speaker.

oral style Visual, vocal, and verbal aspects of the delivery of a public speech or other communication.

As we have seen, dynamism is one dimension of a speaker's credibility. Therefore, an engaging delivery is important. **Oral style** generally should be personal (Wilson & Arnold, 1974). Speakers may include personal stories and personal pronouns, referring to themselves as *I* rather than *the speaker*. Also, speakers may use phrases instead of complete sentences, and contractions (*can't*) are appropriate. Speakers should also sustain eye contact with listeners and show that they are approachable. If you reflect on speakers you have found effective, you will probably realize that they seemed engaging, personal, and open to you.

Effective oral style also tends to be immediate and active (Wilson & Arnold, 1974). This is important because listeners must understand ideas immediately, as they are spoken, whereas readers can take time to comprehend ideas. Speakers foster immediacy by using short sentences instead of complex sentences. Immediacy also involves following general ideas with clear, specific evidence or elaboration. Rhetorical questions ("Would you like to know that a good job is waiting for you when you graduate?"), interjections ("Imagine that!"; "Look!"), and redundancy also enhance the immediacy of a speech (Thompson & Grundgenett, 1999). A Take Action activity at the end of this chapter invites you to notice oral style in a speech.

Four styles of delivery are generally recognized, and each is appropriate in certain contexts. **Impromptu delivery** involves little or no preparation. It can be effective for speakers who know their material thoroughly. Many politicians speak in an impromptu fashion ["impromptu" not an adverb] when talking about their experience in public service and policies they advocate. Impromptu speaking generally is not advisable for novice speakers or for anyone who is not thoroughly familiar with a topic.

Probably the most commonly used presentational style is **extemporaneous delivery**. Extemporaneous speaking involves substantial preparation and practice, but it stops short of memorizing the exact words of a speech and relies on notes. Speakers conduct research, organize materials, and practice delivering their speeches, but they do not rehearse so much that the speeches sound canned. Attorneys, teachers, politicians, and others who engage in public speaking most often use an extemporaneous style of presentation because it allows them to prepare thoroughly and yet engage listeners when speaking.

Manuscript delivery, as the name implies, involves presenting a speech from a complete, written text. Manuscript style requires the speaker to write out the entire speech and to rely on the written document or a teleprompter projection when making the presentation. Few people can present manuscript speeches in an engaging, dynamic manner. However, manuscript delivery is appropriate, even advisable, in situations that call for precision. For instance, U.S. presidents generally use manuscripts for official presentations. In these circumstances, speakers cannot run the risk of errors or imprecise language.

An extension of the manuscript style of speaking is **memorized delivery**, in which a speaker commits an entire speech to memory and presents it without relying on a written text or notes. This style shares the primary disadvantage of manuscript speaking: the risk of a canned delivery that lacks dynamism and immediacy. In addition, the memorized style of delivery entails a second serious danger: forgetting. If a speaker is nervous, or if something happens to disrupt a presentation, the speaker may become rattled and forget all or part of the speech. Without the written text, he or she may be unable to get back on track.

When choosing a style of delivery, speakers should consider the advantages and disadvantages of each speaking style and the constraints of particular communication situations. No single style suits all occasions. Instead, the most effective style is one that suits the particular speaker and the situation. Regardless of which delivery style they use, effective speakers devote thought and practice to their verbal and nonverbal communication. It is important to select words that convey your intended

Extemporaneous speaking allows speakers to be engaged with listeners.

impromptu delivery
A delivery style that involves little preparation; speakers think on their feet as they talk about ideas and positions with which they are familiar.

extemporaneous delivery
A presentational style that includes preparation and practice but not memorization of actual words and nonverbal behaviors.

manuscript delivery
A presentational style that involves speaking from a complete manuscript of a speech.

memorized delivery
A presentational style in which the speech is delivered word for word from memory.

Syracuse Newspapers / S Cannerelli / The Image Works

Harper's careful preparation should make him a highly credible speaker at his graduation.

meanings and that create strong images for listeners. Equally important are effective gestures, paralanguage, and movement. Because public speaking is *enlarged* conversation, nonverbal behaviors generally should be more vigorous and commanding than in personal communication.

"Definitely not memorized or manuscript," Harper decides. "But it's too important an occasion to do impromptu, so extemporaneous is the best choice for this speech." Over the next few weeks, Harper fine-tunes the outline he's been developing throughout his preparation process and uses that to deliver the speech. He practices giving the speech at his desk, then in front of a mirror. Next, he uses his tablet to record himself giving the speech. When he reviews the video, he decides that his gestures are too small and he needs more inflection to speak to the graduation crowd. After making those adjustments, he asks four friends to be his "audience" for another practice speech. Finally, a week before he presents the speech, Harper goes to the stadium where graduation exercises will take place. The stage is not yet set up, but he stands in the stadium, looks up at the empty rafters where the graduating class will sit, and gives his speech.

In the foregoing pages, we've seen Harper go from realizing he has to give an important speech to preparing and practicing delivery of his speech. Table 13.1 summarizes the steps in Harper's process of preparing his graduation speech. Harper's thoughtful preparation and practice make it very likely that his speech will be effective.

Table 13.1

Key Principles of Public Speaking
Generate ideas
Adapt to context
Adapt to audience
Determine purpose
Develop thesis
Build credibility
Organize body of speech
Research supporting material
Build introduction
Build conclusion
Practice delivery

Digital Media and Public Speaking

Digital media can contribute to both the preparation of speeches and to their presentation. Like Harper, many speakers conduct substantial research online. In addition to broad Google searches, the Web provides access to libraries and data banks that offer excellent and up-to-date information on virtually any topic. Another way that Harper could use digital media to enhance his speech is by watching videos of excellent speakers. TED talks offer dynamic, effective speeches on a wide range of topics. In addition, there are speech banks, such as AmericanRhetoric (available with this chapter's online resources), which are recordings of famous speeches such as the Reverend Martin Luther King's "I Have a Dream" speech. Finally, Harper relied on digital media to gain a realistic sense of how his speech sounded. After reviewing the playback of his video, Harper amplified his gestures and inflection.

Digital media can also assist speakers during the actual presentation of speeches. You've probably seen speeches that included excerpts from videos. Television reporting, which is a kind of pubic presentation, frequently includes live or taped interviews

with reporters who are on the scene of a breaking story. Harper might show Power-
Point slides or a video from one of the countries he's visited or he might feature a short
recorded statement from one of his teammates on service trips.

Guidelines for Public Speaking

In this section, we discuss two guidelines for public speaking. The first pertains to
occasions when you might present a speech. The second focuses on effective, critical
listening to speeches given by others.

Adapt Speeches to Audiences

Perhaps the most important guideline for public speakers is to adapt to audiences, a
topic we have discussed throughout this chapter. Listeners are the whole reason for
speaking; without them, communication does not occur. Therefore, speakers should
be sensitive to listeners and should adapt to listeners' perspectives and expectations
(Griffin, 2015; Hamilton, 2015). You should take into account the perspectives of
listeners if you want them to consider your views. We consider the views of our
friends when we talk with them. We think about others' perspectives when we
engage in business negotiations. We use dual perspective when communicating
with children, dates, and neighbors. Thus, audience analysis is important to effectiveness in all communication encounters.

In one of my classes, a student named Odell gave a persuasive speech designed
to convince listeners to support affirmative action. He was personally compelling, his
delivery was dynamic, and his ideas were
well organized. The only problems were
that his audience had little knowledge
about affirmative action, and he didn't
explain exactly what the policy involves.
He assumed listeners understood how
affirmative action works, and he focused
on its positive effects. His listeners were
not persuaded, because Odell failed to give
them the information necessary for their
support. Odell's speech also illustrates our
earlier point that speeches often combine
more than one speaking purpose; in this
case, giving information was essential to
Odell's larger goal of persuading listeners.

The mistake that Odell made was failing to learn about his audience's knowledge
of his topic. It is impossible to entertain,
inform, or persuade people if we do not
consider their perspectives on our topics. To
paraphrase the advice of an ancient Greek
rhetorician, "The fool persuades me with
his or her reasons, the wise person with my
own." This advice—that effective speakers

Adapting to Listeners

On Saturday, January 8, 2011, Representative Gabrielle Giffords of Arizona
was shot in the head when Jared Lee Loughner opened fire during
Giffords' meeting with constituents. Giffords is a popular congress-
person, and many people anxiously awaited news about her injury
and chances of recovery. Miraculously, she survived the head wound.

Her doctors held a press conference to inform the public
of her status. In that public communication, Dr. Dong Kim,
the chair of neurosurgery at UT Health where Giffords was
treated, demonstrated how to adapt highly technical medical
information to listeners without medical expertise. He told
viewers that Giffords had mild hydrocephalus. Since many in
his audience wouldn't know the term *hydrocephalus*, Dr. Kim
translated it by saying, it's like "water in the head." He went on
to explain that patients with brain injury often have difficulty
absorbing fluid in the head, which he made easily understandable by adding that it's like "having a partially clogged
drain." The entire press conference can be found in the online
resources for this chapter.

understand and work with listeners' reasons, values, knowledge, and concerns—is as wise today as it was more than 2,000 years ago.

Although politicians and corporations can afford to conduct sophisticated polls to find out what people know, want, think, and believe, most of us don't have the resources to do that. So how do ordinary people engage in goal-focused analysis? One answer is to be observant. Usually, a speaker has some experience in interacting with his or her listeners or people like them. Drawing on past interactions, a speaker may be able to discern a great deal about the knowledge, attitudes, and beliefs of listeners.

Gathering information about listeners through conversations or surveys is also appropriate. For example, I once was asked to speak on women leaders at a governor's leadership conference. To prepare my presentation, I asked the conference planners to send me information about the occupations and ages of people attending the conference. In addition, I asked the planners to survey the conferees about their experience as leaders and working with women leaders. The material I received informed me about the level of experience and the attitudes and bias of my listeners. Then I could adapt my speech to what they knew and believed.

By taking listeners into consideration, you build a presentation that is interactive and respectful. As we learned earlier in this chapter, listeners tend to confer credibility on speakers who show that they understand listeners and who adapt presentations to listeners' perspectives, knowledge, and expectations.

Listen Critically

A final guideline is to listen critically to speeches you hear. Because we often find ourselves in the role of listener, we should know how to listen well and critically to ideas that others present. As you will recall from Chapter 6, critical listening involves attending mindfully to communication in order to evaluate its merit. Critical listeners assess whether a speaker is informed and ethical and whether a speech is soundly reasoned and supported.

The first step in critical listening is to take in and understand what a speaker says. You cannot evaluate an argument or idea until you have grasped it and the information that supports it. Thus, effective listening requires you to concentrate on what a speaker says. You can focus your listening by asking questions such as these:

◆ What does the speaker announce as the purpose of the talk?

◆ What evidence does the speaker provide to support claims?

◆ Does the speaker have experience that qualifies him or her to speak on this topic?

◆ Does the speaker have any vested interest in what she or he advocates?

You probably noticed that these questions parallel those we identified in our earlier discussion of ways to improve your credibility when you are making speeches. The questions help you zero in on what others say so that you can make informed judgments of their credibility and the credibility of their ideas.

To listen critically, you should suspend your preconceptions about topics and speakers. You need not abandon your ideas, but you should set them aside long enough to listen openly to a speech, especially if you are predisposed to disagree with it. By granting a full and fair hearing to ideas that differ from yours, you increase the likelihood that your perspective and ideas will be well-informed and carefully reasoned.

 **Common Fallacies in Reasoning**

Ad hominem attack	You can't believe what Jane Smith says about voting, because she doesn't vote.
After this, therefore because of this (Post hoc, ergo propter hoc)	The new flextime policy is ineffective because more people have been getting to work late since it went into effect.
Bandwagon appeal	You should be for the new campus meal plan because most students are.
Slippery slope	If we allow students to play a role in decisions about hiring and tenure of faculty, pretty soon students will be running the whole school.
Hasty generalization	People should not be allowed to own pit bulls, because there have been instances of pit bulls attacking children.
Either–or	Tenure should be either abolished or kept as it is.
Red herring argument	People who own pit bulls should switch to cats. Let me tell you why cats are the ideal pet....
Reliance on the halo effect	World-famous actor Richard Connery says that we should not restrict people's right to own firearms.

MindTap Can you find examples of one or more of these fallacies?

Critical listeners recognize fallacies in reasoning and do not succumb to them. To accept a speaker's ideas, critical listeners demand that the ideas be well-supported with evidence and sound reasoning. The ENGAGE! feature on this page provides examples of some of the more common fallacies in reasoning in public communication.

Summary

This chapter opened with Harper, the Student Body President of his college, who realizes he has to give a graduation speech. We traveled with Harper as he considered the speaking context and his listeners in order to generate ideas for his speech and decide on his speaking purpose and thesis. He then worked on organizing and supporting his ideas. When we left Harper, he was practicing his delivery. Every step of Harper's preparation process should enhance his credibility as a trustworthy and dynamic speaker. Like most speakers, Harper conducted some of his research online and he used his tablet to video himself giving the speech. He then reviewed the video and adjusted his delivery.

The final section of the chapter focused on two guidelines related to public speaking. The first guideline is to adapt speeches to listeners. Speakers have an ethical responsibility to consider listeners' perspectives, knowledge, and expectations as they plan, prepare, and present speeches. The second guideline is to listen critically to public speeches by others. Good listeners suspend their views long enough to give a full and fair hearing to what others say. As they listen, they identify and evaluate the quality of speakers' experience, evidence, and reasoning, which allows them to make informed critical assessments of the ideas presented.

Public communication is vital to personal and professional success and to the health of our society. Not reserved for people who have high status or who are in the public limelight, public speaking is a basic skill for us all. In this chapter, we have seen what is involved in presenting and listening to public presentations, and we have identified ways to enhance our effectiveness in this vital realm of social life.

Experience Communication Sample Speech

Together, We Can Stop Cyber-Bullying

Apply what you've learned in this chapter by analyzing the following student speech, using the accompanying questions as a guide. These questions and a video of the speech are also available online with your MindTap Speech for *Communication Mosaics*.

Adam Parrish was an undergraduate, attending University of Kentucky, when he presented this speech. The text of the speech is printed in its entirety. As you read Adam's speech, you should critically assess the choices he made in planning, researching, developing, organizing, and presenting his ideas.

As you read the speech and view it online, consider how it could be made even more effective. Also, think about different ways you might accomplish the speaker's objectives; can you identify alternative organizational structures, kinds of evidence, transitions, and so forth? Following the speech are three questions to guide your thinking about what Adam did and might have done.

© Cengage Learning. All Rights Reserved. The speech was developed and originally presented by Adam Parrish and was presented by Michael Tow.

Together, We Can Stop Cyber-Bullying

By Adam Parrish, University of Kentucky

"I'll miss just being around her." "I didn't want to believe it." "It's such a sad thing." These quotes are from the friends and family of 15-year-old Phoebe Prince, who, on January 14, 2010, committed suicide by hanging herself. Why did this senseless act occur? The answer is simple . . . Phoebe Prince was bullied to death.

Many of us know someone who has been bullied in school. Perhaps they were teased in the parking lot or in the locker room. In the past, bullying occurred primarily in school. However, with the advent of new communication technologies such as cell phones, text messaging, instant messaging, blogs, and social networking sites, bullies can now follow and terrorize their victims anywhere, even into their own bedrooms. Using electronic communications to tease, harass, threaten, and intimidate another person is called cyber-bullying.

As a tutor and mentor to young students, I have witnessed cyber-bullying first hand, and by examining current research, I believe I understand the problem, its causes, and how we can help end cyber-bullying. What I know for sure is that cyber-bullying is a devastating form of abuse that must be confronted on national, local, and personal levels.

Today, we will examine the widespread and harmful nature of cyber-bulling, uncover how and why it persists, and pinpoint some simple solutions we must begin to enact in order to thwart cyber-bullies and comfort their victims. Let's begin by tackling the problem head on.

Many of us have read rude, insensitive, or nasty statements posted about us or someone we care about on social networking sites like MySpace and Facebook. Well, whether or not those comments were actually intended to hurt another person's feelings, if they did hurt their feelings, then they are perfect examples of cyber-bullying.

Cyber-bullying is a pervasive and dangerous behavior. It takes place all over the world and through a wide array of electronic media. According to Keith and Martin's article in the winter 2005 edition of *Reclaiming Children and Youth,* 57 percent of American middle-school students had experienced instances of cyber-bullying ranging from hurtful comments to threats of physical violence. Quing Li's article published in the journal *Computers in Human Behavior* noted that cyber-bullying is not gender biased. According to Li, females are just as likely as males to engage in cyber-bullying, although women are 10 percent more likely to be victimized.

While the number of students who are targets of cyber-bullies decreases as students age, data from the *Youth Internet Safety Survey* indicates that the instances of American high school students being cyber-bullied had increased nearly 50 percent from 2000 to 2005. The problem does not exist in the United States alone.

Li noted that Internet and cell phone technologies have been used by bullies to harass, torment, and threaten young people in North America, Europe, and Asia. However, some of the most horrific attacks happen right here at home.

According to Keith and Martin, a particularly disturbing incident occurred in Dallas, Texas, where an overweight student with multiple sclerosis was targeted on a school's social networking page. One message read, "I guess I'll have to wait until you kill yourself which I hope is not long from now, or I'll have to wait until your disease kills you." Clearly, the cyber-bullying is a worldwide and perverse phenomenon. What is most disturbing about cyber-bullying is its effects upon victims, bystanders, and perhaps even upon bullies themselves.

Cyber-bullying can lead to physical and psychological injuries upon its victims. According to a 2007 article in the *Journal of Adolescent Health,* Ybarra and colleagues noted that 36 percent of the victims of cyber-bullies are also harassed by their attackers in school. For example, the Dallas student with MS had eggs thrown at her car and a bottle of acid thrown at her house.

Ybarra et al. reported that victims of cyber-bullying experience such severe emotional distress that they often exhibit behavioral problems such as poor grades, skipping school, and receiving detentions and sus-pensions. Furthermore, Smith et al. suggested that even a few instances of cyber-bullying can have these long-lasting negative effects.

What is even more alarming is that, according to Ybarra and colleagues, victims of cyber-bullying are significantly more likely to carry weapons to school as a result of feeling threatened. Obviously, this could lead to violent outcomes for bullies, victims, and even bystanders.

Now that we have heard about the nature, scope, and effects of cyber-bullying, let's see if we can discover its causes. Let's think back to a time when we may have seen a friend or loved one being harassed online. Did we report the bully to the network administrator or other authorities? Did we console the victim? I know I didn't. If you are like me, we may unknowingly be enabling future instances of cyber-bullying.

Cyber-bullying occurs because of the anonymity offered to bullies by cell phone and Internet technologies, as well as the failure of victims and bystanders to report incidents of cyber-bullying. You see, unlike schoolyard bullies, cyber-bullies can attack their victims anonymously.

Ybarra and colleagues discovered that 13 percent of cyber-bullying victims did not know who was tormenting them. This devastating statistic is important because, as Keith and Martin noted, traditional bullying takes place face-to-face and often ends when students leave school. However, today, students are subjected to nonstop bullying, even when they are alone in their own homes.

Perhaps the anonymous nature of cyber-attacks partially explains why Li found that nearly 76 percent of victims of cyber-bullying and 75 percent of bystanders never reported instances of bullying to adults. Victims and bystanders who do not report attacks from cyber-bullies can unintentionally enable bullies.

According to De Nies, Donaldson, and Netter of *ABCNews.com* (2010) several of Phoebe Prince's classmates were aware that she was being harassed but did not inform the school's administration. Li suggested that victims and bystanders often do not believe that adults will actually intervene to stop cyber-bullying. However, *ABCNews.com* reports that 41 states have laws against bullying in schools and 23 of those states target cyber-bullying specifically.

Now that we know that victims of cyber-bullies desperately need the help of witnesses and bystanders to report their attacks, we should arm ourselves with the information necessary to provide that assistance. Think about the next time you see a friend or loved one being tormented or harassed online. What would you be willing to do to help?

Cyber-bullying must be confronted on national, local, and personal levels. There should be a comprehensive national law confronting cyber-bullying in schools. Certain statutes currently in state laws should be amalgamated to create the strongest protections for victims and the most effective punishments for bullies as possible.

According to Limber and Small's article titled, *State Laws and Policies to Address Bullying in Schools,* Georgia law requires faculty and staff to be trained on the nature of bullying and what actions to take if they see students being bullied.

Furthermore, Connecticut law *requires* school employees to report bullying as part of their hiring contract. Washington takes this a step fur-ther by protecting employees from any legal action if a reported bully is proven to be innocent. When it comes to protecting victims, West Virginia law demands that schools must ensure that a bullied student does not receive additional abuse at the hands of his or her bully.

Legislating punishment for bullies is difficult. As Limber and Small noted, zero-tolerance polices often perpetuate violence because at-risk youth, i.e., bullies, are removed from all of the benefits of school, which might help make them less abusive. A comprehensive anti-cyber-bullying law should incorporate the best aspects of these state laws and find a way to punish bullies that is both punitive and has the ability to rehabilitate abusers. However, for national laws to be effective, local communities need to be supportive.

Local communities must organize and mobilize to attack the problem of cyber-bullying. According to Greene's 2006 article published in the *Journal of Social Issues,* communities need to support bullying prevention programs by conducting a school-based bullying survey for individual school districts.

We can't know how to best protect victims in our community without knowing how they are affected by the problem. It is critical to know this information as Greene noted, only three percent of teachers in the United States perceive bullying to be a problem in their schools.

Local school districts should create a Coordinating Committee made up of "administrators, teachers, students, parents, school staff, and community partners" to gather bullying data and rally support to confront the problem. Even if your local school district is unable or unwilling to mobilize behind this dire cause, there are some important actions you can take personally to safeguard those you love against cyber-bullying.

There are several warning signs that might indicate a friend or loved one is a victim of a cyber-bully. If you see a friend or loved one exhibiting these signs, the decision to get involved can be the difference between life and death.

According to Keith and Martin's article, *Cyber-Bullying: Creating a Culture of Respect in a Cyber World,* victims of cyber-bullies often use electronic communication more frequently than do people who are not being bullied. Victims of cyber-bullies have mood swings and difficulty sleeping, they seem depressed and/or become anxious; victims can also become withdrawn from social activities and fall behind in scholastic responsibilities. If you witness your friends or family members exhibiting these symptoms there are several ways you can help.

According to Raskauskas and Stoltz's 2007 article in *Developmental Psychology,* witnesses of cyber-bullying should inform victims to take the attacks seriously, especially if the bullies threaten violence. You should tell victims to report their attacks to police or other authorities, to block harmful messages by blocking email accounts and cell phone numbers, and to save copies of attacks and provide them to authorities.

If you personally know the bully and feel safe confronting him or her, do so! As Raskaukas and Stoltz noted, bullies will often back down when confronted by peers. By being a good friend and by giving good advice, you can help a victim report his or her attacks from cyber-bullies and take a major step toward eliminating this horrendous problem. So, you see, we are not helpless to stop the cyber-bulling problem as long as we make the choice NOT to ignore it.

To conclude, cyber-bullying is a devastating form of abuse that must be reported to authorities. Cyber-bullying is a worldwide problem perpetuated by the silence of both victims and bystanders. By paying attention to certain warning signs, we can empower ourselves to console victims and report their abusers.

Today, I'm imploring you to do your part to help stop cyber-bullying. I know that you agree that stopping cyber-bullying must be a priority. First, although other states have cyber-bullying laws in place, ours does not. So I'm asking you to sign this petition that I will forward to our district's State Legislators. We need to make our voices heard that we want specific laws passed to stop this horrific abuse and to punish those caught doing it.

Second, I'm also asking you to be vigilant in noticing signs of cyber-bullying and then taking action. Look for signs that your friend, brother, sister, cousin, boyfriend, girlfriend, or loved one might be a victim of cyber-bullying and then get involved to help stop it! Phoebe Prince showed the warning signs, and she did not deserve to die so senselessly. None of us would ever want to say, "I'll miss just being around her" "I didn't want to believe it," or "It's such a sad thing" about our own friends or family members. We must work to ensure that victims are supported and bullies are confronted nationally, locally, and personally.

I know that if we stand together and refuse to be silent, we can and will stop cyber-bullying.

1. Is Adam's speech persuasive or informative or both?

2. Describe Adam's credibility—initial, derived, and terminal.

3. What organizational pattern did Adam use and to what extent was it effective?

 Key Concepts

Practice defining the chapter's terms by using online flashcards.

comparison (analogy), 260
credibility, 259
derived credibility, 260
evidence, 260
example, 260
extemporaneous delivery, 267
impromptu delivery, 267
initial credibility, 259
manuscript delivery, 267
memorized delivery, 267

oral style, 266
quotation, 260
speech to entertain, 258
speech to inform, 258
speech to persuade, 259
statistics, 260
terminal credibility, 260
thesis statement, 265
transition, 266
visual aids, 260

Review, Reflect, Extend

The Reflect and Discuss, and Take Action features that follow will help you review, reflect on, and extend the information and ideas presented in this chapter. These resources, and a diverse selection of additional study tools, are also available online at the MindTap Speech for *Communication Mosaics*.

Reflect, personalize, and apply what you've learned.

Reflect and Discuss

1. Make a point of listening to students who speak out for causes on your campus. How do the speakers' attempt to establish that they are informed, dynamic, and trustworthy (the dimensions of credibility)?

2. During the next week, pay attention to evidence cited by others in public presentations. You might note what evidence is used on news programs, by professors in classes, and by special speakers on your campus. Evaluate the effectiveness of evidence presented. Are visuals clear and uncluttered? Do speakers explain the qualifications of sources they cite, and are those sources unbiased? What examples and analogies are presented, and how effective are they?

3. Note the use of stories to add interest and effect to public presentations. Describe a speaker who uses a story effectively and one who uses a story ineffectively. What are the differences between them? What conclusions can you draw about the effective use of stories in public presentations?

4. As a class, discuss what makes professors interesting or uninteresting in their classroom communication.

TAKE ACTION

1. Noticing Conversational Speaking Style

Think about the professors who were most effective, and those who were least effective, in communicating course content. For each group of professors, answer these questions:

a. Did the professors use a formal or an informal speaking style?

b. Did the professors state clearly what was important?

c. Did the professors give reasons for ideas and opinions they expressed?

d. Could you follow the professors' trains of thought?

e. Did the professors adapt their ideas to your knowledge and interests?

f. Did you feel engaged?

2. Noticing Oral Style

Attend a speech on your campus. Identify instances of oral style:

| specific ideas and evidence | redundancy | short, simple sentences |
| rhetorical questions | interjections | personal stories and language |

If you perceived the speech as ineffective, was it lacking oral style? If you perceived it as effective, was oral style featured?

Recommended Resources

1. AmericanRhetoric.com provides an online bank of speeches. You can access this resource by going to this chapter's online resources.

2. The online resources for this chapter provide a link to *Vital Speeches* where you may study important public addresses. Select a speech on a topic that interests you. Read the speech to see how it embodies principles discussed in this chapter.

14

Mass Media

Whoever controls the media—the images—controls the culture.
—Allen Ginsberg

How much do media influence what you think and believe?

 MindTap

Learning Objectives

Topics Covered in This Chapter	After studying this chapter, you should be able to . . .
Understanding Mass Media	Given the four media eras identified in your text, discuss the relationship between dominant media and cultural life.
	Reflect on the ways mass media have influenced your personal worldview.
Digital Media and Mass Media	Comment on how the dominance of digital media is affecting human thought, ways of relating, and sense of community.
Guidelines for Engaging Mass Media	Create an action plan to implement the seven guidelines offered in this chapter to improve your engagement with mass media.

MindTap

Start with a quick engagement activity and **review** the chapter Learning Objectives.

Read, highlight, and take notes online.

◆ Police gun down unarmed teen.

◆ Police kill robbery suspect.

◆ White cop kills unarmed black teen.

◆ Black robber taunts white officer.

On August 9, 2014, 18-year-old Michael Brown was shot by 28-year-old Ferguson, Missouri Police officer Darren Wilson. For weeks, the tragedy dominated television news, occupied the front page of most papers, and was the cover story for multiple nationally circulated magazines. The story was framed differently by different mass media outlets. Some reports emphasized that Michael Brown was unarmed and a teenager, which aroused sympathy for Brown and his family. Other reports highlighted Officer Wilson's excellent record—no disciplinary problems, an award for heroism—and the possibility that Brown might have been high on marijuana and had participated in robbing a store prior to the shooting. Some reports focused on the fact that Brown was black and Wilson was white; others gave less attention to the two men's races. Some reports repeatedly showed an interview with eye witnesses who claimed Brown was shot while holding his hands up in surrender. Other reports minimized the eye witnesses' testimony.

◆ Was the shooting of Michael Brown evidence of the problem of urban youth crime? Or was it evidence of persisting racism in America?

◆ Did Brown provoke Wilson? Or did Wilson use excessive force without provocation?

◆ Did Wilson act appropriately, panic, or make an honest error in judgment?

How you answer these questions may reflect the media reports you saw and heard. The way the bare facts were framed by different media outlets fundamentally shaped how viewers and readers perceived the event and whom they judged to be blameworthy. Whether the issue is Michael Brown's untimely death, Hillary Clinton's policy credentials, the Israeli–Palestine conflict, global climate change, or reproductive health policies, mass media shape how we understand the issues, the people involved, and our own feelings about the issues.

This chapter focuses on mass communication, and the next chapter explores the companion system of digital media. The first section of this chapter examines mass communication and discusses features of mass communication that give insight into how it affects our thoughts, attitudes, and sense of identity. In the second section of this chapter, we consider ways that mass media are entwined with social media. We close the chapter with two guidelines for interacting with mass media.

Understanding Mass Media

mass media Communication that addresses large audiences.

Mass media are forms of communication that address large audiences or publics: books, films, television, radio, newspapers, advertising, magazines, and other forms of visual, audio, and print communication that reach multitudes of people. Mass communication includes computer technologies such as the Web and WebTV that reach a great number of people; but it does not include e-mail messages, IMs, tweets, and texting, which are not directed to large publics.

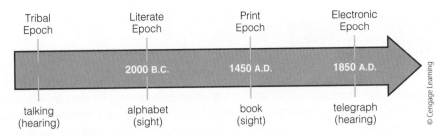

Figure 14.1 Media Epochs in Human History

Despite the popularity of digital media, Americans still engage mass media in their daily lives. In 2013, each day, the average person in the United States watched 4.5 hours of television, listened to 1.5 hours of radio, and read print newspapers and magazines for less than an hour (eMarketer, 2014). Americans' rely on television for national and international news as well as local weather, traffic news, and reports of breaking news ("Pew Media Study," 2011). People also watch TV on mobile devices that now offer traditional and cable TV network shows (Rosman, 2013). Other forms of mass media also remain popular. Most books are still restricted to hard copy. Currently, about 15 percent of the books in the world have been digitized (Darnton, 2011). And most of us continue to watch movies, read magazines, and listen to radio.

In this section, we discuss four premises that help us understand how mass media affect our lives.

Changes in Mass Media Change Human Life

Communication scholar Marshall McLuhan was fascinated by how mass media evolve over time and how changes in mass media transform other aspects of human life. He believed that the dominant media in any era strongly shape both individual and collective life. The Engage feature on page 280 summarizes one of McLuhan's main ideas about the relationship between media and human consciousness.

To explain how media shape our lives, McLuhan identified the media that dominated in four distinct eras in human history (Figure 14.1; McLuhan, 1962, 1964; McLuhan & Fiore, 1967). During the early years of human existence, people lived in tribal communities and the oral tradition reigned. People communicated face to face, giving and getting immediate feedback. Oral cultures were knitted together by stories and rituals that passed along the history and traditions of a culture, as well as by oral transmission of information and forms of entertainment. Reliance on the spoken word fostered cohesive communities and made hearing a dominant sense (McLuhan, 1969). As Derek points out in his commentary, tribal communities and the oral tradition they foster have not disappeared altogether. Although they no longer prevail in the United States, oral cultures continue among insulated communities in regions such as Appalachia and in groups that deliberately isolate themselves from mainstream culture. Oral cultures also prevail in many underdeveloped countries.

 Derek

I spent two years as a Peace Corps volunteer in some of the smaller and poorer countries in Africa. It was an incredible experience to live in societies that had no mass communication. Information was passed along by visitors who traveled into villages or by villagers who traveled to one of the larger cities and returned with news. What I noticed most about these societies is that people interact with each other more and more intensely than in the United States. Talking is living, talking is information, talking is entertainment, talking is history in oral cultures.

ENGAGE!

The Medium Is the Message/Massage

Marshall McLuhan probably is best known for his statement, "The medium is the message." For him, this statement had multiple meanings (McLuhan & Fiore, 1967). It implied, first, that the medium of communication is important in its own right. Before McLuhan, most media scholars focused on the content of mass communication. McLuhan, however, thought the medium by which content was disseminated makes a difference. For example, he argued that watching television shapes how we think, regardless of what we watch on television.

"The medium is the message" had other meanings for McLuhan. By changing only one letter, the statement becomes "The medium is the massage." This implies that media massage our consciousness and transform our perceptions. Finally, McLuhan sometimes made a play on words by saying, "The medium is the mass age," by which he meant that the dominant medium of the era in which he lived had become mass communication.

Invention of the phonetic alphabet ushered in what McLuhan called the literate epoch in human history. Writing allowed people to communicate without face-to-face interaction. They could read when not in the presence of others in their communities. Because we can reread printed materials, reading requires less memory than oral communication. Thus hearing declined in importance and sight ascended as a primary sense.

Writing also established a linear form for communication—letter follows letter, word follows word, sentence follows sentence. According to McLuhan, the continuous sequential order of print cultivated linear thinking and hence the development of disciplines such as mathematics that are based on linear logic.

Although the invention of the alphabet made written communication possible, print did not immediately gain prominence as the medium that reached the masses. Because there was as yet no way to mass-produce the written word, only the elite class of society had access to written media.

When Gutenberg invented the printing press in the 15th century, literacy ascended in human history. The printing press made possible the printing of thousands of copies of a single book at moderate cost. Written media were no longer limited to elite members of society. In addition, mass-produced writing cultivated homogeneity of perspectives and values because the same message could be delivered to many people.

The dominance of print as a medium and the eye as a primary sense organ diminished with the invention of the telegraph, which launched the electronic epoch

The Evolution of Long Distance Communication

Zits © 2007 Zits Partnership King Features Syndicate

in human history. According to McLuhan (1969), electronic media revived the oral tradition and made hearing and touch preeminent.

The telegraph was only the first of a long line of electronic media with the potential to revitalize a sense of community among people. The first television debuted in 1926. Today, assisted by satellite and cable transmissions, television allows us to see and hear around the world. We tune into television news programs to understand what is happening in Iraq or Afghanistan. We watch a live broadcast of a presidential speech and know what our president said and how he looked when he spoke. The increased access to information made possible by electronic communication led McLuhan to claim that electronic media created a **global village** (McLuhan & Fiore, 1967) that resembles the tribal village (Sparks, 2006).

McLuhan died in 1980. He left a partial manuscript that described the computer as a new medium that would change human beings and culture once again. As we will see in Chapter 15, McLuhan was right: Computer-mediated communication has greatly influenced our lives.

> **global village** The modern-day, worldwide community made possible by electronic communication that instantaneously links people all over the world.
>
> **uses and gratification theory** Claims people use mass communication to gratify their interests and desires.

Mass Media Serve Individuals' Needs and Desires

Think about the last time you watched a film. Did you watch because the story mattered to you? Did you want to escape from problems and worries? Did you watch because the film featured stars you like? Did you only pay attention to the parts you liked? If you answered yes to any of these questions, you acted as **uses and gratification theory** would predict. This theory states that we use mass media to gratify ourselves (Reinhard & Dervin, 2009).

Uses and gratification theory assumes that we select media that we think will give us something we value or want. For example, if you are interested in national affairs, you might listen to National Public Radio. If you are concerned about whether a game will be rained out, you might watch The Weather Channel. If you invest in the stock market, you might read *The Wall Street Journal.*

We also use media for pleasure. If you are bored and want excitement, you might watch an action film or read an action novel.

We might choose soft music to enhance romantic feelings, rock to generate excitement, spirituals to inspire or comfort ourselves, and ritualistic chants and folk music to foster a sense of unity among protesters at a rally.

A classic study of how people use mass communication to gratify themselves was conducted by Janice Radway (1991). She investigated what romance novels mean to Midwestern women who read these novels, sometimes as many as 12 in a week. Rather than dismissing romance novels as "mindless drivel," which is how many critics view them, Radway talked with the women who read them to find out why they did. She found that readers gained pleasure by identifying with independent heroines and

Many of us use mass communication for pleasure.

Ringo Chiu/ZUMApress/Newscom

Romance on the Run

If you are a fan of romance novels, you no longer have to choose between reading books and being wired. Harlequin Books, the largest publisher of steamy romance novels, offers electronic books that can be read on cell phones. To fit today's readers, who often have neither long periods of time to curl up with fat novels nor room in briefcases to tote them around, Harlequin has divided books into daily installments that can be read quickly—usually fewer than 10 minutes. Installments are automatically downloaded to subscribers' cell phones for a small monthly fee (Flynn, 2006).

Installment reading isn't restricted to romance novels. Readers who want small segments of stories can download mystery novels too. Of course, presenting novels in installments is hardly new. As Joe Hartlaub (2012) points out, Charles Dickens did that in the 1800s and science fiction magazines published installments of novels in the 1940s.

escaping from the routines of their own lives. Women who frequently read romance novels also explained that to read them was to have personal time, free from the demands of families and housework.

If people use media to gratify themselves, then we might expect that people will also create media if existing media do not satisfy them and others in their communities. That's exactly what happens. Most national and regional newspapers in the United States largely reflect the interests, concerns, and biases of middle-class Caucasian heterosexuals. Typically, they don't offer many stories that speak to the particular concerns of Hispanics, gays, Asian Americans, or other groups. To compensate for this, Spanish-language newspapers and Native American newspapers have been created. These newspapers serve the interests of specific groups that are neglected by mainstream media. Likewise, the exploding number of satellite and cable channels expands our options for choosing media that gratify us.

Mass Media Influence Human Knowledge and Perspectives

As we saw in the accounts of the shooting of Michael Brown that opened this chapter, mass media spotlight some issues, events, people, and aspects of phenomena and downplay others.

Agenda Setting   You set an agenda for a meeting when you decide what issues will be discussed. In a similar fashion, mass media set an agenda for public consciousness when they decide how to distribute media coverage of various issues (Boydstun, 2013; Bryant & Oliver, 2008; McCombs, Ghanem, & Chernov, 2009; Vivian, 2013). In other words, by selecting what events and issues to cover, how to present them, and how much time to give each one, mass communication tells us what we should think about (McCombs, 2014; Vivian, 2013).

Agenda setting directs our attention. First, mass media direct us to pay attention to particular topics by giving those topics coverage. For instance, during the 2008 presidential campaign, mass media devoted a great amount of space and time to the coverage of Sarah Palin's wardrobe and the $150,000+ price tag for it. Media also gave substantial attention to Michelle Obama's and Hillary Clinton's fashion choices. This coverage reinforced the long-standing cultural view associating women and fashion, and it encouraged viewers and readers to see women's appearance as important.

Simultaneously, this media focus diverted attention from these women's substantive stands. And this is the second way that agenda setting works. Mass media lead us to ignore or give minimum attention to some topics and people by covering them barely or not at all. What did Michelle Obama do in her community organizing and her work as a hospital administrator? What were Hillary Clinton's accomplishments as a senator? What fashion choices did John McCain and Barack Obama make? By

agenda setting Media's selection of issues, events, and people to highlight for attention.

giving little or no coverage to these issues, media tell us they are not important to think about. The online resources for this chapter provide a link to an international agenda setting organization and its research.

Gatekeeping   A **gatekeeper** is a person or group that decides which messages pass through the gates that control information flow to reach consumers (McCombs et al., 2009; Shoemaker & Vos, 2009). Gatekeepers screen messages, stories, and perspectives to create messages (programs, interviews, news clips) that shape our perceptions of events and people.

Mass media have many gatekeepers. Editors of newspapers, books, and magazines screen the information that gets to readers; owners, executives, and producers filter information for radio and television programs; advertisers and political groups may also intervene to influence which messages reach end users of mass media. For example, radio and television stations that are owned and financed by conservatives air Rush Limbaugh's comments but not those of Rachel Maddow. Radio and television stations owned and funded by more liberal groups are likely to shut the gate on Rush Limbaugh but include Rachel Maddow. As a result, people who tune into conservative and liberal stations are likely to have different perspectives on issues.

Cultivation of Worldviews   Through gatekeeping, mass media cumulatively promote particular understandings about the world and how it operates. The word *cumulatively* is important to understanding the process of **cultivation** of world views. Researchers don't argue that a particular television program has significant effects on viewers' beliefs or that television viewing directly determines public opinion. However, they claim that watching television over a long period of time affects viewers' basic views of the world. By extension, the more television people watch, the more distorted their ideas about life are likely to be (Gerbner, 1990; Gerbner, Gross, Morgan, & Signorielli, 1986; Robinson, 2009; Signorielli, 2009; Signorielli & Morgan, 1990).

The primary way that television and other forms of mass communication cultivate particular worldviews is by **mainstreaming**. Mainstreaming is the stabilizing and homogenizing of views within a society. For example, commercial programming consistently underrepresents women and casts them in subordinate, often nonspeaking roles. Mass media also overrepresent European Americans and portray them in a range of identities, including upstanding citizens and successful, powerful people. Meanwhile, members of other races are too often depicted as lazy, criminal, highly sexualized, or irresponsible. That is, mass media do this when they include minorities at all. A study of top-grossing films released between 2007 and 2012 found that 76.3 percent of speaking characters were white, 10.8 percent were black, 5 percent were Asian, 4.2 percent were Hispanic, and 3.6 percent were from other or mixed race ethnicities (Smith, Choueiti, & Pieper, 2013). Only 93 of 3,200 children's books published in 2013 were about black people, and only 57 of those books had significant Latino or Latina content (Horning, Lindgren, & Schliesman, 2014; Myers, 2014). The online resources for this chapter provide a link to the Cooperative Center for Children's Books in Wisconsin, which offers detailed information about authors' races and content attentive to different races in children's books.

Another feature of television programming is heavy doses of violence. From Saturday morning cartoons to prime-time dramas, extensive violence is normalized. Given the constant violence on television, it's no wonder that many heavy viewers think the world is more violent than crime reports show it to be. By extension, heavy viewing

gatekeeper A person or group that controls the choice and presentation of topics by media.

cultivation A cumulative process by which the media foster beliefs about social reality, including the belief that the world is more dangerous and violent than it actually is.

mainstreaming The effect of television in stabilizing and homogenizing views within a society.

Testing the Mean World Syndrome

The basic worldview studied by cultivation theorists is exemplified in research on the mean world syndrome (Gerbner et al., 1986). The **mean world syndrome** is the belief that the world is a dangerous place, full of mean people who cannot be trusted and who are likely to harm us. Although less than 1 percent of the U.S. population is victimized by violent crime in any year, television presents the world as a dangerous place in which everyone is at risk.

To test this theory, ask 10 people whether or not they basically agree or disagree with the following five statements, which are adapted from the mean world index used in research. After respondents have answered, ask them how much television they watch on an average day. Do your results support the claim that television cultivates the mean world syndrome?

1. Most public officials are not interested in the plight of the average person.

2. Despite what some people say, the lot of the average person is getting worse, not better.

3. Most people mostly look out for themselves rather than trying to help others.

4. Most people would try to take advantage of you if they had a chance.

5. You can't be too careful in dealing with people.

mean world syndrome
The belief that the world is dangerous and full of mean people.

of mass media may lead some people to view violence as a normal and increasingly acceptable part of ordinary life (Katz, 2013; Pozios, Kambam, & Bender, 2013). Mike's commentary speaks to a concern of many parents.

 Mike

Adults may be able to separate fantasy from real life, but kids aren't. What they see on the TV is real life to them. My wife and I have raised our son not to be aggressive—not a sissy, but not aggressive either. But any time he watches TV, he's picking up sticks and aiming them like they were guns or imitating karate chops he saw some TV character do.

Defining Desirability and Normalcy Mass media also shape mainstream ideas of who and what are desirable and normal. If you watch TV programs and films, you might think that men outnumber women in the population. That is far from true, but mass media consistently overrepresent men and boys and underrepresent women and girls. In fact, the percentage of women in leading roles behind the camera has declined since 1998 (Dowd, 2014). The Geena Davis Institute, which studies gender representations in media states bluntly, "Statistically, there has been little forward movement for girls in media in six decades. For nearly 60 years, gender inequality on screen has remained largely unchanged and unchecked" (Gender in Media, 2012).

Not only are women and girls underrepresented, but they are portrayed in limited and limiting roles. In both programming and advertisements, women—and,

Can Women Talk about Anything Other Than Men?

That obviously ridiculous question is one of three questions in the Bechdel test, named after Alison Bechdel, who won a coveted MacArthur Award in 2014. The Bechdel test asks three simple questions about female characters in films: (1) Does the film feature at least two women? (2) Do they talk to each other? (3) Do they talk about something other than a man? When Bechdel applied those questions to current releases, she found that more than 50 percent of the films nominated for Academy Awards in 2014 failed the test (Dewey, 2014; Hickey, 2014). This chapter's online resources provide a link to a site to information about the Bechdel test.

 MindTap Apply the Bechdel test to a currently popular film you've seen.

Consumer Trends / Alamy

 What is this image's message to women?

increasingly, very young girls—are represented as slender or thin and highly sexual (Gender in Media, 2012; Smith, Choueiti, Scofield, & Pieper, 2013). Judges on *America's Next Top Model* lavish praise on seriously underweight contestants and call normal-sized contestants (130 pounds at 5'8") "plus sized" (Pozner, 2004). The flawless beauty and stunning sexuality that mass media tell women they should have can be achieved only through consumption of products and services. Marketers aim to persuade girls and women to maximize their potential through consumption. The good girl or woman is a serious consumer (Gill, 2008; Kilbourne, 2010; Morreale, 2007). The message that much popular media send to women is clear: Your worth is based on your physical attractiveness; if you aren't superthin and superhot, you should invest in products and procedures to transform yourself.

Media also tell men that they are deficient but can fix that by consuming products. Portraying men with six-pack abs and huge biceps has created unrealistic and unhealthy ideals for masculine bodies and has been linked to the increasing abuse of steroids among men. Although media's idealization of extreme musculature and strength is not the only cause of steroid use, we should not dismiss the influence of portrayals of muscle-bound men as ideal (Katz, 2013). Normal changes in men's sexual vigor are also represented as problems to be solved by buying the right products. The "problem," of course, was not a problem until drug companies decided they could make money by transforming normal changes in male sexual vitality into problems that could be fixed by buying a drug that involves serious health risks (Von Drehle, 2014).

Programs such as *Extreme Makeover* and *The Swan* send the message that women don't have to—and, in fact, shouldn't—settle for how they naturally look. On these shows, ordinary-looking people undergo up to 14 cosmetic surgeries to be transformed into looking like celebrities, and the message is clear: We too can look better. We should look better. It's our job to do what's necessary to make ourselves look like superstars (Morreale, 2007). Economics are deeply linked to the image of ideal

MindTap

TAKE ACTION…activities are located at the end of this chapter and online.

Media-Created Body Ideals

Anthropologist and psychiatrist Anne Becker and her colleagues (Becker, Burwell, Gilman, Herzog, & Hamburg, 2002) reported research suggesting that media are very powerful in shaping—or distorting—body images.

For centuries, Fiji had been a food-loving society. Fijian people enjoyed eating and considered fleshy bodies attractive in women and men. In fact, when someone seemed to be losing weight, acquaintances chided her or him for "going thin." All of that changed in 1995, when television stations in Fiji began to broadcast American programs such as *Melrose Place*, *Seinfeld*, and *Beverly Hills, 90210*. Within three years, an astonishing number of Fijian women began to diet and to develop eating disorders. When asked why they were trying to lose weight, young Fijian woman cited characters such as Amanda (Heather Locklear) on *Melrose Place* as their model.

Sally Steindorf found that as televisions have become common in the quiet village of Kothariya, India, long-standing ethnic and cultural traditions have waned. In their place, villagers have adopted Western values and seek Western products that are advertised on television. Villagers see motorcycles, color TVs, and brand-name shampoo as status symbols (Overland, 2004).

Mainstreaming was also identified among female high school students in South Australia. The students who often read fashion magazines and watched soap operas on television thought it was important to be slim and that bulimia was an acceptable way to keep body weight low (Tiggemann, 2005).

femininity, because achieving that image—or even trying to—requires buying products and services. Thus, programs such as *The Swan* and the advertisers that support them encourage girls and women to believe that their only real power is purchasing power—their power is reduced to what they can buy. The Engage! feature on this page illustrates how mainstream body ideals have been created by what we see on television.

 Kasheta

To earn money, I babysit two little boys four days a week. One day, they got into a fight, and I broke it up. When I told them that physical violence isn't a good way to solve problems, they reeled off a list of TV characters that beat up on each other. Another day, one of them referred to the little girl next door as a "ho." When I asked why he called her that, he started singing the lyrics from an MTV video he'd been watching. In that video, women were called "hos." It's scary what kids absorb.

Mass Media Advance the Dominant Ideology

Mass media advance viewpoints on issues, people, and events. When you read a newspaper article or watch a television news report, you do not get a set of unrelated facts. Instead, you get a narrative—a story that shapes the information into a coherent account that predisposes you to particular conclusions and perspectives on the people and events in the story.

Scholars of mass media point out that gatekeepers' choices of which issues to emphasize and how to frame them are

Consumer Trends / Alamy

Product placement links particular products with celebrities.

often driven by the interests of conservative capitalist values (Liu & Albarran, 2009; McChesney, 1999, 2004, 2008). Making money is the primary goal of multinational corporations such as General Electric, which owns NBC, and Westinghouse, which owns CBS. If making a profit is the key objective, then corporations that own media may not be only, or even primarily, interested in the accuracy of media or serving the general public. How seriously can *Time* magazine criticize AOL when both *Time* and AOL are owned by Time Warner? Should we be surprised that in 1995 CNN, which is owned by Time Warner (a major cable TV operation), refused to run an ad that claimed cable TV rates were likely to rise (Zuckerman, 2002)?

Mass media depend on the revenues generated by advertising, which has become increasingly blurred with content. Years ago, it was easy to spot ads in magazines and commercials on TV. No longer is advertising so clearly distinct from programming. **Product placement**, which is paid for by advertisers and program sponsors, is the practice of featuring products in media and ensuring that viewers recognize the product (for instance, having a character drink Coke from a Coke can) so that the products are associated with particular characters, storylines, and so forth. Because product placement inserts advertising into programs, it blurs the traditional distinction between program content and ads.

If product placement blurs the line between advertising and content, immersive advertising completely erases the line. **Immersive advertising** incorporates a product or brand into actual storylines in books, television programs, and films (Lamb & Brown, 2006). For instance, Naomi Johnson (2007, 2011) analyzed romance novels marketed to young girls. She found that storylines in series such as *A List* and *Gossip Girl* revolved around buying products such as La Perla lingerie and Prada bags. The characters' identities were associated with particular products and services.

product placement A practice, paid for by advertisers and program sponsors, of featuring products in media so that the products are associated with particular characters, storylines, and so forth.

Immersive advertising Incorporating a product or brand into actual storylines in books, television programs, and films.

ENGAGE!   Constructing the News

Many people think news programs present information and news in a factual, neutral way. However, most mass communication scholars think differently (Ghanem, McCombs, & Chernov, 2009). They assert that media construct the news, shaping what is presented and how:

◆ Selecting what gets covered: Only a minute portion of human activity is reported in the news. Gatekeepers in the media decide which people and events will be covered. By presenting stories on these events and people, the media make them newsworthy.

◆ Choosing the frame: Reporters and journalists choose how to focus a story, or how to frame it. In selecting a frame, gatekeepers choose a point of view that shapes how an audience interprets the story. The frame directs our attention to certain aspects of the story and certain ways of seeing those aspects. For example, in a story on a politician accused of sexual misconduct, the focus could be the charges made, the politician's denial, or overall sexual misconduct by public figures.

◆ Choosing how to tell the story: In the foregoing example, media might tell it in a way that fosters sympathy for the person who claims to have been the target of sexual misconduct (interviews with the victim, references to other victims of sexual misconduct), or they might tell it in a way that inclines people to be sympathetic toward the politician (shots of the politician with his or her family, interviews with colleagues who proclaim the politician's innocence).

MindTap™ Compare coverage of one issue in conservative and progressive papers, radio or television programs, TV stations, and online sites. What gets covered and what does not?

Race on Television and in Real Life

Occasionally television's gatekeepers are willing to criticize racism quite overtly. Even in the 1960s, early episodes of *Star Trek* raised questions about stereotypes and bias related to race. Other programs, such as *Sanford and Son* and *The Cosby Show*, offered alternatives to racist portrayals of blacks. A particularly interesting example of media attention to race and racism appeared in 2006 when FX aired a six-part documentary series titled *Black. White.* Professional makeup artists made a white mother, father, and son, the Wurgels, appear black and made a black mother, father, and daughter, the Sparks, appear white. For six weeks, the two families lived as members of the other race and learned, along with viewers, how much difference race still makes in America (Peyser, 2006).

Mass media's dependence on advertisers also explains why they tend to represent the ideology of privileged groups as normal, right, and natural (Hall, 1986a, 1986b, 1988, 1989a, 1989b; Hasinoff, 2008). Television programs, from children's shows to prime-time news, represent white, heterosexual, able-bodied males as the norm in the United States, although they are actually not the majority. Magazine covers and ads as well as billboards portray young, able-bodied, attractive white people as the norm. Despite criticism of bias in media, minorities continue to be portrayed most often as criminals, victims, subordinates, or otherwise less-than-respectable people (Bonilla-Silva, 2013; Hasinoff, 2008; Ramasubramanian, 2010; Robinson, 2009). Even scarcer in the world of television are Latinos and Latinas, the fastest growing ethnic–racial group in the United States (Hartlaub, 2012). Although bias continues to exist, we've also seen an increase in programs, news stories, and popular magazines about groups and lifestyles that are not mainstream. The Engage! feature on this page offers more information on media representation of races.

Let's summarize our discussion of mass communication by restating the four premises we have discussed:

1. Changes in mass communication change human life.

2. Mass communication serves individuals' interests and desires.

3. Mass communication influences human knowledge and perspective.

4. Mass communication advances dominant ideologies.

Taken together, these four premises give us considerable insight into how mass communication affects our thoughts, attitudes, behaviors, and beliefs about ourselves and the world in which we live.

Digital Media and Mass Media

Mass media are not just related to, but, increasingly, intertwined with digital media. At one time, mass media were sharply distinct from computer-mediated communication. Today, however, lines between the two are blurred. When you watch *Orange Is the New Black* or read a novel on a tablet, are you using mass media or digital media? When a video you post on YouTube for friends goes viral, is it social media or mass media? When onlookers at a murder shoot a video on their phone camera and CNN buys the video and shows it, is the video personal media or mass media? These examples make it abundantly clear that mass media and digital media are not distinct, but intertwined.

Not only are the two kinds of communication intertwined, but also they are increasingly responsive to each other. For instance, after the tragic killing of Michael Brown, television news provided reports of both the killing and the aftermath of rioting, looting, and pleas for justice. Immediately, social media were abuzz with responses to reports from mass media. Groups began forming to raise funds for Michael Brown's family and for Officer Wilson, to create a scholarship to honor Brown, and to organize for action to address perceptions of persisting racism in America. The initial reports by mass media fueled a social media firestorm.

A final connection between this chapter's content grows out of McLuhan's keen insight that the dominant media in any era shape individual and collective life. In the next chapter, we will focus on digital media. In advance, ask yourself how McLuhan, if he were alive today, might say the dominance of digital media is affecting human thought, ways of relating, and sense of community.

Guidelines for Engaging Mass Media

Because mass media surround and influence us, we have an ethical obligation to be responsible and thoughtful consumers. Two critical guidelines for interacting with mass media are to develop media literacy and to respond actively.

Develop Media Literacy

The first challenge is to develop media literacy. Just as it takes work to become literate in reading, in communicating orally, and in using technologies, we need to invest effort to develop literacy in interacting with media. Instead of passively absorbing media, cultivate your ability to analyze, understand, and respond thoughtfully to media. Figure 14.2 describes key stages in developing media literacy. How literate we become, however, depends on the extent to which we commit to developing sophisticated skills in interpreting media.

6 Months	3 Years	4 Years	7–8 Years	Throughout Life
Children pay attention to television.	Children engage in exploratory viewing.	Children search for preferred viewing.	Children make clear distinctions between ads and programs.	People who commit to media literacy learn to recognize puffery, hooks, and other devices for directing their attention and behavior.
	Children establish preferred patterns of viewing.	Children develop a viewing agenda.		
	Children do not distinguish between programs and ads.	Children's attention is held by a story line.	Children become skeptical of ads for products with which they are familiar; they are less skeptical of ads for products they haven't tried or don't own.	People who commit to media literacy learn to use media in sophisticated ways to meet their needs and to compensate for media bias and techniques.
		Children begin to distinguish between ads and programs.		
		Children do not realize that ads seek profits.		

Figure 14.2 Stages in the Development of Media Literacy

© Cengage Learning

Realistically Assess Mass Media's Influence   Media literacy begins with understanding how much influence you believe mass media have on people. One view—a rather extreme one—claims that mass media determine individual attitudes and social perspectives. Another view—also extreme—is that mass media don't affect us at all. In between those two radical views is the more reasonable belief that mass media is one of the many influences on individual attitudes and social perspectives.

This last claim represents a thoughtful assessment of the qualified influence of mass media and our ability to exercise control over their effects. Television, individual viewers, and society interact in complex ways. The same argument can be made for the influence of other mass media, such as radio, film, billboards, books, magazines, and newspapers. If this is so, it's inaccurate to presume that a linear relationship exists between media and individuals' attitudes.

Become Aware of Patterns in Media   If you aren't aware of the patterns that make up basketball, you will not be able to understand what happens in a game. If you don't understand how church or synagogue services are organized, you won't appreciate the meaning of those services. In the same way, if you don't understand patterns in media, you can't understand fully the workings of music, advertising, programming, and so forth. Learning to recognize patterns in media empowers you to engage media in critical and sophisticated ways.

As W. James Potter (2004) points out, media use a few standard patterns repeatedly. For example, although there are various genres of music, there are a few basic chords, melody progressions, and rhythms of which all music is comprised. Even the lyrical content of songs tends to follow stock patterns, most often love and sex (Christianson & Roberts, 1998). Most stories, whether in print, film, or television, open with some problem or conflict that progresses until it climaxes in final dramatic scenes. Romance stories typically follow a pattern in which we meet a main character who has suffered a bad relationship or has not had a relationship. The romance pattern progresses through meeting Mr. or Ms. Right, encountering complications or problems, resolving the problems, and living happily ever after (Riggs, 1999).

Actively Interrogate Media Messages   When interacting with mass communication, you should use critical thought to assess what is presented. Rather than accepting news accounts unquestioningly, you should be thoughtful and skeptical. It's important to ask questions such as these:

◆ Why is this story getting so much attention? Whose interests are served, and whose are muted?

◆ What are the sources of statistics and other forms of evidence? Are the sources current? Do the sources have any interest in taking a specific position? (e.g., tobacco companies have vested interest in denying or minimizing the harms of smoking.)

◆ What's the frame for the story, and what alternative frames might have been used?

◆ Are stories balanced so that a range of viewpoints are given voice? For example, does news coverage of regulations for the financial industry include statements from the representatives of banks, investors, auditors, and economists?

◆ How are different people and viewpoints framed by gatekeepers (e.g., reporters, photographers, experts)?

It's equally important to be critical in interpreting entertainment presented by mass media—music, books, magazines, and Web sites. When listening to popular music, ask whose views of society it portrays and who and what it represents as normal or good, and abnormal or bad. Raise the same questions about the images in magazines and on billboards. When considering an ad, ask whether it offers meaningful evidence or merely puffery (see the Engage! feature on this page). Asking questions such as these allows you to be critical and careful in assessing what mass communication presents to you.

Expose Yourself to a Range of Media Sources
Media scholar W. James Potter (2009) regards "mindful exposures" (p. 565) as key to media literacy. Many people choose to view and listen only to what they particularly like. For instance, if you are conservative politically, you might read a conservative daily paper and listen to a conservative radio station. The problem with that is that you don't expose yourself to criticisms of conservative policies and stances, and you don't give yourself the opportunity to learn about more liberal alternatives. If you listen only to popular music, you'll never learn to understand, much less appreciate, classical music, jazz, or reggae. You cannot be informed about any issue or type of media unless you deliberately expose yourself to multiple sources of information and perspectives.

Exposing yourself to multiple media also means attending to more than entertainment. Television focuses primarily on entertainment and popular culture. Tuning into celebrity culture is not sufficient if you want to be media literate.

Focus on Your Motivations for Engaging Media
Sophisticated media users realize that media serve many purposes, and they make deliberate choices that serve their goals and needs at particular times. For example, if you feel depressed and want to watch television, it might be better to watch a comedy or action drama than to watch a television movie about personal trauma and pain.

Respond Actively

People may respond critically or uncritically to mass communication and the world-views that it portrays, depending on how media literate they are (Fiske, 1987; Hall, 1982, 1989b). If we respond uncritically, we mindlessly consume messages and their ideological underpinnings. On the other hand, if we interact critically with media, we recognize that the worldviews presented in mass communication are not unvarnished truth but partial, subjective perspectives that serve the interests of some individuals and groups while disregarding the interests of others.

To assume an active role in interacting with media, you must recognize that you are an agent who can affect what happens around you. You begin to take action by noticing

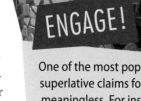

ENGAGE! Puffery: The Best of Its Kind!

One of the most popular advertising strategies is **puffery**—superlative claims for a product that seem factual but are actually meaningless. For instance, what does it mean to state that a particular juice has "the most natural flavor"? Most natural in comparison to what? Other juices, other drink products, the whole fruit from which the juice is made? Who judged it to have the most natural flavor—the corporation that produces it? A random sample of juice drinkers? What is the meaning of an ad that claims a car is "the new benchmark"? Who decided this was the new benchmark? To what is this car being compared? It's not clear from the ad, which is only puffery.

 MindTap Can you identify an example of puffery in contemporary mass media?

puffery Exaggerated, superlative claims about a product that appear to be factually based but are actually meaningless and unverifiable.

what media ask you to think about, believe, and do. Once you become aware of mass communication's efforts to shape perceptions and attitudes, you can then question or challenge the views of reality they advance.

 Manuel

I was really angry about a story in the local paper. It was about Mexicans who come to the United States The story only mentioned Mexican Americans who get in trouble with the law, are on Welfare, or are illegal residents. So I wrote a letter to the editor and said the story was biased and inaccurate. The editor invited me to write an article for the opinion page, and I did. In my article, I described many Mexican Americans who are hardworking, honest citizens who are making this country better. There were a lot of responses to my article, so I know I made a difference.

Manuel's experience demonstrates that speaking out is not just personally empowering; it also enriches cultural life. People have an ethical responsibility to resist and redefine those messages of mass communication that they consider inaccurate or harmful. One of the Take Action features at the end of this chapter lists Web sites for people who are interested in taking a voice in regard to mass communication.

Speaking out can make a difference. In 1995, Calvin Klein discontinued an ad campaign because so many individuals and groups objected to the ads, which a number of people saw as mimicking scenes from vintage pornography. Other companies have withdrawn ads and even products in response to voices of resistance. Power relationships and social perspectives are never fixed in cultural life. They are always open to change and negotiation between voices that offer rival views of reality.

Summary

In this chapter, we began by discussing how the different media epochs have affected individual lives and social organization. Next, we considered how we use media to fulfill our goals and how media shape our worldviews. The second section of this chapter highlighted the ways in which mass media and digital media are interconnected, often seamlessly.

The third section of the chapter focused on two related guidelines for us as we interact with mass media. The first is to develop media literacy. This requires, first, that we develop a realistic, balanced perspective on the power of mass media. Media do not exist in isolation, nor do we as consumers of mass media. Each of us participates in multiple and diverse social systems that shape our responses to mass media and the worldviews it presents. To be responsible participants in social life, we need to question what is included—and what is made invisible—in mass media.

A second guideline is to assume an active voice by responding to mass media. We have an ethical responsibility to speak out against material that we think is inaccurate, hurtful, or wrong. One means of negotiating social meanings is to respond to mass media. Without our consent and support, mass communication cannot exist.

Experience Communication Case Study

The Power Zapper

Apply what you've learned in this chapter by analyzing the following case study, using the accompanying questions as a guide. These questions and a video of the case study are also available online with your MindTap Speech for *Communication Mosaics*.

Charles and Tina Washington are in the kitchen area of their great room working on dinner. At the other end of the room, their six-year-old son, Derek, is watching television. Tina is tearing lettuce for a salad while Charles stirs a pot on the stove.

Tina: One of us is going to have to run by the store tomorrow. This is the last of the lettuce.

Charles: While we're at it, we'd better get more milk and cereal. We're low on those, too.

Tina: I'll flip you for who has to make the store run.

[Charles pulls a quarter out of his pocket, flips it in the air, and covers it with one hand when it lands on his other hand.] "Call it."

Tina: Heads, you have to go by the store.

Charles removes the hand covering the quarter and grins. "Tails—it's your job." She rolls her eyes and says, "Just can't win, some days."

Derek suddenly jumps up from his chair, points his finger at the chair in which he had been sitting, and shouts "Zap! You're dead! You're dead! I win!" Charles goes to Derek. An advertisement for Power Zapper is just ending on the television, and Charles turns down the volume.

Charles: What's going on, Derek? Who's dead?

Derek: The chair is. I zapped it with the Power Zapper, Mom. It's the coolest weapon.

Tina walks over to join Charles and Derek.

Tina: Power Zapper? What's a Power Zapper?

Derek: It's the most popular toy in America, Mom! It's really cool!

Tina: Oh really? Who says so?

Derek: They just said it on TV.

Tina: Does that mean it's true?

Derek points a finger at his mother and shouts, "Pow! I zapped you! You're dead!" At this point, Charles walks over and takes Derek's hand.

© Cengage Learning

Charles: Hold on there, son. Don't go pointing at your mother.

Derek: I was zapping her, Dad.

Charles: I see you were, but we don't hurt people, do we?

Derek: I could if I had a Power Zapper. Can I have one for my birthday? Everybody else has one.

Charles: If everybody jumped off the roof, would you do that?

Derek: I wouldn't need to if I had a Power Zapper because I could zap anyone who bothered me. I'd be so cool.

Charles: But zapping other people would hurt them. You wouldn't want to do that, would you?

Tina [to Charles]: You're overreacting. It's just a toy.

Charles [to Tina]: Kids learn from toys. I don't want Derek to learn that violence is cool.

Tina [to Charles]: He isn't going to learn that with us as his parents. Don't get so worked up over a toy.

1. Identify an example of puffery in the advertisement for the Power Zapper.

2. Are Charles and Tina Washington teaching Derek to be a critical viewer of mass communication?

3. How does this scenario illustrate the process of mainstreaming?

4. Are you more in agreement with Charles or with Tina about whether toys teach important lessons to children?

Key Concepts

Practice defining the chapter's terms by using online flashcards.

agenda setting, 282
cultivation, 283
gatekeeper, 283
global village, 281
immersive advertising, 287
mainstreaming, 283

mass media, 278
mean world syndrome, 284
product placement, 287
puffery, 291
uses and gratification theory, 281

Reflect, personalize, and
apply what you've learned.

Review, Reflect, Extend

The Reflect and Discuss, and Take Action features that follow will help you review, reflect on, and extend the information and ideas presented in this chapter. These resources, and a diverse selection of additional study tools, are also available online at the MindTap Speech for *Communication Mosaics.*

Reflect and Discuss

1. To what extent, if any, should there be control over the violence presented in media? Do you think viewers, especially children, are harmed by the prevalence of violence in media? Are you concerned about the lack of correspondence between the synthetic world of television violence and the actual incidence of violence in social life? If you think there should be some controls, what groups or individuals would you trust to establish and implement them?

2. Make a list of the forms of mass media you use most often. Include newspapers, books, magazines, television, types of films, radio, and so forth. How do your choices of mass media reflect and shape your identity and your social perspectives?

3. As a class, select the current issue of two mainstream magazines. Carefully go through the magazines, both content articles and advertising. After reviewing the magazines, answer this question: If an alien had only these two magazines as evidence of American culture today, what would the alien conclude about who Americans are and what they care about?

TAKE ACTION

1. Detecting Dominant Values in Media

Watch two hours of prime-time commercial television. Pay attention to the dominant ideology that is represented and normalized in the programming. Who are the good and bad characters? Which personal qualities are represented as admirable, and which are represented as objectionable? Who are the victims and victors, the heroes and villains? What goals and values are endorsed?

2. Responding Actively

If you want to learn more about gender and media, or if you want to become active in working against media that foster views of violence as normal, girls and women as subordinate, and buying as the route to happiness, visit the sites for the groups listed below, which you may find in the online resources for this chapter:

- Media Education Foundation
- Media Watch
- The TV Parental Guidelines
- Center for Media Literacy
- The Geena Davis Institute

Recommended Resources

1. Embrace the challenge advanced in this chapter by taking an active role in responding to mass media. Write a letter to the editor of a local paper, or write to a manufacturer to support or criticize its product or the way it advertises its product. Visit the Web sites mentioned in the Take Action activity above to learn about opportunities to become a more involved consumer and controller of mass media.

2. *Miss Representation*. This 90-minute documentary on the hypersexualized representations of girls and women in media premiered at the 2011 Sundance Festival. Jennifer Siebel Newsom is the writer, director, and producer.

15

Digital Media and the Online World

The danger from computers is not that they will eventually get as smart as men, but we will meanwhile agree to meet them halfway.

—Bernard Avishai

On an average day, how much time do you spend using digital media?

🌀 MindTap

Learning Objectives

🌀 MindTap

Start with a quick engagement activity and **review** the chapter Learning Objectives.

Topics Covered in This Chapter	After studying this chapter, you should be able to . . .
Understanding Digital Media	Identify three defining characteristics of digital media.
Uses and Abuses of Digital Media	Given that the use of digital media can have positive and negative consequences, reflect on how you use digital media for identity work, social interaction, and learning.
Guidelines for Interacting with Digital Media	Create an action plan to implement the chapter guidelines for interacting with digital media.

◆ *"Helicopter hovering above Abbottabad at 1AM (is a rare event)."* This tweet, sent by Sonaib Athar, an IT professional living in Abbottabad, was the first unofficial communication about the attack that resulted in the death of Osama Bin Laden (Gilster, 2011). Shortly after Athar's tweet, others followed, telling of high activity—including explosions—in the compound in Abbottabad. As Twitter users got the tweets, they sent questions, updates, and speculations. An average of 3,000 tweets per second were sent as the story developed (Gilster, 2011). Only hours later did President Obama come on national television to announce that he had authorized the attack and that Bin Laden was dead.

◆ On a business trip to Boston, Nisha taps the Lyft app on her phone and says she needs a lift from the MIT campus to the airport. Toni, who is a single mother of two, clicks accept on the Lyft app on her phone and leaves to pick up Nisha. The charge will be $25 of which Toni will net $18.

◆ In June of 2011, Anthony Weiner, a former representative of New York, was forced to resign when provocative online photos and sexually suggestive text messages he had intended to be private became public. Under pressure, he resigned from office.

Digital media profoundly shape our lives. They are seamlessly woven into how we think, work, play, socialize, and learn. Our computers and other media devices influence who we know, how others see us, what we know, and how we interact with people. They also shape how we engage in professional activities, participate in community life, and organize efforts for political and social change.

In the United States, 84.2 percent of individuals use the Internet whereas only about 50 percent of the population used the Internet a decade ago ("Weaving the

Read, highlight, and take notes online.

digital divide The gap between people and communities that do and do not have access to digital technologies.

The Digital Divide

It's easy for college students in the United States to assume that everyone is connected to the online world. In reality, that's not the case—not by a long shot. Worldwide just over one-third of people are connected (Zuckerberg, 2014).

Even within developed countries, there is a **digital divide**, which is the gap between people and communities that do and do not have access to digital technologies. In the United States, many people have limited access to digital media. Income and education are pivotal factors in access to technologies. Lower-income Americans are more likely to have cell phones and, in some cases, smartphones, than computers with broadband connections. Smartphones are great for texting, tweeting, and even going on the Web, but they aren't very useful for creating résumés, filling out job applications, applying for social services, or taking online classes (Sydell, 2014). Disability also limits access. Just over 50 percent of Americans with disabilities own computers and have broadband connection in their homes (Feingold, 2013; Fox, 2011).

Discretionary income also influences data access. Contrary to popular opinion, having a smartphone doesn't necessarily guarantee data access. To have that, you need to purchase a data plan, which costs more than the phone itself (Zuckerberg, 2014). Those who are not connected lose out not only socially but also financially since Internet activity is rapidly overtaking other sectors of economic activity.

MindTap™ Why should the digital divide matter to people who can afford to be fully connected?

Uncle Sam Wants You, PacBot

If one of the soldiers had to be lost, the commanding officer was glad it was the one it was. His hardest job is writing letters to parents, telling them their son or daughter was killed on the battlefield. This soldier had no family—or heart or personality. It was a PacBot, a tactical, mobile robot that takes on some of the most dangerous missions in war. PacBots made their timely debut on September 11, 2001. Their first mission was helping with the cleanup at Ground Zero. Unlike people, PacBots weren't affected by smoke or noxious chemicals, and they weren't traumatized by the sight of dead and dismembered human beings.

Soon after, iRobot, the company that makes PacBots, sent a few PacBots overseas to test how they worked. When iRobot wanted them back, the troops resisted—they didn't want to part with their PacBots, who took the most dangerous and disgusting jobs without complaint. By 2010, 30,000 PacBots had been delivered to serve in the military and domestic public safety units (irobotics, 2010).

PacBot is not the only technology changing war. P. W. Singer, author of *Wired for War* (2009), details how the development of new technologies changes the ways we engage in war. For instance, pilots in Nevada operate remote controls to kill terrorists in Afghanistan. These "drone pilots" engage in remote-controlled warfare for eight or more hours, then leave their offices, get in their cars, and drive home. Interestingly, Singer says that drone pilots suffer a higher rate of posttraumatic stress disorder (PTSD) than conventional pilots do. He thinks it may be because they are removed from seeing the immediate consequences of their actions and later realize those consequences.

Web," 2014). The average U.S. citizen now owns four digital devices and "spends 60 hours a week consuming content across devices" (The Nielsen Company, 2014). While usage is high among all age groups, younger people are the heaviest users: Across devices, usage is approximately 90 percent for 18- to 29-year-olds, 75 percent for 30- to 49-year-olds, 88 percent for 50- to 64-year-olds, and 40 percent for people 65 and older ("Weaving the Web," 2014).

The fact that most Americans are at least somewhat connected doesn't mean we understand how digital media affect us nor does it mean we always make smart choices about their place in our lives. This chapter aims to enhance your insight into digital media so that you may make thoughtful decisions about when, how, and how much you use them. The first section of the chapter defines digital media and discusses their defining features and impact on human thinking. The second section of the chapter explores the ways we use digital media. Next, we consider relationships between digital media and other forms of communication. Finally, we discuss two guidelines that should help you reap the advantages and avoid some of the potential problems of living in a technology-saturated world.

Understanding Digital Media

Many people think that communication technologies are relatively new. Actually, technologies of many types have been with us since humans first inhabited the Earth. A technology is a practical application of knowledge. For example, fire and the wheel are technologies that profoundly changed human life. Paintings on cave walls were a communication technology that allowed cave people to record and share ideas and experiences. Let's review the history of communication technologies, not merely to understand specific technologies but also to grasp the broader idea that humans continuously invent new ways to communicate and connect.

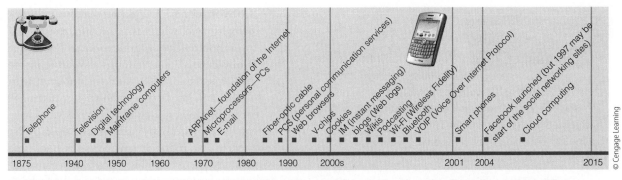

1875   1940   1950   1960   1970   1980   1990   2000s   2001   2004   2015

Figure 15.1 The Evolution of Communication Technologies. What new communication technologies do you think will be invented by 2020?

Communication technologies are means of recording, transferring, sharing, and working with information. Communication technologies include long-established devices, such as the telephone, and newer technologies, such as smartphones and iPads. Figure 15.1 provides a time line so you can appreciate the overall history of communication technologies and notice the speedup in the past few years.

Digital media are electronic modes of communication that store and manage data in digital form rather than analog form. When you communicate face-to-face, you don't have digital, electronic systems mediating between you and the other person or persons. But when you e-mail, tweet, text, talk in chat rooms, post on Facebook, and so forth, your messages are not transmitted directly from you to another person. Instead, they go through computer technologies that digitize, store, and send them. Video games and e-books are also digital media.

Social media are pervasive in our lives.

Features of Digital Media

Older forms of electronic communication, such as the telegraph and radio, rely on analog technology, which transmits messages in continuous numerical form. In contrast, digital media rely on digital technology, which is easier to store and manage because it uses only two numerical values (0 and 1). Three key characteristics of digitization are ease of manipulation, convergence, and speed (Turow, 2008).

Manipulation   The ability to manipulate information is not new; it was possible with analog film and video and film photography. For instance, a photo could be retouched and video could be edited. However, manipulating analog media took a high level of skill that few people had. In contrast, most people who have grown up using digital media know how to manipulate them—for instance, using Photoshop's clone stamping and Despeckle filter allows you to alter photos. The line that divided production and consumption of media in the analog era is blurred, if not erased, in the digital era. We now see homemade videos on television news programs and tweets repeated in newspapers.

communication technologies Means of recording, transferring, sharing, and working with information.

digital media Electronic modes of communication that store and manage data in digital form.

Time Travel

When was the microwave oven invented? How about television or the escalator or the cordless phone? The online resources for this chapter include a link to the PBS technology Web site, which lets you go through the 20th century to find out when various technologies first came on the scene.

Convergence   Digital media also cultivate convergence, which is interconnection of information and communication technologies. For instance, digital platforms allow us to merge print, television, radio, and the Internet with portable and interactive technologies. Just a few years ago, it was difficult and expensive to have a voice-over-Internet (VoIP) phone call. Today, soldiers in Iraq routinely have Skype or FaceTime with family members. This is possible because the technology for transmitting sound and the technology for transmitting visual images are both digital and, thus, they can be managed on a single network. When video, audio (telephone), and computer data are all stored and transmitted as digital signals, they can be managed on the same network.

Convergence of technologies allows interconnectivity, which is the connecting of various devices to each other and to the Internet so users don't have to independently configure each new system. For instance, yesterday's separate technologies of telephone and computer are combined today in phones that allow people to manage e-mail, text, take photos, and visit the Web.

Speed   The third distinguishing feature of digital media is speed. Most obviously, this means that information can travel very quickly: You send an e-mail, tweet, or text and the recipient gets it almost instantly. You turn on your computer, click Facebook, and immediately start checking new posts.

But the speed of digital technology does more than let us send and receive messages quickly. It also affects our expectations for pace in general. Have you ever gotten impatient when you texted a friend and didn't get an immediate reply? Have you ever been irritated by an online site that was slow to load or exasperated by a power outage that prevented you from online contact for hours? If so, you understand how living with digital media affects your expectations of speed. We expect fast responses to our digital communication, and we may feel pressured to answer others' tweets and texts quickly.

A third implication of the increased speed of digital technology is its potential to jeopardize accuracy. Rayford Steele (2009), who studies digital media, points out that "in a world of instant access where everyone can be published or viewed, the time pressure and the volume increase make careful vetting that much harder" (p. 494). Thus, online newspapers and magazines, fearing that they will lose a scoop on a story, publish what they believe to be true before all information has been gathered and critically evaluated.

 Daniel

I love my smartphone. I can stay in touch with all my friends and know what's happening almost before it happens. If I'm tied up, I can check the message when I'm free. That's totally easier than land lines. The only downside is that my grandparents and one of my aunts don't text, which means I don't stay in as much touch with them as other people.

 Kay

Technology is turning human communication into something impersonal. Now people log on and send e-mail about what they are doing—apparently they are too busy doing all of that to pick up the telephone or write a letter. Newer technology has made us lazy. Instead of spelling out words, people write LOL and BRB. Can't we talk to each other anymore?

Digital Media's Impact on Human Thinking

In Chapter 14, we discussed Marshall McLuhan's ideas about media. One of his most important insights is that the dominant media of an era shape human thought and experience. He theorized how oral, audio, and visual media had shaped the thought of the eras in which each was dominant. So how do digital media shape our thinking? As you might expect, there is much controversy about this issue. Research suggests that digital media have the potential for both beneficial and detrimental effects on our thinking.

One of the most obvious and also most important benefits of digital media is access to information and opinion. No longer do we need to rely on newspapers or television to give us news. Along with those sources, we can also choose online sites that we find particularly insightful or fair. In addition, many people follow particular bloggers whom they have decided have expertise in areas that matter to them. The currently wired era gives us unprecedented access to information and perspective.

A second benefit of digital media is their ability to complement human intelligence. In his recent book, *Smarter Than You Think*, Clive Thompson (2013) argues that computers can amplify human intelligence. In other words, Johnson thinks asking whether computers are smarter than humans misses the point. For Johnson, the point is for humans to partner with computers to solve problems, create architecture and literature, and make scientific discoveries. Johnson also asserts that digital devices and social networks encourage collaboration and awareness beyond one's own perceptual world. He believes that outsourcing simple memory tasks such as remembering phone numbers and addresses to our devices frees our minds to engage in more complex reasoning and creativity.

Yet, there are also ways in which digital media are not so beneficial to our thinking. One concern is that the high visual stimulation of digital media (bright colors, cool avatars, flashy images) teaches us to respond to dazzling stimuli and to be less attentive to more subtle phenomenon (Freeman, 2009). If that's the case, we will miss content that does not have immediate vibrancy. Preliminary research also indicates that we may be more likely to forget information we read online than information we read in hard copy books and other offline sources (Cohen, 2011; Sparrow, Liu, & Wegner, 2011).

Perhaps the most worrisome way that digital media affect our thinking is encouraging us to multitask. **Multitasking** is engaging in multiple tasks in rapid sequence and in overlapping and interactive ways. For example, in classes, students often use laptops to take notes while also checking Facebook and playing games; people interrupt face-to-face conversations to answer texts on their smartphones; and people read e-mails and texts during meetings. More and more, we try to do multiple tasks at once.

But can humans really concentrate on more than one thing at a time? No, we can't. In fact, computers can't multitask either. They do one thing at a time—just very, very quickly. A computer can implement millions of instructions in less than a second, but it executes each operation individually in sequence. Because a computer gives its full attention to a single task at a time, it does the task with great accuracy. However, when humans try to do several tasks at once, we're likely to do each one less well than if we concentrated on one thing at a time (Jackson, 2008). Adults who shift between two tasks take longer to do both tasks, and they make more mistakes (Freeman, 2009). The habit of shifting attention moment to moment is so pervasive that Linda Stone, former Microsoft and Apple executive, calls it Continuous Partial Attention (Levy, 2006). Too many people who believe they can multitask have wound up injured or

multitasking Engaging in multiple tasks in rapid sequence or in overlapping and interactive ways.

ENGAGE!

Txtng whl drvng

Reggie Shaw found out the hard way that texting while driving is deadly. When he was 19, Reggie was making an early morning drive through one of Utah's mountain passes. A driver behind him noticed that Reggie's car wandered over the yellow divider line repeatedly before the time when Reggie didn't correct quickly enough. He sideswiped another car, resulting in the deaths of the driver and passenger in the car. Later, it was determined that he had sent and received 11 texts in the moments just before the crash (Richtel, 2014).

Despite story after story about deaths caused by drivers who are texting, people continue to believe they can safely text and drive. At first, those who want to talk while driving argued that talking on a cell or smartphone was no different than talking to a passenger. Once evidence discredited that claim, the new defense was that it was safe to drive and talk if you used a hands-free phone. Now that claim has also been disproved. Substantial research demonstrates that talking on phones—hands-free or not—while driving is dangerous. The problem isn't that "your hands aren't on the wheel. It's that your mind isn't on the road" (Don't Text and Drive, n.d.; Richtel, 2014). Researchers tested drivers' concentration when talking on a hands-free phone, talking with other passengers, and listening to radio or audio books. The results were clear-cut: Phone conversations are more distracting than any of the other activities. Accident statistics bear this out: Drivers talking on phones are four times as likely to have an accident as drivers who are not talking on phones. Twenty-three percent of accidents involved cell phones (Don't Text and Drive, n.d.). That's the same level of risk as driving while legally drunk, which is why texting while driving is sometimes called driving while intexticated.

This chapter's online resources include a link to the Don't Text and Drive site, which provides statistics and other information about the relationship between texting or talking while driving and accidents.

 MindTap Do you text while driving? If so, how do you justify doing so, given the evidence of its dangers?

worse when they texted while driving. The online resources for this chapter provide a link to Brain Facts, which explains what happens when humans try to multitask.

Relying on digital media for entertainment may undermine imaginative thought and sustained mental focus (Begley, 2009). Imagination is ripe to develop at about the age children learn to talk. But today, it's not unusual for two-year-olds to play with smartphones and tablets, and they know how to download apps at that age (Finnerty, 2013; Steiner-Adair, 2013)! Children build their imaginative power by creating make-believe situations and invisible playmates. Many online apps don't encourage children to invent characters' personalities or create the rules for what characters can and cannot do. In short, children are required to use less imagination to participate in high-tech play than in old-fashioned, make-believe activities. And the "one-click gratification" (Finnerty, 2013) of digital media discourages the development of patience.

The instant gratification and high stimulation of digital media may also explain why some people use them excessively. Sherry Turkle (2012), who is an MIT professor well versed in technology, warns that digital media encourage immersion in virtual relationships sometimes at the cost of face-to-face relationships. Her TED talk, "Connected but Alone?," is available in the online resources for this chapter. A similar caution comes from Randi Zuckerberg, also no stranger to digital technology. In her book, *Dot Complicated*, Zuckerberg (2014) warns that online relationships and activities can too easily become more important and more "real" to people than what's happening IRL (in real life).

Does this mean that we should foreswear all digital media? Does it mean that parents should take away video games and the Internet and tell their children to

Rehab

reSTART is America's first rehabilitation program for technology addicts. It includes a 45-day abstinence program to break dependency on technology with individual programs for addiction to smartphones, Internet, and video games. According to Hillary Cash, cofounder of reSTART, digital technology encourages us to respond to our impulses and, as a result, "we end up being controlled by our impulses" (Roberts, 2014). We like the excitement from playing a particular game, so we impulsively keep playing—sometimes for 30-hour binges. And that's when using the Internet morphs into being used by it. When you enjoy playing a video game and then go out with friends, you're in control of your technology use. When you enjoy a game and feel compelled to play it again and again, technology is in control of you. When you check e-mail and Facebook two or three times a day to keep up with friends and colleagues, you're in control of your media use. When you spend more than 10 hours a day massaging your social networks (Levitin, 2014; Steiner-Adair, 2013), the media are controlling you. The online resources for this chapter provide a link to reSTART's site.

MindTap In an average day, how much time do you spend engaged with digital media?

go outside and play? Not necessarily. The wisest conclusion at this time is probably what Dianna advises in her commentary—to encourage activities that allow children to derive the benefits of both technology and old-fashioned play so that they learn to operate within preset virtual worlds and to think beyond prestructured games and contexts and ask, "What if …?"

 *Dianna*

When I was a kid, I played all the time without any fancy toys, much less high-tech ones. Once, when we got a new refrigerator, my sister and I took the box it came in. We thought that box was the greatest thing ever! One day it was a house, another day it was a space ship, another day a pirate ship. Last summer, we got a new stove, and I offered the box to my 5-year-old son. He said, "What do you want me to do with this?" That made me worry that he's not learning to create fantasy worlds. But I see him doing things on his Game Boy that are more sophisticated than anything I did at his age. Some of my friends are huge fans of technology for kids; some are absolutely against it. I'm more of a middle-way person. My son benefits from technology, but he also needs to learn that a big box can be anything in the world.

Uses and Abuses of Digital Media

We use digital media for many of the same reasons we use other modes of communicating. However, the features of digital media that we've discussed affect the nature and the possibilities of interaction (Logan, 2010). We'll look at five prominent ways we use digital media.

Identity Work

In Chapter 9, we discussed how the self develops through interaction with others and through processes such as reflected appraisal and social comparison. Our sense of who we are and can be also develops online as we craft identities that others interact with and respond to. The most basic ways in which we craft online identities are through screen names and e-mail addresses. You must have a screen name to participate in chat rooms and online role-playing games. The name you choose says something about who you are or who you want others to think you are. A screen name such as *dancer* suggests that the person using the name is a dancer or likes dancing. *Tequilaman* and *partygirl* create different impressions of the users. As Steve Duck and David McMahan (2012) note, e-mail addresses also communicate identities. The e-mail address teacher@email.unc.edu tells you that (1) the user is probably a teacher who (2) works at UNC, which is (3) an educational (edu) institution. If the top-level domain in the e-mail address were gov, you would infer that the user is connected to the government.

Digital media allow us to do a great deal more identity work than simply choosing screen names and avatars. Whenever we create a profile on a social networking site, we decide how to present ourselves—which photos to include, which hobbies and interests to highlight, and how to define our relationship and job status. We continue to massage our online identities as we post updates on our lives, edit photos to upload, and respond to others' postings. Many people invest substantial effort in sculpting an online identity (or identities) and keeping people who visit their pages updated on what's happening in their lives (Steiner-Adair, 2013).

Another healthy use of on-screen personalities is to accept limitations or changes in ourselves. One woman lost her leg as a result of an automobile accident. After the amputation, she had difficulty accepting her disability. One way she coped was by logging into a Multi-User Dungeon (MUD) in an online game and creating a one-legged character to represent her. In the MUD, she made friends who accepted her disability, and she became romantically involved with another character in the MUD. For this woman, the virtual character she created helped her accept her real self (Turkle, 2012).

The positive possibilities of online identities are not the whole story. We also have to recognize that online identities hold the potential for hurt or serious harm. People can and do create online identities in a deliberate effort to mislead others, sometimes in dangerous ways. Predators may represent themselves as children's and teens' friends and sometimes seduce children and teens into meeting them in person, which can lead to appalling abuses (Zuckerberg, 2014).

TAKE ACTION…activities are located at the end of this chapter and online.

ENGAGE!   Lez Get Real

Lez Get Real is a popular lesbian news site that claims to offer "a gay girl's view on the world." Readers had come to appreciate the site's author, Paula Brooks, who gave impressions and observation from a lesbian perspective. There's just one problem: Paula Brooks is a man. In 2011, readers learned that Paula is really Bill Graber, who was in the military and, after that, construction (Flock & Bell, 2011). Graber insists that he wanted to be an advocate for gay issues because he was upset when lesbian friends of his were mistreated. He invented the online persona of Paula Brooks because he thought no one would take him seriously if he were a man. The revelation about Graber came just one day after it was discovered that Amina Arraf, author of the Syrian lesbian blog *A Gay Girl in Damascus*, was exposed as Tom MacMaster, an American man.

Connecting with Others

Digital media facilitate social interaction and relationship development and maintenance. Social media allow us to meet potential romantic partners. Many people regard online matching as easier and more productive than face-to-face dating. In part, this is because digital media promote getting to know others on the basis of what they say and do more than how they look. It's not uncommon for people whose relationships began online to admit that they would never have dated one another if they had met face-to-face. We may screen out people with whom we would be very compatible based on superficial qualities such as physical appearance.

Claire

When I wake up in the morning, the first thing I do is check my messages. I respond to the important ones and then get out of bed and take my shower. While I'm fixing my hair and dressing, I update my Facebook page and see who's posted messages on my wall. On the way to classes, I text my three closest friends to see what they're doing and call Mom.

 Ally

Never in a million years would I have gone out with Clifford if I had met him in person first. He is totally not my type. I've always liked guys with dark hair who are tall and wiry. Clifford is blonde and medium height and muscular but a little heavy. Like I said, never in a million years would I have given him a second look. But we met online and talked a lot before we ever saw each other or even exchanged photos. By the time I actually met him, I already liked who he is and what he stands for. We just got engaged!

In addition to meeting people online, many of us use digital media to maintain and develop relationships in which people also interact face-to-face. Perhaps you stay in touch with high school friends that you seldom see face-to-face through a social networking site and texting. Probably you also keep up with friends you do see through online sites as well as in-person interaction. In addition, we text, tweet, and call those we are closest to just to stay in touch throughout the day. At least 25 percent of people report texting partners when both are home in separate rooms (Ellin, 2014). Online apps

 **ENGAGE!**

Job DISqualifications

Be careful what information you put on social networking sites. At least 37 percent of employers now check applicants by searching social networking sites such as Facebook ("37 Percent," 2012). Employers are most likely to dismiss applicants if they find:

1. Information about excessive use of alcohol or other drugs
2. Sexually provocative or photographs or descriptions of inappropriate activity
3. Poor communication skills
4. Speaking negatively about employers or co-workers at previous jobs.

But social networking sites aren't the only source of potential trouble for prospective employees. Santa Barbara start-up company Social Intelligence does what CEO Max Drucker calls "deep searches" of the Internet (Preston, 2011). His company searches not only major social networking sites, but also bulletin boards, YouTube, Flickr, Picasa, Yfrog, Photobucket, blogs, posts on small sites such as Tumblr, and even Craigslist. Social Intelligence gives prospective employers a dossier that includes online records of racist remarks, references to drugs, sexually explicit photos and videos, displays of weapons, and violent activity. Privacy advocates charged that Social Intelligence should not be allowed to operate because it was intrusive in people's personal lives. The Federal Trade Commission investigated Social Intelligence but ruled that the company was compliant with the Fair Credit Reporting Act. Bottom line: Anything online is fair game for background searches (Waters, 2011).

Online Sexuality

Increasingly, we hear about people who are charged with sexting—using their cell phones to send nude photos of themselves or parts of themselves. While some sexting is done to harass, the majority seems to be done either to get attention or to flirt. In most cases so far, the charges have been dropped or reduced, but one consequence of sexting is not going away: File endurance. Once the message is sent, it exists and may resurface at any time such as when a potential employer does an online search of an interviewee!

And sexting is not the only way in which sex and sexuality are online. Many preteen boys have perhaps their first sexual experiences via online pornography, which means they come into their sexuality outside of the context of a relationship with another person (Steiner-Adair, 2013).

such as Couple Counseling and Chatting, Romantimatic, and Embre even help partners make up after arguing (Ellin, 2014).

The most important meaning of much digital communication occurs on the relationship level. At the content level, there's not a great deal going on in text messages such as <r u ok>, <no. boss n bd mood>, and <sad 4 u. be btr>. At the relationship level of meaning, however, they say a lot. They say "I want to stay in touch with you" and "I care what is happening in your life." Digital media facilitate constant connection. We use them to massage relationships with many small strokes instead of one big one.

Digital media may invite excessive sharing and self-promotion (Steiner-Adair, 2013; Zuckerberg, 2013). In part because we aren't getting immediate physical and visual feedback from others, our digital media communication can become quite self-focused, or narcissistic, as we post countless photos of ourselves and comment on trivial, day-to-day moods and happenings (Martin, 2013). Yet, as Zuckerberg (2013) points out, the fact that we can document every moment of our lives doesn't mean we *should*. How many people really need to know or care that it's raining where you live or that you feel bored at 9:18 on Tuesday morning? How many want to see 45 pictures of your new baby or puppy? Is that photo of you looking smashed one you want a potential employer to be able to find? Most of us would be wise to adopt dual perspective when deciding what to post online: Ask yourself whether something you are thinking of posting is consistent with how you want others to perceive you and whether it is of interest or value to others.

Woody

I could never stay in touch with all my old friends without Facebook. Most of them went to in-state colleges but I went across the whole country to come to this school. I get home three times a year so we couldn't make it if we had to do the retro f2f talking. We post on each other's walls weekly or even more often, and we text a lot. That keeps all of us connected and tight like we were in high school.

Learning

Digital media are also venues for learning. Many colleges and universities have course management systems such as Blackboard or Sakai that faculty are encouraged or required to use. These allow faculty to post readings and other course material, record grades, set up discussion forums, and e-mail students. In addition, faculty often post PowerPoint and Pretzi presentations to supplement class lectures and discussions.

The classroom is not the only or even the primary place where learning, including digital learning, occurs. Online sites, including those included in this book's online resources, are rich sources of information. Students use them to extend and complement course material, faculty use them to conduct research, cooks use them to

Digital Media on Campus

Campuses are a prime place to develop new uses for digital. Here are examples of innovative ways to enhance learning.

◆ Stanford's medical school uses iPads to train students. One application allows students to draw anatomical structures with fingers and then annotate the drawings. The iPad is also how students watch videos of medical procedures being performed. Advanced medical students who sometimes confront emergencies can pull up a video that gives them moment-by-moment visual instruction on what they need to do (Keller, 2011).

◆ At the University of Warwick in England, students use smartphones to watch videos that teach about different body organs and take quizzes on anatomy (Young, 2011).

◆ A number of colleges use the location-tracking feature of smartphones to help students, particularly new ones, find their way around campus. For students who ride busses, many campuses have developed an app that lets them know how long they have to wait for the next bus (Young, 2011).

◆ Art departments on many campuses use a Google site to allow students to visit museums around the world and see famous works of art (http://www.googleartproject.com) (Cordell, 2011).

◆ Knewton is a computerized software program that functions as a personal tutor. Knewton gives students immediate feedback on their work and adapts to individual students' learning curves, giving more advanced material to students only when they are ready for it (Fischman, 2011).

◆ Piazza is a platform designed by an enterprising student named Pooja Nath. Piazza allows students to post questions on a course page, and peers and teachers can respond. Compared to rival sites such as Blackboard, Piazza is much faster because it is supported by a system of notification alerts (Rusli, 2011).

find recipes, professionals use them to get information and sometimes to check out opportunities for new jobs, and all of us use them to learn about sports, fashion, politics, and other topics that interest us. As Amy Finnerty (2013) notes, "some 4-year-olds can download apps before they can put on their own shoes" (p. C9).

Professional Communication

Digital media have radically altered how professionals communicate. Many issues that used to require face-to-face meetings can now be handled by e-mail, which remains a primary form of digital media in the workplace. In fact, the average white-collar worker spends 28 percent of work time tending to e-mail (Thompson, 2014). It allows co-workers in different physical locations to plan, review documents, make decisions, and collaborate. Skype and other VoIP protocols allow virtual conferences in which professionals can be visually and verbally present in the same meeting although they are geographically separated. And intranet systems allow posting of documents that can be accessed by members of an organization or organizational unit.

Digital media are integral to professional life.

The Sharing Economy

How would you like a job where you managed yourself, worked only when you wanted to, and set your own schedule? How would you like a job without benefits, credits toward Social Security, unemployment compensation, or the assurance of work on any given day?

If you want either of those jobs, welcome to the sharing economy or the one-gig economy. That's the new term for what was once called piecemeal labor. In this work, individuals contract for one-time jobs such as driving someone to an airport, delivering materials, cooking, and doing chores. The independent contractors have apps they check for offers for their services, which they may accept or decline. The companies that provide connections between customers and independent contractors establish the terms for services, which often include setting prices, and may change those terms with no notice (Singer, 2014).

In addition to increasing productivity, digital media add much convenience to business and professional life. Automated teller machines (ATMs) that operate 24 hours a day may not increase banks' profits, but they make it easier for people to withdraw money when it's convenient for them. People shop online may not spend more than they did in the 1980s, but online shopping saves them a lot of time and facilitates comparison shopping. Many pilots have replaced the 40+ pound flight manuals they used to carry on board with a 1.5 pound iPad that allows them to read aeronautical charts and assess other information (Murphy, 2011). Likewise, towns that provide tablets to officials save the cost of printing agendas, often with extensive appendices and reports (Williams, 2011).

Digital media also have another increasing role in the professional realm. Many employers use them to monitor employees to ensure that they are working while on the job or are reprimanded and perhaps fired if they are not. Recent court rulings have made it clear that employees' communication is not necessarily private. Communication on devices provided by employers is not protected by constitutional privacy rights and may be audited by employers (Liptak, 2011). The Supreme Court has given employers wide power to search and monitor text messages that employees send on pagers.

Organizing

Digital media are also extraordinary tools for social and political organizing. They allow contact, interaction, strategizing, and community building among people who are geographically scattered.

Digital media provide a degree of anonymity that is important for political organizing that challenges powerful forces that could harm those who oppose them. The Initiators and Organizers of the Chinese Jasmine Revolution are a network of educated, young Chinese who use the Internet to encourage Chinese citizens to engage in peaceful protests to persuade the ruling Communist Party to move toward more democratic government. The anonymity of the Internet shields members of the network from punishment by the government (Wong, 2011). These protestors rely on digital media to pass information, plan strategy, and mobilize support for their efforts. Fear of reprisal from the government is minimized because the dissidents' identities can be concealed online (Wong, 2011).

Digital media also feature prominently in organizing for social change in Saudi Arabia. In that country, there are strict governmental regulations that prohibit public gatherings, so Saudis cannot demonstrate in public spaces without risk of grave repercussions. When Manal al-Sharif posted a video of herself driving, which is illegal for women in Saudi Arabia, she was jailed for nine days and clerics urged the government

Who Benefits?

Although digital media enrich our lives in many ways, we would be naïve to think that they exist primarily to please or help us. The people who own and invest in media companies benefit far more than most users. Consider the case of LinkedIn. The initial public offering of LinkedIn stock was priced at $65 and soared to over $100 on its first day of trading. In addition to making stock traders who bought LinkedIn rich overnight, there were other beneficiaries. The team that underwrote the stock, which included financial giants such as Bank of America, JPMorgan Chase, and Morgan Stanley, made a tidy $28.4 million in fees. LinkedIn's primary law firm made $1.5 million, and its accounting firm made $1.35 million. Venture capitalists who had provided financial support when LinkedIn was a start-up company were given stock that soared when the company went public.

Users provide the content that makes LinkedIn valuable, and the owners and venture capitalists profit. The same is true of YouTube and social networking sites such as Facebook. People like you provide the content that makes the sites profitable for others. This doesn't necessarily mean that we shouldn't use and enjoy digital media, but it does suggest that we should be aware that our online activity—such as posting YouTube videos—benefits others handsomely.

Far from being a democratic open space that equalizes all people, the Web is run by elites who profit from what users provide. Tim Wu (2014) puts it bluntly: "The creative masses connect, create and labor, while Google, Facebook and Amazon collect the cash" (p. 20). Users who contribute content in the hope of becoming Internet famous by having their work go viral are deluding themselves: The odds that your work will go viral are about the same as your odds of winning a lottery (Taylor, 2014).

to subject her to public flogging for her crime. Within a few days of her arrest, other Saudis posted more than 30,000 tweets in support of Ms. Sharif (MacFarquhar, 2011). Emboldened by her work and the online support, a handful of Saudi women took driving lessons and posted to Twitter. Activists have posted videos and tweets criticizing other governmental actions with increasing frequency. The greater anonymity that inheres in digital media allows Saudis to organize and build support without risking harsh punishments.

Guidelines for Interacting with Digital Media

There's no chance we are going to return to landlines, typewriters, and hand-written letters. Digital media are here to stay. How they affect us individually and our society as a whole, however, is up to us. We need to think about how we want to integrate digital media into our lives. In this section, we consider two guidelines for doing that.

Consciously Manage Your Engagement with Digital Technologies

One consequence of digital media is extraordinary amounts of information available to us. On a typical day, the average American reads and hears as much content as would be in 174 print newspapers. Nearly 6,000 videos are posted on YouTube every hour (Levitin, 2014). But access to more information doesn't necessarily make us more knowledgeable for at least two reasons. First, human minds have finite processing capacity, so we may not be able to process all of the information that comes our way (Levitin, 2014). Second, knowledge requires more than information. It requires evaluating the credibility of sources of information, thinking about how bits of information fit together, and connecting information to larger contexts in order to draw reasoned conclusions.

It is ironic that technologies designed to save time and increase efficiency often make our lives more frenetic. The sheer amount of information many people receive causes stress and confusion. Smartphones keep us available all the time to everyone, but what if we don't want to be available all the time? A 2011 report (Levy, Nardick, Turner, & McWatters, 2011) noted that more than half of college students surveyed were concerned about their immersion in technology. Many students feel pressure to be connected and responsive all the time. Alexis's commentary makes this point.

 Alexis

The other day I left my phone in my apartment because I was going to be really busy all day and didn't want to be distracted. When I got home I found all of these messages, many really angry because I had not replied to texts immediately. It's like I can't have a life without being available to everyone else 24/7.

The problem of information overload is so serious that the very companies that made information overload possible are now trying to help people cope with it. Tech giants such as Google, Microsoft, and Intel have formed a nonprofit group to study the problem and devise ways to help people cope with the relentless onslaught of information. In addition to concerns about the stress on people, the tech giants are concerned about the costs to business of information overload. Studies of information workers show that the continuous switching from e-mail to smartphone to Internet fractures attention spans. After each interruption or switch, a person has to remember what she or he was doing and get back into that task . . . just in time for the next interruption.

Information overload takes psychological and emotional tolls. We feel compelled to keep up with the blogs we follow, news sites, and social media. And what is required to keep up increases with each new device and app that is developed. Teens, as well as many adults, feel guilty if they don't post updates for friends and respond to friends' texts and tweets (Steiner-Adair, 2013). German automaker Daimler decided to make sure employees used their vacations for what they are intended to be: escapes from work to refresh mind and spirit. When a Daimler employee goes on vacation, her or his incoming office e-mails are handled by others and deleted so that workers don't feel compelled to reply to e-mails while on vacation and don't return from vacation to overflowing inboxes. The program is voluntary, yet nearly 100 percent of employees approve of it ("Giving email," 2014). Volkswagen and Deutsche Telekom, also German companies, have begun restricting work-related e-mails to employees outside of office hours (Thompson, 2014).

The compulsion to stay connected also exacts a toll on face-to-face relationships. Some research reports that teens who are heavy tech users are more likely to be depressed and lonely than peers who spend less time in the digital realm (Finnerty, 2013). Technologies in homes often supplant conversations between family members. White-collar workers who use smartphones receive and respond to e-mail up to 13.5 hours a day, not cutting the devices off even during dinner (Thompson, 2014). Based on interviews with 1,000 children, as well as some parents and teachers, clinical psychologist Catherine Steiner-Adair (2013) reported that many children resent their parents' involvement with digital devices. The children

What Kind of Person Would You Become?

That's a key question Amish people ask when considering whether to adopt technologies ranging from cars to cell phones. Although the Amish still wear homemade clothes and live in homes without electricity, some Amish people use power tools, cell phones, and computers. Although this may sound inconsistent, actually it's not ("Amish," 2009; Umble, 2000). *Wired* magazine's Howard Rheingold (2009) spent some time in an Amish settlement in Pennsylvania to learn how they made decisions about technology.

When considering whether a particular technology belongs in their community, one question the Amish pose is how it would affect them. One Amish man expresses it this way: "It's not just how you use the technology that concerns us. We're also concerned about what kind of person you become when you use it." The Amish don't allow phones in homes. Five or more families may share a phone that is housed in a small structure between homes. Why not in the home? Because people interrupt face-to-face conversations to answer phone calls. Because a ringing phone disturbs family conversation over a meal. Why are cars not allowed by Old Order Amish? Because they allow people to travel greater distances and this undermines the custom of visiting nearby families every other Sunday.

 MindTap   How does your use of digital media affect who you are?

are sad and angry that they can't win in the competition with digital devices for their parents' attention. There are also concerns that parents' attention to digital devices may distract them from adequately supervising children, particularly young ones (Klass, 2014).

Some of the most media-savvy people choose to draw lines about the role of digital media in their lives. The CTO of Cisco unplugs all devices on Saturdays for a "digital detox" and news pro Rachel Maddow unplugs her digital devices on weekends in a country home that has no TV or Cable (Gregoire, 2013).

We too can make deliberate choices about which digital media to use and when and how much to use them. If certain of technologies better our lives and we can afford them, we may choose to have them some of the time and in some of the contexts in our lives. But if they don't fit our lives and don't help us be the people we want to be, we don't have to join the crowd.

> Now available: The Courtesy app. It turns your phone off when you are talking with another person.

Manage Trolls and Other Digital Monsters

In children's stories, trolls are often evil beings who live under bridges and in other dark places where they wait for innocent passersby they can attack. In the online world, trolls are not that different. Trolls are individuals who are intentionally cruel and mean in digital communication. They may operate individually or in groups, they often hide behind a cloak of anonymity, and they often comment on threads and social network postings.

And they cause pain, sometimes serious pain. After actor Robin Williams committed suicide in the summer of 2014, trolls attacked his daughter Zelda. They sent her altered photos of her father with bruises on his neck and the message that he killed himself "because of you" (Manjoo, 2014). The attacks became so vicious that she deleted Twitter from all of her devices (Manjoo, 2014).

ENGAGE! Proactive Strategies for Managing Trolls

It's naïve to think that trolls are going away or even that you personally can escape them. Anyone who is active online is likely to run into a troll or two. But you don't have to let them do the damage they intend to do. Here are some proactive ways to protect yourself (Rosenbloom, 2014):

1. Realize you are more sensitive to negative comments than positive ones. Research shows that we notice and remember criticism and hurtful experiences more than praise and happy experiences (Rosenbloom, 2014). Just being aware of this gives you some perspective if you start to dwell on a troll's comments.

2. Regard criticism as a gift. This sounds hokey or just plain crazy, but it's actually good advice. If a particular insult really gets under your skin, it's likely that there is a grain of truth in it. What can you learn from the criticism that allows you to improve yourself?

3. Challenge comments that are untrue. Out loud. If a troll says "you're fat and ugly," say to yourself, "I am well within the normal weight range for my sex and height and lots of people think I am attractive." If a troll says you're stupid, say out loud, "I make the Honor Roll every semester." Hearing yourself dispute false criticism strengthens your resistance to it.

4. Make fun of trolls' comments. Out loud. Read the trolls' comment aloud in a squeaky or nasal voice. Read them with an upbeat song playing. Pretend the trolls are present and grill them with questions: "Oh yeah, so why do you think I'm stupid? Do you have a Ph.D.? Are you in Mensa? I mean, really, who gave you the right to judge anyone's intelligence?" Asking these questions out loud helps store your resistant messages in your memory. If the trolls are too bothersome, follow Zelda Williams' tactic by disconnecting. The devices and apps are yours. Use them to support yourself.

Trolls don't limit their attacks to celebrities. They also go after regular people, ridiculing their appearance in photos, threatening to stalk or rape, and posting hate messages about their politics. The anonymity of the digital world seems to embolden people to be more cruel, more hateful, than they would in face-to-face conversations.

Cyberbullying differs from face-to-face bullying in two key ways. First, it can be and often is perpetrated anonymously, so victims have no way of confronting their tormentors. Second, cyberbullying has no geographic boundaries. The school-yard bully pretty much stayed on the school yard, so victims could escape. Online bullying can follow the victim anywhere 24-7. It is unremitting.

As far as impact on victims, cyberbullying is every bit as harmful as face-to-face bullying. Either can have devastating effects on self-esteem and can lead to depression, responsive violence, and even suicide. Although people of any age can engage in cyberbullying, it is most common among middle schoolers (Jacobs, 2010). At that age, people are uniquely vulnerable to derision and exclusion by peers. Middle schoolers have online discussions, often with voting, to decide if someone is ugly or stupid or promiscuous. The online group's decisions are typically sent to others, often including the victim who is then publicly humiliated.

The online environment may encourage less personal responsibility for one's actions (Freeman, 2009; Jacobs, 2010). As one eighth-grade student remarked, "It's easier to fight online because you feel more brave and in control. On Facebook, you can be as mean as you want" (Hoffman, 2010, p. A12).

cyberbullying Text messages, comments, rumors, embarrassing pictures, videos, and fake profiles that are meant to hurt another person and are sent by e-mail or posted on social networking sites.

Summary

In this chapter, we've considered what it means to live in an era that is saturated with digital media. After discussing defining features of digital media and their impact on human thinking, we explored the many ways we use them in our daily lives.

The final section of this chapter discussed two guidelines for interacting with communication technologies. One is to make deliberate choices about how to manage the place we give digital media in our lives. Second, we should manage cruel online behavior from trolls and bullies.

Online social interaction is not inherently bad or good, social or antisocial, safe or unsafe. In fact, it is very much like real-world communication. In both the virtual world and real life, there are some people who communicate thoughtfully, ethically, and effectively and some who don't. There are some people online who are mean and even dangerous, but mean and dangerous people also exist offline. This doesn't mean that online communication is without danger. Rather, the reports suggest that it is probably no more (or less) dangerous online than offline.

Experience Communication Case Study

Online Dating

Apply what you've learned in this chapter by analyzing the following case study, using the accompanying questions as a guide. These questions and a video of the case study are also available online with your MindTap Speech for *Communication Mosaics*.

Christina is visiting her family for the holidays. One evening after dinner, her mother comes into her room where Christina is typing at her computer. Her mother sits down, and the following conversation takes place.

Mom: Am I disturbing you?

Chris: No, I'm just signing off on e-mail. [She finishes at the keyboard and turns to face her mom.]

Mom: E-mailing someone?

Chris: Just a guy.

Mom: Someone you've been seeing at school?

Chris: Not exactly.

Mom: [laughs] Well, either you are seeing him or you're not, honey. Are you two dating?

Chris: Sort of. Yeah, you could say we're dating.

Mom: [laughs] What's the mystery? What's he like?

Chris: He's funny and smart and so easy to talk to. We can talk for hours and it never gets dull. I've never met anyone who's so easy to be with. We're interested in the same things and we share so many values. Brandon's just super. I've never met anyone like him.

© Cengage Learning

Mom: Sounds great. When do I get to meet this fellow?

Chris: Well, not until I do. [Laughs] We met online and we're just starting to talk about getting together in person.

Mom: Online? You met this man online? And you act as if you know him!

Chris: I do know him, Mom. We've talked a lot—we've told each other lots of stuff, and . . .

Mom: How do you know what he's told you is true? For all you know, he's a 50-year-old mass murderer!

Chris: You've been watching too many movies on Lifetime, Mom. Brandon's 23, he's in college, and he comes from a family a lot like ours.

Mom: How do you know that? He could be lying about every part of what he's told you.

Chris: So? A guy I meet at school could lie, too. Meeting someone in person is no guarantee of honesty.

Mom: Haven't you read about all of the weirdos that go to these online matching sites?

Chris: Mom, Brandon's not a weirdo, and we didn't meet in a matching site. We met in a chat room where people talk about politics. He's as normal as I am. After all, I was in that chat room, too!

Mom: But, Chris, you can't be serious about someone you haven't met.

Chris: I have met him, Mom, just not face to face. Actually, I know him better than lots of guys I've dated for months. You can get to know a lot about a person from talking.

Mom: This makes me really nervous, honey. Please don't meet him by yourself.

Chris: Mom, you're making me feel sorry I told you how we met. This is exactly why I didn't tell you about him before. Nothing I say is going to change your mind about dating online.

Mom: [Pauses, looks away, then looks back at Chris.] You're right. I'm not giving him—or you— a chance. Let's start over. [Smiles] Tell me what you like about him.

Chris: [Tentatively] Well, he's thoughtful.

Mom: Thoughtful? How so?

Chris: Like, if I say something one day, he'll come back to it a day or so later and I can tell he's thought about it, like he's really interested in what I say.

Mom: So he really pays attention to what you say, huh?

Chris: Exactly. So many guys I've dated don't. They never return to things I've said. Brandon does. And another thing, when I come back to things he's said with ideas I've thought about, he really listens.

Mom: Like he values what you think and say?

Chris: Exactly! That's what's so special about him.

1. Review Chapter 6, which focuses on listening and responding. Identify examples of ineffective and effective listening and responding on the part of Chris's mother.

2. Chapter 10 stated that proximity and similarities are the two most significant influences on initial romantic attraction. Does this statement hold true for the online relationship between Chris and Brandon?

3. If Chris and Brandon meet face-to-face, how will communication on their initial date be different from communication on first dates between people who have not met online?

4. If you were romantically attracted to a person you met online and wanted to have a face-to-face date with her or him, what would you do to maximize your safety?

 MindTap

Key Concepts

Practice defining the chapter's terms by using online flashcards.

communication technologies, 299   digital media, 299
cyberbullying, 312   multitasking, 301
digital divide, 297

 MindTap

Reflect, personalize, and
apply what you've learned.

Review, Reflect, Extend

The Reflect and Discuss and Take Action features that follow will help you review, reflect on, and extend the information and ideas presented in this chapter. These resources, and a diverse selection of additional study tools, are also available online at the MindTap Speech for *Communication Mosaics*.

Reflect and Discuss

1. How do relationships between people who never meet face-to-face differ from relationships between people who can see each other? What are the advantages and limitations of forming and sustaining relationships each way?

2. As a class or in small groups, discuss cyberbullying and, more generally, hurtful online communication. What about the online environment facilitates mean behaviors such as making insults, spreading false rumors, and ridiculing appearance, sexual orientation, ethnicity, and other aspects of identity? Could the factors that facilitate such behaviors be altered or do you think the problem of cyberbullying is inherent in digital media?

3. Reflect on your involvement with digital media. How many devices do you own? How much of the time is at least one device on? How often are you totally disconnected? What is gained and lost by your choices of how much to be connected?

TAKE ACTION

1. Your Professional Image

Spend some time reviewing your home page on Facebook or another social network. Imagine that you are an employer looking at the page. Are there any images, comments, or other postings that might lead an employer to wonder whether you are professional?

Continue with the exercise above by thinking about you're the identity announced by your e-mails, tweets, and texts. How does your name appear? How might that name be perceived by professors and potential employers?

2. Suspending the Digital World

Disconnect—totally, 100 percent—from all forms of digital media for 24 hours. Reflect on your thoughts and feelings during the experiment. What did you miss the most? What, if anything, did you learn about yourself?

Recommended Resources

1. Read the most current issue of *Wired* or a similar magazine that focuses on technologies. Identify technological products and services that are not mentioned in this book, which went to press in the spring of 2015.

2. View the 2014 film *Her*, which features a human-cyborg relationship. What do you find attractive and unattractive about a relationship with a cyborg? Do you imagine there will be cyborgs in the future?

Epilogue

Although this is the final page of this book, what you have learned from it and from the class you are taking will continue to serve you throughout your life. Because communication is central to everything you do, the understandings and skills you have gained will enhance the quality of your personal life, enrich your social and civic involvements, help you succeed professionally, and prepare you to be an informed, active user of mass media and digital media.

In the years ahead, you will find that what we've discussed in this book will help you understand a range of people and communication situations. Whether you are watching television, listening to a friend, participating on a work team, working through conflict with a romantic partner, or communicating online, the ideas and skills we have explored in *Communication Mosaics* will enlarge your insight into yourself, others, and the ways in which communication operates.

I hope that the theories, concepts, processes, and skills we've discussed will increase your effectiveness and pleasure in interacting with others in all the spheres of your life.

Julia T. Wood

© Digital Vision/Getty Images

Glossary

abstract Removed from concrete reality. Symbols are abstract because they refer to, but are not equivalent to, reality.

acknowledgment The second of three levels of interpersonal confirmation; communicating that you hear and understand another's expressed feelings and thoughts.

agape One of the six styles of loving; it is selfless and focused on the other's happiness.

agenda setting Media's selection of issues, events, and people to highlight for attention.

ambiguous Subject to multiple meanings. Symbols are ambiguous because their meanings vary from person to person, context to context, and so forth.

ambushing Listening carefully to a speaker in order to attack her or him.

anxious/ambivalent attachment One of the four styles of attachment; a style, characterized by preoccupation with relationships, in which intimacy is both wanted and feared. It is fostered by inconsistent treatment from a caregiver.

arbitrary Random or not necessary. Symbols are arbitrary because there is no need for any particular symbol to stand for a particular referent.

arbitrator Outside third party who has the authority to make a decision on a conflict between two or more people.

artifact Any personal object with which one announces one's identities or personalizes one's environment.

assimilation The giving up of one's native ways to take on the ways of another culture.

attachment style The pattern of interaction between child and primary caregiver that teaches the child who he or she is, who others are, and how to approach relationships. Four attachment styles have been identified: anxious/ambivalent, dismissive, fearful, and secure.

attribution An explanation of why things happen and why people act as they do; not necessarily correct interpretations of others and their motives.

autonomy/connection One of three relationship dialectics; the tension between the need for personal autonomy, or independence, and connection, or intimacy.

bracketing Identifying and setting aside for later discussion the issues peripheral to a current conflict.

brainstorming A group technique for generating potential solutions to a problem; the free flow of ideas without immediate criticism.

brute facts Objective, concrete phenomena.

chronemics Nonverbal communication involving the perception and use of time to define identities and interaction.

climate communication One of three constructive forms of participation in group decision making; the creating and sustaining of an open, engaged atmosphere for discussion.

cognitive complexity The number of mental constructs an individual uses, how abstract they are, and how elaborately they interact to create perceptions.

cognitive schemata Mental structures people use to organize and interpret experience. Four schemata have been identified: prototypes, personal constructs, stereotypes, and scripts.

cohesion Closeness, or feeling of esprit de corps, among members of a group.

commitment The decision to remain in a relationship. One of three dimensions of enduring romantic relationships, commitment has more influence on relationship continuity than does love alone. An advanced stage in the process of escalation in romantic relationships.

communication A systemic process in which people interact with and through symbols to create and interpret meanings.

communication climate The overall feeling, or emotional mood, between people.

communication network The links among members of an organization. May be formal (e.g., as specified in an organizational chart) or informal (friendship circles).

communication rules Shared understandings of what communication means and what behaviors are appropriate in various situations.

communication technologies Means of recording, transferring, sharing, and working with information.

comparison A form of evidence associating two things that are similar or different in some important way or ways.

confirmation The expressed valuing of another person.

conflict The expression by people who depend on each other of different views, interests, or goals and the perception of differences as incompatible or in opposition.

constitutive rules Communication rules that specify how certain communicative acts are to be counted.

constructive conflict In groups, disagreement that is characterized by respect for diverse opinions, emphasis on shared interests and goals, and a win–win orientation.

constructivism A theory that holds that we organize and interpret experience by applying cognitive structures called schemata.

content level of meaning One of two levels of meaning; the literal information in a message.

covert conflict Conflict that is expressed indirectly; generally more difficult to manage constructively than overt conflict.

credibility The ability of a person to engender belief in what he or she says or does. Listeners confer or refuse to confer credibility on speakers.

critical listening Listening to analyze and evaluate the content of communication or the character of the person speaking.

critical research An approach to research that aims to identify, critique, or change communication practices that oppress, marginalize, or otherwise harm people.

cultivation A cumulative process by which the media foster beliefs about social reality, including the belief that the world is more dangerous and violent than it actually is.

cultural relativism The recognition that cultures vary in thought, action, and behavior as well as in beliefs and values; not the same as moral relativism.

culture The beliefs, values, understandings, practices, and ways of interpreting experience that are shared by a group of people.

cyberbullying Text messages, comments, rumors, embarrassing pictures, videos, and fake profiles that are meant to hurt another person and are sent by e-mail or posted on social networking sites.

defensive listening The perception of a personal attack, criticism, or hostile undertones in communication when none is intended.

derived credibility The expertise and trustworthiness attributed to a speaker by listeners as a result of how the speaker communicates during a presentation.

digital divide The gap between people and communities that do and do not have access to digital technologies.

digital media Electronic modes of communication that store and manage data in digital form.

direct definition Communication that tells us who we are by explicitly labeling us and reacting to our behaviors; usually occurs first in families and later in interaction with peers and others.

dismissive attachment One of the four attachment styles; characterized by a view of others as unworthy of love and the self as adequate yet removed from intimate relationships; fostered by disinterested, rejecting, or abusive treatment by a caregiver.

disruptive conflict In groups, disagreement characterized by competitive communication, self-interested focus on the part of members, and a win–lose orientation.

downer A person who communicates negatively about us and our worth.

egocentric communication An unconstructive form of group contribution that is used to block others or to call attention to oneself.

empathy The ability to feel with another person, to feel what he or she feels in a situation.

endorsement The third of three levels of interpersonal confirmation; the communication of acceptance of another's thoughts and feelings. Not the same as agreement.

environmental distraction In communication situations, any occurrence that interferes with listening.

environmental factor Any nonverbal element of a setting that affects how we think, feel, act, and communicate.

equity theory The theory that people are happier and more satisfied with equitable relationships than inequitable ones. In equitable relationships, partners perceive the benefits and costs of the relationship as about equal for each of them.

eros One of the six styles of loving; passionate, intense, and erotic.

ethics The branch of philosophy that deals with the goodness or rightness of particular actions. Ethical issues infuse all areas of the communication field.

ethnocentrism The tendency to assume that one's own way of life is normal and superior to other ways of life.

ethos One of the three forms of proof; proof based on the speaker's credibility (trustworthiness, expertise, and goodwill).

evidence Material used to support claims; statistics, examples, comparisons, and quotations.

example A form of evidence in which a single instance is used to make a point, to dramatize an idea, or to personalize information. The four types of examples are undetailed, detailed, hypothetical, and anecdotal.

expectancy violation theory A theory claiming that when our expectations are violated, we become more cognitively alert as we struggle to understand and cope with unexpected behaviors.

extemporaneous delivery A presentational style that includes preparation and practice but not memorization of actual words and nonverbal behaviors.

fearful attachment One of the four styles of attachment; characterized by the perception of self as unworthy of love; fostered by dismissive, rejecting, or abusive treatment by a caregiver.

feedback Verbal or nonverbal response to a message. The concept of feedback as applied to human communication appeared first in interactive models of communication.

flaming Excessively insulting another person online, often using language that is derogatory or obscene.

gatekeeper A person, group, or institution that controls the choice and presentation of topics by media.

generalized other The perspective that represents one's perception of the rules, roles, and attitudes endorsed by one's group or community.

global village The modern-day, worldwide community made possible by electronic communication that instantaneously links people all over the world.

grace Granting forgiveness, putting aside our own needs, or helping another save face when no standard says we should or must do so.

group More than two people who interact over time, who are interdependent, and who follow shared rules of conduct to reach a common goal. A team is one type of group.

groupthink The absence of critical and independent thought on the part of group members about ideas generated by the group.

haptics Nonverbal communication involving physical touch.

hate groups Collections of people who advocate and engage in hatred, aggression, or violence toward members of a particular race, ethnicity, gender, sexual orientation, gender identity, religion, or any other selected segment of a society.

hearing A physiological activity that occurs when sound waves hit our eardrums. Unlike listening, hearing is a passive process.

high-context communication style An indirect and undetailed way of speaking that conveys meanings implicitly rather than explicitly; typical of collectivist cultures.

homeostasis A state of equilibrium that systems strive for but cannot sustain.

hypothetical thought Thinking about experiences and ideas that do not exist or are not immediately present to the senses.

I The creative, spontaneous, impulsive aspect of the self. The *I* is complemented by the *me*.

***I*-language** Language that identifies the speaker's or perceiver's thoughts and feelings. (Compare with *you*-language.)

immersive advertising Incorporating a product or brand into actual storylines in books, television programs, and films.

impromptu delivery A delivery style that involves little preparation; speakers think on their feet as they talk about ideas and positions with which they are familiar.

incomprehensibility When a message is not clearly understandable due to language or transmission problems; one of four situational obstacles to listening.

indexing A technique of noting that every statement reflects a specific time and circumstance and may not apply to other times or circumstances.

individualism A predominant Western value that regards each person as unique, important, and to be recognized for her or his individual qualities and behavior.

individualism/collectivism Dimension of cultures that refers to the extent to which members of a culture understand themselves as part of and connected to their families, groups, and cultures.

inference An interpretation that goes beyond the facts known but is believed to logically follow from them.

informational listening Listening to understand information and ideas.

initial credibility The expertise and trustworthiness listeners attribute to a speaker before a presentation begins. Initial credibility is based on the speaker's titles, positions, experiences, or achievements that are known to listeners before they hear the speech.

institutional facts Meanings people assign to brute facts (objective, concrete phenomena) that are based on human interpretation.

interpersonal communication Communication between people, sometimes in close relationships such as friendship and romance.

interpretation The subjective process of creating explanations for what we observe and experience.

intrapersonal communication Communication with ourselves, or self-talk.

investment Something put into a relationship that cannot be recovered should the relationship end. Investments, more than rewards and love, increase commitment.

judgment A belief or opinion based on observations, feelings, assumptions, or other nonfactual phenomena.

kinesics Body position and body motions, including those of the face, that may be used to communicate or may be interpreted as communicating.

leadership A set of behaviors that helps a group maintain a good climate and accomplish tasks in an organized way.

life script A guide to action based on rules for living and identity. Initially communicated in families, scripts define our roles, how we are to play them, and the basic elements in the plot of our lives.

listening The process of receiving, constructing meaning from, and responding to spoken and/or nonverbal messages. The process consists of being mindful, hearing, selecting and organizing information, interpreting communication, responding, and remembering.

literal listening Listening only to the content level of meaning and ignoring the relationship level of meaning.

loaded language An extreme form of evaluative language that relies on words that strongly slant perceptions and thus meanings.

logos One of three forms of proof; proof based on logic and reasoning.

long-term/short-term orientation Dimension of culture that refers to the extent to which members of a culture think about long-term (history and future) versus short-term (present).

lose–lose One of three orientations to conflict; assumes that everyone loses when conflict occurs.

low-context communication style Language that is very explicit, detailed, and precise; generally used in individualistic cultures.

ludus One of the six styles of loving; playful and sometimes manipulative.

mainstreaming The effect of television in stabilizing and homogenizing views within a society.

mania One of the six styles of loving; an obsessive style that often reflects personal insecurity.

manuscript delivery A presentational style that involves speaking from a complete manuscript of a speech.

masculinity/femininity Dimension of culture that refers to the extent to which a culture values aggressiveness, competitiveness, looking out for yourself, and dominating others, which are typically associated with men, versus gentleness, cooperation, and taking care of others and the natural world, which tend to be associated with women. Also called *aggressiveness*.

mass media Communication that addresses large audiences.

matching hypothesis The prediction that people will seek relationships with others who closely match their values, attitudes, social background, and physical attractiveness.

me The reflective, analytical, socially conscious aspect of self. *Me* complements the *I* aspect of self.

mean world syndrome The belief that the world is dangerous and full of mean people.

meaning The significance we attribute to a phenomenon; what it signifies to us.

mediator Outside third party who facilitates discussion between two or more parties who are in conflict but who does not have the power to make a decision.

memorized delivery A presentational style in which the speech is delivered word for word from memory.

message complexity The amount of detailed information or intricate reasoning in a message; can interfere with effective listening.

message overload The receiving of more messages than we can interpret, evaluate, and remember; can interfere with effective listening.

mindfulness The concept of being fully present in the moment; the first step of listening and the foundation of all the other steps.

mind reading The assumption that we understand what another person thinks or how another person perceives something.

minimal encourager Communication that gently invites another person to elaborate by expressing interest in hearing more.

monitoring The observation and regulation of one's own communication.

monopolizing Hogging the stage by continuously focusing communication on oneself instead of on the person who is talking.

multilingual Able to speak and understand more than one language or communication style used in a social group or culture.

multitasking Engaging in multiple tasks in rapid sequence or in overlapping and interactive ways.

neutralization One of four responses to relationship dialectics; balancing or finding a compromise between two dialectical poles.

noise Anything that interferes with the intended meaning of communication; includes sounds (e.g., traffic) as well as psychological interferences (e.g., preoccupation).

nonverbal communication All forms of communication other than words themselves; includes inflection and other vocal qualities as well as several other behaviors such as shrugs, blushing, and eye movements.

norm An informal rule that guides how members of a culture or group think, feel, and act. Norms define what is normal or appropriate in various situations.

novelty/predictability One of three relationship dialectics; the tension between the desire for spontaneous, new experiences, and the desire for routines and familiar experiences.

olfactics The perception of scents and odors; one form of nonverbal communication.

openness The extent to which a system interacts with its surrounding environment.

openness/closedness One of three relationship dialectics; the tension between the desire to share private thoughts, feelings, and experiences with intimates and the desire to preserve personal privacy.

oral style Visual, vocal, and verbal aspects of the delivery of a public speech or other communication.

organizational culture Values, behaviors, practices, and forms of communication that are shared by the members of an organization and that reflect an organization's identity.

overt conflict Conflict expressed directly and in a straightforward manner.

paralanguage Communication that is vocal but not verbal. Paralanguage includes accent, inflection, volume, pitch, and sounds such as murmurs and gasps.

paraphrasing A method of clarifying another's meaning by reflecting one's interpretation of the other's communication back to that person.

participation A response to cultural diversity in which one incorporates some practices, customs, and traditions of other groups into one's life.

particular others Specific people who are significant to the self and who influence the self's values, perspectives, and esteem.

passion Intensely positive feelings and desires for another person. Passion is based on the rewards of involvement and is not equivalent to commitment.

pathos One of the three forms of proof; proof based on appealing to listeners' emotions.

perception An active process of selecting, organizing, and interpreting people, objects, events, situations, and activities.

personal construct A bipolar mental yardstick that allows us to measure people and situations along specific dimensions of judgment, such as "honest– dishonest."

personal relationship A relationship defined by uniqueness, rules, relationship dialectics, commitment, and embeddedness in contexts. Personal relationships, unlike social ones, are irreplaceable.

person-centeredness The ability to perceive another as a unique and distinct individual apart from social roles and generalizations.

physical appearance A form of nonverbal communication; how we look, including the cultural meanings, values, and expectations associated with looks.

policy A formal statement of practice that reflects and upholds an organization's culture.

positive visualization A technique used to enhance success in a variety of situations by teaching people to visualize themselves being effective and successful.

power The ability to influence others; a feature of small groups that affects participation.

power distance Dimension of culture that refers to the size of the gap between people with high and low power and the extent to which that is regarded as normal.

power over The ability to help or harm others. Power over others usually is communicated in ways that highlight the status and influence of the person exerting the power.

power to The ability to empower others to reach their goals. People who use power to help others generally do not highlight their own status and influence.

pragma One of the six styles of loving; based on practical considerations and criteria for attachment.

prejudgment Judging others or their ideas before one has heard them.

preoccupation Absorption in our own thoughts or concerns.

procedural communication One of three constructive ways of participating in group decision making; orders ideas and coordinates contributions of members.

process An ongoing continuity, the beginning and end of which are difficult to identify; for example, communication.

product placement A practice, paid for by advertisers and program sponsors, of featuring products in media so that the products are associated with particular characters, storylines, and so forth.

prototype A knowledge structure that defines the clearest or most representative example of some category.

proxemics A form of nonverbal communication that involves space and how we use it.

pseudolistening Pretending to listen.

psychological responsibility The obligation to remember, plan, and coordinate domestic work and child care. In general, women assume psychological responsibility for child care and housework even when both partners share in the actual doing of tasks.

puffery Exaggerated, superlative claims about a product that appear to be factually based but are actually meaningless and unverifiable.

punctuation Defining the beginning and ending of interaction or interaction episodes. Punctuation is subjective and not always agreed on by those involved in the interaction.

qualitative research Interpretive techniques, including textual analysis and ethnography, used to understand the character of experience, particularly how people perceive and make sense of communication.

quality improvement team A group in which people from different departments or areas in an organization collaborate to solve problems, meet needs, or increase the quality of work life. Also called *continuous quality improvement team*.

quantitative research Techniques such as descriptive statistics, surveys, and experiments, used to gather quantifiable data.

quotation A form of evidence that uses exact citations of others' statements. Also called *testimony*.

reappropriation A group's reclamation of a term used by others to degrade the group's members; the treatment of those terms as positive self-descriptions. Aims to remove the stigma from terms that others use pejoratively.

recognition The most basic level of interpersonal confirmation; the communication of awareness that another person exists and is present.

reflected appraisal The image and estimate of ourselves that others communicate to us.

reframing One of the four responses to relationship dialectics; transcends the apparent contradiction between two dialectical poles and reinterprets them as not in tension.

regulative rules Communication rules that regulate interaction by specifying when, how, where, and with whom to talk about certain things.

relationship culture A private world of rules, understandings, and patterns of acting and interpreting that partners create to give meaning to their relationship; the nucleus of intimacy.

relationship dialectics The tensions between opposing forces or tendencies that are normal parts of all relationships: autonomy/connection, novelty/predictability, and openness/closedness.

relationship level of meaning One of the two levels of meaning in communication; expresses the relationship between communicators.

relationship listening Listening to support another person or to understand how another person thinks, feels, or perceives some situation, event, or other phenomenon.

remembering The process of recalling what one has heard; the sixth element of listening.

resistance A response to cultural diversity; attacking the cultural practices of others or proclaiming that one's own cultural traditions are superior.

respect A response to cultural diversity in which one values others' customs, traditions, and values even if one does not actively incorporate them into one's life.

responding Symbolizing interest in what is being said with observable feedback to speakers during interaction; the fifth of six elements of listening.

rite A dramatic, planned set of activities that brings together aspects of cultural ideology in a single event.

ritual A form of regularly occurring communication that members of an organization perceive as a familiar, routine part of organizational life and that reflects a particular value or role definition.

role The responsibilities and behaviors expected of a person by virtue of his or her position.

rules Patterned ways of behaving and interpreting behavior. All relationships develop rules.

schemata Cognitive structures we use to organize and interpret experiences. The four types of schemata are prototypes, personal constructs, stereotypes, and scripts. (Singular: *schema*)

script One of the four cognitive schemata; scripts define expected or appropriate sequences of action in particular settings.

secure attachment One of the four styles of attachment; a style fostered by a caregiver who communicates with an infant in consistently loving and attentive ways and which inclines people to view themselves and others as worthy and to be comfortable both alone and in intimate relationships.

segmentation One of the four responses to relationship dialectics; segmentation responses meet one dialectical need while ignoring or not satisfying the contradictory dialectical need.

selective listening Focusing only on selected parts of communication; e.g., screening out parts of a message that don't interest us or with which we disagree, or riveting our attention on parts of communication that interest us or with which we agree.

self A multidimensional process that involves forming and acting from social perspectives that arise and evolve in communication with others and ourselves.

self-disclosure The revelation of personal information about ourselves that others are unlikely to discover in other ways.

self-fulfilling prophecy Acting in ways that bring about others' or our own expectations or judgments of ourselves.

self-sabotage Self-talk that communicates that we are no good, that we can't do something, that we can't change, and so forth; undermines belief in ourselves and motivation to change and grow.

self-serving bias The tendency to attribute our positive actions and successes to stable, global, internal influences that we control and to attribute negative actions and failures to unstable, specific, external influences beyond our control.

separation One of the four responses to relationship dialectics, in which friends or romantic partners assign one pole of a dialectic to certain spheres of activities or topics and assign the contradictory dialectical pole to distinct spheres of activities or topics.

silence Lack of sound. Silence can be a powerful form of nonverbal communication.

social climbing The attempt to increase personal status in a group by winning the approval of high-status members.

social community A group of people who live within a dominant culture yet also belong to another social group or groups that share values, understandings, and practices distinct from those of the dominant culture.

social comparison Comparing ourselves with others to form judgments of our talents, abilities, qualities, and so forth.

social loafing Exists when members of a group exert less effort than they would if they worked alone.

social relationships Replaceable relationships that tend to follow broad social scripts and rules and in which participants tend to assume conventional social roles in relation to one another. Contrast with *personal relationship*.

speech to entertain A speech intended to amuse, interest, and engage listeners.

speech to inform A speech intended to increase listeners' understanding, awareness, or knowledge of some topic.

speech to persuade A speech intended to change listeners' attitudes, beliefs, or behaviors or to motivate listeners to action.

standpoint The social, symbolic, and material conditions common to a group of people that influence how they understand themselves, others, and society.

standpoint theory A theory that holds that a culture includes a number of social groups that differently shape the perceptions, identities, and opportunities of members of those groups.

static evaluation An assessment that suggests that something is unchanging or static; e.g., "Bob is impatient."

statistics A form of evidence that uses numbers to summarize a great many individual cases or to demonstrate relationships between phenomena.

stereotype A predictive generalization about a person or situation.

storge One of the six styles of loving; based on friendship; even-keeled.

structure Organizes relationships and interaction among members of an organization. Structures include roles, rules, policies, and communication networks.

symbols Arbitrary, ambiguous, and abstract representations of phenomena. Symbols are the basis of language, much nonverbal behavior, and human thought.

synergy A special kind of collaborative vitality that enhances the energies, talents, and strengths of individual members.

system A group of interrelated elements that affect one another. Communication is systemic.

task communication One of three constructive forms of participation in group decision making; focuses on giving and analyzing information and ideas.

team A special kind of group characterized by different and complementary resources of members and by a strong sense of collective identity. All teams are groups, but not all groups are teams.

terminal credibility The cumulative expertise and trustworthiness listeners attribute to a speaker as a result of initial and derived credibility; may be greater or less than

initial credibility, depending on how effectively a speaker has communicated.

thesis statement The main idea of an entire speech; should capture the key message in a concise sentence that listeners can remember easily.

tolerance A response to diversity in which one accepts differences, although one may not approve of or even understand them.

totalizing Responding to a person as if one aspect of that person were the total of who the person is.

transition A word, phrase, or sentence that connects ideas and main points in a speech so that listeners can follow a speaker.

triangulation Studying phenomena by relying on multiple sources of data, theories, researchers, and/or methodological approaches.

turning point Particular experiences and events that cause relationships to become more or less intimate.

uncertainty avoidance Dimension of culture that refers to the extent to which people want to avoid ambiguity and vagueness.

uncertainty reduction theory The theory that people find uncertainty uncomfortable and so are motivated to use communication to reduce uncertainty.

understanding A response to cultural diversity that assumes that differences are rooted in cultural teachings and that no traditions, customs, or behaviors are intrinsically better than others.

upper A person who communicates positive messages about us and our worth.

uses and gratification theory Claims people use mass communication to gratify their interests and desires.

verbal communication Words and only words; does not include inflection, accent, volume, pitch, or other paralinguistic features of speech.

visual aid A visual image, such as a chart, graph, photograph, or physical object, that reinforces ideas presented verbally or provides information.

vulture A person who attacks a person's self-esteem; may attack others or himself or herself.

win–lose One of the three orientations toward conflict; assumes that in any conflict one person wins and the other(s) loses.

win–win One of the three orientations to conflict; assumes that everyone involved in a conflict can gain.

workplace bullying Recurring hostile behaviors often used by people with greater power against people with lesser power.

***you*-language** Language that attributes intentions and motives to another person, usually the person to whom one is speaking. (Compare with *I*-language.)

References

Acitelli, L. (1993). You, me, and us: Perspectives on relationship awareness. In S. W. Duck (Ed.), *Understanding relationship processes, 1: Individuals in relationships* (pp. 144–174). Thousand Oaks, CA: Sage.

Acker, J. (2013). Is capitalism gendered and racialized? In M. Andersen & P. H. Collins (Eds.), *Race, class, and gender: An anthology* (8th ed., pp. 125–133). Boston: Cengage.

Ackerman, D. (1990). *A natural history of the senses.* New York: Random House.

Adams, S. (2014, April 21). How women breadwinners can save their relationships. *Forbes.* Retrieved August 3, 2014, from http://www.forbes.com/sites /susanadams/2014/04/21/ how-women-breadwinners-can -save-their-relationships/.

Adler, R., & Proctor, R. (2013). *Looking out, looking in* (14th ed.). Stamfort, CT: Cengage.

Afifi, W., & Metts, S. (1998). Characteristics and consequences of expectation violations in three close relationships. *Journal of Social and Personal Relationships, 15,* 365–392.

Agyeman, J. (2007). Communicating "just sustainability." *Environmental Communication, 1,* 119–122.

Alcoff, L. (1991, Winter). The problem of speaking for others. *Cultural Critique,* pp. 5–32.

American Society for Plastic Surgeons. (2014). *Celebrating 15 years of trustworthy plastic surgery statistics.* http://www.surgery .org/media/news-releases/ celebrating-15-years-of -trustworthy-plastic-surgery -statistics. Accessed July 20, 2014.

The Amish flock to small business. (2009, January 9). *New York Times,* p. A3.

Andersen, P., Hecht, M., Hoobler, G., & Smallwood, M. (2002). Nonverbal communication across cultures. In W. Gudykunst & B. Mody (Eds.), *The handbook of international and intercultural communication* (2nd ed., pp. 89–106). Thousand Oaks, CA: Sage.

Anderson, R., Baxter, L., & Cissna, K. (Eds.). (2004). *Dialogue: Theorizing difference in communication studies.* Thousand Oaks, CA: Sage.

Angier, N. (2008, August 5). The nose, an emotional time machine. *New York Times,* pp. D1, D4.

Angier, N. (2013a, November 26). The baby boom for gay parents. *New York Times,* p. D4.

Angier, N. (2013b, November 26). Families. *New York Times,* pp. D1, D2–D3.

Angier, N. (2013c, November 26). The wedding will have to wait. *New York Times,* p. D5.

Argyle, M., & Henderson, M. (1984). The rules of friendship. *Journal of Social and Personal Relationships, 1,* 211–237.

Argyle, M., & Henderson, M. (1985). The rules of relationships. In S. W. Duck & D. Perlman (Eds.), *Understanding personal relationships: An interdisciplinary approach* (pp. 63–84). Thousand Oaks, CA: Sage.

Argyris, C. (2012). *Organizational traps.* New York: Oxford University Press.

Arnett, R. (2004). A dialogic ethic "between" Buber and Levinas: A responsive ethical "I." In R. Anderson, L. Baxter, & K. Cissna, (Eds.), *Dialogue: Theorizing difference in communication studies* (pp. 75–90). Thousand Oaks, CA: Sage.

Arnold, H., & Feldman, D. (1986). *Organizational behavior.* New York: McGraw-Hill.

Ashcraft, K., & Mumby, D. (2004). *Reworking gender: A feminist communicology of organization.* Thousand Oaks, CA: Sage.

Atkinson, P., & Housley, W. (2003). *Interactionism: An essay in sociological amnesia.* Thousand Oaks, CA: Sage.

Atsuko, A. (2003). Gender differences in interpersonal distance: From the viewpoint of oppression hypothesis. *Japanese Journal of Experimental Social Psychology, 42,* 201–218.

Axtell, R. (2007). *Essential do's and taboos: The complete guide to international business and leisure travel.* New York: Wiley.

Baidou, A. (2012). *In pursuit of love.* London: Serpent's Tail.

Bailey, A. (1998, February 29). Daily bread. *The Durham Herald– Sun,* p. C5.

Baird, J. (2014, April 7). Neither female nor male. *New York Times,* p. A21.

Bakalar, N. (2006, May 16). Link is cited between smell and sexuality. *New York Times,* p. D5.

Balcetis, E., & Dunning, D. (2013). Wishful seeing: Desirable objects are seen as closer. *Current Directions in Psychological Science, 22,* 33–37.

Bane, C. M. H., Cornish, M., Erspamer, N., & Kampman, L. (2010). Self-disclosure through weblogs and perceptions of online and "real-life" friendships among female bloggers. *Cyberpsychology, Behavior, and Social Networking, 32,* 131–139.

Bargh, J. (1997). *The automaticity of everyday life*. Mahwah, NJ: Erlbaum.

Bargh, J. (1999, January 29). The most powerful manipulative messages are hiding in plain sight. *Chronicle of Higher Education*, p. B6.

Barstead, M. G., Bouchard, L. C., & Shih, J. H. (2013). Understanding gender differences in co-rumination and confidant choice in young adults. *Journal of Social and Clinical Psychology, 32*, 791–808.

Bartholomew, K., & Horowitz, L. M. (1991). Attachment styles among young adults: A test of a four-category model. *Journal of Personality and Social Psychology, 61*, 226–244.

Bateson, M. C. (1990). *Composing a life*. New York: Penguin/Plume.

Baxter, L. A. (1985). Accomplishing relational disengagement. In S. Duck & D. Perlman (Eds.), *Understanding personal relationships: An interdisciplinary approach* (pp. 243–265). Thousand Oaks, CA: Sage.

Baxter, L. A. (2006). Relational dialectics theory: Multivocal dialogues of family communication. In D. O. Braithwaite & L. A. Baxter (Eds.), *Engaging theories in family communication: Multiple perspectives* (pp. 130–145). Thousand Oaks, CA: Sage.

Baxter, L. A. (2010). *Voicing relationships*. Thousand Oaks, CA: Sage.

Baxter, L. A., & Beebe, E. (2004). *The basics of communication research*. Belmont, CA: Wadsworth.

Baxter, L. A., & Bullis, C. (1986). Turning points in developing romantic relationships. *Human Communication Research, 12*, 469–493.

Baxter, L. A., & Simon, E. P. (1993). Relationship maintenance strategies and dialectical contradictions in personal relationships. *Journal of Social and Personal Relationships, 10*, 225–242.

Becker, A., Burwell, R., Gilman, S., Herzog, D., & Hamburg, P. (2002). Eating behaviours and attitudes following prolonged exposure to television among ethnic Fijian adolescent girls. *British Journal of Psychiatry, 180*, 509–514.

Becker, J. H., Halbesleben, J. B., & O'Hair, H. (2005). Defensive communication and burnout in the workplace: The mediating role of leader–member exchange. *Communication Research Reports, 22*(2), 143–150.

Beckman, H. (2003). Difficult patients. In M. Feldman & J. Christensen (Eds.), *Behavioral medicine in primary care* (pp. 23–32). New York: McGraw-Hill.

Begley, S. (2009, February 16). Will the BlackBerry sink the presidency? *Newsweek*, pp. 36–39.

Belluck, P. (2009, January 6). Creative lift? Find blue room. Better accuracy? Go with red. *New York Times*, pp. A1, A17.

Bendavid, N. (2013, October 31). Countries expand recognition for alternative "intersex" gender. *Wall Street Journal*, p. A9.

Benenson, J., Gordon, A., & Roy, R. (2000). Children's evaluative appraisals of competition in tetrads versus dyads. *Small Group Research, 31*, 635–652.

Berger, C. (1988). Communicating under uncertainty. In M. Roloff & G. Miller (Eds.), *Interpersonal processes: New directions in communication research* (pp. 39–62). Newbury Park, CA: Sage.

Berger, C. K. (1977). The covering law perspective as a theoretical basis for the study of human communication. *Communication Quarterly, 25*, 7–18.

Berger, P. (1969). *A rumor of angels: Modern society and the rediscovery of the supernatural*. New York: Doubleday.

Bergner, R. M., & Bergner, L. L. (1990). Sexual misunderstanding: A descriptive and pragmatic formulation. *Psychotherapy, 27*, 464–467.

Berne, E. (1964). *Games people play*. New York: Grove Press.

Bernstein, E. (2014, January 21). What verbal tics may be saying about us. *Wall Street Journal*, p. D3.

Berry, L. (2014, May 21). "Ideal" body image differs by race. *Medscape Medical News*. http://www.medscape.com/viewarticle/825489. Accessed July 20, 2014.

Beukeboom, C. (2009). "When words feel right: How affective expressions of listeners change a speaker's language use." *European Journal of Social Psychology, 39*, 747–756.

Bevan, J. (2003). Expectancy violation theory and sexual resistance in close, cross-sex relationships. *Communication Monographs, 70*, 68–82.

Bianchi, S. M., Sayer, L. C., Milkie, M. A., & Robinson, J. P. (2012). Housework: Who did, does or will do it, and how much does it matter? *Social Forces, 91*, 55–63.

Bilefsky, D. (2008, June 25). Albanian custom fades: Woman as family man. http://www.nytimes.com/2008/06/25/world/europe/25virgins.html?ex=1372132800&en=8668ba514ff6f5fd&ei=5124&partner=permalink&exprod=permalink. Accessed July 7, 2008.

Birdwhistell, R. (1970). *Kinesics and context*. Philadelphia: University of Pennsylvania Press.

Blanchard, K., Carlos J., & Randolph, A. (1998). *Empowerment takes more than a minute*. San Francisco, CA: Berrett-Koehler Publishers.

Blow, C. M. (2009, February 21). A nation of cowards? *New York Times*, p. A17.

Bocella, K. (2001, January 31). Eating disorders spread among minority girls, women. *Raleigh News & Observer*, p. 5E.

Bodey, K. (2009). *Exploring the possibilities of self work: Girls speak about their lives*. Ph.D. Dissertation. Department of Communication Studies. The University of North Carolina at Chapel Hill.

Bodey, K. R., & Wood, J. T. (2009). Whose voices count and who does the counting? *Southern Communication Journal, 74,* 325–337.

Bolkan, S., & Daly, J. (2009). Organizational responses to consumer complaints: An examination of effective remediation. *Journal of Applied Communication Research, 37,* 21–39.

Bonilla-Silva, E. (2013). *Racism without racists* (4th ed.). Summit, PA: Rowman & Littlefield.

Borchers, T. (2006). *Rhetorical theory: An introduction.* Belmont, CA: Thomson Wadsworth.

Boulding, K. (1990). *Three faces of power.* Thousand Oaks, CA: Sage.

Bowlby, J. (1973). *Separation: Attachment and loss* (Vol. 2). New York: Basic Books.

Bowlby, J. (1988). *A secure base: Parent-child attachment and healthy human development.* New York: Basic Books.

Boydstun, A. (2013). *Making the news: Politics, the media, and agenda setting.* Chicago, IL: University of Chicago Press.

Bradbury, T. N., & Fincham, F. D. (1990). Attributions in marriage: Review and critique. *Psychological Bulletin, 107,* 3–33.

Brady, J. (2013, May 22). Some companies foster creativity, others fake it. *Wall Street Journal,* p. A15.

Braithwaite, C. (1990). Communicative silence: A crosscultural study of Basso's hypothesis. In D. Carbaugh (Ed.), *Cultural communication and intercultural contact* (pp. 321–327). Hillsdale, NJ: Erlbaum.

Braithwaite, D. W., Bach, B. W., Baxter, L. A., Diverniero, R., Hammonds, J. R., Hosek, A. M., Willer, E. K., & Wolf, B. M. (2010). Constructing family: A typology of voluntary kin. *Journal of Social and Personal Relationships, 27,* 388–407.

Braithwaite, S. R., Delevi, R., & Fincham, F. D. (2010). Romantic relationships and the physical and mental health of college students. *Personal Relationships, 17,* 1–12.

Brilhart, J., & Galanes, G. (1995). *Effective group discussion* (8th ed.). Dubuque, IA: WCB Brown & Benchmark.

Brown, J., & Cantor, J. (2000). An agenda for research on youth and the media. *Journal of Adolescent Health, 27,* 2–7.

Brownell, J. (2002). *Listening: Attitudes, principles, and skills* (2nd ed.). Boston: Allyn & Bacon.

Bruess, C. (2015). Yard sales and yellow roses: Rituals in enduring relationships. In D. O. Braithwaite & J. T. Wood (Eds.), *Casing interpersonal communication* (2nd ed., pp. 111–116). Dubuque, IA: Kendall Hunt.

Bruess, C., & Hoefs, A. (2006). The cat puzzle recovered: Composing relationships through family ritual. In J. T. Wood & S. W. Duck (Eds.), *Composing relationships: Communication in everyday life* (pp. 65–75). Belmont, CA: Thomson Wadsworth.

Brunsma, D. L. (Ed.). (2006). *Mixed messages: Multiracial identities in the "color-blind" era.* Boulder, CO: Lynne Reinner.

Bryant, J., & Oliver, M. B. (Eds.). (2008). *Media effects* (3rd ed.). New York: Routledge.

Buber, M. (1957). Distance and relation. *Psychiatry, 20,* 97–104.

Buber, M. (1970). *I and thou* (Walter Kaufmann, Trans.). New York: Scribner's.

Buckley, M. F. (1992). Focus on research: We listen a book a day; we speak a book a week: Learning from Walter Loban. *Language Arts, 69,* 622–626.

Burchell, J. L., & Ward, J. (2011). Sex drive, attachment style, relationship status and previous infidelity as predictors of sex differences in romantic jealousy. *Personality and Individual Differences, 51,* 657–661.

Burgoon, J. (1993). Interpersonal expectations, expectation violations, and emotional communication. *Journal of Language and Social Psychology, 12,* 30–48.

Burleson, B. R., & Rack, J. (2008). Constructivism theory. In L. A. Baxter & D. O. Braithwaite (Eds.), *Engaging theories in interpersonal communication: Multiple perspectives* (pp. 51–63). Thousand Oaks, CA: Sage.

Burney, M. (2012, March 15). Standing up to bullies. *Chronicle of Higher Education,* pp. 50–53.

Buss, A. H. (2001). *Psychological dimensions of the self.* Thousand Oaks, CA: Sage.

Buunk, B., Groothof, H., & Siero, F. (2007). Social comparison and satisfaction with one's social life. *Journal of Social and Personal Relationships, 24,* 197–205.

Buzzanell, P., & Kirby, E. (2013). Communicating work-life issues. In L. Putnam & D. Mumby (Eds.), *The SAGE handbook of organizational communication: Advances in theory, research and methods* (pp. 351–374). Thousand Oaks, CA: Sage.

Cahn, D., & Abigail, R. (2013). *Managing conflict through communication* (5th ed.). Saddle Ridge, NJ: Pearson.

Calero, H. (2005). *The power of nonverbal communication: What you do is more important than what you say.* Los Angeles: Silver Lake.

Callahan, C. (2010). Going home: Deculturation experiences in cultural reentry. *Journal of Intercultural Communication, 22.* Retrieved June 21, 2010, from http://www.immi.se/jicc/index.php/jicc/article/view/175/136.

Campbell, K. (1989). *Man cannot speak for her: II. Key texts of the early feminists.* New York: Greenwood.

Canary, D., Lakey, S., & Sillars, A. (2013). Managing conflict in a competent manner: A mindful look at events that matter. In J. G. Oetzel & S. Ting-Toomey (Eds.), *The SAGE handbook of conflict communication: Integrating research, theory and practice* (pp. 263–289). Thousand Oaks, CA: Sage.

Cancer. (2009, September 1). *New York Times*, p. D6.

Carbaugh, D. (1998). "I can't do that! But I can actually see around the corners": American Indian students and the study of public communication. In J. Martin, T. Nakayama, & L. Flores (Eds.), *Readings in cultural context* (pp. 160–171). Mountain View, CA: Mayfield.

Carbaugh, D., & Buzzanell, P. M. (2009). *Distinctive qualities of communication research*. New York: Routledge.

Carl, W. (1998). A sign of the times. In J. T. Wood (Ed.), *But I thought you meant…: Misunderstandings in human communication* (pp. 195–208). Mountain View, CA: Mayfield.

Carnes, J. (1994, Spring). An uncommon language. *Teaching Tolerance*, pp. 56–63.

Carter, N. M., & Silva, C. (2010). *Broken promises*. New York: Catalyst.

Cassirer, E. (1944). *An essay on man*. New Haven, CT: Yale University Press.

Caughlin, J., Afifi, W., Carpenter-Theune, K., & Miller, L. (2005). Reasons for, and consequences of, revealing personal secrets in close relationships: A longitudinal study. *Personal Relationships, 12*, 43–59.

Caughlin, J., & Ramey, M. (2005). The demand/withdraw pattern of communication in parent-adolescent dyads. *Personal Relationships, 12*, 337–355.

Caughlin, J., & Vangelisti, A. (2000). An individual differences explanation of why married couples engage in the demand/withdraw pattern of conflict. *Journal of Social and Personal Relationships, 17*, 523–551.

Centers for Disease Control and Prevention. (2011). *HIV/AIDS*. Retrieved June 27, 2011, from http://www.cdc.gov/hiv/default.htm.

Chan, Y. (1999). Density, crowding, and factors intervening in their relationship: Evidence from a hyperdense metropolis. *Social Indicators Research, 48*, 103–134.

Chodron, T. (2001). *Working with anger*. New York: Snow Lion Publications.

Choose Your Parents Wisely. (2014, July 26). *Economist*, pp. 21–25.

Christensen, A. (2004). *Patient adherence to medical treatment regimen: Bridging the gap between behavioral science and biomedicine*. New Haven, CT: Yale University Press.

Christensen, A., & Heavey, C. (1990). Gender and social structure in the demand/withdraw pattern in marital conflict. *Journal of Personality and Social Psychology, 59*, 73–81.

Christianson, P., & Roberts, D. (1998). *It's not only rock & roll: Popular music in the lives of adolescents*. Cresskill, NJ: Hampton Press.

Cissna, K. N. L., & Sieburg, E. (1986). Patterns of interactional confirmation and disconfirmation. In J. Stewart (Ed.), *Bridges, not walls* (4th ed., pp. 230–239). New York: Random House.

Classen, C. (2012). *The deepest sense: A cultural history of touch*. Urbana: University of Illinois Press.

Cloven, D. H., & Roloff, M. E. (1991). Sense-making activities and interpersonal conflict: Communicative cures for the mulling blues. *Western Journal of Speech Communication, 55*, 134–158.

Cockburn-Wootten, C., & Zorn, T. (2006). Cabbages and headache cures: Work stories within the family. In J. T. Wood & S. W. Duck (Eds.), *Composing relationships: Communication in everyday life* (pp. 137–145). Belmont, CA: Thomson Wadsworth.

Cohen, P. (2011, July 15). Internet use affects how we remember. *New York Times*, p. A14.

Collier, M. J. (1996). Communication problematics in ethnic friendships. *Communication Monographs, 63*, 314–336.

Collins, F., & Fauci, A. (2010, May 23). AIDS in 2010: How we're living with AIDS. *Parade*, pp. 10–12.

Conrad, C., & Poole, M. (2012). *Strategic organizational communication in a global economy* (7th ed.). New York: Harcourt.

Cooley, C. H. (1912). *Human nature and the social order*. New York: Scribner's.

Coontz, S. (2013). Gender equality. *New York Times*, pp. 1, 6–7.

Coontz, S. (2014, July 27). The new instability. *New York Times*, pp. SR1, 7.

Cooper, M. (2012, December 13). Census: U.S. to have no majority by 2043. *Raleigh News & Observer*, p. 3A.

Coopman, S., & Lull, J. (2015). *Public speaking: The evolving art* (3rd ed.). Belmont, CA: Wadsworth/Cengage.

Cordell, R. (2011, May 13). Resources for teaching with technology. *Chronicle of Higher Education*, p. B10.

Covey, S. (2012). *The 7 habits for managers*. Grand Haven, MI: Franklin Covey Brilliance Audio.

Covey, S. (2013). *The seven habits of highly effective people*. New York: Simon and Schuster.

Cox, J. R. (1989). The fulfillment of time: King's "I have a dream" speech (August 28, 1963). In M. C. Leff & F. J. Kaufeld (Eds.), *Texts in context: Critical dialogues on significant episodes in American rhetoric* (pp. 181–204). Davis, CA: Hermagoras.

Cox, J. R. (2014). Personal communication.

Cox, J. R., & McCloskey, M. (1996). Advocacy and the Istook amendment: Efforts to restrict the civic speech of nonprofit organizations in the 104th U.S. Congress. *Journal of Applied Communication Research, 24*, 273–291.

Cox, J. R., & Pezzullo, P. (2016). *Environmental communication and the public sphere* (4th ed.). Thousand Oaks, CA: Sage.

Crockett, W. H. (1965). Cognitive complexity and impression formation. In B. A. Maher (Ed.), *Progress in experimental personality research* (Vol. 2, pp. 47–90). New York: Academic Press.

Dailey, R. (2006). Confirmation in parent-adolescent relationships and adolescent openness: Toward extending confirmation theory. *Communication Monographs, 73,* 434–458.

Dainton, M. (2006). Cat walk conversations: Everyday communication in dating relationships. In J. T. Wood & S. W. Duck (Eds.), *Composing relationships: Communication in everyday life.* Belmont, CA: Thomson Wadsworth.

Darling, A., & Dannels, D. (2003). Practicing engineers talk about the importance of talk: A report on the role of oral communication in the workplace. *Communication Education, 52,* 1–16.

Darnton, R. (2011, April 22). 5 myths of the "information age." *Chronicle of Higher Education,* pp. B9–B10.

Davies-Popelka, W. (2015). Mirror, mirror on the wall: Weight, identity, and self-talk. In D. O. Braithwaite & J. T. Wood (Eds.), *Casing interpersonal communication* (pp. 25–32). Dubuque, IA: Kendall Hunt.

Davis, R. (1997). *The myth of black ethnicity: Monophylety, diversity, and the dilemma of identity.* Greenwich, CT: Ablex.

DeCremer, D., & Leonardelli, G. J. (2003). Group dynamics. *Theory, Research, and Practice, 7,* 168–174.

DeFrancisco, V. (1991). The sounds of silence: How men silence women in marital relations. *Discourse & Society, 2,* 413–423.

Delbecq, A. L., & VandeVen, A. H. (1971). A group process model for problem identification and program planning. *Journal of Applied Behavioral Science, 7,* 466–491.

Delgado, F. (1998). Moving beyond the screen: Hollywood and Mexican American stereotypes.

In Y. Kamalipour & T. Carilli (Eds.), *Cultural diversity in the U.S. media* (pp. 169–182). Albany: State University of New York Press.

Delgado, R., & Stefanic, J. (2012). *Cricial race theory* (2nd ed.). New York: New York University Press.

Delia, J., Clark, R. A., & Switzer, D. (1974). Cognitive complexity and impression formation in informal social interaction. *Speech Monographs, 41,* 299–308.

Demographics. (2009, January 26). *Newsweek,* p. 70.

Dennis, A., & Wood, J. T. (2012). "We're not going to have this conversation, but you get it.": Black mother-daughter communication about sexual relations. *Women's Studies in Communication, 35*(2), 204–223. doi: 10.1080/07491409.2012.724525.

Derlega, V. J., & Berg, J. H. (1987). *Self-disclosure: Research, theory, and therapy.* New York: Plenum.

Deresiewicz, W. (2009, December 11). Faux friendship. *Chronicle of Higher Education,* pp. B6–B9.

Dewey, C. (2014, January 17). How many of this year's Oscar nominees pass the Bechdel test? Not many. *Washington Post Style Blog.* Retrieved from http://www .washingtonpost.com/blogs/style -blog/wp/2014/01/17/how-many-of -this-years-oscar-nominees-pass -the-bechdel-test-not-many/.

Dickson, F. (1995). The best is yet to be: Research on long-lasting marriages. In J. T. Wood & S. W. Duck (Eds.), *Understanding relationship processes, 6: Understudied relationships* (pp. 22–50). Thousand Oaks, CA: Sage.

Did you know? (1998, September 30). *Raleigh News & Observer,* p. F1.

Dindia, K. (1994). A multiphasic view of relationship maintenance strategies. In D. Canary & L. Stafford (Eds.), *Communication and relational maintenance* (pp. 91–112). New York: Academic Press.

Dindia, K. (2000). Self-disclosure, identity, and relationship

development. In K. Dindia & S. W. Duck (Eds.), *Communication and personal relationships* (pp. 147–162). Chichester, UK: Wiley.

Dirda, M. (2013, August 29). New dictionary words are oh so ugh: "FOMO," "selfie," "squee," "twerk," "jorts," "omnishambles." Srsly? *Washington Post,* p. C3.

Dixson, M., & Duck, S. W. (1993). Understanding relationship processes: Uncovering the human search for meaning. In S. W. Duck (Ed.), *Understanding relationship processes, 1: Individuals in relationships* (pp. 175–206). Thousand Oaks, CA: Sage.

Domingue, R., & Mollen, D. (2009). Attachment and conflict communication in adult romantic relationships. *Journal of Social and Personal Relationships, 26,* 678–696.

Donahue, H., Leonard, J., & Williams, M. (Writers/Directors/Producers). (1999). *The blair witch project* [Motion picture]. United States: Artisan Entertainment.

Donoghue, P., & Siegel, M. (2005). *Are you really listening?* Notre Dame, IN: Ava Maria Press.

Don't Text and Drive. (n.d.). http:// www.textinganddrivingsafety.com /texting-and-driving-stats/. Accessed August 30, 2014.

Douglas, S. (2004, May 10). Confronting the mommy myth. *In These Times,* pp. 28–29.

Douglas, W. (2012, May 17). House Oks anti-domestic violence bill. *Raleigh News & Observer,* p. 3A.

Dowd, M. (2014, March 5). Frozen in a niche? *New York Times,* p. A23.

Duca, L. (2013, December 13). Hollywood's big women problem, in one chart. *Huffington Post.* http://www.huffingtonpost .com/2013/12/13/women-in- film_n_4433968.html?ref=topbar. Accessed July 10, 2014.

Duck, S. W. (2006). The play, playfulness and the players: Everyday interaction as improvised rehearsal of relationships. In

J. T. Wood & S. W. Duck (Eds.), *Composing relationships: Communication in everyday life* (pp. 15–23). Belmont, CA: Wadsworth.

Duck, S. W., & McMahan, D. T. (2012). *The basics of communication: A relational perspective* (2nd ed.). Thousand Oaks, CA: Sage.

Duck, S. W., & Wood, J. T. (2006). What goes up may come down: Sex and gendered patterns in relational dissolution. In M. A. Fine & J. H. Harvey (Eds.), *The handbook of divorce and relationship dissolution* (pp. 169–187). Mahwah, NJ: Erlbaum.

Ean, L. C. (2011). Computer mediated communication and organizational communication: The use of new technology in the workplace. *Journal of South East Asia Research Center for Communication and Humanities, 3,* 1–121.

Eastman, S., & Billings, A. (2000). Sportscasting and news reporting: The power of gender bias. *Journal of Sport and Social Issues, 24,* 192–213.

Eastwick, P., & Hunt, L. (2014). Relational mate value: Consensus and uniqueness in romantic evaluations. *Journal of Personality and Social Psychology, 106,* 728–751.

Egan, G. (1973). Listening as empathic support. In J. Stewart (Ed.), *Bridges, not walls.* Reading, MA: Addison-Wesley.

Eisenberg, E., Goodall, H., & Trethewey, A. (2013). *Organizational communication: Balancing creativity and constraint.* Boston: Bedford/St. Martin's.

Ellin, A. (2014, March 11). After online dating, online making up. *New York Times,* p. D2.

Ellis, A., & Harper, R. (1977). *A new guide to rational living.* North Hollywood, CA: Wilshire.

eMarketer Inc. (2014, April 22). Mobile continues to steal share of U.S. adults' daily time spent with media. Retrieved from http://www.emarketer.com/Article /Mobile-Continues-Steal-Share -of-US-Adults-Daily-Time-Spent -with-Media/1010782.

Eplely, N. (2014). *Mindwise: How we understand what others think, believe, feel and want.* New York: Borzoi/Knopf.

Erbert, L. (2000). Conflict and dialectics: Perceptions of dialectical contradictions in marital conflict. *Journal of Social and Personal Relationships, 17,* 638–659.

Estioko-Griffin, A., & Griffin, P. (1997). Woman the hunter: The Agta. In C. Brettell & C. Sargent (Eds.), *Gender in cross-cultural perspectives* (pp. 123–149). Englewood Cliffs, NJ: Prentice Hall.

Fackelmann, K. (2006, March 6). Arguing hurts the heart in more ways than one. *USA Today,* p. 10D.

Fehr, B. (1993). How do I love thee? Let me consult my prototype. In S. W. Duck (Ed.), *Understanding relationship processes, 1: Individuals in relationships* (pp. 87–122). Thousand Oaks, CA: Sage.

Feingold, L. (2013). The digital divide and people with disabilities. http://lflegal.com/2013/08/digital-divide/. Accessed August 25, 2014.

Feldman, C., & Ridley, C. (2000). The role of conflict-based responses and outcomes in male domestic violence toward female partners. *Journal of Social and Personal Relationships, 17,* 552–573.

Felmlee, D. H. (2001). No couple is an island: A social network perspective on dyadic stability. *Social Forces, 79,* 1259–1287.

Ferrante, J. (2013). *Sociology: A global perspective* (10th ed.). Belmont, CA: Cengage.

Fincham, F. D., & Bradbury, T. N. (1987). The impact of attributions in marriage: A longitudinal analysis. *Journal of Personality and Social Psychology, 53,* 510–517.

Finnerty, A. (2013, September 1). Touchscreen toddlers and instagram teens. *Wall Street Journal,* p. C1.

Fischman, J. (2011, May 13). The rise of teaching machines. *Chronicle of Higher Education,* pp. B12, B14.

Fiske, J. (1987). *Television culture.* London: Methuen.

Fitzpatrick, M. A. (1988). *Between husbands and wives: Communication in marriage.* Thousand Oaks, CA: Sage.

Fletcher, G. J., & Fincham, F. D. (1991). Attribution in close relationships. In G. J. Fletcher & F. D. Fincham (Eds.), *Cognition in close relationships* (pp. 7–35). Mahwah, NJ: Erlbaum.

Flock, E., & Bell, B. (2011, June 13). "Paula Brooks," editor of "Lez Get Real," also a man. http://www.washingtonpost.com/blogs/blogpost/post/paula-brooks-editor-of-lez-get-real-also-a-man/2011/06/13/AGld2ZTH_blog.html. Accessed June 11, 2011.

Flynn, L. (2006, May 3). A romantic read between cell calls. *New York Times,* p. E3.

Foeman, A., & Nance, T. (1999). From miscegenation to multiculturalism: Perceptions and stages of interracial relationship development. *Journal of Black Studies, 29,* 540–557.

Fogg, P. (2008, July 25). Thinking in black and white. *Chronicle of Higher Education,* p. B19.

Foss, S., Foss, K., & Trapp, R. (1991). *Contemporary perspectives on rhetoric* (2nd ed.). Prospect Heights, IL: Waveland.

Foucault, M. (1970). *The order of things: An archaeology of the human sciences.* New York: Pantheon.

Foucault, M. (1972a). The discourse on language. In *The archaeology of knowledge* (Sheridan Smith, Trans., pp. 215–237). New York: Pantheon.

Foucault, M. (1972b). In C. Gordon (Ed.), *Power/knowledge: Selected interviews and other writings 1972–1977* (C. Gordon, L. Marshall, J. Mepham, & K. Soper, Trans.). New York: Pantheon.

Foucault, M. (1978). Politics and the study of discourse (C. Gordon, Trans.). *Ideology and Consciousness, 3,* 7–26.

Fox, S. (2011, January 21). Americans living with disabilities and their technology profile. Pew Research Center. http://www.pewinternet.org/Reports/2011/Disability.aspx.

France, D. (2006, January & February). Domestic violence. *AARP Magazine*, pp. 84–85, 112–118.

Freeman, J. (2009). *The tyranny of e-mail*. New York: Simon & Schuster/Scribner.

Fujishin, R. (2013). *Creating effective groups*. Summit, PA: Rowman & Littlefield.

Furnham, A., & Xenikou, A. (2013). *Group dynamics and organizational culture*. New York: Palgrave Macmillan.

Gabric, D., & McFadden, K. (2001). Student and employer perceptions of desirable entry-level operations management skills. *Mid-American Journal of Business, 16*, 51–59.

Gallagher, C. (2012). Color blind privilege. In E. Higgenbotham & M. Andersen (Eds.), *Race and ethnicity in society* (3rd ed., pp. 57–61). Boston: Cengage.

Galupo, M. P., Bauerband, L. A., Gonzalez, K. A., Hagen, D. B., Heather, S. D., & Krum, T. E. (2014). Transgender friendship experiences: Benefits and barriers of friendships across gender identity and sexual orientation. *Feminism & Psychology, 24*, 193–215.

Galupo, M. P., & Gonzalez, K. A. (2013). Friendship values and cross-category friendships: Understanding adult friendship patterns across gender, sexual orientation, and race. *Sex Roles, 68*, 779–790.

Galvin, K. (2006). Gender and family interaction: Dress rehearsal for an improvisation? In B. Dow & J. T. Wood (Eds.), *Handbook of gender and communication research* (pp. 41–55). Thousand Oaks, CA: Sage.

Galvin, K., Braithwaite, D., & Bylund, C. (2015). *Family communication: Cohesion and change*. Upper Saddle Ridge, NJ: Pearson.

Galvin, K., Dickson, F., & Marrow, S. (2006). Systems theory: Patterns and (w)holes in family communication.

In D. O. Braithwaite & L. A. Baxter (Eds.), *Engaging theories in family communication: Multiple perspectives* (pp. 309–324). Thousand Oaks, CA: Sage.

Gargiulo, T. (2005). *The strategic use of stories in organizational communication and learning*. New York: M. E. Sharpe.

Garner, T. (1994). Oral rhetorical practice in African American culture. In A. Gonzaléz, M. Houston, & V. Chen (Eds.), *Our voices: Essays in culture, ethnicity, and communication* (pp. 81–91). Los Angeles: Roxbury.

Gates, H. L. (1992). *Loose canons: Notes on the culture wars*. New York: Oxford University Press.

Gender in Media. (2012). *Research informs & empowers*. Retrieved from http://www.thegeenadavisinstitute.org/research.

Gerbner, G. (1990). Epilogue: Advancing on the path of righteousness (maybe). In N. Signorielli & M. Morgan (Eds.), *Cultivation analysis: New directions in media effects research* (pp. 250–261). Thousand Oaks, CA: Sage.

Gerbner, G., Gross, L., Morgan, M., & Signorielli, N. (1986). Living with television: The dynamics of the cultivation process. In J. Bryant & D. Zillmann (Eds.), *Perspectives on media effects* (pp. 17–40). Mahwah, NJ: Erlbaum.

Ghanem, S., McCombs, M., & Chernov, G. (2009). Agenda setting and framing. In W. F. Eadie (Ed.), *21st century communication: A reference handbook* (pp. 516–524). Thousand Oaks, CA: Sage.

Gibb, J. R. (1961). Defensive communication. *Journal of Communication, 11*, 141–148.

Gibb, J. R. (1964). Climate for trust formation. In L. Bradford, J. Gibb, & K. Benne (Eds.), *T-group theory and laboratory method* (pp. 279–309). New York: Wiley.

Gibb, J. R. (1970). Sensitivity training as a medium for personal growth and improved interpersonal

relationships. *Interpersonal Development, 1*, 6–31.

Gill, R. (2008). Empowerment/sexism: Figuring female sexual agency in contemporary advertising. *Feminism & Psychology, 18*, 35–60.

Gilster, P. (2011, May 9). Ushered in by the age of Twitter. *Raleigh News & Observer*, p. 1D.

Gitlin, T. (2005). Supersaturation, or the media torrent and disposable feeling. In E. Bucy (Ed.), *Living in the information age: A new media reader* (2nd ed., pp. 139–146). Belmont, CA: Thomson Wadsworth.

Giving Email a Holiday. (2014, August 23). *New York Times*, p. A20.

Global Analytics Workplace.com. Accessed March 18, 2015. http://globalworkplaceanalytics.com/telecommuting-statistics

Goldsmith, D., & Fulfs, P. (1999). You just don't have the evidence: An analysis of claims and evidence in Deborah Tannen's *You Just Don't Understand*. In M. Roloff (Ed.), *Communication yearbook, 22* (pp. 1–49). Thousand Oaks, CA: Sage.

Goleman, D. (2007). *Social intelligence*. New York: Bantam/Dell.

Goleman, D. (2011). *The brain and emotional intelligence*. Florence, MA: More than Sound.

Goleman, D., McKee, A., & Boyatzis, R. (2002). *Primal leadership: Realizing the power of emotional intelligence*. Cambridge, MA: Harvard Business School Press.

González, A., Houston, M., & Chen, V. (Eds.). (2012). *Our voices: Essays in culture, ethnicity, and communication*. New York: Oxford University Press.

Gosling, S. (2008). *Snoop: What your stuff says about you*. New York: Basic Books.

Gottman, J. M. (1993). The roles of conflict engagement, escalation or avoidance in marital interaction: A longitudinal view of five types of couples. *Journal of Consulting and Clinical Psychology, 61*, 6–15.

Gottman, J., & DeClaire, J. (2001). *The relationship cure: A five-step guide for building better connections with family, friends, and lovers*. New York: Crown Books.

Graham, J. M., & Conoley, C. (2006). The role of marital attributions in the relationship between life stressors and marital quality. *Personal Relationships, 13,* 231–241.

Grayling, A. (2013). *Friendship (vices and virtues)*. New Haven, CT: Yale University Press.

Greenberg, S. (1997, Spring/Summer Special Issue). The loving ties that bind. *Newsweek*, pp. 68–72.

Greene, K., Derlega, V. J., & Mathews, A. (2006). Self-disclosure in personal relationships. In A. L. Vangelisti & D. Perlman (Eds.), *Cambridge handbook of personal relationships* (pp. 89–104). Cambridge, MA: Cambridge University Press.

Gregoire, C. (2013, July 26). The surprising weekend habits of highly effective people. *Huffington Post*. http://www.huffingtonpost.com/2013/07/26/weekend-rituals-of-hig_n_3640661.html?icid=maing-grid7%7Chtmlws-main-bb%7Cdll14%7Csec1_lnk2%26pLid%3D350099.

Griffin, C. (2015). *Invitation to public speaking* (5th ed.). Belmont, CA: Wadsworth/Cengage.

Gronbeck, B. E., McKerro, R., Ehninger, D., & Monroe, A. H. (1994). *Principles and types of speech communication* (12th ed.). Glenview, IL: Scott, Foresman.

Groothof, H. A. K., Dijkstra, P., & Bareids, D. P. H. (2009). Differences in jealousy: The case of Internet infidelity. *Journal of Social and Personal Relationships, 26,* 1119–1129.

Gudykunst, W. (1995). Anxiety uncertainty management (AUM) theory: Current status. In R. Wiseman (Ed.), *Intercultural communication theory* (pp. 33–71). Newbury Park, CA: Sage.

Gueguen, N., & De Gail, M. (2003). The effect of smiling on helping behavior: Smiling and good Samaritan behavior. *Communication Reports, 16,* 133–140.

Guerrero, L., Andersen, P., & Afifi, W. (2008). *Close encounters: Communication in relationships* (2nd ed.). Thousand Oaks, CA: Sage.

Guerrero, L., & Farinelli, L. (2009). The interplay of verbal and nonverbal codes. In W. F. Eadie (Ed.), *21st century communication: A reference handbook* (pp. 239–248). Thousand Oaks, CA: Sage.

Guerrero, L., & Floyd, K. (2006). *Nonverbal communication in close relationships*. Mahwah, NJ: Erlbaum.

Guerrero, L., Jones, S., & Boburka, R. (2006). Sex differences in emotional communication. In K. Dindia & D. Canary (Eds.), *Sex differences and similarities in communication* (pp. 242–261). Mahwah, MJ: Erlbaum.

Guerrero, L., La Valley, A., & Farinelli, L. (2008). The experience and expression of anger, guilt, and sadness in marriage: An equity theory explanation. *Journal of Social and Personal Relationships, 25,* 699–724.

Gupta, S. (2012, August 1). More treatment, more mistakes. *New York Times*, p. A21.

Gunns, R., Johnston, L., & Hudson, S. (2002). Victim selection and kinematics: A point-light investigation of vulnerability to attack. *Journal of Nonverbal Behavior, 26,* 129–158.

Hackman, M., & Johnson, C. (2013). *Leadership: A communication perspective* (6th ed.). Long Grove, IL: Waveland.

Hall, E. T. (1968). Proxemics. *Current Anthropology, 9,* 83–108.

Hall, E. T. (1968). *The hidden dimension*. New York: Anchor.

Hall, J. (2006). How big are nonverbal sex differences? The case of smiling and nonverbal sensitivity. In K. Dindia & D. Canary (Eds.), *Sex differences and similarities in communication* (2nd ed., pp. 59–81). Mahwah, NJ: Lawrence Erlbaum.

Hall, J., Coats, E., & Smith-LeBeau, L. (2004). Nonverbal behavior and the vertical dimension of social relations: A meta-analysis. In M. L. Knapp & J. A. Hall (Eds.), *Nonverbal communication in human interaction* (6th ed.). Belmont, CA: Thomson Wadsworth.

Hall, S. (1982). The rediscovery of "ideology": Return of the repressed in media studies. In M. Gurevitch, T. Bennett, J. Curran, & J. Woollacott (Eds.), *Culture, society, and the media* (pp. 56–90). London: Methuen.

Hall, S. (1986b). The problem of ideology: Marxism without guarantees. *Journal of Communication Inquiry, 10,* 28–44.

Hall, S. (1988). *The hard road to renewal: Thatcherism and the crisis on the left*. London: Verso.

Hall, S. (1989a). Ideology. In E. Barnouw et al. (Eds.), *International encyclopedia of communication* (Vol. 2, pp. 307–311). New York: Oxford University Press.

Hall, S. (1989b). Ideology and communication theory. In B. Dervin, L. Grossberg, B. O'Keefe, & E. Wartella (Eds.), *Rethinking communication theory* (Vol. 1, pp. 40–52). Thousand Oaks, CA: Sage.

Hall, J., Park, N., Song, H., & Cody, J. (2010). Strategic misrepresentation in online dating: The effects of gender, self-monitoring, and personality traits. *Journal of Social and Personal Relationships, 27,* 117–135.

Halvorson, H. (2010). *Succeed: How we can reach our goals*. New York: Penguin/Hudson Street Press.

Hamachek, D. (1992). *Encounters with the self* (3rd ed.). New York: Harcourt, Brace, Jovanovich.

Hamilton, C. (2015). *Successful public speaking* (6th ed.). Belmont, CA: Wadsworth.

Harris, G. (2011, July 11). For aspiring doctors, the people skills test. *New York Times*, pp. A1, A12.

Harris, T., & Sherblom, J. (2010). *Small group and team communication*. Boston: Allyn & Bacon.

Harris, T. J. (1969). *I'm OK, you're OK*. New York: Harper & Row.

Hart, P. (1994). *Government: A study of small groups and policy failure*. Baltimore: The Johns Hopkins University Press.

Hartlaub, J. (2012, September 8). Books on the installment plan. *Kill zone*. http://killzoneauthors .blogspot.com/2012/09/books -on-installment-plan.html# .U_dU6UbD_q4. Accessed August 22, 2014.

Hart Research Associates. (2013). It takes more than a major. *Employer priorities for college learning and student success*. Washington, DC: Author.

Hartwig, M., & Bond, Jr., C. (2011). Why do lie-catchers fail? A lens model meta-analysis of human lie judgments. *Psychological Bulletin, 137*, 643–659.

Harvard Business Press. (2010). *Leading virtual teams*. Boston: Author.

Hasinoff, A. (2008). Fashioning race for the free market on *America's Next Top Model*. *Critical Studies in Media Communication, 25*, 324–343.

Hayakawa, S. I. (1962). *The use and misuse of language*. New York: Fawcett.

Hayakawa, S. I. (1964). *Language in thought and action* (2nd ed.). New York: Harcourt, Brace & World.

Haynes, J. (2009). Exposing domestic violence in country music videos. In L. Cuklanz & S. Moorti (Eds.), *Local violence, global media* (pp. 201–221). New York: Peter Lang.

Hegel, G. W. F. (1807). *Phenomenology of mind* (J. B. Baillie, Trans.). Germany: Wurzburg & Bamburg.

Heider, F. (1958). *The psychology of interpersonal relations*. New York: Wiley.

Hellweg, S. (1992). Organizational grapevines. In K. L. Hutchinson (Ed.), *Readings in organizational communication* (pp. 159–172). Dubuque, IA: Wm. C. Brown.

Hendrick, C., & Hendrick, S. (1988). Lovers wear rose-colored glasses. *Journal of Social and Personal Relationships, 5*, 161–184.

Hendrick, C., & Hendrick, S. (1996). Gender and the experience of heterosexual love. In J. T. Wood (Ed.), *Gendered relationships* (pp. 131–148). Mountain View, CA: Mayfield.

Hendrick, C., Hendrick, S., Foote, F. H., & Slapion-Foote, M. J. (1984). Do men and women love differently? *Journal of Social and Personal Relationships, 2*, 177–196.

Hickey, W. (2014, April 1). The dollar-and-cents case against Hollywood's exclusion of women. *FiveThirtyEight Life*. Retrieved from http://fivethirtyeight.com /features/the-dollar-and-cents -case-against-hollywoods-exclusion -of-women/.

Hickson, M., Stacks, D., & Moore, N. (2004). *Nonverbal communication: Studies and applications*. Los Angeles: Roxbury.

Higginbotham, F., & Andersen, M. (2012). *Race and ethnicity: An anthology* (3rd ed.). Boston: Cengage.

Hochschild, A., & Machung, A. (2003). *The second shift* (Rev. ed.). New York: Viking.

Hoffman, J. (2010, June 28). Online bullies pull schools into the fray. *New York Times*, pp. A13–A15.

Hoffman, J. (2012, June 4). A warning to teenagers before they start dating. *New York Times*, pp. A12, A13.

Hofstede, G. (1991). *Culture and organizations: Software of the mind*. New York: McGraw-Hill.

Hofstede, G. (2001). *Cultures' consequences: Comparing values, behaviors, institutions, and organizations across nations*. Thousand Oaks, CA: Sage.

Hofstede, G., Hofstede, G. J., & Minkov, M. (2010). *Cultures and organizations: Software of the mind* (3rd ed.). New York: McGraw-Hill.

Holmberg, D., & MacKenzie, S. (2002). So far, so good: Scripts for romantic relationship development as predictors of relational well-being. *Journal of Social and Personal Relationships, 19*, 777–796.

Holt-Lunstad, J., Smith, T. B., & Layton, J. B. (2010). Social relationships and mortality risk: A meta-analytic review. *PLoS Med, 7*, 1–20.

Honeycutt, J. M., Woods, B., & Fontenot, K. (1993). The endorsement of communication conflict rules as a function of engagement, marriage, and marital ideology. *Journal of Social and Personal Relationships, 10*, 285–304.

Honoré, C. (2005). *In praise of slowness*. San Francisco: Harper.

Hoon, H., & Tan, M. (2008). Organizational citizenship behavior and social loafing: The role of personality, motives, and contextual factors. *Journal of Psychology, 142*, 89–108.

Hoover, E. (2010, January 29). An immigrant learns 2 new languages. *Chronicle of Higher Education*, p. A22.

Horning, K., Lindgren, M., & Schliesman, M. (2014). A few observations about publishing in 2013. Cooperative Children's Book Center. http://ccbc.education .wisc.edu/books/choiceintro14.asp. Accessed August 22, 2014.

Houston, M. (2004). When Black women talk with White women: Why dialogues are difficult. In A. González, M. Houston, & V. Chen (Eds.), *Our voices: Essays in culture, ethnicity, and communication* (4th ed., pp. 119–125). Los Angeles: Roxbury.

Howes, D., & Classen, C. (2013). *Ways of sensing: Understanding the senses in society*. London: Routledge.

Hrabi, D. (2013, June 27). Welcome to the new home office. *Wall Street Journal*. Retrieved March 7, 2014, from http://www.wsj.com/articles/SB 10001424127887324021104578553 533978355660

Hruschka, D. (2010). *Friendship: Development, ecology, and evolution of a relationship.* Berkeley: University of California Press.

Hunter, S. (2012). *Lesbian and gay couples: Lives, issues, and practice.* Chicago, IL: Lyceum Books, Inc.

Hutchby, I. (2005). "Active listening": Formulations and the elicitation of feelings-talk in child counseling. *Research on Language and Social Interaction, 38,* 303–329.

Ihlen, O., Fredrikson, M., & van Ruler, B. (Eds.). (2009). *Public relations and social theory.* New York: Routledge.

ILA. (2008). Priorities of listening research: Four interrelated initiatives. Belle Plaine, MN: ILA.

ILA. (2011). http://www.listen.org/. Accessed June 6, 2011.

Inman, C. C. (1996). Men's friendships: Closeness in the doing. In J. T. Wood (Ed.), *Gendered Relationships* (pp. 95–110). Mountain View, CA: Mayfield.

Irobot Delivers 3,000th Packbot. (2016, February 16). *Robotics Trends.* http://www.roboticstrends .com/security_defense_robotics /article/irobot_delivers_3000th _packbot/. Accessed August 29, 2014.

Isaacs, W. (1999). *Dialogue and the art of thinking together.* New York: Doubleday.

Isay, D. (2008). *Listening is an act of love.* New York: Penguin.

Isikoff, M. (2004, July 19). The dots never existed. *Newsweek,* pp. 36–38.

Islam, G., & Zyphur, M. (2009). Rituals in organizations: A review and expansion of current theory. *Organizational Management, 34,* 114–139.

Italie, L. (2014, July 31). Fashion industry, retailers face gender divide. *Raleigh News & Observer,* p. 8D.

Jackson, M. (2008). *Distracted: The erosion of attention and the coming dark age.* New York: Prometheus.

Jacobs, T. (2010). *Cyberbullying investigated.* Minneapolis, MN: Free Spirit Publishing.

Jaffe, C. (2016). *Public speaking: Concepts and skills for a diverse society* (8th ed.). Belmont, CA: Thomson Wadsworth.

Janis, I. L. (1977). *Victims of groupthink.* Boston: Houghton Mifflin.

Jandt, F. (2012). *An introduction to intercultural communication: Identities in a global community.* Thousand Oaks, CA: Sage.

Janusik, L. (2007). Building listening theory: The validation of the conversational listening span. *Communication Studies, 58,* 139–156.

Jensen, B. (2014, June–July). The new American family. *AARP Magazine,* pp. 34–38.

Jhally, S., & Katz, J. (2001, Winter). Big trouble, little pond. *Umass,* pp. 26–31.

Johnson, A. J., Wittenberg, E., Haigh, M., & Wigley, S. (2004). The process of relationship development and deterioration: Turning points in friendships that have terminated. *Communication Quarterly, 52,* 54–68.

Johnson, F. L. (2000). *Speaking culturally: Language diversity in the United States.* Thousand Oaks, CA: Sage.

Johnson, M. (2006). Gendered communication and intimate partner violence. In B. Dow & J. T. Wood (Eds.), *Handbook of gender and communication research* (pp. 71–87). Thousand Oaks, CA: Sage.

Johnson, N. (2007). *All I want is everything: A feminist analysis of consumption in bestselling teen romance novels.* Ph.D. dissertation. The University of North Carolina at Chapel Hill.

Johnson, N. (2011). The whole package. In D. O. Braithwaite & J. T. Wood (Eds.), *Casing interpersonal communication* (pp. 9–15). Belmont, CA: Wadsworth/Cengage.

Johnson, N., Roberts, M., & Warell, J. (Eds.). (2002). *Beyond appearance:*

A new look at adolescent girls. Washington, DC: American Psychological Association.

Johnson, P. (1999). Reflections on critical White(ness) studies. In T. Nakayama & J. Martin (Eds.), *Whiteness: The communication of social identity* (pp. 1–12). Thousand Oaks, CA: Sage.

Jones, D. (2007, March 30). Do foreign executives balk at sports jargon? *USA Today,* pp. 1B–2B.

Jones, E., & Gallois, C. (1989). Spouses' impressions of rules for communication in public and private marital conflicts. *Journal of Marriage and the Family, 51,* 957–967.

http://pewinternet.org/pdfs/PIP _Generations_2009.pdf. Accessed February 10, 2009.

Kahn, M. (2008, December 2). The six habits of highly respectful physicians. *New York Times,* p. D6.

Katriel, T. (1990). "Griping" as a verbal ritual in some Israeli discourse. In D. Carbaugh (Ed.), *Cultural communication and intercultural contact* (pp. 99–114). Mahwah, NJ: Erlbaum.

Katz, J. (2013). *Tough Guise, 2.* Media Education Foundation.

Kaufman, L. (2013, May 21). For the word on the street, courts call up an online witness. *New York Times,* pp. A1, A3.

Keashly, L., & Newman, J. H. (2005). Bullying in the workplace: Its impact and management. *Employee Rights and Employment Policy Journal, 8,* 335–373.

Keeley, M. P., & Hart, A. J. (1994). Nonverbal behavior in dyadic interaction. In S. W. Duck (Ed.), *Understanding relationship processes, 4: Dynamics of relationships* (pp. 135–162). Thousand Oaks, CA: Sage.

Keith, W. (2009). The speech tradition. In W. F. Eadie (Ed.), *21st century communication: A reference handbook* (pp. 22–30). Thousand Oaks, CA: Sage.

Keizer, G. (2010). *The unwanted sound of everything we want: A book about noise.* New York: Perseus-Public Affairs.

Keller, J. (2011, May 13). The slow-motion mobile campus. *Chronicle of Higher Education*, pp. B4–B6.

Kelley, H. H. (1967). Attribution theory in social psychology. In D. Levine (Ed.), *Nebraska symposium on motivation* (Vol. 15, pp. 192–238). Lincoln: University of Nebraska Press.

Kelly, G. A. (1955). *The psychology of personal constructs*. New York: Norton.

Kendrick, B., & Sooknanan, P. (2014). The impact of computer mediated communication (CMC) on productivity and efficiency in organizations: A case study of an electrical company in Trinidad and Tobago. *Advances in Journalism and Communication*, 2. http://file.scirp.org/Html/1-2840025_46620.htm. Accessed August 14, 2014.

Kennedy, R. (2002). *Nigger: The strange career of a troublesome word*. New York: Pantheon.

Kershaw, S. (2009, April 23). Mr. Moms (by way of Fortune 500). *New York Times*, pp. E1, E6.

Kim, J., & Meyers, R. (2012). Cultural differences in conflict management styles in East and West organizations. *Journal of Intercultural Communication*, 29. Retrieved September 20, 2013, from http://www.immi.se/intercultural.

Kilbourne, J. (2010, summer). Sexist advertising, then & now. *Ms*, pp. 34–35.

Kim, Y. (1995). Cross-cultural adaptation: An integrated theory. In R. Wiseman (Ed.), *Intercultural communication theory* (pp. 170–193). Newbury Park, CA: Sage.

Kimbrough, A. M., Guadagno, R. E., Muscanell, N. L., & Dill, J. (2013). Gender differences in mediated communication: Women connect more than do men. *Computers in Human Behavior, 29*, 896–900.

Kimmel, M. (2013). *Angry white men*. New York: Nation.

Kimmel, M., & Messner, M. (2012). *Men's lives* (9th ed.). Upper Saddle Ridge, NJ: Pearson.

Kimmelman, M. (2014, August 22). In redesigned room, hospital patients may feel better already. *New York Times*, pp. A1, A13.

Kirshenbaum, S. (2011). *The science of kissing*. New York: Grand Central Publishing.

Klass, P. (2014, March 11). Smartphone limits go for parents, too. *New York Times*, p. D8.

Klein, N. (2009). *The shock doctrine*. New York: Macmillan/Picador.

Klein, R. (2001). *Jewelry talks: A novel thesis*. New York: Pantheon.

Klingberg, T. (2008). *The overflowing brain: Information overload and the limits of working memory*. New York: Oxford University Press.

Klopf, D. (1991). *Intercultural encounters: The fundamentals of intercultural communication* (2nd ed.). Englewood Cliffs, NJ: Morgan.

Knapp, M. L., Hall, J. A., & Hogan, T. (2013). *Nonverbal communication in human interaction*. Stamford, CT: Cengage.

Korkki, P. (2013, June 16). Business schools know how you think, but how do you feel? *Wall Street Journal*, p. B1.

Korzybski, A. (1948). *Science and sanity* (3rd ed.). Lakeville, CT: International Non-Aristotelian Library.

Krasnova, H., Wenninger, H., Widjaja, T., & Buxmann, P. (2013). Envy on Facebook: A hidden threat to users' life satisfaction. 11th International Conference on Wirtschaftsinformatik. Retrieved August 5, 2014, from http://warhol.wiwi.hu-berlin.de/~hkrasnova/Ongoing_Research_files/WI%202013%20Final%20Submission%20Krasnova.pdf.

Kristof, N. (2014, March 9). To end the abuse, she grabbed a knife. *New York Times*, pp. SR1, 11.

Krolicki, K. (2007, July 7). U.S. civil rights group holds funeral for "N-word." http://www.reuters.com/article/domesticNews/idUSN0929653620070709. Accessed January 10, 2009.

Kruger, P. (1999, June). A leader's journey. *Fast Company*, pp. 116–138.

Kupfer, D., First, M., & Regier, D. (2002). *A research agenda for DSM-V*. Washington, DC: American Psychiatric Press.

Kurt, J., & Sherker, J. (2003). Relationship quality, trait similarity, and self-other agreement on personality ratings in college roommates. *Journal of Personality, 71*, 21–40.

Kurtzberg, T. (2014). *Virtual teams: Mastering communication and collaboration in the digital age*. Santa Barbara, CA: Praeger.

Lamb, S., & Brown, L. (2006). *Packaging girlhood: Rescuing our daughters from marketers' schemes*. New York: St. Martin's Press.

Landrum, R., & Harrold, R. (2003). What employers want from psychology graduates. *Teaching of psychology, 30*, 131–133.

Langer, S. (1953). *Feeling and form: A theory of art*. New York: Scribner's.

Langer, S. (1979). *Philosophy in a new key: A study in the symbolism of reason, rite, and art* (3rd ed.). Cambridge, MA: Harvard University Press.

Laswell, H. D. (1948). The structure and function of communication in society. In L. Bryson (Ed.), *The communication of ideas*. New York: Harper & Row.

Lawless, B. (2012). More than white: Locating an invisible class identity. In A. González, M. Houston, & V. Chen (Eds.), *Our voices: Essays in culture, ethnicity, and communication* (pp. 247–253). New York: Oxford University Press.

Lazo, A. (2014, January 28). California law gives new options to transgender students. *Wall Street Journal*, p. A4.

Leaper, C., & Ayres, M. (2007). A meta-analytic review of gender variations in adults' language use: Talkativeness, affiliative speech, and assertive speech. *Personality & Social Psychology Review, 11*, 328–363.

Ledbetter, A., Broeckelman-Post, M., & Krawsczyn, A. (2011). Modeling everyday talk: Differences across communication media and sex composition of friendship dyads. *Journal of Social and Personal Relationships, 28,* 223–241.

Lee, J. A. (1973). *The colors of love: An exploration of the ways of loving.* Don Mills, Ontario, Canada: New Press.

Lee, J. A. (1988). Love-styles. In R. J. Sternberg & M. L. Barnes (Eds.), *The psychology of love* (pp. 38–67). New Haven, CT: Yale University Press.

Lee, W. S. (1994). On not missing the boat: A processual method for intercultural understandings of idioms and lifeworld. *Journal of Applied Communication Research, 22,* 141–161.

Lee, W. S. (2000). That's Greek to me: Between a rock and a hard place in intercultural encounters. In L. Samovar & R. Porter (Eds.), *Intercultural communication: A reader* (9th ed., pp. 217–224). Belmont, CA: Wadsworth.

Leeds-Hurwitz, W. (2006). Social theories: Social constructionism and symbolic interactionism. In D. O. Braithwaite & L. A. Baxter (Eds.), *Engaging theories in family communication: Multiple perspectives* (pp. 229–242). Thousand Oaks, CA: Sage.

Levi, D. (2010). *Group dynamics for teams.* Thousand Oaks, CA: Sage.

Levin, D., & Kilbourne, J. (2008). *So sexy, so soon.* New York: Ballantine.

Levin, S., Taylor, P., & Caudle, E. (2007). Interethnic and interracial dating in college: A longitudinal study. *Journal of Social and Personal Relationships, 24,* 323–341.

Levine, M. (2004, June 1). Tell the doc all your problems, but keep it to less than a minute. *New York Times,* p. D6.

Levine, R., & Norenzayan, A. (1999). The pace of life in 31 countries. *Journal of Cross-Cultural Psychology, 30,* 178–205.

Levitin, D. (2014). *The organized mind: Thinking straight in the age of information overload.* New York: Penguin.

Levy, D., Nardick, D., Turner, J., & McWatters, L. (2011, May 13). No cellphone? No internet? So much less stress. *Chronicle of Higher Education,* pp. B27–B28.

Levy, S. (2006, March 27). (Some) attention must be paid! *Newsweek,* p. 16

Lewis, M., Haviland-Jones, J. M., & Barrett, L. F. (Eds.). (2008). *Handbook of emotions.* New York: Guilford.

Lightner, C. (1990). *Giving sorrow words: How to cope with grief and get on with your life.* New York: Warner.

Liptak, A. (2011, June 18). Audit of officer's pager was reasonable, court says. *New York Times,* p. A15.

Liu, F., & Albarran, A. (2009). Media economics and ownership. In W. F. Eadie (Ed.), *21st century communication: A reference handbook* (pp. 851–858). Thousand Oaks, CA: Sage.

Lloyd, S., & Emery, B. (2000). The context and dynamics of intimate aggression against women. *Journal of Social and Personal Relationships, 17,* 503–521.

Logan, R. (2010). *Understanding new media: Extending Marshall McLuhan.* New York: Peter Lang.

Lourogos, A. (2010, August 10). Staying in touch—college students, parents stay connected via technology. *Chicago Tribune.* http://blogs .cofc.edu/parents/2010/08/24 /staying-in-touch-college -students-parents-stay-connected -via-technology/.

Love, D. (2011, June 10). Americans have earned a break. *Raleigh News & Observer,* p. 11A.

Ludden, J. (2014, June 5). Stay-at-home dads on the rise, and many of them are poor. *National Public Radio.* Retrieved from http://www.npr .org/2014/06/05/319214546/stay -at-home-dads-on-the-rise-and -many-of-them-are-poor.

Ludington-Hoe, S. (1993). *Kangaroo care: The best you can do to help your preterm infant.* New York: Bantam.

Luft, J. (1969). *Of human interaction.* Palo Alto, CA: Natural Press.

Lugones, M. (1992). On "Borderlands/ La Frontera": An interpretive essay. *Hypatia, 7,* 31–37.

Lugones, M. (2006). On complex communication. *Hypatia, 21,* 75–85.

Luhrmann, T. J. (2014, September 7). Can't place that smell? You must be American: How culture shapes our sense. *New York Times Sunday Review,* pp. 6–7.

Lumsden, G., Lumsden, D., & Wiethoff, C. (2009). *Communicating in groups and teams* (5th ed.). Belmont, CA: Wadsworth.

Lund, M. (1985). The development of investment and commitment scales for predicting continuity of personal relationships. *Journal of Social and Personal Relationships, 2,* 3–23.

Luttrell, R. (2014). *Social media: How to engage, share, and connect.* Lanham, MD: Rowman & Littlefield.

MacFarquhar, N. (2011, June 16). Social media help keep the door open to sustained dissent inside Saudi Arabia. *New York Times,* p. A5.

MacGeorge, E. (2009). Social support. In W. F. Eadie (Ed.), *21st century communication: A reference handbook* (pp. 283–291). Thousand Oaks, CA: Sage.

Major, B., Schmidlin, A. M., & Williams, L. (1990). Gender patterns in social touch: The impact of setting and age. In C. Mayo & N. M. Henley (Eds.), *Gender and nonverbal behavior* (pp. 3–37). New York: Springer-Verlag.

Makau, J. (2009). Ethical and unethical communication. In W. F. Eadie (Ed.), *21st century communication: A reference handbook* (pp. 435–443). Thousand Oaks, CA: Sage.

Maltz, D. N., & Borker, R. (1982). A cultural approach to male–female miscommunication. In J. J. Gumperz (Ed.), *Language and social identity* (pp. 196–216). Cambridge, UK: Cambridge University Press.

Manjoo, F. (2014, August 15). Web trolls winning as incivility increases. *New York Times*, pp. B1, 2.

Manusov, V. (2006). Attribution theories: Assessing causal and responsibility judgments in families. In D. O. Braithwaite & L. A. Baxter (Eds.), *Engaging theories in family communication: Multiple perspectives* (pp. 181–196). Thousand Oaks, CA: Sage.

Manusov, V., & Spitzberg, B. (2008). Attribution theory. In L. A. Baxter & D. O. Braithwaite (Eds.), *Engaging theories in interpersonal communication: Multiple perspectives* (pp. 37–49). Thousand Oaks, CA: Sage.

Martin, J. (2013, November 3). Don't be a jerk. *New York Times Book Review*, p. 15.

Martin, J., Krizek, R., Nakayama, T., & Bradford, L. (1996). Exploring whiteness: A study of self labels for white Americans. *Communication Quarterly, 44,* 125–144.

Martin, J., & Nakayama, T. (2007). *Intercultural communication in context* (4th ed.). New York: McGraw Hill.

Martin, T. (2007). Muting the voice of the local in the age of the global: How communication practices compromised public participation in India's Allain Dunhangan environmental impact assessment. *Environmental Communication, 1,* 171–193.

Mastro, D. (2003). A social identity approach to understanding the impact of television messages. *Communication Monographs, 70,* 98–113.

McChesney, R. (1999). *Rich media, poor democracy: Communication politics in dubious times.* Urbana: University of Illinois Press.

McChesney, R. (2004). *The problem of the media: U.S. communication politics in the twenty-first century.* New York: Monthly Review Press.

McChesney, R. (2008). *The political economy of media.* New York: Monthly Review Press.

McClure, B. (2005). *Putting a new spin on groups: The science of chaos* (2nd ed.). Mahwah, NJ: Erlbaum.

McClure, M. (1997). Mind/body medicine: Evidence of efficacy. *Health and Healing, 1,* 3.

McCombs, M. (2014). *Setting the agenda: Mass media and public opinion.* Malden, MA: Polity.

McCombs, M., Ghanem, S., & Chernov, G. (2009). Agenda setting and framing. In W. F. Eadie (Ed.), *21st century communication: A reference handbook* (pp. 516–524). Thousand Oaks, CA: Sage.

McCroskey, J., & Teven, J. (1999). Goodwill: A reexamination of the construct and its measurement. *Communication Monographs, 66,* 90–103.

McDonald, M., Phipps, S., & Lethbridge, L. (2005). Taking its toll: The influences of paid and unpaid work on women's well-being. *Feminist Economics, 11,* 63–94.

McGee-Cooper, A., Trammel, D., & Lau, B. (1992). *You don't have to go home from work exhausted.* New York: Bantam.

McKinney, B., Kelly, L., & Duran, R. (1997). The relationship between conflict message style and dimensions of communication competence. *Communication Reports, 10,* 185–196.

McKinney, M. (2006, October). Communication among top-10 fields of study. *Spectra,* p. 8.

McLuhan, M. (1962). *The Gutenberg galaxy.* Toronto, Canada: University of Toronto Press.

McLuhan, M. (1964). *Understanding media.* New York: McGraw-Hill.

McLuhan, M. (1969, March). Interview. *Playboy,* pp. 53–54, 56, 59–62, 64–66, 68, 70.

McLuhan, M., & Fiore, Q. (1967). *The medium is the message.* New York: Random House.

McMurtrie, B. (2011, November 18). International enrollments at U.S. colleges grow but still rely on China. *Chronicle of Higher Education,* pp. A16–A20.

McNees, P. (1999). *YPO: The first fifty years.* Wilmington, OH: Orange Frazier Press.

McNulty, J. K., & Karney, B. R. (2001). Attributions in marriage: Integrating specific and global evaluations of a relationship. *Personality and Social Psychology Bulletin, 27,* 943–955.

McNutt, P. (1997, October/November). When strategic decisions are ignored. *Fast Company,* p. 12.

Mead, G. H. (1934). *Mind, self, and society.* Chicago: University of Chicago Press.

Medhurst, M. (2010). George W. Bush at Goree Island: American slavery and the rhetoric of redemption. *Quarterly Journal of Speech, 96,* 257–277.

Mehrabian, A. (1981). *Silent messages: Implicit communication of emotion and attitudes* (2nd ed.). Belmont, CA: Wadsworth.

Mernissi, F. (2004). Size 6: The Western woman's harem. In J. Spade & C. Valentine (Eds.), *The kaleidoscope of gender: Prisms, patterns, and possibilities* (pp. 297–301). Belmont, CA: Thomson Wadsworth.

Metts, S. (2006). Gendered communication in dating relationships. In B. Dow & J. T. Wood (Eds.), *Handbook of gender and communication research* (pp. 25–40). Thousand Oaks, CA: Sage.

Milbank, D. (2014, August 7). A welcome end to American whiteness. *Raleigh News & Observer,* p. 7A.

Milia, T. (2003). *Doctor, you're not listening.* Philadelphia: Xlibris.

Miller, A. N. (2011, February). Men's and women's communication is different—sometimes. *Communication Currents,* p. 1.

Miller, C. (2014). *Organizing communication: Approaches and processes* (8th ed.). Belmont, CA: Wadsworth/Cengage.

Miller, J. (2006, May 9). Touch. *Raleigh News & Observer,* pp. 1E, 3E.

Miller, J. B. (1993). Learning from early relationship experience.

In S. W. Duck (Ed.), *Understanding relationship processes, 2: Learning about relationships* (pp. 1–29). Thousand Oaks, CA: Sage.

Modaff, D., Butler, J., & DeWine, S. (2011). *Organizational communication: Foundations, challenges, and misunderstandings* (3rd ed.). Boston: Allyn & Bacon.

Monastersky, R. (2001, July 6). Look who's listening. *Chronicle of Higher Education*, pp. A14–A16.

Monastersky, R. (2002, March 29). Speak before you think. *Chronicle of Higher Education*, pp. A17–A18.

Monroe, A. H. (1935). *Principles and types of speech*. Glenview, IL: Scott, Foresman.

Monsour, M. (2002). *Women and men as friends*. Mahwah, NJ: Erlbaum.

Montgomery, B. (1988). Quality communication in personal relationships. In S. W. Duck (Ed.), *Handbook of personal relationships* (pp. 343–366). New York: Wiley.

Mooney, C. (2009). *Theories of attachment*. St. Paul, MN: Readleaf Press.

Morning, A. (2011). *The nature of race: How scientists think and teach about human difference*. Berkeley, CA: University of California Press.

Morreale, J. (2007). Faking it and the transformation of identity. In D. Heller (Ed.), *Makeover television: Realities remodeled* (pp. 6–22). New York: Palgrave Macmillan.

Muehlhoff, T. (2006). "He started it": Everyday communication in parenting. In J. T. Wood & S. W. Duck (Eds.), *Composing relationships: Communication in everyday life* (pp. 46–54). Belmont, CA: Wadsworth.

Mulac, A. (2006). The gender-linked language effect: Do language differences really make a difference? In K. Dindia & D. Canary (Eds.), *Sex differences and similarities in communication* (pp. 219–239). Mahwah, NJ: Erlbaum.

Mumby, D. (Ed.). (1993). *Narratives and social control: Critical perspectives*. Newbury Park, CA: Sage.

Mumby, D. (2006). Constructing working-class masculinity in the workplace. In J. T. Wood & S. W. Duck (Eds.), *Composing relationships: Communication in everyday life* (pp. 166–174). Belmont, CA: Thomson Wadsworth.

Mumby, D. (2007). Introduction: Gendering organization. In B. Dow & J. T. Wood (Eds.), *Handbook of gender and communication research*. Thousand Oaks, CA: Sage.

Murphy, J., & Rubinson, R. (2005). Domestic violence and mediation: Responding to the challenges of crafting effective screens. *Family Law Quarterly, 39*, 177–194.

Murphy, K. (2011, July 5). The paperless cockpit. *New York Times*, p. B6.

Muwanguzi, S., & Musambira, G. (2013). Communication experiences of Ugandan immigrants during acculturation to the United States: A preliminary study. *Journal of Intercultural Communication, 31*. Retrieved July 28, 2014, from http://www.immi.se/intercultural/.

Mwakalye, N., & DeAngelis, T. (1995, October). The power of touch helps babies survive. *APA Monitor*, p. 25.

Myers, L., & Larson, R. (2005). Preparing students for early work conflict. *Business Communication Quarterly, 68*, 306–317.

Myers, W. (2014, March 16). Where are the people of color in children's books? *New York Times*, pp. SR 1, 7.

Nagourney, E. (2006, May 9). Surgical teams found lacking in teamwork. *New York Times*, p. D6.

Nagourney, E. (2008, December 23). Pain is greater if harm seems intentional. *New York Times*, p. D6.

Nanda, S. (2004). Multiple genders among North American Indians. In J. Spade & C. Valentine (Eds.), *The kaleidoscope of gender* (pp. 64–70). Belmont, CA: Wadsworth.

The Nielsen Company. (2014, February 10). The U.S. Digital Consumer Report. Retrieved from http://www.nielsen.com/content/corporate/us/en/insights/reports/2014/the-us-digital-consumer-report.html.

Negra, D. (Ed.). (2006). *The Irish in us: Irishness, performativity, and popular culture*. Durham, NC: Duke University Press.

Nerone, J. (2009). Journalism. In W. F. Eadie (Ed.), *21st century communication: A reference handbook* (pp. 31–38). Thousand Oaks, CA: Sage.

Neuliep, J. (2014). *Intercultural communication: A contextual approach*. Thousand Oaks, CA: Sage.

Nichols, M. (1996). *The lost art of listening*. New York: Guilford.

Noelle, C. (2011). Stay at home fathers and breadwinning mothers: Gender, couple dynamics, and social change. *Gender & Society, 15*, 642–664.

Norton, T. (2007). The structuration of public participation: Organizing environmental control. *Environmental Communication, 1*, 146–170.

Norwood, K., & Duck, S. W. (2009). Friendship. In W. F. Eadie (Ed.), *21st century communication: A reference handbook* (pp. 313–321). Thousand Oaks, CA: Sage.

Notable numbers. (2011, June 11). *Raleigh News & Observer*, p. 16A.

http://www.oxforddictionaries.com/us/words/what-s-new. Recent Updates to Oxford Dictionaries. Retrieved March 6, 2015.

Oetzel, J., & Ting-Toomey, S. (Eds.). (2013). *The SAGE handbook of conflict communication: Integrating research, theory and practice*. Thousand Oaks, CA: Sage.

O'Hair, D., & Eadie, W. F. (2009). In W. F. Eadie (Ed.), *21st century communication: A reference handbook* (pp. 3–11). Thousand Oaks, CA: Sage.

Ohanian, H. (2008). *Einstein's mistakes*. New York: W. W. Norton.

Olds, J., & Schwartz, R. (2010). *The lonely American: Drifting apart in the twenty-first century*. Boston: Beacon.

Olson, J. M., & Cal, A. V. (1984). Source credibility, attitudes, and the recall of past behaviors. *European Journal of Social Psychology, 14*, 203–210.

OMG!!!!! OED ♥ LOL!!!!! (2011, April 5). *New York Times*, p. A20.

Ono, K. A. (2009). Critical/cultural approaches to communication. In W. F. Eadie (Ed.), *21st century communication: A reference handbook* (pp. 74–81). Thousand Oaks, CA: Sage.

Orbe, M. P., & Harris, T. M. (2015). *Interracial communication: Theory into practice* (3rd ed.). Stamford, CT: Cengage.

Ore, T. (2013). *The social construction of difference and inequity*. New York: McGrawHill.

Ornish, D. (1998). *Love and survival: The scientific basis for the healing power of intimacy*. New York: HarperCollins.

Overall, N., Sibley, C., & Travaglia, L. (2010). Loyal but ignored: The benefits and costs of constructive communication behavior. *Journal of Personal Relationships, 17*, 127–148.

Overheard. (2008, August 24). *Raleigh News & Observer*, p. 3E.

Overland, M. (2004, January 9). Tea, TV, and sympathy. *Chronicle of Higher Education*, p. A48.

Overland, M. (2009, January 23). A long time coming. *Chronicle of Higher Education*, p. A6.

Pacanowsky, M. (1989). Creating and narrating organizational realities. In B. Dervin, L. Grossberg, B. O'Keefe, & E. Wartella (Eds.), *Rethinking communication: Paradigm exemplars* (pp. 250–257). Thousand Oaks, CA: Sage.

Pacanowsky, M., & O'Donnell-Trujillo, N. (1982). Communication and organizational cultures. *Western Journal of Speech Communication, 46*, 115–130.

Pacanowsky, M., & O'Donnell-Trujillo, N. (1983). Organizational communication as cultural performance. *Communication Monographs, 30*, 126–147.

Painter, N. (2010). *White people's history*. New York: Norton.

̇ (2008). *The difference: How ⁀r of diversity creates better ⁀s, schools and societies.*

Princeton, NJ: Princeton University Press.

Pappano, L. (2014, November 2). Notes from the pros. *New York Times* supplement, Education Life, p. 6.

Parker, K., & Wang, W. (2013, March 14). Modern parenthood: Roles of moms and dads converge as they balance work and family. *Pew Research: Social and demographic trends*. http://www.pewsocialtrends .org/2013/03/14/modern-parenthood -roles-of-moms-and-dads-converge -as-they-balance-work-and-family/. Accessed June 20, 2014.

Parker-Pope, T. (2010). *For better: The science of a good marriage*. New York: Dutton.

Parker-Pope, T. (2014, August 26). Marital bliss, one decision after another. *New York Times*, pp. D1, D4.

Patterson, M. L. (1992). A functional approach to nonverbal exchange. In R. S. Feldman & B. Rime (Eds.), *Fundamentals of nonverbal behavior* (pp. 458–495). New York: Cambridge University Press.

Pear, R. (2012, May 17). House vote sets up battle on domestic violence bill. *The New York Times*, p. A19.

Pearce, W. B., Cronen, V. E., & Conklin, F. (1979). On what to look at when analyzing communication: A hierarchical model of actors' meanings. *Communication, 4*, 195–220.

Perlow, L. (2013). *Sleeping with your smartphone*. Boston: Harvard Business Review Press.

Peters, M., & Wessel, D. (2013, February 6). More men in their prime are out of work and at home. *Wall Street Journal*, pp. A1, A14.

Petronio, S., & Caughlin, J. (2006). Communication privacy management theory: Understanding families. In D. O. Braithwaite & L. A. Baxter (Eds.), *Engaging theories in family communication: Multiple perspectives* (pp. 35–49). Thousand Oaks, CA: Sage.

Pew media study shows reliance on many outlets. (2011, September 26). *New York Times*, p. B6.

Peyser, M. (2006, March 6). Color us impressed. *Newsweek*, p. 59.

Pezzullo, P. (2007). *Toxic tourism: Rhetorics of travel, pollution, and environmental justice*. Tuscaloosa: University of Alabama Press.

Pezzullo, P. (2008). Overture: The most complicated world. *Cultural Studies, 22*, 3–4.

Pinker, S. (2000). *Words and rules*. New York: HarperPerennial.

Pinker, S. (2008). *The stuff of thought: Language as a window to human nature*. New York: Penguin.

Potter, W. J. (2009). Media literacy. In W. F. Eadie (Ed.), *21st century communication: A reference handbook* (pp. 558–567). Thousand Oaks, CA: Sage.

Potter, M., Gordon, S., & Hamer, P. (2004). The nominal group technique: A useful consensus methodology in physiotherapy research. *New Zealand Journal of Physiotherapy, 32*, 126–130.

Potter, W. J. (2004). *Theory of media literacy: A cognitive approach*. Thousand Oaks, CA: Sage.

Pozios, V. K., Kambam, P. R., & Bender, H. E. (2013, August 25). Does media violence lead to the real thing? *New York Times*, p. SR12.

Pozner, J. (2004, Fall). The unreal world. *Ms.*, pp. 50–53.

Preston, J. (2011, July 21). Social media history becomes a new job hurdle. *New York Times*, pp. B1, B4.

Prevalence of Domestic Violence. (2013, August). *The advocates for human rights*. http://www.stopvaw .org/prevalence_of_domestic _violence. Accessed July 3, 2014.

Putnam, L., & Mumby. D. (Eds.). (2013). *The SAGE handbook of organizational communication: Advances in theory, research and methods*. Thousand Oaks, CA: Sage.

Putnam, R. (2000). *Bowling alone*. New York: Simon & Schuster.

Putnam, R., & Feldstein, L. (2003). *Better together*. New York: Simon & Schuster.

Qin, X. (2014). Exploring the impact of culture in five communicative elements—Case of intercultural misunderstandings between Chinese and American. *Journal of Intercultural Communication, 34*. Retrieved July 28, 2014, from http://www.immi.se/intercultural/.

Quenqua, D. (2014, August 3). Tell me, even if it hurts me. *New York Times*, pp. St1, 8–9.

Quick Facts. (2011). U.S. Bureau of the Census. http://quickfacts.census.gov/qfd/states/00000.html. Accessed July 5, 2011.

Radway, J. (1991). *Reading the romance*. Chapel Hill: University of North Carolina Press.

Rae-Dupree, J. (2008, December 7). Teamwork, the true mother of invention. *New York Times*, p. B3.

Ragan, P. (2003). *The mating game: A primer on love, sex and marriage*. Thousand Oaks, CA: Sage.

Ramasubramanian, S. (2010). Television viewing, racial attitudes, and policy preferences: Exploring the role of social identity and intergroup emotions in influencing support for affirmative action. *Communication Monographs, 77*, 102–120.

Rawlins, W. K. (1981). *Friendship as a communicative achievement: A theory and an interpretive analysis of verbal reports*. Doctoral dissertation, Temple University, Philadelphia.

Rawlins, W. K. (1994). Being there and growing apart: Sustaining friendships during adulthood. In D. Canary & L. Stafford (Eds.), *Communication and relational maintenance* (pp. 275–294). New York: Academic Press.

Ream, Diane Show. (2012, June 25). Aired on NPR 10–11 a.m. EDS.

Reinhard, C. D., & Dervin, B. J. (2009). Media uses and gratifications. In W. F. Eadie (Ed.), *21st century communication: A reference handbook* (pp. 506–515). Thousand Oaks, CA: Sage.

Reinhard, J. (2007). *Introduction to communication research*. New York: McGraw-Hill.

Reis, H. T., Clark, M. S., & Holmes, J. G. (2004). Perceived partner responsiveness as an organizing construct in the study of intimacy and closeness. In D. J. Mashek & A. P. Aron (Eds.), *Handbook of closeness and intimacy* (pp. 201–225). Mahwah, NJ: Erlbaum.

Remland, M. (2000). *Nonverbal communication in everyday life*. Boston: Houghton Mifflin.

Renegar, V., & Malkowski, J. (2009). Rhetorical and textual approaches to communication. In W. F. Eadie (Ed.), *21st century communication: A reference handbook* (pp. 49–56). Thousand Oaks, CA: Sage.

Rheingold, H. (2009, January 9). Look who's talking. *Wired*. http://www.wired.com/wired/archive/7.01/amish_pr.html. Accessed July 25, 2009.

Rhode, D. (2010). *The beauty bias: The injustice of appearances in life and law*. New York: Oxford University Press.

Rhodes, T. (2010, November). Learning across the curriculum. *Spectra*, pp. 12–15.

Rice, R., & Leonardi, P. (2013). Information and communication technologies in organizations. In L. Putnam & D. Mumby (Eds.), *The SAGE handbook of organizational communication: Advances in theory, research and methods* (pp. 425–448). Thousand Oaks, CA: Sage.

Richmond, V. P., & McCroskey, J. C. (1995). *Nonverbal communication in interpersonal relations* (3rd ed.). Boston: Allyn & Bacon.

Richtel, M. (2011, December 15). As doctors uses more devices, potential for distraction grows. *New York Times*, pp. A1, A4.

Richtel, M. (2014, September 14). A texting driver's education. *New York Times*, p. 7 BU.

Riessman, C. (1990). *Divorce talk: Women and men make sense of personal relationships*. New Brunswick, NJ: Rutgers University Press.

Riggs, D. (1999, February 28). True love is alive and well, say romance book writers. *Tallahassee Democrat*, p. 3D.

Riley, P. (1983). A structurationist account of political culture. *Administrative Science Quarterly, 28*, 414–437.

Ritchtel, M. (2010, January 16). Phones drive us to distraction, even when we walk. *New York Times*, p. A4.

Roberts, P. (2014). *The impulse society*. New York: Bloomsbury.

Rosenbaum, L. (2011, November 22). The doctor feels your pain. *Raleigh News & Observer*, pp. 1D, 2D.

Rosenbloom, S. (2014, August 24). Dealing with digital cruelty. *New York Times*, pp. SR1, 7.

Rosman, K. (2013, October 19). How much do people watch TV daily? First, define TV. *Wall Street Journal*, pp. D1–D2.

Rothwell, J. D. (2015). *In mixed company: Small group communication* (9th ed.). Belmont, CA: Thomson Wadsworth.

Rowe-Finkbeiner, K. (2014, April 30). The motherhood penalty. *Politico Magazine*. http://www.politico.com/magazine/story/2014/04/the-motherhood-penalty-106173.html#.U6aurdJOXq4.

Rubin, L. (1985). *Just friends: The role of friendship in our lives*. New York: Harper & Row.

Rudman, L. A., & Glick, P. (2010). *The social psychology of gender*. New York: Guilford Press.

Rusbult, C. E. (1987). Responses to dissatisfaction in close relationships: The exit–voice–loyalty–neglect model. In D. Perlman & S. W. Duck (Eds.), *Intimate relationships: Development, dynamics, and deterioration* (pp. 209–237). London: Sage.

Rusbult, C. E., Drigotas, S. M., & Verette, J. (1994). The investment model: An interdependence analysis of commitment processes and relationship maintenance phenomena. In D. J. Canary & L. Stafford (Eds.), *Communication and relational maintenance* (pp. 115–140). New York: Academic Press.

Rusbult, C. E., Johnson, D. J., & Morrow, G. D. (1986). Impact of couple patterns of problem solving on distress and nondistress in dating relationships. *Journal of Personality and Social Psychology, 50,* 744–753.

Rusbult, C. E., & Zembrodt, I. M. (1983). Responses to dissatisfaction in romantic involvement: A multidimensional scaling analysis. *Journal of Experimental Social Psychology, 19,* 274–293.

Rusbult, C. E., Zembrodt, I. M., & Iwaniszek, J. (1986). The impact of gender and sex-role orientation on responses to dissatisfaction in close relationships. *Sex Roles, 15,* 1–20.

Rusli, E. (2013, June 12). When words just aren't enough some turn to flatulent bunnies. *Wall Street Journal,* pp. A1, A14.

Rusk, T., & Rusk, N. (1988). *Mind traps: Change your mind, change your life.* Los Angeles: Price Stern Sloan.

Rusli, E. (2011, July 4). Homework help site has a social networking twist. *New York Times,* pp. B1, B4.

Sabourin, T., & Stamp, G. (1995). Communication and the experience of dialectical tensions in family life: An examination of abusive and nonabusive families. *Communication Monographs, 62,* 213–242.

Salas, E., & Frush, K. (2012). *Improving patient safety through teamwork and team training.* New York: Oxford University Press.

Samp, J., & Palevitz, C. (2009). Dating and romantic relationships. In W. F. Eadie (Ed.), *21st century communication: A reference handbook* (pp. 322–329). Thousand Oaks, CA: Sage.

Samovar, L., Porter, R., & McDaniel, E. (Eds.). (2013). *Intercultural communication: A reader* (8th ed.). Belmont, CA: Wadsworth.

Samovar, L., Porter, R., McDaniel, E., & Roy, C. (Eds.). (2015). *Intercultural communication: A reader* (14th ed.). Belmont, CA: Wadsworth.

Samp, J., & Palevitz, C. (2009). Dating and romantic partners. In W. F. Eadie (Ed.), *21st century communication: A reference handbook* (pp. 322–330). Thousand Oaks, CA: Sage.

Sandler, R., & Pezzullo, P. (Eds.). (2007). *Environmental justice and environmentalism: The social justice challenge to the environmental movement.* Cambridge, MA: MIT Press.

Sandstrom, K. L., Martin, D. D., & Fine, G. A. (2001). Symbolic interactionism and the end of the century. In G. Ritzer & B. Smart (Eds.), *Handbook of social theory* (pp. 217–231). Thousand Oaks, CA: Sage.

Sawyer, K. (2008). *Group genius: The power of creative collaboration.* New York: Basic.

Scarf, M. (2008). *September song: The good news about marriage in the later years.* New York: Riverhead.

Schiebel, D. (2009). Qualitative, ethnographic and performative approaches to communication. In W. F. Eadie (Ed.), *21st century communication: A reference handbook* (pp. 65–73). Thousand Oaks, CA: Sage.

Schiesel, S. (2006, May 9). The Sims' stimulate kids who play. *Raleigh News & Observer,* p. 8E.

Schmid, R. (2010, July 5). Sense of touch affects behavior in startling ways. *Raleigh News & Observer,* p. 4B

Schmidt, J., & Uecker, D. (2007). Increasing understanding of routine/everyday interaction in relationships. *Communication Teacher, 21,* 111–116.

Schmitt, J. (2014, October 22). Communication studies rise to relevance. *Chronicle of Higher Education.* http://www .huffingtonpost.com/jason -schmitt/communication-studies -ris_b_6025038.html. Accessed October 23, 2014.

Scholz, M. (2005, June). A "simple" way to improve adherence. *RN, 68,* 82.

Schooler, D., Ward, M., Merriwether, A., & Caruthers, A. (2004). Who's that girl: Television's role in the body image of young white and black women. *Psychology of Women Quarterly, 28,* 38–47.

Schramm, W. (1955). *The process and effects of mass communication.* Urbana: University of Illinois Press.

Schroeder, J., & Risen, J. (2014, August 24). Peace through friendship. *New York Times,* p. SR9

Schwartz, N., & Dash, E. (2011, June 14). On college forms, a question of race or races, can perplex. *New York Times,* pp. A1, A12.

Scott, C., & Myers, K. (2005). The socialization of emotion: Learning emotion management at the fire station. *Journal of Applied Communication Research, 33,* 67–92.

Scott, J., & Leonhardt, D. (2013). Shadowy lines that still divide. In M. Andersen & P. H. Collins (Eds.), *Race, class, and gender: An anthology* (8th ed., pp. 117–124). Boston: Cengage.

Searle, J. (1976). *Speech acts: An essay in the philosophy of language.* London: Cambridge University Press.

Searle, J. (1995). *The construction of social reality.* New York: Free Press.

Sedikides, C., Campbell, W., Reeder, G., & Elliot, A. (1998). The self-serving bias in relational context. *Journal of Personality and Social Psychology, 74,* 3763–3864.

Segrin, C., Hanzal, A., & Domschke, T. (2009). Accuracy and bias in newlywed couples' perceptions of conflict styles and the association with marital satisfaction. *Communication Monographs, 76,* 107–233.

Seligman, M. E. P. (1990). *Learned optimism.* New York: Simon & Schuster/Pocket Books.

Seligman, M. E. P. (2002). *Authentic happiness: Using the new positive psychology to realize your potential for lasting fulfillment.* New York: Free Press.

Selingo, J. (2012, September 28). Colleges and employers point fingers over skills gap. *Chronicle of Higher Education*, p. A20.

Sellinger, M. B. (1994, July 9). Candy Lightner prods Congress. *People*, pp. 102, 105.

Setoodeh, R. (2006, May 22). The long goodbye. *Newsweek*, pp. 60–61.

Shannon, C., & Weaver, W. (1949). *The mathematical theory of communication*. Urbana: University of Illinois Press.

Shattuck, T. R. (1980). *The forbidden experiment: The story of the wild boy of Aveyron*. New York: Farrar, Straus & Giroux.

Shellenbarger, S. (2013, September 11). The biggest distraction in the office is sitting next to you. *Wall Street Journal*, pp. D1, D3.

Shiffert, A., & Schwartz, B. (2011). Spouses' demand and withdrawal during marital conflict in relation to their subjective well-being. *Journal of Social and Personal Relationships, 28*, 262–277.

Shimanoff, S. B. (1980). *Communication rules: Theory and research*. Thousand Oaks, CA: Sage.

Shoemaker, P., & Vos, T. (2009). *Gatekeeping theory*. New York: Routledge.

Sias, P. (2013). Workplace relationships. In L. Putnam & D. Mumby (Eds.), *The SAGE handbook of organizational communication: Advances in theory, research and methods* (pp. 375–400). Thousand Oaks, CA: Sage.

Siebold, D., Hollingshead, A., & Yoon, K. (2013). Embedded teams and embedding organizations. In L. Putnam & D. Mumby (Eds.), *The SAGE handbook of organizational communication: Advances in theory, research and methods* (pp. 327–350). Thousand Oaks, CA: Sage.

Signorielli, N. (2009). Cultivation and media exposure. In W. F. Eadie (Ed.), *21st century communication: A reference handbook* (pp. 525–567). Thousand Oaks, CA: Sage.

Signorielli, N., & Morgan, M. (Eds.). (1990). *Cultivation analysis: New directions in media research*. Thousand Oaks, CA: Sage.

Simon, S. B. (1977). *Vulture: A modern allegory on the art of putting oneself down*. Niles, IL: Argus Communications.

Simons, G. F., Vázquez, C., & Harris, P. R. (1993). *Transcultural leadership: Empowering the diverse workforce*. Houston, TX: Gulf.

Singer, N. (2014, August 17). Check app. Accept job. Repeat. *New York Times*, pp. BU 1, 4–5.

Singer, P. W. (2009). *Wired for war*. New York: Penguin.

Smircich, L. (1983). Concepts of culture and organizational analysis. *Administrative Quarterly, 28*, 339–358.

Smith, E., & Hattery, A. (Eds.). (2013). *Interracial relationships in the 21st century* (2nd ed.). Durham, NC: Carolina Academic Press.

Smith, R. (2009). *Strategic planning for public relations* (3rd ed.). New York: Routledge.

Smith, S., Choueiti, M., & Pieper, K. (2013). Race/ethnicity in 500 popular films: Is the key to diversifying cinematic content held in the hand of the black director? Retrieved from http://annenberg.usc.edu/sitecore/shell/Applications/~/media/PDFs/RaceEthnicity.ashx.

Smith, S., Choueiti, M., Scofield, E., & Pieper, K. (2013). Gender inequality in 500 popular films: Examining on-screen portrayals and behind-the scenes employment patterns in mother pictures released between 2007–2012. Retrieved from http://annenberg.usc.edu/Faculty/Communication%20and%20Jour-nalism/~/media/A41FBC3E62084AC8A8C047A9D4A54033.ashx.

Snook, Scott A. (2000). *Friendly fire: The accidental shootdown of U.S. black hawks over northern Iraq*. Princeton, NJ: Princeton University Press.

Spar, D. (2013). *Wonder women: Sex, power and the quest for perfection*. New York: Sarah Crichton Books.

Sparks, G. (2006). *Media effects research: A basic overview* (2nd ed.). Belmont, CA: Thomson Wadsworth.

Sparrow, B., Liu, J., & Wegner, D. (2011). Google effects on memory: Cognitive consequences of having information at our fingertips. *Science*. http://dx.doi.org/10.1126/science.1207745

Spitzberg, B., & Cupach, W. (2015). Unilateral union: Obsessive relational intrusion and stalking in a romantic context. In D. O. Braithwaite & J. T. Wood (Eds.), *Casing interpersonal communication* (pp. 131–136). Dubuque, IA: Kendall-Hunt.

Stafford, L. (2009). Spouses and other intimate partnerships. In W. F. Eadie (Ed.), *21st century communication: A reference handbook* (pp. 295–302). Thousand Oaks, CA: Sage.

Staples, W. (2014). *Everyday surveillance: Vigilance and visibility in post-modern life* (2nd ed.). Lanham, MD: Rowman & Littlefield.

Steiner, C. (1994). *Scripts people live: Transactional analysis of life scripts*. New York: Grove Press.

Steiner-Adair, C. (2013). *The big disconnect*. New York: Harper.

Steinmetz, K. (2014, July 28). Language. *Time*, pp. 52–53.

Stewart, J., Zediker, K., & Black, L. (2004). Relationships among philosophies of dialogue. In R. Anderson, L. Baxter, & K. Cissna (Eds.), *Dialogue: Theorizing difference in communication studies* (pp. 21–38). Thousand Oaks, CA: Sage.

Stolberg, S. (2009, January 29). From the top, the White House unbuttons formal dress code. *New York Times*, pp. A1, A14.

Swain, S. (1989). Covert intimacy: Closeness in men's friendships. In B. Risman & P. Schwartz (Eds.), *Gender and intimate relationships* (pp. 71–86). Belmont, CA: Wadsworth.

Sydell, L. (2014, January 7). Class trumps race when it comes to Internet access. http://www.npr.org/blogs/codeswitch/2014/01/07/260409016/class-trumps-race-when-it-comes-to-internet-access. Accessed July 25, 2014.

Sypher, B. (1984). Seeing ourselves as others see us. *Communication Research, 11,* 97–115.

Tanno, D. (1997). Names, narratives, and the evolution of ethnic identity. In A. González, M. Houston, & V. Chen (Eds.), *Our voices: Essays in culture, ethnicity, and communication* (pp. 28–34). Los Angeles: Roxbury.

Tashiro, T., & Frazier, P. (2003). "I'll never be in a relationship like that again": Personal growth following romantic relationship breakup. *Personal Relationships, 10,* 113–128.

Tavris, C. (1992). *The mismeasure of woman.* New York: Simon & Schuster.

Taylor, A. (2014). *The people's platform: Taking back power and culture in the digital age.* New York: Metropolitan/Henry Holt.

Taylor, M. (1999). *Imaginary companions and the children who create them.* New York: Oxford University Press.

Terlecki, M., Brown, J., Harner-Steciw, L., Irvin-Hannum, J., Marchetto-Ryan, N., Ruhl, L., & Wiggins, J. (2011). Sex differences and similarities in video game experience, preferences, and self-efficacy: Implications for the gaming industry. *Current Psychology, 30,* 22–33.

37 Percent of Employers Use Facebook to Pre-screen Applicants, New Study Says. (2012, April 20). *Huffington Post.* http://www.huffingtonpost.com/2012/04/20/employers-use-facebook-to-pre-screen-applicants_n_1441289.html. Accessed August 29, 2014.

Thompson, C. (2013). *Smarter than you think: How technology is changing our minds for the better.* New York: Penguin.

Thompson, C. (2014, August 29). End the tyranny of 24/7 email. *New York Times,* p. A21.

Thompson, F., & Grundgenett, D. (1999). Helping disadvantaged learners build effective learning skills. *Education, 120,* 130–135.

Tierney, J. (2013, March 19). Good news beats bad on social networks. *New York Times,* p. D3.

Tierney, J. (2014, March 25). Their pants aren't on fire. *New York Times,* p. D3.

Tiggemann, M. (2005). Television and adolescent body image: The role of content and viewing motivation. *Journal of Social and Clinical Psychology, 24,* 361–381.

Timmerman, C., & Scott, C. (2006). Virtually working: Communicative and structural predictors of media use and key outcomes in virtual work teams. *Communication Monographs, 73,* 108–136.

Ting-Toomey, S. (2005). The matrix of face: An updated Face-Negotiation Theory. In W. B. Gudykunst (Ed.), *Theorizing about intercultural communication* (pp. 71–92). Thousand Oaks, CA: Sage.

Tolhuizen, J. H. (1989). Communication strategies for intensifying dating relationships: Identification, use, and structure. *Journal of Social and Personal Relationships, 6,* 413–434.

Toma, C., & Hancock, J. (2011). Looks and lies: The role of physical attractiveness in online dating self-presentations and deceptions. *Communication Research, 37,* 335–351.

Tong, S., & Walther, J. (2011). Just say "no thanks": The effects of romantic rejection across computer mediated communication. *Journal of Social and Personal Relationships, 28,* 488–506.

Tracy, S. J., Lutgen-Sandvik, P., & Albrets, J. (2006). Nightmares, demons, and slaves: Exploring painful metaphors of workplace bullying. *Management Communication Quarterly, 20,* 1–38.

Trees, A. (2006). Attachment theory: The reciprocal relationship between family communication and attachment patterns. In D. O. Braithwaite & L. A. Baxter (Eds.), *Engaging theories in family communication: Multiple perspectives* (pp. 165–180). Thousand Oaks, CA: Sage.

Trees, A. R. (2000). Nonverbal communication and the support process: International sensitivity in interactions between mothers and young adult children. *Communication Monographs, 67,* 239–261.

Trice, H., & Beyer, J. (1984). Studying organizational cultures through rites and ceremonials. *Academy of Management Review, 9,* 653–669.

Tsai, F., & Reis, H. (2009). Perceptions by and of lonely people in social networks. *Personal Relationships, 16,* 221–238.

Tugend, A. (2011, July 2). Comparing yourself to others: It's not all bad. *New York Times,* p. B6.

Turkle, S. (2012). *Alone together: Why we expect more from technology and less from each other.* New York: Basic.

Turow, J. (2008). *Media today* (3rd ed.). New York: Routledge.

Tusing, K., & Dillard, J. (2000). The sounds of dominance: Vocal precursors of perceived dominance during interpersonal influence. *Human Communication Research, 26,* 148–171.

Ueland, B. (1992, November–December). Tell me more: On the fine art of listening. *Utne Reader,* pp. 104–109.

Umble, D. (2000). *Holding the line: The telephone in Old Order Mennonite and Amish life.* Baltimore, MD: Johns Hopkins University Press.

Underwood, A., & Adler, J. (2005, April 25). When cultures clash. *Newsweek,* pp. 68–72.

Van Styke, E. (1999). *Listening to conflict: Finding constructive solutions to workplace disputes.* New York: AMA Communications.

Verderber, R., Sellnow, D., & Verderber, K. (2015). *The challenge of effective speaking*. Belmont, CA: Wadsworth/Cengage.

A Victory for Tolerance. (2014, June 21). *Raleigh News & Observer*, p. 9A.

Virtual Team Challenges. (n.d.). http://onlinemba.unc.edu /research-and-insights/developing -real-skills-for-virtual-teams /virtual-team-challenges/. Accessed August 11, 2014.

Vivian, J. (2013). *The media of mass communication* (11th ed.). Lebanon, IN: Pearson.

Vocate, D. (Ed.). (1994). *Intrapersonal communication: Different voices, different minds*. Mahwah, NJ: Erlbaum.

Von Drehle, D. (2014, July 31). Manopause?! Aging, insecurity and the $2 billion testosterone industry. *Time*. Retrieved from http://time .com/3062889/manopause -aging-insecurity-and-the-2-billion -testosterone-industry/.

Walker, S. (2007). *Style and status: Selling beauty to African American women*. Lexington: University of Kentucky Press.

Waters, J. (2011, July 24). Facebook is fun for recruiters, too. *Raleigh News & Observer*, p. 5E.

Watzlawick, P., Beavin, J., & Jackson, D. D. (1967). *Pragmatics of human communication*. New York: Norton.

Weaver, C. (1972). *Human listening: Processes and behavior*. Indianapolis, IN: Bobbs-Merrill.

Weaving the Web. (2014, July 8). *Wall Street Journal*, p. R3.

Weber, L. (2013, June 13). Why dads don't take paternity leave. *Wall Street Journal*, pp. B1, B7.

Wegner, H., Jr. (2005). Disconfirming communication and self-verification in marriage: Associations among the demand/withdraw interaction pattern, feeling understood, and marital satisfaction. *Journal of Social and Personal Relationships, 22*, 19–31.

Weisinger, H. (1996). *Anger at work*. New York: William Morrow.

Weitz, P., & Weitz, C. (Directors). 2002. *About a boy* [Motion picture]. USA: Universal Studios.

Wen, L., & Kosowsky, J. (2013). *When doctors don't listen*. New York: St. Martins/Thomas Dunne.

Werner, C., Altman, I., & Oxley, D. (1985). Temporal aspects of homes: A transactional perspective. In I. Altman & C. M. Werner (Eds.), *Home environments: Vol. 8: Human behavior and environment: Advances in theory and research* (pp. 1–32). Thousand Oaks, CA: Sage.

Whitman, T., White, R., O'Mara, K., & Goeke-Morey, M. (1999). Environmental aspects of infant health and illness. In T. Whitman & T. Merluzzi (Eds.), *Life-span perspectives on health and illness* (pp. 105–124). Mahwah, NJ: Erlbaum.

Wilco, L. (July 20, 2014). Personal communication.

Williams, J. (2013, June 6). Paygap deniers. *Huffington Post*. http:// www.huffingtonpost.com/joan -williams/pay-gap-deniers _b_3391524.html. Accessed June 22, 2014.

Williams, K. D. (2001). *Ostracism: The power of silence*. New York: Guilford.

Williams, T. (2011, July 23). Town turns to iPads in cost-cutting move. *New York Times*, p. A13.

Wilson, J. F., & Arnold, C. C. (1974). *Public speaking as a liberal art* (4th ed.). Boston: Allyn & Bacon.

Wolvin, A. (2009). Listening, understanding and misunderstanding. In W. F. Eadie (Ed.), *21st century communication: A reference handbook* (pp. 137–146). Thousand Oaks, CA: Sage.

Wong, G. (2011, April 7). China's Internet protestors. *Raleigh News & Observer*, p. 3A.

Wong, N., & Cappella, J. (2009). Antismoking threat and efficacy appeals: Effects on smoking cessation intentions for smokers with low and high readiness to quit. *Journal of Applied Communication Research, 37*, 1–20.

Wood, J. T. (1982). Communication and relational culture: Bases for the study of human relationships. *Communication Quarterly, 30*, 75–84.

Wood, J. T. (1992b). Telling our stories: Narratives as a basis for theorizing sexual harassment. *Journal of Applied Communication Research, 4*, 349–363.

Wood, J. T. (1994c). Saying it makes it so: The discursive construction of sexual harassment. In S. Bingham (Ed.), *Conceptualizing sexual harassment as discursive practice* (pp. 17–30). Westport, CT: Praeger.

Wood, J. T. (1997). Diversity in dialogue: Communication between friends. In J. Makau & R. Arnett (Eds.), *Ethics of communication in an age of diversity* (pp. 5–26). Urbana: University of Illinois Press.

Wood, J. T. (1998). *But I thought you meant…: Misunderstandings in human communication*. Mountain View, CA: Mayfield.

Wood, J. T. (2001b). The normalization of violence in heterosexual relationships: Women's narratives of love and violence. *Journal of Social and Personal Relationships, 18*, 239–261.

Wood, J. T. (2001c). He says/she says: Misunderstandings between men and women. In D. Braithwaite & J. T. Wood (Eds.), *Case studies in interpersonal communication: Processes and problems* (pp. 93–100). Belmont, CA: Wadsworth.

Wood, J. T. (2004b). Monsters and victims: Male felons' accounts of intimate partner violence. *Journal of Social and Personal Relationships, 21*, 555–576.

Wood, J. T. (2005). Feminist standpoint theory and muted group theory: Commonalities and divergences. *Women & Language, 28*, 61–64.

Wood, J. T. (2006). Critical feminist theories of interpersonal communication: Voice and visibility in cultural life. In D. O. Braithwaite & L. A. Baxter (Eds.), *Engaging theories of interpersonal communication: Multiple perspectives* (pp. 197–212). Thousand Oaks, CA: Sage.

Wood, J. T. (2006a). Chopping the carrots: Creating intimacy, moment by moment. In J. T. Wood & S. W. Duck (Eds.), *Composing relationships: Communication in everyday life* (pp. 24–35). Belmont, CA: Thomson Wadsworth.

Wood, J. T. (2010). The can-do discourse and young women's anticipations of future. *Women & Language, 33,* 103–107.

Wood, J. T. (2011). Which ruler? What are we measuring?: Thoughts on theorizing the division of domestic labor. *Journal of Family Communication, 11,* 39–49.

Wood, J. T., & Fixmer-Oraiz, N. (2016). *Gendered Lives* (11th ed.). Boston, MA: Cengage.

Wood, J. T. (2015b). Who's the parent now. In D. Braithwaite & J. T. Wood (Eds.), *Casing communication: Case studies in interpersonal communication* (2nd ed., pp. 175–178). Dubuque, IA: Kendall Hunt.

Wood, J. T., Dendy, L., Dordek, E., Germany, M., & Varallo, S. (1994). Dialectic of difference: A thematic analysis of intimates' meanings for differences. In K. Carter & M. Presnell (Eds.), *Interpretive approaches to interpersonal communication* (pp. 115–136). New York: State University of New York Press.

Wood, J. T., & Duck, S. W. (Eds.). (2006a). *Composing relationships: Communication in everyday life.* Belmont, CA: Thomson Wadsworth.

Wood, J. T., & Duck, S. W. (2006b). Composing relationships: Communication in everyday life (Introduction). In J. T. Wood & S. W. Duck (Eds.), *Composing relationships: Communication in everyday life* (pp. 1–13). Belmont, CA: Thomson Wadsworth.

Wood, J. T., & Fixmer-Oraiz, N. (2017). *Gendered lives: Communication, gender and culture* (12th ed.). Stamford, CT: Cengage.

Wood, J. T., & Inman, C. C. (1993). In a different mode: Masculine styles of communicating closeness. *Journal of Applied Communication Research, 21,* 279–295.

Workers of the World, Log In. (2014, August 16). *Economist,* pp. 51–53.

Workplacebullying.org. (2010).

Workplace Privacy. (2011). Fact Sheet 7. http://management.about.com /gi/o.htm?zi=1/XJ&zTi=1&sdn=man agement&cdn=money&tm=53& gps=464_1035_1001_592&f =00&su=p560.11.336.ip_&tt =2&bt=0&bts=0&zu=http%3A //www.privacyrights.org/fs/fs7 -work.htm. Accessed July 5, 2011.

Wu, T. (2014, July 20). Content and its discontents. *New York Times Book Review,* p. 20.

Yamada, D. (2010). Workplace bullying and American employment law: A ten-year progress report and assessment. *Comparative Labor Law & Policy Journal, 32,* 251–268.

Ye, Z., & Palomares, N. A. (2013). Effects of conversation partners' gender-language consistency on references to emotion, tentative language, and gender salience. *Journal of Language and Social Psychology, 32,* 433–451.

Yerby, J., Buerkel-Rothfuss, N., & Bochner, A. (1990). *Understanding family communication.* Scottsdale, AZ: Gorsuch Scarisbrick.

Yost, B. (2004). We all need someone to lean on. Online edition of *IndyStar.* Retrieved May 21, 2004, from http://www.indystar.com /articles/2/148176-9362-052.html.

Young, J. (2006, June 2). The fight for classroom attention: Professor vs. laptop. *Chronicle of Higher Education,* pp. A27–A29.

Young, J. (2011, May 13). Smartphones on campus: The search for 'killer' apps. *Chronicle of Higher Education,* pp. B6–B7.

Young, S., Wood, J. T., Phillips, G. M., & Pedersen, D. (2001). *Group discussion: A practical guide to participation and leadership* (3rd ed.). Prospect Heights, IL: Waveland.

Zarocostas, J. (2014, May 14). U.S. alone in not paying maternity leave. *Raleigh News & Observer,* p. 3A.

Zorn, T. (1991). Construct system development, transformational leadership, and leadership messages. *Southern Communication Journal, 56,* 178–193.

Zuckerberg, M. (2014, July 8). Everyone will be online. *Wall Street Journal,* p. R3.

Zuckerberg, R. (2013). *Dot complicated.* New York: HarperCollins.

Zuckerman, L. (2002). Questions abound as media influence grows for a handful. In E. Bucy (Ed.), *Living in the information age* (pp. 139–142). Belmont, CA: Wadsworth.

Zuger, A. (2013, April 1). A prescription for frustration. *New York Times,* p. B7.

Index

Note: Boldfaced page numbers refer to definitions of terms. Page numbers followed by the italicized letter *f* refer to figures.